The Fundamentals of Counseling: *A Primer*

Kevin R. Scheel

Revised Edition

DLC Publishing: A division of
Distance Learning Center, LLC
www.DLCPublishing.com

ISBN:978-0-692-25904-7: 7th Edition; 2014; Format: Softcover; Trimsize 8.5x11"; 702 pages.

"*Having taught Addiction Counseling courses for more that 25 years, this is the first text I've seen that covers all of the most up-to-date content material needed for entry level students. It covers (in one text) what used to take two or even three texts thereby providing a significant savings to students, and a comprehensive text for instructional purposes. The 'print upon demand' feature incorporates up-to-date changes, and solves the problem of many traditional texts being out of date before the student gets it.*

I would highly recommend this unique text for use in any instructional program training addiction counselors."

Ed Reading, Ph.D.
President-Elect, International Coalition for Addiction Studies Education (INCASE)

The Fundamentals of Counseling: A Primer

TABLE OF CONTENTS

Section 2: Core Functions

Section 3: Specialty Information

Introduction

The road to becoming a drug and alcohol counselor takes a great deal of hard work and effort. A combination of educational knowledge plus workplace experience will be required in order to become credentialed. One problem though is that at the present time there is no single, unified credentialing process for drug and alcohol counselors. Each state has options that include licensure (state mandated credentials) and/or certification (a credential offered by a private body). Some credentials require college degrees; some only require a certain number of educational and experiential hours to be obtained. Most, regardless of the credential, require some sort of written and/or oral examination before granting the credential.

At this time, most states typically use one of two available national credentialing exams for basic drug/alcohol credentialing - one offered by the National Association of Alcoholism and Drug Counselors (NAADAC), and one by the International Certification & Reciprocity Consortium/Alcohol & Other Drug Abuse, Inc. (IC&RC/AODA). The processes used are very similar - both use a written, multiple-choice examination. NAADAC's written exam is 250 questions in length; IC&RC/AODA's is 150 questions long. IC&RC/AODA may also require a 12-question oral examination, depending on the state where you would become credentialed. (Please note – both groups also offer advanced credentialing and as such, advanced tests for these types of credentials.)

Both written exams test a candidate's knowledge on a variety of topics that have been determined to be the basic knowledge required for drug and alcohol counselors. NAADAC uses the following categories for their information: Pharmacology of Psychoactive Substances; Counseling Practice; Theoretical Bases; and Professional Issues. IC&RC/AODA uses these performance domains: Clinical Evaluation; Treatment Planning; Referral; Service Coordination; Counseling; Client, Family and Community Education; Documentation; Professional and Ethical Responsibilities.

Both require a certain level of proficiency to pass the exam (there is variation in the actual passing level based on certain statistical measures), and depending on the state where you credential, there may be limits to the number of times a candidate may sit for the examination. Regardless, if a candidate is unsuccessful in passing the exam, to take the test again requires additional dollars spent (typically $150 for each time a candidate must take the written exam) as well as the added stress and pressure to succeed.

The purpose of this text then is to help candidates learn much of the basic, need-to-know information that is typically required to perform the skills needed to be a drug/alcohol professional, as well as to obtain a variety of basic knowledge that will be the foundation for the credentialing examinations that will be required. Ultimately, the application of this knowledge will be performed while obtaining in-field experience while serving as an intern or a counselor-in-training at a treatment program or facility.

This text is intended to provide an overview of the more important facts and knowledge used by drug/alcohol professionals. It is comprised of three sections. The first section deals with information that is drug and alcohol specific. It looks at the field in general, reviews the commonly accepted theories of addiction, looks at specific drug and alcohol knowledge, and explores treatment approaches commonly used in the field.

The second section deals with the core functions of counseling. This section is largely presented in an outline format, reviewing such things as screening, assessment, intake, orientation, counseling (individual, group, and family), and other topics. The materials from this section were originally developed for the Project for Addiction Counseling Training, a CSAT program in the early 1990's that was intended to training minority counselors and assist them in entering the drug and alcohol field. The information, therefore, has been tested and used successfully by a variety of individuals across the nation.

The third section deals with more specialized areas of training – for example psychological theories of change, ethics, HIV/AIDS, co-occurring disorders, cultural information, and special populations. While not an all-inclusive set of specialized knowledge, it does represent a major portion of the knowledge base that will be included in the testing process used by both major credentialing bodies.

This text does not review the process of testing for either the IC&RC/AODA (written and oral) or NAADAC (written) examinations. Our website at www.ReadyToTest.com does offer materials to help you prepare for these exams when that time comes. For more information, visit our website at http://www.readytotest.com or e-mail us at readytotest@readytotest.com for more information.

Section 1, Chapter 1:

An Overview of Addiction and its Treatment

The following section is an adaptation of Chapter 1 from "Treatment for Alcohol and Other Drug Abuse, Opportunities for Coordination." The publication is part of the Substance Abuse Prevention and Treatment Block Grant technical assistance program. It has been updated to reflect current findings and information.

DHHS Publication No.(SMA) 94-2075.

Almost everyone has had experience with addictive psychoactive substances. Alcohol is a legal substance that is frequently used in social situations by people from all walks of life. Most people consume it occasionally and experience no adverse effects. Nevertheless, it can be addicting, and for those who reach this level of use, there are potential health and social consequences. In addition to alcohol, mood-altering drugs include a variety of illegal and legal substances that are highly addictive and often result in impaired physical, social, and psychological functioning of users.

The most recent National Survey on Drug Use and Health reports some of the following findings:

- Slightly more than half (52.1 percent) of Americans aged 12 or older reported being current drinkers of alcohol. This translates to an estimated 135.5 million current drinkers.
- An estimated 23.9 million Americans aged 12 or older were current (past month) illicit drug users, meaning they had used an illicit drug during the month prior to the survey interview. This estimate represents 9.2 percent of the population aged 12 or older. Illicit drugs include marijuana/hashish, cocaine (including crack), heroin, hallucinogens, inhalants, or prescription-type psychotherapeutics (pain relievers, tranquilizers, stimulants, and sedatives) used nonmedically.

- In 2012, an estimated 22.2 million persons aged 12 or older (8.5 percent) were classified with substance dependence or abuse in the past year based on criteria specified in the *Diagnostic and Statistical Manual of Mental Disorders*, 4th edition (DSM-IV). Of these, 2.8 million were classified with dependence or abuse of both alcohol and illicit drugs, 4.5 million had dependence or abuse of illicit drugs but not alcohol, and 14.9 million had dependence or abuse of alcohol but not illicit drugs. (Future results will reflect the new DSM-5 standards)
- The specific illicit drugs with the largest numbers of persons with past year dependence or abuse were marijuana (4.3 million), pain relievers (2.1 million), and cocaine (1.1 million).
- An estimated 69.5 million Americans aged 12 or older were current (past month) users of a tobacco product. This represents 26.7 percent of the population in that age range. In addition, 57.5 million persons (22.1 percent of the population) were current cigarette smokers; 13.4 million (5.2 percent) smoked cigars; 9 million (3.5 percent) used smokeless tobacco, and 2.5 million (1 percent) smoked tobacco in pioes.

For a complete review of these findings, visit the website at http://www.oas.samhsa.gov/ and look for the link to the NSDUH Report.

Because of the addictive properties of these substances, and the related physical, social, and psychological consequences they precipitate, treatment will be required for these individuals to recover from their addictions and achieve abstinence. Yet one additional finding from the NSDUH Report raises many concerns:

- 23.1 million persons aged 12 or older needed treatment for an illicit drug or alcohol use problem (8.9 percent of persons aged 12 or older). Of these, 2.5 million (1.0 percent of persons aged 12 or older and 10.8 percent of those who needed treatment) received treatment at a specialty facility. Thus, 20.6 million persons (7.9 percent of the population aged 12 or older) needed treatment for an illicit drug or alcohol use problem but did not receive treatment at a specialty substance abuse facility.

Those who have not had personal experiences using either socially acceptable or illicit drugs still may have been touched by the effects of these substances. Use and abuse of alcohol and other drugs has far-reaching effects. Family members, friends, co-workers, and others often are affected – sometimes tragically – by those who become involved in substance abuse.

In this chapter the process of addiction – progressing from experimental and social use to dependency and addiction – will be examined. This process also includes recovery for many individuals who receive appropriate treatment interventions. Such recovery means a chance to return to productive roles in society that are not focused on procuring and using alcohol and other drugs at the expense of one's physical health and personal well-being. Its chronic and relapsing nature is also recognized as a part of the disorder of addiction. Recovery from addictive illness necessitates sobriety and abstinence, relapse prevention programs, and continuing supportive intervention for those who become dependent on mood-altering chemicals.

The majority of persons who use drugs or alcohol from time to time will not need treatment. Those who are not dependent or addicted may be able to decide to stop using chemicals. However, finding a social climate that is intolerant toward drug use will be important for them. The threat of social, legal, or employer sanctions often is significant enough to persuade them away from continued drug use.

Treatment is for those who cannot or will not stop their use of alcohol or drugs without the help of a special program – usually those who have become physically or psychologically dependent on alcohol or drugs. Without some form of intervention, compulsive alcohol and drug users usually are unable to stop their use for more than a few days at a time. Despite the personal and family consequences, of which they are usually aware, addiction makes it virtually impossible for them to abstain from abusing alcohol or other drugs. Their need for chemicals often forces them to deny the negative consequences they are experiencing.

For youth, the criteria for those needing treatment services are somewhat different. In addition to illicit street drugs, the use of alcohol is also illegal for persons under the age of 21 in most States. Thus, lawfully, any use of these substances by adolescents can be considered abuse. Use of substances is also of particular concern for adolescents who are still developing, physically, socially, and emotionally. For youth, the stance is often taken that if use of alcohol or other drugs are creating problems in one or more areas of functioning, then assessment and intervention services should be provided. This affords a positive opportunity to prevent progression to more serious chemical dependency for many young persons.

Treatment is an essential and cost-effective factor in stemming the tide of substance abuse. Without treatment that is appropriate for the specific needs of individuals, the economic and human costs associated with substance abuse will continue to escalate. Treatment is vital for those whose use of alcohol and other drugs has progressed to the stage of dependence or addiction. This chapter will present a description of the five critical elements necessary for a comprehensive treatment approach.

THE PROCESS OF ADDICTION

No one begins using a mood-altering substance with the intention of becoming addicted to it. For example, the use of alcohol begins with the notion that it will be used only on social occasions, with certain friends, or for specific purposes. In some cases, it is possible to maintain that level of use.

However, for persons who have progressed to dependence on alcohol or other drugs, the sojourn has been difficult. Once past a certain point, there is no turning back. Continuing the journey, with any expectation of health and well-being, will require substance abuse treatment.

Abstinence from alcohol and other drugs is typical for most people most of the time. Occasional use of psychoactive substances may begin because of curiosity or because of the influence of friends. Initial experimental use of mood-altering substances usually occurs during the adolescent years, most often between 12 and 15 years of age. The typical pattern is experimentation with tobacco and alcohol, followed by initial use of marijuana. As use continues, other illicit drugs that can be inhaled or ingested orally may be consumed. Use of more potent drugs, particularly those requiring hypodermic administration, begins somewhat later. During this initial period, use of drugs is intermittent, and most people return to periods of complete abstinence during which they do not seek or consume drugs and experience no adverse consequences from their use. See **Table 1-A** for a brief summary of the characteristics of experimental and social use of alcohol and other drugs.

6

Table 1-A. - Stage 1: Experimental and Social Use of Drugs and Alcohol

Frequency of use: Occasional, perhaps a few times monthly. Usually on weekends when at parties or with friends. May use when alone.

Sources: Friends/peers primarily. Youth may use parents' alcohol.

Reasons for Use:
- ♦ to satisfy curiosity;
- ♦ to acquiesce to peer pressure;
- ♦ to obtain social acceptance;
- ♦ to defy parental limits;
- ♦ to take a risk or seek a thrill;
- ♦ to appear grown up;
- ♦ to relieve boredom;
- ♦ to produce pleasurable feelings; and
- ♦ to diminish inhibitions in social situations.

Effects: At this stage the person will experience euphoria and return to a normal state after using. A small amount may cause intoxication.
Feelings sought include:
- ♦ fun, excitement;
- ♦ thrill;
- ♦ belonging, and;
- ♦ control.

Behavioral Indicators:
- ♦ little noticeable change;
- ♦ some may lie about use or whereabouts;
- ♦ some may experience moderate hangovers; occasionally, there is evidence of use, such as a beer can or marijuana joint.

(Sources: Beschner, 1986; Institute of Medicine, 1990, Jaynes & Rugg, 1988; Macdonald, 1989; Nowinski, 1990).

The metabolic effects of alcohol and other drugs alter the individual's chemistry because psychoactive drugs mimic, displace, block, or deplete specific chemical messengers between nerve cells in the brain. Certain areas of the brain control drives such as hunger, thirst, and sexual libido. When we are hungry we feel uncomfortable; when we eat, we feel satisfied – a positive reward. Psychoactive substances act upon the same areas of the brain and they can produce euphoria, an extremely pleasurable feeling, or cravings for the drug, an unpleasant feeling. With gradually increasing use of a substance, the cycle of euphoria and cravings results in dependence or addiction to the drug.

Problem use or abuse of alcohol or other drugs is the second stage in the process of addiction (see **Table 1-B**). The frequency of administration, as well as the amount of the drug use, increases. Use to the point of intoxication occurs often. The pleasurable, euphoric feelings produced with earlier use are still sought, but after the effects of the drug subside, pain, depression, and discomfort may occur. Unlike earlier stages of use, individuals progressing through this stage are likely to begin encountering consequences for use. These may include:

- work- or school-related difficulties;
- changes in friends;
- family problems;
- physical illnesses;
- weight loss and other physical problems;
- financial and legal complications; and
- personality and emotional changes.

Table 1-B. - Stage 2: Abuse

Frequency of use: Regular; may use several times per week. May begin using during the day. May be using alone rather than with friends.

Sources: Friends; begins buying enough to be prepared. May sell drugs to keep a supply for personal use. May begin stealing to have money to buy drugs/alcohol.

Reasons for Use:
- ◆ To manipulate emotions; to experience the pleasure the substances produce; to cope with stress and uncomfortable feelings such as pain, guilt, anxiety, and sadness; and to overcome feelings of inadequacy.

♦ Persons who progress to this stage of drug/alcohol involvement often experience depression or other uncomfortable feelings when not using. Substances are used to stay high or at least maintain normal feelings.

Effects:
♦ Euphoria is the desired feeling; may return to a normal state following use or may experience pain, depression and general discomfort. Intoxication begins to occur regularly, however.
♦ Feelings sought include:
    - pleasure;
    - relief from negative feelings, such as boredom, and anxiety; and
    - stress reduction.
♦ May begin to feel some guilt, fear, and shame.
♦ May have suicidal ideations/attempts. Tries to control use, but is unsuccessful. Feels shame and guilt. More of a substance is needed to produce the same effect.

Behavioral Indicators:
♦ school or work performance and attendance may decline;
♦ mood swings;
♦ changes in personality;
♦ lying and conning;
♦ change in friendships - will have drug-using friends;
♦ decrease in extra-curricular activities;
♦ begins adopting drug culture appearance (clothing, grooming, hairstyles, jewelry);
♦ conflict with family members may be exacerbated;
♦ behavior may be more rebellious; and
♦ all interest is focused on procuring and using drugs/alcohol.

(Sources: Beschner, 1986; Institute of Medicine, 1990, Jaynes & Rugg, 1988; Macdonald, 1989; Nowinski, 1990).

If substance abuse continues, the individual may reach the stage of dependency/addiction. Dependency occurs when a drug user experiences physical or psychological distress upon discontinuing use of the drug. Addiction implies compulsive use, impaired control over using the substance, preoccupation with obtaining and using the drug, and continued use despite adverse consequences. **Table 1-C** summarizes the characteristics of this stage, including almost continuous use to avoid pain and depression.

Dependent/addicted persons are unlikely to experience euphoria or other pleasant effects from the drug; continued administration is needed to achieve a state of homeostasis – feeling "normal" or not having pain.

Table 1-C. - Stage 3: Dependency/Addiction

Frequency of use: Daily use, continuous.

Sources:
- ◆ will use any means necessary to obtain and secure needed drugs/alcohol;
- ◆ will take serious risks; and
- ◆ will often engage in criminal behavior such as shoplifting and burglary.

Reasons for Use:
- ◆ drugs/alcohol are needed to avoid pain and depression;
- ◆ many wish to escape the realities of daily living; and
- ◆ use is out of control.

Effects:
- ◆ person's normal state is pain or discomfort;
- ◆ drugs/alcohol help them feel normal; when the effects wear off, they again feel pain;
- ◆ they are unlikely to experience euphoria at this state;
- ◆ they may experience suicidal thoughts or attempts;
- ◆ they often feel guilt, shame, and remorse;
- ◆ they may experience blackouts; and
- ◆ they may experience changing emotions, such as depression, aggression, irritation, and apathy.

Behavioral Indicators:
- ◆ physical deterioration includes weight loss, health problems;
- ◆ appearance is poor;
- ◆ may experience memory loss, flashbacks, paranoia, volatile mood swings, and other mental problems;
- ◆ likely to drop out or be expelled from school or lose jobs;
- ◆ may be absent from home much of the time;
- ◆ possible overdoses; and
- ◆ lack of concern about being caught - focused only on procuring and using drugs/alcohol.

(Sources: Beschner, 1986; Institute of Medicine, 1990, Jaynes & Rugg, 1988; Macdonald, 1989; Nowinski, 1990).

The latest edition of the Diagnostic and Statistical Manual of Mental Disorders-5 (DSM-5), published in May of 2013, has removed the distinction between abuse and dependence. The terminology now being used identifies two groups of substance-related disorders: substance use disorders and substance-induced disorders. Substance use disorders are patterns of symptoms resulting from use of a substance which the individual continues to take, despite experiencing problems as a result. Substance-induced disorders include intoxication, withdrawal, substance induced mental disorders, including substance induced psychosis, substance induced bipolar and related disorders, substance induced depressive disorders, substance induced anxiety disorders, substance induced obsessive-compulsive and related disorders, substance induced sleep disorders, substance induced sexual dysfunctions, substance induced delirium and substance induced neurocognitive disorders.

Substance use disorders span a wide variety of problems arising from substance use, and cover 11 different criteria:

1. Taking the substance in larger amounts or for longer than the you meant to;
2. Wanting to cut down or stop using the substance but not managing to;
3. Spending a lot of time getting, using, or recovering from use of the substance;
4. Cravings and urges to use the substance;
5. Not managing to do what you should at work, home or school, because of substance use;
6. Continuing to use, even when it causes problems in relationships
7. Giving up important social, occupational or recreational activities because of substance use;
8. Using substances again and again, even when it puts the you in danger;
9. Continuing to use, even when the you know you have a physical or psychological problem that could have been caused or made worse by the substance;
10. Needing more of the substance to get the effect you want (tolerance);
11. Development of withdrawal symptoms, which can be relieved by taking more of the substance.

The DSM 5 allows clinicians to specify how severe the substance use disorder is, depending on how many symptoms are identified. Two or three symptoms indicate a **mild** substance use disorder, four or five symptoms indicate a **moderate** substance use disorder, and six or more symptoms indicate a **severe** substance use disorder. Clinicians can also add "in early remission," "in sustained remission," "on maintenance therapy," and "in a controlled environment."

The physical, social, occupational, financial, legal, and psychological consequences continue in a downward spiral. Those who persist in drug use to this stage often begin using injectable drugs. On average, it may take from 5 to 10 years following the first experimental use of drugs until a person progresses to the stage of dependency/addiction. This means that many who initiate drug use in their early teens will be addicted by their late teens or early 20s. There are many personal and drug-related variables that can hasten or retard the process, but once dependent, obtaining and using a drug of choice is the focus of one's life.

As the use of mood-altering chemicals progresses through these stages, related physical, social, and psychological problems increase. During earlier stages many people can manage their drug and alcohol use and may move back and forth from abstinence to problem use. Each stage entails some risk of progression to the next, but this course is not inevitable. However, once the stage of dependency/addiction is reached, the individual has acquired chronic relapsing disorder that most professionals believe can never be "cured." Return to earlier stages of controlled use is no longer possible.

However, treatment helps addicted individuals enter a stage of recovery during which they abstain from substance use and experience improved physical, social, and psychological functioning. Because of relapse, the recovery process may be interrupted by periods of return to substance use. This requires attention to relapse prevention and continuing supportive therapeutic interventions. Many treatment modalities (such as methadone maintenance or Alcoholics Anonymous) are viewed as potentially lifelong commitments to maintain the recovery process.

Knowledge of the mechanisms of substance abuse and addiction has not advanced enough to provide a cogent understanding of the reasons some people manage their use of alcohol or drugs while others progress to a problem stage of abuse or addiction. It is likely that a combination of physiological, environmental, and psychological factors converge to exacerbate the problem for some individuals. Although found among all socioeconomic groups, persons already plagued by poverty, disease, and unemployment are over-represented among those afflicted by chemical addiction.

RECOVERY

Research indicates that, while it is not a curable disorder, *treatment for substance abuse does work*. With treatment, substance-dependent persons enjoy healthy and productive lives. Instead of creating health risks, committing crimes, and requiring public support, recovering individuals make positive contributions to society through their work and creativity. Recovery is the process of initiating and maintaining abstinence from alcohol or other drug use. It also involves making personal and interpersonal changes. Whether an individual is addicted to or abusing alcohol, illegal drugs, prescription drugs, or a combination of these, the most important goal is to discontinue the use of alcohol and/or drugs.

With relapse prevention programming and supportive treatment, recovery is a realizable goal. With improved treatment services and adequate resources, society also is protected from further consequences related to drugs and alcohol, including economic, social, health, and crime-related problems.

FIVE CRITICAL COMPONENTS OF EFFECTIVE TREATMENT

Treatment is an effective tool in reducing drug abuse and rehabilitating those affected by it. It is particularly important that treatment strategies incorporate the following five critical components to enhance effectiveness.

1. *Assessment* uses diagnostic instruments and processes to determine an individual's needs and problems. It is an essential first step in determining the possible causes of addiction for the person and the most appropriate treatment modality for his or her needs.

2. *Patient-Treatment Matching* ensure that an individual receives the type of treatment corresponding with his or her personality, background, mental condition, and the extent and duration of substance abuse determined by the assessment.

3. *Comprehensive services* include the range of services needed in addition to specific alcohol or drug treatment. The needs of addicted persons are often very complex, including health problems, financial and legal issues, psychological problems, and many others. Effective treatment must help people access the full extent of additional services needed to make their lives whole.

4. *Relapse prevention* is important because addiction is a chronic and relapsing disorder. Relapse prevention strategies are based on assessing an individual's "triggers" – those situations, events, people, places, thoughts, and activities – that re-kindle the need for drugs. Strategies for coping with these when they occur are then developed.

5. *Accountability* of treatment program is crucial for determining the success of specific approaches and modalities. The need for the program, its integrity, and its results, including abstinence, social adjustment, and reduction of criminal behavior by those treated in the program, must be evaluated.

Treatment programs for AOD addictions vary in style, purpose, philosophy, and type of patients treated. Certain components of treatment, however, are common to all models of treatment programs. The components of CSAT's model comprehensive AOD treatment program are described in **Table 1-E**.

Table 1-E. - Center for Substance Abuse Treatment - Model for Comprehensive Alcohol and Other Drug Abuse Treatment

A model treatment program includes:

♦ **Assessment**, to include a medical examination, drug use history, psychosocial evaluation, and, where warranted, a psychiatric evaluation, as well as a review of socioeconomic factors and eligibility for public health, welfare, employment, and educational assistance programs.

♦ **Same day intake**, to retain the patient's involvement and interest in treatment.

♦ **Documenting findings and treatment**, to enhance clinical case supervision.

♦ **Preventative and primary medical care**, provided on site.

♦ **Testing for infectious diseases**, at intake and at intervals throughout treatment, for infectious diseases, for example, hepatitis, retrovirus, tuberculosis, HIV/AIDS, syphilis, gonorrhea, and other sexually transmitted diseases.

♦ **Weekly random drug testing**, to ensure abstinence and compliance with treatment.

♦ **Pharmacotherapeutic interventions**, by qualified medical practitioners, as appropriate for those patients having mental health disorders, those addicted to heroin, and HIV-seropositive individuals.

♦ **Group counseling interventions**, to address the unique emotional, physical, and social problems of HIV/AIDS patients.

- ♦ **Basic substance abuse counseling**, including psychological counseling, psychiatric counseling, and family or collateral counseling provided by persons licensed or certified by State authorities to provide such services. Staff training and education are integral to a successful treatment program.
- ♦ **Practical life skills counseling**, including vocational and educational counseling and training, frequently available through linkages with specialized programs.
- ♦ **General health education**, including nutrition, sex and family planning, and HIV/AIDS counseling, with an emphasis on contraception counseling for adolescents and women.
- ♦ **Peer/support groups**, particularly for those who are HIV-positive or who have been victims of rape or sexual abuse.
- ♦ **Liaison services** with immigration, legal aid, and criminal justice system authorities.
- ♦ **Social and athletic activities**, to retrain patients' perceptions of social interaction.
- ♦ **Alternative housing** for homeless patients or for those whose living situations are conducive to maintaining the addictive lifestyle.
- ♦ **Relapse prevention**, which combines aftercare and support programs, such as Alcoholics Anonymous and Narcotics Anonymous, within an individualized plan to identify, stabilize, and control the stressors which trigger and bring about relapse to substance abuse.
- ♦ **Outcome evaluation**, to enable refinement and improvement of service delivery.

EXTENT OF SUBSTANCE ABUSE

Although some promising reports indicate a decline in drug use in the general population, other data indicate less encouraging results. Unfortunately, there is no single measurement that provides a clear picture of alcohol and drug use and its complex interaction with individual and social problems. Many large-scale studies use populations that are easily accessed, such as youth in high school or persons living at home who have telephones. However, these methods tend to overlook subgroups that are known to have high rates of substance abuse, such as those in prisons, homeless persons, and high school dropouts. Further, individuals may be reluctant to disclose alcohol and other drug use when they are questioned because they are concerned about potential punishment.

Estimated Drug Use Within the General Population

The National Survey on Drug Use and Health (NSDUH) is an annual survey of the civilian, non-institutionalized population of the United States aged 12 years old or older. Prior to 2002, the survey was called the National Household Survey on Drug Abuse (NHSDA). This brief Overview report provides a concise summary of the main results from the 2007 NSDUH, the most recent reporting period. A more complete presentation of the initial results of the survey is given in the full report, *Results from the National Survey on Drug Use and Health: National Findings.* Both reports present national estimates of rates of use, numbers of users, and other measures related to illicit drugs, alcohol, and tobacco products. Measures related to mental health problems also are included. State-level estimates from NSDUH will be presented in other reports to be released separately. For complete details and for the most current findings, see the SAMHSA website at http://www.oas.samhsa.gov/nhsda.htm.

Highlights of Findings

Illicit Drug Use

- In 2012, an estimated 23.9 million Americans aged 12 or older were current (past month) illicit drug users, meaning they had used an illicit drug during the month prior to the survey interview. This estimate represents 9.2 percent of the population aged 12 or older. Illicit drugs include marijuana/hashish, cocaine (including crack), heroin, hallucinogens, inhalants, or prescription-type psychotherapeutics (pain relievers, tranquilizers, stimulants, and sedatives) used nonmedically.
- The rate of current illicit drug use among persons aged 12 or older increased from 8.1 percent in 2008 to 9.2 percent in 2012. The rate in 2012 was similar to the rates in 2009 to 2011 (ranging from 8.7 to 8.9 percent), but it was higher than the rates in the years from 2002 to 2008 (ranging from 7.9 to 8.3 percent).
- Marijuana was the most commonly used illicit drug. In 2012, there were 18.9 million past month users. Between 2007 and 2012, the rate of current use increased from 5.8 to 7.3 percent, and the number of users increased from 14.5 million to 18.9 million.
- Daily or almost daily use of marijuana (used on 20 or more days in the past month) increased from 5.1 million persons in 2007 to 7.6 million persons in 2012.

- In 2012, there were 1.6 million current cocaine users aged 12 or older, comprising 0.6 percent of the population. These estimates were similar to the number and rate in 2011 (1.4 million persons and 0.5 percent), but they were lower than in 2003 to 2007 (e.g., 2.4 million persons and 1.0 percent in 2006).
- The number of past year heroin users increased between 2007 (373,000) and 2012 (669,000).
- An estimated 1.1 million persons aged 12 or older in 2012 (0.4 percent) used hallucinogens in the past month. These estimates were similar to the estimates in 2002 to 2011.
- The percentage of persons aged 12 or older who used prescription-type psychotherapeutic drugs nonmedically in the past month in 2012 (2.6 percent) was similar to the percentage in 2011 (2.4 percent) and all years from 2002 through 2010.
- The number of past month methamphetamine users decreased between 2006 and 2012, from 731,000 (0.3 percent) to 440,000 (0.2 percent).
- Among youths aged 12 to 17, the current illicit drug use rate was similar in 2011 (10.1 percent) and 2012 (9.5 percent). The rate declined from 11.6 percent in 2002 to 9.3 percent in 2008, increased to 10.1 percent in 2009, and remained at 10.1 percent in 2010 and 2011.
- The rate of current marijuana use among youths aged 12 to 17 decreased from 8.2 percent in 2002 to 6.7 percent in 2006, remained unchanged at 6.7 percent in 2007 and 2008, then increased to 7.9 percent in 2011. The rate declined to 7.2 percent in 2012.
- Among youths aged 12 to 17, the rate of current nonmedical use of prescription-type drugs declined from 4.0 percent in 2002 to 2.8 percent in 2012. The rate of nonmedical pain reliever use declined during this period from 3.2 to 2.2 percent among youths.
- The rate of current use of illicit drugs among young adults aged 18 to 25 increased from 19.7 percent in 2008 to 21.3 percent in 2012, driven largely by an increase in marijuana use (from 16.6 percent in 2008 to 18.7 percent in 2012).
- Among young adults aged 18 to 25, the rate of current nonmedical use of prescription-type drugs in 2012 was 5.3 percent, which was similar to the rates in 2010 and 2011, but it was lower than the rate in the years from 2003 to 2007 (ranging from 5.9 to 6.5 percent).
- There was a decrease from 2005 to 2012 in the use of cocaine among young adults aged 18 to 25, from 2.6 to 1.1 percent.

- Among adults aged 50 to 64, the rate of current illicit drug use increased during the past decade. For adults aged 50 to 54, the rate increased from 3.4 percent in 2002 to 7.2 percent in 2012. Among those aged 55 to 59, the rate of current illicit drug use increased from 1.9 percent in 2002 to 6.6 percent in 2012. Among those aged 60 to 64, the rate increased from 1.1 percent in 2003 to 3.6 percent in 2012. These trends partially reflect the aging into these age groups of members of the baby boom cohort (i.e., persons born between 1946 and 1964), whose rates of illicit drug use have been higher than those of older cohorts.
- Among unemployed adults aged 18 or older in 2012, 18.1 percent were current illicit drug users, which was higher than the rates of 8.9 percent for those who were employed full time and 12.5 percent for those who were employed part time. However, most illicit drug users were employed. Of the 21.5 million current illicit drug users aged 18 or older in 2012, 14.6 million (67.9 percent) were employed either full or part time.
- In 2012, 10.3 million persons aged 12 or older reported driving under the influence of illicit drugs during the past year. This corresponds to 3.9 percent of the population aged 12 or older, which was higher than the rate in 2011 (3.7 percent). The rate had declined steadily between 2002 and 2011, from 4.7 to 3.7 percent, before increasing in 2012. In 2012, the rate was highest among young adults aged 18 to 25 (11.9 percent).
- Among persons aged 12 or older in 2011-2012 who used pain relievers nonmedically in the past 12 months, 54.0 percent got the drug they used most recently from a friend or relative for free, and 10.9 percent bought the drug from a friend or relative. Another 19.7 percent reported that they got the drug through a prescription from one doctor. An annual average of 4.3 percent got pain relievers from a drug dealer or other stranger, and 0.2 percent bought them on the Internet.

Alcohol Use

- Slightly more than half (52.1 percent) of Americans aged 12 or older reported being current drinkers of alcohol in the 2012 survey, which was similar to the rate in 2011 (51.8 percent). This translates to an estimated 135.5 million current drinkers in 2012.
- In 2012, nearly one quarter (23.0 percent) of persons aged 12 or older were binge alcohol users in the past 30 days. This translates to about 59.7 million people. The rate in 2012 was similar to the estimate in 2011 (22.6 percent). Binge drinking is defined as having five or more drinks on the same occasion on at least 1 day in the 30 days prior to the survey.
- In 2012, heavy drinking was reported by 6.5 percent of the population aged 12 or older, or 17.0 million people. This rate was similar to the rate of heavy drinking in 2011 (6.2 percent). Heavy drinking is defined as binge drinking on at least 5 days in the past 30 days.

- Among young adults aged 18 to 25 in 2012, the rate of binge drinking was 39.5 percent, and the rate of heavy drinking was 12.7 percent. These rates were similar to the corresponding rates in 2011 (39.8 and 12.1 percent, respectively).
- The rate of current alcohol use among youths aged 12 to 17 was 12.9 percent in 2012. Youth binge and heavy drinking rates in 2012 were 7.2 and 1.3 percent, respectively. These rates were all similar to those reported in 2011 (13.3, 7.4, and 1.5 percent, respectively).
- In 2012, an estimated 11.2 percent of persons aged 12 or older drove under the influence of alcohol at least once in the past year. This percentage was lower than in 2002, when it was 14.2 percent, but it was similar to the rate in 2011 (11.1 percent). Among persons aged 18 to 25, the rate of driving under the influence of alcohol decreased steadily between 2002 and 2011 (from 26.6 to 18.6 percent), but it did not change from 2011 to 2012 (18.4 percent).
- An estimated 9.3 million underage persons (aged 12 to 20) were current drinkers in 2012, including 5.9 million binge drinkers and 1.7 million heavy drinkers.
- Past month, binge, and heavy drinking rates among underage persons declined between 2002 and 2012. Past month alcohol use declined from 28.8 to 24.3 percent, binge drinking declined from 19.3 to 15.3 percent, and heavy drinking declined from 6.2 to 4.3 percent.
- In 2012, 54.4 percent of current underage drinkers reported that their last use of alcohol occurred in someone else's home, and 31.4 percent reported that it had occurred in their own home. Among current underage drinkers, 28.2 percent paid for the alcohol the last time they drank, including 7.6 percent who purchased the alcohol themselves and 20.4 percent who gave money to someone else to purchase it. Among those who did not pay for the alcohol they last drank, 36.6 percent got it from an unrelated person aged 21 or older, 23.0 percent got it from a parent, guardian, or other adult family member, and 18.8 percent got it from another person younger than 21 years old.

Tobacco Use

- In 2012, an estimated 69.5 million Americans aged 12 or older were current (past month) users of a tobacco product. This represents 26.7 percent of the population in that age range. Also, 57.5 million persons (22.1 percent of the population) were current cigarette smokers; 13.4 million (5.2 percent) smoked cigars; 9.0 million (3.5 percent) used smokeless tobacco; and 2.5 million (1.0 percent) smoked tobacco in pipes.

- Between 2002 and 2012, past month use of any tobacco product among persons aged 12 or older decreased from 30.4 to 26.7 percent, and past month cigarette use declined from 26.0 to 22.1 percent. Rates of past month use of cigars and smokeless tobacco in 2012 were similar to corresponding rates in 2002. However, past month pipe tobacco use increased from 0.8 percent in 2002 to 1.0 percent in 2012.
- The rate of past month tobacco use among 12 to 17 year olds declined from 15.2 percent in 2002 to 8.6 percent in 2012, including a decline from 2011 (10.0 percent) to 2012. The rate of past month cigarette use among 12 to 17 year olds also declined between 2002 and 2012, from 13.0 to 6.6 percent, including a decline between 2011 (7.8 percent) and 2012.
- Among youths aged 12 to 17 who smoked cigarettes in the past month, 54.6 percent also used an illicit drug, compared with only 6.4 percent of youths who did not smoke cigarettes.

Initiation of Substance Use (Incidence, or First-Time Use) within the Past 12 Months

- In 2012, an estimated 2.9 million persons aged 12 or older used an illicit drug for the first time within the past 12 months. This averages to about 7,900 initiates per day and was similar to the estimate for 2011 (3.1 million). A majority of these past year illicit drug initiates reported that their first drug was marijuana (65.6 percent). More than 1 in 4 initiated with nonmedical use of prescription drugs (26.0 percent, including 17.0 percent with pain relievers, 4.1 percent with tranquilizers, 3.6 percent with stimulants, and 1.3 percent with sedatives). In 2012, 6.3 percent of initiates reported inhalants as their first illicit drug, and 2.0 percent used hallucinogens as their first drug.
- In 2012, the illicit drug categories with the largest number of past year initiates were marijuana use (2.4 million) and nonmedical use of pain relievers (1.9 million). These estimates were similar to the numbers in 2011. However, the number of marijuana initiates increased between 2007 (2.1 million) and 2012 (2.4 million).
- The number of past year initiates of methamphetamine was 133,000 in 2012. This number was lower than the estimates in 2002 to 2004, which ranged from 260,000 to 318,000.
- The number of past year initiates of Ecstasy was 869,000 in 2012, which was similar to the numbers in 2010 (949,000) and 2011 (922,000), but it was lower than the number in 2009 (1.1 million). The number had increased from 615,000 in 2005 to 1.1 million in 2009.
- The number of past year cocaine initiates declined from 1.0 million in 2002 to 639,000 in 2012. The number of crack cocaine initiates declined from 337,000 to 84,000 during this period.

- In 2012, there were 156,000 persons aged 12 or older who used heroin for the first time within the past year, which was similar to the estimates from 2007 to 2011. However, this was an increase from the annual numbers of initiates during 2003 (92,000) and 2006 (90,000).
- Most (81.4 percent) of the 4.6 million past year alcohol initiates in 2012 were younger than age 21 at the time of initiation.
- The number of persons aged 12 or older who smoked cigarettes for the first time within the past 12 months was 2.3 million in 2012, which was similar to the estimate in 2011 (2.4 million), but it was higher than the estimate for 2002 (1.9 million). About half of new smokers in 2012 were younger than 18 when they first smoked cigarettes (51.4 percent or 1.2 million). The number of new smokers who began smoking at age 18 or older increased from 623,000 in 2002 to 1.1 million in 2012.
- In 2012, an estimated 778,000 persons aged 12 or older began smoking cigarettes daily within the past 12 months, including 257,000 persons who were under age 18 when they started smoking daily. The annual number of new daily smokers declined from about 1.1 million in 2009 to 778,000 in 2012.
- The number of persons aged 12 or older who used smokeless tobacco for the first time within the past year was 1.0 million, which was lower than in 2009 (1.5 million) and in 2011 (1.3 million).

Youth Prevention-Related Measures

- The percentage of youths aged 12 to 17 perceiving great risk in smoking marijuana once or twice a week decreased from 54.6 percent in 2007 to 43.6 percent in 2012.
- Between 2002 and 2008, the percentage of youths who reported great risk in smoking one or more packs of cigarettes per day increased from 63.1 to 69.5 percent. However, the percentage dropped to 65.5 percent in 2009 and remained steady between 2009 and 2012 (65.7 percent).
- About half (47.8 percent) of youths aged 12 to 17 reported in 2012 that it would be "fairly easy" or "very easy" for them to obtain marijuana if they wanted some. One in six reported it would be easy to get cocaine (16.0 percent), 11.5 percent indicated that LSD would be easily available, and 9.9 percent reported easy availability for heroin. Between 2002 and 2012, there were declines in perceived availability for all four of these drugs.
- A majority of youths aged 12 to 17 (89.3 percent) in 2012 reported that their parents would strongly disapprove of their trying marijuana once or twice. Current marijuana use was much less prevalent among youths who perceived strong parental disapproval for trying marijuana once or twice than for those who did not (4.3 vs. 31.0 percent).

- In 2012, 75.9 percent of youths aged 12 to 17 reported having seen or heard drug or alcohol prevention messages from sources outside of school, which was lower than in 2002 (83.2 percent). The percentage of school-enrolled youths reporting that they had seen or heard prevention messages at school also declined during this period, from 78.8 to 75.0 percent.

Substance Dependence, Abuse, and Treatment

- In 2012, an estimated 22.2 million persons aged 12 or older (8.5 percent) were classified with substance dependence or abuse in the past year based on criteria specified in the *Diagnostic and Statistical Manual of Mental Disorders*, 4th edition (DSM-IV). Of these, 2.8 million were classified with dependence or abuse of both alcohol and illicit drugs, 4.5 million had dependence or abuse of illicit drugs but not alcohol, and 14.9 million had dependence or abuse of alcohol but not illicit drugs.
- The annual number of persons with substance dependence or abuse in 2012 (22.2 million) was similar to the number in each of the years from 2002 to 2010 (ranging from 21.6 million to 22.7 million), but it was higher than the number in 2011 (20.6 million).
- The specific illicit drugs with the largest numbers of persons with past year dependence or abuse in 2012 were marijuana (4.3 million), pain relievers (2.1 million), and cocaine (1.1 million). The number of persons with marijuana dependence or abuse did not change between 2002 and 2012. Between 2004 and 2012, the number with pain reliever dependence or abuse increased from 1.4 million to 2.1 million, and between 2006 and 2012, the number with cocaine dependence or abuse declined from 1.7 million to 1.1 million.
- The number of persons with heroin dependence or abuse in 2012 (467,000) was approximately twice the number in 2002 (214,000).
- In 2012, adults aged 21 or older who had first used alcohol at age 14 or younger were more than 7 times as likely to be classified with alcohol dependence or abuse than adults who had their first drink at age 21 or older (15.2 vs. 2.1 percent).
- Between 2002 and 2012, the percentage of youths aged 12 to 17 with substance dependence or abuse declined from 8.9 to 6.1 percent.
- Treatment need is defined as having substance dependence or abuse or receiving substance use treatment at a specialty facility (hospital inpatient, drug or alcohol rehabilitation, or mental health centers) within the past 12 months. In 2012, 23.1 million persons aged 12 or older needed treatment for an illicit drug or alcohol use problem (8.9 percent of persons aged 12 or older). Of these, 2.5 million (1.0 percent of persons aged 12 or older

and 10.8 percent of those who needed treatment) received treatment at a specialty facility. Thus, 20.6 million persons (7.9 percent of the population aged 12 or older) needed treatment for an illicit drug or alcohol use problem but did not receive treatment at a specialty facility in the past year.

- Of the 20.6 million persons aged 12 or older in 2012 who were classified as needing substance use treatment but did not receive treatment at a specialty facility in the past year, 1.1 million persons (5.4 percent) reported that they felt they needed treatment for their illicit drug or alcohol use problem. Of these 1.1 million persons who felt they needed treatment, 347,000 (31.3 percent) reported that they made an effort to get treatment. Based on combined 2009-2012 data, the primary reason for not receiving treatment among this group of persons was a lack of insurance coverage and inability to pay the cost (38.2 percent).

THE RESPONSE TO SUBSTANCE ABUSE

The incidence of substance abuse remains unacceptably high, and both substance abusers and other persons are adversely affected by this disease. New information about the effectiveness and economic benefits of providing treatment are emerging rapidly. Efforts to evaluate treatment have led the Office of National Drug Control Policy (1990b, p. 30) to state unequivocally, "We now know on the basis of more than two decades of research that drug treatment can work."

Various perspectives have viewed addiction as a matter of personal choice, as a medical illness, or as deviant, criminal behavior. Thus, responses to addicted persons have ranged from ignoring them to hospitalization to imprisonment.

The medical view of addiction understands that addicted persons have a treatable disease, much like other diseases, such as diabetes. Addiction is a chronic disorder that is prone to relapse, even after significant periods of recovery. Thus, the individual needs treatment that is appropriate for his or her particular needs and problems based on an assessment of the cause and course of the disease. The mission of treatment agencies focuses on helping individuals make positive changes. Treatment approaches have evolved in two basic categories:

1. Pharmacological modalities, which affect physiological processes (such as detoxification and methadone maintenance), and

2. Behavioral modalities, which influence behavior or learning processes.

These often are combined to produce a greater effect (NIDA, 2001).

The criminal view of addiction defines drug use as a criminal behavior. The focus of intervention in the criminal justice system is first to protect the health, safety, and welfare of the public, and then to rehabilitate offenders, if possible. Prison crowding and an overwhelming drain on community corrections resources have resulted from increasing numbers of drug-involved offenders. However, as caseloads continue to rise, it is difficult to see that this approach, at least without concomitant treatment, has positively affected the problem of substance abuse.

CONCLUSION

Substance addiction is a chronic, progressive, relapsing disorder affecting all citizens in one way or another. If not directly involved, many have family members with alcohol or other drug-related problems. Highways and places of employment are sometimes unsafe because of the effects of alcohol and drugs on motorists and co-workers. It is a devastating disease to individuals, families, and communities. The exorbitant financial toll includes increased health care costs and reduced productivity, as well as higher law enforcement costs, thefts, and destruction of property. With the onset of HIV/AIDS and other infectious diseases for which transmission is directly or indirectly attributable to substance abuse factors, addiction is truly a deadly disease.

While prevention efforts are successful in lowering rates of substance abuse among some segments of the population, addiction is a pervasive problem among others. However, treatment is a cost-effective strategy for intervening to stop the cycle of destruction and despair. Treatment programs providing comprehensive services and attending to the continuing treatment needs of individuals are most beneficial. These programs include the five critical components of treatment – *comprehensive assessment, patient-treatment matching, comprehensive services, relapse prevention, and accountability.*

With coordination of efforts, appropriate application of resources, and a vision for a better future, great achievements in substance abuse treatment will occur.

Section 1, Chapter 2:

The Neurobiology of Addiction

In understanding the affects of the psychoactive drugs, it is important to understand the nature and function of the nervous system. You don't have to be a scientist or a physician to understand the various elements that make up this system. It is only necessary to develop a basic understanding of how drugs alter nerve functions, mental processes, mood, feelings, consciousness, perception and behavior. This can be done by reviewing the basic aspects of the nervous system.

The nervous system is comprised of the specialized structures that control and coordinate all body activities through the process of stimulus and response. The process of stimulus and response occurs in three stages:
1) sensory reception - some type of stimuli is detected either from outside or within the body,
2) interconnection - the stimuli creates an electrical message that is then transmitted from one part of the system to another, and
3) motor response - an appropriate response is triggered, such as a muscular contraction, as a result of a message being sent back to a body part by a nerve center.

The nervous system consists of three major structures: the brain, the spinal cord, and the peripheral nerves. Each structure is composed mainly of neurons, highly specialized and unique cells which are capable of receiving stimuli and transmitting electrical messages or impulses.

The nervous system (**Figure 2.1**) has two major parts:

1. The central nervous system (CNS), which is composed of the brain and the spinal cord. Psychoactive drugs have their primary effect on the central nervous system;

2. The peripheral nervous system, which consist of all the nerves that branch out from the central nervous system and connect the system to other body parts, including the hands and feet.

Additionally, there are two subdivisions of the peripheral nervous system:

a. The somatic system - comprised of the cranial and spinal nerves which connect the CNS to the skin and the skeletal muscles.

b. The autonomic system - the nerves which connect the central nervous system to the various body organs, including the heart, stomach, intestines, and various glands. These nerves function involuntarily (controlled by the brain automatically, without conscious control or effort). There are two subdivisions of this system:

    1) The sympathetic division, which prepares the body for activities which expend energy, and

    2) the parasympathetic division, which aids the body in returning to normal after a period of expending energy. This division works to counterbalance the activities of the sympathetic division.

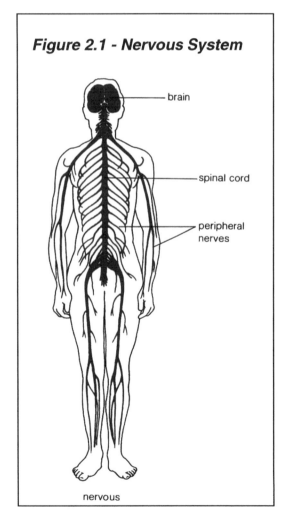

Figure 2.1 - Nervous System

brain

spinal cord

peripheral nerves

nervous

The neuron (**Figure 2.2**) is the basic unit of the nervous system. It is capable of both receiving stimuli and transmitting electrical messages or impulses throughout the system. Extending from the neuron are two types of nerve fibers. Dendrites are fibers that send nerve impulses toward the cell body, while axons carry impulses away from the cell body. Each neuron has several dendrites but only one axon.

Electrical impulses originate in the dendrite and are then transmitted down the axon. Psychoactive drugs do not act primarily on the axon, with the exception of local anesthetics (thus blocking the transmission of pain impulses to the brain). At the junction between the axon of one cell and the dendrite of another (known as the synapse), the electrical impulse must cross a narrow space or gap, called the synaptic cleft. This gap is filled with a special type of fat that acts as an insulator between the cells. The cross-over process is accomplished not by electrical impulse, but by chemical transmission. It is here that other chemicals, specifically the psychoactive drugs, have their major effect. Depressant drugs tend to thicken the medium, thus slowing down the transmission. Stimulant drugs tend to thin the medium, thus causing a more rapid transmission. Certain types of drugs, especially marijuana, have been found to actually fill the gap, thus preventing the transmission from occurring.

When an electrical impulse reaches the end of an axon, tiny, saclike structures known as synaptic knobs manufacture chemicals, called neurotransmitters. The following sequence of events occurs rapidly:

1. A nerve impulse reaches the synaptic knob;

2. A neurotransmitter substance is released into the synaptic cleft;

3. The neurotransmitter substance is diffused across the synaptic cleft;

4. The neurotransmitter reacts with the membranes of the dendrite on the other side of the cleft;

5. The nerve impulse is reestablished in the dendrite and transmission is continued through the cell;

6. The neurotransmitter substance breaks down to prevent continued stimulation of the dendrite.

This process is repeated in each cell until the transmission is complete.

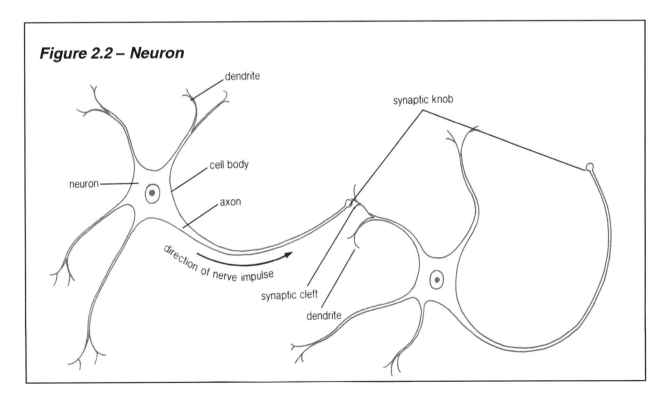

Figure 2.2 – Neuron

There are a variety of neurotransmitter substances within the nervous system. Among these are:

<u>Acetylcholine</u> - an excitatory neurotransmitter released by axons;

<u>Norepinephrine</u> - a neurotransmitter found in the brain, associated with arousal reactions and moods;

<u>Dopamine</u> - a neurotransmitter found in the brain, associated with body movement and pleasure;

<u>Serotonin</u> - a brain neurotransmitter associated with regulation of sensory perception, sleep and body temperature - alterations in the serotonin functioning have been found to be related to mental illness and certain drug-induced hallucinations;

<u>Gamma-aminobutyric acid or GABA</u> - an inhibitory neurotransmitter substance (one that blocks the transfer of a nerve impulse to an adjoining neuron in the brain) - when the normal function of GABA is disrupted, convulsions may occur;

<u>Glycine</u> - an inhibitory neurotransmitter substance found in the spinal cord;

<u>Enkephalins and endorphins</u> - first discovered in 1975, both compounds have been extracted from the brain and pituitary gland - both compounds have pain killing properties that are more powerful than morphine, with endorphins being 40 times more powerful than enkephalins, and 100 times more powerful than morphine.

Current research seems to suggest that the presence or absence of such compounds as endorphins and enkephalins and especially dopamine may explain several conditions including compulsive drug abuse, chemical dependence, pain management, sexual activity, schizophrenia, and the natural "high" of exercise that many people experience. Further research is needed to help us identify exactly how this knowledge may be applied to successful treatment and recovery issues.

The Life Cycle and Action of Neurotransmitters

There is still a great deal that science can not tell us about the brain, especially with regards to the neurotransmitters. There is still uncertainty as to exactly where these substances are produced. It does appear, however, that the neurotransmitters that are used to communicate between neurons are made inside the brain cell from which they are to be released. This would seem to make sense, because if they were freely produced everywhere in the tissues of the brain, the release of a tiny amount from a nerve ending wouldn't be able to have any impact in transferring information from one neuron to another. However, the raw materials, or precursors, from which the neurotransmitter are made are found circulating in the blood supply and in the brain.

A cell that is going to make a particular neurotransmitter may need to bring in the right precursor in a greater concentration than exists in the whole brain. Brain cells apparently have a mechanism built into that cell's membrane for active uptake of the precursor. The precursors themselves are often amino acids that are derived from proteins in the diet, and these amino acids are used in the body for many things besides making neurotransmitters.

After the precursor molecule has been taken up into the neuron, it must be changed, through one or a series of chemical reactions, into the neurotransmitter molecule. This process is known as synthesis. At each step of the synthetic chemical reaction, the reaction is helped along by an enzyme. These enzymes are themselves large molecules that recognize the precursor molecule, attach to it briefly, and hold it in such a way as to allow the synthetic chemical reaction to occur.

When the neurotransmitter molecules have been synthesized, they are stored in the small, round packages in the synaptic knob (which is found at the end of the axon), called synaptic vesicles, from which they will be released. When an electrical signal arrives from the neuron to the synaptic knob, some of the vesicles fuse with the cell membrane and then open, releasing many thousand neurotransmitter molecules at once. This process of neurotransmitter release takes place within a few thousandths of a second after the electrical signal reaches the synaptic knob.

Once the neurotransmitter molecules are released into the small synaptic cleft between neurons, a particular molecule may just float around briefly, or it may be one of the ones that bind to the receptor on the dendrite of the next neuron. This receptor represents the most important recognition site in the entire process, and it is also one of the most important places for drugs to interact with the natural neurotransmitter. With literally thousands of neurotransmitter molecules floating freely in the synaptic cleft, some will come near these receptors, bind to them briefly, and then float away again. In the process of binding, the neurotransmitter may distort the receptor so that a tiny passage is opened through the membrane, allowing an electrical current in the form of charged ions moving through the membrane. This opening does not last long, however, and within a few thousandths of a second the neurotransmitter molecule has left the receptor and the ion channel is closed.

The small, localized electrical current found at a single receptor might not have much effect all by itself. However, these electrical currents do spread, and, if enough receptors are activated at about the same time, then an electrical signal will be sent up the dendrite to the cell body of the neuron, then all the way down the axon to the synaptic knob and a transmitter will be released there. It is this action which takes place over and over that creates the electrical signals which carry information in and around the brain.

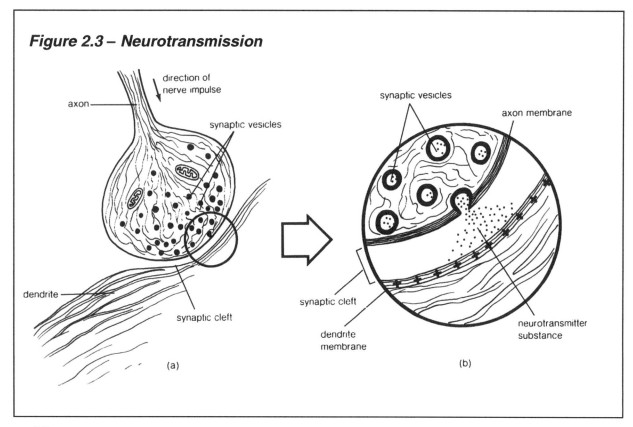

Figure 2.3 – Neurotransmission

Because activity in the nervous system occurs continuously and at a high rate, once a signal has been sent from one neuron to another, it is important to terminate that signal so that a new signal can be transmitted. Therefore, the thousands of neurotransmitter molecules released by a single electrical signal must be removed from the synaptic cleft. Two methods are used for this:

1. In some cells a process of reuptake takes place, in which the neurotransmitter is recognized by a part of the membrane on the neuron from which it was released. The releasing neuron then expends energy to recapture its released neurotransmitter molecules.

2. With other neurotransmitters, enzymes present in the synapse metabolize, or break down, the molecules. (This appears to be especially true with the neurotransmitter dopamine. It is this loss from metabolism, and the body's inability to reproduce all or part of the dopamine that appears to play a significant role in the addiction process.)

In either case, as soon as neurotransmitters are released into the synapse some of them are being removed or metabolized and never get to bind to the receptors on the other neuron. All neurotransmitter molecules may be removed in less than one hundredth of a second from the time they are released (see **Figure 2.3**).

Examples of Drug Actions

The reason for learning about the action and life cycle of a typical neurotransmitter molecule is so that you can understand how foreign molecules, that enter the brain in the form of psychoactive drugs, interact with and alter the normal mechanism for synthesizing, storing, releasing, binding, reuptaking, and metabolizing those neurotransmitters.

One drug that interferes with the synthesis of the neurotransmitters dopamine and norepinephrine is methyldopa, which is used to treat high blood pressure. Methyldopa looks like DOPA, one of the chemicals produced during the synthesis of dopamine and norepinephrine. In the autonomic nervous system, methyldopa is acted on by some of the enzyme molecules that normally act on DOPA. The eventual result is the creation of false norepinephrine (methylnorepinephrine), which the neuron then stores and releases along with some regular norepinephrine molecules. However, the false norepinephrine molecules do not activate the norepinephrine receptors in the heart or the blood vessels. Since norepinephrine usually causes increases in blood pressure, the false norepinephrine molecules reduce this effect.

The majority of drugs have their actions and effects at the receptors sites for neurotransmitters. Because the drug molecule resembles the natural transmitter in its structure, the receptor recognizes the drug molecule. Then the drug molecule may have the same type of action as the neurotransmitter itself does on those receptors. For example, the stimulant drug amphetamine is structurally similar to norepinephrine and dopamine, and one of its effects is to mimic norepinephrine at its receptors. In other cases a drug molecule may bind to the receptor but not activate it (for instance, not distort it so as to open an ion channel). If there are enough drug molecules and they have enough of a tendency to bind to the receptor, they may prevent most of the neurotransmitter molecules from having access to a receptor. The major tranquilizers such as chlorpromazine (Thorazine), which are used in treating psychotic behavior, act by blocking receptors for dopamine in the brain, thus reducing the activity in those dopamine pathways.

Some drugs work by slowing the removal of a neurotransmitter from the synaptic cleft, so that the molecules stay around and continue to bind to the receptors for a longer period than normal. The stimulant drug cocaine interferes with the reuptake of dopamine and norepinephrine, thus effectively increasing the duration and magnitude of each signal in those pathways. However, if too much neurotransmitter is left in the synapse so that the receptors are constantly bound to neurotransmitter molecules, information flow can cease. One of the most dramatic examples of this effect are the nerve gases, which are made up of molecules that bind irreversibly to the enzyme that normally breaks down the molecules of the neurotransmitter acetylcholine. With the enzyme thus tied up, the acetylcholine rapidly builds up in the synapse (there is no reuptake process for acetylcholine). Within minutes of exposure to a lethal dose of a nerve gas, respiration ceases and suffocation results.

The Brain

The brain (**Figure 2.4**) is the most complex structure in the nervous system. It is estimated that there are between 10 and 1,000 billion neurons contained within these tissues. It controls and integrates all human behavior. We are born with all the neurons we will ever have. These specialized cells cannot be reproduced by the body, so once a cell is destroyed it is gone for good. Cells can die during the natural aging process, and various drugs (especially alcohol and inhalant drugs) can destroy several thousand cells at a time. Fortunately, even if we killed off 100,000 neurons each day, we would still die with over 7 billion cells.

Changes in mood and behavior which result from the use of psychoactive chemicals can be best understood when one is aware of the major structural and functional units within the brain:

The Medulla Oblongata - the portion of the brain which connects with the spinal column. It is composed of ascending and descending nerve fibers. The medulla controls the vital centers of the brain - breathing (respiration center), blood pressure (vasomotor center), heart rate (cardiac center), contraction of heart musculature, function of the gastrointestinal tract, sleeping and waking, behavioral alerting, attention and arousal, coughing, sneezing, swallowing, and vomiting. Some drugs can so severely depress these centers that death may occur, often due to respiratory failure. Such drugs include opiates and barbiturates.

A complex network of nerve fibers within the medulla is known as the reticular formation. Part of this formation is known as the ascending reticular activating system, or ARAS. The ARAS is involved in controlling sleeping, waking, and behavioral alerting. It also serves as a filter for incoming sensory impulses. Alcohol and other depressants block normal activity in the ARAS, while amphetamines increase ARAS activity. If nerve stimulation into the ARAS is increased so rapidly as to intensify alertness beyond normal limits, hallucinations often occur. This can happen with both excess stimulation and severe depression of the medulla's ability to filter outside stimuli.

Pons - the pons is a rounded bulge on the underside of the brain stem which connects the medulla to the midbrain. It contains ascending and descending nerve fibers that relay impulses among the cerebrum, cerebellum and spinal cord.

Midbrain - the midbrain is a short segment of the brain stem located just above the pons. It contains bundles of nerve fibers that serve as motor pathways between the cerebrum and lower parts of the nervous system. Within the midbrain are housed the centers which control visual and auditory reflex as well as head movement. Psychedelic drugs work here to create visual or auditory hallucinations.

Cerebellum - a large, convoluted mass of nerve tissue located below the cerebrum and behind the pons and medulla. It serves as a reflex center, coordinating and integrating skeletal muscle movements. When depressed by psychoactive drugs, especially by alcohol intoxication, there is a loss of muscle coordination, staggering and a loss of balance.

Thalamus - located between the cerebrum and the mid- brain, the thalamus, in conjunction with the cerebral cortex, functions as a central relay station of the brain, where all incoming sensory impulses, except for smell, are channeled to the appropriate regions of the cerebrum. It is also responsible for interpreting sensations as either painful or pleasurable and is associated with body temperature and pressure.

Subthalamus - a small area situated beneath the thalamus and above the midbrain, which functions along with the cerebellum in controlling and coordinating motor activity.

Hypothalamus - located near the junction of the thalamus and midbrain, its function is to maintain homeostasis (body normal) by regulating various body activities and by linking the nervous system with the endocrine system. The hypothalamus has several important functions. It controls heart rate, arterial blood pressure, water and electrolyte (chemical) balance, hunger, body weight, movements and glandular secretions of the gastrointestinal tract, sexual behavior, and the synthesis of neurochemical substances that stimulate hormonal production by the pituitary gland. It also functions in the regulation of emotions and behavior. It is a prime site of action of many of the psychoactive drugs.

Limbic System - this system is actually the area where the cerebrum, thalamus and hypothalamus interconnect. It functions in the regulation of emotions, including fear, anger, pleasure and sorrow. It has a significant effect on behavior, especially those aspects which promote survival. Many tranquilizing drugs, especially Librium and Valium, depress the limbic system at doses far below the dose that depresses other brain functions. Rather than behavior being depressed, such drugs result in a tranquilizing and calming effect for the relief of anxiety.

Cerebrum - the largest and most complex part of the brain, which contains billions of neurons as well as nerve centers that have sensory, association and motor functions. It coordinates and interprets internal and external stimuli, and is the site of higher mental functions such as memory and reasoning. It is composed of two large masses or hemispheres, and is divided into various lobes. These lobes, and their functions, are:

Frontal lobes - Motor areas which control movements of voluntary skeletal muscles. Association areas control higher intellectual processes, such as concentration, planning, problem solving, and judgment of the consequences of behavior.

Parietal lobes - Sensory areas which are responsible for temperature, touch, pressure, and skin pain. Association areas function to help us understand speech and to use words to express thoughts and feelings.

Temporal lobes - Sensory areas responsible for hearing. Association areas used to interpret sensory experiences and in the memory of visual scenes, music and other complex sensory impulses.

Occipital lobes - sensory areas responsible for vision. Association areas involved in combining visual images with other sensory input.

The outermost area of the cerebrum, the cerebral cortex, is the gray, wrinkled matter that would be visible if you peered inside the skull and looked at the brain. Beneath the cortex are masses of white matter which contain nerve fibers, as well as more gray matter with neurons that relay impulses between the cortex and spinal cord. Many psychoactive drugs affect cerebral function either directly or indirectly. Stimulants increase neuron activity, sometimes to the point of hallucinations. Depressants decrease nerve cell function, affecting concentration as well as the perception of other stimuli.

For more detailed information on the anatomy of the brain, visit the Digital Anatomist Program of the University of Washington at: http://www9.biostr.washington.edu/da.html.

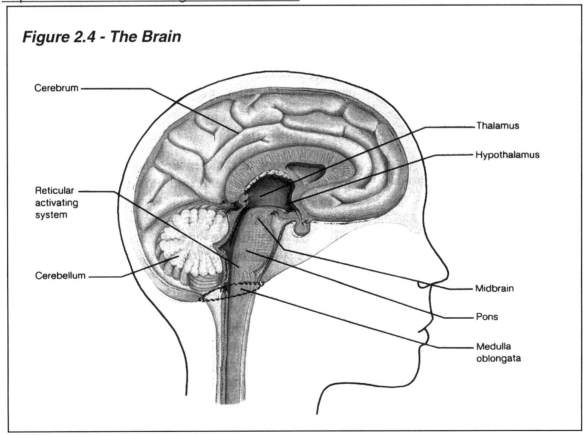

Figure 2.4 - The Brain

Cerebrum

Reticular activating system

Cerebellum

Thalamus

Hypothalamus

Midbrain

Pons

Medulla oblongata

Section 1, Chapter 3:
Drugs of Abuse - Alcohol

Brief Information about Alcohol

Alcohol is a central nervous system depressant

It is the most abused drug in our society - past, present, and probably future

It can cause intoxication, unconsciousness, and in some cases death

It is as potent as many of the illegal drugs and can be potentially fatal when mixed with other drugs

Drinking and driving are a particularly dangerous mix - impairment occurs well before the point of legal intoxication

Alcohol can cause severe damage to a developing fetus

Alcoholism is a very treatable illness

The Facts on Alcohol

Alcohol is the most widely used, the most widely accepted drug known to mankind, past, present and probably future. It is the simplest of all the psychoactive drugs, C_2H_5OH, (comprised of the most basic elements in nature, carbon, hydrogen and oxygen). It is also known as ethanol, ethyl alcohol, or ETOH. Alcohol is a depressant drug, similar to the anesthetic drug ether (if you were to take two molecules of ETOH, add heat [thereby driving away a molecule of water], you would be left with the compound $C_4H_{10}O$, ether).

Alcohol is the only nonmedical drug taken "only" by mouth. Whereas other drugs have multiple methods of use, alcohol is predominately a drug taken orally. You could indeed soak your feet in a vat of brandy and raise your blood alcohol level, but this is not something that could be done with much social grace. You can inject alcohol directly into the vein, but the physical harm this could cause might be life threatening. There are also reported cases of late-stage alcoholics who can no longer drink alcohol due to the destruction of their intestinal system and get drunk by giving themselves vodka "enemas," but again this would not lend itself to the social aspects of drinking.

Alcohol is the only drug with which a large number of those who use it do not become physically dependent upon it - it is estimated that 10% of the drinking population are dependent on alcohol - approximately 15 million Americans. Many other drugs have addiction rates as high as 50 to 60% of those who use them (e.g. marijuana, heroin and cocaine). Because of this fact, the majority of drinkers view alcohol as being relatively safe and tend to <u>not</u> view alcohol as a drug.

By definition, a drug is anything that alters the normal course of body functioning. A psychoactive drug is something that not only changes the way the body works, but also alters the mood, emotions, and psychological process of the brain. Alcohol, being a depressant drug, changes the physical body in many ways. It slows the heart rate, slows breathing. Itcan even put various body systems to sleep, causing them to stop functioning for a period of time. As alcohol depresses the brain, it not only causes changes in the physical activities of the brain, but by causing such depression it actually causes a change in feelings, emotions, and rational thinking.

Alcohol is the only drug that contains calories, yet these are wasted calories. Beers and wines are "clarified". This process removes the vitamins and nutritional value of the beverage. Many late-stage alcoholics who rely solely on alcohol for their daily food intake suffer serious medical problems related to malnutrition because of this.

Types of Alcohol

When we talk about alcohol, we are talking about beverage alcohol, ethanol. The common varieties of beverage alcohol are:

* Beer, both the regular and low-calorie "light beers", made from various cereal grain products such as barley, rye, corn and wheat. The process of making beer is referred to as brewing, in which grains are converted from a cereal broth starch to fermentable sugar, fermented, then stored and aged for a certain period of time. The resulting product contains from 3 to 6% alcohol by volume, with the typical "regular beer" (also known as lager beer) containing approximately 4% alcohol. Light beers generally contain about 3.25% alcohol. Malt liquor has a more delicate, aromatic flavor and contains between 4 and 5% alcohol. Ale, stout and porter beers are bitterer with a "full-bodied" taste and alcohol content between 6 and 7%.

- Wine, made from the fermented juice of grapes or other fruits. A variety of wine products exist on the market today. "Soda pop" wines (Boone's Farm, TJ Swann, etc.) have an alcohol content of about 8%. "Wine coolers" (fruit-flavored wines) range from 4% up to 9% alcohol by volume. Table wines (red, white, rose, sparkling or champagne) contain from 10 to 14%. Fortified wine (e.g. MD 2020) contain up to 21% alcohol. Dessert or cocktail wines (sherry, port, Madeira, vermouth) range from 15 to 24% alcohol by volume by adding neutral distilled spirits or brandy to table wines. Some of the cheapest table wines manufactured in Europe may also have alcohol concentrations of up to 24% by taking wine and "fortifying" it with distilled spirits or some other form of alcohol, most commonly methanol or "wood" alcohol.

- Distilled spirits, made from a variety of fermented mixtures that are heated in a still. Whiskey, vodka, gin and brandy are mixtures of cereal grains or fruits; Rum is derived from molasses, and tequila is made from the fermented juice of the mescal cactus plant. Alcohol has a lower boiling point than the other substances in the fermented mixture. It boils off first; the vapors are then collected, cooled and condensed. These distilled fluids have relatively high alcohol content, along with some water and flavors from the fermented mixture. The alcohol content generally ranges from 40-50%, or 80-100 proof (proof is twice the alcohol content). No distilled beverage can be 100% pure ethanol because alcohol is so toxic it will dilute itself with water from the air around it at about 98% pure.

Box A.1 - Proof

The belief behind the use of the term "proof" comes from sailors of old – to determine the purity of the rum they would buy, they would mix gunpowder with the rum and ignite it. Poor quality rum had more water and less alcohol, therefore the mixture would fizzle. If there was less water and more alcohol, the mixture would explode and go "POOF", thereby signaling a better batch of rum.

As noted, each major type of alcoholic beverage has different alcohol content. Nevertheless, a typical serving of any one of these beverages contains approximately the same amount of ethyl alcohol. Referred to as the "equivalent amount," each of the following drinks contains approximately one-half ounce of ethyl alcohol:

- 1-12 oz. can of beer, 4% alcohol content;

- 1- 4 oz. glass of wine, 12% alcohol content,

- 1 mixed drink containing 1 and one-quarter ounce of 40% liquor (80 proof).

Based on these equivalences, alcohol is alcohol, but a drink is not a drink. Beer is generally prepackaged in cans, but wine and distilled spirits are bottled, meaning the serving size will vary, depending on who pours them. It is important to recognize these equivalences, as alcohol intoxication is dependent upon the amount of ethyl alcohol consumed, not the number of drinks consumed.

Ethyl alcohol is the only form of alcohol that may be consumed with any degree of safety, but it is not the only form of alcohol. These additional types of alcohol are as follows:

- Methyl, Methanol, or wood alcohol (one carbon instead of two, CH_5OH) - drinking methanol can cause blindness because it leaves the body more slowly than ethanol (1/5 as fast) - found in cleaning products, shellac, and is used to make formaldehyde - when methanol is taken into the body, the breakdown element is actually formaldehyde, thus its toxic effect;

- Isopropyl, Isopropanol, or rubbing alcohol (three carbons instead of two, C_3H_5OH) - not as dangerous as methanol but causes serious gastrointestinal distress as well as damage to the lungs. Eight ounces of pure isopropyl can be fatal;

- Butyl alcohol (four carbons instead of two, C_4H_5OH). Made from the molasses of beets - used in lacquer, tanning products, film production;

- Denatured alcohol - ethyl alcohol with additives (methanol or acetone) to make it "undrinkable" - used industrially as a solvent.

The mistaken belief that the term alcohol refers to a single substance rather than a group of related substances has cost many lives in the U.S. Too often, people, especially young drinkers and chronic alcoholics, believe that a product that contains alcohol can be consumed for the purpose of intoxication. This belief can be fatal.

Some Basic Definitions

To understand how people use alcohol, it is first important to define some key terms:

"alcohol use" - the consumption of beverage alcohol within some socially prescribed or ritualistic context.

Societies around the world have many ways of defining the appropriate use of beverage alcohol. Indeed, the term "happy hour" is used to define social use of alcohol, and is also found in Webster's Dictionary. Alcohol is one of three social, legal (when one reaches the correct age) drugs typically associated with fun and good times (caffeine and nicotine are the other two). Wine with communion, champagne on New Years Eve, and a toast to the bride and groom are accepted rituals that center on alcohol.

"alcohol misuse" - unintentional or inappropriate use of beverage alcohol resulting in the impaired physical, mental, emotional or social well being of the user.

While many people consume one or two alcoholic drinks at a sitting with no ill effect, many consume to the point of intoxication. The very nature of alcohol as a toxin and an irritant tends to create physical distress at this level. Additionally, there are a variety of ways that moderate use of alcohol enhances the physical and psychological process, while more than this would actually become harmful. For example, many physicians recommend two glasses of wine with a meal to aid digestion. This amount of alcohol begins to irritate the stomach, causing the release of digestive enzymes and juices. Add food and the digestion is improved. However, three or more drinks would actually prevent the release of these enzymes, thus causing problems with digestion. Similarly, two drinks before bedtime would aid sleep. Three or more, however, actually prevents REM (dreaming) sleep, which is the part of sleep in which we recover.

"alcohol abuse" - deliberate or unintentional use of beverage alcohol which results in any degree of physical, mental, emotional, or social impairment of the user, the user's family, or society in general.

By definition, an adolescent who drinks any form of alcoholic beverage is abusing the drug, simply because of its illegal nature. But what about those who drink legally? Many people who drink socially have tolerance to alcohol, that is, they are able to drink certain amounts with seemingly no adverse effects. Legal intoxication (the level of alcohol in the system that society deems unacceptable to be driving or out in public) is .10 BAC (blood alcohol concentration). Most people reach this level between their third and fourth drink in one hours time. Yet this level does not mean that the person is out of control, falling down drunk. Many people continue to function, and many people drive in this condition. By the very nature of the law, this is alcohol abuse.

Because many people assume that a drink is a drink, there are many problems caused by unintentional abuse. Certain drinks, like Long Island Iced Tea, may actually have up to 7 oz. of distilled spirits. A single drink can cause intoxication above the legal level, resulting in DWI's, arguments, physical discomfort, psychological distress, and so on. Abuse of alcohol is common in our society, but does not mean that the drinker has the more serious problem of alcoholism.

> ***"alcohol dependence" - psychological and/or physical need for beverage alcohol - characterized by compulsive use, tolerance, and physical dependence manifest by withdrawal syndrome.***

This is but one possible definition of alcohol dependence, or alcoholism. One major problem with this definition is with regards to withdrawal syndrome. Many people who have both a physical and psychological need for alcohol do not suffer from physical withdrawal. This fact may allow them to continue to delude themselves into thinking that alcohol is not a problem for them, that they can take it or leave it. Alcoholics tend to return to drinking after going on the wagon, thus having "proved" that they don't have a problem. A more recent definition by the American Medical Association will be given in a later section along with further discussion on the definition of alcoholism.

Today, we know the following facts. Of the total adult population:

- 90% have tried alcohol during their lifetime;

- 60% are classified as regular drinkers (consuming beverage alcohol more than once a month);

- 40% are non-drinkers for a variety of reasons, including religious beliefs, family beliefs, ethnic background, and the like;

- 7% of the drinking population age 18 and older drink alcohol on a daily basis, yet these 7% consume almost half of all alcohol drunk in this country;

- 10 to 11% of those who drink develop the problem of alcoholism.

The History of Alcohol

Alcohol is the oldest drug known to mankind – as old as recorded history. It is made through the simple process of fermentation. All that is required is a source of sugar, yeast, and a source of heat. Probably when ancient man left a bowl of fruit or berries in the sun too long, alcohol was discovered (sugar from the fruit, yeast from the air, and heat from the sun). When he found his bowl now contained a smelly, foul tasting fluid, his curiosity took control. After consuming the liquid and finding the intoxicating effect of the beverage, he found that the beverage was actually quite appealing. From that point on, various sources of sugar were used to make this beverage, and over the years, various refinements took place. Wines and mead (fermented honey) were probably the first alcoholic beverages, with beers to follow.

12-14% alcohol by content is the most that Mother Nature can provide. At that percentage, alcohol kills the yeast, thereby stopping the fermentation process. It was not until the process of distillation was discovered that the percentage of alcohol in a beverage was increased. The use of a still was discovered by an Arabic physician, Rhazes, in the year 800 A.D. He was looking for a way to release *"the spirit of the wine"* when he found that alcohol had a lower boiling point than water. By heating the mixture, collecting, cooling, and condensing the vapor, the more purified form of alcohol was discovered. The term alcohol comes from the Arabic *"al kohl"* which means *"the essential spirit of wine."* Distillation increases the alcoholic content of a beverage by 400-500% (14% to 50%).

The process of distillation was brought to Europe in 1250 A.D. at the end of the Christian Crusades. Europeans coined the term *"aqua vitae"* or water of life for these distilled spirits. During the Middle Ages many of the more traditional forms of hard liquor were discovered. In France, distilling fruit wine made brandy. In England, grain products were distilled and flavored with juniper berries, producing the product gin. In Russia, potatoes were used to create a broth that was fermented and distilled, producing the beverage vodka (vodka is a Russian term which means *"little water"*). The Irish produced distilled spirits using fermented grain, and called the beverage *"usquebaugh"* (Irish for water of life), which was later shortened to the word *"whiskey."* In Scotland, a refinement was made on the process used by the Irish that resulted in the beverage scotch.

Beverage alcohol played an important role in the history of the United States. The Mayflower landed at Plymouth Rock because, as it says in the ship's log, *"We could not now take time for further search or consideration, our victuals having been much spent, especially our beer."* Alcoholic beverages were an important source of fluid and nutrition for early American settlers. The water supplies in America were not considered to be suitable for human consumption. Milk from farm animals was thought to transfer *"milk sickness"* (tuberculosis). Also, wines and beers were not clarified as they are today; so spent yeast (called *"vegamite"*) was not removed, thus providing additional vitamins and minerals.

Spanish missionaries brought grapevines to the New World, and before the United States was a nation, Spaniards were making wine in California. The Dutch opened the first distillery on Staten Island in 1640. A major trade route developed around the production of rum (fermented molasses). Molasses was imported to New England and converted into rum. Rum was then shipped to Europe and to the West coast of Africa. In Africa, rum was traded for slaves, who were then taken to the West Indies and bartered for molasses, with the process continuing.

Whiskey was produced during and after the Revolutionary War as a backwoods substitute for rum. It was also easier to transport distilled grain products rather than the grain itself. A packhorse could only carry four bushel of grain, but the equivalent of twenty-four bushels could be carried by the same packhorse in liquid form. Whiskey became a key trade commodity during the Revolutionary War. It was freely traded with France for guns and ammunition. After the war, it was a major form of barter here in the United States.

Different states became famous for their production and refinement of whiskey. Many church groups became actively involved in whiskey production to fund the parish activities. In one particular case, a parish in a county in Kentucky had a lucrative business as a whiskey distillery. However, one night a fire destroyed a warehouse where the oak barrels were kept. These barrels were used to hold the whiskey while it aged. Because of the fire, they were left with charred oak barrels and could not afford new ones. As a result, they stored their whiskey in these barrels, hoping to earn enough money to replace them. When the whiskey was tasted after some time, they found that the flavor was smoother than traditional whiskey. They continued to store and age whiskey in charred, oak barrels, and named the product after the county in which they lived, Bourbon County, Kentucky.

The importance placed on the production and use of alcoholic beverages caught the attention of the new government after the Revolutionary War. In an effort to raise funds to support the new government, Congress placed a tax on alcoholic beverages in 1791. Needless to say, this did not set well with the American populace. We had just fought a war over the issue of taxation, and alcohol was seen as too important by many people, especially those in the Southern states. It resulted in an uprising that has been called the Whiskey Rebellion of

1794. The uprising actually strengthened the still new government and established its authority regarding the right to make and enforce federal law, as well as its right to tax the populace. From that time forward, taxes on alcohol have been a major source of revenue for both the federal and state governments.

The Jefferson era was known for rampant problems associated with alcohol. Liquor was believed to be healthful, stimulating and nutritious. Whiskey was cheap, often less expensive than coffee or milk, and the early pioneers found that strong drink helped wash down poorly cooked, greasy and sometimes rancid food. The Temperance Movement was founded in this era with the goal of *"moderation"* in the consumption of beverage alcohol.

The movement began to increase their efforts during the 1830's, condemning *"excessive"* drinking and with the call for abstinence from distilled spirits (especially *"demon rum"*). To point out their belief that distilled spirits were bad, the movement promoted the claim that the word alcohol actually came from the Arabic term *"alghul"* which means ghost or *"evil spirit."*

By the middle of the century, consumption of distilled spirits was at an all time high - more than four gallons per person, per year, on average. Beer and wine were less popular, with consumption of beer at 2.7 gallons and wine at less than 1/2 gallon. A variety of groups, including the Independent Order of Good Templars of 1850, grew and expanded across the United States. These groups were convinced that society's evils were caused by the consumption of alcohol. These groups influenced the growth of the Women's Christian Temperance Union and the Anti-Saloon League. By 1869 the movement became known as the National Prohibition Party, advocating political action for the complete suppression of liquor by law.

Pressure was increasingly placed on state and federal officials, and in 1917 the 18th Amendment to the Constitution was passed by Congress. However, it took an additional two years for enough states to ratify the amendment, with Utah being the final state necessary for ratification. The law went into effect on January 1, 1920. The commercial manufacture and distribution of alcohol was outlawed as a result of Prohibition. It did not prohibit use, nor did it ban production for personal use, and it also allowed legal sales for medicinal purposes. During Prohibition, doctors were writing an estimated $40 million dollars worth of prescriptions for whiskey annually. Since fermentation is easy to do, many people began making alcohol at home. During this period, we also saw the rise of *"patent medicines,"* with products coming on to the market with alcohol contents of up to 50%.

Prohibition failed miserably in spite of the fact that during this time alcohol consumption dropped drastically and continued to be low for five years after Prohibition. Deaths related to cirrhosis of the liver dropped from 29.5 per 100,000 in 1919, to 10.7 per 100,000 in 1928. Crime rates did not increase in spite of the rise of organized crime groups who smuggled and manufactured alcohol, filling the supply for the demand. Admissions to mental hospitals for alcoholic psychosis declined during this period as well.

The 18th Amendment was repealed by 21st Amendment in 1933, which was introduced into Congress by Franklin D. Roosevelt. Roosevelt had used the repeal of Prohibition as a main issue in his campaign for the Presidency. The enthusiasm and excitement that greeted the return of alcohol to the masses, as well as the immediate return of the tax revenues generated by the sale of alcohol, would seem to guarantee that "the Great Experiment" would probably never be repeated.

The 1950's are generally referred to as the years of *"the Vodka Revolution."* The liquor industry began a marketing effort to entice more women to drink - studies suggested that women generally did not drink because they did not like the taste of most alcoholic beverages. The Heublein Company in Connecticut purchased the label of a foreign distillery (Smirnoff) and introduced a galaxy of new, alcoholic drinks using vodka. By 1974 Vodka had replaced Bourbon and Whiskey as the number one class of distilled spirits sold in the U.S.

Not to be outdone, the beer industry introduced *"light beers"* in the 1970's to increase the number of beer drinking women, and the wine industry introduced wine coolers in the 1980's for the same purpose (though both deny this emphatically). One of the sad outcomes of these events has been the increase in the number of women who experience the problem of alcoholism. Prior to this period, men outnumbered women in treatment by over 2 to 1. Today, the numbers are virtually identical.

The Business of Alcohol

The liquor industry is big business. Right now, Americans on average are spending in excess of $98 billion on beverage alcohol in bars, taverns, restaurants and take-out stores. Beer is the most popular form of beverage alcohol, followed by wine and distilled spirits. The percentages of beverages consumed are as follows:

- Beer = 47.7% of all alcohol consumed

- Wine = 39.7% of all alcohol consumed

- Distilled Spirits = 12.6% of all alcohol consumed.

Wine and distilled spirits have flip-flopped their percentages in recent years.

The average American typically consumes 20.8 gallons of beer, 2.73 gallons of wine, 3.89 gallons of distilled spirits for a total of 26.92 gallons of alcoholic beverages. (Contrast this to the average consumption of the following products: 20.4 gallons of milk, 10.3 gallons of tea, 18.5 gallons of coffee, 44.7 gallons of soft drinks, 11.5 gallons of juices, 28.3 gallons of bottled water, and 27.5 gallons of tap water)

The liquor industry itself is now spending almost $2 billion annually on advertising alone. Probably more of a concern, however, is the fact that so many adolescents and adults continue to view alcohol as a social drink, not the problem drug that it can be. Drinking is viewed as being a right of passage from adolescence to adult life. There are few places you can go today where alcoholic beverages are not served. There are also few people who recognize the physical and psychological changes that occur when they drink. Many people view alcohol as a stimulant, a quick *"pick me up."* Most people report that they actually act more responsibly, and also drive with greater care when drinking, in spite of medical evidence to the contrary. It's time that society take greater steps to educate people to the drug and its effects, with the hope that knowledge will help people know when to drink, when not to drink, and the problems that drinking can create.

Acute Effects of Alcohol

As a drug, alcohol affects anyone who drinks in virtually the same way. The differences that do occur can be traced to the differences in how alcohol is absorbed, distributed or eliminated by the body.

ABSORPTION - once alcohol is swallowed and enters the stomach, this process begins. Even though it contains calories, alcohol requires no digestion and passes readily through the walls of the stomach, where tiny blood vessels pick up the alcohol. Approximately 20% of alcohol consumed enters the blood in this fashion, while the rest must pass through the stomach into the small intestine to be absorbed. Anything that causes the alcohol to stay in the stomach will delay absorption.

Mixed drinks means the alcohol is more dilute, slowing the absorption. Food in the stomach will delay the absorption, but this in turn may mean that the peak blood alcohol concentration (BAC) won't be reached for several hours. Sweet mixes take longer to digest. The higher the concentration of alcohol, the faster the absorption. The rate of consumption also effects absorption - gulping drinks causes a more rapid rise of blood alcohol. Straight shots of liquor may paralyze the pyloric valve at the base of the stomach, causing it to stay closed and keep the contents of the stomach from moving. Carbonated mixes or sparkling wines may speed up the absorption process by relaxing the pyloric valve.

Mood and emotions may also affect the digestive process. Anger, fear, stress and fatigue can cause the absorption to be delayed, while happiness, excitement and the like can cause the process to speed up.

DISTRIBUTION - once alcohol reaches the bloodstream, it then travels to all body parts. Organs with higher concentrations of water, or dense networks of blood vessels and a richer blood supply (brain, kidneys, liver, and lungs) reach the same blood alcohol concentration (BAC) of the blood very rapidly. Intoxication occurs as the BAC increases faster than the body can remove the alcohol from the blood.

The BAC remains at a peak until equilibration occurs (the equal distribution of alcohol to all body tissues). Body water is the key to an increasing BAC. The more body water, the more dilute the alcohol, the lower the rise in BAC. Therefore women, with more adipos (fatty) tissues and less muscle (water) tissue, generally achieve higher BAC's and a greater level of intoxication, though the climb to this BAC level may be slower than their male counterpart. Body weight is also and important factor in BAC's - the more an individual weighs, the lower the BAC.

ELIMINATION - alcohol is a toxic product - the LD-50 (lethal dose) of alcohol is between 12-19 ounces of pure alcohol (the equivalent of about a fifth and a half of 80 proof spirits or a case of beer). The body will begin to eliminate it immediately upon intake. Since water is the primary mechanism used to dilute and eliminate alcohol, salivation will increase, diluting the alcohol entering the system. This is also why alcohol may burn going down - the cells of the throat burst to give up their water (this effect is most noticeable with straight spirits rather than beer or wine). Two to five percent of all alcohol is eliminated unchanged in urine, perspiration, and respiration. The remainder must be eliminated through the detoxification and oxidation process.

The liver is the only organ that can detoxify alcohol, that is, change ethyl alcohol to acetaldehyde, acetaldehyde to acetic acid. It detoxifies 95 to 98% of all alcohol that enters the system. Once the liver has detoxified alcohol to acetaldehyde, acetaldehyde to acetic acid, all of the organs that possess a dense network of blood vessels can burn (oxidize) the acetic acid. The liver oxidizes about 75% of the alcohol consumed; other body organs eliminate about 20% of the alcohol. The metabolic rate for elimination is typically about 1/2 oz. per hour. This may vary according to age, sex, time of day, race, health of the liver, other drugs in the system, food, menstrual cycle, and oral contraceptives. Since most of the equivalent drinks contain about one-half ounce of ETOH, a good rule of thumb is *"one drink leaves the body every hour."* The breakdown equations for the removal of alcohol are found in **Box A.2**.

BOX A.2 - Detoxification

DETOXIFICATION - the process of making chemical substances non-poisonous.

ETOH + ADH* (ALCOHOL DEHYDROGENASE) ———> ACETALDEHYDE

ACETALDEHYDE + AH* (ACETALDEHYDE HYDROGENASE) ———>   ACETIC ACID
* (ADH and AH are enzymes found in the liver)

OXIDATION - the process in which oxygen is combined with a chemical substance, creating heat.

ACETIC ACID + heat ———> H_2O, CO_2, CO ———>
 Out of System #

Breakdown elements eliminated by urination, perspiration, and respiration.

This process occurs at a fairly constant rate. Nothing, except intravenous administration of fructose or dialysis of the blood, will increase the speed of removal of alcohol. Exercise won't sober you up, just makes you a sweaty drunk. Coffee only allows the stimulant to have greater effect on the body, since the body can only remove one drug at a time (alcohol is always the priority drug when other drugs are present in the body), thus making you more alert but still drunk and impaired. A cold shower does nothing to change the metabolism, just make you cold and wet, but still drunk.

Acute Physical Effects of Alcohol

Alcohol does two things when it comes in contact with the body – it irritates and sedates. It is a depressant drug, not a stimulant. Its primary action is to cause central nervous system depression, which results in change of all body systems. It is an irritant, causing discomfort to all tissues it comes in contact with. There is no system that alcohol does not affect. Some systems show a greater effect than others, but all are impaired by the presence of alcohol in the body. The following are examples of the types of change caused by alcohol in the body.

> *Digestive System* - the lining of gastrointestinal tract is noticeably affected by the presence of alcohol. As an irritant, alcohol causes the stomach to produce a larger than normal flow of hydrochloric acid. This can create gas and indigestion as a short-term effect. Longer exposure to this effect can result in the development of ulcers. Low concentrations of alcohol also stimulate secretion of additional gastric juices that can aid the digestive process. Approximately two glasses of wine before a meal will enhance digestion. More than this amount, however, will actually inhibit these same enzymes, causing poor or improper digestion to occur.

> *Heart and Circulation* - low doses of alcohol initially increase the heart rate and blood pressure, then begins to sedate the heart muscle. As more alcohol enters the system, the pumping power of the heart is reduced and this condition can cause irregular heart rhythms that can be detected on an EKG reading. This effect occurs even in healthy drinkers, and is known as the "Holiday Heart Syndrome," since many social drinkers notice this change in heart rhythm during excess drinking at various holidays. Each year, many hundreds of drinkers report to emergency room settings, fearing a heart attack, but actually suffering from a bout of excess drinking.

Moderate doses of alcohol dilate blood vessels on the surface layer of the skin, causing reddening or a flushed look as well as rapid heat loss. Higher doses actually decrease internal body temperature and impair the body's ability to regulate heat. Many people mistakenly believe that shots of straight spirits during cold weather warm the body, when in actuality the body is losing heat, and the system is more at risk for frostbite and other cold weather conditions.

Each time you drink, red blood cells are killed by the toxic effect of alcohol. Three drinks actually kill as many platelets as the body produces in a given day. As these red cells and platelets float in the system, the body absorbs some and re-uses the components to make new blood cells. However, as the body is doing this naturally each day, the additional die off caused by alcohol cannot always be absorbed. Some of these cells will begin to aggregate in small vessels, particularly the capillaries, slowing or actually stopping circulation in some of these finer vessels. This may cause damage to the nerve endings, the heart, and muscles. This condition is known as *"sludge"* and is irreversible.

Recently, the wine industry has been promoting the health benefits of red wine on the heart. A "Sixty Minutes" story actually talked about the lower rate of heart disease in France as a result of drinking beaucoup red wine (Beaujolais). Apparently, a chemical in red wine called resveratrol, works to lower cholesterol. After the story, sales of red wine showed a 30% increase. The wine council in the United States also released a booklet for distribution at liquor stores called "The Benefit of Wine on the Human Heart."

What they don't tell you is that resveratrol is not unique to wine - you don't have to drink red wine to get the benefit - grape juice also has the chemical, which actually comes from the skin of the red grape. The concentration of the chemical is higher in red wine, but you add the negative benefits of the toxic effect of the ethanol. You just have to consume more juice for the same result, at least until modern science finds a way of concentrating the resveratrol in some other form.

Endocrine - there are noticeable effects on the system of glands and organs that secrete products that regulate our body. In the pancreas, insulin is secreted to control the level of blood sugar. Because of its irritant effect, alcohol causes the pancreas to release additional insulin, which depletes blood sugar, causing a condition known as hypoglycemia (low blood sugar). In mild cases, the symptoms are sweating, nervousness, weakness or confusion. More severe cases show symptoms of abnormal behavior, loss of consciousness, severe confusion or a coma. This is also a critical concern for adolescents who drink because blood sugar is necessary for the brain to function properly. If the blood sugar drops long enough, brain damage or retardation can occur. Children under the age of 10 would be most susceptible to this condition, affecting the intelligence and motor areas of the brain. Even small amounts of alcohol can begin the development of this condition. Alcohol use in any form by pre-teens and teenagers should be discouraged.

When the body suffers from a period of low blood sugar, it responds quickly to stabilize this condition. The liver will begin to produce additional supplies of glycogen, the type of sugar used by the body. Fat cells actually begin to accumulate in the liver because of this, and when the body then overproduces glycogen, a condition called hyperglycemia occurs. In a normal, healthy individual, we may see increased activity, bizarre behavior, and a dry-mouth. If a person is diabetic, coma or death can occur from this condition.

Anyone who drinks notices the increase in trips to the bathroom. This increased urine output is not caused by the effect of alcohol on the kidneys, nor is it caused by the increased fluids in the system. In the pituitary gland, a hormone is released that regulates the action of the kidneys. Alcohol causes the pituitary to release too little of this hormone. As a result, the kidneys produce a larger than normal amount of dilute urine to pass. Without the hormone to regulate the normal flow, the kidneys trigger a response to void, even when there is actually little urine to pass. This effect is most noticeable when BAC is rising.

In women, production of the hormone oxytocin is inhibited by alcohol. This hormone is responsible for stimulating contractions of the uterus, thus its absence may prevent natural labor and delivery. Alcohol has been used to control premature labor, but problems to the fetus caused by the mother drinking have made such use rare and actually discouraged. Oxytocin is also responsible for milk production in a new mother. Its absence can prematurely stop and dry up milk flow.

In men, alcohol lowers testosterone by inhibiting its production as well as causing the liver to remove testosterone more rapidly. Its absence may lead to impotence as well as reduced sperm production. Surprisingly, many problems related to infertility in both males and females are being found to be attributable to the use of various psychoactive chemicals, including alcohol.

Central Nervous System - being the largest water-carrying organ, the effects of alcohol on the brain are most noticeable. The brain is comprised of a variety of sections, each having control over various body aspects. As a depressant drug, alcohol sedates the brain from the outside in, from the cerebral cortex (the outermost area of the brain) to the medullar functions (the deepest brain functions). **Box A.3** shows the various levels of activity that are affected by the presence of alcohol in the brain. As each level is affected, the level below it begins to take charge of the body's control. Many of the behaviors that are exhibited are related to this anesthetic effect.

```
┌─────────────────────────────────────────────────────────┐
│                                                           │
│  BOX A.3 - Functional levels of the brain                 │
│                _____INTELLECT_____                       │
│                                                           │
│                _____EMOTION_____                       │
│                                                           │
│                __MOTOR FUNCTIONS__                         │
│                                                           │
│                ___SEMI-VOLUNTARY__                         │
│                                                           │
│                ____INVOLUNTARY____                        │
│                                                           │
│                _____VITAL_____                       │
│                                                           │
└─────────────────────────────────────────────────────────┘
```

The outermost level controls our intellect, our reasons and our moral codes. In normal situations, this allows us to make rational decisions and keeps us from doing or saying things that are inappropriate. As alcohol puts this area to sleep, we tend to say things we might otherwise not say. We tend to display behavior we do not usually exhibit. We tend to begin acting out in a more sexually provocative manner. For years, alcohol has been believed to be an aphrodisiac, a drug that enhances sexual behavior. Actually, it is the loss of our intellect and moral reasoning that allows us to act on impulses that we have.

The next level houses our emotions. As the intellect is put to sleep, the emotional level takes control. This is why so many people believe alcohol to be a stimulant drug. People who drink usually say and do things with more energy and with more emotion. This is not stimulation, but the fact that the underlying emotions now take charge of the body and the fact that the intellect that controls the flow of emotions is now depressed. This is why some people who drink get wild, crazy, laugh, and generally have a good time. It is also why some people who drink get angry, hostile and violent. The Latin saying, "*en vino veritas,*" – in wine there is truth – relates to the belief that alcohol allows us to see the true nature of the person when they drink. We may see a truer picture of the person inside, but the behaviors are still drug-affected.

The next level controls motor coordination. The effects of alcohol on this area are of great concern, particularly as it relates to driving. As little as two drinks begin to impair motor coordination. People begin to lose balance and judgment, and the ability to perform complex tasks (like driving) is greatly impaired.

At the level where the semi-voluntary systems are controlled, some very noticeable effects occur. The semi-voluntary systems are those that the body controls, but systems that we can consciously control as well. For example, swallowing and blinking are controlled by the body, but we can perform these tasks on command. When alcohol impairs this level, such actions stop. That is why people who drink too much wake up with a dry mouth and red eyes. The alcohol has caused the body to stop salivating, thus we don't lubricate the mouth. It has also stopped the eyes from blinking, thus they dry out and become red and irritated.

The involuntary systems are those which only the body controls, but are not necessary at all times to maintain healthy functioning. Such systems include the gastrointestinal system and the reproductive system. When necessary, the body can stop their actions in order to maintain vital functions. When alcohol sedates this level, the body simply pulls the plug on such systems until the alcohol is dealt with. This is why many people feel nausea and vomit after a period of heavy drinking. The foodstuff in the stomach was not digested appropriately, and the next morning, as the body works to bring the system back to work, it is confronted with a full or partially full stomach. Instead of digesting it, the stomach performs a routine house-cleaning chore and expels the food. In the reproductive system, not only is the libido affected, but the physical ability to perform sexually is also lost. The fact that alcohol reduces inhibitions makes many individuals feel more sexually inclined, but with enough alcohol, the physical ability to perform sexually is lost.

The final level of the brain houses controls for the vital functions - heart, respiration and the action of the brain itself. If alcohol were permitted to sedate this area, death would occur. The body has the ability to stop this process simply by creating a period of unconsciousness or coma if necessary. It would take a high tolerance to alcohol to allow this to occur, and many inexperienced drinkers simply pass out well before reaching this extreme. However, many adolescent drinkers, because of the way they drink to get drunk, put themselves at high risk for this effect. Each year, several hundreds of adolescents nationwide die as a result of acute alcohol poisoning.

The effect on the central nervous system can best be described by looking at the typical effects of alcohol by contrasting the number of drinks consumed with the corresponding blood alcohol concentration (BAC). **Box A.4** shows these effects.

Some important facts come out of this chart:

1. At the three-drink level, motor functions are already being impaired, even before a person reaches the point of legal intoxication. This effect is most pronounced if a person is engaged in more than one task at the same time, e.g. – driving a car and lighting a cigarette. There is also a noticeable decrease in the reaction to visual and auditory stimulus. In other words, being able to see a light turn red and stop safely is greatly impaired, or hearing a train whistle and being unable to realize that a train is coming could prove fatal.

2. At the five drink level, the senses are impaired physiologically - the eye's ability to discriminate intensities of light is reduced, and there is lower resistance to glare (it takes longer to readjust from bright light, thereby causing momentary blindness). With the ears, there is a lesser ability to distinguish sounds, especially high sounds, and a person would be unable to judge distance or direction based on sound.

3. At the seven-drink level, a BAC of .20 and above is considered a key diagnostic aid for alcoholism. While there is no one definitive indicator of alcoholism, a .20 BAC is highly significant in its correlation to alcoholism. It requires a high body tolerance to alcohol to achieve this level. The exception occurs with social drinkers who rapidly ingest large quantities of alcohol. Such a rapid rise may prove fatal to the non-alcoholic individual who lacks body tolerance. Over 400 adolescents die each year due to acute alcohol intoxication.

BOX A.4 - Drinking and Blood Alcohol Levels

# of drinks*	Blood Alcohol Concentration	Psychological/ Physical Effects
1	.02 - .03%	No overt effects, slight mood elevation
2	.05 - .06%	Feeling of relaxation, warmth; slight decrease in reaction time and in
3	.08 - .09%	Balance, speech, vision, hearing increased confidence; loss of motor coordination

.08% - Legal intoxication in United States; some countries have lower limits

4	.11 - .12%	Coordination and balance becoming difficult; distinct impairment of mental faculties, judgment
5	.14 - .15%	Major impairment of mental and physical control: slurred speech, blurred vision, lack of motor skills
7	.20%	Loss of motor control - must have assistance moving about; mental confusion
10	.30%	Severe intoxication; minimum conscious control of mind/body
14	.40%	Unconsciousness, threshold of coma
17	.50%	Deep coma
20	.60%	Death from respiratory failure

Figures based on 150-pound male. For each hour elapsed since the last drink, subtract 0.015% BAC, or approximately one drink.

* Number of drinks based on the following equivalences, each containing approximately one-half ounce of ethyl alcohol:1-12 oz. can of beer, 4% alcohol content; 1-4 oz. glass of wine, 12% alcohol content, 1 mixed drink containing 11/4 ounce of 40% liquor (80 proof).

Alcohol and the Effects on Sleep

For hundreds of years, alcohol has been used to aid in the process or sleep. Even today, many physicians prescribe two drinks of brandy before bedtime to help promote restful sleep. Indeed, alcohol is a depressant drug that causes sedation on the central nervous system. However, the benefits of alcohol on sleep are greatly exaggerated and actually counterproductive.

There are two primary mechanisms that determine our ability to sleep. The first is called the Reticular Activating System (RAS). The job of the RAS is to tell the body when to be alert and active, and it supplies neurochemicals necessary to activate the system. It is a function of the medulla oblongata. Basically, the RAS is our internal clock that knows when we need to wake up and be active, and for what period of time we need to maintain this activity.

Throughout the day, the RAS is triggering messages to the brain that keep a steady flow of energy to help keep our bodies working. As we approach our period of sleep, the RAS begins to slow the release of neurochemicals, allowing the body to begin slowing down in anticipation of sleep. Being a sedative drug, alcohol causes the RAS to function improperly. If the alcohol is present at the time we are normally winding down towards sleep, alcohol may indeed enhance this process. But what happens when this occurs prior to the body's schedule? Basically, as the alcohol sedates the brain, the RAS is forced to slow down in spite of its desire to keep us alert. Then, as the alcohol leaves, the RAS actually works slightly harder than before. It begins triggering a wake up call to the body. A person may then find it difficult to get to sleep, or to stay asleep. We then find that the next day, we are not as alert as we are normally. Even if we spent a full night in bed, we wake up tired.

A more noticeable problem occurs with the second mechanism, the actual sleep mechanism of the body. Sleep is a very complex mechanism. There are several important steps in the sleep process that can impact our ability to recovery during sleep.

The first part of sleep is known as Stage 1 sleep - the period between sleep and wakefulness. It generally lasts from 2-10 minutes in most individuals. This stage makes up 5% of our total night's sleep. From there, we go into Stage 2 sleep - non-dreaming sleep (NREM). This accounts for 40% to 60% of our night's sleep, and is a medium deep and restful sleep. Stage 2 sleep deepens to Stages 3 & 4, which are characterized by specific EEG patterns known as delta waves. This is the soundest sleep we have, which lasts from a few minutes up to 2 hours (elderly to infants) and occurs only during the first 1 to 3 hours of sleep. It accounts for 10 to 20% of our total night's sleep.

Normal sleep almost always begins with NREM sleep. As a person falls asleep, he or she enters Stage 1, then Stage 2, which is followed by Stages 3 & 4. After sleeping for about 70 to 100 minutes, REM sleep occurs (dreaming sleep), which is usually brief (5 to 15 minutes), then alternates with NREM sleep for remainder of night, on cycles of about 90 minutes, with the dreaming periods getting longer as the night progresses. REM constitutes 20 to 25% of total night's sleep, or 90 to 120 minutes per night. REM sleep occurs in approximately 3 to 5 regularly spaced periods.

REM sleep is important, because it is only during REM sleep that the body recovers, physically as well as psychologically. Alcohol can prevent the body's recovery that occurs during REM sleep because REM sleep is suppressed. After a bout of heavy drinking, REM sleep does not occur. This is why so many people, after a night of heavy drinking, report sleeping "like the dead" but wake up tired and irritable. One such episode may actually take upwards of two days before the body is able to recovery fully.

In those people who suffer from alcoholism, REM rebound occurs in recovery as the body forces itself to dream, causing REM sleep to increase dramatically for several days or weeks. It may be associated with vivid dreams or nightmares, usually dreams of using or being intoxicated. On occasion, some depressant drug users also experience so called "daymares" - disturbing nightmare-like visualizations that occur while the person is awake and cause a panic reaction.

Blackouts

Blackouts are probably one of the most curious effects of drinking. A blackout is an amnesia-like period often associated with heavy drinking. It does not mean passing out or losing consciousness. It does not mean psychologically blocking out the memory of an event or situation. Many people assume it to be a sign of alcoholism. Indeed, research does seem to suggest that blackouts more frequently occur with late stage alcoholism than at any other time in the drinking history. However, a blackout can occur to anyone who drinks. It is not always dependent on quantity of alcohol consumed, or on the tolerance to alcohol.

The exact mechanism of a blackout is not fully understood. What we do know is that at some point, alcohol in the body causes the memory-processing activity of the brain to stop working for some period of time. It may only last a few seconds or for several hours, even after the alcohol has left the system. When this occurs, the person continues to function normally, and all other aspects of the brain remain relatively intact. Only the memory of that period of time is lost. People walk, talk and act normally. They may drive a car, fly a plane, or perform surgery without obvious impairment.

Many people may suffer a blackout and never know it. It is only when confronted by another, or when they wake up and don't know where they are or how they got there, that they realize a blackout has occurred. Social drinkers who experience this effect are generally quite concerned and frightened by this. They associate the episode with some specific pattern of drinking, and change the drinking pattern so as to not experience this again. Alcoholics, on the other hand, assume that memory loss is a part of drinking, and in spite of problems or concerns about such episodes, find that they are not able to change the occurrence, especially if they have no desire to stop drinking.

The Hangover

The Germans call it *"katzenjammer"* (wailing of cats), the Italians *"stonato"* (out of tune), the French *"gueulu de boise"* (woody mouth), the Norwegians *"jeg har tommeermenn"* (workmen in my head) and the Swedes *"hont i haret"* (pain in the roots of the hair). While the names may be different, the feelings and effects are universal. If you drink too much, you pay the price with the effects of a hangover.

The hangover - a familiar after effect of over-indulgence that causes fatigue combined with nausea, upset stomach, headache, thirst, depression, anxiety, general malaise, sensitivity to sound, and ill temper. Hangovers aren't much fun. They aren't very well understood, either.

There is no simple explanation for what causes the hangover (other than having had too much to drink). The symptoms are usually most severe many hours after drinking, when little or no alcohol remains in the body.

Theories for why the hangover occurs include the following: accumulation of acetaldehyde (a metabolite of ethanol), dehydration of the tissues, poisoning due to tissue deterioration, depletion of important enzyme systems needed to maintain routine functioning, an acute withdrawal response, and metabolism of the congeners in alcoholic beverages.

Dehydration does seem to have a significant role in creating the hangover effect. When an individual drinks, the body loses fluid in two ways through alcohol's diuretic action (diuretic - a drug or substance that increases the production of urine): (1) the water content, such as in beer, will increase the volume of urine, and (2) the alcohol depresses the center in the hypothalamus of the brain that controls release of a water-conservation hormone (antidiuretic hormone). With less of this hormone, urine volume is further increased. Thus, after drinking heavily (especially the highly concentrated forms of alcohol), the person suffers from thirst. However, this by itself does not explain all of the symptoms of hangover.

The type of alcoholic beverage you drink may influence the hangover that results. Some people are more sensitive to particular congeners than others. Congeners are natural products of the fermentation and preparation process, some of which are quite toxic. Congeners make the various alcoholic beverages different in smell, taste, color, and, possibly, hangover potential.

Beer, with a 4% alcohol content, has only a 0.01% congener level, whereas wine has about 0.04%, and distilled spirits have congener levels of between 0.1% and 0.2%. Gin, being a mixture of almost pure alcohol and water, has a congener content about the same as wine, whereas a truly pure mixture of alcohol and water (vodka) has the same congener level as beer. Whiskey, scotch and rum have higher congener contents, thereby causing people who drink them to often suffer from the hangover effects.

Those who market alcohol beverages often take advantage of peoples' suffering to promote their products. One such example is SKYY vodka. It is typically marketed as an extra-pure form of vodka that will ease the hangover effects without sacrificing the taste.

Aging distilled spirits and wine does not decrease the level of congeners but, in fact, increases their level about threefold. For example, some drinkers have no problem with white wine but an equal amount of some red wine will give them a hangover. Also, there is little evidence that mixing different types of drinks per se causes a worse hangover. What is more likely is that more than the usual amount of alcohol is consumed because of trying a variety of drinks.

A study titled "Experimental Induction of Hangover," provided support for two factors that appear to contribute to the hangover syndrome:

(1) the higher your BAL, the more likely you are to have a hangover, and

(2) with the same BAL, bourbon drinkers were more likely (two out of three) than vodka drinkers (one out of three) to have a hangover.

This fits with the belief that some hangover symptoms are reactions to congeners.

Still other factors contribute to the trials and tribulations of the "morning after the night before."

1. The nausea and upset stomach typically experienced can most likely be attributed to the fact that alcohol is a gastric irritant. The consumption of even moderate amounts causes local irritation of the mucosa covering the stomach.

2. It has been suggested that the accumulation of acetaldehyde, which is quite toxic even in small quantities, contributes to the nausea and headache.

3. The headache may also be a reaction to fatigue. Fatigue sometimes results from a higher than normal level of activity while drinking. Increased activity frequently accompanies a decrease in inhibitions, a readily available source of energy, and a high blood sugar level.

4. One of the effects of alcohol intake is to increase the blood sugar level for about an hour after ingestion. This may be followed several hours later by a low blood sugar level and an increased feeling of fatigue.

How should you treat a hangover? A common technique is to take a drink of the same alcoholic beverage that caused the hangover. This is called "taking the hair of the dog that bit you" (from the old notion that the burnt hair of a dog is an antidote to its bite). This might help the person who is physically dependent, the same way giving heroin to a heroin addict will ease the withdrawal symptoms.

This behavior is not unknown to moderate drinkers, either - it may work to minimize symptoms, since it spreads them out over a longer period of time. The "hair of the dog" method seems to work by depressing the centers of the brain that interpret pain or by relieving a withdrawal response in the central nervous system. Also consider the psychological factors involved in having a hangover; distraction or focusing attention on something else may ease the effects.

Another folk remedy is to take an analgesic compound like an aspirin-caffeine combination before drinking. Aspirin would help control headache; the caffeine may help counteract the depressant effect of the alcohol. These ingredients would have no effect on the actual sobering-up process. Products like aspirin, caffeine, and Alka-Seltzer can irritate the stomach lining to the point where the person may actually feel worse.

There is no evidence that the "surefire this'll-fix-you-up" remedies are effective. The only "surefire" remedy is the time proven method of an analgesic for the headache, rest, and time to recovery from the drinking episode.

Alcoholism

One of the greatest health problems in society today is the problem of alcoholism. It is currently the third leading cause of death in our society, behind cancer and heart disease. It is the most extreme form of problem drinking in our society today. Yet many people do not understand the problem, or don't understand the term.

Many people define alcoholism in relationship with how they themselves drink. If I only drink on weekends, then an alcoholic is someone who drinks every day. If I only drink beer, then an alcoholic is someone who drinks hard liquor. If I only drink after noon, then an alcoholic is someone who drinks in the morning. If I only drink six drinks at a sitting, then an alcoholic drinks more.

Part of the problem in understanding this illness is that many professional groups fail to define it adequately. The American Psychiatric Association uses the following definition:

> Alcoholism: this category is for patients whose alcohol intake is great enough to damage their physical health, or their personal or social functioning, or when it has become a prerequisite to normal functioning.

The World Health Organization uses the following definition:

> Any form of drinking which in extent goes beyond the tradition and customary dietary use, or the ordinary compliance with the social drinking customs of the community concerned, irrespective of etiological factors leading to such behavior, and irrespective also of the extent to which such etiological factors are dependent upon heredity, constitution, or acquired physiopathological and metabolic influences.

Alcoholics Anonymous, while having no official definition, generally cites the concept of Dr. William Silkworth, a friend of AA:

> An obsession of the mind and an allergy of the body. The obsession or compulsion guarantees that the sufferer will drink against his own will and interest. The allergy guarantees that the sufferer will either die or go insane. An alcoholic is a person who cannot predict with accuracy what will happen when he takes a drink.

The American Medical Association in 1956 defined alcoholism as follows:

> Alcoholism is an illness characterized by preoccupation with alcohol; by loss of control over its consumption, such as to usually lead to intoxication or drinking done by chronicity; by progression and by tendency to relapse. It is typically associated with physical disability and impaired emotion, occupational and/or social adjustments as a direct consequence of persistent and effective use.

Because of the reliance we have in using the AMA to define alcoholism as a disease, yet the difficulty which exists in using this definition, a 23-member multidisciplinary committee of the National Council on Alcoholism and Drug Dependence and the American Society of Addiction Medicine recently conducted a 2-year study of the definition of alcoholism in light of current knowledge and concepts. As a result, a new definition has been made which is:

1) scientifically valid,

2) clinically useful, and

3) understandable by the general public.

The following is the currently accepted definition, as published in The Journal of the American Medical Association, August 26, 1992 (reprinted by permission):

> Alcoholism is a primary, chronic disease with genetic, psychosocial, and environmental factors influencing its development and manifestations. The disease is often progressive and fatal. It is characterized by impaired control over drinking, preoccupation with the drug alcohol, use of alcohol despite adverse consequences, and distortions in thinking, most notably denial. Each of these symptoms may be continuous or periodic.

> "Primary" refers to the nature of alcoholism as a disease entity in addition to and separate from other pathophysiologic states that may be associated with it. It suggests that as an addiction, alcoholism is not a symptom of an underlying disease state.

> "Disease" means an involuntary disability. Use of the term involuntary in defining disease is descriptive of this state as a discrete entity that is not deliberately pursued. It does not suggest passivity in the recovery process. Similarly, use of this term does not imply the abrogation of responsibility in the legal sense. Disease represents the sum of the abnormal phenomena displayed by the group of individuals. These phenomena are associated with a specified common set of characteristics by which certain individuals differ from the norm and which places them at a disadvantage.

"Often progressive and fatal" means that the disease persists over time and that physical, emotional, and social changes are often cumulative and may progress as drinking continues. Alcoholism causes premature death through overdose; through organic complications involving the brain, liver, heart, and other organs; and by contributing to suicide, homicide, motor vehicle accidents, and other traumatic events.

"Impaired control" means the inability to consistently limit on drinking occasions the duration of the drinking episode, the quantity of alcohol consumed, and/or the behavioral consequences.

"Preoccupation" used in association with "alcohol use" indicates excessive, focused attention given to the drug alcohol and to its effects or its use (or both). The relative value the person assigns to alcohol often leads to energy being diverted from important life concerns.

"Adverse consequences" are alcohol-related problems or impairments in such areas as physical health (e.g., alcohol withdrawal syndromes, liver disease, gastritis, anemia, and neurological disorders), psychological functioning (e.g., cognition and changes in mood and behavior), interpersonal functioning (e.g., marital problems, child abuse, and troubled social relationships), occupational functioning (e.g., scholastic or job problems), and legal, financial, or spiritual problems. Although alcoholism may theoretically occur in the absence of adverse consequences, we believe that the latter are evident in virtually all clinical cases.

"Denial" is used in the definition not only in the psychoanalytic sense of a single psychological defense mechanism disavowing the significance of events but more broadly to include a range of psychological maneuvers that decrease awareness of the fact that alcohol use is the cause of a person's problems rather than a solution to those problems. Denial becomes an integral part of the disease and is nearly always a major obstacle to recovery. Denial in alcoholism is a complex phenomenon determined by multiple psychological and physiological mechanisms. These include the pharmacologic effects of alcohol on memory, the influence of euphoric recall on perception and insight, the role of suppression and repression as psychological defense mechanisms, and the impact of social and cultural enabling behavior.

It is easy to see why much confusion exists when you look at these definitions. That is why many professionals in the field of chemical dependency today accept the following as a working definition:

> Alcoholism is a chronic, progressive, potentially fatal illness characterized by tolerance <u>and</u> the loss of control over the consumption of beverage alcohol.

Two key issues separate alcohol use/abuse from alcoholism:

1. Tolerance - the need for greater amounts of alcohol to obtain the same desired effect, and

2. Loss of Control - the inability to predict with accuracy what will happen when a person takes a drink. This does not mean getting drunk. Many alcoholics drink without getting drunk. It means not knowing if one drink will be all that is consumed, or if one drink turns into many.

Social drinkers will also develop tolerance, but even with tolerance, they generally lack the ability to consume large quantities of alcohol without noticeable intoxication and effects. Alcoholics tend to look quite normal, even with heavy amounts of the drug.

Section 1, Chapter 4:

Drugs of Abuse - Other Depressants and All-Arounders

The Facts on Sedative-Hypnotics

Sedative-hypnotic drugs are substances that induce depression on the central nervous system. Because these drugs tend to create a calming effect, relax muscles, and relieve feelings of tension, stress, anxiety and irritability, they are commonly referred to as sedatives. At higher doses or if the compound has greater potency, sedatives also produce drowsiness and eventually a state resembling that of natural sleep. Drugs that have a sleep- inducing effect are called hypnotics. Often these drugs are referred to as tranquilizers, sleeping pills, antianxiety drugs, or simply sedatives.

The sedative-hypnotic category of drugs is the single largest category of drugs we will discuss. These drugs are synthetic compounds, prescribed for use under medical supervision. These drugs also have the shortest history of all the drugs in this text. With the exception of potassium bromide, marketed in the 1860's as a treatment for epileptic seizures, the entire history of this category spans less than 100 years. Also, the effects of the drugs in this category vary greatly, depending on their impact on the central nervous system. As a result, we will discuss these drugs by breaking them down into three smaller categories. These categories are:

    1. Barbiturates,

    2. Minor Tranquilizers, and

    3. Other sedative-hypnotics.

For each category we will look at the specific drugs, their history, and the physical effects.

Brief Information about Barbiturates

Barbiturates are central nervous system depressants

They are used to treat anxiety, induce sleep, and control seizures

These drugs can cause intoxication similar to that caused by alcohol

An overdose of barbiturates can cause death by respiratory failure or by seizure

Barbiturates can create both physical and psychological dependence - withdrawal from barbiturates can be dangerous and even fatal

Combining barbiturates with other depressants can cause a synergistic effect that can produce death

Barbiturates

Barbiturates are the single largest category of drugs. There is over 2,500 compounds in this category of which only about 50 derivatives of barbituric acid are marketed for medicinal use, with fewer than 15 in common use today.

The first barbiturate was synthesized in 1862 by Dr. A.H. Bayer of the Bayer Company in Germany. The name barbiturate probably comes from the fact that Dr. Bayer was a great fan of the German military. He undoubtedly used soldiers as volunteers to obtain urine specimens to isolate the uric acid. St. Barbara is the patron saint of the military, so he apparently named his discovery after "Barbara's urates," thus the name barbiturate. In 1903, these barbiturates were first used in medical practice under the name of barbital.

For the next fifty years, a variety of barbiturates were discovered and used in medical practice. They were primarily prescribed to calm nervous individuals, reduce anxiety, or, with larger doses, to induce sleep. Barbiturates can be broken into three smaller categories:

1. Ultrashort-acting barbiturates with rapid onset of effects that are used as surgical anesthetics. These drugs produce anesthesia within one minute of intravenous administration. Due to their rapid onset and brief duration of effect (from fifteen minutes to three hours), these drugs are rarely abused. Examples of ultrashort-acting barbiturates include thiopental (Pentothal®), hexobarbital (Evipal®), and thiamyl (Surital®).

2. Short-intermediate acting barbiturates, used mostly as calming and sleep agents, have an onset of effect from fifteen to forty minutes after oral administration. The duration of effect may last up to six hours, making these compounds highly abusable. These drugs are sold in capsules and tablets, as well as in liquid form or suppositories. Examples of short-intermediate acting barbiturates include secobarbital (Seconal®), amobarbital (Amytal®), pentobarbital (Nembutal®), butabarbital (Butisol®), and aprobarbital (Alurate®). Additionally, amobarbital and secobarbital are combined and sold under the trade name of Tuinal®.

3. Long-acting barbiturates have onset times of up to one hour after use, but their duration of effects is up to sixteen hours. Their slow onset generally discourages abuse. These drugs are used as sedatives, hypnotics, and anticonvulsants (to control seizures), though the non-barbiturate drug Dilantin® is more commonly used as an anticonvulsant today. Examples of long-acting barbiturates include phenobarbital (Luminal®), mephobarbital (Mebaral®), and metharbital (Gemonil®).

Physical effects of barbiturates are similar to alcohol intoxication with a reduction of tension and anxiety, relaxation, slower reaction time, and loss of motor coordination. In addition, these drugs have a high addiction potential as well as a high dependence potential. If physical dependence occurs, withdrawal symptoms occur if the drug is abruptly stopped. Withdrawals from these drugs produce anxiety, tremors, nightmares, insomnia, vomiting and seizures. Medical detoxification is necessary with dependence on barbiturates since the results are often life-threatening.

A high overdose potential exists with the use of barbiturates. As previously noted in other sections of this text, all drugs have what is known as an LD-50, the lethal dose that would kill 50% of the people who took that dosage. As tolerance develops whenever a drug is taken for a long period of time, drug overdoses would occur more commonly if not for the fact that the LD-50 generally increases with tolerance to the drug. This is not the case with barbiturates. As the tolerance increases and as an individual takes more of the drug for the desired effect, the LD-50 remains fairly constant. At some point, the user takes a dosage that exceeds the LD-50 with often fatal results. This is especially true when the barbiturate is combined with alcohol. This combination is responsible for more overdose deaths than any other drug combination known.

Since the early 1970's, barbiturates have been steadily replaced by the use of safer benzodiazepines that are less toxic, do not depress the respiratory centers of the brain, and do not produce sleep as often. There continues to be a large illicit market for the drugs, however, and overdose deaths continue to be quite high.

Brief Information about Minor Tranquilizers

Minor tranquilizers are depressant drugs used to treat anxiety and insomnia

More prescriptions are written annually for tranquilizers than all other prescription drugs combined

Low doses of tranquilizers make the user feel calm, relaxed and drowsy

High doses of tranquilizers can cause loss of coordination and stupor

Tranquilizers can cause both physical and psychological dependence

Tranquilizers are legal when prescribed by a physician, however, they have a high, illicit resale value on the street

Minor Tranquilizers

This group represents the single most popular group of prescribed drugs known today. The term minor tranquilizer, however, is quite misleading. There is nothing minor about the effects and problems associated with these compounds. When compared to the drugs known as major tranquilizers (Thorazine®, Mellaril® and the like), there is a marked difference in effect. Major tranquilizers are often known as "antipsychotic" drugs because they relieve symptoms of a psychotic nature, such as schizophrenia and paranoia. Minor tranquilizers function more like sedative-hypnotics and are useful in treating anxiety and neurotic conditions. A better term for these compounds would be "antianxiety agents."

The first minor tranquilizer was the drug meprobamate, first marketed in the mid 1950's under the names of Miltown® and Equanil®. Initially used as a muscle-relaxant, it was quickly found to have antianxiety effects. During its first month on the market, only about $7,500 worth of the drug was sold. As more and more physicians began prescribing the drug for anxiety, the drug quickly rose to over $500,000 in sales per month within six months.

The success of the drug was related to the fact that it worked to effectively reduce anxiety without causing sedation. It was also less toxic than barbiturates. With excessive use, however, both physical and psychological dependence developed. Its success, however, opened the door for newer, more potent compounds.

In 1960 a new drug was introduced as a more potent, better drug than meprobamate. The drug was chlordiazepoxide (Librium®). It was widely prescribed and marketed as a "wonder drug" to reduce anxiety and allow individuals to cope with the rigors of everyday life. Indeed, the drug has lower dependence potential than meprobamate, and has great value in providing relief from the withdrawal effects of alcohol and other sedative-hypnotics.

Three years later, the first cousin to Librium® was introduced. The drug, diazepam (Valium®) was chemically similar, but 5 to 10 times more potent. Since being introduced, Valium® has been one of the most popular drugs prescribed by physicians, being consistently in the top fifteen drugs sold world-wide. Its place as the number one minor tranquilizer has only been recently replaced by the drug alprazolam (Xanax®).

With the success of Librium® and Valium®, every major pharmaceutical manufacturer around the world began experimenting in an effort to find an antianxiety drug for their stable of drugs. As a result, a variety of compounds (referred to as benzodiazepines) have been introduced in the last forty years, including clorazepate (Tranxene®), lorazepam (Ativan®), oxazepam (Serax®), prazepam (Centrax®), temazepam (Restoril®), alprazolam (Xanax®), triazolam (Halcion®), and flurazepam (Dalmane®). Restoril®, Halcion® and Dalmane® are marketed as sleeping agents, while the others listed are prescribed as anti-anxiety agents.

Controversy continues to exist about the use and benefit of the benzodiazepines. Medical science has been quick to prescribe these drugs for anxiety, stress, and tension, preferring to medicate such complaints rather than encourage patients to seek other, more healthy solutions to such disorders. Also, medical professionals have often been too slow in recognizing the addictive quality of these drugs, as well as other dangerous side-effects.

One such situation involves the drug Halcion®. Touted as being "the perfect sleeping pill," the drug experienced a phenomenal rise in popularity. Introduced in 1982, the drug rocketed to annual sales of more than $250 million by 1988. In 1990, American pharmacists alone filled more than 7 million prescriptions for the drug. In the mid-80's, numerous reports began to surface, suggesting such side effects as amnesia and agitation. Further bad press was encountered when a Utah woman killed her mother while on the drug, blaming the side effects for her actions. The case was settled out of court by the manufacturer, Upjohn, while denying that the drug was to blame for the murder.

In October of 1991, the British Department of Health banned the sales of the drug in Britain. They cited evidence that the drug had a much higher frequency of side effects than previously reported, especially episodes of depression and memory loss. Halcion® works on the limbic system of the brain, which plays a major role in the development of sleep and emotions. While the drug only lasts a few hours in the body, the body's response to its leaving the system is generally the very anxiety that was being treated. This rebound phenomenon is especially true at higher doses. Episodes of violent behavior were also reported as a result of high doses, mixing the drug with alcohol, or long periods of use.

There is no doubt that when taken as prescribed, these drugs work effectively to reduce tension and anxiety. However, the likelihood of misuse and abuse of these drugs is quite high. All of these drugs entered the market with great promise and reports of being "safe, non-addicting" substances. With continued use over a prolonged period, these drugs are quite addicting, and withdrawal symptoms can be quite severe and even fatal with heavy use. Additionally, when combined with alcohol or other central nervous system depressants, the combination is quite deadly.

Physicians cannot prevent patients from misusing such drugs. However, it is important that patients be better educated about the side effects and other dangers of using them. Additionally, it is important that alternatives to stress and anxiety, such as biofeedback, stress reduction, self-hypnosis, meditation and other such methods also be explored as safe alternatives to the use of these products.

Brief Information About Other Sedative-Hypnotics

The euphoriant effect of depressant drugs continues to make them popular on the streets

Because of the problems with the drug Halcion ®, Chloral Hydrate ® is again becoming a popular sleep medication

Quaalude's popularity has not gone away in spite of the fact that it is no longer legally manufactured

It is estimated that 3% of high school seniors have tried Quaalude

Other Sedative-Hypnotics

This category is a "catch-all" category of sedative and hypnotic agents that are nonbarbiturate or nonbenzodiazepines. It includes some of the oldest drugs in the entire category, and also one of the more interesting drugs of abuse. Each drug will be described below:

Paraldehyde® is one of the oldest known sedative-hypnotics. It was discovered in 1829 though not put into use until 1882. It is a compound similar to acetaldehyde, a breakdown product in the detoxification of alcohol. It is a fast acting hypnotic, inducing sleep in 15 to 20 minutes. However, it quickly produces tolerance and physical dependence. Also, it tends to decompose when stored. The resulting product, when consumed, creates a very complex and difficult to manage state of intoxication. Paraldehyde® has an unpleasant taste and leaves the user with a disagreeable breath odor. It has little clinical use today, though was a popular drug for detoxification of alcohol in the 1940's and 50's.

Chloral Hydrate® is another of the older sedative-hypnotics, discovered in 1862, but has continued use today. It was quite popular for the following reasons:

1. It produces less of a "hangover" effect than most other sedative-hypnotics.

2. It affects REM sleep less negatively.

3. When used for sleep, it produces little or no respiratory depression.

4. Its likelihood of producing physical dependence is less than most other sedative-hypnotics.

Chloral Hydrate® is a liquid marketed in syrups and soft, red gelatin capsules. It induces sleep within 30 minutes of use. The sleep generally lasts about five hours. At one time, the drug was notorious as the "Mickey Finn" drug. When mixed with alcohol, the sleep effect occurs more rapidly and for a longer period of time. In the late 1800's, the drug and alcohol combination was used to shanghai potential crewmen for sailing excursions to Hawaii and the Far East. Chloral Hydrate® drops would be slipped into someone's drink, they would quickly fall asleep, and would awaken many miles at sea.

Chloral Hydrate® continues to be prescribed today for sleep. It is especially popular with older populations, and is widely used in nursing home facilities.

Ethchlorvynol (Placidyl®) was introduced in the mid-1950's as a "safe, nonaddicting alternative to the barbiturates." It creates sleep rapidly, but in spite of the claims, it quickly creates tolerance and physical dependence. Side effects, including dizziness, blurred vision, facial numbness, and mild euphoria commonly occur. Also, the drug is quite lethal when combined with alcohol.

Glutethimide (Doriden®, Dormtabs®) was introduced in 1954, again as a safe alternative to barbiturates. In fact, its dependence potential is as great, and the drug has other, more dangerous effects. High doses of the drug, especially once tolerance has developed, often result in seizures and even coma. When an overdose level is taken, the drug is often fatal. This is due to the long duration of action, making it very difficult to reverse overdoses. As a result, it is considered many times more hazardous than barbiturates. It is still in use in medicine today, and is quite popular on the street, especially in combination with codeine. This combination is referred to as "loads" and users claim it produces a high similar to heroin.

Methaqualone (Quaalude®) has been one of the more popular street downer drugs over the past twenty years. It was originally synthesized in 1951 and used in India for the treatment of malaria. It is a fast-acting sedative drug that eventually induces sleep. It was introduced in the United States in 1965, again as a safe, effective, nondependency producing drug to replace barbiturates. By the late 1970's it was the most frequently prescribed sedative-hypnotic.

Because of its alleged safety and widespread availability, the drug was quite popular on the street. Known as "ludes, "sopors," "lemmons," and "714's," it was touted as an aphrodisiac. This effect primarily occurred as a result of the initial sedation caused by the drug, which would then lessen inhibitions by sedation of that portion of the brain that controlled reasoning. With inhibitions lessened, people found they were more inclined towards sexual acting-out than normal. As the drug effects leveled out before continuing towards sleep, people found that unlike alcohol or other sedative drugs, the ability to perform sexually was not lost.

In spite of the belief of their safety, methaqualone has numerous side-effects, including loss of motor coordination, dizziness, and severe hangovers. Tolerance and both physical and psychological dependence occur. Overdose is common and occasionally fatal, especially when combined with alcohol. Without medical supervision, withdrawal is often deadly.

Due to the reputation and problems associated with the drug, the Lemmon Company stopped production of the drug for use in the United States in 1983 after the Federal Government severely limited its medical use. It is still manufactured in the form of an antihistamine, however, and sold in other countries, including Mexico and Canada, under the name Mandrax®. As a result, the drug continues to be available on the street and continues to be quite popular.

Brief Information about Narcotics

Narcotics are derived from naturally occurring substances, and can also be manufactured synthetically

Narcotics, or opiates/opiods, are drugs that cause sedation and euphoria by causing depression of the central nervous system

Narcotics are used medically to relieve pain, suppress cough, and control diarrhea

Some narcotics, such as heroin, have no medical use, and any possession or use is illegal

Overdose can cause death by respiratory depression

Narcotics can cause both physical and psychological dependence

Narcotics impair a person's ability to drive

These drugs can damage the developing fetus

Narcotic abuse is linked with the spread of AIDS due to the use of needles

The Facts on Narcotics

The term narcotic is used to describe the family of drugs that are used as an analgesic (pain-relieving) compound and occasionally to induce sleep. Sometimes referred to as opiates (because they are derived from the opium poppy plant or made synthetically to have the same actions as morphine, a major ingredient in opium), this family of drugs may actually be broken into three classifications:

1. Natural occurring compounds, such as opium, morphine, and codeine;

2. Semisynthetic compounds, such as heroin and hydromorphone (derived by modifying the chemicals produced in opium);

3. Synthetic compounds made entirely in the laboratory, such as Demerol, methadone and Darvon.

Narcotics have a wide range of medical use, including pain relief, treatment of diarrhea, and cough relief. These compounds are also highly addicting. Heavy use of such drugs, or even occasional use over a long period of time will produce tolerance, psychological need and physical dependence, as evidenced by the appearance of withdrawal symptoms upon cessation of use.

Narcotic drugs also depress central nervous system functions. They produce euphoria in the user, provide a sense of well-being, and produce drowsiness that may lead to sleep. Unlike other CNS depressants, there is usually no loss of motor coordination or loss of consciousness with their use, unless the dose is large or the person is ill or fatigued.

The exact effect of most narcotics depends on the individual - if the person is in pain and taking narcotics, they tend to feel less anxious and find relief from pain. If the person is taking the drugs for reasons other than pain-killing, the same dose would produce mental distress, such as fear and nervousness, as well as nausea and possibly vomiting.

Natural Occurring Compounds

Opium is the main source of the natural occurring narcotic drugs. It is produced from the poppy, Papauver somniferum. This poppy is cultivated in many countries of the world, including Turkey, India, China, Thailand, Laos and Mexico. Opium is derived from the unripe poppy pod, prior to the development of seeds. The method of extraction is centuries old - a knife is used to slit the pod; a milky fluid oozes from the seedpod and allowed to bleed overnight; the next day, the dried product is scraped off the leaves, producing a brownish gum known as crude or raw opium.

The dried opium is generally smoked and the vapors inhaled. Occasionally, the crude product is ingested orally. The compound was widely used throughout the world until the beginning of the twentieth century. The drug is not as popular today, due to the strength of action and bulk of the compound, which makes dealing the drug difficult. It is legally imported for the production of other legal derivatives, and is illegally imported for the manufacture of heroin.

Morphine is the main alkaloid ingredient of opium, having a purity of from 4 to 21%. It was isolated from opium in 1803. It is used in medicine as a sedative and a pain killer, being one of the most effective pain killers known (ten times the pain killing properties of opium). Large doses have been used to provide anesthesia in heart surgeries because unlike anesthetic drugs, morphine has no depressant effect on the cardiovascular system. Morphine is also used to control post-operative pain.

Morphine is available in tablets and injectable form. A white crystal form is illegally available on the street. The drug is usually administered IV or IM for the greatest effect. When used non-medically, the drug produces a euphoric high, a sense of well-being, and drowsiness. Tolerance and physical dependence may develop rapidly, depending on the dose and frequency of use.

Codeine is another alkaloid found in opium, though most codeine is manufactured from morphine. Being a derivative of morphine, codeine has pain-killing properties, though it is only about one-tenth as potent. Its greatest effect is as an antitussive (cough-relief), though it is also sold, combined with aspirin or acetaminophen as a pain-killer. Though potentially addictive, it rarely causes problems when taken under medical supervision for a short time. Because of this, it is the most widely used naturally occurring narcotic in medical practice.

Semisynthetic Compounds

Hydromorphone, more commonly known as Dilaudid®, is a chemical variation of morphine. It is sold in tablet and injectable form. It is a shorter-acting and more sedative drug than morphine. Its potency is two to eight times that of morphine, making this compound a highly addicting drug.

Oxycodone is chemically derived from codeine, though it is more potent. It produced potent euphoria, analgesia and sedative effects and has a dependence potential similar to morphine. One of its major advantages in medicine is that, unlike many other powerful narcotics, it retains its potency when administered orally. As a result, it is both widely used and abused. It is generally sold as a combination drug, either as the drug Percodan® (oxycodone, ASA, and caffeine), or as Percocet® (oxycodone and acetaminophen).

Heroin is a chemical derivative of morphine, initially introduced as a "cure" for opium and morphine addiction. It is the most popular narcotic of abuse in the United States, accounting for 90% of all cases of abuse. It is one of the more powerful addicting compounds known to man. Available over-the-counter until 1914, the drug has no medical use today, though is being investigated for possible use as a pain-relieving drug with cancer patients. It is a white powder, with a bitter taste that may also be found in a variety of other colors from black to dark brown, depending on the impurities from the manufacturing process.

Heroin is usually mixed into a liquid solution and injected directly into a vein, or injected just under the skin. It can also be snorted or taken orally when in powdered form. Because of its chemical structure, heroin reaches the central nervous system more rapidly than morphine. Shortly after using the drug, it creates a "rush" of intense euphoria. The faster the drug reaches the central nervous system, the greater the rush. After the effects of heroin wear off, the addict usually has eight to twelve hours in which to find the next dose before withdrawal symptoms appear.

Heroin acts primarily on the CNS and parasympathetic nervous system producing drowsiness, mental clouding and reduced ability to concentrate. Many people report a reduction in feelings of aggression, depressed appetite and sex drive, and a general decline in the level of physical activity. Moderate doses can cause feelings of body warmth, heaviness of the limbs, itchiness (of the nose), constipation, and constriction of the pupils. Larger doses lead to sleep, decreased blood pressure and slowed breathing. Tolerance develops quickly to most of these effects, so addicts are able to take many times the normal lethal dose without significant effects. At this stage, the drug is taken solely to prevent withdrawal.

During early use, there is a great danger of accidental overdose. Combining other drugs with heroin also presents a greater risk for physical problems. A popular combination of heroin and cocaine, called a "speedball" is responsible for a great many deaths, especially some well-publicized cases from Hollywood (e.g. John Belushi). Additionally, heroin is typically cut with other adulterants in order for the dealer to turn a higher profit on sales. Such substances as powdered milk, quinine, starch, sugar, Ajax – any white powdered substance – have been found in batches of the drug. These adulterants can create their own risk to physical health and well-being.

Heroin also possesses a high potential for psychological and physical dependence and may lead to social deterioration, reduced motivation, or infection from the use of non-sterile needles. Because of the user's rapid development of tolerance, larger and larger doses are required to get high. This often results in the user turning to criminal acts to maintain their addiction.

Synthetic compounds

In contrast to the opiate drugs derived either directly or indirectly from naturally occurring compounds, the synthetic narcotics are derived entirely with the laboratory setting. Indeed, the majority of investigation that is occurring in pharmaceutical laboratory settings is in an effort to develop either analgesic compounds that retain the pain-killing properties of morphine (without the dangers of tolerance and physical dependence) or anesthetic agents. As a result, there are several compounds that have been discovered to relieve pain. The more commonly used drugs are described below.

Meperidine (trade named Demerol®) was the very first synthetic narcotic ever produced. Discovered in the early 1930's, it has similar properties of morphine, though less potent, and unlike many of the narcotic drugs, it retains much of its potency when administered orally. Tolerance to the drug's effects develops gradually; therefore it can be used effectively for several weeks at the same dose. In spite of this, both physical and psychological dependence can develop with long-term use. Because of its use in medical settings, meperidine is the most commonly reported drug of abuse among physicians and nursing professionals who are dependent on narcotic agents.

Methadone (trade name Dolophine®) is a synthetic narcotic, similar in potency to morphine. It was first synthesized by a German chemist in 1943 as a substitute for morphine, which was unavailable in Germany during World War II. It has been widely used in the treatment of heroin addiction, and is also useful in managing the withdrawal effects of narcotic drugs. The compound has a longer effect, lasting from 24 to 36 hours, and is highly effective when administered orally. Thus, the drug can be given once a day in detoxification or maintenance programs. Additionally, the drug appears to block the effects of other narcotic drugs, making methadone a valuable tool in the treatment of heroin and other narcotic addictions. As with other narcotics, the drug produces physical and psychological dependence, though such effects develop more slowly and with seemingly less severity.

Buprenorphine is an opioid partial agonist. This means that, although buprenorphine is an opioid, and thus can produce typical opioid agonist effects and side effects such as euphoria and respiratory depression, its maximal effects are less than those of full agonists like heroin and methadone. At low doses buprenorphine produces sufficient agonist effect to enable opioid-addicted individuals to discontinue the misuse of opioids without experiencing withdrawal symptoms. In October 2002, the Food and Drug Administration (FDA) approved buprenorphine monotherapy product, Subutex®, and a buprenorphine/naloxone combination product, Suboxone®, for use in opioid addiction treatment. The combination product is designed to decrease the potential for abuse by injection.

Buprenorphine carries a lower risk of abuse, addiction, and side effects compared to full opioid agonists. In fact, in high doses and under certain circumstances, buprenorphine can actually block the effects of full opioid agonists and can precipitate withdrawal symptoms if administered to an opioid-addicted individual while a full agonist is in the bloodstream.

Propoxyphene (trade name Darvon®) was first marketed in 1959 for the relief of mild to moderate pain. It is only one-fifth to one-tenth as potent as codeine, making it only slightly more potent than two aspirin. In spite of this, it continues to be one of the most prescribed analgesics, with more than 30 million prescriptions written each year. It is favored by physicians because it is less dependence producing than other narcotics. The greatest concern with the drug is the synergistic effect when combined with alcohol - it ranks second to barbiturates in prescription overdose deaths.

Pentazocine (trade name Talwin®) was synthesized in 1961 and introduced as an effective analgesic without the dependency problems associated with other narcotics. In reality, while it does have analgesic properties greater than Demerol®, it is also a weak narcotic antagonist, that is, it can precipitate mild withdrawal symptoms when administered to narcotic dependent users. Talwin has become a popular drug of abuse because of the euphoria it produces as well as pleasant sensations of floating. Many abusers compare the drug to the effects of marijuana. Additionally, when mixed with an over- the-counter antihistamine, pyribenzamine, and injected IV, the drug produces heroin-like effects. This combination is known as T's and Blues.

OxyContin is the brand name for a semisynthetic opioid analgesic prescribed for chronic moderate to severe pain. Its active ingredient is oxycodone, which is also found in drugs like Percodan® and Tylox®. It is more potent than hydrocodone and has a greater potential for abuse. Oxycodone is also found in at least 45 other drugs on the market, including Percocet®. OxyContin contains between 10 and 160 milligrams of oxycodone in a timed-release tablet. Painkillers such as Tylox® contain 5 milligrams of oxycodone and often require repeated doses to bring about pain relief because they lack the timed-release formulation.

Since hitting the U.S. market in 1996, OxyContin has become one of the most popular -- and most abused -- medical painkillers. More than 7.2 million prescriptions were dispensed annually since 2001, according to the company. It is a time-released narcotic which provides continuous relief for up to 12 hours. Like other opioids, it works primarily through interaction with the mu opioid receptors, especially in the brain and spinal cord. It produces a euphoric effect. \

The History of Narcotics

The use of the poppy plant for pain relief, sleep, medicinal and recreational purposes dates back to at least 3000 B.C., when ancient Egyptians cultivated what they called the "joy plant." Ancient Greek, Roman and Arabian cultures all were aware of the benefit and healing power of the plant, as well as the addictive nature of its use. The actual method of extracting raw opium from the poppy plant was well known by the first century A.D.

For the next several centuries, smoking opium was wide-spread in both the Middle East and the Far East. Much of the spread of opium use is credited to the Arabs, who cultivated and traded the plant because of its medicinal benefits. Opium was also an alternative recreational drug to alcohol, whose use was forbidden by the Koran. Arab traders introduced the drug as far west as North Africa, and as far east as China.

The drug was not immediately popular in China, however. Introduced in the eighth century, widespread use did not develop until 400 or 500 years later. Records suggest that the Chinese probably first identified the problems that opium addiction could cause. During this same time period, the drug became popular in India. The Indian government actually controlled the cultivation and sales of opium. Revenue from the sales of opium were an important source of government funds.

Medicinal and recreational use of opium was common in Europe by the seventeenth century. Initially, it was the physicians who praised its ability to treat a variety of ailments. Many others also used the drug recreationally, mixing opium with alcohol (known as laudanum), enjoying the euphoria and dream-like state it induced. A profitable trade was established between the Orient and Great Britain around opium, which resulted in the Opium War (1839-1842) when the Chinese emperors tried to outlaw the sales and use of opium in China. British victory resulted in widespread and free trade in opium.

Until 1803, opium was the sole narcotic product available. Then a German pharmacist, Friedrich Serturner, isolated the principal active ingredient of opium. Because this new drug tended to create sleep in the user, he called the product morphine, named after Morpheus, the Greek god of sleep. Even though the hazards of opium use were well known, the dangers of morphine use were not established for many years. In 1832, a second compound, codeine, was discovered. Less potent than morphine, codeine was found to have great benefit as a cough suppressant. Due to a tuberculosis outbreak in the United States, codeine was widely used to prevent the spreading of the illness.

Throughout the nineteenth century, opium, morphine and codeine use were widespread in the United States. The practice of smoking opium was introduced by Chinese immigrants who migrated to the West Coast of America. Opium dens were established for Chinese immigrants, and many American citizens, especially women, frequented the smoking dens. All three products were also being used more commonly than most people recognized. During this era, a variety of over-the-counter "patent medicines" were being sold, claiming their ability to cure anything from "bowel disorders" to "liver ailments" to "cures for melancholia." Opium, morphine, codeine, alcohol and even cocaine were primary ingredients in such products as "Dr. King's Discovery for Consumption," "Winstar's Balsam of Wild Cherry," "Mrs. Winslow's Soothing Syrup," and "Birney's Catarrh Cure."

The invention of the hypodermic syringe in 1853 took the problem of narcotic addiction to new heights. With its invention, the problems associated with morphine began to increase, and the addictive quality of the drug became more understood. During the Civil War, morphine was freely used in battlefield hospitals. Intravenous morphine was an effective way of providing relief from battlefield wounds. Because morphine and codeine also had a side effect of causing constipation, both were freely used to control dysentery encountered in the crowded, unsanitary army camps. Addiction to morphine increased dramatically, and was often referred to as the "soldier's disease."

During the last half of the century, it was estimated that over one million individuals in the United States were addicted to narcotic drugs. The government began pressuring medical science to develop a cure for this increasing problem. In 1898 A.H.Bayer, founder of the Bayer Company in Germany, introduced a new product that he claimed to be a "heroic drug" which could cure addiction to opium, morphine and codeine. Bayer had been working with a process known as "diacetylation." He had used this process on salicylic acid to make the product less hazardous to the stomach, and marketed his "diacetylated salicylic acid" under the name of "Bayer Aspirin®." He figured that if he could make this product less harmful to the body, then he could also make morphine less harmful in the same fashion. He marketed diacetylmorphine under the trade name of "Heroin" and found that indeed many morphine and opium addicts stopped using those drugs with no problem. It took medical science several years to recognize that those addicted had simply switched one type of addiction for addiction to a more potent narcotic agent.

By the turn of the twentieth century, the United States suffered from an unprecedented drug problem. Not only were all of the narcotic drugs legal and available over-the-counter, but other drugs such as cocaine, marijuana and alcohol were unrestricted as well. It was not until passage of the Federal Food and Drug Act of 1906 that the government began to take steps to control the availability of such products. The Act did not outlaw such drugs, but did require that over-the-counter products be labeled so the consumer was aware of the ingredients they contained.

The federal government finally began controlling access to such drugs with the passage of the Harrison Narcotics Act of 1914. This law established a mechanism of recordkeeping for the importation, manufacture, distribution, sale and prescription of narcotic drugs. It outlawed non-medical use of heroin, severely limited the amounts of opium, morphine, and cocaine used in over-the-counter products, and placed many of the drugs in the hands of medical science to prescribe in a responsible manner.

One major problem that the Act created, however, was that it required narcotic addicts to be registered, and forbided physicians from prescribing narcotics to known addicts. These policies effectively ended the medical profession's involvement in treating drug dependence for nearly forty years. A modification of the Act eventually outlawed heroin in 1924, and coupled with the absence of medical assistance, many addicts turned to the "black market" to maintain their dependency. With the introduction of new, synthetic narcotics drugs, and the growing black market activities of drug dealers, narcotic addictions continued to be a national problem.

During the decade of the 60's, the treatment industry began to establish programming for treatment of drug dependence, with the initial focus being placed on alcohol and narcotic drugs. Unfortunately, with the growing crime rate associated with drug abuse, many efforts towards treatment and rehabilitation were ignored. Instead, both federal and state governments relied on tougher laws to control and punish narcotic abusers. During this period, new, more exotic drugs became readily available, and heroin and other narcotic use peaked during the early 1970's and began to fall. While never disappearing completely, narcotic drug use began to lose favor, particularly due to the fear of illness related to the IV use of narcotics. Interdiction efforts by the federal government were also successful, and the importation of illicit narcotics fell sharply during the 1980's. As we enter the 90's, however, we are again seeing a rise in importation and street trafficking of heroin and other narcotics. It remains to be seen whether or not this trend will continue.

The Physical Effects of Narcotics

After taking a narcotic drug, a person generally becomes less active and finds it difficult to concentrate. They generally become drowsy and may indeed fall asleep for a short period of time. Many users experience a pleasant "high" or euphoria. This effect is the primary reason many users continue to use and abuse narcotics over a long period of time. Many people throughout history have commented on the pleasure associated with drug use, and one author, Thomas de Quincey, wrote the following passage about morphine in 1822:

> *But I took it; and in an hour - oh, heavens! What a revulsion! What an upheaving, from its lowest depths, of the inner spirit! What an apocalypse of the world within me! That my pains had vanished was now a trifle in my eyes; this negative effect was swallowed up in the immensity of those positive effects that had opened before me in the abyss of divine enjoyment thus suddenly revealed. Here was a panacea for all human woes; here was the secret of happiness about which philosophers had disputed for so many ages, at once discovered; happiness might now be bought for a penny and carried in the waistcoat pocket; portable ecstasies might be had corked up in a pint bottle; and peace of mind could be sent down in gallons by the mail coach.*

Not everyone who uses a narcotic drug experiences such effects as described above. Some effects may be less intense with lower potency narcotics such as Talwin®. Some people may not experience euphoria at all, even after using morphine or heroin. They may instead become anxious or frightened. Nausea may occur, which would block the euphoric effects, and is particularly common in novice users. Vomiting often occurs with high doses.

Heart rate and blood pressure are not greatly affected by narcotic drugs. However, the circulatory system is slow to adjust when a person gets up from sitting or lying down. As a result, the user may become dizzy or light- headed. Narcotics have a powerful effect on the respiratory system. With large doses the respiratory centers of the brain are impaired and breathing simply stops. Respiratory failure is the main cause of overdose deaths.

By far the greatest benefit of narcotics is their ability to control pain. Their analgesic actions is stronger and better than any other category of drugs. Narcotics work to change pain sensations as well as to change the response the body has to the pain sensation. While they diminish both, their best effect is on the response the body has to the pain. Many people who use narcotics for pain management report still being aware of the pain, but that it no longer bothers them.

Common side-effects of narcotic use include drowsiness, depressed respiration, nausea, vomiting, increased acid flow in the stomach, constriction of the pupils, and constipation. Tolerance generally develops rapidly with continued heavy use. The withdrawal syndrome is quite pronounced. Indeed, the addictive nature of the most drugs has been measured in relation to the addiction and withdrawal effect of morphine.

Symptoms of withdrawal include watering eyes, nasal discharge, uncontrollable yawning, and heavy sweating. This stage is followed by an agitated sleep. Agitation continues upon awakening and is accompanied by loss of appetite, depression, dilated pupils, and tremor. At the peak of the withdrawal (36 to 72 hours after cessation of use) symptoms include alternating chills and flushing, insomnia, continued loss of appetite, violent yawning and sneezing, "gooseflesh," vomiting, nausea, abdominal cramps, elevated heart rate and blood pressure, pains in the muscles, bones and joints, muscle spasms and jerking motions. The severity of the effects declines in 5 to 7 days. The effects are generally not fatal, unlike alcohol or barbiturate withdrawal, and a user can actually go "cold turkey" (abrupt cessation of use) with no major concern. However, with the availability of medications to lessen the withdrawal effect, especially methadone, the suffering associated with withdrawal can be avoided.

Narcotic Analogs (Designer Narcotics)

Narcotic analogs are designer narcotics made to mimic the effects of narcotic drugs. They were initially produced to skirt existing drug laws, but a change in federal drug laws in 1986 made all analogs of controlled substances Schedule I drugs under the Controlled Substances Act. Today, these designer drugs are sold on the streets as more powerful substances than their illicit counter parts. They are sold under the names China White, Persian White, Mexican Brown, and "new heroin".

There are two primary narcotic analogs - fentanyl analogs (alpha-methylfentanyl (AMF), which is 3-methyl fentanyl, parafluoro fentanyl), and meperidine analogs that include MPPP (1-methyl-4-propionoxy-piperidine) and PEPAP (1-(2-phenylethyl)-4-acetyloxypiperidine).

AMF

AMF was probably the first substance to be called a designer drug. It is an analog of the drug fentanyl, a highly potent narcotic analgesic sold under the trade name of Sublimaze ®. It is an extremely potent compound which has little difference between the dose that produces euphoria and the one that is fatal. AMF has been responsible for a great many deaths due to overdose.

The effects of AMF are fast-acting, but short-lasting. With a typical dose, the use generally will experience the following effects: euphoria; mental confusion; a feeling of warmth; dry mouth; dizziness; drowsiness; constriction of the pupils; constipation; and nausea.

Low doses can also cause rigidity of the muscles, especially those that assist with breathing. As a result, many users suffer from breathing difficulties, including respiratory failure. An additional problem has been found with neurological processes. AMF appears to attack the basal ganglia area in the brain, resulting in a Parkinson's like syndrome even after limited use. As a result, many users suffer from tremors of the hands when they are at rest, difficulty speaking or swallowing, drooling, muscular rigidity which includes a mask-like face, and a shuffling walk. Such damage is permanent and requires the use of medications to control the effects.

MPPP and PEPAP

MPPP first appeared on the streets in the late 1970's. It is a potent analog of the drug meperidine (Demerol ®). The effects of MPPP, as well is its cousin PEPAP, are still not fully known, but presumed to be comparable, though more potent, than meperidine. These effects include: euphoria; disorientation and mild mental confusion; dizziness; drowsiness; visual disturbances; and slight respiratory depression. Such effects may last up to three hours.

Higher doses result in sleep, inability to concentrate, increased respiratory depression, dilation of the pupils, muscle twitches, and tremors.

Probably the greatest danger associated with MPPP is the frequent presence of a compound know as 1-methyl-4-phenyl-1,2,3,6-tetrahydropyridine (MPTP). MPTP is a toxic by-product created when excessive heat or acid is used to make MPPP. Studies reveal that MPTP has no narcotic properties, but instead is metabolized by the brain into a toxic that destroys nerve cells. The result is again Parkinson's like disease as described with AMF.

PEPAP has been found to have a similar by-product known as PEPTP. It produces another neurodegenerative disease similar to Huntington's Chorea. This illness causes spasmodic movements of the limbs and facial muscles as well as progressive deterioration of brain tissue, with a resulting loss of mental functioning. Again, this effect is not reversible.

Brief Information about Inhalants

Inhalants are large group of chemicals which includes solvents, aerosols, gases and nitrites

Inhalants typically are CNS depressants

Inhalants are rarely thought of as drugs

Because inhalants are typically found over-the-counter, many adolescents use these drugs without raising the suspicion of their parents

Moderate use of inhalants can create an effect similar to alcohol intoxication

Inhalants create both physical and psychological dependence

Inhalants can produce immediate death for the user, a term called "sudden sniffing death" syndrome

The Facts on Inhalants

Inhalants are a diverse group of drugs. They are breathable chemicals that produce mind and mood-altering effects. Inhalants include such products as cleaners, cosmetics, paint solvents, glues, motor fuels, and aerosol sprays. Several hundred such products are available in the marketplace and many are available at home. Since most of these products were never intended to be used for medical or recreational use, many people do not even think of them as drugs.

One of the major concerns related to inhalant use is the fact that these products tend to be used and abused by adolescent and preadolescent populations. Many adults either ignore the abuse potential of such substances, or don't understand the reasoning behind such use. The following are some reasons why this population tends to abuse such substances:

1. Inhalants are some of the most readily available "high" producers - While such drugs as alcohol may be readily available at home, there are many more types of inhalants available and their absence from the home may not be noticed. Most households have aerosol cans of paints, gasoline, thinner, or even such products as fingernail polish, polish remover, or various glue products. Inhalants tend to be more reliably intoxicating than even marijuana, without the tell-tale odors and lingering effects.

2. Inhalants are inexpensive - Where as many other types of drugs may cost from a few to many dollars, there are a variety of products that can be inhaled which sell for under $1.

3. Many of the inhalants are legal - Although some states or local communities may have laws related to selling certain aerosol paint products or commercial glues, anyone can buy such products as fingernail polish, polish remover, gasoline, liquid paper and the like.

4. Inhalants are packaged compactly - A tube of plastic cement, a bottle of liquid paper, or a can of lighter fluid fit neatly into a pocket and can intoxicate as readily as a quart of vodka.

5. Inhalants work quickly and don't last too long - A few deep inhalations bring on the intoxicated state. Drugs which are absorbed by the lungs reach the brain in seconds, almost as rapidly as those administered IV. Depending on the dose, inhalant intoxication is over in minutes.

6. The hangover from inhalants is not as bad as most drugs - The most common complaint after using such drugs is generally a headache.

Inhalants are generally divided into three categories, all of which are potentially hazardous to the user:

1. Commercial solvents, such as toluene, xylene, benzene, naphtha, acetone and carbon tetrachloride. Solvents are found in such products as airplane glue, plastic cement, paint thinner, gasoline, cleaning fluids, nail polish, polish remover, lighter fluids and typewriter correction fluids.

2. Aerosols are particles suspended in a gas. These mixtures are generally the propellant gases found in many household and commercial sprays. They contain various hydrocarbons such as freon and are found in products like cooking sprays, glass chillers, spray paints, hair sprays, and aerosol whipped cream. Freon is also used in refrigerators and air conditioners and can be purchased in most automotive supply stores for under $1.

There are two other available products that would fit in the aerosol category. One is a drug called amyl nitrite. Crystals of the drug are placed in a cloth-covered, glass capsule that is snapped in two and inhaled. It is commonly used in the treatment of heart patients to relieve the pain associated with angina by expanding the coronary artery. It also expands arteries in the brain, resulting in a flushing sensation and light-headedness. This drug is commonly referred to as a "popper" or "snapper" and has long been used on the street as an enhancement for sexual orgasm.

The other product is butyl nitrite, a substance which is legally manufactured and sold as a room odorizer or liquid incense. Its cost is around $5. When inhaled it produces a short "high." It is a clear yellow liquid, packaged in small containers, and is sold by the name of "Rush" or "Locker Room." The odor is comparable to the smell of dirty sweat socks or rotting apples. This product is available in many communities, especially in stores known as "Head Shops" which sell a variety of drug paraphernalia.

3. Anesthetics, such as chloroform, ether and halothane, as well as nitrous oxide are abused inhalants. Most are available in doctor and dentist offices, or can be found in medical supply companies. Also, whippets of nitrous oxide can be purchased for home whipped cream machines.

The subtle nature of use and many adults' reluctance to acknowledge such use make inhalants relatively popular with young age groups. The following is an example from my own experience of how easily such abuse is missed:

"While giving a talk to a group of sixth grade students at a local school, I observed a young student in the front row who had a styrofoam cup which was decorated in multiple rings of colors. After the talk, I asked his teacher about this. She reported to me that little Johnny was an artistic student. Every day, at the start of school, he would obtain a large, styrofoam cup from the teachers' lounge. Then he would proceed to decorate the cup with magic markers. He would carry the cup all day, and continue to decorate the cup until the end of school. She thought this was "cute" and thought nothing of it. I pointed out to her that this wasn't cute, that the child was inhaling the vapors from the magic markers which were soaked into the styrofoam. While giving my talk, he had placed his nose over the cup and taken several deep breaths. The teacher wanted to disagree, but in reviewing the child's progress in school during the semester, it was obvious that his grades and conduct had changed."

Greater awareness of the abuse potential of such products is important if we are to assist youngsters who are involved in such behavior. Many chemical dependency specialists see inhalant use as being the most dangerous form of drug use we deal with, particularly because of the immediate effect they have on the body as well as the long-term damage to the brain.

The History of Inhalants

Inhalant abuse has a relatively short history compared to other drugs of abuse, even though there are reports of the use of inhalants in ancient Greek cultures. The majority of reports focus more on the last two hundred years. Ether was discovered in the late 18th century. It was used as both a solvent and a medicine. It also became a popular alternative to alcohol. A few drops, either inhaled or drunk, would produce intoxication. Nitrous oxide and chloroform were discovered in the 19th century and also used as a more fashionable form of intoxication.

Reports of sniffing gasoline began to appear in the 1930's, but it was not until the 1960's that more widespread use of many additional products was reported. Due to the expanding use of many types of drugs, inhalants became a cheap high, and many products were experimented with. Such products included:

- Adhesives such as rubber cement, which contain such products as benzene, naphthalene, toluene and xylene;
- Aerosol sprays, which may contain ethanol, isopropanol, toluene and xylene;
- Antifreeze, composed of glycols, methanol and isopropanol;
- Degreasers, which may contain isopropanol, acetate, methyl ethyl ketone, benzene, toluene, xylene, methylene chloride and trichloroethylene;
- Fingernail polish, which may contain acetone and alcohol;
- Foam dispensers, which may be propelled by nitrous oxide;
- Gasoline;
- Glue products, which may contain naphtha, petroleum distillates, toluene, or ethyl acetate;
- Lacquer and paint removers, which may contain naphtha, toluene, methanol, benzene and acetone;
- Lighter fluid, which contains naphtha;

- Model cements, which contain ethanol, isopropanol, acetone, toluene and xylene;

- Nail polish remover, which contain acetone;

- Paint thinners, which contain methanol, ethanol, isopropanol, acetone, naphthalene, and toluene;

- Room deodorizers or odorizers which may contain isoamyl nitrite or isobutyl nitrite;

- Spot removers and cleaning fluids, containing trichloroethylene, trichlorethane and petroleum distillates;

- Typewriter correction fluid, primarily containing trichloroethylene and carbon tetrachloride.

During this time, inhalants predominately became the domain of adolescents and preadolescents. The quick, cheap high, as well as the ability to use the compounds without detection (fingernail polish or airplane glue in the bedroom do not draw attention like a bottle of beer or a joint of marijuana) seem to appeal to this population.

The Acute Physical Effects of Inhalants

A variety of effects are noticed, but may vary depending on the inhalant used. Generally, the effects are similar to alcohol intoxication, except that most inhalants produce an excitability and delirium. The effects on the central nervous system are those of depression, similar to anesthesia. The initial use may produce nausea and vomiting. Further inhalation results in more progressive CNS depression, with disorientation and confusion. Use will result in decreased inhibitions, increased impulsiveness, and a sense of invulnerability.

As the inhalation progresses, depression deepens leading to decreased coordination, ataxia, stupor, seizure or cardiac or respiratory arrest. During and shortly after inhalant use, the sniffer may exhibit abusive and violent behavior. Visual and auditory hallucinations, which can occur in susceptible individuals, are very colorful and vivid and often revolve around themes of fire and heat. Recovery from lower doses is usually complete in 15 minutes to a few hours.

There is a high risk of sudden death from inhalants. This is referred to as SSD or "Sudden Sniffing Death." Inhalants interfere directly with the respiratory centers in the brain, and this interference may produce irregular heart beats, leading to direct heart failure and death. Risk of death by suffocation also increases when users sniff fumes from plastic bags.

Studies of long-term users of inhalants have reported bone marrow damage, dramatic weight loss, impaired vision, muscle paralysis, loss of memory and inability to think clearly. These dysfunctions generally cease when sniffing stops. One effect which does not clear, however, is the potential damage to the brain. Many of the inhalants, especially the solvents, have the potential of washing away the very specialized fat compounds found in the brain. This fat is the covering around each of the brain cells. When this fat is lost, the brain cell dies. Long-term use can result in permanent brain damage, some of which may seriously impact on the long-term development of the user.

The volatile solvents possess moderate to high psychological dependence ability, and moderate to low physical dependence ability, although symptoms such as nausea, depression, insomnia, and loss of appetite have been noted in users after discontinuation, an indication of possible withdrawal.

Brief Information about Marijuana

Marijuana is the most frequently used illicit drug in the U.S.

The potency of the active ingredient in marijuana, THC, has increased dramatically since the early 1960's

Marijuana has depressant, stimulant, some analgesic, and even hallucinogenic effects

Marijuana has from four to ten times the amount of tar and carcinogenic substance found in cigarettes, creating a high risk of lung damage

Marijuana does have both physical and psychological dependency potential

Marijuana does cross the placenta and creates fetal effects

The Facts on Marijuana

Marijuana is probably the most controversial of all of the psychoactive drugs. There are more myths and misconceptions about the drug, its nature, its addiction potential, and the physical and psychological problems associated with its use than any other drug we deal with. It is the most popular drug of abuse, behind alcohol. It is estimated that better than 25% of the total population of the United States have tried the drug at least once, and between 3 to 5 million Americans are daily users.

Marijuana is a mixture of the crushed leaves, flowers, small branches, stems, and seeds of the hemp plant, Cannabis sativa. It grows wild in temperate and tropical areas throughout much of the world, and is cultivated in many countries. If it were legal, marijuana would be the largest cash crop grown in the United States.

Marijuana is a depressant drug, though it does have psychedelic effects at high doses. As a result, it is classified in both categories, though most professionals classify it as a psychedelic. Unlike sedatives, marijuana does not produce anesthesia or death. Unlike psychedelics, there is little cross-tolerance between marijuana and other psychedelics (in other words, using marijuana does not seem to lessen the impact of using other psychedelics).

Marijuana is not a single chemical. At the present time there are at least 426 known compounds in the plant, 61 which are unique to marijuana. In addition, when marijuana is burned, an additional 1,500 compounds are formed. Chemical compounds found only in marijuana are referred to as cannabinoids. They are the most active and principal mind-altering ingredients of marijuana. The primary cannabinoid that has been identified is delta-9-tetrahydrocannabinol, or THC for short.

The amount of THC present in marijuana determines the potency of the drug. Various parts of the plant have different concentrations of THC, so the potency of the drug sold on the street is determined by the type of plant materials in the mixture, as well as the conditions in which the plant is grown. The parts of the plant, along with their THC concentrations is as follows:

Root - the plant has a long tap root which has no THC value

Stalk - the stalk is hollow and fibrous and may grow up to 4 inches in diameter. The fibers were once used to make hemp rope. There is very little THC in the stalk.

Branches - branching depends on how the plant is grown. When crowded together, there are few branches on the stalk - if uncrowded, there are many branches. Some THC is found in the branches.

Leaves - the male plant is well known for its five leaflets per leaf. The female plant may have seven or more leaflets per leaf. A moderate amount of THC is found in the leaves.

Buds, flowers, seeds - the male plant produces flowers that pollinate the female plants. These buds and flowers have little THC value. The female plant buds, then flowers (if pollinated), then seeds. The buds of the female plan contain the highest concentration of THC.

The THC concentration of marijuana has dramatically increased over the past 40 years. In the 1960's, the purity of THC was less than .2% (two tenths of one percent). Today, THC concentrations average between 5-8% pure, with some concentrations of over 18%, making the marijuana today 25 to 40 times more potent. This is highly significant, because the drug we studied and tested in the 60's is not the same drug that people are using today.

Marijuana is sold in a variety of forms. The common forms are as follows:

Bhang - the dried leaves and flowering shoots of the cannabis plant, containing small amounts of THC.

Ganja - the resinous mass derived from the small leaves and branches of the cannabis plant.

Hashish - the resinous secretions of the female cannabis plant that are collected from the flowering tops, dried, then compressed into various forms, such as balls or cakes. This form of cannabis is generally more potent than marijuana, having THC concentrations of up to 10%. Hash is the major form of marijuana used in the Middle East and in North Africa. In the Far East, this product is referred to as Charas.

Hashish oil - a dark viscous liquid produced by a process of repeated extraction of cannabis plant materials. A solvent, such as ether, is mixed with the marijuana mixture, removing more of the existing THC. This product has the highest THC concentrations, upwards of 60%.

Marijuana - the general term for the most common form of the drug used on the streets. It contains all forms of the cannabis plant, which are dried, chopped and mixed into a tobacco-like product.

Sinsemilla - a seedless variety of high-potency marijuana, originally grown in California and prepared from the unpollenated female marijuana plant.

Thai sticks - a cannabis preparation common in Southeast Asia, consisting of marijuana buds bound onto short sections of bamboo.

Few psychoactive drugs have as many names as marijuana. The name "marijuana" is likely derived from the Mexican slang for cheap tobacco. One street name is the English equivalent, "Mary Jane." Some of the more commonly applied names are: Acapulco Gold, ace, bhang, Colombian, ganja, grass, hemp, Indian, Jamaican, joint, Mexican, Maui wowie, Panama Red, Panama Gold, pot, reefer, sativa, sinse, tea, Thai, weed. "Roach" refers to the remainder of a marijuana cigarette after most of it has been smoked. A "roach clip" is some type of commercial product or a simple bobby pin that allows the user to consume virtually all of the marijuana joint.

The History of Marijuana

The history of the drug marijuana dates back to 2700 B.C. in ancient China. The plant was known as "ma," a Chinese word that meant valuable or endearing. The plant was valued for its fibers, which were used to manufacture rope, cloth, and paper. It was also discovered that the resins, flowers and leaves had some medicinal value, and potions were made and used to treat gout, malaria, and gas pains. By the year 500 B.C., the Chinese virtually banned the use of the plant due to its unpredictable intoxicating effects. They replaced marijuana with opium, preferring opium's smooth, tranquil and predictable sedation.

Marijuana was introduced in ancient India specifically for its mind-altering effects. It was used in religious ceremonies for its euphoria-producing ability and was cultivated commercially. In due time, the plant was known for its intoxicating effects, as well as for its value in the production of rope and cloth. Commercial cultivation spread throughout Asia, Africa and Europe.

By the time Europeans were exploring the New World, the cannabis plant had great commercial success. As a result, English settlers brought the plant to colonies in America during the early seventeenth century, making marijuana our first cash crop. Before long, cannabis plants were abundant and the hemp fiber industry was flourishing.

Though the intoxicating and psychoactive properties of the plant were well known, the general American public showed relatively little interest in marijuana as a nonmedical, recreational drug. It was predominately used in medicines, with cannabis preparations being prescribed legally for numerous physical and mental ailments until 1940. When the Harrison Narcotics Act was passed by Congress in 1914, many available drugs were removed from the marketplace, but the Act excluded marijuana from any control.

Marijuana smoking did not become prominent until the era of Prohibition. Mexican immigrants and West Indian sailors introduced the practice in states along the Mexican border and in Gulf states. With the absence of alcohol as a intoxicant, marijuana smoking became popular in urban populations.

During the 1930's, allegations of marijuana abuse and increased violence associated with its use began to spread. Tales of bizarre effects, murder, rape, sexual excesses, and memory loss began to circulate. The federal government produced a film entitled "Reefer Madness" in an effort to educate the public of the growing concern for marijuana addiction. (The film did little to help raise awareness, and instead remains as an example of how scare tactics actually did more harm than good in educating the general population.)

By 1935 most state governments enacted laws against the nonmedical use of marijuana. There was a growing concern as to the "epidemic" of marijuana use. It was during this time that cannabis and its extracts were inaccurately classified as narcotics in scientific literature as well as legal provisions. Such classification was responsible for some of the harsher penalties associated with possession of marijuana, including life in prison and the death penalty. In 1937 the federal government enacted the Marijuana Tax Act, which in effect, banned the nonmedicinal possession and use of cannabis on a national level.

During the World War II era, marijuana was again commercially grown in the United States. Hemp rope had been replaced with rope made from fibers of the sisal plant, grown in the Philippines. Because of the Japanese invasion of the Philippines, sisal rope was no longer available. Farmers in the United States were encouraged to cultivate the plant for rope production. As a result, the plant again became widespread in its growth across the United States, even after the war. Birds apparently like the seeds of the marijuana plant, and by eating the seeds and passing them in bird droppings, marijuana plants began to grow wild across the United States.

Because of its availability, marijuana became one of the most popular drugs of use during the late 1950's and through much of the 1960's. Its popularity remains today. Many scientific studies were performed to determine the health hazards associated with its use, but the majority of studies were inconclusive or contradictory. As a result, many users of the drug used this uncertainty to advocate changes in drug laws that outlawed recreational use of the drug. Many states have decriminalized marijuana, reducing the penalty for possession and use of small amounts of the drug. There continues a national effort by some groups to legalize the drug, claiming that the drug is no worse than alcohol or tobacco.

Because of the refinements in the production of marijuana, marijuana today is not the same marijuana studied in the 1960's. The THC concentrations are 25 to 50 times more potent, with some forms of hashish being up to 100 times more potent. Since much of the research was based on less powerful varieties of the drug, the findings and conclusions have little relevance to the use of the stronger marijuana now available.

The Acute Physical Effects of Marijuana

When smoked, marijuana is rapidly absorbed into the bloodstream, reaching the brain in less than 30 seconds. Its physical and psychological effects appear quickly, and reach their peak about the time smoking is completed. If the drug is taken orally, absorption would take much longer, and the effects would develop more slowly over two to three hours, and last longer.

In a relatively short period of time, the liver begins to break THC down into many chemical by-products known as metabolites. Because marijuana is a fat soluble drug, 25 to 30% of the original THC consumed, along with various metabolites, remains in the human body for up to one week after the initial dose is taken. The average half-life of marijuana is 36 hours, with some forms of THC having a half-life of 72 hours. A single use of marijuana may require 30 days or longer to clear the system. As a result, marijuana can be detected more accurately and for a longer period of time than most other drugs, up to 6 weeks, depending on the specific test used.

It is this fat solubility that is also at the heart of the greatest debate about marijuana – is it addicting. We do not see any rapid development of physical dependence – many users will smoke the drug sporadically for many months and years. Tolerance does occur, but this is a natural occurrence with any type of drug use and this alone does not indicate addiction. Also, there is not life-threatening abstinence syndrome. There is, though, a noticeable withdrawal syndrome upon stoppage of use. It may not manifest itself for many weeks, but we do see irritability, restlessness, and even nausea and vomiting in individuals with high-frequency use.

A single use of marijuana impairs motor coordination, specifically, hand steadiness, body sway, accuracy of carrying out body movements, and maintaining stable body posture. Although an individual under the influence of marijuana may feel fluid and graceful, they are actually quite clumsy.

Reaction time, that is, the time lag between a signal and a person's reaction to that signal, may actually increase, though not for all who use the drug. The ability to follow a moving stimulus is significantly and consistently diminished lasting for 4 to 8 hours beyond the point of intoxication. Such a disability would interfere with driving skills significantly. Additionally, the ability to perceive a brief flash of light is significantly impaired. This impaired visual perception also constitutes a major risk for users who operate cars or heavy machinery.

The Physical Effects of Marijuana

Recent studies seem to indicate that there are greater physical concerns related to the use of marijuana than previously believed. The effects on the respiratory system of a single joint are equivalent to smoking fifteen cigarettes. Marijuana has at least 50% more tar and carcinogenic materials than cigarettes, and contains the compound benzopyrene – a proven cancer causing agent. The unfiltered marijuana smoke is drawn into the lungs at a temperature that is hotter than cigarette smoke, causing drying and irritation of tissues in the lung.

Initially, marijuana causes the vessels of the lungs to dilate, possibly improving the quality of breathing. However, in time, the marijuana acts to constrict the air passages, causing asthmatic and similar types of respiratory distress.

Marijuana smoke also causes damage to the body's immune systems located in the lungs. The anti-infection white blood cells of the lungs, known as the "alveolar macrophages" are either paralyzed or destroyed. As a result, smokers tend to have higher incidence of laryngitis, pharyngitis, bronchitis, cough, hoarseness and dry throat. Additionally, recent studies suggest that marijuana may depress T-lymphocyte functions (known as the killer T cells).

Marijuana has been shown to increase the heart rate by as much as 50%, as well as increasing the blood pressure in some people. However, research suggests that these changes do not create permanent harmful effects on normal hearts and blood vessels and are virtually insignificant among healthy people. Individuals with heart disease, hypertension or coronary disease, however, should avoid use of marijuana at any time.

Marijuana has been widely used as an aphrodisiac, with some users reporting an increased interest in sex. In reality, this increased interest is related to the loss of inhibitions due to the depressant effect of the drug. Tests actually suggest that major changes develop in the reproduction and sexual function of both males and females. In the male body, marijuana causes a decrease of the male hormone testosterone. Actually, marijuana prevents the male body from changing estrogen, the female sex hormone, to testosterone. As a result, we have seen reports of what is considered (and reported as) a humorous side-effect of males developing breast tissue and losing facial and body hair. Additionally, marijuana impairs male fertility by reducing sperm, causing the production of abnormally shaped sperm, and changing the ability of the sperm to move normally.

In females, marijuana suppresses the function of the ovaries, thereby stopping ovulation, production of estrogen and progesterone (the female sex hormones), and menstruation itself. As in males, such problems may impair fertility. There is nothing in the research, however, to suggest such effects are chronic, and the effects seem to reverse with abstinence.

A greater concern is the fact that marijuana is a drug that can cross the placenta of a pregnant female and affect a developing embryo. Studies suggest an effect similar to fetal alcohol syndrome resulting from the use of marijuana by a pregnant female. Further research is being conducted, but pregnant females are cautioned to avoid smoking marijuana.

As with most drugs, some of the most profound effects occur in the brain. As a depressant drug, marijuana produces a sense of euphoria, but also produces anxiety, confusion and in heavy use, a form of drug-induced psychoses. It affects reflexes, vision, and motor coordination.

Short-term memory is diminished by a single moderate dose of marijuana. Remembering a sequence of numbers or memorizing and following a series of directions become difficult to accomplish. The memory deficit is especially evident in obtaining and storing information, tasks that require attention. By impairing memory, the continuity of speech is also impaired. Irrelevant words and ideas are often introduced into conversations, and the ability to conduct a sequential dialogue is impaired.

Current studies suggest that marijuana actually fills the synaptic gap between brain cells, causing the flow of electrical energy to stop. This is of particular concern for the processing of long-term memory. With short-term memory impaired, and the ability to process long-term memory lost, learning becomes extremely difficult. Because this is dose related, and because it may take upwards of one week to clear a single dose of marijuana from the body, even casual smokers may suffer this effect. There is an interesting correlation between the rise of marijuana use in the 60's, 70's, 80's and 90's, and the parallel decline of SAT scores during this same time span.

The problem of "burn-out" is also reported among marijuana users. More appropriately known as the amotivational syndrome, it refers to the pattern of personality changes observed in some daily users of marijuana. It is characterized by apathy, lack of concern for the future, and loss of motivation. The syndrome tends to persist beyond the period of intoxication. Other aspects of this condition include loss of ambition, loss of effectiveness, dullness, diminished ability to carry out long-term planning, difficulty in concentration, intermittent confusion, impaired memory, and a decline in work or school performance. When regular use of marijuana stops, the condition usually disappears over a period of several weeks.

Current studies suggest that there are actually some medical benefits associated with the use of marijuana. In 1965, THC was synthesized and experiments proved the compound to be useful in treating glaucoma, nausea and vomiting caused by chemotherapy, and asthmatic conditions, due to its initial effect as a bronchodilator. It has shown benefit in helping prevent weight loss in cancer patients, can prevent muscle spasms or spasticity, can help prevent chemotherapy side effects, and can help prevent convulsions and seizures. Additional testing and research is needed to determine any long-term benefit of such treatments, or treatment for other physical health needs.

Though marijuana remains controversial and research seems to suggest that the drug is not as poisonous or lethal as alcohol or tobacco, marijuana by no means should be considered harmless or safe. Only time will tell whether or not the efforts by many individuals to decriminalize or actually legalize the drug will prove successful. Greater research and study of the drug is needed to destroy some of the myths and misconceptions.

A Word about "All-Arounders"

Many texts classify psychoactive drugs by the physical action that they cause on the human body – either depression or stimulation of the central nervous system (CNS). This tends to keep the classification fairly simple. However, there are those group of drugs known as hallucinogens or psychedelics that have the capability of acting as both a stimulant and depressant at the same time, making their classification more difficult. As a result, in this text we will include the description of "all-arounders" to include those hallucinogenic/psychedelic drugs that can fit either category, and include specific reference to the more general physical effects where appropriate.

Brief Information about Hallucinogens/Psychedelics

Hallucinogens alter mood, thought, and perception

Though they typically create CNS depression, hallucinogens can also cause stimulation

With the exception of LSD and PCP, hallucinogens are naturally occurring substances

Hallucinogen use dates back thousands of years

When used in large quantity, many hallucinogens produce toxic effects that can be fatal

Hallucinogens create psychological dependence, but apparently no physical dependence

Driving while under the influence of hallucinogens is extremely dangerous

The Facts on Hallucinogens/Psychedelics

The hallucinogens/psychedelics are a diverse group of drugs, the majority of which are naturally occurring compounds. These drugs have been referred to by such labels as hallucinogens (drugs which induce hallucinations), and psychotomimetics (drugs which mimic a psychotic condition). The term psychedelic fits the category better as it refers to mind expansion or mind manifestation - the ability of the mind to perceive more than it can tell and to experience more than it can explain. The current version of the Diagnostic Statistical Manual refers to the category as hallucinogens. For the purposes of this text, we will refer to the category as hallucinogens/psychedelics.

Characteristics of the hallucinogenic or psychedelic state include:

- Heightened awareness of sensory input, experienced as a flood of sensory experiences;

- Experiencing vivid but unreal imagery;

- Enhanced sense of clarity or clearness;

- Diminished control over what is experienced;

- Heightened perception of the surrounding environment;

- Overlapping of sensory inputs (the term for this effect is **"synesthesia"** - due to the overload of sensory inputs to the brain, the normal sensory response areas begin to overlap, causing one sensation to be translated into another - e.g., sound may be seen, smell may be felt, sight may be heard, etc.).

As a group, hallucinogenics/psychedelics tend to distort perception of reality, decrease logical thought, heighten sensation, and change or modify one's state of consciousness. The psychological effects of psychedelics can vary greatly from one user to another, and typically depend upon the expectations of the user, the mental state of the user, and the circumstances under which the drug is used. These drugs create central nervous system excitation that affects the senses, time, feelings, moods, experience and mental processes. The change to the CNS is a result of the overproduction or deactivation of various neurotransmitters in the brain. In large doses, such drugs can also produce hallucinations and delusions (referred to as a "bad trip"), though such responses are relatively rare.

Many who use psychedelics do so because of the appearance that they are not as dangerous as other types of drug use. While repeated use of psychedelics can lead to tolerance, the physical side effects are relatively dull. And though there may be a psychological dependence that develops over the course of using, there is no evidence of physical dependence that these drugs create.

The various hallucinogenics/psychedelics have very diverse histories. One of the most interesting aspects of such drugs is the fact that they are found over most of the world and are naturally occurring. Many cultures have a history of some type of psychedelic drug use during some stage of development. It has been suggested that man began using such drugs after noticing the change and effects such products created in animals. Because of the variety of drugs in this category, we will review both the history and the physical effects of each drug discussed.

Hallucinogenic Mushrooms

Fly agaric (amanita muscaria) is a hallucinogenic mushroom common to many parts of Europe and Asia. Its use dates back hundreds, perhaps thousands of years. Various legends report its use across a variety of cultures. It was used in ancient India and referred to as "soma" in their poetry. It was used medicinally and recreationally by people in the area that is the modern-day Afghanistan. The Vikings of Norway were said to use the mushroom to create their ferocity in battle. Interestingly enough, the active ingredient of the mushroom, muscimole, is excreted unchanged in the urine. Because of this, and due to the relative scarcity of the mushroom, people often saved their drug-containing urine and reused it. Such practices have been reported among people in Siberia and eastern Europe.

Another variety of mushroom called <u>teonacatl</u> was used in religious ceremonies by Central American Indians. Stone carvings found in the region suggest that the use of the mushrooms dates back to at least 1000 B.C. Spanish explorers reported that Indians used it both socially and in religious ceremonies, referring to the mushroom as "God's Flesh." Teonacatl is a member of the Psilocybe genus.

More popular in North America is the <u>psilocybin mushroom</u> (Psilocybe caerulescens, Stropharia cubensis, and several other members of the Psilocybe genus). Native American Indians noted that the mushroom only grew in the excrements of grain feed animals, and that when consumed by animals there was profound behavior change. As a result, they were used in religious ceremonies and manhood rites by a variety of Native American tribes.

Psilocybe mushrooms effect perception and cognition similar to the effects of mescaline and LSD, but to a lesser degree. They produce very strong visual distortions, as well as vivid and colorful illusions. In the body, the chemicals in the mushroom are changed to psilocyn, which then enters the brain. There it depletes the neurochemical serotonin. One to five grams of the dried mushroom would be required for its psychedelic effect, the equivalent of 20 to 60 milligrams of active ingredient. The compound has been synthesized in laboratory settings. The effects begin within 30 minutes and have a duration of 3 to 6 hours. Tolerance develops rapidly, though physical dependence does not appear.

Peyote and Mescaline

<u>Peyote</u> from the peyote cactus, Lophophora williamsii, has been used by Mexican Indians for thousands of years. The plant is native to Central America, though is also found in the southwest deserts of the United States. It creates visual and kaleidoscopic illusions, thus the belief that the plant would allow one to communicate directly with their gods.

The fleshy green cactus tips – the mescal buttons – are harvested during November and December. They are sliced and allowed to dry. They are then chewed or swallowed for the effect, though the bitter taste has caused some who use it to smoke the ground up product, brew a peyote tea, or swallow capsules containing the powdery form (a more modern method of use). Two or three buttons are chewed for the psychedelic effects, which will peak in 2-3 hours, but have a duration of 8-12 hours.

Peyote use spread to the North American Indians in the nineteenth century. It has become a sacrament of the Native American Church, an amalgamation of Christianity that espouses traditional beliefs and practices. Peyote use is an important part of the church's activities, and the cactus is believed to be a gift of God to man. The United States government has allowed sacramental use of peyote by members of the church, though various states have attempted to restrict its use. It is currently legal in Texas to harvest and sell the cactus, which grows in the western part of the state, provided the seller has the necessary permits.

Mescaline is the major psychoactive ingredient in the peyote cactus and is responsible for the psychedelic effect. The alkaloid was identified in 1886 along with 30 other psychoactive chemicals. The average dose that is required for the psychedelic effect is 300-600 milligrams, about the size of an aspirin tablet. Mescaline has been synthesized in the laboratory, the chemical name being 3,4,5-trimethoxyphenethylamine. Available as capsules, tablets or in liquid form, synthetic mescaline usually produces less intense nausea and vomiting than does peyote. The psychedelic effects of the synthetic form are virtually identical to LSD.

Peyote and mescaline act on the central nervous system by activating the release of the neurochemical norephinephrine, thus interfering with the stimulus filtering mechanism of the brain. They alter perceptions and tend to create less mental or cognitive disorganization than other psychedelics. Neither produces physical dependence, but tolerance develops rapidly.

Morning Glory Seeds

Another hallucinogen used by the Aztec and North American Indians was the Ololiuqui - or seeds of the morning glory plant. The seeds contain ergot alkaloids that is similar to LSD but only one-tenth as potent. A dose of between 200 to 300 seeds will induce the effects within 30 minutes and have a duration of 3 to 4 hours. The seed can be chewed or pulverized and made into a liquid preparation.

The initial effect is a period of apathy and irritability, which is followed by a state of elation and serenity as a result of the release of serotonin in the brain. The seeds are called "pearly gates" and "heavenly blues" on the street, but are not an ideal psychedelic unless a natural source of the seed can be located. Commercially available seeds are treated with a fungicide (to discourage their recreational use) that is poisonous. The toxic substance of the coating induces dizziness, nausea, vomiting, chills and diarrhea.

Nightshade

Since ancient times, five plants and related members of the nightshade family have been used for psychedelic effects as well as for the toxic effects of the poisons they contain. They are belladonna (Atropa belladonna), jimson weed (Datura strammonium), henbane (Hyocyamus niger), mandrake root (Mandragora) and Angel's Trumpet (Datura sauveolens).

These plants contain related alkaloids: atropine, scopolamine and hyocyamine - all of which inhibit the neurochemical acetylcholine. Physically, they make the skin hot, dry and red, sometime a bright scarlet. The pupils become dilated and do not react to light or accommodation. Vision is therefore blurred. The tongue, mouth and lips are dry and coated. Complaints of thirst are frequent. The pulse is rapid, and the blood pressure and temperature are elevated.

The psychological symptoms fall into one of two patterns and are dose related:

1. Wild delirium, disorientated, loudly hallucinating, restless and irritable, or

2. A muttering delirium, confusion, stuporous, uncoordinated, and unable to concentrate or respond appropriately to outside stimulation.

Belladonna derives its name from the medieval practice of using the drug as a cosmetic. Women used the plant compounds to make the cheeks rosy and the eyes wide and bright. Thus the term belladonna (beautiful lady). In the United States, belladonna was the primary ingredient of Witches' Brew. The plants were made into a liquid compound. Sticks would be dipped in the liquid and straddled while dancing around a fire. The compound would actually absorb through the vaginal cavity or the muscles of the thigh and create a sensation of floating, thus giving rise to the legend of witches flying on broomsticks. The toxic effect of the compounds was also well known and a common ingredient in poisons used by professional poisoners of the Middle Ages - most notably the Borgia family of Italy during the 1400's and 1500's.

Jimson weed, or more properly Jamestown weed, is so named because a troop of English soldiers, who were sent to Jamestown in 1676 to put down Bacon's Rebellion, found some of the young plants and ate them as greens. Historical accounts of the episode report the following:

"They turned into natural fools for several days. One would blow up a Feather, another would dart Straws at it, another, stark naked, sat in a Corner grinning and making Mows (mooing sounds), another would fondly kiss and paw his companions. In this frantik Condition they were confined lest they in their Folloy should destroy themselves. They would have wallowed in their own Excrements if they had not been prevented." (After eleven days they recovered, not remembering anything that had occurred.)

From "The Substance Abuse Problems," by Sidney Cohen, M.D.

Outbreaks of Jimson weed use and poisonings continue today. The weed grows widespread, and commonly is found in vacant lots and garbage dumps. Adolescents commonly hear of the plant and try it for its hallucinogenic effects. Often the plant is sold on the streets as a form of marijuana, but when smoked creates shortness of breath and occasionally can paralyze the respiratory system. In large doses it also creates psychotic conditions, delirium, and confusion.

Mandrake root, henbane and Angel's Trumpet also have a long history of use. All have been used as hallucinogenics, allowing one to hear God (thus the name Angel's Trumpet). They also have been commonly used as aphrodisiacs due to the heightening effect on the sensation of touch. Mandrake root was the primary ingredient in love potions during Shakespeare's time and was referred to in "Romeo and Juliet." Both henbane and mandrake root are referred to in the Bible, especially in the book of Ruth. Henbane was also a favorite among the Romans and used in orgies.

DMT

Dimethyltryptamine, or DMT, is both a naturally occurring compound and has been synthesized since the 1960's. It is a derivative of a certain South American shrub. It is a powerful, fast-acting drug that produces psychedelic effects of an extremely short duration. It can be snorted, smoked (usually on marijuana or parsley) or injected.

Psychedelic effects often begin and reach their peak within ten minutes of ingestion. The trip lasts between 30 and 60 minutes, with the visual and time-sense distortions subsiding rapidly. In essence, it is a compact version of LSD without the side effects of LSD. Because of this effect, it is commonly referred to as "The Businessman's Lunch."

As with most other psychedelics, DMT produces tolerance but no physical dependence. One great concern, however, is that the drug may cause life-threatening blood pressure changes when combined with other drugs or even with various foods and liquids such as pickled herring, salami and pepperoni, sharp or aged cheeses, yogurt and sour cream, beef and chicken livers, fava beans, canned figs, bananas, avocados, soy sauce, beer, Chianti wine, sherry, cola beverages, coffee, chocolate and raisins.

Nutmeg and Mace

Nutmeg is a commercial spice derived from the tropical evergreen Myristica fragrans, which contains the active ingredient myristican. It appears as either a whole, dried seed, or as a preparation of coarsely ground powder. The seed and powder can be eaten, and the powder is occasionally snorted. It requires 10 to 20 grams of the product to produce the psychedelic effects, but produces vomiting and nausea at a much lower dose. Two to five hours after ingestion, confusion occurs as well as mild euphoria and illusions. It is rarely used as a psychedelic except when other, more potent forms are not available, and many times is predominately used by adolescents and those incarcerated in jail or prison.

Mace is the outer skin of the nutmeg shell. It can be used alone, or in combination with nutmeg. Its effects are less potent than nutmeg itself.

Brief Information about LSD

Pure LSD is a white, odorless crystalline substance

LSD is one of the most potent drugs known

LSD is one of the few drugs that can be absorbed into the system directly through the skin

LSD is relatively easy to make, and is inexpensive when compared to other illicit drugs, making it popular with adolescents

LSD-25

By far and away, when people think of psychedelic drugs, they most commonly think of the drug LSD. Derived from a fungus that grows on rye or from lysergic acid amide, which is found in morning glory seeds, LSD is an abbreviation for the chemical name lysergic acid diethylamide. It is probably the most potent drug known to man. It has been estimated to be 100 times more potent than psilocybin and 4,000 times more powerful than mescaline. Because it is so powerful, the drug is measured in micrograms (millionths of a gram) as compared to milligrams or grams. The average effective oral dose is from 30 to 50 micrograms, with street doses running as high as 400 micrograms. The drug is primarily ingested, though this can be accomplished in many ways. As blotter acid, a drop of LSD in liquid form is placed on paper and placed under the tongue. The liquid can be mixed with any beverage and ingested. It is sold in capsule or tablet form. It is even so potent that the drug can actually absorb directly through the skin. Numerous tales exist of the drug being placed on children's' stickers and tattoos, causing unsuspecting youth to be subjected to the hallucinogenic effects of the drug. (NOTE: The vast majority of such tales have been found to be false - the drug has been sold in such forms on the street, but rarely have we experienced this problem with the population at large)

LSD is sold in a variety of forms and as a variety of products. It is sold as tablets, capsules, and liquid. It is known as "windowpane," "blotter acid," "micro-dots," "acid," "barrels," "California sunshine." The hallucinogenic effect of the drug, known as a "trip," varies greatly from one user to the next. As with any psychedelic drug, the effects are generally determined by the user's environment. Such drugs cause the normal stimulation from the outside world to be changed and altered. The power and potency of this drug makes it more responsive to such outside stimulation. As a result, if the environment is calm and pleasant, the experience of the drug is viewed as being pleasant. If the environment is loud and disturbing, the experience is usually referred to as a "bad trip."

The drug was discovered in 1943 by Dr. Albert Hoffman and Dr. W.A. Stoll in a Swiss pharmaceutical laboratory. They had been working with ergot compounds from plant fungus, looking for an anesthetic agent as well as a drug which could cause uterine contractions and control hemorrhaging. The experimentation actually began in 1938, but was unproductive. Upon reviewing their experiments in 1943, Dr. Hoffman accidentally ingested a small amount of the 25th combination of drugs they had prepared. He experienced restlessness, dizziness, and delirium, characterized by excited fantasies and intense kaleidoscopic play of colors. A few days later, he took 250 micrograms in a controlled experiment to see if the drug had any potential in modern medicine. The trip lasted over 9 hours, and his assistant recorded the psychedelic experience.

At first, psychiatrists and scientists felt that LSD would assist the medical community in the study and treatment of mental illness. Many physicians were encouraged to try the drug by the manufacturer, so as to better understand the nature of their patients' problems. During the 1950's it was used to treat mental illness, including schizophrenia, with the belief that the effects would reverse the illness suffered by an individual. It was even used to treat alcohol withdrawal, but with no success.

By the 1960's, many individuals were using the drug recreationally. Students, writers and philosophers became intrigued with the drug's mind-altering and nonaddicting qualities. By the mid 60's, Dr. Timothy Leary and Richard Alpert of Harvard University were advocating the use of the drug among young people, with the phrase "turn on, tune in, drop out" being their rally cry. The resulting media coverage increased national interest in the drug. As a result, the drug became a symbol of the 60's. The drug remained legal and readily available until 1965. At that time, the drug did not disappear. It is relatively easy and cheap to synthesize, and the formula for making the drug was widely circulated in various underground cookbooks. The drug continues to have widespread popularity among today's youth.

Although the effects of LSD are unpredictable and vary considerably from person to person as well as from one use to another, there are several common experiences:

Low dose - 25 to 50 micrograms - characterized by restlessness, heightened awareness of objects and nature, enhanced rapport with others. Emotional clarity and relaxation are often experienced and persist for several hours. The trip lasts for 4-6 hours.

Moderate dose - 75 to 150 micrograms - characterized by noticeable physical effects including dizziness, weakness, drowsiness, nausea, rapid pulse, increased heartbeat and blood pressure, loss of appetite. Psychedelic effects involve alterations in perception and thought, spatial distortion, intense imagery when the eyes are closed, changes in sound perception as well as thought and mood, and intensification of emotions. Time is distorted, making time seem to drag on forever. Visual illusions are colorful and generally include geometric figures. Synesthesia (over-lap of senses) is common. Sounds are seen, colors are smelt, walls begin to breathe. The trip lasts from 8 to 12 hours.

High dose - 200 to 500 micrograms - similar to moderate dose effects. However, at the peak of the trip, people report a loss of ego boundaries, a self-fragmentation or even a disintegration of the self. Feelings of euphoria and philosophical insight are also reported. The potential of having hallucinations, mystical or even psychotic experiences is great. The trip lasts from 15 to 20 hours.

LSD continues to be quite controversial. Scientific information suggests few long-term problems with the drug. There are no indications of physical dependence, though there are numerous accounts of psychological dependence. Reports during the 60's of chromosome damage related to the use of LSD are unfounded. Pregnant women should never use the drug, however, because LSD causes contractions of the uterus. More problems occur due to the impurity of street LSD and to the mental changes and images that can occur during a trip.

Reports of suicides, homicides, accidental injury and death abound in current literature.

Brief Information about PCP

PCP creates stimulation, depression, analgesia and hallucinations

A more common term for the effects of PCP is disassociative anesthetic

Many illicit drugs on the streets today are actually PCP

PCP can cause death by overdose

PCP can re-enter the system from the bloodstream, causing an unpredictable length of effect

Many homicides, suicides, and accidental deaths are related to the use of PCP

Phencyclidine (PCP)

In 1957, a new anesthetic was brought onto the market by a leading drug manufacturer. Called Sernyl, the drug was touted for its analgesic and anesthetic properties. However, before the drug was given final approval for widespread use, numerous reports of postoperative agitation and delirium were reported. As a result, the drug was deemed unfit for human consumption and removed from the market in 1965.

The drug's manufacturer returned the drug to the laboratory and continued their experiments. A new anesthetic was developed from the compound, ketamine, which is still used today. The original formula was also found to have benefits as an animal tranquilizer, and the product was renamed Sernylan.

Because of the numerous reports and scientific knowledge of the drug's psychedelic effects, the drug became popular during the psychedelic era of the late 60's. Known on the street as "angel dust," "PeaCe Pill," "Hog Heaven," and "embalming fluid," phencyclidine (PCP) enjoyed tremendous popularity.

Numerous problems exist with this drug, however. One problem is how to classify the drug. It is a rare drug indeed, having depressant, stimulant, analgesic, hallucinogenic, anesthetic, and convulsant effects in the body, all effects being dose dependent. The scientific community even today is greatly divided on its classification, though there is common acceptance of classifying the drug a "dissociative anesthetic."

Of greatest concern are the behavioral problems and bizarre activities or violence which occurs when the drug is used. Numerous accounts of extreme violence, suicides, impulsive homicides, or individuals suffering serious physical injury while on the drug and continuing to function normally continue to surface. An individual may use the drug on several occasions and experience nothing more than the psychedelic effects. Then the drug may be taken and have profound change on the person's personality. Much of this is dependent on the dose or the purity of the drug being taken. The drug is also misrepresented - many people who have heard the horror stories of the drug might never buy it, but buy various forms of LSD or marijuana which are laced with PCP.

The Effects of PCP

PCP is another substance which is manufactured in illicit laboratory settings. The Psychotropic Substances Act of 1978 banned the production of PCP, even as an animal tranquilizer. As a result, the illicit compound appears on the street in a variety of forms and colors. Originally, PCP was produced as a white crystalline powder and continues to appear in this form. It also appears in various colors of powder, capsule or tablet form, or as a liquid. PCP can be snorted, taken orally, smoked, or injected IV. It is most commonly smoked as a "Sherman", "Sherm", or "Superkool" (hand rolled cigarettes which are dipped in liquid PCP), as a "Bogart" (commercially manufactured cigarettes dipped in liquid PCP), or as "dusted weed" (marijuana joints which are sprinkled with PCP powder).

When taken orally, PCP produces a high which lasts between 5 and 8 hours; when smoked or snorted, the effects can last from 3 to 5 hours. Small doses (under 5 mg) lead to a state of drunkenness, a sense of floating, and numbness to the extremities (due to its anesthetic effect). Feelings of strength, power and invulnerability may coexist within this state.

In moderate doses (10 to 15 mg), analgesia and anesthesia are both produced - as a result, the user is unaware of burns, cuts, muscle strains, broken bones, etc. A psychic state resembling sensory deprivation is also produced. As a result, the user disconnects from reality and has no awareness of their surroundings. Changes in body image, disorganized thoughts, drowsiness, as well as hostile and aggressive behavior may occur.

In larger doses (greater than 20 mg), CNS depression occurs. Increased salivation, sweating, repetitive movements, and muscle rigidity may occur. Analgesia and anesthesia are more pronounced, and stupor or coma may develop, though the eyes of the PCP user will remain open even while in a coma. It may also produce seizures and convulsions at this level. Deaths from acute overdose of PCP have occurred at amounts estimated to be between 150 and 200 mg.

Part of the unpredictability of the drug centers around how the body removes it. The effects of a small dose of PCP will generally last one to two hours, while a large dose may last up to 48 hours. Normally, the body begins to detoxify a substance and remove it as it is circulating through the blood stream. PCP, however, can be recirculated from the brain, to the blood, to the stomach, back to the intestines, then be reabsorbed into the blood for recirculation, making the drug more potent than normal. Also, the drug is a fat-soluble drug which the body may store in fatty cells for many months. The stored PCP may then be released during exercise or fasting, resulting in a true chemical reaction weeks or months after the last use.

In spite of all the problems and all the reports of difficulties that users experience, PCP remains quite popular on the street. Whether people do not remember the bad experiences, or because the problems occur infrequently, the widespread use of this drug continues to be of major concern to treatment professionals across the country.

Brief Information about Designer Drugs

Designer drugs are synthetic products, chemically related to illegal mind-altering drugs, but manufactured to produce greater effects

Designer drugs originally were manufactured to be legal forms of illicit substances - current laws make drugs that are chemically similar to controlled substances illegal

Because they are manufactured in back-room chemistry labs, these drugs, as well as their impurities, can be highly dangerous and unpredictable

Designer drugs are available that mimic any psychoactive effect

Designer drugs are not a new phenomena - many were created during the 1960's

The Facts on Designer Drugs

Designer drugs, or analogs, are synthetic substances which are similar to illegal street drugs in their chemical formula and psychoactive effects. Street chemists initially began producing these products in the 1960's in an effort to combine certain types of psychoactive properties (i.e., design a special high). Then in the 1970's the drugs were being made to circumvent existing drug laws. While the molecular structures of these preparations might differ only slightly from those of the drugs they mimic, these drugs were actually legal until the mid-1980's. The uproar caused by the drug MDMA caused a change in federal drug laws in 1986. Laws were rewritten to classify any analogs of a controlled substance as Schedule I drugs under the Controlled Substances Act.

Designer drugs can be dangerous because of their direct effects, as well as from impurities and unknown byproducts that may result from their preparation by unskilled street chemists. Also, these analogs may actually be hundreds of times more potent that the drugs they mimic. As a result, an unsuspecting user may ingest the same quantity of an analog, and suffer from an accidental overdose.

Designer drugs should not be confused with drugs called "look-alike" drugs - combination drugs with ephedrine, caffeine, and phenylpropanolamine (PPA). Look-alike drugs are packaged to look like commonly used illicit drugs (e.g., black beauties, white cross, pink hearts, etc.), but are legal and sold over-the-counter. Designer drugs are more powerful and sold illegally on the streets.

There are actually two categories of designer drugs at the present time: narcotic analogs (related to fentanyl and meperidine), and the hallucinogenic amphetamine analogs (MDMA, MDA, DOM). The latter category is covered below. For more information on the narcotic analogs, see Section 1.4.

MDMA

MDMA is often referred to as the "LSD of the 80's" due to its popularity. Yet the drug is not a new one. It was discovered in 1914, a combination of amphetamine and mescaline. Its chemical name is 3,4-methylenedioxymethamphetamine. It is known on the street as "Ecstasy," "X," "the Big E," "XTC." As with MDA, even though it is a combination drug with stimulant qualities, its predominate action on the CNS is one of depression associated with extreme physical fatigue which can last up to two days.

From the 1920's to the 1980's, MDMA was legal and available over-the-counter. It was popular with psychologists and other therapists because it reduced a person's anxieties, intensified feelings, improved self-insight, promoted positive changes in attitudes and feelings, and encouraged close interpersonal relationships. It therefore facilitated the therapeutic process.

However, as the drug gained popularity, particularly with the high school and college crowds, numerous reports began to surface regarding its negative side. It creates amphetamine-like effects on the body - dilated pupils, dry mouth and throat, lower jaw tension, grinding of the teeth, CNS stimulation, as well as mind-expanding qualities of psychedelics, without the scary visual distortions. It also creates mental confusion, depression, anxiety, panic situations and paranoia.

During the summer of 1985, the national media began talking about the availability of this drug. Many who had never heard of the drug found that health food stores had legal supplies of it. The Food and Drug Administration quickly acted, and by July 1, 1985, the drug became a Schedule I controlled substance, meaning that it cannot be manufactured and it cannot be prescribed by physicians. Because of the popularity of the drug, however, many street chemists began designing compounds which were sold as MDMA. Few if any of such compounds proved to be the real thing, and many of the problems associated with the drug today are due to the fact that people who use the drug may be getting any number of different chemicals, or other powerful psychedelics that are sold to represent MDMA.

MDMA has show a recent rise in popularity, causing many of the federal agencies involved in drug/alcohol research and education to post new information about its use, availability, and effects.   Current research from the National Institute on Drug Abuse shows that MDMA can affect the brain by altering the activity of chemical messengers, or neurotransmitters, which enable nerve cells in many regions of the brain to communicate with one another. Research in animals has shown that MDMA in moderate to high doses can be toxic to nerve cells that contain serotonin and can cause long-lasting damage to them. Further, MDMA can interfere with the body's ability to control its temperature, which has on rare occasions led to severe medical consequences, including death. Also, MDMA causes the release of another neurotransmitter, norepinehrine, which is likely what causes the increase in heart rate and blood pressure that often accompanies MDMA use.

Although MDMA is known universally among users as Ecstasy, researchers have determined that many Ecstasy tablets contain not only MDMA but a number of other drugs or drug combinations that can be harmful as well. Adulterants found in MDMA tablets purchased on the street include methamphetamine, caffeine, the over the counter cough suppressant dextromethorphan, the diet drug ephedrine, and cocaine. Also, as with many other drugs of abuse, MDMA is rarely used alone. It is not uncommon for users to mix MDMA with other substances, such as alcohol and marijuana.

MDA

MDA, or "mellow drug of America," is a synthetic drug derived from various plant oils, including sassafras. Its chemical name is 3,4-methylenedioxyamphetamine. It was one of the popular "alphabet soup" drugs of the 1960's. It is chemically similar to both mescaline and amphetamine. Even though MDA is a combination drug with stimulant qualities, its predominate action on the CNS is one of depression. It produces an euphoric, peaceful, dreamlike state about 60 minutes after ingestion. It cam be taken orally, snorted or injected as a solution. The duration of effect is about eight hours.

Few physical reactions occur, except at high dosages or when injected, which may result in seizures and convulsions. The most notable effect seems to be tranquility and internal warmth. The drug was commonly promoted as a sexually enhancing drug. No physical dependence seems to develop with use of the drug, though tolerance does occur.

DOM (STP)

Another synthetic variation of mescaline and amphetamine, DOM (4-methyl-2,5-dimethoxyamphetamine) was introduced in 1967 as STP ("Serenity, Tranquility and Peace"). Taken at low dosages, it produces amphetamine-like euphoria as well as feelings of enhanced self-awareness. At higher doses, LSD-like effects occurred. The drug is not metabolized rapidly by the body, and remains in the body much longer than most other psychedelics (from 12-24 hours with a small dose, up to 72 hours with a large dose). More physical difficulties occur with this drug as well, including nausea, sweating, tremors, and convulsions. The length and intensity of the experience contribute to the unusually high rate of bad trips produced by the drug.

Synthetic Cannabinoids

(K2, Spice, Demon, Genie, Bayou Blaster, Spike Gold, Armageddon, and others)

Synthetic cannabinoids are chemically engineered substances similar to THC that, when smoked or ingested, can produce a high similar to marijuana. Initially developed for research related to treatment of pain and the effects of cannabis on the brain, these substances have recently become a popular alternative to marijuana. When sprayed onto dried herbs, the substances are marketed under names such as "Spice," "K2" or "Genie" and sold legally in local convenience stores or through the Internet.

These products produce effects that are quite different from marijuana's mellow high and produce less of a mental high and more of a "body" high that lasts 3 to 5 hours. The use of these products can cause agitation, paranoia, vomiting, and high blood pressure. The compounds are 10 times more active than THC.

Synthetic Psychedelics (2C-"X" Family)

(Aca Ice, Europa)

The 2C family of compounds are powerful synthetic psychedelic/hallucinogens similar to LSD and Ecstasy. They typically come in powder form and have been available for sale in convenience stores and through the Internet. Though thought of as a recent phenomenon, most of the currently known 2C compounds were first synthesized by Alexander Shulgin (a pharmacologist and chemist who previously worked for Dow Chemical) in the 1970s and 1980s, and published in his book, *PiHKAL* (*Phenethylamines i Have Known And Loved*). Dr. Shulgin also invented the term 2C, being an acronym for the 2 carbon atoms between the benzene ring and the amino group in each of these compounds.

The death by overdose of 2C-E of a user in Minnesota in March of 2011 (along with the hospitalization of 10 others), has drawn attention specifically to this particular compound, but there are a number of these products available over-the-counter, of which 2C-T-2, 2C-T-7, 2C-E, 2C-I, and 2C-B are most well known. Methods of use include snorting, eating, injecting, and smoking it. Effects vary wildly from person to person – they can cause nausea, paranoia, and vivid hallucinations for 8 to 12 hours from doses of 10-255 mg.

Flashbacks

Before we leave the psychedelic category of drugs, it is important to talk about flashbacks. Long after a psychedelic drug has been eliminated from the body, many users report partial reoccurrence of psychedelic effects, such as the intensification of colors, the apparent motion of a fixed object, or the mistaking of one object for another. In effect, the flashback seems to be a "free trip" - a repeat of the drug's effects without taking the drug. In many situations, this is wholly unexpected and therefore quite frightening. For years, many believed that some of a psychedelic drug was deposited in brain tissue, released at a future time. Indeed, with PCP this is actually the case. However, PCP is the exception. For the majority of other psychedelics, what appears to happen is nothing more than a stimulus-response mechanism.

During the course of a psychedelic experience, the memory is continuing to work. Memory is a chemical and electrical process which occurs in the brain. An experience is coded both chemically and electrically, transferred to a brain cell, and encoded with a key that allows us to recall the event. Normally, such keys are commonly used stimulation, and memory flows easily. "Two plus two equals four" can be recalled without problem. However, the key that allows a person to recall the memory of a psychedelic experience may be rather strange and unique. It may be that the key is never activated again, and memory of trips and psychedelic experiences may never be recalled. Or it may be that in a certain setting at some future point, a combination of shadows, noises, sounds or the like may fit the memory and allow the recall to flood into consciousness. The intensity is generally as great as if the individual was experiencing the high once again.

Flashbacks do not pose any true physical problem for the drug user. However, the time and place that such an event occurs may create potential problems. Many people who experience flashbacks tend to lose control and panic. If infrequent, the event may just be seen as a nuisance or accepted as interesting or even amusing. It is estimated that 25% of psychedelic drug users experience a flashback at some point in time.

Section 1, Chapter 5:

Drugs of Abuse - Stimulants

Brief Information about Caffeine

Caffeine is the most widely consumed central nervous system stimulant

It is a naturally occurring substance that is found in many beverages, chocolates, and over-the-counter medications

Caffeine can produce effects that range from mild feelings of alertness to extreme nervousness and insomnia

Caffeine does produce tolerance as well as withdrawal effects

Caffeine can produce both physical and psychological dependence

Caffeine in the system of a mother, can cross the placenta - however, its effects on the fetus are unknown

The Facts on Caffeine

Caffeine is the most widely used and most regularly consumed psychoactive stimulant compound in the world. It is a bitter tasting, odorless compound found naturally in a number of plants including:

1. Seeds of Coffee arabica and related species (coffee),
2. Leaves of Thea sinensis (tea),
3. Seeds of Theobroma cacao (cocoa, chocolate),
4. Leaves of the South American mate plant Ilex paraguariensis (yerba mate, a South American tea),
5. Kola nuts from the tree Cola acuminata (cola drinks),
6. Seeds of the Cassina, or Christmas Berry Tree (a caffeine beverage used among Indians in colonial America).

The most common source of caffeine in America today is coffee. It is estimated that the average American coffee drinker consumes almost 1,000 cups each year. Another popular source of caffeine for many adults is tea, both hot and cold. Young populations obtain the majority of their caffeine in the form of colas or chocolates.

Another source of caffeine is found in a variety of over-the-counter preparations. Some of these products are sold as drugs that increase one's alertness and contain nothing but caffeine. Many products sold as analgesics contain caffeine as one of their primary ingredients. A new concern centers on the use of over-the-counter diet aids. These drugs not only contain a large quantity of caffeine, but also contain many other forms of legal stimulants.

Americans consume a surprisingly large amount of caffeine each day. The average American consumes about 227 milligrams of caffeine each day. Many, however, consume more, primarily because most people are not aware of what products contain caffeine, or how much caffeine is found in a particular item. Depending on the product, brand and method of preparation, a single cup of coffee contains at least 66 milligrams (mg) and as much as 150 mg. of caffeine. Cola products contain between 32 mg and 65 mg per 12-ounce container. Alertness tablets contain from 100 to 200 mg. Analgesics deliver 32 to 65 mg per tablet. **Table C.1** shows the caffeine content of a variety of products.

TABLE C.1 Common Sources of Caffeine*

	Average Milligrams	Caffeine Range
Coffee (8 oz. cup):		
Brewed, Drip Method	135	60-180
Instant	95	30-120
Decaffeinated, brewed	5	2-5
Decaffeinated, instant	2	1-5
Tea (8 oz. cup):		
Brewed, U.S. brands	50	20-90
Brewed, imported brands	60	25-110
Instant	30	25-60
Iced (12-oz cup)	70	67-76
Chocolate:		
Hot Cocoa (8 oz. cup)	5	2-20
Chocolate milk (8 oz.)	5	2-7
Milk chocolate (1.5 oz.)	10	1-15
Dark chocolate (1.5 0z.)	31	5-35
Chocolate syrup (1 oz.)	4	4

Soft Drinks	**Milligrams Caffeine (12 0z.)**
Jolt	71
Mountain Dew	55
Diet Mr. Pibb	52
Coca Cola	46
Diet Coke	46
Tab	44
Dr. Pepper	41
Royal Crown Cola	36
Pepsi Cola	36
Mr. Pibb	34
7-Up, Sprite	0
Fresca	0
Sunkist Orange	0

Nonprescription Drugs:	**Milligrams Caffeine**
Dexatrim	200
Vivarin	200
No Doz	100
Excedrin	65
Bromo Seltzer	32.5
Triaminicin	30

- Sources: National Coffee Drinking Trends survey; National Coffee Association of U.S.A.; Nutrition Action Healthletter; Center for Science in the Public Interest.
- Specific amounts of caffeine subject to change as manufacturers reformulate their products.

The History of Caffeine

The exact origin of caffeine use is rather obscure. It is believed that coffee was the first caffeine containing product to be used. The plant was native to Ethiopia and natives apparently chewed the beans, or made an infusion with the leaves of the plant. Until the fourteenth century, the coffee plant was used as a medicine. At that time, the practice of roasting the beans, grinding them and making a drink from them was developed in Arabia.

One of the primary uses in the Arabian culture was of a religious nature. Coffee was consumed to allow worshipers to maintain their alertness in all night prayer. This lead to the practiced use of coffee in many religious ceremonies. Later, in the fifteenth century, coffee houses began to appear as a place to gather, talk, and drink coffee. However, many rulers in Arabia began to fear the gatherings that took place, branding them as acts of sedition. This led to the banning of coffee from many parts of the Arab world.

After the period of the Crusades, coffee and coffee houses appeared in European countries. The history of such houses was colorful and full of debate regarding the European monarchies. Many rulers, including Charles II of England, banned coffee houses. The resulting protest was so great, that many switched courses, instead levying taxes on coffee that actually had greater success in curbing its use.

Interestingly enough, another source of opposition to coffee came from the alcohol industry in that day. Coffee was cheaper than alcohol and many people reduced their use of alcohol as they increased their use of coffee. Many governments increased taxes again on coffee to make it more costly than alcohol, and several governments actually encouraged consumption of alcohol over that of coffee.

A further decline in the use of coffee was the result of the increasing popularity of tea. Tea use began in China, several thousand years B.C. The first recorded history was in the fourth century, A.D. By the eighth century, the use of tea was so widespread that taxes were imposed on it.

Tea was introduced to Europe in the seventeenth century. Dutch traders brought tea leaves back from the Orient, along with the method of brewing tea. The British actually developed a world-wide network of sales and trade, particularly through the British East India Company. Revenues generated by tea helped fund the British Empire.

Tea was a popular drink in America. There was much unhappiness, however, over the taxes levied on tea by the British government. Prior to the Revolutionary War, the British government actually rescinded the tax on tea. However, in doing so, they allowed the East India Company to sell tea directly to the consumer, bypassing the colonial merchants. The Boston Tea Party was actually an act of rebellion aimed at overturning this policy, not the issue of taxation. It then became a patriotic duty for Americans to abstain from tea drinking, which resulted in an increase in the popularity of coffee.

Coffee and tea are universally accepted today, with the majority of tea being produced in China and India, while coffee production is world-wide, with the South American countries being the largest producers. Caffeine use from other products has a less colorful history, with the exception of cola products.

Few if any such products existed prior to the end of the nineteenth century. Then, John Pemberton concocted a coca product, containing both coca leaf flavoring (cocaine) and caffeine from the kola nut. He sold his product as a nerve tonic, but had little luck in developing a large following. It was only after he carbonated the beverage and sold it as a soft drink, that Coca-Cola was born. As a result of this product's popularity, we have frequently been witness to the "Cola Wars" as various manufacturers try to capitalize on the popularity of such drinks. (By 1906, Pemberton's successors had removed cocaine from Coca-Cola. The beverage is still flavored with extracts from decocainized coca leaves.)

The Acute Physical Effects of Caffeine

Caffeine acts on the central nervous system fairly rapidly. Its psychological impact is probably greater than its physical effect. All of us know someone, who, after just three or four sips of their early morning "fix" begins to feel better and is better able to start off the day. Tolerance and psychological dependence can occur in some people drinking five or more cups of coffee or tea per day. If the person abruptly discontinues the beverage and all other sources of caffeine, a depression will follow similar to that caused by withdrawal from other CNS stimulants.

Caffeine has a mild accelerating effect on metabolic rate. Three or four cups of coffee or tea can increase the metabolic rate from 10 to 25 per cent for up to four hours. Being a CNS stimulant, caffeine will offset a fatigue-induced drop in performance of motor tasks. However, caffeine may not improve motor skills involving muscular coordination. Heavy use of caffeine leads to irregular heart- beat, tinnitus, restlessness, extreme nervousness and inability to sleep.

Caffeine stimulates the heart, acts to speed up the production of urine, and increases the capacity for muscular work. It is not considered to be particularly hazardous, with the LD-50 being in excess of 4 grams. However, with many over-the-counter products containing large amounts of caffeine, the condition known as caffeinism is becoming increasingly common. This condition is a result of chronic toxicity or poisoning from long-term caffeine use. It is characterized by mood changes, anxiety, disruption of sleep, various bodily complaints, and other medical and psychological problems. Symptoms include wakefulness, insomnia, restlessness, irritability, muscle twitching, tremulousness, headache, sensory disturbances (e.g., ringing ears), dry mouth, lethargy, depression, irregular heartbeat, vomiting, stomach pain, gastric ulcers and diarrhea. (By contrast, if tea is the predominate beverage, instead of diarrhea, constipation would occur. All other symptoms would be similar.)

New research also suggests that pregnant women should avoid the use of caffeine during and immediately after pregnancy. Studies on lab animals show birth defects with heavy use. Additionally, caffeine is a drug that can cross the placenta. Babies born to heavy caffeine-using mothers are found to be more irritable and suffer from sleeplessness. Pregnant women should be cautious about consumption of large amounts of caffeine.

A study published in the New England Journal of Medicine (October 15, 1992) raises additional concerns about the use of caffeine. The study reports that withdrawal symptoms were present in people who consumed even the average daily dose of caffeine (227 mg.). Symptoms of anxiety, depression, sluggishness and moderate to severe headache appeared for even moderate users who missed their caffeine intake for a single day. Some also exhibited sick-in-bed symptoms worse than the flu. Symptoms appear to reach their worst after a day or two and usually taper off within a week of abstinence. Researchers recommend that to avoid withdrawal symptoms, users should taper off their caffeine use, or simply not stop using the drug.

So what does this mean with regards to the concept of "addiction" to caffeine? So far available research indicates that caffeine is not able to switch the brain from "pleasure" to "chemical dependence" because it does not powerfully and selectively affect DA (dopamine activating) functions in the shell of the main "addictive" center of the brain that is affected by the more powerful CNS stimulants. The public and news media are much more likely to state that caffeine is "addicting" than are scientists. Further, the National Institute on Drug Abuse does not recognize caffeine as a harmful or "addicting" drug.

Synthetic Caffeine

Phenylpropanolamine, or PPA, is a synthetic stimulant used in a variety of over-the-counter and many caffeine-free products. It is a mild stimulant, chemically related to amphetamine. It has properties as an appetite suppressant and a nasal decongestant. Because the Food and Drug Administration initially ruled the drug to be safe and effective and did not impose any limit on the dosage used. As a result, it has been found in virtually all of the diet aids at one time or another, and has also been found in the bulk of cough and cold remedies. Additionally, when many in society became concerned about their daily intake of caffeine, many products were marketed as being "caffeine free." Instead of caffeine, these products often contain PPA. (The claim is to be caffeine free, not stimulant free.)

Brief Information about Nicotine

Nicotine, found in tobacco products, is a powerful CNS stimulant

Tobacco products which contain nicotine also contain thousands of other chemicals, many of which are known to cause cancer

Nicotine is a highly addictive compound whose addictive qualities are enhanced by the method of delivery - a smoker will ingest 10-20 hits per cigarette

A past report by the Surgeon General of the United States calls nicotine more physically addicting that cocaine and heroin

60 milligrams of nicotine can be fatal - a cigarette typically contains from .05 to 2.5 milligrams, and a cigar contains about 120 milligrams

The Facts on Nicotine

Though smoked by Native American Indians for centuries prior to the discovery of the New World, tobacco was America's contribution to the world. One of the nightshade family of plants native to the Western Hemisphere, tobacco leaves have been smoked, chewed and sniffed in the Western world for only 400 years.

Tobacco farming is the fifth largest, legal cash crop in the United States. The leaves of Nicotiana tabacum have become a popular source of altering one's mood throughout the modern world. Cigarette smoking, however, is also credited with being the "largest single preventable cause of illness and premature death in the United States," according to the U.S. Surgeon Generals Office.

Nicotine is the main psychoactive compound in tobacco. It is the second most used stimulant, behind caffeine. The nicotine content ranges from 0.3% to 7% depending on the variety of tobacco, as well as the leaf position on the stalk (the higher the leaf position, the higher the concentration). This alkaloid was not isolated from tobacco until 1828. About 60 milligrams is the LD-50, although tolerance to nicotine builds rapidly in the user. A cigar contains twice the LD-50, about 120 mg of nicotine. The average cigarette contains between 0.05 to 2.5 mg of nicotine. The smoker who inhales the smoke gets about 90% of the nicotine in the bloodstream, compared to 20 to 50% from smoke taken only into the mouth then exhaled. Nicotine from inhaled tobacco reaches the brain in only seven seconds - twice as fast as from intravenous administration in the arm.

The History of Nicotine

As previously noted, Native Americans used tobacco in a variety of forms for hundreds of years. Tobacco was used in folk medicines and in religious rituals in the Mayan, Aztec and other tribes from Quebec to Paraguay. It was smoked in the form of cigars (chopped tobacco wrapped in tobacco leaves), cigarettes (chopped tobacco wrapped in corn husks), and in pipes. It was made into a syrup and swallowed or applied to the gums. It was chewed, snuffed, and even administered rectally in religious ceremonies.

Tobacco reached Europe after the return of Columbus from the New World. It is believed that one of his crewmen brought the practice of smoking back to Portugal. When observed smoking, many people believed this seaman to be possessed by the devil. He was placed in jail for several years as a result.

Slowly, the practice of smoking took hold. Portuguese sailors were avid smokers, and their practice led to the introduction of tobacco to many parts of the world. They are also responsible for the development of a world-wide tobacco industry. Portugal set up trade with India, Brazil, Japan, China, Arabia and Africa.

As early as 1520, the addictive qualities of tobacco were recognized. Many people who smoked reported great difficulty in giving the habit up. Smoking was quite controversial, with medicinal use of tobacco being widely accepted, but smoking for pleasure was frowned upon. By 1574, the use of tobacco was recommended for over 36 different illnesses.

Tobacco was described as a holy, healing herb, a remedy sent by God to man. It was also described as an evil plant, an invention of the devil. King James I of England was fanatically opposed to smoking. In an effort to limit its use, he raised the import tax on tobacco, making its use more costly. Nevertheless, tobacco use increased. By 1614 there were over 7,000 tobacco shops in London alone. The demand for tobacco outstripped the supply. It was literally worth its weight in silver.

The cultivation of tobacco played a significant role in the successful colonization of the United States. In 1610, John Rolfe was sent to Virginia to develop a tobacco industry. It only took three years to establish the success of the industry and the Virginia colony. Its value as a cash crop increased during the Revolutionary War, as tobacco, along with rum, funded much of the war effort. So vital was the tobacco industry, General Cornwallis made the destruction of the Virginia tobacco plantations one of his major campaign objectives during the war.

Until the turn of the twentieth century, chewing and snuffing tobacco were the most common methods of use in the United States. In 1897, half of all tobacco grown was prepared for chewing. Spittoons were required by law in all public buildings until 1945. Cigar smoking was also popular, and remained the dominate form of smoking tobacco until about 1920 when the cigarette became popular. In 1885 a billion cigarettes a year were being produced. In 1985, over 615 billion cigarettes were consumed, about 4,000 per person aged 18 or older.

The most important chapter in the history of tobacco took place in the early 1960's. After years of study, the U.S. Surgeon General reported in 1964 that "cigarette smoking is causally related to lung cancer in men; the magnitude of the effects of cigarette smoking far outweighs all other factors." Congress established the National Clearinghouse for Smoking and Health in 1965. This organization has been responsible for monitoring, compiling, and reviewing medical literature that bears on the health consequences of smoking. After their first three annual reports, Congress passed laws which have required warning labels be placed on cigarette packages since November 1, 1970. Further pressure on Congress resulted in legislation that prohibited tobacco advertising on radio and television after January 2, 1971.

More recently, a report was issued by the Surgeon General's Office which suggests that nicotine "is more addicting than cocaine or heroin." Over one-third of all adults in the United States have a tobacco habit. An individual who smokes only one pack per day can average over 7,000 cigarettes, resulting in over 70,000 "hits" of nicotine. As a result, tobacco not only has a physical addiction associated with its use, but the psychological stimuli of the taste, sight, and feel of the cigarette, as well as the many social settings in which smoking takes place is of as great a concern.

The Acute Physical Effects of Nicotine

Nicotine is the substance in tobacco that causes dependence. Nicotine first stimulates and then depresses the central nervous system. Stimulation occurs due to the release of norepinephrine and because it mimics the action of acetylcholine (both neurochemicals). It stimulates nerve endings rapidly, but is not removed from the receptors very quickly. As a result, it then creates depression of the CNS, caused by blocked nerve activity.

Nicotine increases the respiration rate and stimulates the cardiovascular system by the release of epinephrine, causing increases in coronary blood flow, heart rate, and blood pressure. Cigarette smoking tends to inhibit hunger contractions in the stomach for about an hour.

The tar and nicotine contents of cigarettes affect mortality rates. The risk of premature death in men who smoke is about 70% higher than for non-smokers. Not only do they die sooner, but they also have a higher probability of certain diseases such as cancer of the lungs, larynx, lips, esophagus, and bladder; chronic bronchitis and emphysema; disease of the cardiovascular system and peptic ulcers.

Pregnant women who smoke have a significant harmful effect on the fetus, the survival of the newborn infant, and the continued development of the child. Adverse effects range from spontaneous abortion, impaired fetal growth, premature and still births, to neonatal death. Women, especially adolescent females, form the highest number of new smokers each year. As a result, women are also showing increases in reported deaths due to cancers and heart disease.

Long-term effects include higher chances of diseases such as emphysema and bronchitis, cancer of the mouth, lungs, esophagus and bladder, and cardiovascular disease. Additionally, due to many smoking related illnesses, smokers may expect to experience increased absenteeism from the work place - up to 33% for men and 45% for women, compared to non-smokers.

There has been a great deal of controversy recently about the addiction and health problems associated with tobacco. Reports now confirm that the tobacco industry was aware of the addictive nature of tobacco back in the 1960's in spite of industry claims that said there was no link between nicotine and addiction. Additionally, a list of many of the chemical additives used in making cigarettes was recently released that raises additional fears about health related concerns. Without a doubt, smoking is responsible for a great many deaths and health related problems. While difficult to do, there is a great deal of benefit gained by people who quit smoking. **Table N.1** shows the benefits to an individual's health that occur when he or she quits smoking.

Table N.1 - REASONS TO QUIT SMOKING

According to the American Cancer Society , within 20 minutes of smoking that last cigarette, the body begins a series of changes that will continue for years. However, all benefits are lost by smoking just one cigarette a day.

AFTER NOT SMOKING FOR:

20 MINUTES:
* Blood pressure drops to normal
* Pulse rate drops to normal
* Body temperature of hands and feet increases to normal

8 HOURS:
* Carbon monoxide level in blood drops to normal
* Oxygen level in blood increases to normal

24 HOURS:
* Chance of heart attack decreases

48 HOURS:
* Nerve endings start regrowing
* Ability to smell and taste is enhanced

2 WEEKS TO 3 MONTHS:
* Circulation improves
* Walking becomes easier
* Lung function increases up to 30 percent

1 TO 9 MONTHS:
* Coughing, sinus congestion, fatigue, shortness of breath decrease
* Cilia regrow in lungs, increasing ability to handle mucus, clean the   lungs, reduce infection
* Body's overall energy increases

1 YEAR:
* Excess risk of coronary heart disease is half that of a smoker

5 YEARS:
* Lung-cancer death rate for average former smoker (one pack a day) decreases by almost half
* Stroke risk is reduced to that of a non-smoker 5-15 years after quitting
* Risk of cancer of the mouth, throat and esophagus is half that of a smoker's

10 YEARS:
* Lung-cancer death rate is similar to that of non-smokers
* Precancerous cells are replaced
* Risk of cancer of the mouth, throat, esophagus, bladder, kidney and pancreas decreases

15 YEARS:
* Risk of coronary heart disease is that of a non-smoker

Brief Information on Naturally Occurring Plant Stimulants

The euphoria created by stimulant drugs continues to cause widespread popularity in their use

Natural products are appealing to a greater number of people than ever before

Natural stimulants have always been popular in such countries as Africa and Asia

Current events in Africa have triggered the introduction of many of these products here in the United States

Many of the over-the-counter "look-alike" drugs contain natural plant stimulants

The FDA is taking a more serious look at the availability of such products

The Facts on Miscellaneous, Naturally Occurring Plant Stimulants

When talking about naturally occurring plant stimulants, most people think of caffeine, nicotine and cocaine. However, there are several substances worldwide which create stimulation on the central nervous system, many of which have been used for years, and used as commonly as coffee, tea, and tobacco are used in the United States. The following are some of the more common substances that are becoming favorite drugs of abuse on the streets today.

Betel Nuts

Historical reference to the use of betel nut dates back more than 15 centuries. It has a wide history of use in such nations as India, Malaysia, the Philippines and New Guinea, as well as widespread use in the Arab world. The adventurer Marco Polo introduced betel nuts to Europe in 1300.

Worldwide, more than 200 million people use betel nuts not only as a recreational substance but also as a form of folk medicine. The effects of this substance are similar to that of nicotine or very strong coffee and include a mild sensation of euphoria, excitation, decrease in fatigue, and lowered levels of irritability. Some users chew this compound from morning until night, while others use it only as a recreational substance in social situations. Many who use betel nuts liken the practice to that of gum-chewing or the drinking of soft drinks (especially colas) in the west.

The husk and/or meat of the betel nut is usually chewed in combination with another plant leaf (peppermint, mustard, etc.) and some slaked lime (because of the bitter, sickening taste of the nut). Unfortunately, while making the substance tastier, the juice of this mixture tends to blacken the teeth of the user over time. When consumed in large quantities or high doses, one of betel nuts primary ingredients, muscarine, can be toxic. Of greater concern, however, is the principal danger of tissue damage to the mucous linings of the mouth. The continuous contact of the substance to these tissues tends to cause sores and scarring. In addition, reports indicate that up to 7% of regular users develop cancer in the mouth and esophagus. While there is still some question as to the potential for the development of physical dependence, the drug tends to rapidly produce psychological dependence.

Yohimbe

Yohimbe is a bitter, spicy extract derived from the African yohimbe tree. It is generally used by brewing it into a stimulating tea or used as a form of medicine. It also has great popularity due to reports of its mild aphrodisiac effects. This effect seems to be as a result of the drug causing increase in the brain of the neurotransmitter acetylcholine, which results in more penile blood inflow. It also causes an increase in blood pressure and heart rate. Yohimbe is also reported to produce a mild euphoria and occasional hallucinations, but in larger doses it can be quite toxic. The bark can be bought at some herbal stores.

Ephedra

The ephedra bush, found in desert climates throughout the world, contains the drug ephedrine, a mild stimulant that is used medicinally over-the-counter and by prescription to treat asthma, allergies, low blood pressure, and narcolepsy (sleeping sickness). Ephedrine, which is also known as marwat, was recognized as a stimulating tonic over 4,000 years ago in China. A medicinal tea from herbs the Chinese call "ma huang" was used to relieve breathing problems and increase alertness. The product is still available today in health food stores - many people use it to brew a stimulating tea for quick energy, and also as a weight-loss aid. Religious groups such as the Mormons and Seventh Day Adventists brew the leaves of the ephedra as a substitute for coffee, which is forbidden by their respective religion.

On Feb. 6, 2004, the U.S. Food and Drug Administration issued a ruling prohibiting the sale of dietary supplements containing ephedra "because such supplements present an unreasonable risk of illness or injury." The rule was made effective on April 12, 2004. Companies that fail to stop distribution of dietary supplements that contain ephedrine alkaloid products, such as ephedra, Ma huang, Sida cordifolia and pinellia, by Monday will face any number of FDA enforcement possibilities, including "seizure of the product, injunction against the manufacturers and distributors of such products and criminal prosecution." The rule does not include traditional Chinese herbal remedies and generally does not apply to products like herbal teas that are regulated as conventional foods.

KHAT

A substance gaining popularity in the United States today is the drug known as khat. References to Khat can be found in Arab journals as far back as the 13th century. The leaves were used by some physicians as a treatment for depression. Though not a new drug, current awareness of its intoxicating and euphoric effects did not have widespread recognition until late 1992. When the United States government sent troops to Somalia, they discovered that a large percentage of the population were chewing the leaves, twigs, and shoots of the khat shrub in order to get an amphetamine-like rush and stimulation. In Yemen, another country on the Arabian peninsula, more than half the population uses khat, and many people spend over a third of their family income on the drug. It is the driving force of the economy in Somalia, Yemen, and other countries in East Africa, Southern Arabia, and the Middle East.

Khat is a shrub that grows 10 to 20 feet tall. The fresh leaves and tender stems are chewed, then retained in the cheek as a ball and then either chewed some more or swallowed to release the active drug. Dried leaves and twigs are not as potent as the fresh leaves, but can be crushed for tea or made into a chewable paste. Many homes in some of the Middle East or African countries mentioned actually have a room in their house dedicated for the purpose of khat chewing.

The main active ingredient, cathinone, is most potent in fresh leaves which are less than 48 hours old. Cathinone is a naturally occurring amphetamine-like substance that produces a similar euphoric effect along with a sense of exhilaration, energy, talkativeness, hyperactivity, wakefulness , and loss of appetite. Unfortunately, it also causes chronic insomnia, anorexia, gastric disorders, tachycardia, hypertension, and dependence. When khat is utilized to excess, users become irritable, angry, and often violent. Chronic khat abuse results in symptoms similar to those seen with amphetamines addiction, including physical exhaustion, violence, suicidal depression upon withdrawal, and there are rare reports of paranoid hallucinations, and even of overdose deaths.

Recently, cathinone has been synthesized in illegal laboratories, particularly in the Midwest United States, and is being sold on the street as a more powerful alternative to methamphetamine. Since it is relatively cheap to manufacture, and because the necessary ingredients are more readily available than those needed to make methamphetamine, a large number of labs have sprung up. From late 1992 to the fall of 1993 alone, 17 laboratories were raided in Michigan. Khat, itself, is also being smuggled into the United States in large quantities.

While the use of khat and its effects has been blamed for some of the constant factional battles in Somalia which have devastated the country, much of the blame is focused on the infighting between rival clans trying to control the money involved in the trade (not unlike a gang battle trying to control drug trade here in the United States). Hundreds of millions of dollars are spent on the drug, even in poor countries. In Muslim countries where alcohol is banned, khat is used in a number of social situations. Such a thriving, lucrative trade is enough to create the type of conflict being seen.

Brief Information about Amphetamines

Amphetamines are strong central nervous system stimulants

Amphetamines can be legally prescribed by a physician - any other use is illegal

They are drugs which increase alertness and induce a sense of well-being when initially used

Heavy doses or the long-term use of stimulants can lead to extreme anxiety, malnutrition, paranoia, physical health problems, and even death

People with high blood pressure, heart disease, diabetes, thyroid disease, or difficulty in urination should not take this drug in any form

Users can become both physically and psychologically dependent

Amphetamine use in pregnancy can harm the developing fetus, especially in its neurological development

Driving while using amphetamines is dangerous

Use of amphetamines can reduce one's resistance to disease by lowering the white blood count

The Facts on Amphetamines

Amphetamine drugs are powerful CNS stimulants with cocaine-like effects. Unlike such naturally occurring stimulants like cocaine, caffeine and nicotine, amphetamines are synthetic substances. Amphetamine itself is actually a collective term for three closely related drugs: amphetamine or levoamphetamine (Benzedrine), dextroamphetamine (Dexedrine), and methamphetamine (Desoxyn, "meth" or "speed"). Such stimulants are manufactured, both legally and illegally, as tablets or capsules that come in a variety of colors, as well as basic white. They can be sniffed, taken orally, or injected intravenously.

Commonly referred to as "uppers," "pep pills," "whites," "bennies," "white cross," "hearts," "pink ladies," "speed," "meth," "crystal," and "crank," amphetamines are the third most commonly used stimulants nationwide. These stimulant drugs allow the user to work harder and longer than normal. The effects of amphetamines typically last for several hours after administration of the drug.

The History of Amphetamines

Amphetamines were first produced in Germany by the Romanian chemist Lazar Edeleanu in 1887. It was not until 1927, however, that physicians discovered the drugs' ability to stimulate the CNS, alleviate fatigue, reduce the appetite, and relieve congested nasal passages. One of the first drugs marketed was Benzedrine in 1932, in the form of a nasal inhaler. In 1935, amphetamines were used to treat narcolepsy, a condition of uncontrolled sleeping. In 1937, amphetamines were also found to have a paradoxical calming effect on children with hyperkinetic disorders. These drugs were initially thought to be the answer for a variety of other medical problems such as obesity, depression and addiction to other drugs such as opiates. Such beliefs were found to be false. As a result, use and further investigation of the amphetamines remained somewhat dormant until World War II.

During the period of World War II, amphetamines were used as stimulants by soldiers and prisoners of war. Large amounts of amphetamines were produced in Japan during this time to aid in the war effort, including use by factory workers and by the famed "Kamikaze" pilots. After the war, large supplies of methamphetamines were released into the Japanese marketplace to be sold without a prescription. Oral and intravenous use of the drugs spread rapidly among the residents of Japan, with a peak use in 1954 of about two percent of the population. Tighter controls decreased the magnitude of the problem but illicitly synthesized products filled the remaining demand.

In the United States, methamphetamine (white cross) was introduced, and nonprescription Benzedrine inhalers were extremely popular. Intravenous amphetamine abuse became prominent in the late 60's. In the San Francisco Bay area, "speed" users displaced the users of L.S.D., the so called mind expanding drug.

Amphetamines were prescribed widely for the control of depression and as an aid in dieting right up to 1970. They were also used in treating epilepsy, asthma, sedative overdose, and nausea in association with pregnancy. The abuse of such drugs was so widespread, that the Controlled Substances Act of 1970 placed amphetamines under Schedule II, thus restricting their manufacture and distribution.

The illicit synthesis of amphetamines, which initially developed in the San Francisco area, became more popular as a result, and has continued to this day. Over the years, several manuals have been published with instructions for the secret synthesis of many illicit drugs, including methamphetamine. Many pre-1960 college chemistry books contained the formulas and method of amphetamine production, since the method practices several chemistry techniques that are routinely taught in laboratory settings. Currently, Texas leads the nation in the production and distribution of illicit amphetamines.

With the increasing demand for stimulants in the late 80's, we saw not only an increase in the use of cocaine and crack cocaine, but also a marked rise in the use of amphetamines. In 1987, the national overdose rate for methamphetamine (known by street names such as crystal, crank and methadrine) jumped thirty percent.

Amphetamines are making a resurgence primarily because they are cheap, available and effective for hours longer than cocaine. They can be inhaled or swallowed, but are more commonly injected for the "rush".

The Acute Physical Effects of Amphetamines

Amphetamines stimulate the central nervous system, leading to increased wakefulness, alertness, arousal, activity, talkativeness, restlessness, pleasure, and reduced appetite. Larger doses may produce irritability, aggressiveness, suspiciousness, anxiety, excitement, auditory hallucinations, and paranoid fears (delusions, psychotic reactions). Amphetamines also dilate the pupils, increase sweating, quicken breathing, raise blood pressure and produce tremors of the hands. These drugs have high potential for psychological dependency, tolerance develops quickly to their use, and withdrawal effects may occur as long as twenty-one days after cessation of use.

There are some great dangers associated with amphetamine use. The drugs produce high levels of pleasurable feelings, and, occasionally, feelings of greatly increased power. They also produce sensations comparable to sexually orgasmic experiences when taken IV. Overdose can be rapidly achieved, with marked impairment of judgment, greatly increased suspiciousness (paranoia), aggressive behavior and serious interruption of normal patterns of eating and sleeping (which produces physical deterioration). Chronic heavy use often leads rapidly to psychotic-like behavior which can be indistinguishable from paranoid schizophrenia. Suicides have occasionally been triggered by the prolonged depressions of mood which often follow the intense stimulation produced by continued use of high doses of amphetamines. IV amphetamine users learn, in time, that heroin produces similar orgasmic feelings when injected with none of the deteriorative effects of amphetamines on health and performance. Thus, there is some tendency to switch from amphetamines to heroin use (which is biologically safer) but the higher prices of heroin ultimately forces many into criminal activity.

Cessation of use by the psychologically dependent user may lead to severe depression, collapse from exhaustion, severe cramping of the abdominal muscles, symptoms resembling asthmatic attacks and changes in brain wave patterns. These signs can usually be reversed by another dose of amphetamines or relieved by such other drugs as Thorazine or Mellaril.

Even small infrequent doses of amphetamines can produce toxic effects in some people. Panic, circulatory and cardiac disturbances, hallucinations, and convulsions and coma have all been reported. Heavy and frequent doses of stimulants can produce brain damage resulting in speech disturbances and difficulty in turning thoughts into words. Users who inject stimulants intravenously can contract serious and life-threatening infections from non-sterile equipment.

Long-term users often have acne, and a rash resembling measles. They develop sores on the arms, legs and face from picking and digging at "bugs" believed to be crawling under the skin (the term for this condition is "formication"). As the body requires calcium to detoxify amphetamines, many users develop trouble with teeth, gums, fingernails, and dry lifeless hair. Other problems can include liver disease or damage, cerebral hemorrhage, and kidney damage.

Substituted Cathinones
(Vanilla Sky, Ivory Wave, Ocean, White Lightning, Cloud-9, White Dove)

Substituted cathinones – referred to by their street name, "bath salts" – are derivatives of cathinone, a psychoactive substance with stimulant properties that occurs in nature, for example in the leaves of *Ephedra* and khat plants. The effects of synthetic cathinones are similar to amphetamines like ecstasy and cocaine.

According to the U.S. Department of Justice's "Drug Alert Watch: Increasing Abuse of Bath Salts" from Dec. 17, 2010:

> *Law enforcement officials throughout the country are reporting that products promoted as bath salts have become prevalent as a drug of abuse. Bath salts have recently appeared in some of the same retail outlets that previously sold synthetic cannabinoid products such as K2 and Spice, and also are available via the Internet. Bath salts are abused as recreational drugs typically by injection, smoking, snorting, and, less often, by the use of an atomizer. Effects include agitation, an intense high, euphoria, extreme energy, hallucinations, insomnia, and making abusers easy to anger. Preliminary testing indicates that the active ingredients in many brands contain MDPV (3,4-methylenedioxypyrovalerone) and/or mephedrone.*

Brief Information about "Ice"

"Ice" is a smokable form of methamphetamine

"Ice" is extremely pure, with few additives

The smoke from "Ice" is colorless and odorless

"Ice" is less expensive to manufacture than crack

One gram of "Ice" usually sells for around $400 and yields 10-15 hits

"Ice" is highly addictive

Physical damage from "Ice" is similar to the damage from amphetamines, but occurs more quickly and with greater intensity

The high from "Ice" can last up to 30 hours

The effects on the unborn fetus from the use of "Ice" by the mother are still unknown

"ICE"

Since first surfacing in the fall of 1989 in Hawaii, Korea and California, "Ice" has been discovered in the suburbs of major cities throughout the world. This potent form of freebase amphetamine is a powerful, highly seductive euphoriant – a smokable/inhalable stimulant drug.

"Ice" owes its appeal to several factors: the high from smoking "Ice" endures for 12-24 hours; "Ice" can be manufactured in clandestine speed labs; because it is odorless, "Ice" can be smoked in public virtually without detection; "Ice" reverts to its solid state when it cools, thus becoming reusable and highly transportable; "Ice" costs two to three times more than crack - where crack sells for $2,000 an ounce, "Ice" commands $4,000 to $6,000 per ounce, but because it last longer, the user gets "more bang for the buck." Common side effects include depression, insomnia, paranoia, increased blood pressure and heart rate, nausea, faintness, chills, sweating, blurred vision and rapid eye movements, muscle tension and narrowing of coronary arteries.

"Ice" is produced by allowing methamphetamine to stand in water or alcohol until it crystallizes. It has the potential of destroying serotonin producing neurons as well as causing the degeneration of neurons containing dopamine. This type of brain damage can result in alterations of the brain's regulatory mechanisms dealing with aggression, mood, sexual activity, loss of sleep and sensitivity to pain, resulting in distortion of these types of behaviors, including a sense of heightened sexual experience. As with many other drugs, the prospect of increased sexuality has been a major reason for many to try the drug.

"Ice" has all of the physical, psychological and behavioral toxicity associated with crack cocaine. Many users of stimulants prefer "Ice" because it is longer acting, requires less frequent use, and produces less interference with work or other activities requiring prolonged performance. While the largest increase of crack use has taken place in the inner-city, "Ice," so far, has had its greatest increase in the white, blue-collar populations. This could rapidly expand the number at risk for abuse of such a highly addictive, rapid delivery drug.

Typically, cocaine users have considered amphetamines to be inferior drugs. "Ice" may yet change that thinking, though the drug has not captured the popularity that the field was most concerned about, or the levels of use that seemed to spike in the late 1990's. Only time will tell how widespread and dangerous this form of smokable methamphetamine will truly be, or if it is just one more in a long list of potential illicit drugs for some users to experiment with.

Brief Information about Cocaine

Cocaine is the most powerful naturally occurring central nervous system stimulant

It creates a short-lived sense of euphoria

Heavy use of this drug can be both physically and psychologically harmful

Cocaine does create physical dependence, as well as psychological dependence

Cocaine users are at an increased risk of infectious diseases, both because of injecting the drug and because of the reduction of white blood cells

Cocaine is used in multiple ways, including snorting, swallowing, smoking, and injecting

Binge use, or cocaine runs, frequently lead to anxiety, irritability, panic, and paranoid psychosis

Even short term use of cocaine can cause damage to the heart and neurological functioning of the brain, which can result in death

Cocaine use can cause hazards when driving, particularly due to impaired judgment, poor concentration, and impaired motor coordination and vision

The Facts on Cocaine

Cocaine is a white crystalline powder extracted from the leaves of the coca (not cocoa) plant. It is the most powerful central nervous system stimulant of natural origin. The plant, Erythroxylon coca, grows in the mountainous regions of Columbia, Bolivia, Peru and Argentina at altitudes many other plants will not withstand. A shrub or small tree which grows to six or eight feet, it is usually kept smaller when cultivated. The leaves of the plant contain a variety of chemicals, including about 1% of cocaine hydrochloride.

The drug is probably one of the most widely recognized psychoactive compounds used today. Even those who don't use the drug know of its power and seductive appeal. It is known by a variety of names including "coke," "C," "snow," "flake," "happy dust," "Peruvian marching powder," and "white lady." As it is sold on the streets, this drug is a mixture of the cocaine hydrochloride and various adulterants which are added to increase the quantity of the drug, usually to the advantage of the seller. Adulterants include such substances as sugars (lactose, sucrose, mannitol), local anesthetics (procaine, novacaine, lidocaine), or any other type of white powder.

Cocaine is one of the most expensive drugs we deal with. The cost of an ounce of powder ranges from $1,400 to $2,800, or from $50 to $100 a gram. The recent introduction of crack cocaine, however, has brought the price of smokable cocaine down to $5 to $20 per vial (approximately 300 milligrams, sufficient for one or two intoxicating doses).

Cocaine is one of the most effective euphoria producing drugs ever discovered. Originally a favorite of the "upper class," cocaine is now a favorite drug of all socioeconomic groups. Its popularity is directly related to its guarantee of immediate pleasure, well-being and alertness. It has gained an unjustifiable reputation as being a drug of pleasure with no addictive qualities or undesirable health effects. Only recently have we begun to understand its addictive nature as well as the serious medical concerns related to its use.

The History of Cocaine

The precise origin of chewing the leaves of the coca plant are not known, but many authorities date its widespread use to pre-Columbian Indians who inhabited the Andes Mountains. Early beliefs suggested the drug was of divine origin and was thus used by the Inca Indians as a part of their religious ceremonies. The use of coca leaves was tightly controlled by the ruling class, and the emperors apparently gave the leaves to subjects as a reward for services to the empire. The ability to extract the cocaine was not known, but the leaves still provided some euphoria, as well as various vitamins and nutrients that supplemented their diets.

When the Spanish explorers reached South America in the sixteenth century, coca leaves were no longer a symbol of political authority or social status. The use was more widespread, and the Spanish used coca leaves to trade the Incas for their gold and silver. When introduced to Europe, it never became popular. Europeans believed the claims of the Inca Indians as to the benefits and euphoria of the leaves was greatly exaggerated. There is reason to believe that in transporting the leaves to Europe, the potency of the cocaine was lost. By the time they reached Europe, very little cocaine remained.

It was not until 1860 that a physician by the name of Dr. Albert Neiman isolated the alkaloid representing cocaine as we know it today. Once cocaine was isolated, storage and transport of the drug were easy. Use spread rapidly in the second half of the century as many drinks and elixirs made with cocaine were introduced. One of the most popular was "Mariani's wine," made by a Corsican monk and endorsed by a variety of political and religious leaders of that time. In the United States, John Pemberton introduced a product similar to Mariani's wine, promoting his "French Wine Cola" as a nerve tonic and stimulant.

The very next year, Pemberton developed another coca product, a syrup made from coca leaf flavoring (cocaine) and caffeine from the kola nut. He marketed the product as a "remarkable therapeutic agent" and "sovereign remedy" to be used when thirsty, tired or "head-achey." He named this product Coca-Cola. The drink did not catch on until it was carbonated and sold exclusively as a soft drink. All reference to the medicinal properties of the drink were dropped. The active ingredient, cocaine, was kept in the formula until 1906 when introduction of the Pure Food and Drug Act required labeling of the ingredients of various over-the-counter products. Coca-Cola is still flavored by extracts of decocainized coca leaves.

Methods of administration of cocaine by other routes developed in the second half of the century as well. Both intranasal use and injection became popular. Various companies, including Sears and Roebucks, sold "cocaine kits" which contained vials and syringes for administering cocaine. Physicians touted its benefits as a curative for asthma, colds, corns, eczema, neuralgia, opiate and alcohol addiction, and even venereal disease. The product was legally available over-the-counter, and cheaper than many other drugs which were being sold at that time.

One of the more famous advocates of the use of cocaine was Dr. Sigmund Freud, who used cocaine himself to treat his own depression. He prescribed the drug to many of his patients and even wrote a set of papers entitled "The Cocaine Papers" on the drug's benefit. It was only after evidence of cocaine's health liabilities that Freud and other physicians began to lose their enthusiasm for the drug.

During the mid 1880's, a very famous piece of literature was written by an author who was reported to have used cocaine on a regular basis. Apparently, while on a three-day cocaine binge, he wrote a story about a doctor who takes a drug that changes him into a new person, physically ugly and psychologically evil. The book, "The Strange Case of Dr. Jekyll and Mr. Hyde," may well have been Robert Lewis Stevenson's story of his own experiences with the drug. Stevenson died only a few short years after writing this book in a sanatorium in Philadelphia, Pennsylvania. He died of complications from alcohol and drug addiction.

By the turn of the twentieth century, both the federal government and the medical profession were greatly concerned with the widespread use and abuse of many drugs, including cocaine. The Pure Food and Drug Act of 1906 began regulating patent medicines, requiring labeling of ingredients and stopping various claims of medicinal benefit. It was not until the Harrison Narcotic Act of 1914 that the sale and distribution of cocaine and various other drugs were controlled or stopped. This loss of respectability, together with the high cost of illicit cocaine, reduced the use of cocaine for the next forty years.

The popularity of amphetamines during the 40's and 50's led to the reemergence of cocaine in the 60's. When the federal government stepped in to reduce the use and production or amphetamines, cocaine was again in high demand. Cocaine became an emblem of wealth and status during the 60's and 70's. The smuggling and sales of illicit cocaine suddenly became profitable, and drug dealers have continued to promote the use which is at record levels today.

Patterns of Use

There are several patterns of use for the drug cocaine. Each method is unique and determines the effect of the drug on the body. The patterns are described as follows:

Snorting or sniffing through the nose has been the most common method of use until the recent availability of crack cocaine. Typically, the cocaine powder is chopped fine with a razor blade on a hard, flat surface. It is then arranged into thin lines or columns. A line of cocaine is then inhaled intranasally, often through a rolled dollar bill or straw. It can also be snorted from a "coke spoon." The inhaled cocaine penetrates the mucous membranes of the nasal cavity, enters the blood- stream, and is circulated to the brain within one to three minutes. One line usually provides 20 to 40 minutes of stimulation and euphoria.

Oral use or cocaine can still be found, especially in South America. Many Andean Indians still chew the leaves for mild stimulation. Members of the upper social class brew tea made from coca leaves. This pattern of use is not typical in the United States, but there has been a recent trend among some groups toward the use of organic or natural drugs, away from synthetic ones.

Intravenous injection of a cocaine solution induces an intense, initial "rush" not often experienced when cocaine is taken orally or snorted. This "rush" of intense pleasure is relatively short-lived, lasting only about 10 minutes. After this high, there is a rebound phenomenon that results in the user experiencing a "crash" toward physical and psychological depression. There has been a trend away from the IV use of cocaine, predominately due to the very real danger of contracting AIDS from contaminated needles. Injecting cocaine also carries additional hazards of other serious infections, formation of blood clots, and possible adverse reactions to additives which were mixed with the cocaine.

Freebasing is a method of smoking cocaine which was popular before crack arrived. It is a "do-it-yourself" chemical process of extracting pure grains of cocaine from an adulterated batch of cocaine powder. The powder is mixed with water and a powerful base chemical, like ammonia, is added to the mixture. Ether is then added to the mixture, which collects the cocaine hydrochloride, raising it to the surface. The ether is then removed and allowed to dry, or is heated, leaving a smokable "base" or "freebase" behind. This is then smoked in a water pipe or sprinkled on marijuana or tobacco. Within seven seconds the cocaine reaches the brain, producing a sudden and intense high. This euphoria quickly subsides and is generally followed by restlessness, irritability and depression. The process is both dangerous and costly. The presence of the ether creates fire hazards, as witnessed by the accident involving comedian Richard Pryor. Smokers also tend to smoke until exhausted or they run out of cocaine and money in an effort to avoid the crash that follows using.

Crack smoking will be covered later in this chapter.

Acute Effects of Cocaine

It is estimated that approximately 22 million people in this country have used cocaine. The widespread nature of use is creating some alarming problems in society. Both deaths and emergency room visits attributable to cocaine use are up over 200% since 1976. Because of increased availability, there is a significant increase in the number of high school students who use the drug. Due to the demand for the drug, thousands of tons of the drug are smuggled into the country each year. The problems associated with crime and violence is showing an alarming increase.

A variety of myths about cocaine seem to prevail. Here are a few examples:

1) Cocaine is not addictive.

Fact: Cocaine is an extremely addicting drug (both physically and psychologically) with a specific withdrawal syndrome associated with it. Most books and articles published before 1984 state that cocaine is psychologically addicting, but not physically addicting. With the release of the Diagnostic Statistical Manual, Fourth Edition, the issue of physical addiction was clearly identified.

2) Cocaine will improve your sex life.

Fact: With initial use the stimulating effect of the drug may indeed enhance sex; however, a tolerance to this aspect of the drug quickly occurs.

3) Practically everyone is using it.

Fact: Although there has been a significant increase in the number of people using cocaine, not everyone is using it.

4) Using cocaine is a symbol of success.

Fact: The converse is frequently true. Many successful people have lost everything due to their cocaine use.

Cocaine apparently has its effect at the neural synapses located in the brain. Cocaine appears to stimulate the release of neurotransmitters into the synaptic cleft between cells. The increased release of neurotransmitters is responsible for the "high" associated with cocaine. With this release there is a heightening of body senses and an intensity of feelings such as fear, passion, and flight or fight. The increase of the neurotransmitter Dopamine, in particular, gives the body "chemical rewards." The body feels as if it has had food, sex or drink even if it has not.

Cocaine then inhibits the re-uptake of the neurotransmitters. Because they are not reabsorbed, they stay free at the synaptic cleft. Eventually there is a depletion of the neurotransmitters. The decrease of Dopamine in particular is thought to cause the feelings of dysphoria in cocaine withdrawal. Since Dopamine is so closely associated with pleasure, it is thought that this process has a great deal to do with the addictive nature of the drug, especially as it relates to the craving and desire for continued use of the drug.

Acute Physical Effects of Cocaine

As with any drug, the effects of cocaine are dependent upon the dosage, the drug's purity and the route of administration. The initial effects are quite euphoric and quite intense but subside quickly. Users report feelings of self-confidence and super-charged energy. Physically, they experience an increased heart rate and blood pressure, dilation of the pupils, constriction of peripheral blood vessels, and a rise in body temperature and metabolic rate. There is a reduction of fatigue (masked by stimulation of the central nervous system), mental alertness, and increased sociability.

Frequent users report feelings of restlessness, irritability, anxiety and sleeplessness. In addition, initial episodes of use may create various psychological problems and mood swings, while long-term use may result in hallucinations of touch, sight, taste or smell. Prolonged snorting tends to dry the mucous membrane linings of the nose until they crack, bleed and develop ulcerlike sores. Long-term use produces cold-like symptoms with a running nose, dull headaches, and a loss or cartilage separating the nostrils.

Regardless of the route of administration, prolonged use results in malnutrition due to the suppression of the appetite. Chronic abusers often lose weight and develop a variety of vitamin deficiencies. Loss of calcium, which is needed to detoxify cocaine from the system, results in tooth and gum disease, hair loss, dry, itchy skin, and joint aches and pains.

Among the more alarming problems of prolonged use are confusion, anxiety, and cocaine psychosis, characterized by paranoia and hallucination of tactile, visual, olfactory, and auditory nature. This can occur both during and after use of the drug. One particular hallucination is referred to as formication - the belief that bugs are crawling on or under one's own skin.

In looking at the use of cocaine it is also important to understand the symptoms of cocaine intoxication. The signs of cocaine intoxication include: increased blood pressure, increased pulse, dilated pupils (wide eyes), anxiety and euphoria. These symptoms are due to the effect of the release of the neurotransmitter norepinephrine. Occasionally, cocaine users will also experience hallucinations, paranoid ideations and psychosis. These symptoms are associated with increased amounts of Dopamine present in the brain.

There is a growing concern related to pregnant women's use of cocaine and the effects on the unborn child. We are seeing an increase of "cocaine babies" who are born experiencing withdrawal symptoms, have an increased number of respiratory and kidney problems, visual problems, and lack of coordination. Recent reports also show that as these children grow up, they suffer from hyperactivity and neurological disorders, as well as suffer from learning disabilities. There will be a tremendous impact on society for years to come as additional problems are identified.

Brief Information about Crack Cocaine

Crack is a more potent form of cocaine

It is one of the most highly addicting drugs known

Crack is absorbed immediately when smoked and enters the brain within seven seconds

Crack is manufactured simply by mixing cocaine with baking soda and water

Crack use does harm the developing fetus

Crack has become a serious social problem in the United States

Crack Cocaine

Crack is a form of freebased cocaine. It is a less volatile form of smokable cocaine (it does not have the explosive nature of freebased cocaine which is mixed with ether) as well as a cheaper form of the drug, made by combining cocaine with baking soda and water. This combination removes impurities and frees the cocaine hydrochloride. As a result, many forms of crack cocaine may be as much as 90% pure.

The name crack comes from the sound that is heard when the drug is smoked. Lumps of crack are smoked in a two-chambered glass pipe. The drug is burned in the top section. As the user inhales, the smoke is cooled and filtered through water in the lower chamber.

Crack is considered one of the most dangerous and addicting drugs around because it reaches the pleasure centers of the brain in 8 to 10 seconds. Once in the brain, crack produces a short, intense, electrifying feeling of euphoria as it causes a sudden release of neurotransmitters, especially Dopamine, in the brain. Its effects are much more intense and pleasurable than snorting or IV use of cocaine. The high generally lasts only 3 to 5 minutes, followed by a crushing depression which may persist for 10 to 40 minutes or longer. The depression is caused by the body's inability to resupply Dopamine.

Crack resembles hard shavings which are similar to slivers of soap. It is often sold in small vials, in folding papers, or in heavy tinfoil. Sometimes, crack is broken into tiny chunks that are sold as rocks or chips. Crack is relatively cheap, costing as little as $5, up to $20, making it affordable to school age children as well as lower socioeconomic groups.

On the street, crack is referred to by some of the following names:

Crack, rocks, Roxanne, ready-rock, gravel, French Fries, space crack (mixed with PCP), moon rock (crack and heroin), geek, fry daddy, primo (crack and marijuana), cocktail (cigarette laced with crack).

The History of Crack

While most people believe crack to be a phenomenon of the 1980's, in actuality the history of crack dates back to the mid 1970's. Underground cookbooks reported a method of making "rock" cocaine that could be smoked. Freebasing was the popular form of smokable cocaine use. "Rock" cocaine was viewed as being poor in quality and not as pleasurable as freebasing. However, it was not possible to keep freebase cocaine around, so dealers were forced to make batches of the drug for those who wished to purchase the drug, causing them to be in longer contact with the buyer than they preferred. Also, freebasing itself is dangerous due to the use of ether in the process.

As a result, crack cocaine was reintroduced in 1981 and quickly spread to many of the major cities in the United states. By 1985, the government declared crack use to be at an epidemic level. The introduction of crack cocaine into society has been responsible for an increase in crime across America. Many youth, once addicted, have turned to stealing, prostitution and drug dealing in order to support their compulsive use of the drug. Daily habits of $150 to $200 are not uncommon.

The use of crack has also signaled a rise in cocaine related deaths. Like cocaine in any form, crack can cause high blood pressure that may lead to brain hemorrhage. It may block the heart's electrical system causing cardiac arrest and death by interruption of the brain's control over the heart and respiratory system.

Short Term Physical Effects

Crack produces the same short-term effects as other forms of cocaine as well as amphetamines. The dose used, tolerance and user sensitivity may also influence the effects. Because it is smoked, the drug reaches the brain within 7 seconds, with an "afterglow" that may last as long as ten minutes. Large doses create a feeling of enhanced sexuality, particularly in males. The "rush" that is experienced is generally compared to sexual orgasm.

Though it has a shorter high than traditional cocaine, it produces the same feelings of enhanced energy, increased self-esteem, mental alertness and heightened sensory awareness. The user is more sociable, with increased motor activity and arousal, but a reduced need for food and sleep.

Crack increases heart rate, blood pressure, respiratory rate, and body temperature. Crack also changes heart rhythm, dilates pupils, and produces sweating, restlessness and excitement. High doses create more intense euphoria and create some adverse reactions that include:

- bizarre and violent behavior,

- extreme anxiety and restlessness,

- twitches, tremors, spasms and loss of coordination,

- hallucinations and delusions, and

- chest pain and nausea.

It can also cause seizures, respiratory arrest, cardiac arrest, and high fever - all of which can prove fatal.

Once the "afterglow" wears off, the user will experience intense craving sensations. They will often repeat doses of the drug quickly over the next several hours, going on a binge that lasts until all of their money is gone.   Binge use often creates the following effects:

- extreme alertness and watchfulness,

- disinhibition,

- impaired judgment,

- grandiose behavior,

- impulsivity,

- compulsivity,

- hypersexual and atypical sexual behavior.

Binges also lead to anxiety, panic, paranoia, and often attempts at suicide. Homicidal behavior has also been exhibited during such use.

Long-term Effects

Long-term crack usage can create serious physical and psychological problems for the user. Symptoms include restlessness, extreme excitability, tremors, anxiety, insomnia, and a form of paranoid psychosis. Other effects include:

- massive weight loss,

- dehydration,

- constipation,

- tooth decay,

- urinary tract problems.

Due to smoking the drug, other effects include:

- chronic sore throat,

- lung congestion,

- hacking cough,

- black sputum discharge,

- lung damage.

Chronic use may also cause hypertension, seizures, respiratory arrest, and cardiac failure. Withdrawn social behavior and total abstinence from sex, as well as impotence, may also occur.

Section 1, Chapter 6:

Causes of Addiction and Treatment Approaches

The following section is an updated adaptation of Chapter 3 from "Treatment for Alcohol and Other Drug Abuse, Opportunities for Coordination." DHHS Publication No.(SMA) 94-2075, First printed 1994

For some persons substance abuse progresses from experimental or social use to dependency and addiction. Major consequences ensue for individuals, their families, and society. Addicted persons usually experience increasingly debilitating or dysfunctional physical, social, financial, and emotional effects. Treatment is essential for those who become chemically dependent and are unable to control their use of alcohol or other drugs.

As long as mood-altering, or psychoactive, substances have resulted in personal and social problems, people have tried to understand the causes of dependency and addiction. Two overriding questions abound:

1. *What causes people to initiate and continue behaviors that are often very self-destructive?*

2. *How can these behaviors be changed or controlled to help the involved persons achieve better health and well-being?*

The way in which causes of addiction are understood helps determine the focus of assessment and treatment of substance abuse disorders. Treatment professionals and political and judicial decision makers must have an understanding of the causes of substance abuse and their implications for treatment and other interventions.

This chapter will briefly summarize several prevailing concepts about the causes of substance abuse. The ways in which different perspectives influence treatment are reviewed, and a synopsis of major treatment modalities and techniques also is presented.

CAUSES OF ALCOHOL AND DRUG ADDICTION

Many assumptions and beliefs about the causes of substance abuse have been espoused. As the amount of knowledge gained through research expands, some of these explanations have been discounted or proved false. For example, the moral model attributes the cause of drug and alcohol problems to moral weakness in the character of individuals. Proponents of this model believe change is possible only through personal motivation and efforts. While there is currently little support for the moral model within the drug treatment community, it is, unfortunately, still a widely held belief among significant segments of the general population.

Substance abuse, like other physical or mental disorders, is multifaceted and complex. Many viewpoints have been developed that appear to have validity in advancing an understanding of alcohol and other drug addictions. Most researchers and practitioners agree that a single comprehensive understanding of addiction that applies to all persons and circumstances has not yet evolved. There are no "magic bullets" or miracle cures for substance abuse that can help an addicted person achieve sobriety without the structure, discipline, and personal resolve needed to help him or her remain drug-free. Similarly, in alcohol and other drug treatment modalities, "one size does not fit all." Rather, patient-treatment matching considers the characteristics of treatment programs and the personality, background, mental condition, and substance abuse patterns of individuals to realize the best fit and the greatest chance of successful treatment .

Research has shown that certain factors correlate strongly with the early initiation of drug use. Studies have found that among youth with histories of drug and alcohol involvement and delinquent behavior, these factors are proportionately more prevalent. A given youth may experience several of these problems and not become involved in delinquency or substance abuse. However, a combination of several of these factors is a stronger indicator of the possibility of such behavior.

The quest by medical scientists to comprehend the complex phenomenon of substance abuse continues, and with each additional piece of knowledge, a better understanding develops. As research continues, it is likely that current knowledge and concepts will be expanded, modified, or rejected. Perhaps new hypotheses will be developed.

Concepts about the causes of addiction often are grouped in various categories because of their similarities and differences. In this text, some concepts that are currently considered valid will be labeled and discussed in four categories:

- biopsychosocial;
- medical;
- clinical; and
- social.

Major contributions to each of these areas will be summarized, and implications for treatment will be considered.

Biopsychosocial Model

As an understanding of addiction has evolved and knowledge has been gained through research, the complexity of the causes for and persistence of substance abuse has been compounded. It now appears that a constellation of factors can be correlated with initiation and continuation of chemical use and dependency. No single explanation appears adequate in most cases. Similarly, across the range of persons affected by substance abuse, there are wide variances in precipitating factors and motivations for continued use.

The *biopsychosocial model* has emerged to provide a broader, more holistic view of substance abuse and its treatment. It is the model that is most widely endorsed by treatment researchers because it can most adequately explain the intricate nature of addiction. This model incorporates elements of all the other more narrowly focused models described later in this chapter.

Biological causes of substance abuse include a possible hereditary predisposition, especially for alcoholism. As research progresses, there also is evidence that use of chemical substances may actually alter brain chemistry. With habitual substance abuse, natural chemicals may no longer be produced in the brain, resulting in dependency on alcohol or other drugs to avoid discomfort. Substance abuse also may be initiated and continued because individuals experience emotional and psychological problems. Initially, chemicals can produce positive sensations that help counteract painful events and underlying problems. Alcohol and other drug use often begin in social situations. It is through social interactions that substance use often is learned and reinforced. Addiction also is often correlated with various social problems such as unemployment, poverty, racism, and family dysfunction.

Variables affecting substance use often interact with each other and cut across multiple levels. When assessing and intervening with an individual troubled by problems related to chemical dependency, the individual's uniqueness, level of functioning, and attraction toward and susceptibility to addictive behavior must be considered. Multiple measures of biological, psychological, and social functioning must be collected, integrated, and interpreted. Addiction, then, is impacted by physiological, social, behavioral, and environmental factors.

The most important implication of the biopsychosocial model for treatment is the realization that a single treatment approach is unlikely to be sufficient. Rather, as biological, psychological, and social needs are assessed, an integrated, comprehensive treatment response must be implemented to meet the entire range of needs of the individual. The first stage of this response requires a comprehensive assessment to determine the entire range of strengths, needs, and problems presented by the individual.

A biopsychosocial approach necessitates comprehensive services and appropriate patient-treatment matching. For individual patients, this often requires multidisciplinary teams of treatment professionals to provide the array of treatment and case management services needed. A continuum of treatment and supportive services is needed for adequately meeting the extent of needs presented by addicted persons. At community and State levels, an array of adequately funded treatment resources and coordination of policies and services are essential.

Medical/Biological Causes of Substance Abuse

From this perspective, drug addiction is seen as an illness comparable to other diseases, such as diabetes or heart disease. Alcohol or drug addiction is considered a chronic, progressive, relapsing, and potentially fatal disease. Although persons may choose whether or not to initiate the use of psychoactive substances, *alcohol or drug dependence is an involuntary result.* Common characteristics include impaired control over drinking or taking drugs, preoccupation with a substance of abuse, continued use despite adverse consequences, and distortions in thinking.

Being a chronic disease, the management of behavior is a central feature for the improvement of functioning. The client enters treatment in order to get into remission and begin the process of recovery. A course of care is developed, but it is important to understand that relapse can and does occur. Recovery then represents the long-term management of the addictive disease and is life-long. As such, the field must treat not just the acute symptoms that clients present with, but the long-term needs that exist.

The following medical/biological causes of substance abuse have evolved and are supported by some research findings.

Genetic Causes

Research into the biological causes of addiction has resulted in convincing evidence that there is a hereditary vulnerability to alcoholism. Alcohol-related disorders have been found in multiple generations of families and have been studied over time. It is believed that many people with a genetic predisposition to alcoholism will progress to dependency if they begin using alcohol. Although a similar assumption is often made about other drugs of abuse, research evidence is much more difficult to obtain. Mood-altering drugs produce various pharmacological effects. The use of drugs over time is often influenced by fads and availability. Thus, different generations of families may be exposed to different types of drugs, whereas use of alcohol has been consistent over several generations. This makes the multigenerational study of drug abuse more difficult than similar studies of alcoholism.

Brain Reward Mechanisms

Certain areas of the brain, when stimulated, produce pleasurable feelings. Psychoactive substances are capable of acting on these brain mechanisms to produce these sensations. These pleasurable feelings become reinforcers that drive the continued use of the substances.

Altered Brain Chemistry

Because of long-term use of alcohol or other drugs, the normal release of various types of natural chemicals in the brain that produce pleasurable sensations may be disrupted. Habitual substance abuse can alter brain chemistry, requiring continued use of psychoactive substances to avoid discomfort created by brain chemistry imbalance.

Self-Medication

Some individuals who have psychiatric conditions, such as anxiety or depression, use psychoactive substances to alleviate the symptoms they experience. If their emotional discomfort is relieved by alcohol or other drugs, they may persist in using chemicals to continue achieving such results.

Concepts of the medical/biological causes of substance abuse influence treatment in two important ways. First, according to these concepts, *abstinence* is viewed as the only feasible way to avoid the negative consequences of substance abuse. If alcohol- or drug-dependent persons are unable to control their use of chemical substances (whether because of genetic factors, metabolic imbalance, or altered brain chemistry), they must refrain from any use of psychoactive substances. It is impossible for them to use any alcohol or other drugs without experiencing physical, social, and emotional effects.

Second, *pharmacotherapeutic interventions* have been developed or are being sought to meet the following needs:

- substitute for abused drugs and provide a more controllable form of addiction;
- block the effects of abused drugs;
- reduce cravings for drugs; and
- alleviate drug withdrawal symptoms and block the toxic effects of drugs.

Use of pharmacological modalities is regulated by the United States Food and Drug Administration (FDA). Programs providing this type of treatment must have medical staff who administer medications and supervise the program and patients.

Methadone is a chemical substance used to replace abused narcotic drugs. Methadone prevents the physical withdrawal symptoms experienced by opiate addicts, does not deliver the mood-altering experience of opiates, and, therefore, allows dependent persons to focus on activities other than procuring and using heroin. It is also valuable in the treatment of infectious diseases and mental health problems. The incidence of HIV/AIDS and other infectious diseases (**see Section 3.5**) is escalating among drug-involved persons, especially injection drug users. Methadone treatment can help these persons control their use of illicit injection drugs and improve their general health. In so doing, they will reduce the probability of becoming infected. If they are already infected, cessation of illicit drug use will likely boost the functioning of their immune systems and delay the onset of AIDS.

All treatment modalities to be discussed in this document stress abstinence from all psychoactive substances. In some instances, pharmacotherapeutic interventions offer the best course of treatment for addictions. These treatment approaches often are coupled with behavioral or psychosocial interventions. More information on treatment modalities will be provided later in this chapter.

Clinical Causes of Substance Abuse

Clinical or psychological causes of addiction focus on personal needs or personality traits of those abusing substances. They can be divided into two categories: (1) those emphasizing the rewards derived from the use of mood-altering drugs that tend to perpetuate their use, and (2) those stressing that substance abusers have different personalities from those who abstain.

Reinforcement Processes

People tend to seek rewards and minimize negative consequences through their behaviors. If past behaviors have brought a response that is perceived as reinforcing, persons tend to repeat those behaviors to obtain similar rewards. Drug use may be rewarded in several ways, as described in the following list.

- *Positive reinforcement.* Persons abusing drugs and alcohol have found their use rewarded and, therefore, continue use. Without a positive reward, substance abuse would not likely continue, according to this perspective. There are many types of positive rewards that may accrue to someone using psychoactive substances, including their pharmacological effects (e.g., euphoria), social rewards, peer acceptance and esteem.

- *Avoidance of pain.* Behaviors also may be motivated by a need to seek relief or avoid pain. If using alcohol or other drugs helps someone who is suffering (physically or emotionally), he or she is likely to use the substance again when experiencing the same distress, and a strategy for coping with pain or stress develops that is dependent on the use of alcohol and other drugs. Some drugs produce painful withdrawal symptoms when use of them is discontinued. Persons dependent upon a drug may find that taking a dose will diminish their pain. Substance abuse also may be motivated by a desire for relief from pain, anger, anxiety of depression, and alleviation or boredom.

- *Drug cues.* Another aspect of reinforcement pertains to the anticipation of rewards. Certain stimuli can be associated with a drug and its rewards. These stimuli may act as triggers for drug seeking and use. Physiological responses, sometimes called cravings, may result from the introduction of a cue or stimulus. Cues vary from one individual to another, but may include being with specific people, engaging in particular activities, or going to certain places.

Personality Traits

The use of drugs is linked with emotional problems and personal inadequacies according to this school of thought. Substance abuse may provide the individual with an escape from the problems of life through euphoria and drug-induced indifference. Although such drug use may mask certain difficulties temporarily, the underlying problems are not solved, and addiction generates new, and often more serious, problems.

As a response to psychological suffering, substance abuse is sometimes viewed as an adaptive effort for survival. Associations have been found between drug use and psychological characteristics such as low self-esteem, low self-confidence, low self-satisfaction, need for social approval, high anxiety, low assertiveness, greater rebelliousness, and self-regulatory deficiencies. The causes of these characteristics have been attributed variously to factors such as peer rejection, parental neglect, high achievement expectations, school failure, social and physical stigma, and poor coping ability, among others. Deviant activity, such as substance abuse, may be chosen by some as a way of achieving group acceptance, status, and membership or escaping the realities of rejection. Some research indicates that Antisocial Personality Disorder and Borderline Personality Disorder may place persons at increased risk of substance abuse.

Based on the concept of reinforcement, behavioral treatment approaches often try to help individuals find significantly greater rewards from legitimate activities. Involvement in a variety of activities, depending on individual interests and abilities, may help some persons achieve greater peer acceptance and self-esteem. Substituting other activities to achieve feelings of happiness and well-being also are recommended. For example, some persons claim to get a "high" from running or other physical activities. Virtually all of the prevailing psychosocial treatment approaches emphasize helping chemically dependent persons learn new ways to structure their time and social relationships through drug-free activities.

Relapse prevention, a critical component of treatment, is closely tied to drug cues. Approaches are recommended for helping individuals control or change their reactions to drug cues. Avoiding people, places, and activities formerly associated with substance abuse is one example. Relapse prevention is a critical element of any treatment approach.

Aversive conditioning is a technique that involves pairing a negative stimulus with drug cues. Some methods that have been tried include chemically or hypnotically induced nausea or electric shocks paired with the sight, taste, smell, or other reminders of specific substances. Another approach, sometimes called extinction or cue exposure, consists of presenting the drug cue repeatedly. However, in controlled settings, where this cue cannot be followed by alcohol or drug use, reaction to the stimulus is gradually reduced. Substance abusers also may receive skills training and cognitive behavioral counseling to provide them with tools to avoid relapsing to alcohol or other drug use.

A variety of therapeutic interventions may be implemented in addressing the personal and emotional problems thought to underlie substance abuse. Traditional mental health approaches may include building self-esteem, lowering anxiety, and resolving other distressful problems through individual, group, and family counseling.

Behavioral or psychosocial treatment approaches often are linked to a clinical understanding of addiction. These methods include self-help and individual, group, and family counseling. All rely heavily on changing the individual's self-concept and dealing with distressing situations and relationships thought to underlie substance abuse.

Social Causes of Substance Abuse

These perspectives focus on situations, social relations, or social structures related to substance abuse. Virtually any factor outside the individual, such as peers, family, or the media, could be associated with social causes of addiction.

Social Learning

In group settings, individuals are exposed to persons who model certain behaviors, and they receive rewards or punishments for their own behaviors from group members. When one associates with groups that define drug use as desirable and whose members model drug-related behavior, drug use by the individual is learned and rewarded.

Subculture Perspectives

This viewpoint indicates that drug use is expected and encouraged in certain social circles, while it is discouraged, and even punished, in others. There is not a single drug subculture; rather, there are several of them. For example, there might be a drug subculture of white, high school youth, or young adult black males, and some drug subcultures are formed according to the drug of choice (e.g., groups for alcohol, marijuana, cocaine, or heroin users). Members of a subculture teach new members how to use a particular drug, supply the drug initially, and provide role models.

Socialization

According to this perspective, potential drug users are attracted to other drug-involved individuals and drug subculture groups because their own values and activities are compatible with those of persons who use drugs. The four main agents of socialization for adolescents are parents, peers, school, and the media. The greater the youth's affinity for drug use, the more likely he or she is to choose to participate with others having similar values and norms. Alienation from parents and friendships with drug-using peers is an especially strong factor in the socialization of youth into drug use.

Social Control

This approach claims that absence of the social control requiring conformity leads to drug abuse. Those more attracted to conventional society are less likely to engage in behavior that violates societal values and norms. Socially detached persons will not feel the constraint of these norms and values.

Social, Economic, and Political Factors

Elements of unemployment, poverty, racism, sexism, family dissolution, and feelings of powerlessness and alienation are associated with the problem of substance abuse. Although not universal by any means, some persons consistently subjected to these conditions are drawn into drug activity to escape their painful life circumstances.

One approach to treating substance abuse from the social perspective involves changing the substance abuser's environment and peer associations. The behavioral treatment approaches emphasize positive peer associations and pro-social lifestyles and activities. For example, therapeutic communities are based on group support and confrontation to help members learn new attitudes and behaviors toward drugs and other persons. Self-help strategies similarly encourage drug-free activities and association with others in recovery.

Working to strengthen social values and norms that preclude drug dependency also is important. Our society generally is committed to eliminating pain, suffering, and discomfort. Millions of dollars are spent on advertising products such as patent medicines, alcohol, and tobacco as "quick cures" for physical and emotional distress. Promoting and glamorizing the use of such substances contributes to an attitude that drinking and other drug use is acceptable and even desirable. Instant gratification is an underlying theme throughout most of American society.

Treatment strategies must consider more than just the individual affected by substance abuse. Considerations of economic, political, and social changes are also important concerns of treatment professionals and decision makers.

THE ROLE OF DETOXIFICATION

Detoxification is not a treatment modality, but is the necessary first step in the treatment process. Detoxification provides medical and supportive services needed to alleviate the short-term symptoms of physical withdrawal from chemical dependence, including physical discomfort and cravings, as well as mood changes. Once symptoms of craving and withdrawal are controlled, treatment can begin.

The purpose of detoxification is to help the patient stabilize physically and psychologically until the body becomes free of drugs or the effects of alcohol. Within this broad goal there are several additional objectives that can be targeted. Promoting the health of the individual can be accomplished through measures to reduce and control seizures that occur with some drugs. It also includes screening for and treating infectious diseases and other medical problems. Drug education and relapse prevention programming can begin during detoxification. Some attention may even be given to family, vocational, religious, and legal problems in some settings. It is also important that detoxification be used as an opportunity to recruit and prepare persons for appropriate longer-term treatment programs.

There are three major categories of abused substances that often require detoxification: (1) alcohol and other central nervous system (CSN) depressants; (2) opiate drugs; and (3) cocaine. Some of the major considerations for each are described.

Alcohol Detoxification

Following withdrawal from alcohol, a dependent person may experience several symptoms, including:

- eating and sleep disturbances;

- tremors (involuntary trembling motion of the body);

- sweats;

- clouding of the sensorium;

- hallucinations and agitation;

- elevated temperature;

- change in pulse rate; and

- convulsions.

Some of these symptoms can be life-threatening. In addition, the potential for suicide must be considered. Because of the possibility of these extreme consequences, there should be clearly defined procedures to follow when an individual is experiencing alcohol detoxification. These should be implemented in a variety of settings, including jails, shelters, and other congregate living situations.

Alcohol detoxification is usually provided in a hospital setting for five days or less. Medical supervision is needed to provide medications, vitamin therapy, and, in some cases, measures to correct water and electrolyte imbalances. Alcohol detoxification also may be provided in nonhospital settings, but the rates of successful completion have been much lower. Patients who need medical or psychiatric care, have no housing, have coexisting drug dependence, are unemployed, or come to the initial visit intoxicated are less likely to succeed in outpatient treatment and are more likely to need hospitalization.

Medications that can be useful in the treatment of alcohol withdrawal include benzodiazepines and other CNS depressants such as barbiturates. Clonidine and beta blocking drugs may help decrease symptoms of tremor, fast heart rate, and hypertension.

Detoxification from Other CNS Depressants

This category includes sedative drugs (such as barbiturates), hypnotic drugs (such as methaqualone), and anxiolytics, used for the treatment of anxiety. These drugs have legitimate medical uses, but they are also subject to misuse. Signs of abuse and dependency include:

- gradually increasing use;

- periods of intoxication;

- functional impairment; and

- unsuccessful attempts to decrease or discontinue use.

Sudden discontinuation of these drugs may result in life-threatening withdrawal. Again, procedures should define steps to be taken to ensure the safety of individuals withdrawing from CNS depressants. Signs of withdrawal include:

- tremor (involuntary trembling);

- hyperreflexia (increased/heightened sense of reflex);

- agitation;

- hypertension (high blood pressure);

- tachycardia (excessively rapid heart beat);

- insomnia;

- vomiting, nausea;

- diaphoresis (excessive perspiration);

- cognitive impairment (memory loss, decreased ability to concentrate);

- seizures;

- weakness;

- anorexia;

- irritability;

- anxiety, restlessness;

- headache;

- muscle aches;

- depression;

- tinnitus (buzzing, whistling, or ringing sound in the ears);

- depersonalization (a state of impersonality, not of one's usual character);

- paranoid delusions; and

- hypersensitivity to touch, light, and sound.

Detoxification from these drugs is achieved by gradually reducing the amount of the substance used or by substituting a similar acting drug and then gradually withdrawing it by decreasing the dosage. Phenobarbital is an often-used drug substitute for this purpose.

Detoxification From Opiate Drugs

Detoxification from opiate drugs is needed as an initial treatment for opiate dependence (usually heroin) when addicts are entering a drug-free rehabilitation program. Detoxification also may be implemented when a person who has been stabilized on methadone wishes to discontinue its use. According to recent regulations by the FDA, methadone can be used for detoxification for up to 180 days.

Some of the more common symptoms of opiate withdrawal include the following:

- increased blood pressure, pulse rate, and temperature;

- piloerection ("gooseflesh");

- increased pupil size;

- rhinorrhea (nasal drainage/mucus, can be excessive);

- lacrimation (excessive secretion of tears, heavy tearing);

- tremor;

- insomnia;

- vomiting, nausea;

- muscle aches;

- abdominal cramps;

- irritability;

- anorexia;

- weakness/tiredness;

- restlessness;

- headache;

- dizziness/lightheadedness;

- sneezing;

- hot or cold flashes; and

- drug craving.

The most common approach to detoxification from opiate drugs is the substitution of a longer-acting opioid, such as methadone, which blocks symptoms of withdrawal and drug cravings. The amount of methadone can then be gradually reduced. Combined with counseling services, methadone can help addicts quit using illicit drugs. It has reduced criminal behaviors associated with obtaining and taking illicit drugs. Vocational and educational services, coupled with cessation of illegal drug use, can help individuals lead more stable and productive lives. Clonidine is another drug that is used sometimes because it can block many of the signs and symptoms of opiate withdrawal. Acupuncture and electrostimulation of the central nervous system have also been used as adjunct therapies to alleviate withdrawal symptoms of opiate drugs. Reducing injection drug use and needle sharing among heroin addicts also diminishes the risk of contracting or spreading HIV and other substance abuse-related infectious diseases.

Detoxification From Cocaine

Cocaine dependence results in a period of physical and mental instability upon discontinuation of use. The usual pattern of cocaine use involves "binges" or "runs" lasting from 12 to 36 hours during which the person consumes all the cocaine available. Following this are periods usually lasting several days during which no cocaine is used and detoxification occurs. The effects of withdrawal include:

- irritability;

- weakness;

- reduced energy;

- hypersomnia (an excessive feeling of sleepiness, fatigue);

- depression;

- loss of concentration;

- diminished capacity to experience pleasure;

- increased appetite; and

- paranoid ideations.

In addition, the cocaine-dependent person will experience cravings for the drug, leading to another episode of binging on the drug.

Detoxification efforts have focused on ways of managing withdrawal symptoms and cravings long enough to disrupt the cycle of binging and craving. Drugs that have been used to counteract cocaine withdrawal problems include:

- desipramine hydrochloride;

- amantadine;

- bromocriptine;

- flupenthixol decanoate; and

- buprenophine.

These are usually administered on an outpatient basis and accompanied by counseling. However, for persons with concomitant psychiatric or medical problems (e.g., pregnancy, myocardial damage) inpatient care is recommended. Patient dropout rates for these treatments (especially outpatient programs) tend to be high, because it usually takes one to two weeks for the therapeutic effects of medications to begin. In the interim, the cycle of craving and cocaine use may continue.

Addiction is considered a medical illness with related psychological and social dimensions. As reviewed in **Section 1.1**, substance abuse problems progress from experimental to addictive use for some people. This process occurs more quickly for some people than it does for others. Detoxification is *necessary* to prepare patients for the treatment process. It is particularly important for those who have become dependent on alcohol and other CNS depressants, opiate drugs, and cocaine. Until the body is free of the effects of the drugs and the distorted thoughts and feelings they produce, it is difficult for recovery to begin.

Studies have shown that rapid relapse is likely to follow detoxification unless patients become engaged in additional treatment and transition services. Persons completing a detoxification program without continuing treatment are no more likely to succeed in reducing future drug use than persons achieving unassisted withdrawal.

The use of methadone has been well researched, and its effectiveness as part of the detoxification process for opiate drugs has been supported. However, many other drug treatments for alleviating withdrawal symptoms either have not been well researched or have resulted in contradictory findings. Thus, this is an area requiring additional medical research. As with any medical problem, when medications, such as methadone, Antabuse, and others, are used, supervision by a physician is required.

There also are varied findings regarding the preference of inpatient or outpatient care. Inpatient care is clearly necessary when the individual has associated psychiatric or medical problems. Because of the potential for life-threatening withdrawal symptoms, alcohol detoxification often takes place in a hospital or other medical facility. Patient retention in detoxification programs also has been significantly greater with inpatient programs compared to outpatient care. However, some research findings are emerging indicating that outpatient alcohol detoxification may be as beneficial in many cases and is much more cost-effective.

The Institute of Medicine recommends that hospital-based drug detoxification be used only if medical complications occur or when appropriate residential or outpatient facilities are not available. The conditions for which hospital-based drug detoxification is recommended include:

- serious concurrent medical illness such as tuberculosis, pneumonia, or acute hepatitis;

- history of medical complications such as seizures in previous detoxification episodes;

- evidence of suicidal ideation;

- dependence on sedative-hypnotic drugs; and

- history of failure to complete earlier ambulatory or residential detoxification.

TREATMENT FOR ALCOHOL AND OTHER DRUG PROBLEMS

Some persons who *use* drugs do not need drug treatment. Many people can use alcohol and some illicit drugs without encountering adverse consequences. Some grow weary of a lifestyle in which the pursuit of drugs and managing the varied consequences of substance use predominates. Most people who have not progressed to the point of dependency or addiction are able to decide to stop using drugs and maintain this resolve. However, a social climate that is intolerant toward substance abuse and the risk of social, legal, or employer sanctions may be needed for them to make and maintain their decision to stop or limit their drug use.

For those who are dependent or addicted, treatment for substance abuse is crucial in controlling their substance abuse and improving their health and social functioning. Without treatment, substance abuse may ultimately be fatal because of the risk of overdose, related suicides and homicides, and infectious diseases and other assaults to one's health. Yet few voluntarily seek treatment. Cessation of drug use is very difficult and treatment programs can be demanding and intense.

However, for those who enter and remain in treatment, the news is often positive. Research indicates that treatment is effective and many drug-and alcohol-involved persons respond favorably to a diversity of treatment approaches.

MAJOR TREATMENT MODALITIES

There is no "magic bullet" for effectively treating persons with substance abuse problems. Different people respond to various approaches in diverse ways. The effects of various substances of abuse produce different symptoms and needs among users. As indicated earlier, there are diverse ways in which the causes and progression of drug and alcohol addiction may be understood. This makes it critically important that individuals be matched appropriately with the treatment program or modality that is most likely to attack the problems resulting in their particular needs; the most successful treatment is individualized. Many factors must be considered, including personality, background, mental condition, and drug use experience.

There are several ways to categorize treatment programs and modalities. In this text they will be grouped into two broad categories:

1. Those that are biologically based, including:

    - medication-assisted treatment (MAT)

    - acupuncture

2. Those that are behaviorally or psychosocially based, including:

    - residential or inpatient treatment programs, such as:

        - inpatient hospitalization

        - therapeutic communities

    - outpatient nonmethadone treatment

Various treatment components and approaches are used in these treatment programs and modalities, including:

- self-help programs;

- individual counseling;

- group counseling/treatment;

- family therapy; and

- behavior modification.

The remainder of this section will provide a brief description of each of the major treatment approaches commonly found in the United States. General information about each treatment method will be provided, realizing that approaches can vary markedly because of differences in settings, professional staff, and client characteristics. Available information about the effectiveness of each of these modalities also will be provided.

Medication-Assisted Treatment (MAT)

Substance abuse, by definition, is a chronic disease in which the use of psychoactive substances may result in both physical and psychological addiction. Thus, one treatment approach that has shown favorable outcomes is medication-assisted treatment — the use of approved medications with medical supervision. Such pharmacotherapies are designed to be adjunctive to formal treatment and are not intended to be used as an independent or solo therapy. The goals of medication-assisted treatment include:

- reduction in the use of illicit drugs or alcohol;

- reduction in criminal behavior; and

- improvement of social behavior and psychological well being.

A further goal is the urgent imperative to control and prevent the spread of substance abuse-related infectious diseases, such as HIV/AIDS and tuberculosis. For those already infected, treatment for alcohol and other drug addictions may stabilize their physical condition, boost the immune system, and delay or prevent the onset of serious illness.

More research has been conducted on drug therapies for opiate drugs and alcohol than on other categories of abused substances. There are four categories of pharmacological treatment for substance abuse. Each will be defined, followed by some examples of the more common pharmacotherapeutic agents.

Agonists

These drugs can be substituted for the drug of abuse to provide a more controllable form of addiction. The properties and actions of these drugs are similar to those of particular abused drugs. Using them alleviates many of the withdrawal symptoms often experienced by persons addicted to various psychoactive substances. Examples of drugs in this category include methadone and clonidine.

Methadone, a synthetic narcotic analgesic compound, is the most commonly used form of pharmacotherapy for opiate drugs. It is medically safe and has few side effects. It produces a stable drug level and is not behaviorally or subjectively intoxicating. It blocks the cravings for opiate drugs and does not produce euphoria, as heroin and other drugs do. The characteristics of methadone patients have changed considerably over the past decade because of increased rates of HIV infection among intravenous drug abusers, concomitant use of cocaine and crack, and homelessness. These changes have resulted in methadone programs' needs for enlarged and more sophisticated physical facilities, better trained staff, and more funding.

Among the various pharmacotherapies, methadone maintenance has been studied most thoroughly. Methadone maintenance is generally successful in meeting treatment goals. When appropriate doses of methadone are administered, heroin use decreases markedly. However, in some cases other drugs, such as cocaine and alcohol, continue to be used. A substantial reduction in criminal behavior has been documented by several studies, and this reduction increases with length of time in methadone treatment. Socially productive behavior, such as employment, education, or homemaking, has also been shown to improve with the length of time in treatment.

Clonidine can partially suppress many withdrawal symptoms of opiates, alcohol, and tobacco. It is most effective for persons who are motivated and involved in their treatment program. It is not as useful in maintaining abstinence after withdrawal from opiate drugs has been achieved.

Antagonists

These drugs occupy the same receptor sites in the brain as specific drugs of abuse. However, they do not produce the same effects as the abused drugs, and they are non-addicting. Thus, when they are present, the effects of the abused drug are blocked because they cannot act on the brain in the usual way. Therefore, they do not produce the expected mood-altering experiences. Antagonists may be used for persons who do not want to be maintained on drug substitutes (i.e., agonists, like methadone); they also are used, at times, for persons leaving other drug-free treatment programs and re-entering the community, to diminish their risk of relapse.

Naltrexone is an opiate antagonist, also approved for the treatment of alcoholism (under the name Revia®). It does not result in euphoria as do opiate drugs.

Buprenorphine is a mixed agonist-antagonist agent. It is long-acting and blocks the effects of other opiate drugs. It produces less physical dependence than methadone, but some withdrawal symptoms do occur with its use. In October 2002, the Food and Drug Administration (FDA) approved the buprenorphine monotherapy product, Subutex®, and a buprenorphine/naloxone combination product, Suboxone®, for use in opioid addiction treatment. The combination product is designed to decrease the potential for abuse by injection. The maximum number of patients a physician may treat with buprenorphine is limited by law. As such, SAMHSA has created a physician and treatment locater website to assist programs and clinicians in finding available resources. To learn more, visit the following website: http://buprenorphine.samhsa.gov/bwns_locator/index.html.

Antidipsotropics

These drugs create adverse physical reactions when the person consumes the substance of abuse. These drugs are used to develop an aversion to the abused drug.

Antabuse (disulfiram) interferes with the metabolism of alcohol, causing unpleasant side effects when alcohol is ingested. Facial flushing, heart palpitations and a rapid heart rate, difficulty in breathing, nausea, vomiting, and possibly a serious drop in blood pressure are the major effects produced by the combination of alcohol and Antabuse. Paired with other treatment approaches, Antabuse has been successful in preventing relapse.

Psychotropic Medications

These control various symptoms associated with drug use and withdrawal. Antianxiety drugs, antipsychotics, antidepressants (for major depressions), and lithium have been tested. However, further research is needed on the effectiveness of these agents, as current research is produced conflicting results in some cases or has been inconclusive.

Researchers conceptualize two categories of therapeutic medications. Those that help patients *stop abusing drugs* include medications that reduce acute drug withdrawal symptoms, medically maintain patients, decrease drug craving, and block the drugs' reinforcing effects. Methadone, clonidine, buprenorphine, desipramine, bromocriptine, and naltrexone are included in this category. Medications that help *prevent relapse* are able to reduce prolonged withdrawal syndromes, decrease drug craving, alter the drug's reinforcing effects, treat underlying psychopathology, and treat drug-induced psychopathology. Included in this category are antidepressants, desipramine, bromocriptine, naltrexone, and disulfiram.

Most research and development of medications used in the treatment of addictive diseases has been fostered by the federal government. In treating most diseases, clinical trials of new medications usually are undertaken by pharmaceutical companies. However, these companies have been reluctant to associate their organizations and medications with drug addiction. This is, in part, due to the negative stereotypes of drug abusers. The number of persons who could benefit from a particular pharmacological treatment for addiction is also comparatively small. Thus, if involved in developing medications for addictive disorders, the pharmaceutical industry would not realize the degree of profit or recover its investment for research and development to the extent desired. There is also concern that medications will be used in combination with other illegal drugs. Pharmaceutical companies worry that the drugs or their companies will gain a bad reputation if this occurs.

Acupuncture and Transcutaneous Electrical Nerve Stimulation

Acupuncture applies a treatment method developed in China and other Far Eastern countries to the problem of alcohol and drug addiction. Addiction represents an adaptation of the central nervous system's activity in response to chronic drug administration, resulting in withdrawal symptoms when drug use is discontinued. Acupuncture or transcutaneous electrical nerve stimulation can modulate central nervous system activity in those regions of the brain affected by substances of abuse. Therefore, acupuncture may serve as a useful adjunct to comprehensive treatment for addiction.

Acupuncture involves placing needles at strategic body points (usually the outer ear). The treatments generally last for 45 minutes and are administered daily for the first few weeks and then are decreased. It is most commonly used to help drug users detoxify. The effect is a reported reduction in withdrawal symptoms and the physical craving for drugs and alcohol. Ideally, acupuncture treatment is combined with a comprehensive treatment approach, including counseling, drug testing and other interventions. Two significant advantages of this approach, at least in some programs, are its low cost and lack of waiting lists. Transcutaneous electrical nerve stimulations produce similar results but uses a different technology. Both therapeutic techniques can provide physiologic relief without toxicity or the potential for abuse that may be inherent in the use of medications.

Residential or Inpatient Treatment Programs

Programs in which the individual lives in the facility while participating in treatment can be defined as inpatient or residential programs. Some detoxification programs as well as therapeutic communities, and hospital-based programs are in this category. These programs are most appropriate for individuals who have not been successful in outpatient settings, those who have a very serious substance abuse problem, those needing concomitant medical or psychiatric care or observation, and those without a stable social support system in the community. Inpatient programs are the most restrictive, structured, and protective types of programs.

Inpatient Hospital Treatment

Inpatient treatment programs may be located in hospitals or in specialized chemical dependency centers. Chemical dependency treatment, Minnesota Model, 28-day programs, or Hazelden-type treatments are terms that may be used to denote this type of treatment approach. Many of these programs are privately financed; thus, patients are usually employed persons (or have employed spouses or parents) with private insurance. The goal of treatment is abstinence from alcohol or other drugs.

A variety of treatment techniques and strategies are usually employed in these programs, including the Twelve-Step model (the basis of Alcoholics Anonymous and other self-help programs), individual, group and family counseling, drug education, and medical management. Long-term aftercare and transitional services, especially for opiate addicts, are an important part of treatment, but many programs do not devote significant resources to them. These programs may be especially appropriate for persons with concomitant psychiatric disorders, persons assessed to be suicidal, those addicted to more than one chemical, or persons with serious medical complications. Inpatient treatment provides comprehensive treatment services, constant support during the early stages of sobriety, and close supervision to prevent relapse and respond to medical emergencies. Most inpatient programs have a multidisciplinary staff team, representing a range of training and experience and capable of offering a variety of services.

Several studies have consistently found that chemical dependency (inpatient) treatment is more effective for persons with alcohol addiction than for those whose presenting problem is another drug addiction. Those addicted to more than one substance (polydrug users) have the poorest prognosis.

Therapeutic Communities

Therapeutic communities are self-contained residential programs that emphasize self-help and rely heavily on ex-addicts as peer counselors, administrators, and role models. They provide a highly structured milieu, with program stages through which members must progress; this advancement is noted with special tasks and ceremonies. The stages progressively demand more responsibility and provide more freedom. Group encounter sessions often are confrontational, focusing on openness and honesty. Social and vocational skills also are taught.

The goals of therapeutic communities include:

- habilitation or rehabilitation of the total individual;

- changing negative patterns of behavior, thinking, and feeling that predispose drug use; and

- development of a drug-free lifestyle.

Because of costs, availability, and insurance reimbursement, several adaptations of the therapeutic community model have been developed. These include:

- *Modified therapeutic communities, where stays last an average of six to nine months.* The goals of treatment are more limited, but the primary objective is to help residents achieve a drug-free state and acquire practical living skills. This model is appropriate for persons with minimal social support systems.

- *Short-term therapeutic communities, where residents remain an average of three to six months.* The primary goal of this approach is to help persons attain a drug-free lifestyle; much less emphasis is placed on re-socialization. This model is appropriate for persons from a stable social and family environment.

- *Adolescent therapeutic communities for juveniles.* Modifications needed for youth include: increased supervision to prevent youth from leaving the program or engaging in antisocial behavior and negative peer activities; more recreational activities to promote leisure skill-building and prevent boredom; greater family involvement; academic education; increased staff-to-youth ratio; separation of youth by gender except for occasional program activities; and limiting the size of the program to 45 or fewer youth.

- *Therapeutic communities in correctional facilities to begin the treatment process in jails and prisons.* These focus on socialization, positive value formation, and education. When released, inmates are referred to other treatment agencies in the community. This approach attempts to form a strong, positive, anti-drug culture; develop work teams; and provide referral and transitional services. Successful programs must have good working relationships between treatment and correctional personnel.

This modality has been considered appropriate for hard-core drug users involved in criminal activities. The treatment approach is not a specific to any particular class of drugs. Individuals dependent on any illicitly obtained drug or combination of drugs are accepted in therapeutic communities. Characteristically, participants in therapeutic communities have experienced problems with social adjustment to conventional family and occupational responsibilities because of drug seeking (and, in some cases, before initiating drug use). Therapeutic communities often are seen as a next step for persons who continue to relapse in less restrictive treatment settings.

Because of these programs' use of confrontation and prohibition of psychotropic drugs, the use of therapeutic communities is *not* appropriate for individuals with psychopathology or with substance abuse-related neurological damage. For some persons, especially those who have low levels of self-esteem and impaired neurological functioning, the confrontational approach of the modality may be too intense.

The length of stay in traditional therapeutic communities ranges from 6 to 24 months. Research has shown that the longer clients remain in therapeutic communities, the more likely they are to have positive results. However, traditionally, dropout rates are high. Approximately 15 to 25 percent of those admitted to therapeutic communities complete the program and graduate. About 25 percent drop out within two weeks, and about 40 percent, by three months.

One study found that early dropouts from long-term therapeutic communities had common psychosocial characteristics, including:

-   low self-esteem and self-value;

-   poor concept of self-identity;

-   low self-acceptance;

-   low evaluation of self-behaviors;

-   low evaluation of physical attributes, health, and sexuality;

-   low assessment of self-worth and self-adequacy;

-   low evaluation of self in relation to family/friends and primary group;

-   high levels of self-criticism and lack of adequate defenses; and

-   a tendency to overemphasize negative features.

Evaluations of therapeutic communities demonstrate that they are cost-effective when compared with prisons. While persons are in the program, criminal activity is significantly reduced compared with pre- or post-treatment criminal activity. For those who complete the program, illicit drug use and criminal activities are diminished, while employment status improves. Approximately 15 percent of therapeutic community graduates qualify to be trained for staff counseling positions. Of those, approximately half continue their employment for more than one year.

Some studies have reported that less severe criminal activity is correlated with longer retention in therapeutic community programs, while lower lifetime criminality has been correlated with better treatment outcomes. More positive treatment outcomes have also been noted with higher levels of education and lower levels of drug and alcohol use.

Outpatient Nonmethadone Treatment

Outpatient nonmethadone treatment programs involve trained professionals working with addicted persons to achieve and maintain abstinence while living in the community. Community mental health centers, private clinics, and professional therapists in private practice are examples of settings in which outpatient treatment is offered. Outpatient treatment programs offer a range of services and treatment modalities, including pharmacotherapy, and individual, group, and family counseling. They often incorporate a Twelve-Step philosophy.

Outpatient treatment allows individuals to live at home, continue working, and be involved in family activities while receiving treatment. Outpatient treatment is usually less expensive than residential treatment alternatives. It also allows for longer-term support of the individual than is possible with inpatient programs.

Considerations for referring individuals to outpatient treatment programs include their motivation for treatment, ability to discontinue use of drugs or alcohol, social support system, employment situation, medical condition, psychiatric status, and past treatment history. Those who remain in outpatient (nonmethadone) treatment longer tend to have better outcomes than shorter-term clients. However, dropout rates are high.

Combined Settings

Some treatment programs have been developed to attempt to capitalize on the advantages of both inpatient and outpatient treatment approaches. They provide elements from each type of setting, attempting to maximize benefits while reducing costs.

Two by Four Programs are two-phase approaches. The individual is hospitalized first for a short time (usually two weeks). This ensures complete detoxification. This is followed by outpatient treatment. However, there is the option to return to inpatient care if he or she is unable to function in the less restrictive outpatient program.

Day or partial hospitalization involves treatment in the program during normal working hours, but the person returns home during the evening hours. The individual lives at home and has to assume more responsibility than would be the case in inpatient treatment. A prerequisite for this type of treatment is a supportive, stable family.

Halfway houses provide an intermediate step between inpatient treatment and independent living. It is a good alternative for persons who do not have a stable social support system. Halfway house programs generally have a small patient population, emphasize Twelve-Step programs, and have a minimum of rules and few professional staff members. Usually residents must find employment or work within the house.

Sober living houses play an important role in supporting treatment and recovery from drug and alcohol addiction. Sobering living helps individuals in recovery to maintain and alcohol and drug free lifestyle by establishing a living environment that supports sobriety and recovery. When living in a sober environment, recovering addicts are surrounded by others who share a common experience and who all support one another in their sobriety.

Individuals in such drug and alcohol free houses often become residents after being in a licensed non-medical residential alcohol or drug recovery or treatment facility. Sober living usually serves to help those individuals transition from a residential treatment facility back into their daily lives. For some individuals, returning home to their old environments where they used drugs would be stressful and triggering, so sober living serves as a way to help those individuals to transition back into daily life while helping them to maintain their recovery.

As with other treatment programs, length of stay for some subgroups of residents has been correlated with successful treatment outcomes. Other evaluations of effectiveness have been contradictory, however.

TREATMENT COMPONENTS

A variety of techniques are used in all the treatment modalities just presented. These include self-help or Twelve-Step approaches; individual, group, and family counseling; and behavior modification approaches. Each of these will be discussed briefly.

Self-Help Programs

Self-help or Twelve-Step organizations involve mutual help among peers experiencing similar problems. With the development of the first Alcoholics Anonymous group in 1935, a long tradition of the use of self-help groups for substance abusers was launched. Self-help groups often meet in churches, community facilities, prisons, and other locations, but they generally claim no political or religious affiliation. Alcoholics Anonymous (AA) describes itself as a voluntary, self-run fellowship. Its membership is multiracial and there are no age, educational, or other requirements for members. It is nonprofessional and has no dues or outside funding sources. An important characteristic for many persons is its promise of anonymity, protecting the right to privacy of its members.

Members of AA believe that addiction is a disease that can never be cured. However, they maintain that progression of the disease can be arrested, and those in remission are *recovered* alcoholics. Groups function to reinforce social and cognitive behaviors that are incompatible with addictive behaviors. The Twelve Steps provide a concrete, tangible course of action.

The primary goals of AA and similar self-help groups are to:

- achieve total abstinence from alcohol or other drugs;

- affect changes in personal values and interpersonal behavior; and

- continue participation in the fellowship to both give and receive help from others with similar problems.

Self-help groups may be the only intervention used by some persons to end chemical dependency. However, self-help groups often are used in tandem with other treatment modalities, such as residential or outpatient treatment programs.

Alcoholics Anonymous developed the Twelve-Step tradition that has been adopted and adapted by many other self-help groups. These steps consist of a series of cognitive, behavioral, and spiritual tasks, including:

- an admission of powerlessness;

- assessment of character defects;

- overcoming shortcomings that contributed to addiction, learning the tools of nondrug-centered living, and restructuring damaged relationships; and

- commitment to a higher power.

Often, experienced members act as "sponsors" to newer members, creating a person-to-person guidance system in times of crisis and creating bonds between members.

AA groups are autonomous and traditionally are open to all members. Some groups may be directed to special-interest groups, such as women, minority groups, gays, or physicians. There are several types of meetings.

- *Closed meetings* are for AA members/prospective members only.

- *Open meetings* are for non-alcoholics as well.

- *Speaker meetings* involve AA members who describe their experiences with alcohol and their recovery.

- *Discussion meetings* are those in which an AA member describes personal experiences and leads a discussion on a topic related to recovery.

- *Step meetings* (usually closed) consist of discussion of one of the Twelve Steps.

The self-help approach was first applied to drug addiction in the U.S. Public Health Service Hospital in Lexington, Kentucky, In 1947. Narcotics Anonymous (NA) is modeled on the Alcoholics Anonymous concept, and although the two programs are not affiliated, they use the same Twelve-Step program. NA is a different organization with diverse jargon, style, substance, and social traditions. It is concerned with the problem of *addiction,* and members may have had experience with any or all of the entire range of abusable psychoactive substances. *Thus, referrals to the two organizations should be made with care.* Alcoholics Anonymous focuses on alcohol dependence and behaviors, while Narcotics Anonymous focuses on drug addictions and uses drug-specific language and approaches. Narcotics Anonymous developed more recently and reflects the milieu of the late 1970s and 1980s. Most clinicians believe this makes it a more applicable organization for the needs of many drug-involved persons.

Alcoholics Anonymous is now a world wide organization with groups in the United States and 114 other countries. Its membership is estimated at 1.5 million. Narcotics Anonymous is international as well, with groups in at least 36 countries. Estimates of its membership total approximately 250,000.

Although there is ample anecdotal testimony to the effectiveness of self-help organizations, especially Alcoholics Anonymous, there is little in the way of objective data to support these claims. However, opinions of many clinicians and individuals who have been helped by the approach strongly support it for the recovery for some substance abusers. Scientific research of these groups is very difficult because of the anonymity promised to members and self-selective membership practices. It is difficult to arrange studies with appropriate sampling techniques, control groups, or experimental design.

Various studies of the outcomes for persons attending AA have found that, overall, 46.5 to 62 percent of active AA members had at least one year of continuous sobriety. Thirty-five to forty percent of subjects reported abstinence of less than one year. Twenty-six to forty percent were sober from one to five or six years, and 20 to 30 percent maintained abstinence five or six years or more.

Self-help or Twelve-Step programs may be useful adjuncts to treatment for alcohol and other drug abuse. Persons who attend AA *and* other treatment programs have a more favorable outcome in regard to drinking. Those who attend more than one meeting per week, have a sponsor and/or sponsor others, lead meetings, and work Steps 6 through 12 tend to have more favorable outcomes.

Individual Counseling

Individual counseling approaches assume a one-to-one encounter between a client and a counselor. Counselors are usually trained professionals, but they may be paraprofessional or peer counselors. The specific counseling approach or methods used in individual treatment of substance abusers come from modalities originally developed to treat other conditions. Regardless of the particular counseling model endorsed, there are some tasks or goals of individual treatment that usually are seen across all approaches, although the emphasis placed on each may vary. These include:

- helping the individual resolve to stop using psychoactive substances;

- teaching coping skills to help the person avoid relapse after achieving an initial period of abstinence;

- changing reinforcement contingencies;

- fostering management of painful feelings; and

- improving interpersonal functioning and enhancing social supports.

Substance abusers typically enter treatment with a goal of controlled use, especially for alcohol. Therapists help patients explore their motivation and set appropriate treatment goals, including a goal of abstinence. Identifying circumstances that increase the likelihood of resuming drug use and practicing strategies for coping with these high risk situations are other parts of the treatment process. For many substance abusers, drug use has been the entire focus of their lives. When it stops, they need help in filling their time and finding rewards that replace those derived from drug use. Many drug-involved persons have never achieved satisfactory adult relationships or vocational skills because drug abuse was initiated during adolescent or early adult years. Individual interventions can help them maintain their motivation during the processes of learning new skills and recovery. Individual therapy often includes techniques to elicit strong feelings and help the individual learn acceptable means of managing them within the protected environment of the therapeutic setting. For some persons who have emotional or anxiety disorders, combined treatment with medications and individual counseling may be appropriate. Encouraging the person to participate in self-help groups can provide a source of social support outside of individual counseling sessions.

Individual therapy provides privacy to those persons who are not willing to disclose their substance abuse publicly or fear that doing so may damage their careers and reputations. In individual treatment, the pace can be flexible to meet the needs of the individual. Compared to group therapy, much more time can be spent on issues that are unique to the individual involved. In situations where caseloads are not large enough to have appropriate groups, individual therapy is more practical and can begin immediately. Some patients have particular personality disorders that do not lend themselves to group involvement.

Individual therapy is more expensive than group therapy because of the one-to-one relationship of the therapist and patient. Involvement in group treatment approaches also can have the advantage of mutual support and modeling of coping strategies. Group members often provide external control for an individual, as they may be able to detect each other's attempts to conceal relapse or early warning signals that relapse is beginning.

Reviews of several empirical studies of individual treatment of drug abusers have reached the following conclusions:

- Most studies indicate that persons involved in individual treatment, either as a single modality or in combination with other approaches, do better than those in control groups (not receiving individual treatment).

- No specific type of individual treatment approach has been shown consistently to produce better results.

- Individual treatment is especially appropriate and effective for persons with other psychiatric problems.

Group Therapy

Group therapy is often combined with other treatment modalities to provide a structured, comprehensive treatment program for substance abusers. Group therapy can be defined as:

> ... an assembly of chemically dependent patients, usually five to ten in number, who meet regularly (usually at least once a week) under the guidance of a professional leader (usually a professional therapist or addiction counselor) for the purpose of promoting abstinence from all mood-altering chemicals and recovery from addiction.

The treatment goals of group therapy may include:

- establishing abstinence;

- integration of the individual into the group;

- stabilization of individual functioning;

- relapse prevention; and

- identifying prevention and working through long-standing problems that have been obscured or exacerbated by substance abuse.

There are several types of group approaches used with alcohol- and drug-involved persons. These include the following categories.

Exploratory groups explore and interpret members' feelings and help them develop greater ability to tolerate distressing feelings without resorting to mood-altering substances.

Supportive groups help addicted members tolerate abstinence and assist them in remaining drug- or alcohol-free by enabling them to draw on their own resources.

Interactional groups create an environment of safety, cohesion, and trust, where members engage in in-depth self-disclosure and affective expression.

Interpersonal problem-solving groups teach an approach to solving interpersonal problems, including recognizing that a problem exists, defining the problem, generating possible solutions, and selecting the best alternative.

Educational groups provide information on issues related to specific addictions, such as the natural course and medical consequences, implications of intravenous drug use, and availability of community resource. Methods used may include material such as videotapes, audio cassettes, or lectures followed by discussion.

Activity groups provide occupational and recreational means for socialization and self-expression.

Groups are often an especially important aspect of treatment for youth, as peer association is particularly important during adolescence. Their developmental tasks include separating from family and forming their own identities. Peer groups have a significant effect on attitudes and behaviors. This influence can be either positive or negative. Peer groups may be located in schools, community agencies, residential programs, churches, and on the streets (such as gangs). Four categories of peer group programs have been identified:

1. *Positive peer influence programs* emphasize group interaction and positive influence of the group on the individual member.

2. *Peer teaching programs* emphasize youth conveying information to their peers.

3. *Peer counseling, facilitating, and helping programs* focus on peers helping peers. Through these programs, youth who provide this help will develop a sense of responsibility. The "helper" often benefits more than the peer who is helped.

4. *Peer participation programs* create new roles for youth, giving them decision-making power and responsibility. These programs emphasize youth empowerment and accountability.

Despite the persistent use and popularity of group treatment approaches, few studies of effectiveness have been done. Some advantages of group therapy include its cost-effectiveness, allowing one professional to work with several different individuals at once; shared learning among group members; and the potential to work through problems from earlier stages of growth because group members may reflect characteristics of a member's family of origin.

Family Therapy

In many cases addictive disorders are multigenerational within families. A full assessment of the identified substance abuser and his or her family is important to determine the range of bio-psychosocial factors influencing the person's addiction. Within family systems drug use behavior has a purpose, and it is important to assess this. Family therapy is usually not sufficient as the sole means of treatment for substance abuse. Rather, it is a valuable, and often essential, adjunct to other treatment modalities. The opportunity to observe the total family is always valuable in the diagnostic process.

There are three parts of the family system (often traversing three or more generations) that are important to include, if applicable and available. These include the substance abuser's family of origin, spouse, and children. At times it can be helpful to broaden the definition of family to include significant others and employers.

The dysfunctional patterns manifested by families of substance abusers may include denial of the problem, scapegoating all family problems on the identified abusers, the use of guilt by the addict to coerce the family into supporting his or her habit, negative communication, and lack of consistent limit setting by parents. Children of alcoholics are more likely to develop emotional and psychosocial problems, including substance abuse. Adult children of alcoholics tend to have poor communication skills, difficulty expressing feelings, role and identity confusion, and problems with trust and intimacy. Approximately 30 percent of children from alcoholic families marry alcoholics. Alcoholic fathers are apt to abuse their children through violence, sexual seduction, or assault, and alcoholic mothers are more likely to neglect their children.

Family treatment priorities include persuading the family to work together to initiate detoxification of the identified person. Also important is helping the family initiate and support the person's involvement in an appropriate treatment program (e.g., Twelve Steps, therapeutic community, methadone maintenance). Family members may need to be coached by the therapist to confront the addicted person with care and concern. The family also may need to be educated about the deadly consequences of substance abuse, and they may need help in setting limits. Behavior techniques may be used to eliminate family members' responses that trigger drug use; in their place, methods of reinforcing positive behavior may need to be taught. Communication-centered therapy may be needed to teach people to state messages clearly and correct discrepancies in communication among family members.

As juveniles are not yet independent, family interventions are especially important in addressing the basis of their drug and alcohol involvement. Some juveniles may not be living with their families of origin, but may be in adoptive families, foster family placements or other family surrogate situations. Regardless of the definition of family used, involving those who are significant in the youth's life is important. Family interventions may include classes to help parents, siblings, and others understand substance abuse. Both educational and counseling interventions to improve coping and parenting skills may be beneficial.

Although continuing research efforts are needed, available data do support the efficacy of family therapy interventions. Adolescents involved in family therapy have been shown to have half the recidivism rate of those not receiving this service. There is also evidence that family therapy improves adolescent retention in residential treatment programs. Family treatment has also been favorably correlated with days free of methadone, illegal opiates, and marijuana. It has been found that alcoholic persons who received treatment with their spouses, including both alcohol-related interventions and marital therapy, were more compliant, decreased their drinking more rapidly, and relapsed more slowly than study participants who received only alcohol-focused treatment with their spouses. They also maintained better marital satisfaction and were more likely to stay in treatment than persons receiving treatment with minimal spouse involvement. In general, family involvement enhances assessment and intervention and increases motivation in treatment.

Behavior Modification

Behavior modification is often incorporated in various treatment modalities. Behavior modification increases rewards for positive, pro-social behavior. Rewards may include praise, attention, activities, and material items. For negative or antisocial behavior, responses that are unpleasant or withhold rewards may help to extinguish the unwanted behavior. Programs that gradually give participants increased freedom as they show responsibility are using positive rewards. Some programs have levels, steps, or phases that participants must earn through appropriate behavior. With each advancement there are rewards of privileges, increased freedom, and decreased supervision.

Aversive Conditioning

Aversive conditioning is an example of providing negative rewards to extinguish unwanted behaviors. Unpleasant stimuli, such as chemically or hypnotically induced nausea or paralysis, electrical shock, and noxious imagery, are paired with the sight, smell, and taste of the abused drug. When the person has contact with the abused substance, the same response is triggered and he or she experiences repulsion instead of craving or the desire to use the drug.

Programs using this approach have claimed high rates of success. However, research studies often have been flawed, and follow-up studies have found inconsistent results. Additional studies are needed to assess the usefulness of this approach.

CONCLUSION

In this chapter both the causes of substance abuse and current treatment approaches have been reviewed. One's point of reference concerning the causes of addiction often influences decisions about treatment practices.

Addiction to alcohol and other drugs is multifaceted. For most people there is not a single cause of addiction; rather, there is a complex set of biological, social, and psychological influences that contribute to the initiation of substance use and progression to addiction. The combination of causal factors is unique for each person. Treatment programs also have particular philosophies about addiction. Thus, a comprehensive assessment is required to identify the causes of each individual's addiction and plan for appropriate patient-treatment matching. Treatment is likely to be more effective when program philosophies are considered in comparison to an individual's specific needs and characteristics.

Substance abuse treatment occurs in a variety of settings under the auspices of various agencies and organizations. Both the treatment modality and the treatment setting are important considerations. Some individuals will be more successful with the restrictions of a residential setting while others may do well in outpatient treatment. Pharmacotherapy has been proven effective for treating some drug addiction problem.

Relapse prevention programming, another critical element of treatment, has been emphasized through the information provided about treatment effectiveness of each modality. Rates of relapse for most current treatment modalities are high, and increased attention to relapse prevention is needed to mitigate this trend. Finally, the meager evaluation studies of many treatment modalities emphasize the need for continuing research and greater program *accountability,* the fifth critical element.

In the continuing quest to discover ways to change the behavior of drug-involved persons and help them achieve better health and well-being, current approaches can be improved and new approaches should be sought to enhance drug abuse treatment. Coordination among all systems that interact to provide and promote treatment is of vital importance. Treatment providers and local, State, and federal decision makers can have a significant impact on the future role of treatment. Solutions for many of the problems related to alcohol and drug addiction are possible, and treatment is an important part of the response.

References - Section 1

Section 1, Chapter 1

Adirim, T.A., & Gupta, N.S. (1991). A national survey of state maternal and newborn drug testing and reporting policies. *Public Health Reports*, 106(3), 292-296.

Beck, A.J., Kline, S.A., & Greenfeld, L.A. (1988). *Survey of youth in custody, 1987*. Washington, DC: Bureau of Justice Statistics.

Beschner, G. (1986). Understanding teenage drug use. In G. Beschner & A.S. Friedman (Eds.), *Teen drug use*. Lexington, MA: D.C. Health and Company.

Califano, J.A. (1992, December 21). Three-headed dog from hell: The staggering public health threat posed by AIDS, substance abuse and tuberculosis. *Washington Post*, A21.

Centers for Disease Control and Prevention (1993, February). HIV/AIDS *Surveillance Report*. Atlanta, GA: Author.

Dackis, C.A., & Gold, M.S. (1992). Psychiatric hospitals for treatment of dual diagnosis. In J.H. Lowinson, P. Ruiz, R.B. Millman & J.G. Langrod (Eds.), *Substance abuse: A comprehensive textbook* (Second edition). Baltimore: Williams & Wilkins.

Daley, D.C., & Marlatt, G.A. (1992). Relapse prevention: Cognitive and behavioral interventions. In J.H. Lowinson, P. Ruiz, R.B. Millman & J.G. Langrod (Eds.), *Substance abuse: A comprehensive textbook*. Baltimore: Williams & Wilkins.

Dembo, R., Williams, L., Wish, E.D., & Schmeidler, J. (1990, May). *Urine testing of detained juveniles to identify high-risk youth*. Washington, DC: National Institute of Justice.

Did you know . . . (1992, March/April). *The Counselor*, 10(2), 7.

Doweiko, H.E. (1990). *Concepts of chemical dependency*. Pacific Grove, CA: Brooks/Cole Publishing Company.

Frances, R.J., & Miller, S.I. (1991). Addiction treatment: The widening scope. In R.J. Frances & S.I. Miller (Eds.), *Clinical textbook of addictive disorders*. New York: The Guilford Press.

Graham, M. (1989, April 17). One toke over the line. *The New Republic*.

Gropper, B.A. (1985, February). *Probing the links between drugs and crime*. Washington, DC: National Institute of Justice.

Group for the Advancement of Psychiatry, Committee on Alcoholism and the Addictions (1991, October). Substance abuse disorders: A psychiatric priority. *American Journal of Psychiatry*, 148(10), 1291-1300.

Hawkins, J.D., Lishner, D.M., Jenson, J.M., & Catalano, R.F. (1987). Delinquents and drugs: What the evidence suggests about prevention and treatment programming. In B.S. Brown & A.R. Mills (Eds.), *Youth at high risk for substance abuse*. Rockville, MD: National Institute on Drug Abuse.

Institute of Medicine (1990). *Treating drug problems* (Volume 1). Washington, DC: National Academy Press.

Jaynes, J.H., & Rugg, C.A. (1988). *Adolescents, alcohol, and drugs*. Springfield, IL: Charles Thomas, Publisher.

Knott, D.H. (1986). *Alcohol problems: Diagnosis and treatment*. New York: Pergamon Press.

Larsen, J., & Horowitz, R.M. (1992). *Judicial primer on drug and alcohol issues in family cases*. State Justice Institute, American Bar Association, National Association for Perinatal Addiction Research and Education.

Macdonald, D.I. (1989). *Drugs, drinking and adolescents*. Chicago: Year Book Medical Publishers.

McLellan, T., & Dembo, R. (1992). *Screening and assessment of alcohol-and other drug (AOD)-abusing adolescents* (Treatment Improvement Protocol Series 3). Rockville, MD: Center for Substance Abuse Treatment.

Messalle, R. (1992, November 15). Meeting the challenge: A judicial perspective on substance abuse and the role of the courts. Presentation at Oakland, CA.

Morse, R.M., & Flavin, D.K. (for the Joint Committee of the National Council on Alcoholism and Drug Dependence and the American Society of Addiction Medicine to Study the Definition and Criteria for the Diagnosis of Alcoholism) (1992). The definition of alcoholism. *Journal of the American Medical Association*, 268(8), 1012-1014.

National Institute on Drug Abuse (2001). *Drug abuse and drug abuse research*. Rockville, MD: U.S. Department of Health and Human Services, Alcohol, Drug Abuse, and Mental Health Administration.

Nowinski, J. (1990). *Substance abuse in adolescents and young adults: A guide to treatment*. New York: W.W. Norton & Company.

Nurco, D.N., Hanlon, T.E., & Kinlock, T.W. (1990, March). *Offenders, drugs, crime and treatment: Literature review*. Washington, DC: U.S. Department of Justice, Bureau of Justice Assistance.

Office of National Drug Control Policy (1990a, September). *Leading Drug Indicator*s (White Paper). Washington, DC: Author.

Office of National Drug Control Policy (1990b, June). *Understanding drug treatmen*t (White Paper). Washington DC: Author.

Portenoy, R.K., & Payne, R. (1992). Acute and chronic pain. In J.H. Lowinson, P. Ruiz, R.B. Millman & J.G. Langrod (Eds.), *Substance abuse: A comprehensive textbook* (Second Edition). Baltimore: Williams & Wilkins.

Primm, B.J. (1992). Future outlook: Treatment improvement. In J.H. Lowinson, P. Ruiz, R.B. Millman & J.G. Langrod (Eds.), *Substance abuse: A comprehensive textboo*k (Second Edition). Baltimore: Williams & Wilkins.

Ray, O., & Ksir, C. (2003). *Drugs, society, and human behavior, 10ᵗʰ Edition*. New York, NY: McGraw-Hill.

Schnoll, S. (1986). *Getting help: Treatments for drug abuse*. New York: Chelsea House Publishers.

Schuckit, M.A. (1989). *Drug and alcohol abuse: A clinical guide to diagnosis and treatmen*t (Third Edition). New York: Plenum Medical Book Company.
Singer, A. (1992). *Effective treatment for drug-involved offenders: A review and synthesis for judges and other court personnel*. Newton, MA: Education Development Center, Inc.

Substance Abuse and Mental Health Services Administration. (2003). *Overview of findings from the 2002 National Survey on Drug Use and Health* (Office of Applied Studies, NHSDA Series H-21, DHHS Publication No. SMA 03–3774). Rockville, MD.

Yazigi, R.A., Odem, R.R., & Polakoski, K.L. (1991, October 9). Demonstration of specific binding of cocaine to human spermatozoa. *Journal of the American Medical Association*, 266 (14), 1956-1959.

Section 1, Chapters 2-6
Alling, F.A. (1992). Detoxification and treatment of acute sequelae. In J.H. Lowinson, P. Ruiz, R.B. Millman & J.G. Langrod (Eds.), *Substance abuse: A comprehensive textbook* (Second Edition). Baltimore: Williams & Wilkins.

Alterman, A.I., O'Brien, C.P., & McLellan, A.T. (1991). Differential therapeutics for substance abuse. In R.J. Frances & S.I. Miller (Eds.), *Clinical textbook of addictive disorders*. New York: The Guilford Press.

Anthenelli, R.M., & Schuckit, M.A. (1992). Genetics. In J.H. Lowinson, P. Ruiz, R.B. Millman & J.G. Langrod (Eds.), *Substance abuse: A comprehensive textbook* (Second Edition). Baltimore: Williams & Wilkins.

Arbiter, N. (1988, Summer). Drug treatment in a direct supervision jail: Pima County's Amity Jail Project. *American Jails, 35-40*.

Brehm, N.M., & Khantzian, E.J. (1992). A psychodynamic perspective. In J.H. Lowinson, P. Ruiz, R.B. Millman, & J.G. Langrod (Eds.), *Substance abuse: A comprehensive textbook* (Second Edition). Baltimore: Williams & Wilkins.

Bullock, M.L., Umen, A.J., Culliton, P.D., & Olander, R.T. (1987). Acupuncture treatment of alcoholic recidivism: A pilot study. *Alcoholism: Clinical and Experimental Research, 11*(3), 292-295.

Centers for Disease Control. (1989, March 17). Update: Acquired immunodeficiency syndrome associated with intravenous-drug use—United States, 1988. *Morbidity and Mortality Weekly Report*, 38(10), 165-170.

Chan, Y. (1991, December 15). Getting the point. *Daily News*.

Childress, A.R., Ehrman, R., Rohsenow, D J., Robbins, S.J., & O'Brien, C.P. (1992). Classically conditioned factors in drug dependence. In J.H. Lowinson, P. Ruiz, R.B. Millman, & J.G. Langrod (Eds.), *Substance abuse: A comprehensive textbook* (Second Edition). Baltimore: Williams & Wilkins.

Dembo, R., Williams, L., Wish, E.D., Dertke, M., Berry, E., Getreau, A., Washburn, M., & Schmeidler, J. (1988). The relationship between physical and sexual abuse and illicit drug use: A replication among a new sample of youth entering a juvenile detention center. *International Journal of the Addictions*, 23(11), 1102-1123.

Donovan, D.M., & Marlatt, G.A. (1988). *Assessment of addictive behaviors*. New York: The Guilford Press.

Doweiko, H.E. (1990). *Concepts of chemical dependency*. Pacific Grove, CA: Brooks/Cole Publishing Company.

Emrick, C.D. (1987, September/October). Alcoholics Anonymous: Affiliation processes and effectiveness as treatment. *Alcoholism: Clinical and Experimental Research*, 11(5), 416-423.

Galanter, M., Castaneda, R., & Franco, H. (1991). Group therapy and self-help groups. In R.J. Frances & S.I. Miller (Eds.), *Clinical textbook of addictive disorders*. New York: The Guilford Press.

Gardner, E.L. (1992). Brain reward mechanisms. In J.H. Lowinson, P. Ruiz, R.B. Millman & J.G. Langrod (Eds.), *Substance abuse: A comprehensive textbook* (Second Edition). Baltimore: Williams & Wilkins.

Geller, A. (1992) Rehabilitation programs and halfway houses. In J.H. Lowinson, P. Ruiz, R.B. Millman & J.G. Langrod (Eds.), *Substance abuse: A comprehensive textbook* (Second Edition). Baltimore. Williams and Wilkins.

Gifford, P.D. (1989). A.A. and N.A. for adolescents. In P. B. Henry (Ed.), *Practical approaches in treating adolescent chemical dependency: A guide to clinical assessment and intervention*. New York: The Haworth Press.

Goode, E. (1972). *Drugs in American society*. New York: Knopf Publishing.

Goodwin, D.W. (1992). Alcohol: Clinical aspects. In J.H. Lowinson, P. Ruiz, R.B. Millman, & J.G. Langrod (Eds.), *Substance abuse: A comprehensive textbook* (Second Edition). Baltimore: Williams & Wilkins.

Greenstein, R.A., Fudala, P.J., & O'Brien, C.P. (1992) Alternative pharmacotherapies for opiate addiction. In J.H. Lowinson, P. Ruiz, R.B. Millman, & J.G. Langrod (Eds.), *Substance abuse: A comprehensive textbook* (Second Edition). Baltimore: Williams & Wilkins.

Haddock, B.D., & Beto, D.R. (1988, June). Assessment of drug and alcohol problems: A probation model. *Federal Probation* pp. 10-15.

Hawkins, J.D., Lishner, D.M., Jenson, J.M., & Catalano, R.F. (1987). Delinquents and drugs: What the evidence suggests about prevention and treatment programming. In B.S. Brown & A.R. Mills (Eds.), *Youth at high risk for substance abuse*. Rockvillle, MD: National Institute on Drug Abuse.

Hollandsworth, J.G. (1990). *The physiology of psychological disorders*. New York: Plenum Press.

Institute of Medicine. (1990). *Treating drug problems* (Volume 1). Washington, DC: National Academy Press.

Jaffe, J.H. (1992). Current concepts of addiction. In C.P. O'Brien & J.H. Jaffe (Eds.), *Addictive states*. New York: Raven Press, Ltd.

Jaynes, J.H., & Rugg, C.A. (1988). *Adolescents, alcohol and drugs*. Springfield, IL: Charles Thomas, Publishers.

Katims, J.J., Ng, L.K.Y., & Lowinson, J.H. (1992). Acupuncture and transcutaneous electrical nerve stimulation: Afferent nerve stimulation (ANS) in the treatment of addiction. In J.H. Lowinson, P. Ruiz, R.B. Millman & J.G. Langrod (Eds.), *Substance abuse; A comprehensive textbook* (Second Edition). Baltimore: Williams, & Wilkins.

Kaufman, E. (1992). Family therapy: A treatment approach with substance abusers. In J. H. Lowinson, P. Ruiz, R.B. Millman & J.G. Langrod (Eds.), *Substance abuse: A comprehensive textbook* (Second Edition). Baltimore: Williams & Wilkins.

Knott, D.H. (1986). *Alcohol problems: Diagnosis and treatment*. New York: Pergamon Press.

Lowinger, P. (1992) Drug abuse: Economic and political basis. In J.H.
Lowinson, P. Ruiz, R.B. Millman, & J.G. Langrod (Eds.), *Substance abuse: A comprehensive textbook* (Second Edition). Baltimore: Williams & Wilkins.

Lowinson, J.H., Marion, I.J., Joseph, H., & Dole, V.P. (1992). Methadone maintenance. In J.H. Lowinson, P. Ruiz, R.B. Millman, & J.G. Langrod (Eds.), *Substance abuse: A comprehensive textbook* (Second Edition). Baltimore: Williams & Wilkins.

MacDonald, D.I. (1989). *Drugs, drinking and adolescents* (second Edition). Chicago: Year Book Medical Publishers, Inc.

McCrady, B.S., Noel, N.E., Abrams, D.B., Stouts, R.L., Nelson, H.F., & Hay, W.M. (1986). Comparative effectiveness of three types of spouse involvement in out-patient behavioral alcoholism treatment. *Journal of Studies on Alcohol*, 47(6), 459-467.

Mirin, S.M., & Weiss, R.D. (1991). Substance abuse and mental illness. In R.J. Frances, & S.I. Miller (Eds.), *Clinical textbook of addictive disorders*. New York: The Guilford Press.

Mullen, R., Arbiter, N., & Glider, P. (1991). A comprehensive therapeutic community approach for chronic substance-abusing juvenile offenders: The Amity model. In T.L. Armstrong (Ed.), *Intensive interventions with high-risk youths: Promising approaches in juvenile probation and parole*. Monsey, NY: Criminal Justice Press, a Division of Willow Tree Press, Inc.

Nace, E.P. (1992). Alcoholics Anonymous. In J.H. Lowinson, P. Ruiz, R.B. Millman, & J.G. Langrod (Eds.), *Substance abuse: A comprehensive textbook* (Second Edition). Baltimore: Williams & Wilkins.

National Institute on Drug Abuse. (1991). *Drug abuse and drug abuse research*. Rockville, MD: Author.

Nowinski, J. (1990), *Substance abuse in adolescents and young adults: A guide to treatment*. New York: W.W. Norton & Company.

O'Brien, W.B., & Biase, D.V. (1992). Therapeutic community (TC): A coming of age. In J.H. Lowinson, P. Ruiz, R.B. Millman, & J.G. Langrod (Eds.), *Substance abuse: A comprehensive textbook* (Second Edition). Baltimore: Williams & Wilkins.

Office of National Drug Control Policy. (1990, June). *Understanding drug treatment* (While Paper). Washington, DC: Author.

Resnik, H.S. & Gibbs, J. (1988) Types of peer program approaches (Chapter III). In *Adolescent peer pressure: Theory, correlates, and program implications for drug abuse prevention*. Rockville, MD: Alcohol, Drug Abuse, and Mental Health Administration.

Rounsaville, B.J., & Carroll, K.M. (1992) Individual psychotherapy for drug abusers. In J.H. Lowinson, P. Ruiz, R.B. Millman, & J.G. Langrod (Eds.), *Substance abuse: A comprehensive textbook* (Second Edition). Baltimore: Williams & Wilkins.

Schinke, S.P., Botvin, G.J., & Orlandi , M.A. (1991). *Substance abuse in children and adolescents: Evaluation and intervention*. Newbury Park: Sage Publications.

Schuckit, M.A. (1989). *Drug and alcohol abuse: A clinical guide to diagnosis and treatment* (Third Edition). New York: Plenum Medical Book Company.

Serban, G. (1984). Social stress and drug abuse. In G. Serban (Ed.), *The social and medical aspects of drug abuse*. New York: Spectrum Publications, Inc.

Shaffer, H.J. (1992). The psychology of staff change: The transition from addiction to recovery. In J.H. Lowinson, P. Ruiz, R.B. Millman, & J.G. Langrod (Eds.), *Substance abuse: A comprehensive textbook* (Second Edition). Baltimore: Williams & Wilkins.

Siegel, S. (1988). Drug anticipation and the treatment of dependence. In B.A. Ray (Ed.), *Learning factors in substance abuse* (NIDA Research Monograph 84). Rockville, MD: National Institute on Drug Abuse.

Thomason, H.H., & Dilts, S.L. (1991). Opioids. In R.J. Frances & S.I. Miller (Eds.), *Clinical textbook of addictive disorders*. New York: The Guilford Press.

Washton, A.M. (1992). Structured outpatient group therapy with alcohol and substance abusers. In J.H. Lowinson, P. Ruiz, R.B. Millman, & J.G. Langrod (Eds.), *Substance abuse: A comprehensive textbook* (Second Edition). Baltimore: Williams & Wilkins.

Wesson, D.R., & Ling, W. (1991, October-December). Medications in the treatment of addictive disease. *Journal of Psychoactive Drugs*, 23(4), 365-370.

Additional References

"Alcohol," 2nd Edition, Hafer, B.Q., with Brog, M.J., West Publishing Co., St. Paul, MN., 1983.

"Alcohol Abuse Curriculum Guide for Nurse Practitioner Faculty," Hasselblad, J., U.S. Department of Health & Human Services, Publication # (ADM) 84-1313, 1984.

"Alcohol and the Addictive Brain," Blum, K., and Payne, W., The Free Press, 1991.

"Alcohol and Your Unborn Baby," Sandmaier, M., National Institute on Alcohol Abuse and Alcoholism, 1986.

"Alcoholics Anonymous," 4th Edition, Alcoholics Anonymous World Services, Inc., NY, NY., 2000.

"Alcoholism and the Family: A Guide to Prevention and Treatment," Lawson, G., Peterson, R., and Lawson, A., Aspen Publishers, Inc., Rockville, MD., 1983.

"Alcoholism and Substance Abuse in Special Populations," Lawson, G. and Lawson, A., Aspen Publishers, Inc., Rockville, MD., 1988.

"Alcoholism and Substance Abuse: Strategies for Clinical Intervention," Bratter, M. and Forrest, D., The Free Press, NY, NY., 1985.

"Alcohol Problems and Alcoholism," Royce, R., The Free Press, NY, NY., 1981.

The Bottom Line on Alcohol in Society: ARIS Publications, 1106 East Oakland, Lansing, MI 48906

"Diagnosis and Treatment of Alcoholism," Mendelson, R. and Mello, D., 2nd Edition. McGraw-Hill, NY, NY., 1985.

"The Disease Concept of Alcoholism," Jellinek, E.M., Hillhouse Press, New Haven, CT., 1965.

"Drugs of Abuse," DEA. Office of Public Affairs, 1975.

"Drugs in Modern Society," Carroll, C., 5th Edition, Wm. Brown Publishers, Dubuque, Iowa, 2001.

"Drugs: Issues for Today," Payne, W. A., Hahn, D.B., and Pinger, R. R., 2nd Edition, Mosby Year Book, 1995.

"Drugs, Society and Behavior," Guilford, C.T., Dushkin Publishing Group, 1986.

"Drugs, Society, and Human Behavior," Ray, O. and Ksir, C., 10th Edition, McGraw-Hill, New York, NY, 2003.

"The Facts about Drugs and Alcohol," Gold, M., Bantom Books, New York, NY., 1988.

"A Handbook on Drug and Alcohol Abuse; the Biomedical Aspects," Hofmann, F.G., Oxford University Press, New York, N.Y., 1983.

"I'll Quit Tomorrow," Johnson, V., Harper & Row, Publishers, Inc., New York, NY., 1973.

"Learning About Alcohol, A Resource Book for Teachers," Miles, S.S., American Association for Health, Physical Education, and Recreation, Washington, D.C., 1974.

"Loosening the Grip," Kinney, J. and Leaton, G. , 7th Ed. Times Mirror/Mosby College Publishing, 2003.

"Mind-altering Drugs - A Guide to the History, Uses and Effects of Psychoactive Drugs," Kaminski, A., Wisconsin Clearinghouse, Board of Regents of the University of Wisconsin System, 1992.

"Prevention of Alcohol Abuse," Miller, D. and Nirenbeg, M., Plenum, Philadelphia, PA., 1984.

"Treatment for Alcohol and Other Drug Abuse - Opportunities for Coordination," Crowe, A.H., and Reeves, R., DHHS Publication No. (SMA) 94-2075, Printed 1994.

"Uppers, Downers, All Arounders," Inaba, D.S., and Cohen, W. E., 4th Edition, CNS Productions, Inc., 2000.

"Women and Alcohol," Yourcha, G., Crown Publishers, Inc., NY, NY., 1986.

Section 2, Chapter 1:

The Functions of Counseling - Screening, Intake, Orientation, and Assessment

A Definition of Screening

The International Certification and Reciprocity Consortium/Alcohol and Other Drug Abuse, Inc. (IC&RC/AODA) defines the core function of screening as follows:

> "Screening: the process by which a client is determined appropriate and eligible for admission to a particular program. The eligibility criteria are generally determined by the focus, target population and funding requirements of the counselor's program or agency. Many of the criteria are easily ascertained. These may include the client's age, sex, place of residence, legal status, veteran status, income level, and the referral source."

The following supplemental expansion of this definition of "screening" may be useful in understanding this core function:

> "Additionally it is imperative that the counselor use appropriate diagnostic criteria to determine whether the applicant's alcohol or other drug 'use' constitutes abuse. All counselors must be able to describe the criteria they use and demonstrate their competence by presenting examples of how the use of alcohol and other drugs has become dysfunctional for a particular client."

> "The determination of a potential client's appropriateness for a program requires a greater degree of judgment and skill by the counselor and is influenced by the program's environment and modality (i.e., inpatient, outpatient, residential, chemotherapy, detoxification or day care). Important factors include physical condition of the client, the psychological functioning of the client, outside supports/resources, previous treatment efforts, motivation, and the philosophy of the program."

I. Eligibility Criteria

    A. Eligibility criteria are determined by the program's:
        1. goals and objectives
        2. target population
        3. funding requirements

    B. Criteria related to the client might include:
        1. age
        2. sex
        3. residence
        4. legal status
        5. veteran status
        6. income level
        7. referral source
        8. physical condition
        9. psychological functioning
        10. outside support available
        11. previous treatment efforts

    C. Criteria related to the program might include:
        1. environment and philosophy of the program
        2. whether program is:
            a. detoxification unit
            b. inpatient
            c. residential
            d. outpatient

II. Diagnostic Criteria

    A. Counselor must utilize subjective criteria to determine:
        1. whether or not substance abuse is present
        2. the client's level of dysfunction
        3. key issues and problem areas
        4. degree of denial

III. Establishing Rapport

    A. Screening is the first step in establishing rapport with a potential client
        1. may be client's first attempt to seek help
        2. an opportunity to provide needed emotional support and guidance

    B. Skills which help establish rapport include:
        1. warm tone of voice
        2. encouraging prompts
            a. for example, "tell me more about that"
        3. non-threatening questions
            a. that is, questions which do not appear to threaten or attack the client
        4. appropriate self-disclosure
            a. that is, sharing some small piece of personal information which will invite openness without shifting the focus away from the client
        5. clarifying confusing information
            a. that is, asking clarifying or follow-up questions to insure that the client's response is clear
            b. for example, "can you tell me more about the frequency in which you are smoking marijuana?"

IV. Screening Information

    A. Screening forms generally ask for:
        1. patient data (age, sex, residence, etc.)
        2. referral source
        3. presenting problems
        4. insurance availability
        5. whether to accept into the program or refer elsewhere

V. Screening Tasks for the Counselor

A. Assemble screening forms

B. Collect and analyze information from referral sources

C. Interview the prospective client, with specific questions about:
   1. general client date
   2. presenting problems
   3. previous treatment efforts
   4. outside support available
   5. level of commitment to change

D. Analyze all information to determine client appropriateness for program.   Apply criteria from Sections I and II.

E. If client is appropriate, begin arrangements for intake

F. If client is inappropriate, investigate referral options and discuss with client

VI. Referral

A. Screening process sometimes ends in referral if client is not appropriate

B. Counselor needs to be well-informed about other appropriate Programs

196

A Definition of Intake

The International Certification and Reciprocity Consortium/Alcohol and Other Drug Abuse, Inc. (IC&RC/AODA) defines the core function of "intake" as follows:

"Intake: the administrative and initial procedures for admission to a program."

The following supplemental expansion of this definition of "intake" may be useful in further understanding this core function:

"The intake usually becomes an extension of the screening, when the decision to admit is formally made and documented. Much of the intake process includes completion of various forms. Typically, the client and the counselor fill out an admission or intake sheet, document the initial assessment, complete appropriate releases of information, collect financial data, sign consent for treatment, and assign the primary counselor."

I. Tasks

A. Intake is an extension of the screening process; it occurs after a client is accepted into treatment

B. The intake interview is instrumental in engaging a client in the treatment process and beginning to develop a relationship between client and counselor/treatment program

C. The intake interview consists primarily of the completion of admission forms

D. The information collected during the intake will form the basis of the client's treatment plan

E. The primary counselor is generally assigned to the client at this time

F. The counselor and client discuss confidentiality at this point

II. General Types of Forms

A. Admission/intake form
1. basic information: name, address, employer, family composition, who to contact in an emergency, etc.

B. Initial assessment form
1. brief statement about the presenting problems and immediate client needs, i.e. detox, residential, outpatient

C. Consent for treatment form
1. the client's agreement to the general terms of the treatment, i.e., type of treatment, number of sessions, cost, name of counselor, etc.

D. Financial form
1. summary of the client's financial status, generally used to determine the cost and for necessary billing to insurance companies

E. Release of information forms
1. the required written permission of a client for the release of information to a specific outside party or to receive any information from an outside party, i.e., former treatment provider or therapist, probation or parole officer, family physician, etc.

III. Confidentiality

A. State and federal regulations protect the client's identity and the content of the counseling sessions

B. Confidentiality is a therapeutic, ethical and legal issue

C. The client is often anxious about "who will find out"; this anxiety should be addressed in the first session in order to:
1. reduce client's anxiety
2. build rapport and trust

D. The regulations should be explained to the client in the first session and in writing; should be presented in a way that lets the client know that they are in his/her best interest

E. The federal regulations:
1. cover any program providing alcohol/drug abuse diagnosis, treatment or referral for treatment which is directly or indirectly federally assisted
2. allow disclosure of information about a client only under certain circumstances:
    a. when the client has consented in writing
    b. in a medical emergency
    c. when the client commits or threatens to commit a crime on program premises or against program personnel
    d. to qualified persons conducting audit, research, or program evaluation
    e. if required by court order
3. even under these circumstances, the requirements are strict regarding the redisclosure of client information
4. there are criminal penalties for violation of the regulations

A Definition of Orientation

The International Certification and Reciprocity Consortium/Alcohol and Other Drug Abuse, Inc. (IC&RC/AODA) defines the core function of "orientation" as follows:

"Orientation: - Describing to the client:

- the general nature and goals of the program;
- the rules governing client conduct and infractions that can lead to disciplinary action or discharge from the program;
- in a nonresidential program, the hours during which services are available;
- treatment costs to be borne by the client, if any; and
- client's rights.

The following supplemental expansion of this definition of orientation may be useful to help further understand this function:

"The orientation may be provided before, during and/or after the client's screening intake. It can be conducted in an individual, group, or family context. Portions of the orientation may include other personnel for certain specific parts of the treatment, such as medication."

I. When/How Orientation Takes Place

    A. Depending upon the nature of the program, orientation may take place before, during or after screening and intake

    B. It can be conducted in individual, group, or family contexts

    C. It may include other program personnel for specific parts of treatment; for example, the agency's physician or nurse may be present for a client who is on medication

II. When Designing an Orientation Program, One Should Consider the Following:

    A. What the client needs to know about the program in order to assimilate as quickly as possible

    B. The best methods to present information

    C. How to handle problems or questions which might arise during the orientation

    D. How to present rules, regulations and consequences for infractions
        1. this is especially important because clients may be upset and/or confused when they enter the program; they need a clear presentation
        2. presenting verbally and following up with a written guidebook is a good choice

III. Other Goals of Orientation

    A. Client's fears and misconceptions about treatment can be discussed

    B. Questions about rules, regulations, and expectations can be fully discussed

    C. Begin to develop a relationship with the primary counselor

    D. Present client's rights

IV. Orientation Tasks for the Counselor:

A. Introduce the program, rules, and regulations
1. verbal presentation by counselors or other clients
2. slide show or video
3. written guides

B. Present client's rights—as recommended by the Joint Commission on Hospital Accreditation of Healthcare Organizations, clients must receive a written statement of client rights, which include:
1. impartial access to treatment
2. recognition of personal dignity
3. individualized treatment provided by qualified, competent staff
4. the assurance of personal privacy
5. visits, mail and telephone calls from family and friends, when appropriate and not clinically contraindicated
6. the right of review of treatment plan
7. explanation of client rights in a language the client understands
8. documentation of the explanation of client rights. State requirements should also be considered and included - some states have more stringent patient rights requirements - know what your state requires

C. Provide tour of facility

D. If residential or inpatient program, assignment to a bed and screening of clothing and personal belongings

E. Many programs will assign another patient to be the client's "buddy"

V. Forms

A. Clients must be presented with a statement of client's rights, which should be read and signed by the client in order to indicate receipt and understanding

B. Most programs have a pre-printed orientation checklist to use - has areas to be checked to insure proper orientation is completed as well as a space for the client and counselor to sign

A Definition of Assessment

The International Certification and Reciprocity Consortium/Alcohol and Other Drug Abuse, Inc. (IC&RC/AODA) defines the core function of assessment as follows:

"Assessment: Those procedures by which a counselor/program identifies and evaluates an individual's strengths, weaknesses, problems, and needs for the development of the treatment plan."

The following supplemental expansion of this definition of "assessment" may be useful in helping you understand this core function:

"Although assessment is a continuing process, it is generally emphasized early in treatment. It usually results from a combination of focused interviews, testing, and/or record reviews."

"Many counselors use a General Systems perspective, which is analytic, synthetic, dynamic, and historic, simultaneously. Using this approach, the counselor would separately evaluate major life areas (i.e., physical health, vocational development, social adaptation, legal involvements, and psychological functioning). At the same time, the counselor assesses the extent to which alcohol or drug use has interfered with the client's functioning in each of these areas. Next, the counselor would attempt to determine the relationship of functioning between these life areas. The result of this assessment should suggest the focus for treatment."

I. When/How Assessment Takes Place

A. Although emphasized strongly early in treatment, assessment is a continuing process

B. It results from a synthesis of information such as records, interviews, testing

C. It is necessary to use a multidisciplinary approach in order to gain a broad spectrum of information

II. Goals of Assessment

A. To determine whether the client has a chemical dependency problem

B. To identify other conditions associated with addictions and other problems in these areas:
1. psychological
2. physiological
3. behavioral
4. family
5. economic
6. environmental
7. interpersonal
8. other drug use; multiple addictions

C. To increase the client's likelihood of entering and remaining in treatment by:
1. identifying barriers to treatment
2. reducing client's anxiety about treatment

D. To satisfy the demands of insurance companies for determining diagnosis and prognosis

III. Tasks/tools

A. As addiction is a complex behavioral problem, assessment should take a multidisciplinary approach, looking at these components:
1. behavioral
2. physiological
3. sociological
4. psychological

B. Assessment tools used can be
1. self-administered surveys such as the Michigan Alcoholism Screening Test (MAST)
2. a verbal drug abuse history from the client, which includes:
   a. age at first use of drugs/alcohol
   b. heaviest time of use
   c. pattern of use up to the present time
   d. whether tolerance developed
   e. whether dependence developed
   f. history of convulsions/hallucinations

       g. current drugs being used - be sure to include both licit and illicit drugs, as well as over-the-counter drugs
       h. current dose/amounts
       i. current frequency
       j. route of use
       k. why client is seeking help now
    3. drug abuse history from the family and significant others:
       a. reveals information about family dynamics
       b. reveals the impact of addiction on family members and significant others

C. Structuring the verbal history setting and establishing rapport:
    1. allow no interruptions
    2. give client undivided attention
    3. make eye contact with the client
    4. provide for the client's physical comfort
    5. don't sit behind a desk, as it presents a physical barrier between client and counselor
    6. keep the interview on track if the client digresses
    7. do not be judgmental
    8. be accepting and encouraging
    9. ask for clarification when necessary
    10. use a combination of yes-no and open-ended questions
    11. don't be uncomfortable with client silence

IV. Barriers to assessment

A. The client's denial that a problem exists

B. The client's memory disturbance and possible cognitive impairment as a result of addiction can lead to a vague, inaccurate history

C. Repression/Suppression of behaviors and using activities

D. Blackouts

E. Euphoric recall

F. Enablers

G. Co-existing mental disorders

V. Special Populations

A. Women
1. special emphasis has been placed recently on the unique problems of women substance abusers, which may include:
   a. sexual abuse
   b. difficulties with male counselors
   c. poor self-esteem
   d. lack of independence, which may keep women in abusive relationships
   e. medical problems different from those of men
2. these issues must be addressed in treatment, but will also impact the assessment process

B. Ethnic minorities
1. experience shows that minority males, especially Hispanics, have difficulty with treatment which requires confrontation; this results from cultural conditioning
   a. these clients respond best to a caring environment
   b. it is important that the staff include minority or ethnic group members
2. some cultures place a stigma on addiction, which may result in limited support from family members
3. these issues have implications for treatment, but, again, they will also affect the assessment process

VI. Matching the Client with Appropriate Treatment

A. The best approach for treatment of addiction is a multidisciplinary approach, tailored to the client's particular needs

B. Treatment should involve the family

C. Treatment should be focused on long-term process of recovery - may require multiple levels of care

D. Treatment requires a change in the client's lifestyle and behavior

E. Treatment should start with the least restrictive level of intervention but one that insures structure and safety, both physical and psychological, for the client

Additional Information on Screening and Assessment

A significant number of questions asked on the two national credentialing examinations center on the area of screening and assessment. We therefore present an expanded section on this important topic area. The information for this material comes from Chapter 4 of TAP 11: Treatment for Alcohol and Other Drug Abuse: Opportunities for Coordination. TAP 11 is a publication of the Substance Abuse and Mental Health Services Administration: Center for Substance Abuse Treatment. DHHS Publication No. (SMA) 94-2075. Printed 1994.

Screening and Assessment

Assessment is one of the five critical elements of effective substance abuse treatment. It is the first stage of intervention with persons who are chemically dependent. A comprehensive appraisal of the individual's alcohol or drug problem, and how it affects his or her health and functioning, is vital for selecting treatment resources that best meet his or her needs. Assessment includes a determination of many factors, including:

- the severity of the problem;
- possible influences that have perpetuated chemical use, culminating in addiction;
- related difficulties; and
- the individual's perceptions of and attitude toward treatment.

This chapter will provide information about the purpose of assessment, as well as screening and assessment processes, methods, and instruments.

The Purpose of Assessment

Screening, assessment, and diagnosis are important in the treatment of any illness. Consider two people who go to a doctor with pain in their left arm. A variety of medical problems could result in such pain, including cardiovascular disease, a broken bone, arthritis, an infected wound, or cancer of the bone marrow, among others. Each of these conditions would call for a different type of treatment, ranging from the possibility of taking aspirin and doing some exercises for mild arthritis to possible surgery for severe heart disease or aggressive chemotherapy for cancer. If the physician prescribed the same treatment for both patients, without assessing and diagnosing the problem carefully, the odds of the treatment being appropriate for the problem would be minimal.

Instead, the doctor will ask each patient questions about how and when the pain started, how intense it is, the exact location of the pain, and other physical symptoms. He or she also will examine each patient and may request some medical tests. It may be necessary to have a specialist conduct part of the medical evaluation because of his or her greater expertise in a particular field. For example, a radiologist might be consulted to read x-rays of the affected area. Before determining the treatment needed for each person, the physician will review and analyze all of the information gathered. Once a diagnosis has been made, the doctor may provide the treatment needed or may refer either or both of the patients to a specialist who is more knowledgeable about treatment of the specific problem. Often, the doctor will ask the patient to return for a follow-up visit so that the accuracy of the diagnosis and the effectiveness of the treatment can be evaluated.

If the prescribed treatment has not alleviated the pain, additional tests may be done to further assess the cause of the problem. If the treatment has resulted in improvement or recovery from the problem, the physician will document that the diagnosis was accurate and the treatment was effective. This information will be useful if the doctor sees the same patient again for a similar problem. If another patient presents with the same symptoms and, after assessment, the diagnosis is the same, it is likely that the same course of treatment will be used again. However, if another patient with pain in the arm is diagnosed differently, the treatment prescribed is likely to be very different from that for another patient with the same presenting problem.

The Purpose of Assessment for Substance Abuse

There are at least five objectives for conducting appropriate and comprehensive assessments of persons with substance abuse problems or chemical dependency:

1. Identify those who are experiencing problems related to substance abuse and/or have progressed to the stage of addiction.
2. Assess the full spectrum of problems for which treatment may be needed.
3. Plan appropriate interventions.
4. Involve appropriate family members or significant others, as needed, in the individual's treatment.
5. Evaluate the effectiveness of the interventions that are implemented.

Why Is Assessment Important?

The assessment of persons with alcohol or drug problems is very much like the diagnosis of other disorders. Assessment is one of the five critical elements of effective treatment, and it is the first stage of the treatment process.

The assessment process includes gathering information from a variety of sources. These sources may include the patient's own statements, previous records, and significant others. When the information is collected, it is reviewed and evaluated by a trained professional. The information and the treatment professional's interpretation of it are then used to develop plans for treatment.

A variety of instruments have been developed as *tools* for the assessment process. There is a list of some currently available assessment instruments at the end of this chapter. Assessment instruments should be evaluated for validity (Do they measure what they say they measure?) and reliability (Do they consistently provide the same results?). When assessment instruments are used, it is important to ascertain that research has been conducted to determine their validity and reliability on populations similar to those on whom the instrument will be used. For example, an instrument might be a valid and reliable assessment tool for white adult males, but it may not necessarily be useful for assessing adolescent females.

Without a comprehensive assessment, there is a risk of treating the wrong set of problems or failing to provide any intervention for some problems. The general disorder of chemical addiction is very global. An assessment that delineates causative influences, types of substances abused and related health, social, and behavioral factors is necessary for appropriate patient-treatment matching. The treatment of an adolescent who has an alcohol problem is markedly different from the treatment of an adult addicted to opiate drugs.

Each person with a substance abuse problem is likely to have a unique constellation of symptoms and factors. Several areas must be included in a comprehensive assessment, including:

- physical development and medical problems (including both general health conditions and possible infectious diseases such as HIV, tuberculosis, hepatitis, and sexually transmitted diseases);
- history of drug use and any prior treatment received;
- psychosocial problems (either precipitating chemical use or resulting from the abuse of drugs or alcohol), such as family- and peer-relationships, school or vocational difficulties, and legal and financial problems;
- psychiatric disorders; and
- current socioeconomic status and eligibility for various programs.

Who Should Be Assessed?

Substance abuse is not a selective illness; it is found among all segments of the population. People of either gender, from all age cohorts, racial and ethnic groups, and socioeconomic strata, are subject to the destructive impact of alcohol and other drug abuse and addiction. Thus, the identification of those who have a substance abuse disorder requires attentiveness and sensitivity to the range of complex indicators that might signal the need for assessment and possible treatment. There are many clues that can alert health professionals, educators, employers, family members, criminal and juvenile justice system personnel, and others that the use of alcohol or other drugs is a problem for an individual. For example:

- a physician might become suspicious of frequent injuries, liver damage, weight changes, certain diseases, and a variety of other physical symptoms for which one explanation could be substance abuse;
- a teacher or employer might be alerted by changes in performance or attendance at school or on the job;

- family members, significant others, and peers might become concerned over changes in mood, friendship patterns, and relationships; or
- criminal and juvenile justice personnel might infer associations between substance use and criminal or delinquent behavior such as income-generating crimes (e.g., thefts, prostitution), violent crimes, and drug-related crimes (e.g., possession, sales of controlled substances).

When these or other problems become apparent it is vital that the person be evaluated and referred for appropriate treatment, if needed. A thorough assessment for substance abuse is important because it can identify not only chemical dependency, but other medical, psychosocial, or psychiatric problems that may underlie the symptoms. Even if problems are not caused by substance abuse, it is just as vital that the person receives other appropriate interventions, such as primary health care or human services.

A Comprehensive Assessment Process

A comprehensive assessment consists of five consecutive stages. These stages are:

- Recognition of Risk Factors;
- Initial Screening;
- Comprehensive Assessment;
- Appropriate Interventions; and
- Evaluation of Process and Outcome.

Each part of this process will be discussed briefly in the following sections.

Recognition of Risk Factors

There is often a precipitating event that brings alcohol or drug-involved persons to the attention of those concerned about them. An automobile accident or DUI arrest, being fired from a job, an arrest for shoplifting, or a head injury from a fall might all result from the effects of alcohol or other drugs. On the other hand, the indicators of problem drinking or drug abuse might be pieced together over time. For example, a teacher might notice a steady decline in a student's grades and school attendance or an employer might notice changes in productivity. A parent or spouse might notice that an individual's habits, grooming, and disposition have changed, and there may be increasing tensions and difficulties in the person's relationships.

These signs often are consistent with substance abuse. All too often, however, no action is taken until the disease has progressed to the point of full addiction which is irreversible, but treatable. Declining social functioning and increasing involvement with the criminal or juvenile justice system are typical indicators of substance abuse. The consequences to the person's health and personal functioning can be devastating. As pointed out in Chapter 1, it is estimated that approximately 6.5 million Americans are addicted to chemicals, but only about 300,000 persons are receiving treatment (Primm, 1992).

Education and coordination are very important for this stage of the assessment process. Health care providers, mental health professionals, educators, employers, criminal and juvenile justice personnel, and many others must know how to recognize factors that may be associated with substance abuse. It is also important that they conduct, or refer the person for, an initial screening to determine whether or not alcohol or drug use is a likely cause of the problems noticed.

Throughout the assessment and treatment process, coordination, collaboration, and communication among all responsible individuals and organizations is vital. At the State level, planners, legislators, funding sources, and other factions must recognize and underscore the importance of comprehensive assessments. This can be done by mandating that assessments be conducted and providing sufficient resources to accomplish this goal. State level decision makers also may provide guidelines related to appropriate assessment processes, techniques and instruments.

Community coordination is also critical. Agencies and professionals representing health and mental health care, education, the courts, and many other interests need to evaluate the problem of substance abuse in the community and the resources available for intervening. If not already in place, the services and funding needed to provide comprehensive assessments should be developed. The return on such an investment can be extremely valuable in both human and economic terms. Comprehensive assessment will facilitate more appropriate patient-treatment matching, more efficient use of scarce treatment resources, and more positive treatment outcomes. It is also important that agencies and professionals have open communication, are aware of the services available, and understand how to make referrals for assessment services.

Within agencies, such as hospitals, school systems, and the like, coordination of assessment and other substance abuse services is also important. For example, many persons are treated in hospitals for illnesses or injuries related to alcohol or drug abuse, but never receive a comprehensive substance abuse assessment or needed treatment. Ways of coordinating services to ensure that all personnel are alert to risk factors and follow through with appropriate screening and referrals for assessment should be developed.

Initial Screening

Screening refers to brief procedures used to determine the presence of a problem, substantiate that there is reason for concern, or identify the need for further evaluation. Screening may occur in several community and correctional settings. Private physicians, public health clinics, hospitals, mental health programs, and educational programs are among those that might screen individuals for substance abuse. Within the criminal and juvenile justice systems, screening should occur throughout the individual's contact. It should begin upon entry into the system and continue until release. This may include screening at points such as diversion, detention, pretrial, presentencing, sentencing, probation, incarceration, parole or aftercare, and revocation hearings.

Screening Interviews and Instruments

Interview techniques and screening instruments may be designed to attempt to get alcohol-or drug-involved persons to reveal information about their substance abuse. These self-reports can be helpful in determining whether there is a need for further assessment and intervention. Screening interviews and instruments may be developed by a given agency, or they may be obtained from other sources providing them as a service or for profit.

Screening interviews might include a few brief questions asked during intake procedures that query the individual about the use of alcohol or other drugs. Screening instruments include brief tests (usually self-administered) that individuals take to provide information about their abuse of substances. In both cases, the alcohol- or drug-involved person is asked to give a self-report of his or her substance abuse.

Denial is a common facet of substance abuse disorders, as individuals (and often other significant persons in their lives) tend to minimize both the nature and the amount of their drug or alcohol use. Often, persons in denial actually convince themselves that substance abuse is not a serious problem, though objective indicators suggest serious consequences. Persons who are drug-involved are more likely to be truthful about their use in settings they perceive as non-threatening. Thus, reports from persons in treatment often are more credible than those from individuals in the criminal justice system. Assurance of confidentiality is an important factor that enhances self-reporting, while potential of prosecution and other sanctions is likely to diminish disclosures. While screening interviews and instruments may not give a true picture of drug and alcohol use in all cases, there are some persons who will be truthful. Coupled with other screening methods, such as chemical tests, these measures help distinguish users from nonusers.

Drug Recognition Techniques

Drug recognition techniques are a systematic and standardized evaluation process to detect observable signs and symptoms of drug use. These include, among others, indicators such as dilated or constricted pupils, abnormal eye movements, elevated or lowered vital signs, muscle rigidity, and observation of behavioral indicators of drug use, such as speech, affect, and appearance. All the areas evaluated in these procedures are observable physical reactions to specific types of drugs. The three key elements in the drug recognition process are:

- verifying that the person's physical responses deviate from normal;
- ruling out a non-drug-related cause of the deviation; and
- using diagnostic procedures to determine the category or combination of drugs that is likely to cause the impairment.

These techniques originally were developed by the Los Angeles Police Department as a result of frequent encounters with impaired drivers. However, when tested for blood alcohol levels, these motorists did not have high enough concentrations of alcohol to result in the impairments the officers observed. In response to this problem, drug recognition techniques were developed to help officers identify drug-impaired drivers. Subsequently, personnel at the Orange County, California, Probation Department applied drug recognition techniques to their clients and have used their findings to expand the period for detecting drug use. The techniques are based on documented medical findings about the effects of alcohol and various drugs of abuse on the body.

Drug recognition techniques can be very useful in identifying persons who are under the influence of alcohol or illegal substances or who have used drugs recently. They may be used appropriately at many points of contact with individuals. Based on evaluations conducted in several settings, trained personnel are capable of accurately detecting current or recent drug use with these techniques with high degrees of accuracy.

Drug recognition techniques are cost-effective. Although initial staff training can be costly, the techniques require only a few pieces of equipment and few continuing costs. They provide immediate information about current or recent drug use, and they are minimally intrusive. They rely on observations of body parts and functions that are visible to anyone at any time, rather than the collection of body fluids and the observation of bodily functions that are considered private. The techniques also are systematic and standardized, and they collect information about several observable signs and symptoms that are reliable indicators of drug use.

With drug recognition techniques, categories of drugs can be detected, but specific drugs cannot be determined. For example, it is possible to conclude that someone has used a central nervous system (CNS) stimulant, but it would not be possible to decide whether it was cocaine or amphetamines. Not all drugs are equally detectable with these techniques. Some categories of drugs cause pronounced physical symptoms while others provide few observable clues. Chemical testing is needed to determine more specific information about the types of drugs used. This is especially true when an individual is abusing more than one drug. If the person denies use, or if court actions or sanctions are to be taken, toxicological evidence may be necessary. However, drug recognition techniques are a good screening device before chemical testing. Sometimes, when confronted by the findings of a drug recognition expert, individuals may acknowledge their drug use and cooperate with the treatment process more readily. The techniques also can be used to rule out the presence of certain categories of drugs, thereby reducing the costs of testing for all possible substances.

Chemical Testing

Chemical testing is the most accurate method of determining current or recent drug use. Chemical testing can delineate the specific drug or drugs being used, but it cannot replace the assessment process to diagnose the addictive disorder. Many addicted persons use more than one mood-altering substance. It is especially common for alcohol to be used in combination with other drugs. Proper determination of the specific drugs being used is crucial in the patient-treatment matching process. The abuse of differing substances often requires varied treatment approaches. When multiple substances are being abused, it is important to combine appropriate treatment modalities and components.

Scientific methods of chemical testing include:

- breath analysis;
- saliva tests;
- urinalysis;
- blood analysis; and
- hair analysis.

Additional methods are being developed and investigated, such as the analysis of perspiration.

Currently breathanalysis, saliva tests, and urinalysis are the most practical, accurate, and cost-effective methods of chemical testing available, especially for the criminal justice system and many community agencies. Blood analysis is sometimes used in medical settings, but is much more costly. Breathanalysis and saliva tests are used to detect alcohol consumption, while urinalysis is employed to detect other drugs of abuse.

These tests can accurately reveal drugs in the system, but the time frame for detection is limited. Alcohol is eliminated from the body within a few hours of ingestion. Other drugs remain in the system longer, but detection limits can range from a few hours to about 30 days. Thus, chemical testing is dependable for identifying frequent users, but less frequent users of some drugs may test negative despite continuing use. Urinalysis cannot determine when drugs were actually ingested, nor can the level of intoxication be identified, as it can be with breath analysis for alcohol. It addition to identifying drug use, chemical testing can be a useful monitoring device and therapeutic agent in treatment when used with other interventions. As addiction is a chronic relapsing condition, chemical testing is a therapeutic tool to help prevent relapse.

Chemical testing is a highly reliable method of determining alcohol or drug use, but it also is a more intrusive process–especially urinalysis. To prevent adulteration of urine samples, the collection of specimens should be observed.

Selection of urinalysis methodologies also is important. For initial tests, immunoassays are generally used. All immunoassay tests operate in basically the same way, but differ from one manufacturer to another in the chemical "tag" used to identify the drug.

Specimens for testing may be sent to laboratories for analysis; however, reliable products are available for on-site testing in agencies. Whether using laboratory or on-site testing, agencies need to have well-defined chemical testing policies that delineate procedures, including the following areas:

- specimen collection;
- chain of custody (e.g., handling, documentation, storage, transportation);
- cutoff levels for initial and confirmation tests;
- scheduling of tests and selection of persons to be tested;
- quality assurance and quality control;
- safety procedures;
- interventions/treatment referrals; and
- other applications of findings, such as legal actions.

Gas chromatography/mass spectrometry (GC/MS) is considered the "gold standard" in urinalysis. It is highly accurate and is the only method of urinalysis that reliably produces quantitative results. It is frequently used as a confirmation method if initial immunoassay tests produce positive results.

Technological Innovations

New developments in drug detection technologies are currently being researched. The National Institute of Corrections (NIC) and the National Aeronautics and Space Administration (NASA) have formed a partnership to explore ways in which space-age technology can benefit the corrections community. The VIPER (Visual Identification of Pupillary Eye Responses) Project is developing an instrument called the optical funduscope which can evaluate the eye, pupil, and retina. This instrument can measure involuntary eye movements associated with drug use impairment, like those used with drug recognition techniques discussed previously. The VIPER Project is currently working with private companies to develop the instrument.

A second development, called the Telemetered Drug Use Detection system, is evaluating the feasibility of a drug detection device worn on the wrist. Through analysis of perspiration, the device could detect drug use and send results to a central control station. This technology combines position identification (similar to electronic monitoring), chemical and biological processes, and microcommunications and signaling. It is a noninvasive method of chemical testing for drug use.

Other Sources of Information

The screening processes already described in this section are those which attempt to obtain information directly from the person believed to be using drugs or alcohol. It also may be important to collect data from other sources during the screening process. Among others, this may include obtaining facts from family members, teachers, and employers; reviewing available records (e.g., health, psychosocial, legal); and considering the observations made by professionals.

Advantages and Disadvantages of Screening Methods

Drug recognition techniques and chemical testing methods can provide reliable information on current or recent drug use. However, self-reports through interviews and tests are the only screening devices that will provide information about alcohol and drug use over time. The accuracy of self-reports relies upon the motivation of the individual to disclose drug use. Chemical testing is the most expensive of the three methods but provides the most scientifically valid information. Chemical testing also is the most intrusive of the three methods, requiring observed specimen collection procedures to ensure accurate results.

Key Issues in Screening for Alcohol and Drug Involvement

There are several considerations in selecting screening methods and instruments and conducting screening procedures. These should be deliberated carefully by those who will be endorsing or conducting screenings. **Table 4-A** provides a summary of key areas.

Screening should detect specific indicators of substance abuse, such as health factors, educational or job-related problems, relationship difficulties, or financial and legal consequences of substance abuse. If screening procedures indicate that substance abuse or dependency is probable, the person should be referred for a more comprehensive assessment.

Table 4-A: Key Considerations in Screening for Alcohol and Drug Abuse

- Screening should be conducted on persons recognized to be at risk, in a variety of settings, by a range of professionals.
- There should be collaboration among agencies and professionals on screening processes, techniques, and instruments.
- All instruments and processes should be sensitive to racial, cultural, socioeconomic, and gender-related concerns.
- Initial screening procedures should be brief.
- Information should be gathered from various sources

Comprehensive Assessment

Screening is useful in differentiating persons who are alcohol-or drug-involved from those who are abstainers or whose use is limited and is not creating any problems for them. *Assessment*, on the other hand, indicates a process to determine the nature and complexity of the individual's spectrum of drug abuse and related problems. A comprehensive assessment uses extensive procedures that evaluate the severity of the substance abuse problem, elicit information about cofactors, and assist in developing treatment and follow-up recommendations. In addition to assessing substance abuse *per se*, a comprehensive assessment will probe related problem areas, such as:

- medical status and problems (including both general health conditions and infectious diseases such as HIV, tuberculosis, hepatitis, and sexually transmitted diseases);
- psychological status and possible psychiatric disorders;
- social functioning; family and peer relations;
- educational and job performance;
- criminal or delinquent behaviors and legal problems; and
- socioeconomic status and problems.

There are three basic steps in the assessment process:

1. Information
2. Data analysis
3. Treatment plan development

Each of these will be discussed in the following sections.

Information Gathering

There are three sources of information that can be helpful in conducting a comprehensive assessment:

1. Existing information
2. Individual and collateral interviews
3. Testing instruments

Investigation of existing information. Table 4-B contains several categories of information that may already be available about an individual. Confidentiality requirements, to protect the privacy of individuals, require the person to sign a release of information form before much of the information listed in **Table 4-B** can be requested.

Self-reports, interviews, and collateral contacts. Interviews with individuals are much more extensive than the self-reports that were described as a method for screening. The interview can reveal valuable information about the person, to complement other information and obtain an accurate evaluation of problems. An assessment interview also may be the foundation for a positive, trusting working relationship during future interventions.

As with screenings, collateral interviews involve gathering information from other persons who are, or have been, associated with the person being assessed. Collateral sources should be asked to provide descriptive information rather than to form judgments about the person. As with patient interviews, information received is not always accurate. Possible collateral sources include family members, peers, teachers, employers, and others who might have helpful information.

Information gathering may involve one professional obtaining information in all areas. However, when particular areas raise concern, an interviewer or case manager may request consultation from other professionals. For example, if an individual discloses that he or she is bothered by certain physical symptoms, and the assessor is not a physician, a referral should be made for a medical examination. Similarly, it might be necessary to obtain psychological or psychiatric evaluations if it is determined that in-depth assessments in these areas are needed and the person conducting the assessment is from a different discipline. *A multi-disciplinary assessment team is recommended for obtaining the range of information needed for comprehensive assessment and treatment planning.*

Interviews should be adapted to the age and culture of the patient. Cognitive abilities can affect the interview process; thus, the interviewer must be aware of the patient's cognitive ability level and try to structure the interview accordingly. Language may present another barrier in the assessment process. If the individual being assessed is not fluent in the same language as the interviewer, an experienced interpreter who is familiar with the patient's culture and the interview questions should be used.

Some of the information to be probed during interviews with the individual and collateral sources will include, but is not limited to, the following areas. Often, these overlap with information gathered from existing records.

Testing instruments. Testing instruments can include:

- standardized interviews,
- structured interviews; and/or
- self-administered tests.

These techniques have been developed to assess individuals in multiple areas (e.g., personality, aggressive tendencies, social skills, stress factors, risk for substance abuse, intellectual capacity). Most of the instruments have been formulated and standardized through a systematic research and validation process.

An advantage of using standardized instruments is that information regarding their reliability and validity may be available. If an instrument has high *validity,* it will accurately measure what it intends to measure. An instrument that has high *reliability* will produce stable results; the test's outcome will not be significantly influenced by fluctuating or extraneous factors (such as a person's mood or the time of day). The instrument should be normed, or validated, with a population similar to those with whom it will be used. For example, an instrument used with adolescents should be normed on other adolescents. An instrument to be used with criminal offenders should have been normed on other offender populations. However, even when the credibility of these tests has been proved, test outcomes may be affected by other factors, including:

- attempts by individuals using them to "slant" the outcome by deliberately answering questions incorrectly;
- ability of individuals to read and understand the test items;
- motivation of persons to take the test seriously; and
- cultural sensitivity of the test.

The assessment process is likely to be most helpful and informative when a variety of techniques are used. Testing instruments are a tool to guide decision-making efforts. As with all other techniques, the limitations of these tests must be realized. Staff members who are given the responsibility of administering and interpreting them should be fully trained.

Standardized and Structured Interviews. The *standardized interview* differs from the *structured interview* in that it limits the interviewer to a prescribed style and list of questions. Using the standardized interview, the interviewer is restricted from freely probing beyond conflicting or superficial answers, sometimes considered a disadvantage of this technique. An advantage is that this interview may be more credible than the structured interview, an important consideration when results are used to support significant decisions (e.g., treatment referrals or legal actions).

Table 4-B.-Information From Existing Sources

- **Drug history.** Health and mental health treatment agencies and criminal or juvenile justice agencies may have records containing information about previous drug-related treatment or charges. These records also may contain some information about the age at which substance use was initiated, the type of chemicals used, the frequency and amount of alcohol or drugs used, and other important data.
- **Medical history and current status.** This will provide information about medical treatment for substance abuse, medical conditions, substance abuse-related infectious diseases, medical emergencies that may have been related to substance abuse, current prescribed medications, recent illnesses or injuries, and possible family history of substance abuse.
- **Mental health history and current status.** This information may identify past or current emotional, psychological or psychiatric problems and previous treatment for substance abuse.
- **Criminal or delinquency history.** Criminal or juvenile justice records may provide information about prior offenses and drug involvement at the time of prior arrests and a history of offenses that may be related to income-generating crimes or expressive behaviors associated with the effects of certain types of drugs. It also may be important to obtain information on any current legal problems, of either a criminal or civil nature.
- **Educational history and current status.** This may include information about enrollment in or completion of education programs, attendance records, identified learning disabilities, and behavior problems at school. This information may be important for both juvenile and adult offenders.
- **Employment history and current status.** This may include current and previous employment, attendance problems, and reasons for termination.

Table 4-C.-Areas of Assessment Through Patient and Collateral Interviews

- **Drug history and current patterns of use:** When did alcohol or other drug use begin? What types of alcohol or other drugs does the individual currently use? Does the person use over-the-counter medications, prescription drugs, tobacco, and caffeine? How frequently are the substances used and in what quantity?
- **Substance abuse treatment history:** Has the individual ever received treatment for substance abuse? If so, what type of treatment (inpatient, outpatient, methadone maintenance, Twelve-Step programs, etc.)? Were these treatment experiences considered successful or unsuccessful and why? Has the person been sober and experienced relapse, or has s/he never attained recovery?
- **Medical history and current status:** What symptoms are currently reported by the patient? Are there indicators of infectious and/or sexually transmitted diseases? Has the individual been tested for HIV and other infectious diseases? Are there indicators of risk for HIV or other diseases for which testing should be done? What kind of health care has been received in the past? The causes and effects of various illnesses and traumas should be explored.
- **Mental status and mental health history:** Is the individual orientated to person, place, and time? Does s/he have the ability to concentrate on the interview process? Are there indicators of impaired cognitive abilities? What is the appropriateness of responses during the interview? Is the person's affect (emotional response) appropriate for the situation? Are there indicators from collateral sources of inappropriate behavior or responses by the person? Is there evidence of extreme mood states, suicidal potential, or possibility of violence? Is the individual able to control impulses? Have there been previous psychological or psychiatric evaluations or treatment?
- **Personal status:** What are this person's critical life events? Who constitute his/her peer group? Does the individual indicate psychosocial problems that might lead to substance abuse? Does the person demonstrate appropriate social, interpersonal, self-management, and stress management skills? What is the individual's level of self-esteem? What are the person's leisure time interests? What are his/her socioeconomic level and housing and neighborhood situation?

- **Family history and current relationships:** Who does the individual consider his/her family to be; is it a traditional or nontraditional family constellation? What role does the individual play within the family? Are there indicators of a history of physical or sexual abuse or neglect? Do other family members have a history of substance abuse, health problems or chronic illnesses, psychiatric disorders, or criminal behavior? What is the family's cultural, racial, and socioeconomic background? What are the strengths of the family and are they invested in helping the individual? Have there been foster family or other out-of-home placements?

- **Positive support systems:** Does the person have hobbies, interests, and talents? Who are his/her positive peers or family members?
- **Crime or delinquency:** Have there been previous arrests and/or involvement in the criminal or juvenile justice system? Has the person been involved in criminal or delinquent activity but not been apprehended? Is there evidence of gang involvement? Is the person currently under the supervision of the justice system? What is the person's attitude about criminal or delinquent behavior?
- **Education:** How much formal education has the person completed? What is the individual's functional educational level? Is there evidence of a learning disability? Has s/he received any special education services? If currently in school, what is the person's academic performance and attendance pattern?
- **Employment:** What is the individual's current employment status? What employment training has been received? What jobs have been held in the past and why has the person left these jobs? If currently employed, are there problems with performance or attendance?
- **Readiness for treatment:** Does the patient accept or deny a need for treatment? Are there other barriers to treatment?
- **Resources and responsibilities:** What is the individual's socioeconomic status? Is the person receiving services from other agencies, or might s/he be eligible for services?

(Doweiko, 1990; McLellan & Dembo, 1992; Tarter, Ott & Mezzich, 1991)

Minimal training is usually required to administer standardized interviews. To administer structured interviews, interviewers must have knowledge and experience in working with similar populations, as well as expertise in interviewing. The goal of this interview is to obtain as much information as possible about the person. Therefore, the interviewer is *expected* to probe beyond superficial or conflicting answers. Structured interviews usually take more time to administer and interpret than standardized interviews.

Self-Administered Tests. Usually, less staff skill is required with *self-administered* tests than with structured or standardized interviews. On the other hand, these tests require some motivation and reading ability on the part of the individual being assessed. Many instruments are written at the fourth or fifth grade reading level. Moreover, self-administered tests are only credible if the person is willing to answer the questions honestly. However, written tests can be helpful for those who have difficulty speaking directly about themselves. These instruments provide an indirect and, for some, less threatening method of self-disclosing information. They also prevent interviewer bias and, like other standardized instruments, can be scored and quantified. Reliability and validity measures usually are available as well.

Data Analysis

Once information is gathered, it is interpreted for use in decision making. During this phase, professional service providers determine the severity of the person's alcohol or drug problem, possible contributing factors, and his or her readiness for intervention.

The professional conducting or managing the assessment process will use all of the collected data to arrive at an opinion about the individual's substance abuse problem. The question to be answered is: Do the data indicate that the person is addicted to or dependent on one or more chemicals, an abuser of chemicals, or not adversely affected by occasional use of drugs and/or alcohol?

The analysis must encompass the range of problems, strengths and sources of support available to the person. It also should address factors that have contributed to or are related to alcohol and other drug abuse.

Treatment Plan Development

The findings from the assessment process and monitoring of treatment should be documented to enhance clinical case supervision. The data derived from the screening and assessment processes form the basis of a treatment plan. This plan must recognize the unique constellation of problems and other factors that have been identified for the individual. The treatment plan will recommend a course of action that attempts to address the patient's unique needs. Implementation of the plan will involve providing or referring the person to appropriate treatment programs and monitoring his or her progress. A single treatment modality or a combination of services may be needed. The treatment plan should be comprehensive, containing information about the following categories:

- the identified problems to be addressed;
- the goals and objectives of the treatment process (e.g., to help the individual abstain from use of drugs, to help the patient resolve underlying self-esteem problems, to help the person achieve full employment);
- the resources to be applied (i.e., treatment programs, funding, other services, etc.);
- the persons responsible for various actions (e.g., making referrals, attending treatment sessions, follow-up reports);
- the time frame within which certain activities should occur; and
- the expected benefits for the person who will participate in the treatment experience.

Appropriate Interventions

Based on the recommendations made in the treatment plan, appropriately matched treatment interventions should be provided to the drug-involved individual. This may include:

- preventive and primary medical care;
- testing for infectious diseases;
- random drug testing;
- pharmacotherapeutic interventions;
- group counseling interventions

- substance abuse counseling;
- life skills counseling;
- general
- health education;
- peer/support groups
- liaison services;
- social and athletic activities;
- alternative housing; and
- relapse prevention.

These may be provided on either an outpatient or an inpatient/residential basis depending on the needs of the person. More information on these interventions and services will be given in later chapters.

Evaluation of Process and Outcome

As with the example of the treatment of arm pain at the beginning of this chapter, the assessment and intervention process includes evaluation of the process and outcomes. Process evaluation indicates whether or not the appropriate procedures were used. Were the needed assessment procedures performed and did they result in a timely and appropriate treatment plan? Did the individual attend the treatment programs and services recommended in the treatment plan? Were the services that were promised delivered?

The outcome evaluation will examine whether or not the individual benefited from the assessment and the interventions. It will indicate whether or not the assessments were accurate in correctly defining the problem and matching the person with appropriate treatment resources. If so, and if the patient is cooperative, there should be indicators of improvement or recovery when follow-up evaluations are conducted. If not, it will be necessary to use the feedback information to initiate additional assessment procedures or change the treatment plan. Outcome evaluation also may indicate problems in service delivery.

Process and outcome evaluation data also may provide documentation of service needs. Although assessments may indicate needs for specific services, often they do not exist in particular communities, they are not affordable for all persons who need them, or there is not sufficient room in programs for new referrals. These data are extremely important for community and State decision makers who must determine program priorities and funding resources.

Assessment Instruments

There are standardized testing instruments available to assess individuals in a variety of areas. When selecting these instruments, consideration should first be given to the areas to be assessed, and options should be limited to instruments that are designed to address those areas. The following factors should then be considered in reviewing the various instruments:

- ease of use;
- expertise and time required of staff to administer and score test;
- training required to administer and score the instrument, and whether or not such training is available;
- possibility of bias (cultural or in administration of the test);
- validity (Have studies proved that it accurately measures what it was intended to measure?);
- reliability (Have studies shown that if the test were repeated with the same person, the results would be the same?);
- credibility of test among members of the judiciary and treatment professionals;
- adaptation of test to management information system input and retrieval;
- whether the test has been normed with a population similar to the client group;
- availability of test in languages other than English;
- motivation level, verbal and reading skills required of persons to be assessed;
- propensity for test to be manipulated; and
- average cost per test.

Sources of Assessment Instruments

Proprietary instruments are developed and copyrighted by individuals or organizations. There is usually a cost for their use. Some instruments are developed by local agencies. They often are program-specific and may or may not be useful in other settings. Often they have not been validated to determine their accuracy. Many agencies are willing to share such instruments without a charge. Instruments developed by federal agencies are in the public domain and may be used without a fee. Validity and reliability studies for them are documented.

Brief information about several available assessment instruments (both interviews and self-administered) is included at the end of this chapter. The instruments included in this list do not represent an exhaustive exploration of such instruments, nor does incorporation in this list represent an endorsement of particular instruments. Rather these are offered as a compilation of those instruments located through literature review. Because the needs of various agencies and systems vary, service providers and decision makers should examine an array of instruments and select those best suited to their particular needs.

Conclusion

Assessment is the beginning of the treatment process. It is a critical element of treatment, for without comprehensive assessment, appropriate patient-treatment matching is not possible. Just as it would be inappropriate to treat arthritis with chemotherapy intended for cancer patients, it is similarly unsuitable to provide a drug-involved adolescent with treatment intended for an adult male alcoholic. Thus, scarce treatment resources may not be used wisely if patients are not assessed carefully before treatment plans are formulated. Comprehensive assessment improves the overall cost-effectiveness of providing treatment.

Assessment is important in the coordination of services, as well. Valuable information can be gained so that the most appropriate services for individuals are delivered at the community level. Aggregated information is also beneficial for State and local decision makers needing to determine priorities, set standards, and allocate funding according to the areas of greatest need.

Substance Abuse Screening & Assessment Instruments

Instrument Name	Description	Contact/Source
Addiction Severity Index (ASI)	The ASI is most useful as a general intake screening tool. It effectively assesses a client's status in several areas, and the composite score measures how a client's need for treatment changes over time. It has been used extensively for treatment planning and outcome evaluation. Outcome evaluation packages for individual programs or for treatment systems are available. Designed for adults of both sexes who are not intoxicated (drugs or alcohol) when interviewed. Also available in Spanish.	A. Thomas McLellan, Ph.D. Building 7 PVAMC University Avenue Philadelphia, PA 19104 Phone: (800) 238-2433
Adolescent Drinking Index	This is a 24-item paper and pencil test self-report rating scale intended to measure the severity of drinking problems. Completion time is about 5 minutes; youth need fifth grade reading skills.	Psychological Assessment Resources, Inc. P.O. Box 998 Odessa, FL 33556 1-800-331-TEST
Adolescent Drinking Inventory	This is a 25-question self-report instrument to screen adolescents. It focuses on drinking-related loss of control and social, psychological and physical symptoms of alcohol problems.	Psychological Assessment Resources, Inc. P.O. Box 998 Odessa, FL 33556 1-800-331-TEST
Adolescent Drug Involvement Scale	Paper and pencil drug abuse screening instrument adapted from the Adolescent Involvement Scale.	D. Paul Moberg Center for Health Policy and Program Evaluation 433 West Washington Ave., Suite 500 Madison, WI 53703
Alcohol Dependence Scale (ADS)	This is a 25-item multiple-choice questionnaire to assess the Alcohol Dependence Syndrome. It is derived from the Alcohol Use Inventory. It yields an index of severity of alcohol dependence.	Addiction Research Foundation 33 Russell St. Toronto, Ontario M5S-2S1, Canada (800) 661-1111

230

Alcohol Expectancy Questionnaire	Used to gauge high risk circumstances that may lead to alcohol use.	Dr. Mark Goldman Alcohol and Drug Abuse Research Institute Department of Psychology BEH 339 University of South Florida Tampa, FL 33620 (813) 974-6963
Alcohol Use Disorders Identification Test (AUDIT)	The purpose of the AUDIT is to identify persons whose alcohol consumption has become hazardous or harmful to their health. The AUDIT screening procedure is linked to a decision process that includes brief intervention with heavy drinkers or referral to specialized treatment for patients who show evidence of more serious alcohol involvement. It has been used with adults, particularly primary care, emergency room, surgery, and psychiatric patients; DWI offenders; criminals in court, jail, and prison; enlisted men in the armed forces; and workers in employee assistance programs and industrial settings.	Can be downloaded from Project Cork Web site: www.projectcork.org
American Drug and Alcohol Survey (ADAS)	This is a 57-item self-report instrument. It requires 20 to 25 minutes to complete. It develops a typology of 9 styles of use of drugs that are listed in order of increasing severity of drug involvement.	RMBSI, Inc. 2100 W. Drake Rd., Suite 144 Fort Collins, CO 80526 1-800-447-6354

Assessment of Chemical Health Inventory (ACHI)

This 128-item self-administered instrument assesses the nature and extent of substance abuse and associated psychosocial problems and facilitates communication between treatment providers. It can be taken and scored on a computer. There is also a paper and pencil format. It screens for random, inattentive, or inconsistent test-taking behavior and for defensiveness, exaggeration, or social desirability tendencies. The test requires a sixth grade reading level and takes 15 to 25 min. to complete.

Recovery Software, Inc.
7401 Metro Blvd., Suite 445
Minneapolis, MN 55439
(612) 831-5835

Beck Depression Inventory-II (BDI-II)

The BDI-II consists of 21 items to assess the intensity of depression. The BDI-II can be used to assess the intensity of a client's depression, and it can also be used as a screening device to determine whether there is any current indication of the need for a referral for further evaluation. Each item is a list of four statements arranged in increasing severity about a particular symptom of depression. These new items bring the BDI-II into alignment with Diagnostic and Statistical Manual for Mental Disorders, 4th edition (DSM-IV) criteria. Items on the new scale replace items that dealt with symptoms of weight loss, changes in body image, and somatic preoccupation. Another item on the original BDI that tapped work difficulty was revised to examine loss of energy. Also, sleep loss and appetite loss items were revised to assess both increases and decreases in sleep and appetite.

The Psychological Corporation
19500 Bulderve
San Antonio, TX 78259
Phone: (800) 872-1726
www.psychcorp.com

CAGE Questionnaire	A self-report screening instrument consisting of 4 yes-no questions. Requires approximately 1 minute to complete.	J.A. Ewing (1984, October 12), "Detecting Alcoholism: The CAGE Questionnaire" (*Journal of the American Medical Association,* 252[14], 1905-1907; see p. 1906) Also available by downloaded from the Project Cork Web site: www.projectcork.org
Chemical Dependency Assessment Profile (CDAP)	This is a 235-item multiple-choice and true-false self-report instrument to assess alcohol and other drug use and chemical dependency problems. Can be administered by computer or in paper and pencil format. A computerized report can be generated.	Multi-Health Systems (MHS) Publishers 908 Niagara Falls Blvd. North Tonawanda, NY 14120 1-800-456-3003
Circumstances, Motivation, and Readiness Scales (CMR Scales)	The instrument is designed to predict retention in treatment and is applicable to both residential and outpatient treatment modalities. Consists of four derived scales measuring external pressure to enter treatment, external pressure to leave treatment, motivation to change, and readiness for treatment. Developed from focus groups of recovering staff and clients and retain much of the original language. Clients entering substance abuse treatment perceive the items as relevant to their experience.	George De Leon, Ph.D., or Gerald Melnick, Ph.D. National Development and Research Institutes, Inc. 71 West 23rd Street 8th Floor New York, NY 10010 Phone: (212) 845-4400 Fax: (917) 438-0894 E-mail: gerry.melnick@ndri.org www.ndri.org

Comprehensive Addiction Severity Index for Adolescents (CASI-A)	This structured interview was designed to evaluate drug and alcohol use and psychosocial severity in adolescent populations in a variety of settings. It is administered by an assessor to the youth and takes approximately 45 to 60 minutes. A computerized scoring technique takes about 45 minutes to enter and 10 minutes to score (Schaefer, 1992).	Kathleen Meyers Penn/V.A. Center for Studies of Addiction PVAMC Bldg. 7 University & Woodland Aves. Philadelphia, PA 19104 (215) 823-5809
Comprehensive Drinker Profile (CDP)	This is an 88-item structured interview questionnaire. It is designed to provide a history of drinking practices and problems. It incorporates the Michigan Alcoholism Screening Test. It requires from 1 to 2 hours to administer.	Psychological Assessment Resources P.O. Box 998 Odessa, FL 33556 1-800-331-TEST
Drug Abuse Screening Test (DAST)	The purpose of the DAST is (1) to provide a brief, simple, practical, but valid method for identifying individuals who are abusing psychoactive drugs; and (2) to yield a quantitative index score of the degree of problems related to drug use and misuse. It is especially useful in screening and case finding; level of treatment and treatment/goal planning. There is both an adult and an adolescent version.	Addiction Research Foundation 33 Russell St. Toronto, Ontario M5S-2S1, Canada 1-800-661-1111
Drug Offender Profile Evaluation/ Referral Strategies (DOPERS)	Assesses suspected drug-involved adult probationers. Helps determine specific supervision and treatment recommendations. It is an interview format that takes approximately 25 minutes to complete. A 2 1/2 day training session is required to use the instrument.	Bob Lynch Texas Department of Criminal Justice Community Justice Assistance Division 8100 Cameron Rd., Bldg. B, Suite 600 Austin, TX 78754 (512) 835-7745

Drug Use Screening Inventory (DUSI)	This 149-item instrument evaluates adolescent drug use and the youth's health, psychiatric, and psychosocial problems, identifies problem areas, and quantitatively monitors treatment progress and outcome. It consists of a Personal History Form, Drug Use Screening Instrument, and demographic, medical, and treatment/prevention summary plan. A sixth grade reading level is needed and completion takes 20 to 40 minutes. Scoring takes 15 to 20 minutes.	Ralph E. Tarter, Ph.D. Department of Psychiatry University of Pittsburgh School of Medicine 3811 O'Hara St. Pittsburgh, PA 15213 (412) 624-1070 *Distributed by:* The Gordian Group P.O. Box 1587 Hartsville, SC 29550 (803) 383-2201
Global Appraisal of Individual Needs (GAIN)	The GAIN was developed to implement an integrated biopsychosocial model of treatment assessment, planning, and outcome monitoring that can be used for evaluation, clinical practice, and administrative purposes. It embeds questions for documenting substance use disorder, attention deficit/hyperactivity disorder, oppositional defiant disorder, conduct disorder, and pathological gambling; dimensional patient placement criteria for intoxication/withdrawal, health distress, mental distress, and environment distress to guide movement among and between levels of care; treatment planning; reporting requirements related to the State client data system; and measures of a core set of clinical status and service utilization outcomes used in the Drug Outcome Monitoring Study.	The Lighthouse Institute Chestnut Health Systems 720 West Chestnut Bloomington, IL 61701 www.chestnut.org/li/gain/
Inventory of Drinking Situations	Used to identify emotional, cognitive, and social factors that may precipitate drinking.	Addiction Research Foundation 33 Russell St. Toronto, Ontario M5S-2S1, Canada (800) 661-1111

Juvenile Automated Substance Abuse Evaluation (JASAE)	This is a computer-assisted instrument for assessing alcohol and other drug use behavior in adolescents. It is suggested for use with follow-up interviews to provide focus and conserve the amount of time necessary to conduct the interview. It is a 102-item self-administered questionnaire written at the fifth grade level. It can be given individually or in groups. Available in English and Spanish and on audio tape for those with reading difficulties. Personnel key responses into a computer. Administration takes approximately 20 minutes. Keying in responses takes 5 minutes.	ADE, Inc. P.O. Box 660 Clarkston, MI 48347 1-800-334-1918
Level of Care Utilization System (LOCUS)	This tool is used to assess immediate service needs (e.g., for clients in crisis); to plan resource needs over time, as in assessing service requirements for defined populations; to monitor changes in status or placement at different points in time LOCUS is divided into three sections. The first section defines six evaluation parameters or dimensions: (1) risk of harm; (2) functional status; (3) medical, addictive, and psychiatric co-morbidity; (4) recovery environment; (5) treatment and recovery history; and (6) engagement. A five-point scale is constructed for each dimension and the criteria for assigning a given rating or score in that dimension are elaborated. In dimension IV, two subscales are defined, while all other dimensions contain only one scale.	American Association of Community Psychiatrists www.wpic.pitt.edu/aacp/find.html

MACH Drug Involvement Scale (MDI)	This is a standardized interview in computer format that can be self-administered. It takes about 30 minutes to administer and results are generated immediately. The MDI scale is used to identify adolescent drug involvement. It is available in English and Swedish.	Minnesota Assessment of Chemical Health 110709 Kings Lane Chaska, MN 55318 (612) 887-0332
Michigan Alcoholism Screening Test (MAST)	Quantifies the severity of alcohol problems for adults, using a 24-item self-administered questionnaire calling for "yes" and "no" responses.	Melvin L. Selzer, M.D. 4016 Third Ave. San Diego, CA 92103 (619) 299-4043
Offender Profile Index (OPI)	This is an interview format that can be completed in approximately 30 minutes. It is designed to be used with suspected drug-involved adult defendants/offenders to determine specific drug intervention disposition.	Robert Anderson Director of Criminal Justice Programs National Association of State Alcohol and Drug Abuse Directors 444 North Capitol Street, NW. Suite 642 Washington, DC 20001 (202) 783-6868
Personal Experience Inventory (PEI)	This two-part instrument is designed to assess the extent of psychological and behavioral issues with alcohol and drug problems; assess psychosocial risk factors associated with teenage chemical involvement; evaluate response bias or invalid responding; screen for the presence of problems other than substance abuse; and aid in determining appropriateness of inpatient or outpatient treatment. A sixth grade reading level is needed to take the self-administered assessment which takes 45 to 60 minutes (McLellan & Dembo, 1992). The 147-item questionnaire is available in pencil and paper and computerized versions.	Western Psychological Services 12031 Wilshire Blvd. Los Angeles, CA 90025 (310) 478-2061

Personal Experience Screening Questionnaire (PESQ)	This is a self-report screening questionnaire for use with adolescents suspected of abusing alcohol or other drugs. It is a 40-item questionnaire. It requires a fourth grade reading level and can be administered to individuals or in groups. It takes about 10 minutes to administer and score it.	Western Psychological Services 12031 Wilshire Blvd. Los Angeles, CA 90025 (310) 478-2061
Prevention Intervention Management and Evaluation System (PMES)	Items related to both alcohol and other drug problems constitute this 150-item instrument designed to assess substance abuse and other life problems of adolescents; assist in treatment planning; and provide follow-up assessment and evaluation data on treatment outcome. There is a Client Intake Form and the Information Form on Family, Friends, and Self. It requires a sixth grade reading level and takes approximately 1 hour to administer and 10 to 15 minutes to score.	D. Dwayne Simpson, Ph.D. Institute of Behavioral Research P. O. Box 32880 Texas Christian University Fort Worth, TX 76129 (817) 921-7226
Problem Oriented Screening Instrument for Teenagers (POSIT)	The POSIT provides a brief screening of adolescents for treatment and other service needs. It is intended to identify troubled youths and can be used in a variety of settings. It is useful for developing treatment and referral plans. It is a 139-item self-administered questionnaire designed for use with youth 12 to 19 years old. It requires a sixth grade reading level.	Elizabeth Rahdert, Ph.D. NIDA 5600 Fishers Lane, Rm. 10A-30 Rockville, MD 20857 (301) 443-4060 *Or available from:* NCADI 1-800-729-6686
Problem Severity Index (PSI)	This is a structured interview developed to identify, document, and respond to drug/alcohol abuse as well as problems in other important areas of functioning among adolescents entering the juvenile court system. Administration takes 45 to 60 minutes.	Jim Boylan Juvenile Court Judges Commission P.O. Box 3222 Harrisburg, PA 17105 (717) 787-6910

Psychiatric Research Interview for Substance and Mental Disorders (PRISM)	The instrument was designed to maximize reliability and validity in community samples, alcohol, drug, and co-occurring disorder treatment samples. Although primarily designed as a research instrument, the PRISM provides systematic coverage of alcohol- and drug-related experiences and symptoms that may be useful in identifying areas of focus for treatment. Additionally, the unusually high reliability of the depression diagnoses in individuals with heavy drinking may provide a better basis for treatment decisions than less consistent methods for assessing major depression and dysthymia.	Dr. Deborah Hasin New York State Psychiatric Institute Box 123 722 West 168th Street New York, NY 10032 Phone: (212) 960-5518
Quantitative Inventory of Alcohol Disorders (QIAD)	Each item on this 22-item self-report instrument is rated on a 5-point scale. It takes 10 to 12 minutes to complete. It assesses the severity of alcohol problems during the month before administration of the test.	T.D. Ridley & S.T. Kordinak (1988), "Reliability and Validity of the Quantitative Inventory of Alcohol Disorders (QIAD) and the Veracity of Self-Report by Alcoholics" (*American Journal of Drugs and Alcohol Abuse* , 14[2], 263-292; see pp. 279-287)
Readiness to Change Questionnaire	Designed to assist the clinician in determining the stage of readiness for change among problem drinkers or people with alcohol use disorders. Assesses drinker's readiness to change drinking behaviors; may be useful in assignment to different types of treatment.	Center for Alcohol and Drug Studies Plummer Court, Carliol Place Newcastle upon Tyne NE1 6UR UNITED KINGDOM Phone: 44(0)191219 5648 Fax: 44(0)191219 5649

Recovery Attitude and Treatment Evaluator (RAATE)	Designed to assist in placing patients into the appropriate level of care at admission, in making continued stay or transfer decisions during treatment (utilization review), and documenting appropriateness of discharge. The RAATE provides objective documentation to assist in making appropriate treatment placement decisions; it strengthens individualized care and facilitates more individualized treatment planning; it measures treatment process; and it assesses the need for continuing care and discharge readiness.	Evince Clinical Assessments P.O. Box 17305 Smithfield, RI 02917 Phone: (401) 231-2993 Toll-free in USA: (800)-755-6299 www.evinceassessment.com
Self-Administered Alcoholism Screening Test (SAAST)	This is a 34-item questionnaire or interview with a yes-no format. There is also an abbreviated 9-item version. Considered useful for screening medical patients for alcoholism.	W.M. Swenson & R.M. Morse (1975), "The Use of a Self-Administered Alcoholism Screening Test (SAAST) in a Medical Center" (*Mayo Clinic Proceedings,* 50[4], 204-208; see pp. 207-208)
Short Michigan Alcohol Screening Test (SMAST)	This is a 13-item questionnaire to identify alcohol problems. It reviews an individual's drinking habits, history, and alcohol-related problems. Takes approximately 15 minutes to complete and requires a seventh grade reading level.	M.L. Selzer, A. Vinokur & L. van Rooijen (1975), "A Self-Administered Short Michigan Alcoholism Screening Test (SMAST)" (*Journal of Studies on Alcohol,* 36[1], 117-126; see p. 124)
Structured Clinical Interview for DSM-IV Disorders (SCID-IV)	Obtains Axis I and II diagnoses using the DSM-IV diagnostic criteria for enabling the interviewer to either rule out or establish a diagnosis of "drug abuse" or "drug dependence" and/or "alcohol abuse" or "alcohol dependence."	American Psychiatric Publishing, Inc. 1400 K Street, N.W. Washington, DC 20005 www.appi.org

Substance Abuse Questionnaire (SAQ)	This self-administered instrument targets adult probationers. It assesses risks and needs and presents treatment recommendations. Requires computer and is available in English or Spanish.	Herman Lindeman 2601 N. Third St., Suite 108 Phoenix, AZ 85004 (602) 234-2888
Substance Abuse Relapse Assessment (SARA)	This is a structured interview developed for use by substance abuse treatment professionals to help recovering individuals recognize signs of and avoid relapse. Used mostly with adult populations. Contains 41 questions administered in paper and pencil format. Takes approximately 60 minutes to complete. The results are interpreted individually by the assessor.	Roger Peters Florida Mental Health Institute Dept. of Mental Health Law and Policy University of South Florida 13301 Bruce B. Downs Blvd. Tampa, FL 33612-3899 (813) 974-4510
Substance Abuse Subtle Screening Inventory (SASSI)- Adult or Adolescent Version	This is a 52-item self-administered true-false questionnaire. Many items appear to be unrelated to substance abuse, but items allow clients to self-report negative consequences of substance use. May be administered in booklet or computer form. Can be given to individuals or groups. Requires about a third grade reading level. Requires 10 to 15 minutes to complete and about 1 minute to score.	SASSI Institute P.O. Box 5069 Bloomington, IN 47407 1-800-726-0526
T-ACE Questionnaire	This instrument is designed to identify pregnant women who consume quantities of alcohol that potentially can damage the fetus. It takes approximately 1 minute to complete and incorporates three items of the CAGE Questionnaire. In addition, it assesses alcohol tolerance (NIAAA, 1990).	
TASC, Inc. Illinois	Interview format that takes 90 to 120 minutes to complete. It assesses need, motivation, and level of treatment for drug-involved offender populations. Should be performed by a trained clinician (Singer, 1992).	Melody Heaps, Eve Weinberg TASC, Inc. 1500 N. Halstead Chicago, IL 60622 (312) 787-0208
University of Rhode Island Change	The URICA defines four theoretical stages of change—precontemplation,	Carlo C. DiClemente University of Maryland

Assessment (URICA)   contemplation, action, and   Psychology Department
maintenance—each assessed by eight   1000 Hilltop Circle
items. Assessment of stages of   Baltimore, MD 21250
change/readiness construct can be   Phone: (410) 455-2415
used as a predictor, treatment
matching, and outcome variables.

Section 2, Chapter 2:

The Functions of Counseling - Individual, Group, and Family Counseling

A Definition of Counseling

The International Certification and Reciprocity Consortium/Alcohol and Other Drug Abuse, Inc. (IC&RC/AODA) defines the core function of counseling as follows:

> "Counseling: (Individual, Group and Significant Others) - The utilization of special skills to assist individuals, families, or groups in achieving objectives through:
> - explorations of a problem and its ramifications;
> - examination of attitudes and feelings;
> - consideration of alternative solutions; and
> - decision-making."

The following supplemental expansion of this definition of "counseling" may be useful to help you better understand this skill:

> "Counseling/Therapy is basically a relationship in which the counselor helps the client mobilize resources to resolve his/her problem and/or modify attitudes and values. The counselor must be able to demonstrate a working knowledge of at least three counseling approaches. These methods may include Reality Therapy, Behavior Therapy, Systemic Counseling, Transactional Analysis, Strategic Family Therapy, Client Centered Therapy, etc. Further, the counselor must be able to explain the rationale for using a specific approach for the particular client. For example, a behavioral approach might be suggested for clients who are resistant, manipulative, and having difficulty anticipating consequences and regulating impulses. On the other hand, a cognitive approach may be appropriate for a client who is depressed, yet insightful and articulate."

"Also, the counselor should be able to explain his/her rationale for choosing a counseling approach in an individual, group, or significant other contact. Finally, the counselor should be able to explain why a counseling approach or context changed during treatment."

I. Six Stages of Counseling

    A. Information Gathering
        1. The counselor gathers as much information as is realistically possible in order to make a valid assessment and treatment plan
        2. The type of information collected is:
            a. Client's perception of the problem
            b. Motivation for seeking help
            c. Duration of the problem
            d. Previous ways of coping: adaptive responses, defense, and support system
            e. Relevant past history
            f. Expectations of how counseling will help
            g. Time and energy commitment

    B. Evaluation - There are five issues involved in evaluating the information the client provides
        1. Nature and severity of the presenting symptoms
            a. The symptoms can be used to determine progress in counseling
            b. Symptoms will decrease as the person resolves his/her problem
        2. Cause of the symptoms
            a. Medical, psychological, or both
            b. The needs that are not being met are causing the symptoms - Maslow's hierarchy of needs includes:
                1) Physiological needs: hunger, thirst, and sex drive
                2) Safety needs: security and absence of danger
                3) Belongingness and love needs: acceptance by others and affection
                4) Esteem needs: achievement, competency, approval, and recognition
                5) Self-actualization needs: meaningful life and purpose

3. Relief of the symptoms - are there possible solutions to the problem which will relieve the symptoms?
4. Client's readiness for counseling
    a. Not all people with symptoms are ready to do the work necessary to resolve the problem or are capable of solving the problem
    b. It may be necessary to refer the client for:
        1) Medical assistance
        2) Food and shelter assistance
        3) Self-help group support
5. Client - counselor match
    a. Personalities should not clash unreasonably
    b. Counselor's style of therapy is appropriate
    c. Difficulty with the client's issues and lifestyle
    d. If the counselor is inappropriate for the client, he/ she needs to refer the client to another counselor who is more appropriate

C. Feedback
    1. The counselor provides information to the client so he/she can decide if counseling is a good thing to do - provided counseling is not mandatory
    2. There are four guidelines to giving feedback
        a. Present the feedback information in simple, concrete terms
        b. The intention is to provide information, not impress the client with the counselor's profound knowledge
        c. Identify the client's strengths that will help resolve the problem and weaknesses that cause the problem and/or will get in the way of resolving it
        d. Be open to questions during or after the feedback
        e. Make recommendations regarding the start of counseling
            1) Begin individual, marital, family, or group counseling
            2) Suggest another counselor who may be more helpful
            3) Refer to an alternate form of help, medical attention, self-help group, or a class

        4) Suggest no further counseling because:
            a) The client's concerns are normal and there is no problem to resolve
            b) The intake session provided the necessary information for the client to handle things alone
            c) The client would not be helped by counseling at this time

D. Counseling Agreement - There are three issues that the counselor and client must talk through and come to agreement upon
    1. Practical issues which set limits
        a. Length of sessions
        b. Typical number of sessions, if appropriate
        c. Meeting time - Example: "Our meetings will consist of four 50 minute sessions at 10:00 a.m. each Wednesday."
        d. Later in counseling, this information can be discussed again if the client keeps switching appointments - Example: "I don't understand this constant switching. I need you to choose a regular time for our meetings."
    2. Expectations
        a. Counselor explains what he/she expects of the client - punctuality; honesty; effort to resolve problem; no use of alcohol and drugs at the sessions
        b. If these expectations are not met (e.g., client arrives for a session under the influence), the counselor will need to confront him/her with the problem - Example: "It seems you are having difficulty keeping to our agreement about drinking before sessions. We need to talk about this."
        c. It is important for the client to share his/her expectations so the counselor can correct any misperceptions
            1) Hope of "quick fix"
            2) Hope of becoming friends and socializing
            3) Things that may be helpful or unhelpful
        d. Other issues that set limits that the counselor needs to discuss are
            1) The extent of the counselor's availability
            2) The extent and nature of confidentiality
            3) The particular focus of the helping process
            4) The counselor's theoretical orientation
        e. A frequent mistake that beginning counselors make with clients is the failure to openly discuss each other's expectations - this can later interfere with establishing trust and rapport

3. Goals
    a. In order to turn a vague concept of "the helping process" into a concrete system of change, it is important to set goals that are specific and measurable
    b. The large problem and possible solution must be broken down into small pieces that allow the client to meet them one step at a time
    c. These small successes will eventually add up to a large success and help to keep the client's motivation high
    d. The goals must be realistic and healthy
    e. The client must agree on and "own" goals to make them work

E. Changing Behavior
    1. The client and the counselor work toward resolving problems and meeting goals
    2. The counselor uses a variety of techniques to facilitate this change

F. Termination
    1. Termination is a stage in the counseling process, not the last session - it is the agreement between counselor and client that:
        a. Things have improved for the client
        b. He/she is on the way toward meeting goals or has met them
        c. He/she does not need to continue the special supportive-confrontive relationship because he/she is capable of handling life without it
    2. The question of termination can be introduced by the counselor or the client
        a. The counselor should carefully explain to the client his/her recommendations for the termination of treatment
        b. The counselor may use appropriate levels of self-disclosure to assist the client in handling termination issues - the client may act out these issues or show anger or fear at the thought of termination

    c. Usually the number of sessions in non-group work are tapered off to decrease the discomfort of an abrupt ending
        1) Tapering may involve going from 4 sessions per week to 2 sessions per week to monthly sessions over a period of several months
        2) In group therapy, members do not taper termination because it is disruptive to the members who are continuing

II. Counseling Skills of Stage I: Responding to the Client's Frame of Reference

    A. Attending Skills
        1. Attending skills develop the trusting relationship between the client and counselor
        2. Physical attending techniques include:
            a. Being at a comfortable working distance with no objects to act as a barrier between counselor and client
            b. The counselor facing the client and maintaining a relaxed, open body posture
            c. The counselor leaning toward the client indicating interest
            d. The counselor maintaining eye contact - a client who seems uneasy when the counselor maintains eye contact, may have difficulty with interpersonal relationships
        3. Psychological attending skills include:
            a. Observation of the client's grooming, posture, speed of movement, and facial expressions
                1) To gain more information
                2) To look for the matching of verbals with non-verbals (congruency)
                3) To identify feelings
            b. Listening for the client's:
                1) Verbalizations
                    a) Generalizations
                    b) Deletions
                    c) Distortions
                2) Tone of voice - whining, demanding, seductive, or sad
                3) Recurring themes

              4) Feelings
              5) Representational mode
                  a) People perceive the world through their senses
                  b) Often one sense becomes the dominant way of perception - this dominance is reflected in speech, hearing, and touch
                      (1) Sight - "I see what you mean."
                      (2) Hearing - "I hear you."
                      (3) Touch - "I've got a feel for what you mean."
                  c) When the counselor begins to respond to the client using words from the same representation mode, the client feels understood and supported
              6) Good listening requires an objective attitude

4. Self-attending skills, by which the counselor is in touch with him/herself, include:
    a. Awareness of counselor's own message - especially, if the client's material is activating the counselor's personal issues
    b. Awareness of counselor's own physical and emotional needs and ways to get them met outside the session so the focus remains on the client
    c. Remaining centered regardless of the client's material - by practicing relaxation techniques

5. Responding skills, to let the client know the counselor is listening, include:
    a. Minimal encouragers - Examples: "Uh huh"; "And"; "Go on"; "Oh"
    b. Silence - indicates the counselor has the time to let the client proceed at his/her own pace and is not going to jump in with questions and comments

6. As the counselor utilizes attending skills, the client relaxes and begins to trust the counselor
    a. The trust that develops when a counselor listens, shows interest and understanding, and provides background information can be jeopardized by:
        1) The counselor not being aware of his/ her own countertransferential reactions
        2) The counselor constantly reassuring the client

        b. When a client has a high level of trust in the counselor, he/she indicates it is safe to feel pain in front of the counselor

        c. In trying to build rapport with a client in denial who has been referred for a suspected alcohol problem, the counselor may want to, for example, focus on his excellent employment and gradually work through the denial

B. Concreteness
1. Means identifying specific feelings, behaviors or situations relevant to the problem - prevents vagueness which allows the problem to continue because vagueness cannot be challenged
   Example of vagueness: "I always blow things."
   Example of concreteness: "I watched TV all night instead of studying for the exam, and I failed it."
2. May involve asking the client for more information to clarify general statements
3. Can involve not allowing the client to ramble

C. Distinguishing Content from Feelings
1. Content is what the client talks about in session
   Example: "I went to a new A.A. meeting last night"
2. Content may be what is implied or what isn't said in a session
   Example: "I'm being transferred next month," implies the client will miss the aftercare group members
3. Feelings are body-mind reactions that the client experiences but may not be able to express because he or she:
     a. Does not have the feelings vocabulary
     b. Denies feelings
     c. Is unaware of feelings
3. Feelings color and give flavor to the content and are shown in nonverbal behavior and manner of delivery
4. Feelings may enhance the content
   Example: "It hurts so much that he left me" is said with tears in eyes and shaking voice
5. Feelings may contradict the content
   Example: "I am pretty content with my life as it is" is said without eye contact in a flat voice

D. Probing
    1. It is important not to turn a counseling session into a question and answer period
        a. Puts the focus on the counselor who is seeking the "right" questions to ask which will solve the problem
        b. Client does not assume responsibility because:
            1) The counselor is the authority with the "right" questions
            2) The client is not given the opportunity to explore and find his/her own answers
    2. Open-ended questions are a useful means of gathering information because they don't limit the choice of answers and are less directive
        a. They don't ask for a "yes" or "no" or one word answer
        b. They force the client to explore issues that the counselor decides need further detail
        c. They typically include the words "are," "is," or "do"
        d. They do not begin with "why" because "why questions" are difficult to answer and frequently lead to excuse making
        Examples:
        * Counselor: "What are your concerns about your health?"
        Not: "Is your health getting worse?"

        * Counselor: "Tell me about your new job?"
        Not: "Do you like your new job?"

E. Primary Level: Accurate Empathy
    1. Is the ability to feel with the client and sense what his/her world is like
    2. Is talking to the client, not at the client, to communicate understanding and support for the person, not necessarily the behavior
    Example:
    Client: "I just wanted to borrow a few dollars for lunch and he turned on me in front of the whole crowd and said if I wasn't such a spend thrift I wouldn't have to borrow money."

    Counselor: "It's painful to be embarrassed in front of others - that must have felt awful."

F. Genuineness
    1. Is being oneself in the role of counselor
    2. The counselor does not become a different person when counseling but maintains his/her own personality while conducting oneself in a professional manner
    3. The counselor does not use excessive professional jargon but uses everyday terms to put the client at ease and facilitate communication
    4. The counselor is spontaneous yet tactful, not rigid
    5. The counselor is able to express thoughts and ideas at the appropriate time

G. Respect
    1. Is treating the client with dignity, as a human being not a case
    2. Is treating the client with warmth but without the intimacy that is reserved for friends; avoids artificial warmth
    3. Is non-judgmental and non-exploitative

III. Counseling Skills of Stage II: Stimulating the Client to Alternative Frame of Reference

A. Advanced Accurate Empathy
    1. Provides congruency, support, and understanding for the client
    2. The counselor tries to give additional meaning to the client's words and behavior based on the counselor's observation and experience
    3. The goal is to increase client self-awareness
    4. Some therapies such as psychoanalysis, rely heavily on interpretation while others, such as Gestalt, minimize its use
    5. Summarization
        a. Ties together the main points the client discussed
        b. Encourages the client to further explore an issue identified in the summary
        c. Allows the counselor to check out his/her perceptions of the content of the session
        d. Can help end a session in an orderly manner

B. Self-Disclosure
  1. The counselor shares personal information with the client: ideas, values, attitudes, and experience
     a. Must relate directly to the client's situation
     b. Can build a sense of trust and rapport between counselor and client
  2. When used appropriately, can enable the counseling relationship to move to deeper levels
     a. Excessive self-disclosure shifts the focus from client to counselor
     b. Minimal self-disclosure, gives the appearance of aloofness
     c. Inappropriate self-disclosure can be seen as phony and manipulative
  3. Involves a certain amount of risk to the counseling relationship because the information may threaten the client

C. Confrontation
  1. The pointing out of discrepancies in three areas
     a. Between a client's ideal and real self
     b. Between a client's verbal and nonverbal expression
     c. Between a client's view and the counselor's view of the client
  2. A way for the counselor to act as a role model for direct, honest, and open communication
     a. It may involve giving honest feedback about what is actually happening
     b. It does not include solutions to problems
     c. It is not an accusation
     d. A common way to confront is to use the sentence, "You say... but you do..."
  3. Though confrontation is uncomfortable for the counselor and the client, it pushes the helping process past client blocks
     a. Forces the client to talk about deeper underlying emotions
     b. Does not allow chatting about superficial recent events

4. Does not have to be done in a solemn or combative manner
   a. This is appropriate with some clients
   b. Other clients respond better to a lighter, more humorous approach
      1) The intent, which clients understand, is just as serious
      2) Helps them laugh at themselves while they also get the counselor's message
      3) Humor also conveys the impression that the counselor is human
5. Is an effective means of motivating the substance abuser to accept help because it is difficult for the client to deny his/her job performance, problems, and the resultant disciplinary action
6. Forces the person to accept more responsibility for his/ her own behavior

D. Immediacy
   1. The counselor leads the discussion as to what is happening at the moment between the counselor and the client
   2. Enables resolution of an immediate issue between the counselor and client
   3. Role models healthy behavior that the client can use in other relationships

IV. Counseling Skills of Stage III: Helping to Act

A. Role-Playing
   1. Is a process where participants pretend to be in a particular situation - the situation is not real but the feelings that come up are real
      a. The client can then address the feelings
      b. The counselor or other participants can let the client know how the behavior affected him/her with discussion of possible alternate behavior

2. Allows the client to practice new and scary behavior in a safe place
   a. Elicits potential responses from others so the client can identify likely consequences of the new behavior
      Example: A client is having difficulty saying "No" to co-workers who want him/her to join them for an after-work drink - role play allows him/her to replicate and rehearse responses to the situation
   b. Allows the client to work through old issues that may not be possible or safe to do in real life

B. Values Clarification
1. The process of helping the client decide what is important to him/her and the order of priorities
2. It is helpful to access the client's internal frame of reference to understand the importance of the client's values
3. It may be part of the counseling process to help the client modify his/her values

C. Goal Setting
1. Important to keep the counseling process focused and moving
2. Based on the client's values, the goals reflect what is important to him/her
   a. Goals are broken down into small steps that are not overwhelming
   b. Goals are specific and measurable
   c. Goals are realistic and healthy
3. Goals are re-evaluated periodically to make sure they are still what the client wants

D. Problem Solving
1. Clients can use a problem solving approach on their own
2. Problem solving can be broken into the following steps
   a. Defining the problem in concrete terms so it is solvable
   b. Thinking of all the possible solutions
      1) Realistic, unrealistic, and fantasy
      2) Sometimes a solution that looks unrealistic at first, may be the best answer with/without adjustments
   c. Weighing the pluses and minuses to each solution
   d. Deciding on the best alternative
   e. Making an action plan with goals broken into small steps (if applicable)
   f. Putting the solution into action
   g. Evaluating the results

E. Homework - Homework enables the client to:
   1. Practice new behavior
   2. Gain insight into old behavior by recording it as it occurs
   3. Be exposed to new concepts by reading
   4. Become part of a self-help group by attending meetings

F. Advice Giving
   1. When a client asks for advice, it is usually to help him/her explore available alternatives and their consequences
   2. If the counselor chooses to give advice, it is helpful to find out what the client has already thought about and then offer more than one solution so if the client chooses to follow the advice, there is still some shared client responsibility
   3. Summarization is a technique that helps keep the exploring manageable

V. Counseling Skills of Termination

A. Timing
   1. There is no clear time to terminate because the ideal of a client resolving all problems usually does not happen
   2. Client behaviors that indicate whether it is time to terminate or not include:
      a. Saying he/she wants to end
      b. Saying he/she has made a lot of progress
      c. Feelings of loss at the approaching end of the relationship
      d. Bringing back old, unproductive behavior so counseling won't end
      e. Creating new problems so counseling won't end
   3. While the counselor and the client agree that it is time to terminate, it is important to allow for time to reach closure on issues such as:
      a. Unfinished business between the counselor and client
      b. Planning ways for the client to keep growing after therapy is over
      c. Discussing feelings about ending the client-counselor relationship
      d. Reviewing client progress

B. Re-entering Counseling
  1. It is important for the client to feel that he/she can re-enter counseling without feeling like a failure
  2. At some point after termination, many clients discover that other issues surface that counseling can help resolve more quickly

VI. Alcohol/Drug Counseling

A. Three Stages of Drug/Alcohol Treatment
  1. Medical - physical intervention
  2. Psychosocial rehabilitation
  3. Aftercare

B. Goals of Counseling
  1. To help the client accept and admit that alcohol/drugs are a problem and he/she needs help to stop using
  2. Acceptance is the most important issue in early treatment - if the client maintains his/her denial that chemicals are not a problem, then it is difficult to make progress in counseling
  3. To determine the necessity for medical treatment
     a. Alcohol and drug dependence can be both psychological and physical
     b. The counselor must accurately assess whether the client has reached the stage of physical dependence
        1) This is important because of the danger of unsupervised withdrawal
        2) It is necessary to refer to inpatient treatment if physical dependence is determined
        3) If no physical dependence is determined, the client is maintained in outpatient treatment
  4. To help the client accept that he/she cannot use alcohol and drugs - in order to prevent the reactivation of the dependence cycle

5. To help the client reorganize his/her life without alcohol and drugs
    a. It is important for the client to understand the losses in his/her life caused by alcohol and drugs
        1) In order to fully accept the impact that substance abuse has had
        2) In order to accept responsibility for:
            a) The losses
            b) Gaining back what was lost (if possible)
            c) Substituting a healthy alternative for unregainable losses
        3) The counselor can help by:
            a) Speaking the client's language
            b) Rephrasing problems in a way that minimizes the client's resistance
            c) Showing empathy without allowing the client to wallow in self-pity
        4) Some of the losses include:
            a) Loss of self-respect
            b) Loss of respect by others
            c) Loss of an important relationship
            d) Loss of promotions, career advancement, or jobs
            e) Loss of health
    b. At all times, the client must accept responsibility for putting his or her life back together without alcohol and drugs
    c. The focus during early counseling sessions will be on becoming clean and sober and staying clean and sober - it is normal for a recovering person to still feel the urge to drink/use drugs
        1) The counselor can help by telling the client this is normal and encouraging him/her to continue working the program to prevent relapse

2) It is helpful to maintain sobriety by:
  (a) Attending A.A. or N.A. and other supportive meetings
  (b) Explaining to the spouse the importance of the recovering alcoholic's need to attend A.A. or N.A. meetings
  (c) Getting and working with a sponsor
  (d) Joining other activities that the client enjoyed before alcohol took over his/her life
  (e) Getting these support systems in place early in outpatient counseling or before leaving in patient treatment
d. As sobriety lengthens, the client can shift some attention in counseling to:
  1) Repairing relationships
  2) Starting new relationships
  3) Improving job performance
  4) Finding enjoyable leisure activities
  5) Living a normal life without alcohol
e. It is important for the counselor to maintain some focus on the dependence or abuse throughout treatment so the client will not forget that the cause of the problems he/she is solving is alcohol/drugs

VII. Examples of Counseling Skills in Action

A. Feelings
  1. For the client who has a long-term goal of improving self-esteem, the counselor determines that the inability to talk openly and express feelings may be an obstacle to reaching this goal
  2. If a treatment goal for a client is to learn to deal with his/her feelings without using a drug, the counselor could consider progress is being made when the client:
    a. Reports that he/she shared his/her anger with his/her wife by describing how he/she felt
    b. He/she cried openly in group when talking about guilt feelings
    c. Has an angry confrontation with a group member
    d. Hits a punching bag when feeling tense

       3. Able to say "No - I always feel taken advantage of," the counselor interprets this to mean that he/she has difficulty asserting and expressing feelings

       4. When a client says that he/she feels it is dangerous to express feelings, the counselor can assume that having close relationships with others causes conflicts

       5. To assess a client's underlying feelings, the counselor often must rely upon:

          a. The client's body posture

          b. The verbal content of the discussion

          c. The client's information and tone of voice

          d. Themes that repeat during a session

B. Sensitive Issues

       1. In dealing with sensitive issues such as abuse, violence, and incest, the counselor must:

          a. Be able to communicate empathy

          b. Be able to focus on the client and put aside his/her own value system

          c. Understand personality theory to help organize the information about why people behave in particular ways

          d. Not deny the client's feelings and concerns

       2. When a client says that as a child he/she was punished severely by an alcoholic father, was constantly told he/she was no good, and was never shown affection, the counselor can expect the client to have:

          a. A poor self-image

          b. Difficulty trusting others and sharing feelings

C. Treatment Issues

       1. When a client tells the counselor a long story about a friend who told others about the client's drinking problem, the counselor can assume that he/she is concerned that the counselor will also betray his/her confidence

       2. During the last session, a long-term client talks with down cast eyes about his/her father's death 16 years ago and how difficult it was to run the family without him - the counselor can guess that he/she is expressing his/her concern about his/her ability to get along without the counselor's help

       3. During an initial interview, a client reports that his/her brother died one month ago, he/she is unproductive and has been in the streets since his wife threw him out last week – the counselor should begin the helping process with the most immediate issue of housing

4. During a session, the counselor notices that the client is getting progressively more agitated and suspects a potential for violence - he/she should:
   a. Continue to reflect and interpret the client's behavior using extra caution
   b. Empathetically self-disclose, let the client know of his/her own feelings and concerns when the client behaves like this
   c. Reassure the client of a commitment to him/her and continue trying to problem solve
   d. Think of his/her own safety and an escape plan if the agitation increases

D. Cultural Issues
   1. A counselor who works with clients from various cultural backgrounds must be able to adjust the treatment so that it is accepted by the culture (without causing it to be ineffective) and be aware of personal bias
   2. A counselor working with a Hispanic client needs to realize that the client's claim he can't stop drinking because he needs to socialize with his friends may be either a reflection of the culture or resistance to treatment
   3. A counselor working with an African-American client must realize the historical influence of oppression as it relates to the development of trust in a therapeutic relationship
   4. A counselor working with a Native American should be aware of the cultural barriers that exist which impact on seeking and receiving treatment

COMMUNICATION SKILLS

I. Introduction

A. Definition of Communication
   1. Transmission of ideas, feelings, and attitudes by verbal, nonverbal, and written methods
   2. Reception of these ideas, feelings, and attitudes which creates a response

B. Purpose of Communication
  1. To be understood as the speaker intended
  2. To receive a favorable response to the message sent
  3. To maintain pleasant relationships
  4. Sometimes all of these goals are attained - sometimes none of them are

C. Dynamics - Each person brings to each communication two sets of dynamics
  1. Intrapersonal (within oneself) consists of
    a. All past and current experiences and feelings
    b. Cultural and ethnic background
    c. Ideals, self-concept, loyalties, prejudices, obligations, and goals
  2. Interpersonal (between or among people) consists of
    a. Each person's intrapersonal material
    b. Organization of the material presented
    c. Listening ability

II. Barriers to Communication

A. Barriers
  1. Differences in perception
    a. A lack of the experience and knowledge of an other, combined with an unwillingness to understand, leads to miscommunication
    b. These differences include age, sex, experience, and cultural and ethnic background
  2. Lack of basic knowledge
  3. Emotions can impede receiving and sending messages clearly
  4. Appearance
    a. A striking appearance, rather than the message, can become the focus of attention
    b. It may stir up prejudices and biases
  5. External distractions, e.g., physical discomfort, noise, and lighting

6. Poor listening
    a. Preconceived ideas of what the speaker is saying
    b. Thinking of responses while the speaker is still talking
    c. Listening for details rather than the entire message
    d. Evaluating the right or wrong of the message (and sender) before fully understanding the message
7. Poor organization by the speaker leads to confusion
8. Language
    a. Differences in interpreting words
    b. Inadequate vocabulary hinders sending a precise message
    c. Using emotionally charged words that create intense emotions in the listener and therefore reduce clarity
    d. Speaking errors which draw attention to grammar or pronunciation rather than the message
    e. Talking down to people or over their heads
9. Lack of interest by speaker or listener

B. Responsibilities of the Speaker
1. Choose a time and place with as few distractions as possible
2. Request the listener's attention
4. Organize the message and provide a brief but complete message - tell who, what, where, when, and how
5. Use an appropriate level of language and define terms
6. Repeat and clarify the main point
7. Request feedback
8. Maintain eye contact
9. Decrease distracting mannerisms and gestures

C. Responsibilities of the Listener
1. Concentrate on listening which requires tuning out distractions
2. Show interest
3. Listen for the whole message not details
4. Make sure you understand the message and ask for clarification before commenting on it
5. Do not interrupt the speaker but make a note, mental or written, on points to clarify or discuss

III. Communication Skills

A. The Ladder of Active Listening Skills
   1. Attentive listening
      a. Purpose
         1) To truly hear and understand the speaker
         2) To help the speaker feel valued and open up more
      b. Technique
         1) No commenting from the listener
         2) Eye contact and appropriate facial expression
   2. Minimal encouragers
      a. Purpose - to encourage the speaker to continue by indicating that the listener is understanding the messages
      b. Understanding is communicated via small verbals such as "yes," "I see," and "uh huh"
   3. Parroting
      a. Definition - repeating in whole or in part the speaker's own words
      b. Purpose
         1) To refer a point back to the speaker for further clarification or explanation
         2) To buy the listener time before speaking
            Example:
            Client: "I was so angry I wanted to punch him."

            Counselor: "Punch him!?!"

            Client: "Really punch him, because you know what else he did?..."

            Client: "I don't have a problem with alcohol. I just get drunk now and then."

            Counselor: "Now and then."

            Client: "Yeah, a few times a month."

4. Paraphrasing
    a. Definition - reflecting back the gist of what was said in the listener's own words with no interpretations
    b. Purpose
        1) To show the speaker that the listener is paying attention and understands
        2) To enable the speaker to clarify any misunderstandings on the spot
        3) To help the speaker clarify and expand thoughts
            Example:

            Client: "My boss doesn't understand me at all; he doesn't realize I'm always shaky in the morning."

            Counselor: "Sounds like mornings are bad for you, and you wish he understood."

            Client: "My wife always nags me about my drinking. It's gone too far...I think I'm going to move out."

            Counselor: "Sounds like things have gotten so bad that you are thinking about leaving."

5. Reflecting with interpretations
    a. Definition - reflecting what was said and unsaid, and picking up on feelings and attitudes
    b. Purpose
        1) To provide the speaker with feedback on how the listener has heard and interpreted what was said
        2) To build understanding and develop intimacy
    c. Caution - if reflecting with interpretation is done unskillfully, the speaker does not feel listened to or understood and may react with anger or frustration
        Example:

        Client: "I've spent 15 years trying to make a good life for us. And now all she does is nag me about drinking. A man deserves some relaxation."

        Counselor: "Sounds like you feel resentful that your wife doesn't accept your drinking as a way to relax after a hard day's work."

Client: "After my husband left me, my whole world collapsed and I've had more problems than I can handle. I found a couple of drinks helped."

Counselor: "Sounds like you are blaming your husband for getting you started in drinking.

6. Confrontation
    a. Definition - the pointing out of the noted discrepancies in three areas
        1) Between client's ideal and real self
        2) Between client's verbal and nonverbal expressions
        3) Between client's view and counselor's view of the client
    b. Though confrontation is uncomfortable to the client and the counselor, growth often gets blocked unless the client is confronted face to face and deals with an issue.
    c. It forces the client to talk about deeper underlying emotions that will lead to the resolution of the issue rather than focusing on shallow experiences
    d. Confrontation is a way for the counselor to act as a role model for direct, honest, and open communication
    e. It may involve giving honest feedback about what is real vs. imagined

B. Sending Effective Messages
    1. Speak in the first person "I"
    2. Send complete and specific messages
    3. Make verbal and nonverbal messages congruent (matching) - the nonverbal will be believed over the verbal if they are not congruent
    4. Ask for feedback and questions
    5. Tailor the message to the receiver
    6. Describe feelings to reduce ambiguity
    7. Describe other people's behaviors without judging or interpreting

C. Communicating feeling - the components of an "I" message
1. "I" - to own the message
2. "Feel _____ about"
3. Identify the feeling, "because it makes me feel _____ "
4. Identify the consequences of continuing the behavior

Example: "I am frustrated with you because you say 'yes' when you mean 'no' and if you continue to do this, I am going to ignore your whining when you have to meet your commitment."

Example: "I feel so proud that you stood up for yourself that I'd like to treat you to lunch."

Additional Information on Basic Counseling Skills

Overview

A significant number of questions asked on the two credentialing examinations center on the area of counseling. We therefore present an expanded section on this important topic area. *Counseling Alcoholic Clients: A Microcounseling Approach to Basic Communication Skills* is a federal publication originally printed in 1974. It still contains the best view of counseling skills that has ever been presented. It was designed to help practicing alcoholism counselors upgrade their abilities to use eight basic communication skills-- attending paraphrasing, reflection of feeling, summarizing, probing, counselor self-disclosure, interpreting, and confrontation -- in one-to-one interaction with a client. Unfortunately, the materials are no longer in print and difficult to find.

Fortunately, a search of my old files (see, they sometimes do come in handy!) turned up a copy of these materials. We were able to have the materials transcribed and included in this section on counseling skills.

On completion of this information, you will be able to:

- define each skill;
- recognize when each skill is being practiced effectively; and
- demonstrate the ability to use each skill and to integrate all skills appropriately and effectively in a simulated counseling situation.

The eight skills as defined in this program are:

- Attending. Demonstration of the counselor's concern for and interest in the client by eye contact, body posture, and accurate verbal following.

- Paraphrasing. A counselor statement that mirrors the client's statement in exact or similar wording.

- Reflection of Feeling. The essence of the client's feelings, either stated or implied, as expressed by the counselor.

- Summarizing. A brief review of the main points discussed in the session to insure continuity in a focused direction.

- Probing. A counselor's response that directs the client's attention inward to help both parties examine the client's situation in greater depth.

- Counselor Self-Disclosure. The counselor's sharing of his/her personal feelings, attitudes, opinions, and experiences for the benefit of the client.

- Interpreting. Presenting the client with alternative ways of looking at his/her situation.

- Confrontation. A counselor's statement or question intended to point out contradictions in the client's behavior and statements, or to induce the client to face an issue the counselor feels the client is avoiding.

These skills can be classified under the broader headings of listening, processing, and feedback, three elements that comprise communication between two individuals. This program addresses communication from the counselor's perspective.

- Listening is defined as receiving messages from a client by focusing attention on what the client is expressing, both verbally and nonverbally.

- Processing is the complex series of events that take place within the counselor between his or her listening and responding to the client. Processing may include mentally cataloging data, categorizing, comparing, hypothesizing on significance, exploring implications, and selecting a response on the basis of the counselor's life experience, beliefs, knowledge, attitudes, feelings, self-acceptance, and other factors that influence judgment and performance.

- Feedback is the verbal or nonverbal response that the counselor makes as a result of processing the information received from listening to the client.

Attending can be classified as a listening skill; the remaining seven can be classified as feedback, and as such, provide evidence of the quality of the listening and processing that precede the feedback. Processing skills are not covered explicitly in this course.

Paraphrasing, reflection of feeling and summarizing are primarily the feedback skills that demonstrate to the client that the counselor is paying attention to what the client is expressing verbally and nonverbally. The counselor can also use these skills to help the client recognize and clarify his/her own understanding of what he/she says and the feelings related to these messages. The counselor applies the other four skills--probing, counselor self-disclosure, interpreting, and confrontation--to promote a mutual identification and understanding of the client's problems and ways to deal with those problems.

These eight skills constitute only a partial listing of skills that can be subsumed under the heading of listening, processing, and feedback. Other dimensions of processing include the counselor's knowledge about alcohol and alcoholism; specific treatment techniques (behavior shaping, modeling, goal setting, assertiveness training, relaxation training); various theories of psychological development and human behavior; self-awareness of feelings, values, and attitudes; and past personal and professional experiences. Other feedback skills include advising, information giving, directing, supporting, and structuring.

Mastery of all the listening, processing, and feedback skills and others such as maintaining confidentiality, record keeping, crisis intervention, and referral are necessary for effective counseling. Mastery of all these skills depends on both training and experience and requires the same focused attention that is being given to the eight basic communication skills in this program.

Feedback and Assumptions

Feedback

Feedback was described in the Overview as the verbal or nonverbal response that the counselor makes as a result of processing the information received from listening to the client. With the exception of attending, the communication skills covered in this program are classified as feedback.

Feedback used in another sense is an important aspect of this training program. During skill practice sessions, participants will take turns as counselor, client, and observer. Client and observer will give the counselor feedback dealing with his or her performance of the skill in question.

The definition of feedback as used in the context of the practice sessions is: telling the counselor what you (as observer) heard and saw as he or she practiced a particular skill, or what you (as client) felt in response to his or her practice of the skill.

The extent to which you give each other feedback and the quality of the feedback may be the critical factor in determining whether or not this workshop will be productive for you. For example, if in practice sessions neither the observers nor the clients give you significant feedback about your performance as a counselor, you might complete your training, having gone through all the prescribed activities, and have gained nothing. You may perhaps even take away a more distorted rather than a clearer picture of your capabilities. In addition being a recipient of feedback can help sharpen your perception of what constitutes useful feedback.

When giving feedback, whether positive or negative, keep these guidelines in mind. They apply to both counseling and skill practice situations.

- The purpose of feedback is to be helpful to other people by giving them useful information about what they are doing or the effect they are having on you.
- Timing is important. If feedback is given so long after an event that the recipient can't remember it clearly, it is not likely to be helpful. Feedback is most helpful when given as soon as possible.

- Be specific rather than general. Generalities often raise people's defenses so that they don't get the message you are trying to give. It's much easier to hear and acknowledge "I felt annoyed when you were late for our appointment today," than it is to hear and acknowledge "You're always late and I'm sick and tired of it." (Even if the other person *is* always late and you are sick and tired of it, it's more constructive to deal with specific situations as soon as possible, rather than not give feedback and sit on your feelings until you finally explode.)
- Being descriptive rather than judgmental is also less likely to raise people's defenses and is more helpful. "You just went through a stop light and you're driving at 40 mph in a 20 mph school zone, and I feel nervous," is more constructive than "You're really a lousy driver."
- The last point to remember about feedback is that it should be directed toward behavior, which is something the receiver can do something about. While you may find you simply have to tell someone the effect that his/her height, or age, or color of eyes has on you, this is not feedback. In effect, you're not telling that person anything about himself/herself but something about yourself. Even if it's positive, such as "Darling, I just love your green eyes," you're talking about your own likes or dislikes rather than something someone else has control over and could change if he/she wanted to.

Assumptions

Despite earnest intentions to give accurate and meaningful feedback, we may sometimes unconsciously erect barriers to doing so. These barriers may derive from our own needs, beliefs, prejudices, preferences, values, or fears, and they may frequently take the form of assumptions about others. Sometimes our assumptions are on target; quite often they are far from reality. However, they are accurate often enough to encourage us to keep making assumptions.

Making assumptions often takes the form of taking observable facts about another person, developing a theory to explain those facts, and then treating the other person as if your theory is proven. In alcoholism counseling, this process might mean observing that a client's eyes are bloodshot, assuming that he/she has been drinking, and reacting to the client with anger and disappointment on the basis of your assumptions. The client, however, may actually have hay fever or may not have been able to sleep. This kind of assuming is sometimes called pigeonholing or stereotyping.

Making assumptions can also take the form of making another person responsible for our feelings. For example, I may feel frightened; if I assume that some other person is threatening to me, then this assumption justifies or rationalizes my fear. This process could easily take place with a client who may, in reality, be dangerous only to himself/herself or not dangerous at all.

Three things to remember about assumptions are:

- Recognize that you probably have some.
- Don't take them too seriously. You can't know another person's experience, only your own perceptions of that experience. Any conclusions or theories that you may have about another may be accurate or they may be *only* your assumptions.
- Check them out. Using nonjudgmental words and tentative phrases, share your assumptions with the recipient and see whether they are accurate or not--for example, "It seems like you may have been drinking today." Remember, the object in counseling another is not for the counselor to be right (and the client wrong) but rather to establish communication, build a relationship, and help the client develop the capacity to deal more effectively with his/her life.

Attending

Definition of Attending

Attending is fundamental to the use of all other counseling skills. As used here, attending implies a concern by the counselor with all aspects of the client's communication. It includes listening to the verbal content, hearing and observing the verbal and nonverbal cues to the feelings that accompany the communication, and then communicating back to the client the fact that the counselor is paying attention.

Purposes of Attending

1. It encourages the client to continue expressing his/her ideas and feelings freely.

2. It allows the client to explore ideas and feelings in his/her own way and thus provides the client with an opportunity to direct the session.

3. It can give the client a sense of responsibility for what happens in the session by enabling him/her to direct the session.

4. It helps the client relax and be comfortable in the counseling session.

5. It contributes to the client's trust of the counselor and sense of security.

6. It enables the counselor to draw more accurate inferences about the client.

Components of Attending

Effective attending has two components: (1) listening and observing and (2) communicating to the client that listening and observing is going on.

The first component of attending behavior is listening effectively and observing carefully. For many people, listening is a difficult task to learn. Although society does place great emphasis on spoken exchanges, many people have not learned to listen effectively. Often, people may think they are listening when they are actually thinking about something else or are debating a subject in their head while waiting for the other person to pause so that they can present some comment of their own. A client can usually sense when the counselor is listening with "half an ear."

Effective listening by itself, however, is not enough. Counseling occurs in a face-to-face situation where both participants watch, as well as listen to, each other. The difference in information gathered from seeing and hearing as opposed to hearing alone is illustrated vividly by contrasting television with radio.

The counselor learns much about the feelings of the client through observation. Frequently, nonverbal behavior that expresses feelings may appear to alter or even negate verbal messages. It is common for people to communicate much more than they intend by their body language. As a matter of fact, the nonverbal message is more likely than the spoken words to transmit the real message--for example, a facial expression showing disgust may contradict the statement, "I'm not bothered by the thought of a drunken women."

Conversely, many of the skills, attitudes, and feelings of the counselor are conveyed to the client through nonverbal behavior such as facial expressions, posture, eye contact, and gestures. The first component of attending occurs when the counselor stays attuned to what the client is expressing verbally and nonverbally. He/she listens closely and observes carefully.

The second component of attending behavior is *letting the client know that he/she is really being heard*. The counselor communicates his/her attentiveness to the client generally through three methods.

a. Eye Contact--The counselor should initiate and maintain eye contact with the client. Strong impressions--favorable and unfavorable--are formed depending on the kind and amount of eye contact. In ordinary social interaction, it is considered courteous to look at the person with whom one is speaking. In counseling, this behavior is almost imperative. However, in some cases continuous eye contact might cause the client to feel uncomfortable, as could a fixed stare or an intense gaze. Varied use of eye contact is the most effective and natural behavior for the counselor and the most likely to put the client at ease.

It is important to note that these comments on eye contact are not applicable to all cultures. For instance, maintaining direct eye contact is a hostile act to some Native Americans and may be taken as a lack of respect by some Orientals.

b. Posture--Body language reveals a great deal about people; posture and gestures convey distinct messages. Impression of others are formed even from the way they sit. The counselor wants to communicate to the client by his/her body posture that he/she is interested. An upright seated position with the upper body leaning slightly forward is generally considered to convey attentiveness, but the counselor should adopt a posture in which he/she will feel relaxed and comfortable. The first position the counselor assumes won't necessarily be the only one. The counselor will undoubtedly shift positions during the counseling session, for comfort and as a reflection of his/her feelings.

Again, a word of caution is offered regarding cultural differences in acceptable attending. In some culture, sitting too close to a client might be considered offensive or threatening; sitting too far away might convey detachment or withdrawal, and individuals vary in the amount of distance or closeness they need. By watching how the client uses space in relation to the counselor, the counselor will probably have an indication of what is comfortable for the client.

c. Accurate verbal following--The counselor communicates to the client by verbal responses that listening and observing are occurring. The most important characteristic of accurate verbal responses is that they relate directly to what the client is expressing. This means the counselor doesn't jump to new topics or interrupt the client but follows the client in what he/she is saying. The counselor takes his/her cues from the client and indicates involvement by simply nodding, using encouraging phrases such as "um-hm'" or "I see," repeating key words, or posing one-word questions, such as "Oh?" or "Yes?"

Later in this training program, the counselor will practice more specific types of responses (for example, paraphrasing, reflection of feeling, and summarizing) that convey to the client that the counselor has listened and observed. At this point in the program, the counselor can demonstrate accurate verbal following by offering minimal verbal responses, making head movements, and staying with the topic.

Summary of Attending

In attending, the counselor's goal is to listen effectively, to observe the client, and to communicate his/her interest and attentiveness through direct eye contact, relaxed body posture, and accurate verbal following. The skill of attending is the foundation on which all the other skills in this program are built.

Paraphrasing

Definition of Paraphrasing

Paraphrasing is a counselor response that restates the content of the client's previous statement. Paraphrasing concentrates primarily on cognitive verbal content, that is, content which refers to events, people and things. In paraphrasing, the counselor reflects to the client the verbal essence of his/her last comment or last few comments. Sometimes, paraphrasing may involve simply repeating the client's own words, perhaps emphasizing one word in particular. More often, paraphrasing is using words that are similar to the client's, but fewer in number.

Paraphrasing and reflection of feeling are very similar and therefore are easy to confuse. In both skills, the counselor must identify the client's basic message, either cognitive or affective (pertaining to feeling or emotion), and give that message back to the client using his/her (the counselor's) own words.

The distinguishing feature between paraphrasing and reflection of feeling is the focus of the counselor's response. A paraphrase focuses on the words the client is speaking. Reflection of feeling focuses on the associated feeling or emotion as expressed in the client's tone of voice, rate and volume of speech, posture, and other nonverbal behavior as well as verbal content.

In actual counseling it is neither realistic nor therapeutic to perform only one skill at a time. However, for the purpose of refining the individual skills in this workshop, it is helpful to concentrate on each skill separately. Reflection of feeling will be discussed and practiced in a separate session.

Purposes of Paraphrasing

1. It communicates to the client that the counselor understands or is trying to understand what he/she is saying. Paraphrasing can thus be a good indicator of accurate verbal following.

2. It sharpens a client's meaning to have his/her words rephrased more concisely and often leads the client to expand his/her discussion of the same subject.

3. It often clarifies confusing content for both the counselor and the client. Even when paraphrasing is not accurate, it is useful because it encourages the client to clarify his/her remarks.

276

4. It can spotlight an issue by stating it more succinctly, thus offering a direction for the client's subsequent remarks.

5. It enables the counselor to verify his/her perceptions of the verbal content of client's statements.

Components of Paraphrasing

Paraphrasing has two components: determining the basic message and rephrasing.

The counselor uses his/her judgment to *determine the basic message* that is being expressed in the client's verbal content. Much of the time clients tend to speak in short paragraphs. They seldom state a single thought and wait for a reply. So the counselor must attend to all of the client's verbal content, but decide on the basic message being expressed in the "paragraphs."

After the counselor determines the basic message to be responded to, he/she attempts to give this content back to the client in a more precise way by *rephrasing* it. The counselor may want to combine several of the client's related comments into one response to the client.
To paraphrase effectively, then, the counselor determines the basic message from the content and rephrases it, usually in similar, but fewer words.

Checking Out

To minimize the possibility of the counselor's letting his/her assumptions distort what the client is saying, the counselor should get in the habit of checking out his/her paraphrasing. This can be done by adding phrases such as, "Is that right?" "Am I correct?" or "Have I heard you correctly?" to the paraphrase. This procedure will usually evoke a response from the client, and the counselor can then judge whether he/she is making assumptions or is accurately attending to the client. Checking out may not be necessary, however, if the client is clearly indicating agreement either verbally or nonverbally.

Assessing the Outcome of Paraphrasing

How effectively a counselor has used paraphrasing can best be judged by the client's next response after a paraphrase. If the paraphrase is effective, the client may indicate agreement by a word or gesture and may continue to talk further on the same subject.

Sometimes the counselor will not succeed in accurately distilling the client's comments, and the client may reply, "No, that's not what I meant." When this occurs, the counselor's attempt at paraphrasing has still been useful because it allows the counselor to see immediately that he/she has erred either in determining the basic message or in rephrasing the content.

In other instances the client may confirm the accuracy of the counselor's paraphrase, but, having heard his/her meaning expressed in different words, decide to modify or even reverse the meaning entirely to reflect a changed point of view.

Each of these outcomes can be regarded as evidence that the counselor's paraphrase has been effective.

Summary of Paraphrasing

To paraphrase is to determine the basic message in the client's cognitive statements and concisely rephrase it. The rewording should capture the essence of cognitive verbal content. Occasionally, an exact repetition of the client's remarks may be an appropriate paraphrase. More commonly, the counselor determines and rephrases the basic message of the verbal content using similar, but fewer words.

Reflection of Feeling
Introduction

Dealing with feelings and emotions--one's own or others'--is probably the most difficult part of human relations. One cause of this difficulty is that the dominant American culture does not value open and free expression of feelings and emotions.

At an early age, we learn to control, mask, or deny our feelings. Unfortunately, with most of us, this process is learned well and reinforced continuously in our schooling. Through primary emphasis on intellectual achievement, we are conditioned to restrain, and even deny, our emotions. However, denied or suppressed feelings do not just disappear. Depending on the intensity of the feelings and how long they have been suppressed, they manifest their presence both psychologically and physically in such ways as difficulty in communicating with others, depression, fatigue, tension headaches, and psychosomatic illness. A more constructive approach is to recognize that feelings and emotions exist, accept them as part of ourselves, and learn to express them in ways that promote individual growth and mutually satisfying relationships.

In counseling, we must communicate with the client not only on the factual, or cognitive level (meaning events, people, things), but also on the affective level (meaning feelings about events, people, and things). Frequently, we may have as clients people who have controlled, inhibited, or denied their feelings and emotions for years. One of our tasks is to help them understand that it is acceptable, even necessary, to be aware of and express their feelings in the counseling relationship. The ability of the counselor to transmit that message is based on the assumption that the counselor can get in touch with, identify, and express his/her own feelings. Our primary focus here is on helping the client to become aware of, identify, and express his/her feelings.

An important concept to understand with regard to reflection of feeling is *empathy,* which has been identified as one of the essential conditions in counseling. Empathy, in everyday language, means putting oneself in the other person's shoes. More formally, it might be defined as a counselor's attempt to perceive the world through the client's frame of reference. Thus the counselor manifests empathy through his/her ability to perceive what is happening in regard to the client's feelings and to communicate this perception to the client. Reflection of feeling is one of the ways empathy can be communicated.

Definition of Reflection of Feeling

Reflection of feeling is the counselor's expressing the essence of the client's feelings, either stated or implied. In contrast to paraphrasing, reflection of feeling focuses primarily on the emotional element of the client's communication, whether it is verbal or nonverbal. The counselor tries to perceive the emotional state or condition of the client and feed back a response that demonstrates his/her understanding of this state. Reflection of feeling, then, is an empathic response to the client's emotional state or condition.

Purposes of Reflection of Feeling

1. It conveys to the client that the counselor understands or is trying to understand what the client is experiencing and feeling. This empathy for the client usually reinforces the client's willingness to express feelings to the counselor.
2. It clarifies the client's feelings and attitudes by mirroring them in a nonjudgmental way.

3. It brings to the surface feelings of the client that may have been expressed only vaguely.

4. It gives the client the opportunity to recognize and accept his/her feelings as part of himself/herself. Sometimes the client may refer to "it" or "them" as the source of a problem, when he/she really means "I was feeling angry."

5. It verifies the counselor's perceptions of what the client is feeling. That is, it allows the counselor to check out with the client whether or not he/she is accurately reflecting what the client is experiencing.

6. It can bring out problem areas without the client feeling pushed.

7. It helps the client infer that feelings are causes of behavior.

Components of Reflection of Feeling

The reflection of feeling skill consists of two components: identification and formulation.

The counselor must first *identify* the basic feeling(s) being expressed verbally or nonverbally by the client. To be able to identify feelings in clients, a counselor must be able to recognize feelings in himself/herself. Although the counselor can't feel the client's feelings, he/she can infer what they might be by processing the verbal and nonverbal information the client is communicating. The counselor matches the information he/she gains with his/her experiences in order to label the feelings the client seems to be experiencing. Since the counselor has experienced feelings such as joy, anger, pain, fear, and boredom, he/she can remember how they felt.

To recognize or be aware of feelings in the client, the counselor attends to both verbal and nonverbal cues. When he/she is listening effectively to the client's statements, the counselor may perceive feelings that are either directly expressed or implied. Sometimes the verbal indications of feelings may not be as straightforward as they seem. Often "I think" and "I feel" are used interchangeably, although they have different meanings, particularly in counseling. For example, if a client says, "I felt overjoyed at the news," the counselor can infer that the client was happy. However, if the client says, "I feel he is too strict," the counselor can not reliably infer what the client feels, but only what he/she thinks.

Distinct messages of emotional content also will come from nonverbal cues. Nonverbal indicators of feeling include such things as head and facial movements, posture, gesture, and voice tone and quality. Some examples of specific nonverbal cues are lowered head, folded arms, restlessness, crying, and slowness of speech.

Think back for a moment. When you're depressed, how does your voice sound? When you're angry, what happens to your face, mouth, eyes, jaw, and voice? When you're afraid, what happens to your eyes, your body posture, your gestures? Of course, different people will display different degrees and amounts of emotional intensity in different ways. Only after observing and interacting with a person over time can anyone begin to decide what that individual's nonverbal behavior might really be saying about how he/she is feeling.

In general, though, the counselor can be alert to such facial and body expressions as smiles, eyes widening or narrowing, worry wrinkles, drooping shoulders, or tightly clenched hands. Voice quality is an important area to attend to for signs of emotion. Loudness or softness, changes in tone or inflection, and emphasis on one word are indications of feelings. Sometimes the client may convey conflicting messages with his/her verbal and nonverbal behavior. He/she may say "I'm not upset," when his/her hands are shaking and his/her face is red.

Thus, in identifying feelings, the counselor attempts to enter the client's frame of reference by drawing on his/her own experiences with feelings. The counselor must identify the feelings the client is communicating before he/she can reflect them accurately to the client.

The second component of an effective reflection of feeling response is to *formulate a response* that captures the essence of the feeling expressed by the client. Although the counselor tries to understand and identify the client's feelings as well as he/she can, it is not possible to *be* the client, so any conclusions drawn should be considered tentative and presented as tentative reflections. By remaining tentative and open-minded in formulating verbal responses, the counselor avoids dogmatic-sounding responses that might alienate the client if they are inaccurate.

Examples of appropriate phrases with which a counselor might begin a reflection-of-feeling response are:

It seems that you feel . . .
Are you saying that you feel . . .
You seem to feel . . .
Is it possible that you feel . . .
I'm picking up that you feel . . .
You appear to be feeling . . .
Perhaps you're feeling . . .
I sense that you feel . . .

Often, counselors find reflection of feeling one of the harder skills to master. Some common errors counselors tend to make in using this skill follow in the next section. These errors may also occur in using some of the other skills in the program.

Common Errors in Formulating Reflection of Feeling Responses.

1. Stereotypical language--The counselor can fall into a pattern of always beginning reflections in the same way with a phrase such as "You feel . ." Some of these phrases were listed above as appropriate, but the counselor should avoid using any one of them too often. The counselor should vary his/her style of reflecting.

2. Timing--Sometimes the inexperienced counselor attempts to reflect feelings after every statement the client makes. This can give an impression of insincerity and may dilute the effect of the technique. At the other extreme, the counselor waits until the client has finished a long series of comments and tries to reflect many feelings in one response. Another error in timing involves pauses. Counselors often don't wait out pauses. Long pauses can mean that the client is trying to say things that are difficult for him/her to say, but the uncomfortable counselor may jump in and respond immediately, in effect interrupting and breaking off the client's struggle to express a complex or painful thought or feeling.

3. Too-shallow or too-deep responses--The counselor should strive to feed back to the client the essence of what he/she is expressing. The counselor should avoid either reflecting a feeling at a level that is more intense than the client is feeling or taking away from the client's meaning by merely labeling the feeling. The goal is to communicate to the client that he/she is understood on the level where he/she is. For example, a client may say, "I feel bad. I had some drinks at the office party last night after I promised myself I wouldn't." A too-shallow response from the counselor might be, "You mean you're sorry." A too-deep response might be, "You feel *really* guilty about your drinking."

Checking Out

Checking out perceptions is as important in reflection of feeling as it is in paraphrasing, even though the reflection of feeling is phrased tentatively. The addition of a questioning phrase, usually at the end of the reflection of feeling statement, will ensure that the counselor is not making unfounded assumptions about the client. For example, "I sense that you feel discouraged today. Is that right?"

Assessing the Outcome of Reflection of Feeling

In reflection of feeling, as in paraphrasing, the effectiveness of the activity can be determined by the client's response. The client may confirm or disclaim the reflection. If the reflection is accurate, the client is more likely to continue discussing the feeling reflected. An inaccurate reflection will often bring a correcting response from the client, which results in clarification. In either case, the net result of reflection of feeling responses made by the counselor should be an increased focus on feelings by the client as he perceives that discussing feelings is acceptable in counseling.

Summary of Reflection of Feeling

Reflection of feeling involves identifying the essence of the feeling the client is expressing and formulating a response that indicates that the counselor understands. Usually the counselor offers fresh words that capture the basic verbal or nonverbal feeling message of the client.

Summarizing

Definition of Summarizing

Summarizing is the tying together by the counselor of main points discussed in a counseling session. Summarizing can focus on both feelings and content and is appropriate after a discussion of a particular topic within the session or as a review at the end of the session of principal issues discussed. In either case, a summary should be brief, to the point, and without new or added meanings.

In many respects, summarizing is similar to, or an extension of, paraphrasing and reflection of feeling in that the counselor seeks to determine the basic meanings being expressed in content of feelings and gives these meanings back to the client in fresh words. Summarizing differs primarily in the span of time it is concerned with. In paraphrasing, a statement or brief paragraph occurring over a short period of time is rephrased. In summarizing verbal content, several of the client's statements, the entire session, or even several sessions are pulled together.

In reflection of feeling, the counselor responds to the last feeling or feelings expressed or displayed. In summarizing feelings, the counselor reviews numerous feelings expressed or displayed over a longer period of time.

Purposes of Summarizing

1. It can ensure continuity in the direction of the session by providing a focus.

2. It can clarify a client's meaning by having his/her scattered thoughts and feelings pulled together.

3. If often encourages the client to explore an issue further once a central theme has been identified.

4. It communicates to the client that the counselor understands or is trying to understand what the client is saying and feeling.

5. It enables the counselor to verify his/her perceptions of the content and feelings discussed or displayed by the client during the session. The counselor can check out whether he/she accurately attended and responded without changing the meanings expressed.

6. It can close discussion on a given topic, thus clearing the way for a new topic.

7. It provides a sense of movement and progress to the client by drawing several of his/her thoughts and feelings into a common theme.

8. It can terminate a session in a logical way through review of the major issues discussed in the entire session.

Components of Summarizing

Accurate summarizing has two components: selection and tying together.

The counselor uses his/her judgment to select the key points discussed. As the counselor picks out the highlights of content and feelings, general themes usually begin to emerge. When deciding what materials to summarize, the counselor should note consistent and inconsistent patterns that have evolved in the session. For example, the client may keep coming back to one particular issue, implicitly emphasizing its importance, or the client may seem to contradict himself/herself by making conflicting statements at different times during the session.

After selecting the principal points discussed or displayed, the counselor attempts to *tie together* these points and to feed them back to the client in a more concise way. In drawing together the content and feelings, the counselor should avoid adding his/her own ideas, which could well be assumptions. The idea is to give back to the client essentially what he/she has said concisely, using fresh words.

Assessing Outcomes of Summarizing

The outcome of a summarization depends to a large extent on where in the counseling session it occurs. If the summarizing of a particular topic occurs during the session, it is likely to encourage the client to talk further. If summarizing occurs at the close of the session, it is more likely to terminate further discussion.

How effectively a counselor has summarized the essence of the verbal content and feelings the client has expressed can best be determined by the client's response to the summary. The client may affirm that the counselor has tied together points already discussed and, depending on where in the session the summary is made, continue to explore the topic, begin a related or new topic, or accept the counselor's remarks as a wrap-up of the session.

Sometimes the counselor may not have accurately pulled together the essential content and feelings of the client, or may have added assumptions of his/her own to the exchange. In that case, the client might say, "That isn't quite what I said," or "I agree with that except for . . . " The counselor and client can then resolve areas in question before proceeding or ending the session.

As with paraphrasing and reflection of feeling, the counselor should make a practice of checking out the accuracy of a summary with the client to minimize the chances of making unwarranted assumptions.

Examples of Summarizing

To a divorced woman exploring problems that she is having with a teen-age son, who is drinking heavily:

> As I understand what you've been saying during the past few minutes, you seem to be struggling with three possible ways to handle the situation: you might continue trying to reason with your son yourself;
>
> you might ask his father to help you deal with the boy; or you might stop discussing the problem with your son and punish him by taking away his privileges.

At the end of a session with a male client:

> Let's take a look at what we've covered in today's session. It sounds like you've felt inadequate in dealing with several areas of your life--your family, your job, and now your drinking.

Summary of Summarizing

To summarize is to select the key points or basic meanings from the client's verbal content and feelings and succinctly tie them together. The summarization should accurately reflect the essence of the client's statements and feelings and should not include assumptions of the counselor. Summarizing then, is a review of the main points already discussed in the session to ensure continuity in a focused direction.

Probing

Definition of Probing

Probing is a counselor's use of a question or statement to direct the client's attention inward to explore his/her situation in more depth. A probing question, sometimes called an "open-ended question," requires more than a one-word (yes or no) answer from the client.

When phrased as a statement, the probe contains a strong element of direction by the counselor; for example, "Tell me more about your relationship with your parents," or "Suppose we explore a little more of your ideas about what an alcoholic is."

Purposes of Probing

1. It can help focus the client's attention on a feeling or content area.

2. It may help the counselor better understand what the client is describing by giving him/her more information about the client's situation.

3. It may encourage the client to elaborate, clarify, or illustrate what he/she has been saying.

4. It sometimes enhances the client's awareness and understanding of his/her situation or feelings.

5. It directs the client's attention to areas the counselor thinks need attention.

Components of Probing

The two components of probing are identification and open-ended phrasing.

The counselor uses his/her judgment to *identify* a subject or feelings area touched on by the client that needs further exploration. As with the other skills practiced in this training program, it is important that the counselor use probing only after attending to the client. By listening to and observing the client, the counselor may identify matters that either seem unresolved or seem to need further development.

In probing, the counselor decides what areas might need further attention, whereas in paraphrasing, reflection of feeling, and summarizing, the counselor attempts to feed back to the client in a more concise way the same material or feelings the client presented or displayed.

After identifying the area that needs to be explored further, the counselor attempts to *phrase an open-ended question or statement* to help include such words as what, where, when, or how. For example, "When do you feel that way?" "Where does that occur for you?" It is generally best to avoid asking questions beginning with the words are, is, do, or why. The first three words tend to elicit one-word answer. "Why" frequently poses a question that the client cannot answer. As a result, the client may feel defensive and resist further exploration of the topic, or may indulge in vague speculation unrelated to the topic under discussion.

Assessing the Outcomes of Probing

As with the other skills studies, how effectively a counselor has probed can best be determined by the client's response. If the probe encourages the client to talk in greater depth about his/her feelings or the content identified by the counselor, then the technique has probably been helpful. Similarly, if the probe seems to make the client more aware of a situation he/she has tended to avoid or ignore, and more apt to discuss it specifically, then the probe has been effective. In general the probe may be seen as effective when the client responds by talking further about the subject or feeling on what seems like a deeper level (as opposed to a superficial, intellectualizing level).

Sometimes, the counselor may probe an area that the client is not yet ready to discuss or deal with. In that case, the counselor might encounter extended silence or some other form of resistance on the part of the client. Or the client may simply say "I'd rather not talk about that." The probe might still be considered effective in this case, because the counselor may have succeeded in directing the client's attention to the problem area which either the client or the counselor might come back to later.

Summary of Probing

Probing is the use of a counselor question or statement to direct the client's attention inward to explore his/her situation in depth. The counselor identifies an area which seems to need exploration and then openly phrases a response. Used effectively, probing should help both the client and counselor to better understand the client's situation.

Counselor Self-Disclosure

Introduction

The importance of identifying and responding to feelings has been stressed throughout this program. Although our focus has been on the feelings of the client, the feelings of the counselor are just as important. The counselor should be aware of his/her feigns during the counseling session, and this awareness should lead to congruency between the counselor's verbal and nonverbal behavior.

If the counselor becomes impatient with the client's evasive statements, this impatience will probably show in his/her own nonverbal behavior. Therefore, it should be constructively expressed. Showing honest and open involvement with the client by being congruent is one way the counselor can be genuine. When the counselor provides a model of genuineness, the client is more likely to perceive that being genuine is acceptable and necessary in counseling. It may also establish a pattern that the client may apply to his other social interactions.

For the counselor to be genuine and congruent in counseling, he/she must be aware not only of feelings, but also of aspects of himself/herself that others may see. In an attempt to clarify the kinds of information available about all people, Joe Luft and Harry Ingham contributed their names and ideas to the concept of Johari Window. The Window is a visual way of describing information available about any person. The four "panes" of the Window are:

1. Information known by all about a person (open area).

2. Information known by the person, but not by other (hidden area).

3. Information known by others, but not by the person (blind area).

4. Information not known by the person or by others (unknown area).

Individual awareness, which contributes to genuineness and congruency, depends on any person's increasing the information in his/her open area while reducing the blind and hidden areas.

---

[*] For a diagram of the Joharl Window and a discussion of the related concept, see: Hanson, P.G. "The Johari Window: A Model for Soliciting and Giving Feedback," J. William Pfeiffer and John E. Jones, Editors. *The Annual Handbook for Group Facilitators*. Lajolla, Calif.: University Associates, 1973, pp. 114-119.

Definition of Self-Disclosure

Self-disclosure is a sharing by the counselor of his/her own feelings, attitudes, opinions, and experiences with a client *for the benefit of the client*. Self-disclosure should include significant content and be relevant to the client's situation. Self-disclosure *in the present* (the here and now of the counseling session) occurs when the counselor communicates his/her feelings about the client or the session, such as by saying, "I'm pleased that you can talk about these things." Self-disclosure may also include revealing experiences the counselor has had *in the past* that seem relevant to the client's current situation.

Purposes of Self-Disclosure

1. It tends to build a sense of trust and rapport between the counselor and the client.

2. It helps reduce the client's feelings that he/she is unique and alone in the situation he/she is experiencing.

3. It often enables the counseling relationship to move to deeper levels.

4. It fosters a feeling of empathy in the counseling relationship when the client perceives that the counselor may indeed be able to see things from the client's point of view.

5. It tends to promote the expression of feelings by the client in the counseling relationship.

6. It may create an atmosphere in which the client feels free to express content that he/she had previously avoided.

7. It may encourage the client to explore further a particular subject or feeling by sharing the counselor's experience with a similar situation.

Guidelines for Self-Disclosure

Self-disclosure requires knowledge of principles to guide the appropriate timing and content of the self-disclosure.

1. *The counselor's disclosure should relate directly to the client's situation.*-- This principle pertains primarily to disclosures about the counselor's past experiences. To help decide whether an experience is relevant to the client's situation, the counselor may first use paraphrasing, reflection of feeling, summarizing, and probing responses to ensure that he/she does understand the client's situation.

2. *The counselor should disclose only experiences that have actually happened to him/her.*--Using a personal pronoun such as I, me, my, or myself in a self-disclosure can give a clear message to the client that the counselor is telling about an experience that happened to him/her and is not merely relating the hearsay experience of a third party. This principle is most appropriate to the "past" type of self-disclosure.

3. *The counselor has the option of revealing information about himself/herself on various levels of intimacy.*--The counselor could reveal information that is in the open area of the Johari Window and probably known to many. Or, if the counseling relationship has produced a deep level of mutual trust, empathy, and genuineness, the counselor might reveal to the client an aspect of himself/herself that few others know. The guiding principle as to what level of information to reveal lies in the answers to two questions: Will it benefit the client and will the counselor feel comfortable in revealing that information?

Problems of Self-Disclosure

There are also some problems associated with self-disclosure of which the counselor should be aware.

1. *Self-disclosure in the present (the here and now of the session) can have an immediate and sometimes extreme effect on the client.*--When the counselor reveals a current feeling about the client (for example, that the counselor feels bored), the client may feel rejected or belittled. In deciding whether to disclose what might be perceived by the client as a negative feeling, the counselor must ask himself/herself whether he/she is disclosing for the sake of the client or out of a personal need. Positive feelings (pleasure, happiness, pride) revealed by the counselor usually do not result in as obvious reactions in the client as do negative feelings. The counselor should recall that he/she is attempting to be a genuine, honest person in the counseling relationship and therefore must consider revealing positive and negative feelings if such disclosures would benefit the client.

2. *The use of counselor self-disclosure shifts the focus of the session away from the client to the counselor.* --The counselor must guard against allowing subsequent responses to leave the focus on the counselor and thus tend to deny or downgrade the experiences of the client. The counselor should keep in mind that the self-disclosure is for the benefit of the client. The client is not likely to be helped if the counselor proceeds to work through a need of his/her own.

3. *The premature use of an intimate past experience or a threatening present feeling could make the client anxious and could damage the counseling relationship.*--If the counselor is quite sure that he/she understands the client's situation and that the conditions of trust, empathy, and genuineness are present in the relationship, the self-disclosure will probably be appropriate.

4. *There is a certain amount of risk to the counseling relationship any time the counselor uses self-disclosure.*--The counselor reveals something personal about himself/herself that the client may ignore, deny, or ridicule. In exposing himself/herself, the counselor stands to gain by being perceived as an honest, genuine person but runs the risk that the client's perception of him/her may change and thus change the dynamics of the counseling relationship. If the client's perception of the counselor has changed negatively because of an inappropriate self disclosure, the counseling relationship may be disrupted.

Not all counselors may feel comfortable sharing personal experiences, but all counselors should recognize the value of the "here and now" self-disclosures that foster a climate of trust and openness. Each counselor makes his/her own decision about whether to use self-disclosure in counseling. When self-disclosure is used appropriately, the benefits, in the form of a deeper counseling relationship, can be great. The counselor will probably be using self-disclosure appropriately if he/she continually asks the question "Is this disclosure for the sake of the client?"

Summary of Self-Disclosure

Self-disclosure involves the counselor sharing his/her own feelings, attitudes, opinions, and experiences with a client for the benefit of the client. The self-disclosure of the counselor might be revealing a present feeling or relating a relevant past experience. Both timing and appropriateness of content are central to effective self-disclosure. Used, appropriately, counselor self-disclosure should increase the level of trust, genuineness, and empathy in the counseling relationship and reduce the client's feeling of being unique in his/her problems or difficulties.

Interpreting

Introduction

Most people place limits on how they will look at problems or situations. As a result of this restricted outlook, people make comments like "I could never do that." When asked why they couldn't, they often don't know. They just know that they have never considered doing such a thing. This kind of thinking produces narrow vision, which hinders people from arriving at other ways of looking at problems or situations. People thus become further entrenched in the one position rather than trying to open up their vision or perspective.

The counselor, as well as the client, is subject to falling into the trap of restricted thinking. After learning the skill of interpreting, the counselor will be able to help clients broaden their perspectives. To do so, the counselor has to broaden his/her own way of viewing problems and situations.

Definition of Interpreting

Interpreting is a technique used by the counselor to present the client with alternative ways of looking at his/her situation. For example, the counselor might use a different perspective to explain events to a client so that he/she might be able to see the problem in a new light and perhaps generate his/her own fresh ways of looking at it.

Interpreting differs from reflection of feeling, paraphrasing, and summarizing in that it usually involves the addition of the counselor's ideas to the basic messages being expressed or manifested by the client. In other words, in reflection of feelings, paraphrasing, and summarizing, the counselor attempts to understand and maintain the client's frame of reference. In interpreting, the counselor offers a new frame of reference to the client. Interpreting, as defined here, is not the "in-depth" type of interpretation that psychoanalysis might do. In this training program, the emphasis in interpretation is not on digging into the client's psyche but on offering alternative points of view in regard to his/her immediate problem or situation.

Purposes of Interpreting

1. It helps the client realize that there is more than one way to look at most situations, problems, and solutions.

2. If offers the client a role model of the counselor seeking alternative ways of viewing events in life.

3. It can teach the client how to use self-interpretation to explore new points of view.

4. It can help the client understand his/her problems more clearly.

5. It often generates new and distinctive solutions to problems.

6. It may prompt the client to act more effectively when he/she sees other solutions to problems.

7. It often enables the client to gain a better understanding of his/her underlying feelings and how these might relate to verbal messages he/she has expressed.

Components of Interpreting

Effective interpreting has three components: determining and restating basic messages; adding counselor ideas for a new frame of reference; and "checking out" these ideas with the client.

The basic framework on which all of the counseling skills presented thus far have been built is the ability to listen effectively and observe carefully. It is especially important that the counselor employ the skills of attending, paraphrasing, reflection of feeling, and summarizing prior to and in conjunction with interpreting. The first step in interpreting *is to determine the basic messages* the client has expressed or displayed and restate them. The counselor seeks to determine the essence of what the client is saying or doing (the client's frame of reference) and then restates this in a paraphrase, reflection of feeling, or summary.

As the counselor is determining the basic messages and restating them, he/she probably will have some ideas or hunches about alternative ways of viewing the client's situation, or may begin to see connections, relationships, or patterns in the events the client describes. When these ideas are included in the material being restated to the client, the counselor is *adding his/her ideas* to offer the client a new frame of reference from which to view his/her situation.

Because the counselor is departing from the client's frame of reference and offering alternative viewpoints, it becomes very important to phrase any interpretation tentatively or *to check out directly* with the client his/her reaction to any new points of view. Tentative phrases such as "The way I see it. . . " or "I wonder if . . ." are appropriate ways to begin an interpretation. Sometimes the counselor might want to phrase the interpretation as a question--for example, "do you think, then, that you might be uncomfortable with older men because of your poor relationship with your father?" This form of interpretation is more tentative than a statement and thus there is a greater possibility that the client will see the offered interpretation as a possibility rather than as a fact. Whether the counselor is on target or completely off, the client is more likely to react to an interpretation openly if it is offered tentatively.

Another way of checking out how the interpretation is received by the client is to add a question onto the end of the new point of view such as, "How does that hit you?" or "Am I really far off?" However the counselor relays the tentativeness of his interpretation, it is imperative that the counselor let the client know it is merely an alternative way of looking at the situation and not necessarily the only or right way.

Guidelines for Effective Interpreting

Interpreting is a more complex and subtle skill than other included in this program. Because it can be a potent promoter of behavior change, however, it is worth the effort required to learn interpreting and use it effectively. Some general guidelines follow:

1. In formulating interpretations, the counselor should use simple language, close to the level at which the client is operating. He/she should avoid jumping too far ahead of the client, indulging in speculation, or stating the interpretation in such a way as to seem to be showing off psychological expertise. An example of not staying at the same level as the client's is one in which the counselor replies to the client's remark that he wishes his dad would lose some weight, with, "You're suffering from typical castration anxiety complicated by Oedipal conflicts."

2. Added ideas or explanations that the counselor offers to the client are often expressed to the client in terms of a particular theory of behavior and personality, such as Gestalt, behavioristic, rational emotive, or psychoanalytic. Such a theory will probably provide some of the labels the counselor will tend to put on feelings and events in the client's life. The counselor should, of course, be aware of what theoretical position he/she operates from. However, in this training program, no discussion of various theoretical positions is given.

3. The counselor should encourage the client to get in the habit of considering a range of alternative ways to view his/her situation. The counselor may serve as a model for this kind of unfettered thinking by presenting an alternative and then asking the client to suggest others. For example, to a client who has said that feelings of loneliness have caused him to drink in the past, the counselor might say, "Let's look at some things you might do to deal with that lonely feeling, other than drink. One thing you could do is call your A.A. sponsor and talk to him for a while. What are some other things you might do?"

Outcomes Expected from Interpreting

The effectiveness of interpretation can be determined by the client's reaction to any frame of reference offered. If the alternative point of view is close to what the client has expressed, the client might immediately accept the interpretation as a useful way to rethink the problem. In fact, the client might seem to get a sudden recognition of what the problem is. A response such as "I just realized that's it," could be a typical reply.

If the interpretation varies somewhat from what the client has expressed, several reactions are possible. The client might accept a new frame of reference tentatively--"I'll have to think about that one." On the other hand, he/she might reject the interpretation completely or say "Yes, but . . . " Or the client might accept it too uncritically. The counselor should be cautious in proceeding in the direction of an interpretation that the client accepts without any hesitation, because it could mean that the client does not feel free to challenge anything the counselor says. However, if the counselor keeps in mind the procedure of checking out perceptions with the client, the counselor's interpreting and subsequent responses will be made tentatively or cautiously.

If the interpretation is too extreme, the client might become anxious or threatened and the session could be disrupted. Or the client, again, might accept the interpretation at a cautious or tentative level.

Although the client will usually make some sort of response immediately after an interpretation (as opposed to saying nothing), the actual effect of the attempt to offer an alternative point of view may not be realized by either client or counselor until later. The client may come back to the next session, after having given the new point of view some thought and report that he/she wishes to explore that or other alternatives to the way he/she had been thinking.

Summary of Interpreting

Interpreting is presenting the client with alternative ways of looking at his/her situation. It involves determining and restating the basic messages of the client, adding counselor ideas to this material for a news frame of reference, and checking out with the client the acceptability of the new point of view. Used effectively, interpreting should assist the client to realize that there is more than one way of viewing most situations and to help him/her apply this kind of unrestricted thinking to all aspects of his/her life.

Confrontation

Definition of Confrontation

Confrontation is the deliberate use of a question or statement by the counselor to induce the client to face what the counselor thinks the client is avoiding. The client's avoidance is usually revealed by a discrepancy or contradiction in his/her statements and behavior. Thus, confrontive responses point out discrepancies either within the client or in the client's interaction with the environment. In confrontation, the counselor frequently identifies contradictions that are outside the client's frame of reference, whereas paraphrasing, reflection of feeling, and summarizing involve responding within the client's frame of reference. In using confrontation, the counselor gives honest feedback about what he/she perceives is actually happening with the client. Confrontation should not include accusations, evaluations, or solutions to problems.

Purposes of Confrontation

1. It helps the client become more congruent (what he/she says corresponds with how he/she behaves) when the client sees how he/she is being perceived by the counselor.

2. It establishes the counselor as a role model in using direct, honest, and open communication.

3. It tends to focus on problems about which the client might take action or change his/her behavior.

4. It often breaks down the defenses of the client which he/she has consciously or unconsciously put up.

5. It tends to enrich the condition of empathy in the counseling relationship when the client perceives the confrontation as being done by a concerned counselor.

6. It encourages the client to acknowledge his/her feelings and behavior by bringing to the surface those he/she has denied. Once the client has accepted ownership of these feelings and behavior, he/she is more likely to accept responsibility for them.

Types of Discrepancies

A discrepancy or contradiction in the client is often a clue to the counselor that confrontation is indicated. A discrepancy or contradiction might be one of the following general types:

1. A discrepancy between how the client sees himself/herself and how others see him/her for example, the client may describe himself as an outgoing, talkative person, but the counselor perceives the client as extremely quiet and reserved.

2. A contradiction between what the client says and how he/she behaves--for example, the client says she is not depressed, but she is talking slowly, sitting in a slumped posture, looking as if she is ready to cry.

3. A discrepancy between two statements by the client--for example, a client may say he wants to be treated for his drinking problem, but later says the only important thing to him is saving his driver's license.

4. A discrepancy between what the client says he/she is feeling and the way most people would react in a similar situation--for example, a client may say that if his wife leaves he doesn't care if he ever gets to see his children again.

5. A contradiction between what the client is now saying he/she believes and how he/she has acted in the past--for example, a client may say she has no trouble staying away from the bottle, but she has had three slips in a month.

Using Confrontation Effectively

There are a few guidelines that the counselor should keep in mind when formulating a confrontive response. First, and perhaps most important, mutual trust and empathy must already be firmly established as part of the counseling relationship. Confrontation should come across as a positive and constructive act by a caring counselor, not as a negative and punitive act of a judgmental counselor. This attitude of empathy and caring can be transmitted not only by what the counselor says but also by his/her tone of voice and facial expression when the confrontive response is introduced into session.

The counselor should also keep in mind that the most effective confrontive responses are those that address specific, concrete attributes of the client's behavior that the client can do something to change. It isn't very helpful to confront general behavior, for example, "You're always talking about changing your behavior, so why don't you do it?' An example of a specific confrontation would be, "You say you want to quit drinking, but what I see you doing is figuring out how to get a pint to get through the day."

Confrontation may be directed toward the client's assets (strengths) or his/her limitations (weaknesses). The counselor should be wary of always identifying contradictions that point up weaknesses in the client. Confrontive responses can be used constructively by focusing on strengths of the client. For example, to the client who expresses lack of confidence in his ability to handle stressful situations without drinking, the counselor might say, "Last time this happened you called me and did most of the work of sorting things out and deciding what to do."

In practical application, the confrontive response often takes the form of a compound statement that sets up a "you say . . ., but you do . . ." format. The second part of the statement points out the discrepancy or contradiction in the client's behavior or message. For example, "You say you don't want to see him again, but you go to places where you know he'll be." In using confrontation, then, the counselor listens to the client's feeling and content messages, observes the client's behavior, and presents evidence of a contradiction or discrepancy to the client.

Risks Involved in Confrontation

Because confrontation is an extremely powerful tool for the counselor to use, there are certain risks involved. Whenever the counselor becomes aware of a discrepancy or contradiction in the client's behavior or messages, the benefits of using confrontation must be weighed against the risks.

Risks to the Client
If trust and empathy have not been firmly established in the counseling relationship, the premature use of a confrontive response could harm the relationship. The client could become distrustful of the counselor or decide that the counselor cannot be of any help to him/her. The use of confrontation can be very threatening and anxiety-producing for the client, and if the proper conditions aren't there to begin with, it can damage or end the counseling relationship.

The use of confrontation may precipitate a crisis in the client's life. Especially if a client seems emotionally unstable about certain areas of his/her life, it might not be wise to confront him/her on those particular areas. For example, if a client has just been fired from his job and is very upset about it, the counselor should probably not confront him at that moment with his job performance.

Risks to the Counselor

Sometimes the counselor does not confront the client because the counselor is protecting himself/herself from risk. The counselor may be hesitant to point out a discrepancy for fear he/she might be wrong and would not be able to substantiate the contradiction to the client. Or the counselor might not like to deal with the extreme emotional reactions that could follow a confrontation. The counselor may not be comfortable with anger, anxiety, or tears. The counselor may pass over an appropriate confrontation situation because he/she would be uncomfortable if the usual defenses were dropped and thus wants to prevent the relationship from getting too close or intense.

In deciding whether to confront or not, the counselor must weigh the possible benefits to the client against the possible harm. In addition, if the counselor is hesitating to confront, he/she should ask himself/herself whether this reluctance is out of concern for the client or out of self-concern. If the counselor recognizes that the reluctance to confront is out of concern for himself/herself, the counselor should search himself/herself to see whether the cause of the apprehension is a legitimate concern, such as fear of physical harm from an intoxicated client, or whether it is a fear the counselor should try to resolve within himself/herself.

The Outcomes of Confrontation

If the counselor's confrontation has been effective, it could lead to exploration of previously blocked or denied feelings or behavior. In addition, an effective confrontation can often bring about a kind of break-through in the client's recognition that a behavior change is needed.

In practice, the counselor often may not know whether the confrontation has been effective or helpful until after several more exchanges in the session or until a later session. The client's immediate response to the confrontation sometimes does not indicate its effectiveness.

Frequently, the beginning counselor does not know what to do after he/she attempts a confrontive response. The following general guide might help:

1. If the client accepts the confrontation and agrees with the discrepancy pointed out, the counselor can use the opportunity to reinforce positive behavior. The counselor might say, "It's really a step in the right direction that you can recognize and accept this contradictory behavior so easily."

2. If the client denies the confrontation, the counselor is probably wisest to return to an empathic response, such as "My even suggesting that seems to bother you a lot." The client may not be ready to deal with the discrepancy at that time and it would not be helpful to persist in the confrontation.

3. The client may simply act confused or ambivalent after a confrontive statement. In that case, the counselor could focus on the current feeling by saying, "You seem to feel confused by my saying that."

Summary of Confrontation

In confrontation, the counselor uses a question or statement to induce the client to face what the counselor thinks the client is avoiding. The counselor may, for example, point out discrepancies between the client's verbal and nonverbal behaviors, between two of the client's statements, or between the client's past behavior and his/her position or behavior in the counseling session.

Used effectively, confrontation should help the client become more congruent and accept responsibility for his behavior. It can also reinforce the climate of trust, empathy, and genuineness in the counseling relationship. Because it is one of the most potent techniques the counselor can use, there are also some risks involved in using it. In deciding whether to use it or not, the counselor must determine whether the benefits of confrontation outweigh the possible harm to the client.

OVERVIEW: Group Counseling

In a majority of alcohol and drug treatment settings, group counseling is seen as one of the most effective means of promoting change and personal growth. The reasons for this are numerous, but the central factor involved, which makes group counseling powerful, is the aspect of denial. For the chemically dependent individual whose defense system is often very strong, the peer support and peer pressure that occurs in a group can be quite effective in breaking through the denial.

As in any group counseling situation, there are a number of factors that allow the group setting to instill change. (See outline for Yalom's curative factors). The one therapeutic factor that seems to have the most profound effect on the chemically dependent individual is that of "universality". The first step one takes in eliminating denial is to recognize that he or she is not alone. This recognition, known as universality, helps eliminate the isolation and perhaps demoralization that the individual is feeling.

Through peer support and peer pressure, the individual can begin to identify with others and admit his or her problem. This admission can come about through the power that universality gives to combat the cultural forces that lead to denial. Through confrontation, the group can assist in altering the substance abuser's defensive style and help eliminate his or her distortions that lead to denial.

Another important therapeutic factor that occurs in group for the chemically dependent person involves interpersonal learning. Alcoholics and drug dependent individuals commonly share difficulties in interpersonal relationships. The group setting provides a safe environment to learn new ways of communicating needs and feelings. Members tend to be accepting of one's expressions of feelings in the group and are free to give feedback to each other.

Although the feedback may be confrontational at times, a trusting relationship among group members will foster the acceptance of the feedback and allow the individual to gain self-understanding and psychological growth. Hence, the group can be seen as a microcosm of society and provide a safe arena for each member to "try out" new behavior. These changes are crucial for the chemically dependent person as he or she adjusts to a new life without alcohol or drugs.

A skilled group counselor will know what to look for as well as how and when to intervene. He or she is given the opportunity to observe patterns of communications for each member, something not possible in an individual setting. By being directive in his or her interventions, a counselor will guide the group's interaction in order to promote trust and risk taking. By closely observing each member, the group leader will be able to help appropriately integrate each individual into a group that when skillfully molded, will be mutually effective for all participants.

Good group facilitation is much more than conducting therapy with a number of individuals in a group. It requires an active counselor who is constantly observing all of the nuances of the members' interactions. It requires a skill that can only be mastered through supervised group experience and an understanding of group process and group dynamics.

I. Introduction to group counseling

A. Advantages of group counseling
1. Some people feel a sense of safety because there are other people that the counselor can focus on - thus the individual can "hide" for a while until he/she can risk joining the group discussions or activities
2. There is intense learning experience
    a. Vicarious
        1) Through observation and identification with learning, the group member:
            a) Sees and feels the struggle and resolution
            b) Internalizes the message
        2) Through observation of healthy behavior modeled by the leader and strived for by the members, the individual learns, remembers and can later initiate behavior that he/she has observed
    b. Direct
        1) Support and acceptance by a group of people provides a strong sense of belonging
            a) Helps to meet intimacy and relatedness needs
            b) Promotes growth

2) Interactions with others in a safe environment can:
- a) Promote the learning of healthy interpersonal relationships
- b) Allow the practice of new behavior before trying it in the "real" world
- c) Permit honest feedback that guides the individual
3. In group, an individual is expected to be concerned about other members
  - a. Prevents an unhealthy self-centeredness
  - b. Prevents blowing a problem out of proportion because others are sharing equally trying or more difficult problems
4. Groups are cost-efficient because more people can be seen and helped by one counselor

B. Disadvantages of group counseling
1. Each member actually receives less attention
2. Without proper leadership, the group may choose a member as a scapegoat and vent hostility upon him/her, thus harming the individual
3. The counselor has less control and power as compared to individual sessions
   - a. There is more stimuli to process and react to
   - b. Group peer pressure can move an individual toward negative values that he/she is struggling against
   - c. Members may challenge the counselor for the leadership role through verbal attack, insults, and patronizing
   - d. The counselor may suffer from a sense of exclusion
   - e. The counselor's influence may appear to be less powerful

C. A.A. and group counseling
1. A counselor can help a client understand interpersonal relationships in A.A.
2. The group explores other issues and teaches about alcohol
3. Being in A.A. and in group counseling at the same time should not create a problem for the client
4. Encouragement from a group to join A.A. is helpful in deciding to attend A.A. meetings
5. A.A. is an effective aid to group counseling for most alcoholics

D. Assumptions of new group members
    1. New members frequently have expectations that are not the same as those of the leaders or other members
        a. To prevent either dropping out or disruptive behavior, these expectations must be explored and clarified before the client is accepted into a group or during the first session
        b. To decrease misunderstandings, an orientation should be held before the new client reaches the group or during the first session - the orientation should include:
            1) Establishing group ground rules
            2) Statements about the purpose of the group
            3) Statements about expectations of group members, and the leaders
    2. Assumptions about the leader
        a. The leader is seen as a trained expert who is not a group member - though the leader is a trained professional, he/she must make it clear that he/she is human and still has normal problems so he/she won't be seen as god-like and someone whom members can't relate to
        b. Leadership styles
            1) He/she may choose to remain an uninvolved observer with little self-disclosure
            2) He/she may actively participate in the group with a lot of self-disclosure
            3) No matter how much the leader shares, he/she still has the role of leader
            4) He/she will never be truly just another member
    3. The need for confidentiality needs to be addressed directly
        a. There is no way to enforce confidentiality among members so they need to realize its importance and maintain it based on its own value, not outside punishment
        b. Broken confidentiality leads to broken trust
    4. The client needs to recognize that uncomfortable thoughts and feelings are often necessary if a person is to grow
        a. Many people want to be better but do not want to pay for it in effort, pain, or discomfort
        b. It is important for the client to realize that there will be some uncomfortable moments during the growth process

E. Therapeutic factors
1. There are dynamic forces within the group that promote a healthy change
2. According to the works of Yalom, there are 12 factors that help group members change - these are all factors that need to be part of a group to help group members grow
   a. Instillation of hope - the person must feel there is hope to solve his/her problems
   b. Universality - the person must feel he/she has a problem common to others
   c. Imparting information - an informed person is better able to cope and think through new problems
   d. Altruism - caring about others decreases an unhealthy self-absorption
   e. Corrective recapitulation of one's family-members behave the way they did while growing up in their families - through group process, they learn healthier ways to behave
   f. Development of socializing techniques - the person learns how to interact with people
   g. Imitative behavior - the leaders and senior group members act as role models of healthy behavior for newer members
   h. Interpersonal learning
   i. Notice new interpersonal skills
   j. Group cohesiveness - when members feel a sense of togetherness, they are more willing to attend, participate, help other members, and defend group rules
   k. Catharsis - after a person has a release of intense emotions, he/she may be freer to use information and new experience to grow
   l. Existential factors (self-responsibility) - the person owns responsibility for his/her own thoughts, feelings, and behaviors
3. Critical to group participant outcome is:
   a. Commitment to participation
   b. Commitment to sobriety (if appropriate)
   c. Regular and timely attendance
   d. Completion of the group

4. It is important for a group to release energy and interest through activity such as:
    a. Active verbal participation in discussions
    b. Structured exercises which:
        1) Can be used as decelerating devices to calm the group
        2) Can help people get in touch with some suppressed emotions
    c. Role-playing, e.g., acting out dialogue and situations

II. Stages of group development

A. Initial stage
    1. Each member is concerned about:
        a. Acceptance
        b. Identity
        c. Power
        d. Intimacy

    2. To begin answering these concerns, each member begins to test the group
        a. Participation is hesitant
        b. Members depend on the leader for guidance
        c. Discussion tends to be more superficial for example, the small talk of a cocktail party
        d. Giving and seeking advice frequently occurs
        e. Members are sized up and tested
            1) Members sense motivation in one another and this seems to be very important for mutual acceptance - trust must be established before the group can move on to other business
            2) To facilitate the resolution of members' concerns and promote the development of trust, the leader must model
                a) Caring
                b) Genuiness
                c) Openness
                d) Acceptance and respect
                e) Listening
                f) Instilling hope

B. Transition stage
    1. Though members continue to struggle with issues from Stage One, the focus shifts to:
        a. Dominance
        b. Control
        c. Power
    2. As members struggle to become a group, conflicts arise
        a. Each person wants his/her needs met
        b. Some feel uncomfortable in a non-leadership position which is a less powerful and less controlling one than the leadership position
            1) Some try to gain power by challenging the leader
            2) Some try to gain power by allying with (befriending) the leader
        c. There tends to be a lot of defensiveness, resistance, and anger
        d. There is a lot of attack-withdrawal behavior among some members
    3. Throughout this process, members become more committed to the group and more open
    4. To facilitate members passage through this stage and onto greater trust, the leader must:
        a. Remain nondefensive, especially when attacked
        b. Help the group see what is going on
        c. Encourage healthy behavior
            1) Acceptance of others
            2) Respect
            3) Helpful feedback
            4) Healthy disagreement
            5) Self-disclosure
            6) Self-exploration
C. Working stage
    1. The group has emerged from its conflicts with a sense of oneness and cohesiveness
    2. Members show
        a. Spontaneity
        b. Honesty
        c. Acceptance
        d. Responsibility
        e. Self-disclosure
        f. Constructive expression of hostility and resentment
        g. Encouragement of others
        h. Less dependence on the leader
        i. More equality among members

3. Group members address these issues
    a. Responsibility
    b. Taking risks
    c. Becoming more open
    d. Group cohesiveness
    e. Trying new attitudes and behaviors to resolve problems
4. The group develops its standards for membership, and all members are willing to meet these standards
    a. Group patterns of behavior are determined by the norms that have been described and accepted with the group acting as the agent of change
    b. A sense of feeling valued, understood, and accepted has developed
        1) There is a genuine concern for others
        2) There is a commitment to solve ones own problems and help others solve theirs
        3) There is less tendency for members to terminate before it is appropriate
5. The leader needs to
    a. Help members do more self-exploration
    b. Focus appropriately on "here and now" issues within the group and model healthy confrontation
    c. Facilitate discussions
    d. Propose alternatives and examine consequences
    e. Help shift learning from inside to outside of the group
    f. Encourage risk taking in the real world

D. Final stage
1. Termination is an integral part of the counseling process and is an important force in the process of change because it prepares the members for post-group independence, emphasizing process not an event (i.e., the last meeting)
2. The group or individual members terminate when its or his/her goals have been achieved
    a. However, a group can place subtle pressure on a member not to terminate
    b. Some socially isolated clients may postpone termination because they use the group as a social group
    c. In a group with a preset number of sessions, the client's goals may not be met

3. When a group is nearing termination, members may
    a. Deny that the group is ending
    b. Resort to old, unproductive behavior with original symptoms

        Example: The member expresses fears of resuming drinking to which the leader asks him/her to review the ways he/she handled situations that have triggered past desires to drink

    c. Review significant events of the group
    d. Assess what the group has accomplished
    e. Indicate that the group is more important than ever
4. The leader needs to help members
    a. Finish any business
    b. Express feelings about termination but not a catharsis - usually includes a feeling of loss
5. The leader does not
    a. Ignore members' concerns in group and deal with them in individual sessions - concerns should be handled as a group
    b. Ask the group how they want to end the group
    c. Provide opportunities for the group to socialize afterwards to renew relationships - the group's purpose is not socialization but problem solving over a limited period of time
6. When the group is over, the members will look back on the experiences and remember the counselor's presence and support, not individual intervention

III. Group process

A. Definition - Group process is the continuing development of the individual member and the group as a whole which involves many changes

B. The Role of the Individual - There are three necessary processes an individual must go through in order to allow the group to be helpful
    1. Compliance
        a. The new member decides to allow the leader and other members to help him/her
        b. He/she decides to join in the work of the group

    2. Identification

        a. As the new member starts to form relationships with the leader and other members, he/she begins to identify with their issues, concerns, and solutions

    3. Internalization

        a. By working through emotionally-laden issues with the help of the group, the individual learns new attitudes, concepts, and behaviors - a client's ability to reorganize and identify feelings has a great deal of impact on other members of the group

        b. When he/she is able to reorganize harmful behaviors and self-correct them, he/she has transferred these lessons to the real world

C. The counselor's role

    1. To move the individual through the three processes, the leader attempts to help him/her accept the following truths

        a. "Only I can change the world I have created for myself."

        b. "There is no danger in change."

            1) Some clients do not change their behaviors, even though they want to, because they fear their worlds will collapse if they do

            2) The leader works toward helping the individual perform the feared behavior in group (if appropriate) so that the client will learn that the world will continue after the behavior

        c. "To attain what I really want, I must change." The leader helps the client clarify what is important to him/her and see how his/her current behavior is self-defeating

        d. "I can change, I am powerful."

            1) If the client has accepted that he/she is responsible for him/herself, there is nothing to fear from change

            2) Change will lead to fulfilling his/her needs

            3) He/she feels capable of making the necessary changes

2. At this point the counselor leads the client through four steps that promote change
    a. "Here is what your behavior is like."
    b. "Here is how your behavior makes others feel."
    c. "Here is how your behavior influences the opinion others have of you."
    d. "Here is how your behavior influences your opinion of yourself."
    e. Changes occur by the counselors (or other members) making process statements through
        1) Feedback
        2) Questions
        3) Self-observation
3. To understand the dynamics of group process, the counselor needs to
    a. Attend the issues such as
        1) Seating arrangements
        2) Posture
        3) Behavioral cues
        4) Nonverbal expressions
        5) What is not said
        6) The "meta communication" which is the how and why of communication
    b. Assess the mood of the group by focusing on
        1) The "here and how" of the group
        2) Power issues
        3) Overcoming resistance to change
        4) The verbal and nonverbal communications

IV. Leadership

A. Styles of leadership
 1. Authoritarian
   a. The leader is viewed as an expert
   b. Communication is directed through the leader - there is no direct interaction with other members
   c. Used by leader who
    1) Takes a psychoanalytical approach
    2) Uses an educational model
   d. Leader is responsible for the success of the group
 2. Democratic
   a. The leader is viewed as a facilitator
   b. Communication flows both ways
    1) Between leaders and members
    2) Among members
   c. Used by leader who takes a humanistic approach
   d. Leader shares responsibility with members for direction and success of the group
 3. Laissez-faire
   a. The leader does not take on the leadership role but acts as a member - this is, in essence, a leaderless group
   b. Communication flows among the members
   c. Used by leader who
    1) Is uncomfortable in the leadership role
    2) Is imitating a Tavistock model in which group members fend for themselves and in the process come to terms with authority issues and other childhood issues
   d. Frequently this type of group is unproductive because the group has no guidance through the development stages - the exception to the unproductiveness is Tavistock workshops for individuals who are prepared for the leaderless approach

B. Functions of the leader
   1. Emotional stimulation - to provide:
      a. Challenge
      b. Confrontation
      c. Self-disclosure
      d. Caring
      e. Support
      f. Acceptance
      g. Praise
   2. Meaning attribution (explanation of the world)
      a. Concepts (thought framework)
      b. Explanation
      c. Interpretation
   3. Execution function
      a. Limit setting
      b. Time management
      c. Interceding
   4. Yalom's writings suggest that the most successful groups are conducted by leaders who show
      a. a high caring level
      b. a high meaning attribution level
      c. a moderate emotional stimulation level
      d. a moderate executive function level

C. Leadership techniques
   1. In order to effectively lead a group, a leader should
      a. Be able to guide group interaction and structure
      b. Volunteer to be a participant in a group experience
      c. Encourage members to behave in a particular way
      d. Provide feedback on a member's behavior
      e. Arouse tension in the group in order to uncover hidden conflicts and resolve them
   2. The leader intervenes in group process to counteract such nonfunctional behavior as
      a. Verbal abuse of another member - by careful monitoring of the group, the leader can often prevent inappropriate expressions of anger, hostility, and scapegoating
      b. Rambling and story telling which prevents genuine self-disclosure
      c. Harmful gossiping - especially about missing members, which leads to decreased trust
      d. Rescuing so another member cannot finish working out an issue

  e.   Invasion of privacy which leads to decreased safety

  f.   Withdrawal which blocks individual and group

  g.   Boredom - if the counselor is bored, so is the group

  h.   The subverting of group discussion by a member requesting a one-to-one session or refusing to talk except to his/her own counselor

  i.   Domination by one member which leads to resentment within the group

  j.   Minimizing the problem so the group or individual doesn't have to work on it

  k.   Rationalizing - all thoughts, no feelings

 3.   The leader may use several techniques that are helpful in group

  a.   Group commentary

   1)   Useful when the majority of members are engaged in counterproductive behavior such as silence, silliness, chatting, and scapegoating

   2)   Statements such as the following make the group address the issues it is avoiding

    a)   "What's going on in the group right now?"

    b)   "What is this silence saying?"

    c)   "What are we avoiding by talking about the World Series?"

  b.   "Here and now" focus

   1)   Since the dynamics of the group reflect the member's interpersonal skills and issues that he/she uses in the real world, it is often helpful to direct the group's attention to a presently occurring situation to learn from it; gaining the insight and skills to resolve the situation within the group will allow carry-over into the real world

  c.   Questions directed to individual members

   1)   To resolve interpersonal issues

    a)   "What do you feel about what Max said about not trusting you?"

    b)   "What do you want from the group right now?"

   2)   To include members into the process

    a)   "What is your reaction, Ted, to the conflict between Al and Bill?"

    b)   "How does it make you feel, Joe, when I laugh at your problem?"

d. Role-playing new behavior
    1) Groups provide a safe place to practice new behaviors so the leader can direct members to perform certain tasks
    2) A member may be resolving a conflict that is causing difficulty both in the group and outside
        a) "John, I want you to tell Paul how his laughing at you has hurt you and made you angry."
        b) "Tell each member, Sue, if I trust you . . ."
    3) A member may also practice for an upcoming situation in the real world via role-playing
e. Seeking insight
    1) Members are often not aware of their own thoughts and feelings and the impact of their behavior on others
    2) Requesting them to pause for assessment can lead to insight and behavior change
        a) "When you do this, how do other people react to you?"
        b) "When you do this, what are you hoping will happen?"
f. Commonality
    1) A leader can take on a member's problem and either ask if others have had a similar experience or generalize about it so others can relate to it – this includes the other members in discussion
    2) Shifts the focus from one-to-one back to group
    3) Helps the members feel connected and not alone
g. Self-disclosure by the leader
    1) To enhance discussions
    2) To express feelings of anxiety or uncertainty about what's happening in the group

        Example: "I'm feeling confused about what was just said."

    3) To express anger toward a group member

        Example: "I'm finding myself getting angry with your continual put downs of the group, Harry."

    4) To admit personal conflicts that are similar to those of the group members

      5) To share positive feelings about the progress of the group

      Example: "This group has really worked hard today."

D. Interventions
  1. Leader interventions are dependent on picking out the point of urgency at the appropriate moment to move the group forward
  2. Interventions include
    a. Focusing the attention of the group on process issues
    b. Encouraging the group to stay in the "here and now"
    c. Putting responsibility for growth on the group
    d. Encouraging members to express feelings
    e. Suggesting the group move on to another topic if the discussion has become unconstructive
    f. Focusing attention on difficulties in the group's functioning
    g. Remaining silent to raise the tension level
    h. Provoking a discussion about a hostile atmosphere that exists in the group
    i. Interpreting
    j. Self-disclosing
    k. Eliciting responses
    l. Directing members to activity
  3. When faced with group denial, the counselor needs to directly confront the denial in order to work through it so growth can continue
  4. When conducting groups and making interventions, co-facilitation (2 leaders) can be useful
    a. The leaders complement and support one another
    b. The leaders can assume different roles
    c. It provides objectivity for each leader
    d. It can lessen the initial anxiety of the group

V. Problematic client behavior

A. Problematic client types
1. Silent client
   a. Silence is a behavior
   b. Silence may be saying that the client
      1) Fears self-disclosure
      2) Is a perfectionist and will speak only when he/she can be perfect (which is never)
      3) Feels threatened by a member, the situation, or large groups of people
      4) May fear losing control
      5) May be trying to manipulate and control the group
   c. In general, the silent client does not grow and change as much as the client who actively participates
   d. The counselor can encourage participation by
      1) Inviting the client to speak
      2) Commenting on his/her nonverbal behavior
         a) It is important that the counselor and other members do not get caught up in a manipulative power struggle of "Talk!" - "You can't make me!"
         b) After a number of weeks of silence, if there is no movement toward some involvement, the counselor may choose to
            (1) See the client in individual counseling also
            (2) Terminate the client from group
2. Boring client
   a. The boring client is frequently a frightened, inhibited individual who rarely takes risks and feels badly about him/herself
   b. He/she craves attention - but by demanding, timidly pleading, or droning, he/she drives people away
   c. Since the client wants to be accepted by the group, he/she is rarely actively disruptive, says safe and predictable things, and is rarely spontaneous

        d. The counselor and other members can be encouraging to the client by
            1) Reinforcing small risky displays of spontaneity
            2) Cheering the members on as he/she works toward release of inhibition by physical activity such as screaming or hitting a punching bag - this lets the client know that spontaneity and inhibition release (for this very inhibited person) is good and others will still accept him/her

3. Monopolizing client
    a. This person must have the majority of the counselor's attention
        1) He/she does not seem to notice other members' negative reactions
        2) He/she may belittle another's problem to regain attention

          Example: "You think that's bad, you should hear what happened to me."

        3) He/she feels that he/she has the most difficult problems of anyone in the group
    b. He/she may tag along on another member's statements by claiming some similarity and then shifting attention to him/herself

        Example: "I also went to a doctor once but what he told me was far worse!"

    c. He/she cannot stand silence and will chatter or ramble to avoid it
        1) He/she will ask another member a series of questions
         2) He/she will ask for help and advice and then proceed to say why that won't work in this situation

d. Other members may initially be relieved that there is a "talker" in the group so they don't have to self-disclose
   1) Soon they come to resent having little time and attention
   2) They may act out this resentment by dropping out of the group, making veiled attacks on the monopolizer, and missing group sessions
   3) Eventually, one member will usually attack the monopolizer in a fairly brutal attack releasing weeks of frustration
   4) The rest of the group is supportive of the attacks
   5) The monopolizer feels demolished and possibly drops out
e. To prevent the frustration - attack cycle, the counselor must address the issue early on
   1) It is appropriate for the leader to ask the group why they are letting the person do all the talking and work in the group

      NOTE: The leader's non-threatening, tactful approach places responsibility for allowing the monopolizer's inappropriate behavior on the group

   2) In discussing the monopolizing behavior, the counselor must point out that compulsive talking "hides" the client - less talking and more substance is the goal in the group session
4. Self-righteous client
   a. The goal of this client is to be right at any cost
   b. He/she has often struggled with life yet has little to show for it
      1) Results in a sense of failure and shame
      2) These feelings are covered up by moral self-righteousness

      c. The client frequently appears poised and calm - does not get involved in group process until he/she can take a moral stand which attempts to prove everyone else is wrong

      d. In time, the group members become resentful and often attack the client who refuses to be shaken from his/her conviction of being right

      e. If the counselor can catch onto this client's behavior style before the hostility solidifies, he/she can help tune the group in to the client's inferior feelings

            1) The need to be right and the patterns of generating hostility are typical of adults who grew up in alcoholic or other dysfunctional families

            2) Knowing this information at the onset of the group can key the counselor into this potential behavioral pattern

   5. Hostile client

      a. Most hostile clients use anger as a way to cover up fear

         1) Hostility can also be the result of

            a) Excessive stress

            b) The counselor or group member reminds him/her of someone threatening

            c) Inappropriate treatment by the counselor or group members

      b. It is not helpful to the client for the counselor to

         1) Avoid the hostility

         2) Allow inappropriate expression of the hostility

      c. The counselor must guide the client into appropriate expressions for the hostility and to deal with the underlying fears

B. Problematic client defense mechanisms - Client behavior which is meant to interfere with group progress is called blocking

   1. Type 1: The client doesn't believe he/she can relate to the other members

      a. The client is relating to the superficial aspects of others in the group who seem different from him/herself

      Example: *"If these people are all alcoholics, I can't possibly be one. I don't drink as much as they do."*

      Example: *"I can spend time helping others in group since my problems aren't as severe."*

b. If the client will stay for a few sessions, he/she will begin to see that underneath the different problems and faces, the feelings are similar and he/she can relate to them - he/she may still choose to run away using the excuse of "being different"

c. A variation on the theme is the client who feels his/her problems are so different no one could possibly understand

2. Type 2: The quick thinker is valued in society but if he/she refuses to move from thoughts to feelings, he/she will not grow

   a. Some "intellectualizers" play the role of assistant
      1) Wants to let others know of his/her vast knowledge of psychology
      2) Clarifies and summarizes for the group but does not share personal material

   b. This type of client needs to be helped to turn off thinking and get into feelings
      1) Sometimes he/she must be taught the difference between a thought and a feeling
      2) Use of nonverbal exercises designed to bring out feelings

3. Type 3: The client enjoys irritating others
   a. He/she does this by
      1) Not understanding
      2) Not remembering
      3) Breaking rules and pretending innocence

   b. This is essentially passive-aggressive behavior which people have learned to adopt when feeling helpless

   c. Confrontation usually does not work well because the client will outwardly profess innocence and inwardly delight in "Gottcha!"

   d. Teaching healthier ways to express anger, get attention, and get needs met may work if the client is willing to change his/her behavior

4. Type 4: The client brings confusion to the group
   a. In a hidden way, his/her intent is to control and manipulate the group
   b. He/she is usually in crisis - when one issue is resolved, another is raised that is even more important
   c. As with the monopolizing client, it is important for the counselor to identify this behavior pattern early in order to confront it and not let the individual dominate the group - otherwise, the client will continually create a crisis
5. Type 5: At times a client will arrive at an alcoholic and drug group intoxicated
   a. The group leader asks the individual to leave immediately
      1) The alcohol/drug use of the client is not the responsibility of the counselor or the group
      2) It is the responsibility of the intoxicated client
   b. The inebriation may be a way of acting out conflicts
   c. The strongest clue that a group member may be at risk to relapse is when he/she shows a rigid compliance to the suggestions of the group regarding sobriety
      1) It shows little thought on the client's part so there is no owning of the problem or solution
      2) It is impossible to do everything that everyone suggests so it is easy to become frustrated and toss it all away
   d. The appropriate use of a discussion on drinking, which may occur as the result of an intoxicated member, is to express feelings regarding use, society, and slips

Counseling the Family and Significant Others

In the counseling process, even when only one individual is being seen, family dynamics and family issues are predominant. They are central to the screening and assessment, the ongoing counseling process, and in the client's ongoing recovery. When we refer to family, we are referring to many dynamics, many interpersonal relationships, and in most cases, different family systems for each individual. These family systems include families of origin, extended families and immediate families, as well as other combinations of individuals who may not even be related to the individual.

Every individual in a family affects that family's dynamics. It is no surprise then that alcoholism and drug dependency affect family dynamics. Family systems are a complex integration of relationships between members. The multiplicity of these dynamics warrants much family exploration when counseling an alcoholic or drug dependent individual.

Alcoholism and drug dependency are called family diseases. The effects of chemical dependency vary with each family member, but nonetheless, they are present since every family member is affected. Each member takes on a role within the family. This role can have a profound effect on his or her interactions within the family as well as with those outside of the family. Family members become "co-dependent" and as a result have a "disease" themselves because their personalities and their abilities to deal with the substance abuser are affected. Co-dependent people often become enablers both with the substance abusing family member and in other relationships. in or outside of the family. Children of alcoholics usually carry their co-dependency with them into adulthood. Adult children of alcoholics (ACOAs) commonly experience low self-esteem, impulsiveness, and difficulties in intimate relationships.

In the counseling process, it is important to explore family issues so that they can be appropriately dealt with. A skilled counselor will be sensitive to the additional burden ACOAs bring with them into treatment and will know the importance of not expecting too much too soon.

Regarding the involvement of the client's family, it is important for the counselor to know when to involve the family, when and where to refer the family, and how to use the family for making an intervention. For those ACOAs who become alcoholics or drug abusers, an extra challenge is facing them if and when they seek treatment. The impact that this client's dysfunctional family may have had on him/her is often significant and needs to be addressed in counseling. It is important that a counselor recognize these issues and have a good understanding of the possible resulting behavior. If these issues aren't taken into account, a client may be mistakenly labeled resistant or into denial when a further understanding of the individual's past would have given the counselor a therapeutic opportunity to build rapport. This opportunity can allow the counselor to give the client more time to deal with the issues of his or her dysfunctional family while showing empathy regarding the client's situation. A client who has difficulty forming relationships, for example, may be therapeutically harmed if confronted inappropriately about his or her denial. Many ACOAs require additional time and education before they can begin to understand what impact their parents' disease may have had on their personalities.

I. The Family and Alcoholism

A. The alcoholic
1. The alcoholic's behavior creates a disturbed environment for those who live with the alcoholic
2. As alcoholism progresses, the alcoholic becomes more preoccupied with alcohol:
   a. Maintaining a supply
   b. Covering up
   c. Despairing about getting drunk again
   d. Though the family is loved, they take a back seat to alcohol
3. The alcoholic feels good about alcohol which is an object, not about people:
   a. When the alcohol wears off, he/she feels lonely and isolated because he/she no longer has meaningful relationships with people
   b. These feelings are compounded by additional feelings of shame, fear, and guilt
   c. To survive the alcoholic denies these feelings and places the blame for them on others; family, friends, and co-workers
4. Eventually, the alcoholic becomes a bundle of unresolved feelings, all of which leave him/her continually aching

B. The Family is Drawn in
1. Since the alcoholic cannot bear to feel, he/she cannot tolerate family members expressing honest feelings
2. The alcoholic may deny it to him/herself but he/she knows that he/she is the source of the family's anger, shame, and disgust
3. As the alcoholic loses control over his/her own life, he/she demands and gains control over the family's life:
   a. The weapon of power is alcohol
   b. The family learns to plan its life around the drinker and alcohol
      1) Nothing must be done to upset the alcoholic, to provide a reason for drinking
      2) Though it is not possible, the family thinks it can control the alcoholic's drinking - as the family increasingly fears alcohol and tries desperately to control its effects, it sinks deeper and deeper into the alcoholic web

C. The Family Rules
1. Every family has rules that keep family life running smoothly - some rules are spoken, others are unspoken but understood
2. In an alcoholic family, the rules are made by the person in power, the alcoholic - the rules reflect the disease: inhumane; rigid; designed to maintain the status quo, so drinking can continue
3. The rules are:
   a. Alcohol is the most important thing in the family's life
      1) The alcoholic struggles to continue drinking
      2) The family plots to stop him/her
      3) No other family events or issues can ever be more important
   b. The alcoholic is not to blame for the drinking - the blame is placed on someone else in the family, usually the spouse or a child who is acting out
   c. Everyone must protect the alcoholic from the consequence of drinking
   d. Don't talk to anyone about the family situation
      1) To other family members
      2) To outsiders
      3) Letting no information out or new information into the family keeps the alcoholic's grip on family members strong
      4) A rigid insistence on family loyalty

       e. Don't feel
         1) Those who live at the whim of the alcoholic learn that he/she cannot be trusted
         2) Since the family members are not being genuine, they can't be trusted
         3) Outsiders are not even considered because of rules c & d

D. The Family Roles of Sharon Wegscheider-Cruse (adapted from the work of Virginia Satir and others)
  1. As the family follows the rigid, inhumane rules, each member becomes:
    a. More isolated
    b. More out of touch with feelings
    c. More desperate
    d. More disturbed
  2. For survival, each person learns to play a role, consisting of a set of behaviors, attitudes, and feelings
  3. Each person believes that he/she is limited to playing his/her role and cannot act any other way - this reduces stress and maintains a fragile family balance
  4. The roles are forced on the family member and based upon:
    a. Position in the family
    b. Gender
    c. Age
    d. Birth order
    e. Ethnic custom
    f. Social class
  5. The enabler
    a. Is assumed by the person who is emotionally closest to the alcoholic, usually the spouse
    b. The enabler provides protection that enables the alcoholic to keep drinking:
      1) By making excuses
      2) By taking over responsibilities
      3) By rescuing the alcoholic from negative consequences
        a) Initially protects out of love or loyalty
        b) Later protects from habit, shame, and guilt
        c) The person appears capable and strong to outsiders

                    d) Inside, the enabler is
                        (1) Tired
                        (2) Resentful
                        (3) Worried
                        (4) Suffering from low self-esteem
                        (5) Obsessed with alcohol
                        (6) Feeling helpless
                        (7) At greater risk of developing a
                             physical illness than the spouse of a
                             non-alcoholic
                        (8) At greater risk of being depressed
                        (9) At greater risk of becoming
                             chemically dependent
                       (10) At greater risk of having problems
                             with co-workers
                    e) Though the enabler feels helpless, he/she
                       holds the key to family recovery
                        (1) Once the enabler stops protecting
                             the alcoholic and forces him/her to
                             face the negative consequences of
                             drinking, the pain may be intense
                             enough to cause the alcoholic to
                             seek recovery
                        (2) He/she can create a healthy
                             environment for the children
        6. The hero
            a. Usually the oldest child
            b. Provides self-worth to the family
                1) An achiever and successful
                2) Appears to "have-it-all-together"
            c. The hero knows something is wrong and feels obligated
               to "fix" it - tries to fix the problems between parents by
               achieving some thing that will make them proud and
               forget the problem
                1) Each achievement is only a temporary cure
                2) Hero tries compulsively harder for the next
                   curing achievement
                3) Feels like a failure, guilty, and not good enough
                   when unable to fix everything

        d. Beneath the "perfect" facade, the hero is angry
          1) He/she has tried hard, but no one really appreciated the effort in an acceptable way
          2) He/she gets tired of trying, but leaves the family in an acceptable way
            a) Joins the military
            b) Goes off to college
            c) Gets married
            d) Takes a job in a distant city
          3) Heroes are perfectionists and without help may become:
            a) Workaholics
            b) Abusers of prescription medication (example: valium)
            c) The next generation of enablers

7. The scapegoat
    a. Usually the second child
    b. Since the hero has the family's positive attention, the second child seeks what is left, i.e., negative attention - this child's role is to take the attention away from the alcoholic by accepting blame for the family's trouble
    c. Usually seeks acceptance from peers who are also having trouble with parents - frequently becomes involved in alcohol, drug abuse, vandalism, and sexual promiscuity which leads to trouble with school authorities and police
    d. Beneath the hostile facade, the scapegoat is hurt, lonely, and often ashamed of his/her actions
    e. Scapegoat often becomes the next generation of alcohol and drug abusers

8. The lost child
    a. Usually the youngest child
    b. This child's role is to cause no trouble for the family
    c. Receives little positive or negative attention from the family
      1) Needs are not attended to
      2) No praise for achievements

3) Not reassured about fears
   a) Creates a fantasy world where things are as he/she would like them to be
   b) Has little interpersonal experience so makes humiliating mistakes when he/she goes to school causing more withdrawal
   c) Becomes a loner who has trouble with intimacy
   d) If he/she enters treatment, the prognosis is good
d. The self-reliance developed in isolation is a strength
e. Addressing the repressed anger of being ignored, increasing self-esteem, feeling accepted, and learning interpersonal skills will break the prison of isolation
f. Without treatment, the lost child looks toward leading a lonely life sometimes seeking relief in alcohol, drugs, and over-the-counter medication

9. The mascot
a. Usually the third or a middle child
b. Senses that something is wrong in the family but receives reassurance from other family members that nothing is wrong - this discrepancy between one's own perception and the reassurance of others causes a continual conflict that leads to anxiety and feelings of "going crazy"
   1) He/she feels less frightened when others give him/her attention
   2) Develops behaviors, such as clowning around or being cute, that will draw attention to him/herself
   3) Attention provides reinforcement to continue these behaviors
      a) Child does not continue to grow and mature but remains stuck in babyish behavior that has brought attention
      b) No one takes the mascot seriously leading him/her to feel unimportant and inadequate and to suffer from low self-esteem with anxiety
c. The compulsive need for attention is often misunderstood and misdiagnosed as:
   1) Hyperactivity
   2) Schizophrenia
   3) Paranoia

    d. In helping the mascot, it is important to reassure him/her that the fear that some thing was wrong with the family was a fact, not a crazy notion - with support, reassurance and training in interpersonal skills, the mascot can finally grow up

E. The family roles of Claudia Black
1. The responsible one
    a. Usually the oldest child
    b. Take on responsibility for making the family run as smoothly as it can
        1) Takes over many household chores
        2) Directs the activity of the younger children
        3) Learns to set realistic, short term goals
    c. Joins only structured activities
    d. As an adult, he/she continues to be very responsible and frequently a leader
        1) He/she has learned not to trust others or depend on them - feels it is better to do it oneself - has unequal relationships because he/she does not know how to trust, become intimate, and have fun
        2) Often is tense, anxious, fearful, lonely, and depressed
2. The adjuster
    a. Learns to get along by denying that trouble some events bother him/her
        1) Does not think or feel
        2) Does not draw attention to him/herself, just gets by
    b. Does not question situations but adapts to them with no fuss and then does not think about it
    c. As an adult, he/she frequently lacks direction, a sense of responsibility or personal power, and stable relationships or work history - he/she seeks out chaos and chooses to remain ignorant of feelings
3. The placater
    a. Is considered the "sensitive" child yet is always trying to make others feel better
    b. Does not seem to be disappointed or upset because he/she will express these feelings only in privacy

c. Seems to be a warm, caring, problem-free child
   1) Directs attention away from him/herself so no one sees any problems
   2) Feels guilty because he/she can't really fix things
d. As adults, they do not have equal relationships because they always give more than they take, seeking out people who do not take emotional responsibility
4. The acting-out child
   a. This child draws negative attention to him/herself through behavior such as delinquency
   b. Feels angry
   c. As an adult, continues to get involved in conflicts and chemical abuse

F. Adult Children of Alcoholics - A General Statement
1. They carry over into adulthood their childhood problems related to alcohol
2. They need help in dealing with their feelings
3. They tend to have difficulty with intimate relationships
4. They are at a higher risk for developing alcohol/drug dependence
5. They continually seek approval or flaunt contempt
6. They are either super-responsible or super irresponsible

G. Violence
1. Violence in an alcoholic home is not an isolated phenomenon affecting only one member
   a. Child abuse appears to be related to spousal abuse
   b. Wives are often the recipients of serious injury
2. Child abuse
   a. Can occur in any social class
   b. Families of violence may also have times of caring and tenderness
   c. Alcohol and child abuse related arrests are linked
   d. A child abuser may not have severe psychological problems but he/she may have decreased inhibitions due to the influence of alcohol/drugs
3. When a counselor is informed of domestic physical abuse of the client's children, he/she has a legal obligation to inform the appropriate state or social service agencies

II. Intervention

A. Introduction
   1. Intervention is the creation or use of a crisis involving the alcoholic that is so emotionally painful that he/she will stop denying that alcohol/drugs is a problem before he/she has lost everything
   2. The goal of intervention is treatment for the alcoholic
   3. Intervention can work if:
      a. It is prepared for carefully under the guidance of a trained person
      b. It is conducted in a loving, honest, and non-hostile manner
      c. There is a treatment system in place that will accept the client
      d. The family is committed to recovery and will continue treatment for themselves regardless of the outcome of the intervention
   4. Sometimes a crisis naturally occurs involving a family member - this can be an indirect cry for help that will eventually focus on alcoholism

B. Preparation for Intervention
   1. Someone must reach out for help
      a. Frequently it is the enabler, hero, or an outside friend
      b. The person reaching out needs to be reassured by the counselor that breaking the family rule of silence is a healthy and loving thing to do
   2. During the first meeting, the counselor discusses with the individual what important issues are facing the alcoholic, e.g., a drunk driving charge, marital problems, job performance, and health problems
   3. A list is made of the important people in the alcoholic's life who have seen the chemical induced behavior or the consequences
      a. It is decided who would be willing to participate in a Confrontation
      b. A meeting is arranged with the counselor and those who are willing to participate
         1) The counselor provides more information on chemical dependency and the intervention process
         2) The counselor can assess the family's damage

c. It is appropriate to include the spouse in an intervention especially:
   1) When the alcoholic's police record indicates a history of spousal abuse
   2) When the client appears to be heavily into denial but admits his wife has complained about his drinking and that there are some problems in the marriage
   3) If the work supervisor, when making a referral, said the potential client's wife has called him on several occasions complaining about the husband's behavior
4. A training is set up to teach the family how to intervene
   a. The family must realize that alcohol/drugs is the primary problem - most other problems result from it
   b. The session helps family member realize the importance of denial and understand why the alcoholic will not seek help without the intervention
   c. The family must learn how its own behavior enables the alcoholic to continue drinking and have the motivation to change the behavior
   d. The family must learn how drinking has affected each member - each member must resolve his/her own denial before attempting to confront the alcoholic's denial
   e. A plan for the intervention day is made
      1) A time is chosen when the alcoholic is sober, but feeling the effects of a hangover or drunk driving charges, so he/she will be more vulnerable and unable to deny the problem
      2) Each member lists concrete examples of the alcoholic's behavior that caused pain, danger, and humiliation
         a) The wording is checked for directness, honesty, caring, and lack of hostility
         b) Each member practices reading his/her own list so it can be delivered calmly during the intervention
      3) Prior to the intervention, the family decides on a course of action and makes arrangements with a treatment facility

4) A date is set for the intervention
 a) So all family members will be there
 b) So the counselor can attend as the neutral party
 c) The place can be home or the counselor's office

C. The Intervention
 1. During the intervention, each family member reads his/her list that was rehearsed during the preparation
 2. As the alcoholic hears detail after detail of how his/her alcoholic behavior has harmed the people he/she loves, it is difficult to maintain the denial that alcohol is not a problem
 3. The leader of the confrontation proposes the treatment plan that the family has agreed to
  a. The alcoholic may accept with no argument
  b. He/she may request doing it "my way"
   1) It is almost impossible to stop drinking without professional help
   2) Before the family members agree to "my way", they clearly state that if the alcoholic takes just one drink then he/she will go to the treatment facility the family is requesting
 4. If the intervention is well-prepared and the family has made some recovery before the confrontation, there is a greater than 75% chance that the intervention will be a success
 5. In some cases, the alcoholic will cling to denial in the face of all the evidence
  a. The family must make it clear that they plan to continue treatment and indicate as concretely as possible how life will change
  b. These changes will make the alcoholic more uncomfortable because no one will be protecting him/her any longer
  c. At times, it may be necessary for the family to leave the alcoholic if treatment is refused - life would be too harmful to the family to continue living with drinking

6. Supervisors at work can play a big role in intervention
    a. A supervisor's threat of discipline is often more effective in getting the alcoholic into treatment than a spouse's threat to leave
    b. Unfortunately, not all supervisors are aware of the destructive effects of alcohol because:
        1) The employer may be an enabler who believes that covering up is helping the employee
        2) The alcoholic employee has a job which he can adequately do under the influence of alcohol
        3) The workplace is sometimes the last to be affected by alcoholism
7. All that has been stated about alcoholism, holds true for drug dependence - simply substitute the appropriate word

D. Post-Intervention Treatment
    1. The family needs to continue in treatment, joined by the newly sober substance abuser
        a. To begin experiencing the feelings that were previously forbidden
        b. To clarify and document the problems caused by the abuser
        c. To begin changing the pathological relationships that exist
            1) Helping each person step out of his/her role
            2) Helping to develop a healthy, balanced family system which includes a functional former abuser
            3) Developing new family rules that are flexible and humane
            4) Developing trust among family members
    2. The family may become temporarily more unstable as the family pushes to become normal

III. Support for Families

A. Self-help Groups
1. Al-Anon: the purpose is to offer support to non-alcoholic friends and relatives coping with alcoholism
2. Alateen: the primary purpose is to offer support to the teenage children of alcoholics to help them cope with the alcoholic
3. ACOA.: the primary purpose is to help adults who grow up in an alcoholic or otherwise dysfunctional home to understand and "heal" the emotional wounds of their upbringings
4. Nar-Anon: the primary purpose is to offer support to family and friends of drug users

B. Community Mental Health Centers
1. The purpose of the center is to offer a variety of services to the individuals and families
2. These services can include
    a. Crisis counseling
    b. Marital counseling
    c. Family counseling
    d. Financial counseling
    e. Information and referral
    f. Education in such areas as
        1) Stress management
        2) Re-entry workshop
        3) Financing a college education
        4) Resume writing
        5) Parenting skills
        6) Retirement
        7) Smoking cessation

Section 2, Chapter 3:

The Functions of Counseling - Treatment Planning, Case Management, and Crisis Intervention

A Definition of Treatment Planning

The International Certification and Reciprocity Consortium/Alcohol and Other Drug Abuse, Inc. (IC&RC/AODA) defines the core function of treatment planning as follows:

"Treatment Planning: the process by which the counselor and the client:

- identify and rank problems needing resolution;
- establish agreed-upon immediate and long-term goals; and
- decide on treatment methods and the resources to be used."

The following expanded definition of "treatment planning" may be useful to help you better understand this definition:

"The treatment contract is based on the assessment and is a product of a negotiation between the client and counselor to assure that the plan is tailored to the individual's needs. The language of the problem, goal, and strategy statements should be specific, intelligible to the client, and expressed in behavioral terms. The statement of the problem concisely elaborates on the client the need identified previously. The goal statements refer specifically to the identified problem and may include one objective or a set of objectives ultimately intended to resolve or mitigate the problem. The goals must be expressed in behavioral terms in order for the client and counselor to determine progress in treatment. The plan or strategy is a specific activity that links the problem with the goal. It describes the services, who will provide them, where they will be provided, and at what frequency. Treatment planning is a dynamic process, and the contracts must be regularly reviewed and modified as appropriate."

I. Tasks

A. The basis of the client's treatment plan is the assessment

B. The Joint Commission on Accreditation of Health Care Organizations requires that:
1. a treatment plan be formulated on the basis of intake information
2. a treatment plan based on presenting problems, physical, behavioral and emotional status be developed within 72 hours of intake

C. The treatment plan should be individualized, based on the client's particular problems and needs
1. should identify strengths and limitations
2. should involve the family where appropriate

D. To create the treatment plan, the client and the primary counselor list the significant problems and issues and then rank them in terms of priority. Some examples of issues identified in a treatment plan might include:
1. alcohol dependence
2. other drug dependence
3. withdrawal history/concerns
4. unemployment
5. sexual abuse
6. marital difficulties
7. adult child of alcoholic parent(s)
8. lacking drug-free peer group
9. recent death of significant other

E. Once the problems are identified, the client and counselor negotiate long term and short term goals. Some examples are:
1. Long term goal: Mary Smith will remain alcohol and drug free with the help of an ongoing support group

   Short term goals: She will remain in weekly individual counseling sessions; she will attend AA meetings 4 times weekly; she will begin to utilize the AA tools (slogans, sponsor, phone numbers)

2. Long term goal: Mary Smith will develop vocational skills that will enable her to maintain consistent employment

   Short term goal: She will make an appointment with the Department of Vocational Rehabilitation within the next 2 weeks

3. Long term goal: Mary Smith will appropriately resolve the grief resulting from the death of her alcoholic mother

   Short term goals: She will attend 1 Al-Anon meeting weekly; she will read 1 book about co-dependency; she will express her feelings about her mother to her counselor in their individual sessions

F. Goals should be expressed clearly and in concrete, measurable, behavioral terms, and should include expected date of achievement

G. Specific counseling strategies and services should be identified, as well as who will perform tasks, where they will take place, and how often; outside referrals may be considered

H. Client progress notes should regularly reflect attention being paid to the areas outlined in the treatment plan - documentation of progress and struggles in these specific areas should be noted

I. Resolution of problem areas specified in the treatment plan should be documented in the progress noted and/or on the treatment plan itself

J. Treatment plans should be reviewed regularly (every 7- 10 days) by the client and counselor, and by the clinical supervisor and/or treatment team. JCAHO requires:
   1. at minimum, review at "major key points in each patient's treatment course", i.e., admission, transfer, discharge, or major change in condition

K. Treatment plans should always allow for flexibility and for changes in addressing client problems, needs and goals

A Definition of Case Management

The International Certification and Reciprocity Consortium/Alcohol and Other Drug Abuse, Inc. (IC&RC/AODA) defines the core function of case management as follows:

"Case Management: Activities which bring services, agencies, resources, or people together within a planned framework of action toward the achievement of established goals. It may involve liaison activities and collateral contacts."

The following supplemental expansion of this definition of "case management" may be useful in helping understand this core function:

"Case Management is the coordination of a multiple-service plan. By the time any alcohol and other drug abusers enter treatment, they tend to manifest dysfunction in a variety of areas. For example, a heroin addict may have hepatitis, lack job skills, and have a pending criminal charge. In this case, the counselor might monitor his medical treatment, make a referral to a vocational rehabilitation program, and communicate with representatives of the criminal justice system."

"The client may also be receiving other treatment services, such as family therapy and chemotherapy, within the same agency. These activities must be integrated into the treatment plan, and communication must be maintained with the appropriate personnel."

I. Tasks

A. Case management is one of the most critical tasks of the addictions counselor; it includes aspects of the following activities:
   1. treatment planning
   2. counseling
   3. referral
   4. consultation
   5. report and recordkeeping
   6. crisis intervention
   7. client education

B. Case management involves the coordination of individuals and services in order to assist the client to achieve the goals outlined in the treatment plan

C. The case manager/counselor receives input from other members of the treatment team including:
   1. his/her clinical supervisor
   2. other counselors who have contact with the client
   3. other professionals, such as doctors or educators, who have contact with the client

D. Major areas that may require case management attention
   1. health and medical services
   2. psychological testing
   3. family therapy
   4. vocational counseling
   5. special therapy groups
   6. self help groups

Crisis Intervention in Addiction Counseling

A crisis can be defined as any significant event during the rehabilitation process that threatens to jeopardize or destroy the treatment effort. Crises have many causes and can be directly related to alcohol and or other drug use (e.g. relapse) or indirectly related. Suicidal gestures, divorce or separation, psychotic episodes, or outside pressure to terminate treatment can all bring about a crisis.

In crisis intervention, the counselor needs to master the ability to resolve or diminish the crisis and to use it as a therapeutic opportunity. An understanding of what behaviors indicate that a crisis is imminent can lead to crisis prevention which for the substance abuser is a key to continued sobriety.

In developing crisis intervention skills, the counselor will become alert to any attitudinal or mood changes that may indicate a pending crisis. It is also crucial that the counselor be aware of what he or she is equipped to deal with. Some situations may warrant consultation with an appropriate resource. Examples include crises which are the results of cultural issues or a medical problem. The counselor needs to know what his or her limitations are so that an appropriate referral can be made at the appropriate time.

Through crisis intervention counseling, a skilled counselor has the ability to relate the current situation to a past experience thus providing the client with an opportunity to gain insight. In some cases, this may have the effect of turning the crisis into a more positive growth experience. Knowing what to look for, when to probe, and when to make interventions are all important skills to master in the crisis intervention process.

A Definition of Crisis Intervention

The International Certification and Reciprocity Consortium/Alcohol and Other Drug Abuse, Inc. (IC&RC/AODA) defines the core function of crisis intervention as follows:

"Crisis Intervention: Those services which respond to an alcohol and/or other drug abuser's needs during acute emotional and/or physical distress."

The following supplemental expansion of this definition of "crisis intervention" may be useful in understanding this core function:

"A crisis is a decisive, crucial event in the course of treatment that threatens to compromise or destroy the rehabilitation effort. These crises may be directly related to alcohol and/or drug use (i.e., overdose or relapse) or indirectly related. The latter might include the death of a significant other, separation/divorce, arrest, suicidal gestures, psychotic episode, or outside pressure to terminate treatment."

"It is imperative that the counselor be able to mitigate or resolve the immediate problem and use the negative events to enhance the treatment effort, if possible."

I. Causes and Reactions to Crises

A. Definition
1. A crisis is a state of mental and emotional confusion that is caused by the perception of threat
2. It involves a sense of urgency
3. It may last a few hours to a few weeks

B. Traumas that set off crises
1. A trauma is an objective event that damages a person's sense of well-being and creates anxiety
2. For a trauma to set off a crisis, the person has to perceive the traumatic event as very threatening
3. There are four types of traumas that set off crises
   a. Situational - the circumstance causes the upset
   Examples: the death of a loved one; the break up of an important relationship; serious illness; serious financial problems; spouse military deployment; family violence, etc.
   b. Developmental - the process of growing through life stages can cause upset
   Examples: peer pressure; marriage; children leaving home; retirement

      c. Intrapsychic - thoughts and feelings can create upset
          Examples: identity confusion; thoughts and feelings created during interpersonal friction; suicidal thoughts
      d. Existential - a sense of emptiness and lack of purpose in life causes upset
          Example: recognition that daily activities don't provide meaning and satisfaction in life and a void or feelings of emptiness results

C. Reactions to crises
  1. People in crisis perform some form of reactive behavior or to reduce emotions
  2. Common reactions
    a. Shock
      1) Trauma may stun some people into a dazed and numb state
      2) This numbness prevents other feelings from being felt
      3) A person in shock may appear zombie-like have difficulty concentrating, feel helpless, and demonstrate increased suggestibility
    b. Anxiety
      1) The trauma may overwhelm some people they feel like they are falling apart
      2) Trauma causes some people to act agitated or perform useless activity such as pacing, hand wringing, smoking, or drinking
      3) Some people have symptoms of increased nervous system arousal: rapid heart beat, chest pains, difficulty breathing, dizziness, and sweating
    c. Depression
      1) The traumas may "flatten" some people creating a sense of hopelessness
      2) Some people are immobilized - they are preoccupied with the event, don't attend to daily needs, have a low energy level, or cry frequently
      3) Some people may become suicidal

d. Anger
  1) The trauma may outrage some people
  2) They direct the anger outward onto others
    c) The cause of the trauma
    d) An easy target
  3) They direct the anger inward leading to self-destructive actions
e. Intellectualization
  1) The trauma may cut off thoughts and feelings in some people
  2) They use rational thinking to get through the crisis
  3) They are cut off from painful feelings
  4) This will leave the trauma unresolved after the crisis has passed

II. Crisis Intervention
  A. Goals of crisis intervention
    1. To stabilize the individual so no further deterioration in functioning occurs
    2. To relieve the individual of as much pressure as possible
    3. To convert the emergency to a solvable problem and resolve it
    4. To return the person to his/her pre-crisis level of functioning
  B. Process of crisis intervention
    1. Establish rapport - this must be done rapidly at the beginning of the interview - the client must feel he/she has a knowledgeable ally who will see him/her through the crisis
    2. Gather relevant data
      a. To assess risk of danger to self and others
      b. To become informed about current problem
        1) Medical
          a) Current symptoms
          b) Precipitating event
          c) History of this medical problem (brief)
          d) If alcohol and drugs are involved
            (1) Include what drug, dose, and when taken
            (2) Provide information immediately to medical personnel
            (3) Allow enough time to observe the client and then interview him/her after the substance level has decreased in order to collect history and plan treatment

      e) If the client presents with psychotic symptoms, a medical evaluation is needed

        (1) Anti-psychotic medication may be given to control the psychotic symptoms

        (2) Can assess that the client is out of crisis when he/she shows a marked decrease in thought disorder

  2) Psychological

      a) Current symptoms

      b) Precipitating event

      c) History of a psychological problem (brief)

      d) The following comments may be helpful in deciding if there is a psychological crisis

        (1) "Describe your present mood."

        (2) "Tell me about the changes in your lifestyle."

        (3) "Have you ever thought of harming yourself?"

        (4) "Describe your eating and sleeping habits."

c. To assess client's ability to cope with the crisis

  1) Strengths

      a) Personal

      b) Support network: family, friends, and employer

      c) Physical: finances, housing, and transportation (when relevant)

      d) The fewer the resources, the greater the danger

  2) Weaknesses - same categories as strengths

d. To form a realistic treatment plan

3. Reframe the crisis into a solvable problem and potential growth situation
    a. Decreases the pressure on the client when a solution is possible - helps to increase level of functioning
    b. Enables the counselor to point out:
        1) What the client is doing that worsens the problem and makes it less solvable
        2) What the client is doing that lessens the problem and makes the problem more solvable
    c. Clarifies the focal problem that caused the crisis
4. Help the client examine realistic options for solving the problem
    a. Weigh the advantages and disadvantages of each option
    b. Choose the most workable option
    c. Make a plan of action
5. Contact necessary support individuals who can help carry out the plan of action - possible contacts include:
    a. Family
    b. Friends
    c. Employer
    d. Physician or psychiatrist
    e. Service agencies
6. Arrange for a follow up interview, if appropriate, many clients fail to follow through with counseling because the counselor did not get a commitment to treatment

C. Counselor danger zones
    1. Taking responsibility for the client
        a. Once the intensity of emotions has decreased, most people are capable of making choices - the counselor assists in decision making but does not make the decision
        b. Family and friends need to be called upon to make choices for a person who is not capable of decision making - the counselor would make the decision if there is no one else to turn to for help

2. Giving false assurance
    a. It is not appropriate to paint a brighter picture than really exists
        1) The client will feel the counselor does not understand which leads to lack of rapport and trust
        2) It sets up false expectations that may not come true leaving the client potentially more devastated
    b. A realistic assessment, phrased in a tactful manner, is more useful
3. Becoming anxious
    a. It is sometimes difficult to remain calm when dealing with an anxious, panicky individual - it is especially difficult when dealing with potential injury to self or others
    b. Knowing one's limits and asking for help from other colleagues is a way to ensure appropriate help for the client and a clear head for the counselor
4. Focusing on problems, not solutions to resolve the crisis. It must be reformed as a problem with solutions
    a. Data is needed on the current crisis and some times past events
    b. Excessive focus on the crisis will fuel the client's upset and produce no solutions
5. Projecting one's own interpretation of the trauma
    a. The intense feelings the client is experiencing are based on his/her thoughts and belief system the counselor needs to investigate these thoughts to understand the feelings
    b. It is not appropriate to interpret the thoughts based on the counselor's personal experience - one feeling can be caused by many different and conflicting thoughts

D. Factors affecting crisis outcome
   1. Duration
      a. The sooner the person requests help after reaching the breaking point, the better the prognosis - because there has been little time for maladaptive behaviors to set in
      b. 10-14 days is the average length of time people struggle with a crisis before seeking help
   2. Nature of the trauma
      a. Generally the less severe the trauma is, as viewed by an uninvolved observer, the better the prognosis
      b. The counselor must remember that individuals have different abilities to cope -what appears to the uninvolved observer to be a mini-trauma may have a profound impact on an individual with few coping skills
   3. Client personality - a person who is normal and healthy prior to trauma has a better prognosis than someone who has had previous emotional difficulties, adjustment problems, and crises
   4. Support network - the person who has good relationships with people who can be called upon during difficult times has a better prognosis than the individual who is alone

E. Qualities of an effective crisis counselor
   1. Empathy
      a. Helps to rapidly develop rapport
      b. Helps client to relax
   2. Good questioning skills
      a. Ability to gather information quickly for an individual who is in the midst of intense emotions
      b. Able to be direct yet tactful
   3. Rapid assessment
      a. Quickly and accurately pinpoints the big issues
      b. Determines risk factors
      c. Discovers options to solve the problem
   4. Realistic viewpoint
      a. Does not make false promises to the client
      b. Knows own limits in being able to help so does not feel responsible for the client beyond professional duties
      c. Asks for help when needed to assure client will receive the best help available
   5. Uses resources available
      a. Client's network
      b. Professional network
      c. Agency network

III. Suicide

  A. Risk factors

      1. Many people think about suicide but would never actually attempt it - others are potential suicide victims

      2. Certain circumstances increase the potential for suicide

         a. Suicide is associated with depression

            1) The signs of depression are not always obvious

               a) Sadness

               b) Guilt

               c) Inadequacy

               d) Hopelessness

               e) Weight loss

               f) Loss of appetite

               g) Loss of sexual desire

               h) Sleeplessness

               i) Fatigue

         b. Men commit suicide more frequently than women though women attempt it more often

            1) At greater risk are:

               a) Teenage boys

               b) Men older than 50 years

               c) Older people rather than younger people

               d) One who suffered a recent, permanent loss

               e) Someone who is seriously ill

               f) Someone who does not have a network of caring people

               g) People who have unstable relationships

               h) Alcohol and drug dependent people

               i) Impulsive people

               j) Emotionally "burned out" individuals

B. Cues to suicide potential
1. In talking with an individual, the counselor needs to be alert to the above listed risk factors
2. The counselor must also note the following cues of immediate danger:
   a. The client has decided on a method, time and place - lethality increases with such methods as shooting, jumping off a bridge, and fast-acting drugs
   b. Suddenness of the desire to kill oneself
   c. Depression
      1) Especially if sudden
      2) If combined with:
         a) Psychotic thinking
         b) Alcohol and drug use
         c) Confused thinking
         d) Anger and aggression
      3) Sudden improvement in depression
   d. Confused thinking and feeling, indicating inability to cope
   e. Use of phrases like:
      1) "Tired of living - won't be long now"
      2) "Want out"
      3) "Family is better off without me"
   f. Previous suicide attempts - as a person gets older, the chances of succeeding increase
   g. Talking about suicide
      1) It is not true that those who talk suicide never do it
      2) Threats must be taken seriously

C. Dealing with a suicide crisis
  1. The counselor should form a relationship with the client so the individual will talk about suicide
      a. Prepare him/herself for the flood of emotional confusion that will pour out
      b. Don't interrupt client to relieve his/her own feeling of discomfort about suicide - take care of own needs later with a colleague
      c. Act calm - keep any inner upset hidden because it will only agitate the client
  2. Do not attempt:
      a. To cheer up the client by minimizing his/her loss or pointing out what good things are left - he/she will feel the counselor does not understand and possibly terminate the conversation
      b. To talk the client out of committing suicide
          1) Request he/she postpone the deed for a day or so
          2) Ask to discuss the situation again to be sure suicide is what the client really wants to do
  3. Identify the key issues
      a. Clarify what the precipitating event was
      b. Address the current problem in concrete terms - don't shift focus to past problems which will minimize the importance of the current suicide issue
  4. Assess lethality based on
      a. Concreteness of plan
      b. Sex
      c. Age
      d. Depression
      e. Resources
      f. Important relationships
      g. Losses
  5. Evaluate the client's strengths and resources which can be called upon to decrease the threat of suicide

6. Design a treatment plan and put it into action
   a. Ask the client to postpone suicide and set a time to talk again - make yourself or agency available for contact before the date if the client finds it necessary
   b. Help the client begin to reduce stress by action, if appropriate
   c. Contact resources
      1) Psychiatrist for evaluation
      2) Inpatient hospitalization
      3) Client's network
   d. Plan for follow-up treatment
      1) Provide hope that someone cares
      2) Provide hope that something can be done to make life bearable
7. If a client informs the counselor that he/she has frequent thoughts of suicide and a definite plan which he/she will carry out if the counselor tells anyone, the counselor should:
   a. Immediately notify his/her clinical supervisor
   b. Formulate a protective treatment plan

Section 2, Chapter 4:

The Functions of Counseling - Education, Referral, Reports and Recordkeeping, and Consultation

A Definition of Education

The International Certification and Reciprocity Consortium/Alcohol and Other Drug Abuse, Inc. (IC&RC/AODA) defines the core function of education as follows:

"Education: provision of information to individuals and groups, concerning alcohol and other drug abuse and the available services and resources."

The following expanded definition of "education" may be useful in understanding this core function:

"Client education is provided in a variety of ways. In certain inpatient and residential programs, for example, a sequence of formal classes may be conducted using a didactic format with reading materials and films. On the other hand, an outpatient counselor may provide relevant information to the client individually and informally. In addition to alcohol and drug information, client education may include a description of self-help groups and other resources that are available to the clients and their families."

I. How and What is Provided

    A. Client education can be provided in a variety of ways, such as:
        1. formal, didactic classes with readings and films, etc., for small groups, large groups, or family groups
        2. information given informally to individual client by counselor
    B. Types of information given varies widely and may include:
        1. information on alcohol and drugs
        2. descriptions of self-help groups
        3. other resources available for clients and families

II. Availability of Client Educational Materials

    A. Availability of materials has increased in recent years, enabling facilities to expand and upgrade educational programs
    B. The advent of videotape and VCR's has been a boon to even the smallest treatment agencies
        1. National TV programs and movies
        2. PBS broadcasts
        3. National Clearinghouses for Alcohol and Drug Information
        4. Private companies (Hazelden, Johnson Institute, FMS Films, etc.)
    C. New books on substance abuse treatment have begun to emerge

III. Tasks: What to do When Designing a Client Education Program

    A. Tailor the educational material to meet the needs of the clients, considering:
        1. the range of presenting problems in your population
        2. the range of learning abilities in your population
        3. the types of materials available
        4. your budget constraints
    B. What's the best method of presentation?
        1. to individual clients
        2. to groups of clients
        3. to clients and families
        4. to family members only
        5. during individual or group therapy sessions

C. What's the best format for the topic?
   1. books
   2. videotapes
   3. cassette tapes
   4. pamphlets
   5. films
   6. speakers
   7. lecture
   8. group discussions

D. Issues to consider as a "lecturer" or presenter
   1. be careful not to present information that is too "dry" or overly technical
   2. maintain a relaxed and personal presentation style
   3. pay attention to your audience response and take cues from them
   4. allow for flexibility in your presentation to accommodate audience's learning needs

E. The most appropriate time to introduce information
   1. consider when clients are ready for the material, i.e., when it wouldn't be distracting or harmful

F. How to evaluate your program in order to:
   1. receive feedback from clients on content and means of presentation
   2. continually make needed changes to ensure client understanding and participation
   3. keep materials current

IV. Content of Educational Programs

A. The "Planning Alcoholism Counseling Education" (PACE) curriculum guide from the U. S. Department of Health and Human Services suggests that the following topics be included in educational programs:
   1. current statistics on prevalence and incidence of alcohol/drug abuse
   2. physical, psychological and social effects of alcohol/drugs
   3. stages and characteristics of alcoholism/drug addiction
   4. dynamics of addiction
   5. alcohol/drug interactions; multiple and cross dependence

B. Other topics to include:
1. information on self-help groups such as:
    a. Alcoholics Anonymous for recovering alcoholics
    b. Narcotics Anonymous for recovering drug addicts
    c. Adult Children of Alcoholics for adult offspring of alcoholics
    d. Al-Anon for spouses or other significant others of recovering alcoholics
    e. Alateen for teen-age children of recovering alcoholics
    f. Overeaters Anonymous for overeaters
2. resource listings of books, tapes and films which might be of further interest

A Definition of Referral

The International Certification and Reciprocity Consortium/Alcohol and Other Drug Abuse, Inc. (IC&RC/AODA) defines the core function of referral as follows:

"Referral: identifying the needs of the client that cannot be met by the counselor or agency and helping the client to utilize the support systems and community resources available."

The following supplemental expansion of this definition of "referral" may be useful in helping you better understand this core function:

"In order to be competent in this function, the counselor must be familiar with community resources, both alcohol/drug and others, and be aware of the limitations of each service. In addition, the counselor must be able to demonstrate a working knowledge of the referral process, including the confidentiality requirements."

"Referral is obviously closely related to case management when integrated into the initial and ongoing treatment plan. It also includes, however, aftercare or discharge referrals that take into account the continuum of care."

I. Referral Preparations

    A. Site visit

        1. Before referring a client to an outside agency, the counselor should visit the agency and meet with key staff members

        2. The counselor should ask questions that will enable him/her to make appropriate referrals, answer questions, and calm the client's anxiety. The reason for early termination of treatment in many cases is a referral error

        3. It is typical to collect adequate information in the following areas:

            a. Agency philosophy

                1) Primary conditions treated

                2) Approach to addictions - medical model, primary illness, psychiatric problem, holistic, chemical dependency, and/or A.A. model

                3) Predominant therapies used - Reality Therapy, Rational Emotive Therapy, Behavior modification, etc.

                4) Predominant treatment method - one-on-one, groups, lectures, A.A. meetings, etc .

                5) Views on medication - can a person on medication, especially psychotropic drugs, be admitted and function well

                6) Acceptance of clients with psychiatric and medical problems

            b. Program structure

                1) Length of the program

                2) Hours of the program

                3) Size of the program

                4) Staff including availability of medical and psychiatric services

                5) Frequency of the treatment meetings

                6) Length of the treatment meetings

                7) Staff participation in treatment meetings

            c. Admissions criteria - sex, age, types of problems, issue of the medicated client, and other criteria

            d. Finances - cost, criteria for sliding scale, responsibility for payment, and time period for payment

4. To ensure that the agency has maintained its standards and has not drastically changed, the counselor should check back with the referred client and make ongoing site visits - semiannually to most agencies and more frequently to agencies that receive many referrals

5. Since self-help groups are an important part of treating chemical dependency, the counselor should visit as many groups as possible in the local area and collect the following information in a referral file:
   a. Smoking or non-smoking meetings
   b. Predominantly male, female, or equal
   c. Predominantly white collar, blue collar, or mixed
   d. Predominantly young, older, or mixed
   e. Gay, Lesbian, and Trans-gender groups
   f. Do several types of meetings occur simultaneously or not

B. Referral file
   1. The referral file should have information, where available, on resources in each of these areas:
      a. Marital counseling
      b. Family counseling
      c. Sexual counseling
      d. Education counseling
      e. Financial counseling
      f. Legal counseling
      g. Religious counseling
      h. Career counseling
      i. Dietitians/nutritionists
      j. Psychiatric assistance
      k. Family planning and birth control
      l. Veterans Administration
      m. Public health facilities
      n. Alcoholics Anonymous
      o. Narcotics Anonymous
      p. Al-Anon
      q. Nar-Anon
      r. Alateen
      s. Adult Children of Alcoholics (ACOA)
      t. Overeaters Anonymous

2. Sample of information a referral card on file might contain:
   Agency: New Hope Counseling Center
   Address: 12 Spanish Oak, Austin, TX
   Telephone: (512) 344-9896
   Contact: Billy Richards
   Services: Programs in marital, family, and sexual counseling
   Cost: $30-70/hours; Insurance accepted
   Hours of operation: 9 AM - 5 PM, Mon.- Fri.
   Information Materials: Free pamphlets in reception area
   (On back of card, note the counselor's initials and date of most recent site visit)

II. Making the Referral

A. The choices
   1. The counselor may decide at any point in treatment (screening, rehabilitation, aftercare) that the client's problems exceed the counselor's ability to handle them
   2. The counselor must find an organization or agency that can handle the client's problems
   3. To find the appropriate resource, the counselor matches the client's needs to the information collected about agencies to find the "best fit"

B. The process
   1. When the counselor decides that a referral is necessary, he/she must talk with the client about the need for a referral
   2. The counselor should discuss the agency/organization to familiarize the client with the resource and calm any anxieties
   3. To assure that the client will follow through on the referral, the most appropriate thing for the counselor to do is to contact the referral source in the client's presence and tell them a referral is being made, and then have the client call to make an appointment
   4. If the counselor cannot contact the referral source, it is important to give the client the agency/organization name, a contact person, and a telephone number

C. Specific situations
    1. If the counselor is uncertain what referral to make, he/she should consult with the clinical supervisor
    2. Referrals to medical personnel should be made when clients exhibit psychotic symptoms and/or have such physical problems as:
        a. Chronic low energy
        b. Chronic difficulty in concentrating
        c. Unexplained weight loss
        d. Difficulty sleeping

OVERVIEW: Reports and Recordkeeping

Recordkeeping is one of the most critical tasks of the addictions counselor. In terms of quality and continuity of treatment, frequent and careful attention should be paid to this task.

Recordkeeping begins with the first contact that is made by the client with a treatment program (typically called a screening) and continues through the evaluation and treatment process. The intake, assessment and treatment planning tasks all require thorough and thoughtful documentation in order to adequately form the basis of the client's treatment experience. Once these are in place, the progress notes should objectively summarize the client's activities and progress towards identified goals. Progress notes are also written following individual sessions, group therapy, family sessions and other activities which have clinical significance. Any other critical incidents or crises should also be noted. Progress notes must always be dated and signed.

The discharge plan is created just prior to a client's discontinuation of treatment and generally specifies post-treatment recommendations. The discharge summary presents an overview of the client's treatment experience with a statement of prognosis for the future.

It is critical that all reports and record inclusions be written legibly and with correct spelling and usage of grammar and punctuation. Records are often reviewed by supervisors and other staff members and must be readable to be useful. It is imperative that the client's progress and significant activities be accurately documented. Records must also include appropriate Releases of Information forms for information that is requested from or revealed to others.

Finally, accurate recordkeeping is necessary from the legal, funding and ethical perspectives. The client's treatment and recovery, as well as the good standing of the treatment program rely on responsible documentation.

A Definition of Report and Recordkeeping

The International Certification and Reciprocity Consortium/Alcohol and Other Drug Abuse, Inc. (IC&RC/AODA) defines the core function of report and recordkeeping as follows:

> "Report and Recordkeeping: Charting the results of the assessment and treatment plan, and writing reports, progress notes, discharge summaries, and other client-related data."

The following supplemental expanded definition of "report and record keeping" may be useful in helping you better understand this core function:

> "The report and record keeping function is extremely important. It can benefit the counselor by documenting the client's progress in achieving his/her goals. It can facilitate adequate communications between co-workers. It can assist the counselor's supervisor in providing timely feedback. It can be valuable to other programs that may provide services to the client at a later date. It can enhance the accountability of the program to its funding sources. Ultimately, if properly performed, it can enhance the client's treatment experience."

I. Tasks

A. Documentation of client goals and progress made toward achieving those goals is important for both the client and the counselor

B. Documentation is critical for maintaining clear communication with other treatment team members regarding client progress

C. Reports can be very useful for others working with the client, i.e. physician, parole or probation officer, future treatment provider. A signed Release of Information form is required for sending client information to them

D. Funding and licensing agencies pay close attention to recordkeeping and often have particular recordkeeping requirements

E. The clinical supervisor should regularly review all client records and provide feedback to the counselor regarding content, format, etc.

II. Typical Forms

A. Intake

B. Assessment

C. Treatment plan

D. Treatment plan reviews

E. Progress notes - JCAHO requires that progress notes:
1. be a part of client's record
2. document the implementation of the treatment plan
3. serve as the basis for plan review
4. document all treatment delivered to the client
5. describe the client's response to treatment, change in conditions, outcome of treatment, and achievement of goals
6. include written reports from outside service providers

F. Discharge plan
1. developed by client and counselor
2. becomes permanent part of client's record, and may be shared with future service-providers after discharge
3. specifics might include:
   a. where client will live after discharge
   b. whether or not client will receive outpatient counseling
   c. whether or not client should attend self-help groups
   d. how client will obtain work or return to school
   e. financial plan for self-support, if necessary
   f. recommendation for continuation of prescribed medication, if appropriate (i.e., Antabuse, methadone)

G. Discharge summary - JCAHO requires:
  1. discharge summary entered into client's record within 15 days after discharge
  2. inclusion of the results of the intake assessment and diagnosis
  3. inclusion of summaries of:
      a. significant findings
      b. achievement of goals
      c. course of treatment
      d. final assessment
      e. recommendations for further treatment
      f. written aftercare plan based on client's needs as reassessed, to be developed by counselor with input from client and family

A Definition of Consultation

The International Certification and Reciprocity Consortium/Alcohol and Other Drug Abuse, Inc. (IC&RC/AODA) defines the core function of consultation as follows:

"Consultation: Relating with our own and other professionals to assure comprehensive, quality care for the client."

The following supplemental expanded definition of "consultation" may be useful in helping you better understand this core function:

"Consultations are meetings for discussions, decision-making and planning. The most common consultation is the regular in-house staffing in which client cases are reviewed with other members of the treatment team. Consultations also can be conducted in individual sessions with the supervisor, other counselors, psychologists, physicians, probation officers and other service providers connected with the client's case."

I. Why and How We Consult with Others

A. Goals of consultation
1. provides a firmer foundation for comprehensive treatment of addictions
2. in concert with other professionals, the maximum benefit can accrue to the client
3. consultation meetings are for discussion, decision-making and planning

B. The most common type of consultation is the required in-house staff meeting during which cases are reviewed with other members of the treatment team

C. Meetings can also be with other counselors, psychologists, physicians, probation officers, educators and other service providers in connection with the client's case

II. The Benefits of Consultation

A. Counselor benefits by the experiences and education of other professionals in the field

B. Client benefits by additional input, information, and insight of other professionals applied to the treatment of his/her problems

III. Tasks: What to do when Seeking Consultation

A. Know your reason for seeking consultation

B. Decide on the best person to talk to

C. Obtain necessary Releases of Information

D. Think about the desired result of the consultation

E. Think about how you will utilize the information obtained

F. Document your conversations

References - Section 2

American Academy of Pediatrics (1988). *Substance abuse: A guide for health professionals.* Elk Grove Village, IL: Author.

American Psychiatric Association (1987). *Diagnostic and statistical manual of mental disorders* (Third Edition). Washington, DC: Author.

Basic Attending Skills, Leader Manual. Amherst, Massachusetts: Microtraining Associates, 1974.

Basic Influencing Skills, Participant Manual. Amherst, Massachusetts: Microtraining Associates, 1976.

Basic Influencing Skills, Leader Manual. Amherst, Massachusetts: Microtraining Associates, 1976.

Beattie, M. *Co-Dependent No More.* Center City, MN. Hazelden. 1987.

Black, C., Ph.D., MSW. *It Will Never Happen to Me.* Denver, CO. MAB Publishing. 1982.

Bramer, L. *The Helping Relationship.* Englewood Cliffs, New Jersey: Prentice-Hall, 1973.

Center for Substance Abuse Treatment (1993a, April). *Criminal justice treatment planning chart.* Rockville, MD: Author.

Center for Substance Abuse Treatment (1993b, April). *Juvenile justice treatment planning chart.* Rockville, MD: Author.

Cermak, T., M.D. Diagnosing and Treating Co-Dependence. Minneapolis, MN. Johnson Institute. 1988.

Corey, G., Corey Schneider, M., Callanan, P. *Group Techniques*; 3rd Edition. Belmont, CA. Wadsworth Publishing. 2004.

Corey, G. *Theory and Practice of Group Counseling*; 6th Edition. Belmont, CA. Wadsworth Publishing. 2003.

Crawford, J., Stancavage, F., and Jimenez, C. *Individual Counseling for Alcoholism Counselors, Participant's Manual.* Rockville, Maryland: National Institute on Alcoholism and Alcohol Abuse, 1975.

Crist, D.A., & Milby, J.B. (1990). Psychometric and neuro-psychological assessment. In W.D. Lerner & M. A. Barr (Eds.), *Handbook of hospital based substance abuse treatment.* New York: Pergamon Press.

Doweiko, H.E. (1990). *Concepts of chemical dependency.* Pacific Grove, CA: Brooks/Cole Publishing Company.

Ellenhorn, M.J., & Barceloux, D.G. (1988). *Medical toxicology-diagnosis and treatment of human poisonings.* New York: Elsevier Science Publishing Co.

Giannini, A.J., & Slaby, A.E. (1989). *Drugs of abuse.* Oradell, NJ: Medical Economics Books.

Gilman, A., & Goodman, I. (1985). *The pharmacological basis of therapeutics* (Seventh Edition). New York: MacMillan Publishing Co.

Grinspoon, L., & Bakalar, J.B. (1990). *Drug abuse and dependence* (Mental Health Review No. 1). Boston, MA: Harvard Medical School.

Hackney, H., and Nye, S. *Counseling Strategies and Objectives.* Englewood Cliffs, New Jersey: Prentice-Hall, 1973.

Haley, J. *Uncommon Therapy*, 2nd ed. New York, NY. Norton & Co. 1987.

Herdman, J. Global Criteria: The 12 Core Functions of the Substance Abuse Counselor. 3rd Edition. Lincoln, NE. Learning Publications. 2000.

Hoshino, J. (1992). Assessment of adolescent substance abuse. In G.W. Lawson & A.W. Lawson (Eds.), *Adolescent substance abuse: Etiology, treatment and prevention.* Gaithersburg, MD: Aspen Publishers, Inc.

Inciardi, J. (1993, in development). Screening and Assessment of Alcohol and Other Drug (AOD) Abusers in the Criminal Justice System (Treatment Improvement Protocol). Rockville, MD: Center for Substance Abuse Treatment.

Ivey, A., and Gluckstern, N. *Basic Attending Skills, Participant Manual.* Amherst, Massachusetts: Microtraining Associates, 1974.

Jackson, K.M. (1992, Winter). NIC/NASA project identifies promising technologies for corrections. *Large Jail Network Bulletin.*

Johnson, V. Intervention: How to Help Someone Who Doesn't Want Help. Minneapolis, MN. Johnson Institute. 1987

Julien, R.M. (1992). *A primer of drug action.* San Francisco: W.H. Freeman Co.

Kulewicz, S. *The Twelve Core Functions of a Counselor.* 4th Edition. Marlborough, CT. Counselor Publications. 1996.

McCabe, T., Ph.D. Victims No More. Center City, MN. Hazelden . 1978 .

McLellan, T., & Dembo, R. (1992). *Screening and assessment of alcohol- and other drug (AOD)-abusing adolescents* (Treatment Improvement Protocol 3). Rockville, MD: Center for Substance Abuse Treatment.

Miller, N.S. (1991). Special problems of the alcohol and multiple-drug dependent: Clinical interactions and detoxification. In R.J. Frances & S.I. Miller (Eds.), *Clinical textbook of addictive disorders.* New York: The Guilford Press.

National Institute on Alcohol Abuse and Alcoholism (1990, April). Screening for alcoholism. *Alcohol Alert.* U.S. Department of Health and Human Services.

National Institute on Alcohol Abuse and Alcoholism (1991, April). Assessing alcoholism. *Alcohol Alert.* U. S. Department of Health and Human Services.

National Task Force on Correctional Substance Abuse Strategies (1991). *Intervening with substance-abusing offenders: A framework for action.* Washington, DC: U.S. Department of Justice, National Institute of Corrections.

Nurco, D.N., Hanlon, T.E., & Kinlock, T.W. (1990, March). *Offenders, drugs, crime and Treatment: Literature review.* Washington, DC: U.S. Department of Justice, Bureau of Justice Assistance.

O'Brien, R., & Cohen, S. (1984). *Encyclopedia of drug abuse.* New York: Facts on File, Inc.

Okun, B. *Effective Helping: Interviewing & Counseling Techniques.* N. Scituate, Massachusetts: Duxbury Press, 1976.

Primm, B.J. (1992). Future outlook: Treatment improvement. In J.H. Lowinson, P. Ruiz, R.B. Millman & J.G. Langrod (Eds.), *Substance abuse: A comprehensive textbook* (Second Edition). Baltimore: Williams & Wilkins.

Project for Addiction Counselor Training. Internship: Counselor Workbook. Washington, D.C. 1991.

Schaefer, P.J. (1992). *Summaries of assessment instruments for identifying and diagnosing adolescent drug involvement.* Lexington, KY: American Probation and Parole Association (unpublished).

Schuckit, M.A. (1989). *Drug and alcohol abuse: A clinical guide to diagnosis and treatment.* New York: Plenum Medical Book Co.

Seixas, J., & Youcha, G. Children of Alcoholism: A Survivors Manual. New York, NY. William Morrow and Co. 1985.

Shertzer, B., and Stone, S. *Fundamentals of Counseling.* Boston: Houghton-Mifflin, 1968.

Singer, A. (1992). *Effective treatment for drug-involved offenders.* Newton, MA: Education Development Center, Inc.

Small, J. *Becoming Naturally Therapeutic: A Handbook on the Art of Counseling, with Special Application to Alcoholism Counselors.* Austin, Texas: Texas Commission on Alcoholism, 1974.

Straus, M., ed., Abuse, Victimization Across The Life Span. Baltimore, MD. The Johns Hopkins University Press. 1988.

Steinglass, P., M.D. The Alcoholic Family. New York, NY. Bouc Books. 1987.

Tarter, R.E., Ott, P.J., & Mezzich, A.C. (1991). Psychometric assessment. In R.J. Frances & S.I. Miller (Eds.), *Clinical textbook of addictive disorders.* New York: The Guilford Press.

Wegscheider, D. If Only My Family Understood Me. Center City, MN. Hazelden. 1979.

Wegscheider, S. Another Chance: Hope and Health for the Alcoholic Family. Palo Alto, CA. Science and Behavior Books. 1981.

Wegscheider-Cruse, S. Choice Making. Center City, MN. 1978.

Woititz, J., Ed.D. Adult Children of Alcoholics. Pompano Beach, FL. Health Communications. 1983.

Section 3, Chapter 1:
Psychological Based Therapies

Most of us have experienced a time or situation in our lives when we were dramatically helped by "talking things over" with a relative or friend. Such discussions usually resolve the need that many of us feel. Sometimes, however, such informal conversations fail to resolve certain types of conflicts. At such times, a more formalized therapeutic intervention may be needed.

Formal psychotherapy as practiced by a mental health professional shares many aspects in common with the more familiar informal experience. Most therapists, like all good listeners, rely on a common repertoire of receptiveness, warmth, empathy, and a nonjudgmental approach to the problems their clients present. Most, however, also introduce into the relationship certain psychological interventions that are designed to promote new understandings, behaviors, or both on the client's part. The fact that these interventions are deliberately planned and guided by certain theoretical preconceptions is what distinguishes professional therapy from more informal helping relationships.

Psychotherapy is based on the assumption that, even in cases where physical pathology is present, an individual's perceptions, evaluations, expectations, and coping strategies also play a role in the development of the disorder and will probably need to be changed if maximum benefit is to be realized. The belief that individuals with psychological or even chemical dependency problems can change - can learn more adaptive ways of perceiving, evaluating, and behaving - is the conviction underlying all psychotherapy. The goal of psychotherapy, then, is to make this belief a reality.

To achieve this goal, a trained psychotherapist may attempt a variety of strategies that can open new directions to the client so they can experience a more meaningful and fulfilling existence. Such strategies might include: (a) change maladaptive behavior patterns; (b) minimize or eliminate environmental conditions that may be causing or maintaining such behavior; (c) improve interpersonal and other competencies; (d) resolve handicapping or disabling conflicts among motives; (e) modify individuals' cognitions, their dysfunctional beliefs about themselves and their world; (f) reduce or remove discomforting, or disabling emotional reactions; and (g) foster a clear-cut sense of self-identify.

Achieving these changes is by no means easy. Sometimes an individual's distorted view of the world and unhealthy self-concept are the end products of faulty parent-child relationships reinforced by many years of life experiences. In other instances, inadequate occupational, marital, or social adjustment may require major changes in a person's life situation. With the problem of chemical dependency, many times it becomes an issue of which came first - did the drinking and drug using create the life problems, or did the life problems create the belief on the part of the individual that drinking or drugging would solve their problems, or at least make them feel better.

A significant problem in providing help to an individual exists in that it is often easier to hold to one's present problem filled but familiar lifestyle rather than to risk change and the unpredictability it brings with it. It would be too much to expect that a therapist, even a highly skilled and experienced one, could in a short time undo an individual's entire past history and prepare him or her to cope with a difficult life situation in a fully adequate manner. Therapists can offer no magical transformations for the realities in which people live their lives. Nevertheless, a well-formulated and executed plan of therapy holds promise in even the most severe of problems, and indeed for certain of them may provide the only realistic hope for significant and lasting life change.

It has been estimated that several hundred "therapeutic approaches" exist, ranging from psychoanalysis to Zen meditation. Indeed, the last few decades have witnessed a stream of "new therapies" - each winning avid proponents and followers for a time. The faddism in the popular literature on self-help and self-change might give the casual reader the idea that the entire field of psychotherapy is in constant flux. In reality, the professional field of psychotherapy has shown both considerable stability over time and coherence around a few basic orientations, albeit ones that vary appreciably in the "visions" they embody of the world and of human nature.

The field of chemical dependency services offers a significant challenge to using the more time-tested theoretical bases of change. Not all have easy application to the population. Others are more widely used and accepted. In order to help the counselor better know and understand what therapies are used, we will offer a broad review of many of the standard, well documented approaches to therapy. Immediately following, you will find an outline that references these therapies, providing a broad overview of "need to know" information. A more detailed review of "behavior therapy" follows the outline.

Many of the behavior approaches have greater application to the field of chemical dependency treatment. As a result, they are presented to assist the counselor in gaining greater understanding to their approaches and application. Finally, a quick review of each of the major theories ends our look at psychological based therapies. It is adapted from the work of Gerald Corey in his book *"Theory and Practice of Counseling and Psychotherapy,"* 6th Edition, 2000.

A. What is psychology?

1. Psychology is the study of people - understanding why they think, feel, and behave as they do
2. A branch of psychology studies personality
   a. Personality is defined as a unique and enduring set of psychological tendencies that a person reveals in the course of interacting with the environment
   b. Theories of personality have been developed to explain
      1) The consistency of an individual
      2) The difference between people
      3) The ability to adapt to the environment
3. Counseling theories are personality theories that are applied to help people
   a. There are several goals of the helping process
      1) Assessment of the problem
      2) Relationship development and maintenance
      3) Action to make the situation better
   b. The helping process involves
      1) Helping the individual understand his/her impact on others
      2) Learning new ways of thinking about a situation
      3) Learning new skills
      4) Experimenting with new ways of behaving
   c. Each counseling theory has a set of beliefs about people
      1) The action part of the helping process will be based on these beliefs
      2) Different beliefs will be more comfortable to different counselors

B. Psychodynamic Theory

1. Sigmund Freud was the founder of psychodynamic/psychoanalytic theory
2. View of person
   a. The mind is composed of three parts
      1) Id
         a) The collection of instincts and basic urges
         b) Wants immediate gratification regardless of consequences
         c) It is totally unconscious
      2) Ego
         a) The rational, reasoning part of the mind
         b) Deals with reality
         c) Negotiator between the wants of the id and the rules of the super ego
         d) Uses defense mechanisms to handle negotiations - it is partially conscious
      3) Super ego
         a) The conscience, ideals, rules - learned from parents and other adults
         b) Frequently in conflict with the id
         c) It is unconscious
   b. An individual is in constant battle between the id's desire for immediate gratification and the super ego's restraint
      1) The id always seeks pleasure
      2) The super ego seeks what it has been taught is right
      3) The ego tries to find a compromise
         a) Satisfy some of the id's desire for pleasure in a way that will not upset the super ego
         b) If this conflict between id and super ego is too great for the ego to handle, it resorts to using defense mechanisms
      4) All people use defense mechanisms some times
      5) They help keep the unacceptable thoughts and impulses from the awareness where they would have to be looked at by
         a) The individual
         b) Other people
         c) The counselor who will use the information to move along the progress of treatment by helping the individual understand the nature of the defense mechanism

c. The defense mechanisms are
1) Repression - forcing unacceptable thoughts and feelings from the conscious mind into the unconscious mind
   a) "Forget" it but still act from it because it is not resolved

   Example: The child may hate his/her parent for abuse during childhood, but the hate creates so much anxiety that the child pushes it out of his/her conscious mind so he/she is no longer anxious - but because the hate is not resolved, he/she acts with hostility toward the parent

   b) The client may show the counselor he/she has repressed feelings by behaving inappropriately, such as laughing when it is not appropriate

2) Projection - accusing others of motives and traits that the person senses are true about him/herself but he/she finds unacceptable

   Example: A client calmly describes to his counselor that his father physically abused him and then later in the session, for no apparent reason, asks if the counselor is angry with him, projecting his anger onto the counselor

3) Displacement - discomfort is created by one person but there is too much anxiety to talk directly with the person, so the individual takes out his/her feelings on someone or something less threatening

   Example: A parent reprimands the child unjustly but the child feels too threatened to correct the parent. He/she goes out to play and starts a fight with a friend over a trivial incident

4) Reaction formation - exchanging an unacceptable urge or feeling for a more acceptable one - often expressed in excess

   Example: A woman dislikes and resents her younger brother who is the family favorite - but to express these feelings may cause rejection by her parents, so she replaces these uncomfortable feelings and acts nauseatingly affectionate toward her brother

5) Regression - returning to more immature behavior that used to be satisfying - occurs more frequently when under extreme pressure

   Example: Under pressure to make a decision about continuing a difficult intimate relationship, a man sleeps away the day just as he did when he was a teenager

6) Rationalization - finding a satisfactory reason for doing something unacceptable

   Example: When a teenager shoplifts some clothes from a large department store, he/she tells him/herself the store can afford the loss, besides the clothes were over-priced

7) Intellectualization - understanding a difficult situation with the mind but not allowing any feelings about it

   Example: A woman calmly describes being sexually abused by her drunken father and explains to the counselor it was because her father had a disease - she cannot allow herself to feel the anger, hurt, and fear she feels toward her father because she feels she would fall apart

d. Freud's theory suggests that by the time a child is five years old, the personality is already formed
   1) The rest of life is an acting out of unresolved conflicts
   2) Solution is long term psychoanalysis during which conflicts are discovered and resolved
e. Each person develops through a series of stages, each with its own conflicts to resolve
   1) If there is no resolution to the conflict at a particular stage, the individual will remain stuck (fixated) there
   2) The only options available will be those related to that stage

      Example: A 25-year-old remaining emotionally at a 3-year-old level

C. Client-Centered Therapy

1. Carl Rogers was the Founder of client-centered therapy
2. View of the person
   a. A person is essentially good
   b. A person is capable of living a meaningful life
   c. An individual integrates experiences into a consistent picture of him/herself
   d. The self continually changes through the interaction of the person with the environment
   e. A person gets out of touch with him/herself and has impaired relationships when he/she places unrealistic demands on him/herself and denies feelings
   f. Each person has a natural healing ability so that in a safe environment, he/she can explore without fear of criticism
   g. As he/she learns more about him/herself, he/she will reorganize the picture of him/herself into a healthier, more fulfilling one
3. Goal of therapy - self healing through self-discovery and self-acceptance
4. Techniques of treatment
   a. The therapist creates a safe, accepting environment by expressing:
      1) Genuineness - the counselor is him/herself, not playing the role of therapist
         a) May involve self-disclosure and sharing
         b) As the counselor learns more about the client, it is easier for him/her to be genuine
      2) Empathy - the ability to feel with the client and sense what his/her world is like
         a) It is important to communicate this understanding of the client's feelings back to the client
         b) Empathy is expressed not only in words, but by tone and manner
         c) Counselor can often begin to empathize with the client by observing the client's nonverbal behavior
         d) Listening with empathy can be a therapeutic response to a sensitive issue a client shares with the counselor

3) Unconditional positive regard - shows respect and acceptance of the client without judgment
   a) This is communicated to the client by words and nonverbals but mostly in the way the counselor orients him/herself (general approach) to the client
   b) Being nonjudgmental is best communicated through nonverbal behavior
      (1) Uncrossed arms and legs indicating openness and lack of threat
      (2) No frowning or shocked looks at client disclosure
   b. The therapist does not interpret but reflects thoughts and feelings back to the client for further examination and clarification

Examples:

* Client: "I don't like people getting too close. When they do, I really get burned up."

Counselor: "You get mad when people get too personal."

* Client: "I've been having thoughts of drinking, possibly because my youngest son moved out last month. It's just me now; you know my wife died many years ago."

Counselor: "It seems to upset you to be thinking so much about drinking."

* Client: "It's awful to admit but I used to hit my wife, ignore the kids, and lie to my boss when I was drinking."

Counselor: "Sounds like you really regret having done these things."

* Client: "I didn't want to come here. There is nothing wrong with me. I only came to see you because my wife insisted."

Counselor: "Sounds like you feel resentful about being here."

* Client: "I'm afraid I influence his drinking...like he may drink because I bother him so much."

Counselor: "You worry that you may contribute to his drinking."

* Client: "I just can't tell my buddies that I don't drink anymore. You know, we spent a lot of time together at Joe's bar."

Counselor: "That sounds tough. You may feel guilty thinking that you're breaking a loyalty to them."

* Client: "My wife said she'd leave me if I resume drinking."

Counselor: "She's really serious about your sobriety."

D. Gestalt

1. Fritz Perls was the Founder of Gestalt therapy
2. View of the person
   a. A healthy person is one whose experiences form a meaningful and balanced pattern
   b. A healthy person continues to grow and experience genuine interactions with people, objects, and the environment
   c. A healthy person lives in the present, responsible for his/her own thoughts, feelings, and actions
   d. A healthy person accepts pain as well as pleasure
3. Goal of therapy - integration of experiences into a whole personality
4. Techniques of treatment
   a. The client actually does the changing and integrating
   b. The counselor acts as a catalyst to speed up the process
      1) Creates a safe, caring environment
      2) Provides a "here and now" challenge to speed up growth
         a) May be pointing out parallels between a client's interpersonal relationships and the client/counselor interaction
         b) May be analysis of dreams
         c) May be discussing something the client said
         d) May be focusing on body language

            Example: A female client regularly wears her coat and keeps her purse on her lap during sessions - she may be indicating she is mistrustful of people and very guarded in new relationships

c. The counselor designs exercises that force the client to experience rather than just talk about him/herself

d. The counselor acts as a guide and helps the client make appropriate choices that will integrate the self into a whole and help him/her interact more effectively with the environment

E. Rational-Emotive Therapy

1. Albert Ellis is a Founder of Rational-Emotive Therapy (R.E.T.)
2. View of the person
   a. Thinking and feeling are two processes but are closely linked together
      1) Event—>person's thoughts and feelings about event —>action
         a) The event does not cause the action
         b) The person's thoughts and feelings about the event cause the action
   b. In childhood, the person is taught to think and feel certain things about him/herself, others, and the world
      1) Then a judgment is placed on each thing
      2) A collection of these judgments becomes the person's belief system from which he/she experiences life
      3) Some belief systems are distorted because of irrational thinking

      Examples:

      * "Everyone must love me for me to be lovable."

      * "I must succeed at everything I do, or I am a failure."

      * "I must be capable in everything I do, or I am a failure."

      * If I become angry, no one will like me."

      * "If I am 'together,' I will never feel afraid.'"

3. Goal of therapy - teaching a client to analyze his/her belief system and correct the irrational distortions
4. Techniques of treatment
   a. The counselor engages in active dialogue with the client
   b. The counselor does not need to "feel" with the client, but needs to identify and understand the client's irrational beliefs

   Example:
   * Client: "I've ruined my chances with my son by drinking so much. He calls me, but I know he'll never forgive me. I could never make it up to him."

   Counselor: "His telephone calls seem to say that he really does care about you."

   c. The counselor creates new judgments that are rational (logical) based on data from the client's life

   1) The client is instructed to practice saying these messages so in time they will replace the old messages
   2) The client is instructed to practice new behaviors that act out the new messages and reinforce them

F. Reality Therapy

1. William Glasser is the Founder of Reality Therapy
2. View of the person
   a. A healthy person is a responsible person
   b. A healthy person satisfies his/her own needs: to love and be loved and to feel worthwhile
      1) Satisfaction occurs without harming others
      2) There is a sense of purpose in life and a connection with others
      3) Child is taught right from wrong

4) Problems occur when behavior, in trying to meet needs, is in conflict with this moral code
a) This behavior is irresponsible
b) Conflict causes unhappiness and leads to more difficulty in meeting needs
c) Conflict causes person to lose more contact with objective and moral reality
3. Goal of therapy - helping the individual get back in touch with objective and moral reality by making responsible choices
4. Techniques of treatment
a. The counselor establishes a warm, caring relationship with the client - the client must feel the counselor cares or the rest of the therapy will not progress
b. The counselor helps the client evaluate how successful his/her behavior is in meeting needs without harming anyone else
1) Little time is spent on past history because it leads to excuse making
2) Focus is on the present
c. The counselor teaches the client
1) What the objective and moral reality is
2) How to get one's needs met within reality because reality does not adapt to the individual
d. The counselor makes a plan for change and gets a commitment to it
1) The client learns to act responsibly which leads to increased self-worth
2) The counselor accepts no excuse for irresponsible behavior

Examples:
* Client: "I'm having a difficult time accepting responsibility for changing."

Counselor: "You're having a tough time deciding between..."

* Client: "When I was drinking a few years ago, I did something awful. I had sex with my 14-year-old daughter."

Counselor: "I'm not condoning what you did, but I'm willing to help you deal with it."

* Client: "How can I continue to stay sober when my wife keeps nagging me? And you'd think the guy at work could have the decency not to drink around me."

Counselor: "These situations sound tough even for a sober person. What are some ways to deal with them?"

G. Transactional Analysis

1. Eric Berne is the Founder of Transactional Analysis (T.A.)
2. View of the person
   a. Each person has three ego states that are continuously functioning
      1) Parent - a collection of unquestioned messages the person received while growing up: values, rules, and judgments and messages about self, others, and the world
         a) Acts as a conscience
         b) Similar to Freud's super ego
      2) Adult - information is processed without distortion because this state is rational and reality oriented
         a) Not influenced by the past
         b) Similar to Freud's ego
      3) Child - a collection of feelings, thoughts and behaviors that the individual experienced as a child (2 - 5 years old)

   b. These ego states interact with the ego states of another person
      1) This is a "transaction"
      2) Transactions can be complimentary - the sender gives a message in one ego state and it is received by a receiver in the same ego state

         Example:
         John: "Where are the intake forms, Jane?"

         Jane: "In the third drawer on the right."

      3) Transactions can be crossed - the sender gives a message in one ego state and it is received by a receiver in a different ego state

         Example:
         John: "Where are the intake forms, Jane?"

         Jane: "You should know by now that they are always kept in the third drawer on the right."

      4) Based on life experiences, a person develops one of four life positions from which he/she views him/herself, others, and the world.
         a) "I'm not OK - you're OK" - the infant initially feels this while realizing that most of the world and people in it are bigger than he/she is and he/she must depend on others for survival
            (1) With proper nurturing, the infant grows out of this life position
            (2) If an individual remains stuck in this position, he/she is a dependent person who feels helpless
         b) "I'm not OK - you're not OK"
            (1) Without enough nurturing, the child will come to view him/herself and others as bad
            (2) If the person becomes stuck here, he/she feels hopeless

       c) "I'm OK - you're not OK"
          (1) If a child does not receive enough nurturing, never develops trust, and may have been abused, he/she doesn't trust anyone
          (2) This is a position of survival
          (3) If the person remains stuck here, he/she will blame others for all that goes wrong and will not accept any responsibility
       d) "I'm OK - you're OK"
          (1) Is the result of a child receiving enough nurturing and having developed trust
          (2) Person is able to feel good about him/herself, and others and form successful interpersonal relationships
    5) All of the positions are unconscious, though, "I'm OK - you're OK" also has a component that is in the conscious awareness
  c. Some transactions develop into "games"
      1) A game is a complementary transaction of a short-term nature
      2) It maintains the relationship at a superficial level
      3) The players hide the real meaning of the interaction
      4) There is a payoff - the players gain something through the interaction, but they do not gain genuine intimacy
  d. Each person has a "script"
    1) A script is the theme of the person's life
      a) Developed in childhood
      b) Strongly influenced by parents and other important family members as well as childhood culture
      c) It contains the person's life choices and problems
    2) People act out these scripts through the games they play as well as through genuine encounters
3. Goal of therapy
  a. The goal is to identify the types of transactions in which the client participates
  b. The transactions are interpreted in light of the client's script
    1) Games are identified
    2) The client's role in the script is defined
    3) The client is helped to function from the rational adult position which is considered the healthiest place
4. Techniques of treatment
  a. The counselor analyzes the client's transaction in terms of his/her script - a diagram may be used to facilitate understanding
  b. The counselor identifies the script's theme and problems
  c. The counselor helps the client rewrite the script to become healthier and more representative of the person

H. Behaviorism

1. Pavlov is the name associated with classical conditioning - B.F. Skinner is the name associated with operant conditioning
2. View of the person
   a. Behaviorists are interested only in observable behavior, not the client's inner being
   b. All people are subject to "conditioning"
      1) Conditioning is learning a particular response to a certain stimulus
      2) Classical conditioning paradigm (model)
         a) An unconditioned stimulus leads to a specific response

            Example: food leads to salivation in dogs

         b) An unconditioned stimulus is paired with a conditioned stimulus
         c) Conditioned stimulus alone leads to response
   c. Operant conditioning – four types
      1) Positive reinforcement - a particular behavior is strengthened by the consequence of experiencing a positive condition
         a) Subject performs desired behavior
         b) Subject is rewarded by the addition of something they desire = positive reinforcement
         c) Subject will repeat behavior in hopes of getting another reward

            Example:
            A child has been struggling with schoolwork, resulting in low grades. The parent offers the child a monetary reward in return for getting good grades. The child brings home a report card with all A's and receives $5 for each A. The child's behavior of getting good grades is strengthened by the addition of the monetary reward.

2) Negative reinforcement - a particular behavior is strengthened by the consequence of stopping or avoiding a negative condition.
   a) Subject performs a desired behavior
   b) Subject is rewarded by subtraction of something they do not like = negative reinforcement
   c) Subject gradually displays new behavior in order to avoid consequence they don't like

   Example:
   A child brings home a report card with all grades of A. The parent, wanting to strengthen this behavior, rewards the child by removing all household chores for the next week. The child continues to strive for good grades in order to avoid doing household chores. The child's behavior of getting good grades is strengthened by the consequence of avoiding household chores.

3) Punishment - a particular behavior is weakened by the consequence of experiencing a negative condition.
   a) Subject has learned an undesirable behavior
   b) Subject is given an unpleasant stimulus
      (1) Consequence of giving the subject something undesirable
      (2) Consequence of removing something desirable
   c) Behavior tends to not be repeated to avoid unpleasantness = extinction

   Example:
   A child fails English at school. The parent responds by requiring the child to study an additional 2 hours each day until the grade is brought back to a passing level.

   Or, the child fails English at school. The parent responds by taking away their driving privilege for a period of one month.

   In either example, the child's behavior will be weakened as they strive to avoid the consequence of either having to do additional homework or restoring their driving privilege.

4) Extinction - a particular behavior is weakened by the consequence of not experiencing a positive condition or stopping a negative condition

Example:
A child brings home a report card with all A's and B's. The parent, expecting the child to always strive for good grade, does nothing to acknowledge the child's efforts. Neither a positive nor a negative condition exists for the child. During the next reporting period, the same thing happens. The child's behavior of striving for good grades is weakened by the consequence of not experiencing anything positive or stopping anything negative.

3. Goal of therapy - client learns new responses to old stimulus
4. Techniques of treatment
   a. The counselor discusses with the client what specific behavior the client wants to change - it is made clear about what new behavior is wanted
   b. Behavior modification
      1) Is clear and specific about what is rewarding = pleasant to the client
      2) When the desired behavior is performed, then, and only then, the client gets the reward
      3) Repetition eventually makes the desired behavior automatic
      4) May also include a punishment aspect
   c. Contracting
      1) The above behavior modification model can be formalized between the client and counselor into a contract
      2) All the details are carefully written out and both parties sign the contract
      3) Contracting prevents misunderstanding and can be used as a tool in confrontation when the client has broken the contract
      4) Some form of contracting, not necessarily for behavior modification, is often used with alcohol and drug dependent clients

    d. Systematic desensitization
        1) The client is taught a method to relax the mind and body
        2) A list of anxiety producing stimuli is decided upon and rated from least to most upsetting
        3) Desensitization works on the assumption that a person cannot be anxious and relaxed at the same time
            a) The client relaxes
            b) The client visualizes or imagines the first anxiety producing stimulus until he/she starts to feel anxious
            c) The client stops visualizing and relaxes
            d) The client repeats visualizing and relaxes until he/she is able to visualize the stimulus without becoming anxious
            e) Then the client repeats the process with the next more anxiety producing stimulus, through the entire list; at this point the stimulus should not cause any anxiety
    e. Modeling - client observes and mimics the counselor or another expert in the desired behavior

BEHAVIOR THERAPY

Although the use of conditioning techniques in therapy has a long history, it was not until the 1960s that behavior therapy, the use (as originally formulated) of therapeutic procedures based on the principles or respondent and operant conditioning, really came into its own. The major reason for the long delay was the dominant position of psychoanalysis in the field. In recent years, however, the therapeutic potentialities of behavior therapy techniques have been strikingly demonstrated in dealing with a wide variety of maladaptive behaviors, and literally thousands of research publications have dealt with the systematic application of behavior-change principles to modify maladaptive behavior.

In the behavioristic perspective, a maladjusted person (unless suffering from brain pathology) is seen as differing from other people only in (a) having failed to acquire competencies needed for coping with the problems of living, (b) having learned faulty reactions or coping patterns that are being maintained by some kind of reinforcement, or (c) both. Thus a behavior therapist specifies in advance the precise maladaptive behaviors to be modified and the adaptive behaviors to be achieved, as well as the specific learning principles or procedures to be used.

Instead of exploring past traumatic events or inner conflicts to bring about personality change, behavior therapists attempt to modify behavior directly by extinguishing or counter- conditioning maladaptive reactions, such as anxiety, or by manipulating environmental contingencies - that is, by the use of reward, suspension of reward, or, occasionally, punishment to shape overt actions. Indeed, for the strict behaviorist, "personality" does not exist except in the form of a collection of modifiable habits. Behavior therapy techniques seem especially effective in altering maladaptive behavior when a reinforcement is administered contiguous with a desired response, and when a person knows what is expected and why the reinforcement is given. The ultimate goal, of course, is not only to achieve the desired responses but to bring them under the control and self-monitoring of the individual.

Extinction

Because learned behavior patterns tend to weaken and disappear over time if they are not reinforced, often the simplest way to eliminate a maladaptive pattern is to remove the reinforcement for it. This is especially true in situations where maladaptive behavior has been reinforced unknowingly by others, an extremely common occurrence.

Billy, a 6-year-old first grader, was brought to a psychological clinic by his parents because he "hated school" and his teacher had told them that his showing-off behavior was disrupting the class and making him unpopular. It became apparent in observing Billy and his parents during the initial interview that both his mother and father were noncritical and approving of everything he did. After further assessment, a three-phase program of therapy was undertaken: a) the parents were helped to discriminate between showing-off behavior and appropriate behavior on Billy's part; b) the parents were instructed to show a loss of interest and attention when Billy engaged in showing-off behavior while continuing to show their approval of appropriate behavior; and c) Billy's teacher was instructed to ignore Billy, insofar as it was feasible, when he engaged in showing-off behavior, and to devote her attention at those times to children who were behaving more appropriately.

Although Billy's showing-off behavior in class increased during the first few days of this behavior therapy program, it diminished markedly thereafter when it was no longer reinforced by his parents and teacher. As his maladaptive behavior diminished, he was better accepted by his classmates, who, in turn, helped reinforce more appropriate behavior patterns and changed his negative attitude toward school. Billy's therapy, thus, was direct modification of his abnormal behavior, combined with changing the environmental reaction of his parents and teacher to the behavior.

Two techniques that rely on the principle of extinction are implosive therapy and flooding. Both focus on extinguishing the conditioned avoidance of anxiety-arousing stimuli and can thus be used to treat anxiety disorders. Accordingly, they are primarily Type A therapies in focusing on the modification of affect. The techniques are roughly similar, except that implosive therapy involves having a client imagine anxiety-arousing situations, usually with much coaching and dramaturgical hype provided by a therapist; flooding, on the other hand, involves inducing a client to undergo repeated exposures to his or her real-life anxiety-arousing situations.

In implosion, clients are asked to imagine and relive aversive scenes associated with their anxiety. However, instead of trying to banish anxiety from the treatment sessions, as in the older technique of systematic desensitization, a therapist deliberately attempts to elicit a massive "implosion" of anxiety. This is somewhat reminiscent of psychodynamic approaches because it often deals with past trauma and with an internal conceptualization of anxiety, though most traditional analysts would doubtless strongly disapprove of the procedure. With repeated exposure in a "safe" setting, the stimulus loses its power to elicit anxiety and the neurotic avoidance behavior is extinguished. Hypnosis or drugs may be used to enhance suggestibility under implosive therapy. The following is an example of implosive therapy:

> A young woman who could not swim and was terrified of water - particularly of sinking under the water. Although she knew it was irrational, she was so terrified of water that she wore a life preserver even when she took a bath. She was instructed by the therapist to imagine in minute detail taking a bath without a life preserver in a "bottomless" tub, and slipping under the water. Initially, the client showed intense anxiety, and the scene was repeated over and over. In addition, she was given a "homework" assignment in which she was asked to imagine herself drowning. Eventually, after imagining the worst and finding that nothing happened, her anxiety diminished. After the fourteenth therapy session, she was able to take baths without feelings of anxiety; the maladaptive behavior had been effectively extinguished. Implosion techniques are sometimes referred to as "in vitro desensitization."

Flooding, or "in vivo procedures," involve placing an individual in a real-life situation as opposed to a therapeutic setting, may be used with individuals who do not imagine scenes realistically. For example, a client with a phobia of heights may be taken to the top of a tall building or bridge. This is another means of exposing the client to the anxiety-eliciting stimulus and demonstrating that the feared consequences do not occur. In a study of clients with agoraphobia (fear of open spaces), prolonged exposure in vivo plainly proved superior to simple reliance on the imagination, and in the past few years the flooding procedure seems to have gained a definite ascendancy over that of implosion.

Reports on the effectiveness of implosive therapy and flooding have generally been favorable, and they may be considered the treatments of choice for simple phobias. Some investigators, however, have reported unfavorable as well as favorable results. These mixed results appear to be particularly true of flooding in vivo. In one case, the agoraphobic client "hid in a cellar out of fear of being sent into the street for 90 minutes by the therapist." On the other hand, the flooding procedure can be made relatively bearable without diminished effectiveness for even a severely fearful client by increasing therapist support and active guidance during exposure.

In general, it appears that while many clients respond favorably to implosion or flooding, some do not respond, and a few suffer an exacerbation of their phobias. This finding suggests a need for caution in the use of these techniques, particularly because they involve experiences that may be highly traumatic.

A modified form of flooding that involves repeated exposure to the somatic cues - "false alarms" - usually preceding panic (for example, heart palpitations), rather than to traumatizing situations themselves, may provide a key to circumventing undesirable reactions to exposure treatment. Accumulating evidence shows that it is these sorts of cues that in fact trigger full-blown anxiety attacks. Effective procedures for extinguishing this type of chain reaction teach clients to self-induce their false alarm symptoms repeatedly. In a recent study in which the exposure to anticipatory cues procedure was a centerpiece in a treatment package for panic disorder, effectiveness was demonstrated to be far superior to drug treatment with alprazolam (Xanax), a benzodiazepine compound touted as having strong antipanic properties.

Systematic Desensitization

The process of extinction can be applied to behavior that is positively reinforced or negatively reinforced. Of the two, behavior that is negatively reinforced - reinforced by the successful avoidance of a painful situation - is harder to deal with. Because an individual with negatively reinforced maladaptive behavior becomes anxious and withdraws at the first sign of the painful situation, he or she never gets a chance to find out whether the expected aversive consequences do in fact come about. In addition, the avoidance is anxiety-reducing and hence is itself reinforced.

One technique that has proven especially useful in extinguishing negatively reinforced behavior involves eliciting an antagonistic or competing response. Because it is difficult if not impossible to feel both pleasant and anxious at the same time, the method of systematic desensitization is aimed at teaching an individual to relax or behave in some other way that is inconsistent with anxiety while in the presence (real or imagined) of the anxiety-producing stimulus. The term systematic refers to the carefully graduated manner in which the person is exposed to the feared stimulus, the procedure opposite of implosion and flooding. It should be pointed out that systematic desensitization is not used exclusively to deal with avoidance behaviors brought about by negative reinforcement - that is, by successfully avoiding aversive experience. It can be used for other kinds of behavioral problems as well. In general, however, it is a therapeutic procedure aimed at anxiety reduction.

The following is a brief description of systematic desensitization. A client is first taught to induce a state of relaxation, typically by progressive concentration on the relaxing of various muscle groups. Meanwhile, in collaboration with the therapist, an "anxiety hierarchy" is constructed consisting of imagined scenes graded as to their capacity to elicit anxiety. For example, were the problem one of disabling sexual anxiety, a low-anxiety scene might be a candlelight dinner with the prospective partner, while a high-anxiety scene might be imagining the penis actually entering the vagina.

Following these preliminaries, active therapy sessions consist of repeatedly imagining the scenes in the hierarchy under conditions of deep relaxation, beginning with the minimum anxiety items and gradually working toward those rated in the more extreme ranges. A session is terminated at any point where the client reports experiencing significant anxiety, the next session resuming at a lower point in the hierarchy. Treatment continues until all items in the hierarchy can be tolerated without notable discomfort, at which point the client's real-life difficulties will typically have shown substantial improvement. The usual duration of a desensitization session is about 30 minutes, and the sessions are often given two to three times per week. The overall therapy program may, of course, take a number of weeks or even months. Even clients who have progressed only 25 to 50 percent of the way through their anxiety hierarchy show significant therapeutic gains, as evidenced by a marked reduction in specific avoidance behaviors when compared with their pretreatment levels.

Several variants of systematic desensitization have been devised. One variation involves the use of a tape recorder to enable a client to carry out the desensitization process at home. Another utilizes group desensitization procedures - as in "marathon" desensitization groups, in which the entire program is compressed into a few days of intensive treatment. One of the present authors routinely employs hypnosis to induce relaxation (the standard relaxation training can be quite tedious) and to achieve vividness in the imagining of hierarchy scenes. Perhaps the most important variation is in vivo desensitization, which is essentially similar to flooding but typically involves graduated exposure to the feared situations after a state of relaxation has been attained.

The truly essential element in the behavioral treatment of anxiety is repeated exposure of a client to the stimuli, even if only imaginarily, that elicit the fear response, regardless of the methods employed in achieving that end. Despite some continued wrangling among proponents of one or another specific procedure, that conclusion appears to be fair and accurate. Where a therapist has a choice - that is, dependent on client cooperation and tolerance - in vivo procedures seem to have an edge in efficiency and possibly in ultimate efficacy over those employing imagery as the mode of confrontation. Overall, the outcome record for exposure treatments is impressive.

Aversion Therapy

Aversion therapy involves modifying undesirable behavior by the old-fashioned method of punishment. Punishment may involve either the removal of desired reinforcers or the use of aversive stimuli, but the basic idea is to reduce the "temptation value" of stimuli that elicit undesirable behavior. The most commonly used aversive stimulus is electric shock, although drugs (such as Antabuse with alcoholics) may also be used. Punishment is rarely employed as the sole method of treatment.

Apparently the first formal use of aversion therapy was made by a physician named Kantorovich in 1930, who administered electric shocks to alcoholics in association with the sight, smell, and taste of alcohol. Since that time, aversion therapy has been used in the treatment of a wide range of maladaptive behaviors, including smoking, drinking, overeating, drug dependence, gambling, sexual variants, and bizarre psychotic behavior.

The use of electric shock as an aversive stimulus, however, has generally diminished in recent years because of the ethical and "image" problems involved in its use and because the new behaviors induced by it do not automatically generalize to other settings. Also, less dangerous and more effective procedures have been found. The method of choice today is probably differential reinforcement of other responses (DOR), in which behaviors incompatible with the undesired behavior are positively reinforced. For example, for a child who indulges in antisocial, destructive behavior, positive reinforcement might be used for every sign of constructive play. At the same time, any reinforcement that has been maintaining maladaptive behavior is removed. Even where there are reports of successful use of electric shock therapy, many clinicians recommend the use of nonpunitive treatment for self-injurious behavior.

Aversion therapy is primarily a way - often a very effective one - of stopping maladaptive responses for a period of time. With this interruption, an opportunity exists for substituting new behavior or for changing a life-style by encouraging more adaptive alternative patterns that will prove reinforcing in themselves. This point is particularly important because otherwise a client may simply refrain from maladaptive responses in "unsafe" therapy situations, where such behavior leads to immediate aversive results, but keep making them in "safe" real-life situations, where there is no fear of immediate discomfort. Also, there is little likelihood that a previously gratifying but maladaptive behavior pattern will be permanently relinquished unless alternative forms of gratification are learned during the aversion therapy. A therapist who believes it possible to "take away" something without "giving something back" is likely to be disappointed. This is an important point with regard to the treatment of addictions and paraphilias, one often not appreciated in otherwise well-designed treatment programs.

Modeling

Learning would be exceedingly laborious, not to mention hazardous, if people had to rely solely on the effects of their own actions to inform them what to do. Fortunately, most human behavior is learned observationally through modeling: from observing others one forms an idea of how new behaviors are performed, and on later occasions this coded information serves as a guide for action. Because people can learn from example what to do, at least in approximate form, before performing any behavior, they are spared needless error.

Although reinforcement of modeled behavior can influence whether an observer-learner attends to a model's actions and strengthens the response imitated, observational learning does not seem to require extrinsic reinforcement. Rather, reinforcement functions as a facilitative condition to learning. Anticipation of a reinforcement may also make an individual more likely to perform a behavior.

As the name implies, modeling involves the learning of skills through imitating another person, such as a parent or therapist, who performs the behavior. A client may be exposed to behaviors or roles in peers or therapists and encouraged to imitate the desired new behaviors. For example, modeling may be used to promote the learning of simple skills, such as self-feeding in a profoundly mentally retarded child, or more complex ones, such as being more effective in social situations for a shy, withdrawn adolescent.

Modeling and imitation are used in various forms of behavior therapy, especially in the treatment of phobias. For example, it has been found that live modeling of fearlessness combined with instruction and guided participation is the most effective desensitization treatment resulting in the elimination of snake phobias in over 90 percent of the cases treated.

Systematic Use of Reinforcement

Systematic programs involving the use of reinforcement to elicit and maintain effective behavior have achieved notable success, particularly in institutional settings. Response shaping, token economies, and behavioral contracting are among the most widely used of such techniques.

Response Shaping: Positive reinforcement is often used in response shaping; that is, in establishing by gradual approximation a response that is not initially in an individual's behavior repertoire. This technique has been used extensively in working with children's behavior problems. The following case is illustrative:

> An 8-year-old autistic boy lacked nominal verbal and social behavior. He did not eat properly, engaged in self-destructive behavior, such as banging his head and scratching his face, and manifested ungovernable tantrums. He had recently had a cataract operation, and required glasses for the development of normal vision. He refused to wear his glasses, however, and broke pair after pair.

> The technique of shaping was decided on to counteract the problem with his glasses. Initially, the boy was trained to expect a bit of candy or fruit at the sound of a toy noisemaker. Then training was begun with empty eyeglass frames. First the boy was reinforced with the candy or fruit for picking them up, then for holding them, then for carrying them around, then for bringing the frames closer to the eyes, and then for putting the empty frames on his head at any angle. Through successive approximations, the boy finally learned to wear his glasses up to twelve hours a day.

<u>Token Economies</u>: Approval and other intangible reinforcers may be ineffective in behavior therapy programs, especially those dealing with severely maladaptive behavior. In such instances, appropriate behaviors may be retarded with tangible reinforcers in the form of tokens that can later be exchanged for desired objects or privileges. In working with hospitalized schizophrenic clients, for example, using the commissary, listening to records, and going to movies were considered highly desirable activities by most clients. Consequently, these activities were chosen as reinforcers for socially appropriate behavior. To participate in any of them, a client had to earn a number of tokens by demonstrating appropriate ward behavior.

Token economies have been used to establish adaptive behaviors ranging from elementary responses, such as eating and making one's bed, to the daily performance of responsible hospital jobs. In the latter instance, the token economy resembles the outside world where an individual is paid for his or her work in tokens (money) that can later be exchanged for desired objects and activities. The use of tokens as reinforcers for appropriate behavior has a number of distinct advantages: (a) the number of tokens earned depends directly on the amount of desirable behavior shown; (b) tokens, like money in the outside world, may be made a general medium of currency in terms of what they will "purchase"; hence they are not readily subject to satiation and tend to maintain their incentive value; (c) tokens can reduce the delay that often occurs between appropriate performance and reinforcement; (d) the number of tokens earned and the way in which they are "spent" are largely up to the client; and (e) tokens tend to bridge the gap between the institutional environment and the demands and system of payment that will be encountered in the outside world.

The ultimate goal in token economies, as in other programs of extrinsic reinforcement, is not only to achieve desired responses but to bring such to a level where their adaptive consequences will be reinforcing in their own right - thus enabling natural rather than artificial rewards to maintain the desired behavior. For example, extrinsic reinforcers may be used initially to help children overcome reading difficulties, but once a child becomes proficient in reading, this skill will presumably provide intrinsic reinforcement as the child comes to enjoy reading for its own sake.

Although their effectiveness has been clearly demonstrated with chronic schizophrenic clients, mentally retarded residents in institutional settings, and children, the use of token economies has declined in recent years. In part, this decline is a result of budget-inspired reductions in trained hospital treatment staffs, which are required for the effective management of such programs. Ironically, the corollary excessive reliance on medication, which in our judgment has little likelihood of enhancing independent living skills, is probably far more expensive in the long run. Token economies are also poorly understood by lay persons, many of whom see them as inhumane or easily manipulative. If these people are "sick," so the thought goes, they should have medicine and not be expected to "perform" for simple amenities. Unfortunately, such thinking makes for chronic social disability.

Behavioral Contracting: A technique called behavioral contracting is used in some types of psychotherapy and behavior therapy to identify and agree on the behaviors that are to be changed and to maximize the probability that these changes will occur and be maintained. By definition, a contract is an agreement between two or more parties - such as a therapist and a client, a parent and a teenager, or a husband and a wife - that governs the nature of an exchange. The agreement, often in writing, specifies a client's obligations to change as well as the responsibilities of the other party to provide something the client wants in return such as tangible rewards, privileges, or therapeutic attention. Behavior therapists frequently make behavioral contracting an explicit focus of treatment, thus helping establish the treatment as a joint enterprise for which both parties have responsibility.

Behavioral contracting can facilitate therapy in several ways: (a) the structuring of the treatment relationship can be explicitly stated, giving the client a clear idea of each person's role in the treatment; (b) the actual responsibilities of the client are outlined and a system of rewards is built in for changed behavior; (c) the limitations of the treatment, in terms of the length and focus of the sessions, are specified; (d) by agreement, some behaviors (for example, the client's sexual orientation) may be eliminated from the treatment focus, thereby establishing the "appropriate content" of the treatment sessions; (e) clear treatment goals can be defined; and (f) criteria for determining success or failure in achieving these goals can be built in to the program.

Assertiveness Therapy

Assertiveness therapy or training has been used as an alternative to relaxation in the desensitization procedure and as a means of developing more effective coping techniques. It appears particularly useful in helping individuals who have difficulties in interpersonal interactions because of anxiety responses that may prevent them from speaking up, claiming their rights, or even from showing appropriate affection. Such inhibition may lead to continual inner turmoil, particularly if an individual feels strongly about a situation. Assertiveness therapy may also be indicated in cases where individuals consistently allow others to take advantage of them or maneuver them into uncomfortable situations.

Assertiveness is viewed as the open and appropriate expression of thoughts and feelings, with due regard to the rights of others. Assertiveness training programs typically follow stages in which the desired assertive behaviors are first practiced in a therapy setting. Then, guided by the therapist, the individual is encouraged to practice the new, more appropriately assertive behaviors in real-life situations. Often attention is focused on developing more effective interpersonal skills. For example, a client may learn to ask the other person such questions as "Is anything wrong? You don't seem to be your usual self today." Such questions put the focus on the other person without suggesting an aggressive or hostile intent on the part of the speaker. Each act of intentional assertion is believed to inhibit the anxiety associated with the situation and therefore to weaken the maladaptive anxiety. At the same time, it tends to foster more adaptive interpersonal behaviors.

Although assertiveness therapy is a highly useful procedure in certain types of situations, it does have limitations. For example, it is largely irrelevant for phobias involving nonpersonal stimuli. It may also be of little use in some types of interpersonal situations; for instance, if an individual has in fact been rejected by someone, assertive behavior may tend to aggravate rather than resolve the problem. However, in interpersonal situations where maladaptive anxiety can be traced to lack of self-assertiveness, this type of therapy appears particularly effective.

Biofeedback Treatment

For many years it was generally believed that voluntary control over physiological processes, such as heart rate, galvanic skin response, and blood pressure, was not possible. In the early 1960s, however, this view began to change. A number of investigators, aided by the development of sensitive electronic instruments that could accurately measure physiological responses, demonstrated that many of the processes formerly thought to be "involuntary" were modifiable by learning procedures - operant learning and classical conditioning (operant learning - form of learning in which a particular response is reinforced and becomes more likely to occur; classical [respondent] conditioning - basic form of learning in which a previously neutral stimulus comes to elicit a given response). For example, galvanic skin response could be conditioned by operant learning techniques.

The importance of the autonomic nervous system in the development of abnormal behavior has long been recognized. For example, autonomic arousal is an important factor in anxiety states. Thus many researchers have applied techniques developed in the autonomic conditioning studies in an attempt to modify the internal environment of troubled individuals to bring about more adaptive behavior - for instance, to modify heart rates in clients with irregular heartbeats, to treat stuttering by feeding back information on the electric potential of muscles in the speech apparatus, and to reduce lower-back pain and chronic headaches.

This treatment approach - in which a person is taught to influence his or her own physiological processes - is referred to as biofeedback. Several steps are typical in the process of biofeedback treatment: (a) monitoring the physiological response that is to be modified (perhaps blood pressure or skin temperature); (b) converting the information to a visual or auditory signal; and (c) providing a means of prompt feedback - indicating to a subject as rapidly as possible when the desired change is taking place. Given this feedback, the subject may then seek to reduce his or her emotionality, as by lowering the skin temperature. For the most part, biofeedback is oriented to reducing the reactivity of some organ system innervated by the autonomic nervous system - specifically, a physiological component of the anxiety response.

Biofeedback treatment is a popular treatment approach that requires the investment of capital to purchase complicated equipment and, in larger centers, a cadre of semiprofessional biofeedback technicians to perform the treatment. Whether its effectiveness justifies this expense is not an easily answered question. Although there is general agreement that many physiological processes can be regulated to some extent by learning, the application of biofeedback procedures to alter abnormal behavior has produced varied results.

The effects of biofeedback procedures are generally small and often do not generalize to situations outside the laboratory, where the biofeedback devices are not present. In addition, biofeedback has not been shown to be any more effective than relaxation training, leading to the suggestion that biofeedback may simply be a more elaborate (and usually more costly) means of teaching clients relaxation. As with almost any treatment procedure, however, a small percentage of clients may show an unusually good response with biofeedback.

Evaluation of Behavior Therapy

As compared with psychoanalytic and other psychotherapies, behavior therapy appears to have three distinct advantages. First, the treatment approach is precise. The target behaviors to be modified are specified, the methods to be used are clearly delineated, and the results can be readily evaluated. Second, the use of explicit learning principles is a sound basis for effective interventions as a result of their demonstrated scientific validity. Third, the economy of time and costs is quite good. Not surprisingly, then, the overall outcomes achieved with behavior therapy compare favorably with those of other approaches. Behavior therapy usually achieves results in a short period of time because it is generally directed to specific symptoms, leading to faster relief of an individual's distress and to lower financial costs. In addition, more people can be treated by a given therapist.

As with other approaches, the range of effectiveness of behavior therapy is not unlimited, and it works better with certain kinds of problems than with others. Generally speaking, the more pervasive and vaguely defined the client problem, the less likely is behavior therapy to be useful. For example, it appears to be only rarely employed to treat Axis II personality disorders, where specific symptoms are rare. On the other hand, behavioral techniques are the backbone of modern approaches to treating sexual dysfunctions. The meta-analysis of therapeutic outcomes confirms the expectation that behavior therapy has a particular place in the treatment of "neurotic" disorders, particularly where anxiety is a manifest feature, and therefore where the powerful Type A exposure techniques of behavior therapy can be brought to bear. Thus, although behavior therapy is not a cure-all, it has earned in a relatively brief period a highly respected place among the available psychosocial treatment approaches.

AN OVERVIEW OF PSYCHOLOGICAL THEORIES

Adapted from *"Theory and Practice of Counseling and Psychotherapy,"* **7th Edition, 2004, by Gerald Corey.**

PSYCHOANALYTIC THERAPY

Key Figure:
Sigmund Freud

Philosophy:
Human beings are basically determined by psychic energy and by early experiences. Unconscious motives and conflicts are central in present behavior. Irrational forces are strong: the person is driven by sexual and aggressive impulses. Early development is of critical importance, for later personality problems have roots in repressed childhood conflicts.

Key Concepts:
Normal personality development is based on successful resolution and integration of psychosexual stages of development. Faulty personality development is the result of inadequate resolution of some specific stage. Id, ego, and superego constitute the basis of personality structure. Anxiety is a result of repression of basic conflicts. Ego defenses are developed to control anxiety. Unconscious processes are centrally related to current behavior.

Goals of Therapy:
To make the unconscious conscious. To reconstruct the basic personality. To assist clients in reliving earlier experiences and working through repressed conflicts. Intellectual awareness.

The Therapeutic Relationship:
The therapist, or analyst, remains anonymous, and clients develop projections toward the analyst. Focus is on reducing the resistances that develop in working with transference and on establishing more rational control. Clients experience intensive, long-term analysis and engage in free association to uncover conflicts. They gain insight by talking. The analyst makes interpretations to teach them the meaning of current behavior as related to their past.

BEHAVIOR THERAPY

Key Figures:
B.F. Skinner; Arnold Lazarus

Philosophy:
Humans are shaped and determined by socio-cultural conditioning. The view is basically deterministic, in that behavior is seen as the product of learning and conditioning.

Key Concepts:
Focus is on overt behavior, precision in specifying goals of treatment, development of specific treatment plans, and objective evaluation of therapy outcomes. Therapy is based on the principles of learning theory. Normal behavior is learned through reinforcement and imitation. Abnormal behavior is the result of faulty learning. This approach stresses present behavior and has little concern for past history and origins of disorders.

Goals of Therapy:
To eliminate clients' maladaptive behavior patterns and help them learn constructive patterns. To change behavior. Specific goals are selected by the client. Broad goals are broken down into precise subgoals.

The Therapeutic Relationship:
The therapist is active and directive and functions as a teacher or trainer in helping clients learn more effective behavior. Clients must be active in the process and experiment with new behaviors. Whereas a personal relationship between them and the therapist is not highlighted, a good working relationship is the groundwork for implementing behavioral procedures.

RATIONAL-EMOTIVE THERAPY (RET)

Key Figure:
Albert Ellis

Philosophy:
Humans are born with potentials for rational thinking but also with tendencies toward crooked thinking. They tend to fall victim to irrational beliefs and to reindoctrinate themselves with these beliefs. Therapy is cognitive/ behavior/ action oriented and stresses thinking, judging, analyzing, doing, and redeciding. This model is didactic and directive. Therapy is a process of reeducation.

Key Concepts:
Neurosis is irrational thinking and behaving. Emotional disturbances are rooted in childhood but are perpetuated through reindoctrination in the now. A person's belief system is the cause of emotional problems. Thus, clients are challenged to examine the validity of certain beliefs. The scientific method is applied to everyday living.

Goals of Therapy:
To eliminate clients' self-defeating outlook on life and assist them in acquiring a more tolerant and rational view of life.

The Therapeutic Relationship:
The therapist functions as a teacher, and the client as a student. A personal relationship is not essential. Clients gain insight into their problems and then must practice actively in changing self-defeating behavior.

CLIENT-CENTERED (PERSON-CENTERED) THERAPY

Key Figure:
Carl Rogers

Philosophy:
The view of humans is positive; humans have an inclination toward becoming fully functioning. In the context of the therapeutic relationship the client experiences feelings that were previously denied to awareness. The client actualizes potential and moves toward increased awareness, spontaneity, trust in self, and inner directedness.

Key Concepts:
The client has the potential for becoming aware of problems and the means to resolve them. Faith is placed in the client's capacity for self-direction. Mental health is a congruence of ideal self and real self. Maladjustment is the result of a discrepancy between what one wants to be and what one is. Focus is on the present moment and on the experiencing and expressing of feelings.

Goals of Therapy:
To provide a safe climate conducive to clients' self-exploration, so that they can recognize blocks to growth and can experience aspects of self that were formerly denied or distorted. To enable them to move toward openness to experience, greater trust in self, willingness to be a process, and increased spontaneity and aliveness.

The Therapeutic Relationship:
The relationship is of primary importance. The qualities of the therapist, including genuineness, warmth, accurate empathy, respect, and permissiveness, as well as the communication of these attitudes to clients are stressed. They use this real relationship with the therapist for translating self- learning to other relationships.

GESTALT THERAPY

Key Figure:
Frederick (Fritz) Perls

Philosophy:
The person strives for wholeness and integration of thinking, feeling, and behaving. The view is antideterministic, in that the person is seen to have the capacity to recognize how earlier influences are related to present difficulties.

Key Concepts:
Focus is on the what and how of experiencing in the here and now to help clients accept their polarities. Key concepts include personal responsibility, unfinished business, avoiding, experiencing, and awareness of the now. Gestalt is an experiential therapy that stresses feelings and the influence of unfinished business on contemporary personality development.

Goals of Therapy:
To assist clients in gaining awareness of moment-to-moment experiencing. To challenge them to accept responsibility for internal support as opposed to depending on external support.

The Therapeutic Relationship:
The therapist does not interpret for clients but assists them in developing the means to make their own interpretations. They are expected to identify and work on unfinished business from the past that interferes with current functioning. They do so by re-experiencing past traumatic situations as though they were occurring in the present.

EXISTENTIAL THERAPY

Key Figures:
Viktor Frankl; Rollo May

Philosophy:
The central focus is on the nature of the human condition, which includes capacity for self-awareness, freedom of choice to decide one's fate, responsibility and freedom, anxiety as a basic element, the search for a unique meaning in a meaningless world, being alone and being in relation with others, finiteness, and death, and a self-actualization tendency.

Key Concepts:
Essentially an approach to counseling and therapy rather than a firm theoretical model, it stresses core human conditions. Normally personality development is based on the uniqueness of each individual. Sense of self develops from infancy. Self-determination and tendency toward growth are central ideas. Psychopathology is the result of failure to actualize human potential. Distinctions are made between "existential guilt" and "neurotic guilt" and between "existential anxiety" and "neurotic anxiety." Focus is on the present and on what one is becoming; that is, the approach has a future orientation. It stresses self-awareness before action. It is an experiential therapy.

Goals of Therapy:
To provide conditions for maximizing self-awareness and growth. Removal of blocks to fulfillment of personal potential. To help clients discover and use freedom of choice by expanding self-awareness. To enable them to be free and responsible for the direction of their own lives.

The Therapeutic Relationship:
The therapist's main tasks are to accurately grasp client's being-in-the-world and to establish a personal and authentic encounter with them. They discovery their own uniqueness in the relationship with the therapist. The human-to-human encounter, the presence of the client/therapist relationship, and the authenticity of the here-and-now encounter are stressed. Both the client and the therapist can be changed by the encounter.

TRANSACTIONAL ANALYSIS (TA)

Key Figure:
Eric Berne

Philosophy:
The person has potential for choice. What was once decided can be re-decided. Although the person may be a victim of early decisions and past scripting, self-defeating aspects can be changed with awareness.

Key Concepts:
Focus is on games played to avoid intimacy in transactions. The personality is made up of Parent, Adult, and Child. Clients are taught how to recognize which ego state they are functioning in with given transactions. Games, rackets, early decisions, scripting, and injunctions are key concepts.

Goals of Therapy:
To help clients become script-free, game-free, autonomous people capable of choosing how they want to be. To assist them in examining early decisions and making new decisions based on awareness.

The Therapeutic Relationship:
An equal relationship exists, with de-emphasis on the status of the therapist. The client contracts with the therapist for the specific changes desired - when the contract is completed, therapy is terminated. Transference and dependence on the therapist are de-emphasized.

REALITY THERAPY

Key Figure:
William Glasser

Philosophy:
The person has a need for identity and can develop either a "success identity" or a "failure identity." The approach is based on growth motivation and is antideterministic.

Key Concepts:
This approach rejects the medical model and its concept of mental illness. Focus is on what can be done now, and rejection of the past is a crucial variable. Value judgments and moral responsibility are stressed. Mental health is equated with acceptance of responsibility.

Goals of Therapy:
To guide clients toward learning realistic and responsible behavior and developing a success identity. To help them make value judgments about behavior and decide on a plan of action for change.

The Therapeutic Relationship:
The therapist's main task is to get involved with clients and encourage them to face reality and make a value judgment regarding present behavior. After clients decide on specific changes desired, plans are formulated, a commitment to follow through is established, and results are evaluated. Insight and attitude change are not deemed crucial.

ADLERIAN THERAPY

Key Figure:
Alfred Adler

Philosophy:
A positive view of human nature is stressed. Humans are motivated by social interest, by striving toward goals, and by dealing with the tasks of life. People are in control of their fate, not victims of it. Each person at an early age creates a unique style of life, which tends to remain relatively constant throughout life.

Key Concepts:
Based on a growth model, this approach emphasizes the individual's positive capacities to live in society cooperatively. It also stresses the unity of personality, the need to view people from their subjective perspective, and the importance of life goals that give direction to behavior. People are motivated by social interest and by finding goals to strive for. Therapy is a matter of providing encouragement and assisting clients in changing their cognitive perspective.

Goals of Therapy:
To challenge clients' basic premises and goals. To offer encouragement so they can develop socially useful goals. To change faulty motivation and help them feel equal to others.

The Therapeutic Relationship:
The emphasis is on joint responsibility, on mutually determining goals, on mutual trust and respect, and on equality. A cooperative relationship is manifested by a therapeutic contract. Focus is on examining lifestyle, which is expressed by the client's every action.

Section 3, Chapter 2:

Addressing Diverse Populations in Treatment

Treatment programs increasingly are called on to serve individuals with diverse backgrounds. Roughly one-third of the U.S. population belongs to an ethnic or racial minority group. More than 11 percent of Americans, the highest percentage in history, are now foreign born (Schmidley 2003).

Culture is important in substance abuse treatment because clients' experiences of culture precede and influence their clinical experience. Treatment setting, coping styles, social supports, stigma attached to substance use disorders, even whether an individual seeks help, all are influenced by a client's culture. Culture needs to be understood as a broad concept that refers to a shared set of beliefs, norms, and values among any group of people, whether based on ethnicity or on a shared affiliation and identity.

In this broad sense, substance abuse treatment professionals can be said to have a shared culture, based on the Western worldview and on the scientific method, with common beliefs about the relationships among the body, mind, and environment (Jezewski and Sotnik 2001). Treating a client from outside the prevailing United States culture involves understanding the client's culture and can entail mediating among U.S. culture, treatment culture, and the client's culture.

This chapter contains

- An introduction to current research that supports the need for individualized treatment that is sensitive to the client's culture
- Principles in the delivery of culturally competent treatment services
- Topics of special concern, including foreign-born clients, women from other cultures, and religious considerations
- Clinical implications of culturally competent treatment

- Sketches of diverse client populations, including
    - Hispanics/Latinos
    - African-Americans
    - Native Americans
    - Asian Americans and Pacific Islanders
    - Persons with HIV/AIDS
    - Lesbian, gay, and bisexual (LGB) populations
    - Persons with physical and cognitive disabilities
    - Rural populations
    - Homeless populations
    - Older adults
- Resources on culturally competent treatment for various populations

What It Means To Be a Culturally Competent Clinician

It is agreed widely in the health care field that an individual's culture is a critical factor to be considered in treatment. The Surgeon General's report, *Mental Health: Culture, Race, and Ethnicity,* states, "Substantive data from consumer and family self-reports, ethnic match, and ethnic-specific services outcome studies suggest that tailoring services to the specific needs of these [ethnic] groups will improve utilization and outcomes" (U.S. Department of Health and Human Services 2001, p. 36). The *Diagnostic and Statistical Manual of Mental Disorders*, Fifth Edition (DSM-5) (American Psychiatric Association 2013) calls on clinicians to understand how their relationship with the client is affected by cultural differences and sets up a framework for reviewing the effects of culture on each client.

Mental Health: Culture, Race, and Ethnicity is the first comprehensive report on the status of mental health treatment for minority groups in the United States. This report synthesizes research data from a variety of disciplines and concludes that

- Disparities in mental health services exist for racial and ethnic minorities. These groups face many barriers to availability, accessibility, and use of high-quality care.
- The gap between research and practice is worse for racial and ethnic minorities than for the general public, with problems evident in both research and practice settings. No ethnic-specific analyses have been done in any controlled clinical trials aimed at developing treatment guidelines.

- In clinical practice settings, racial and ethnic minorities are less likely than Whites to receive the best evidence-based treatment. (It is worth noting, however, that given the requirements established by funders and managed care, clients at publicly funded facilities are perhaps *more* likely than those at many private treatment facilities to receive evidence-based care.)

Because verbal communication and the therapeutic alliance are distinguishing features of treatment for both substance use and mental disorders, the issue of culture is significant for treatment in both fields. The therapeutic alliance should be informed by the clinician's understanding of the client's cultural identity, social supports, self-esteem, and reluctance about treatment resulting from social stigma. A common theme in culturally competent care is that the treatment provider — not the person seeking treatment — is responsible for ensuring that treatment is effective for diverse clients.

Meeting the needs of diverse clients involves two components: (1) understanding how to work with persons from different cultures and (2) understanding the specific culture of the person being served (Jezewski and Sotnik 2001). In this respect, being a culturally competent clinician differs little from being a responsible, caring clinician who looks past first impressions and stereotypes, treats clients with respect, expresses genuine interest in clients as individuals, keeps an open mind, asks questions of clients and other providers, and is willing to learn.

This chapter cannot provide a thorough discussion of attributes of people from various cultures and how to attune treatment to those attributes. The information in this chapter provides a starting point for exploring these important issues in depth. More detailed information on these groups, plus discussions of substance abuse treatment considerations, is found in the resources listed at the back of this chapter. The following resources may be especially helpful in understanding the broad concepts of cultural competence:

- *Mental Health: Culture, Race, and Ethnicity* (U.S. Department of Health and Human Services 2001) (www.mentalhealth.org/cre/default.asp). Chapter 2 discusses the ways in which culture influences mental disorders and mental health services. Subsequent chapters explain the historical and sociocultural context in which treatment occurs for four major groups — African-Americans, American Indians and Alaska Natives, Asian Americans and Pacific Islanders, and Hispanic/Latino Americans.
- The forthcoming TIP *Improving Cultural Competence in Substance Abuse Treatment* (CSAT forthcoming *a*) will include an in-service training guide.

Principles in Delivering Culturally Competent Services

The Commonwealth Fund Minority Health Survey found that 23 percent of African-Americans and 15 percent of Latinos felt that they would have received better treatment if they were of another race. Only 6 percent of Whites reported the same feelings (La Veist et al. 2000). Against this backdrop, it clearly is important for providers to have a genuine understanding of their clients from other cultures, as well as an awareness of how personal or professional biases may affect treatment.

Most counselors who provide treatment services are White and come from the dominant Western culture, but nearly half of clients seeking treatment are not White (Mulvey et al. 2003). This stark fact supports the argument that clinicians consider treatment in the context of culture. Counselors often feel that their own social values are the norm — that their values are typical of all cultures. In fact, U.S. culture differs from most other cultures in a number of ways. Clinicians and program staff members can benefit from learning about the major areas of difference and from understanding the common ways in which clients from other cultures may differ from the dominant U.S. culture.

Treatment Principles

Members of racial and ethnic groups are not uniform. Each group is highly heterogeneous and includes a diverse mix of immigrants, refugees, and multigenerational Americans who have vastly different histories, languages, spiritual practices, demographic patterns, and cultures (U.S. Department of Health and Human Services 2001).

For example, the cultural traits attributed to Hispanics/Latinos are at best generalizations that could lead to stereotyping and alienation of an individual client. Hispanics/Latinos are not a homogeneous group. For example, distinct Hispanic/Latino cultural groups — Cuban Americans, Puerto Rican Americans, Mexican Americans, and Central and South Americans — do not think and act alike on every issue. How recently immigration occurred, the country of origin, current place of residence, upbringing, education, religion, and income level shape the experiences and outlook of every individual who can be described as Hispanic/Latino.

Many people also have overlapping identities, with ties to multiple cultural and social groups in addition to their racial or ethnic group. For example, a Chinese American also may be Catholic, an older adult, and a Californian. This individual may identify more closely with other Catholics than with other Chinese Americans. Treatment providers need to be careful not to make facile assumptions about clients' culture and values based on race or ethnicity.

To avoid stereotyping, clinicians must remember that each client is an individual. Because culture is complex and not easily reduced to a simple description or formula, generalizing about a client's culture is a paradoxical practice. An observation that is accurate and helpful when applied to a large group of people may be misleading and harmful if applied to an individual. It is hoped that the utility of offering broad descriptions of cultural groups outweighs the potential misunderstandings. When using the information in this chapter, counselors need to find a balance between understanding clients in the context of their culture and seeing clients as merely an extension of their culture. Culture is only a starting point for exploring an individual's perceptions, values, and wishes. How strongly individuals share the dominant values of their culture varies and depends on numerous factors, including their education, socioeconomic status, and level of acculturation to U.S. society.

Differences in Worldview

A first step in mediating among various cultures in treatment is to understand the Anglo-American culture of the United States. When compared with much of the rest of the world, this culture is materialistic and competitive and places great value on individual achievement and on being oriented to the future. For many people in U.S. society, life is fast paced, compartmentalized, and organized around some combination of family and work, with spirituality and community assuming less importance.

Some examples of this worldview that differ from that of other cultures include

- **Holistic worldview.** Many cultures, such as Native-American and Asian cultures, view the world in a holistic sense; that is, they see all of nature, the animal world, the spiritual world, and the heavens as an intertwined whole. Becoming healthy involves more than just the individual and his or her family; it entails reconnecting with this larger universe.
- **Spirituality.** Spiritual beliefs and ceremonies often are central to clients from some cultural groups, including Hispanics/Latinos and American Indians. This spirituality should be recognized and considered during treatment. In programs for Native Americans, for example, integrating spiritual customs and rituals may enhance the relevance and acceptability of services.
- **Community orientation.** The Anglo-American culture assumes that treatment focuses on the individual and the individual's welfare. Many other cultures instead are oriented to the collective good of the group. For example, individual identity may be tied to one's forebears and descendants, with their welfare considered in making decisions. Asian-American and Native-American clients may care more about how the substance use disorder harms their family group than how they are affected as individuals.

- **Extended families.** The U.S. nuclear family consisting of parents and children is not what most other cultures mean by family. For many groups, family often means an extended family of relatives, including even close family friends. Programs need a flexible definition of family, accepting the family system as it is defined by the client.
- **Communication styles.** Cultural misunderstandings and communication problems between clients and clinicians may prevent clients from minority groups from using services and receiving appropriate care (U.S. Department of Health and Human Services 2001). Understanding manifest differences in culture, such as clothing, lifestyle, and food, is not crucial (with the exception of religious restrictions on dress and diet) to treating clients. It often is the invisible differences in expectations, values, goals, and communication styles that cause cultural differences to be misinterpreted as personal violations of trust or respect. However, one cannot know an individual's communication style or values based on that person's group affiliation.
- **Multidimensional learning styles.** The Anglo-American culture emphasizes learning through reading and teaching. This method sometimes is described as linear learning that focuses on reasoned facts. Other cultures, especially those with an oral tradition, do not believe that written information is more reliable, valid, and substantial than oral information. Instead, learning often comes through parables and stories that interweave emotion and narrative to communicate on several levels at once. The authority of the speaker may be more important than that of the message. Expressive, creative, and nonverbal interventions that are characteristic of a specific cultural group can be helpful in treatment. Cultures with this kind of rich oral tradition and learning pattern include Hispanics/Latinos, African-Americans, American Indians, and Pacific Islanders.

Common issues affecting the counselor-client relationship include the following:

- **Boundaries and authority issues.** Clients from other cultures often perceive the counselor as a person of authority. This may lead to the client's and counselor's having different ideas about how close the counselor-client relationship should be.
- **Respect and dignity.** For most cultures, particularly those that have been oppressed, being treated with respect and dignity is supremely important. The Anglo-American culture tends to be informal in how people are addressed; treating others in a friendly, informal way is considered respectful. Anglo Americans generally prefer casual, informal interactions even when newly acquainted. However, some other cultures view this informality as rudeness and disrespect. For example, some people feel disrespected at being addressed by their first names.

- **Attitudes toward help from counselors.** There are wide differences across cultures concerning whether people feel comfortable accepting help from professionals. Many cultures prefer to handle problems within the extended family. The clinician and client also may harbor different assumptions about what a clinician is supposed to do, how a client should act, and what causes illness (U.S. Department of Health and Human Services 2001).

Clinical Implications of Culturally Competent Treatment

Programs should take the following steps to ensure culturally competent treatment for their clients:

- Assess the program for policies and practices that might pose barriers to culturally competent treatment for diverse populations. Removing these barriers could entail something as simple as rearranging furniture to accommodate clients in wheelchairs or as involved as hiring a counselor who is from the same cultural group as the population the program serves. Section 2 provides more information about assessing program needs.
- Ensure that all program staff receives training about the meaning and benefits of cultural competence in general and about the specific cultural beliefs and practices of client populations that the program serves.
- Incorporate family and friends into treatment to support the client. Although family involvement is often a good idea in any program, it may be particularly effective given the importance of family in many cultures. Some clients left families and friends behind when they came to the United States. Helping these clients build support systems is critical.
- Provide program materials on audiotapes, in Braille, or in clients' first languages. All materials should be considerate to the culture of the clients being served.
- Ensure that client materials are written at an appropriate reading level. People who are homeless and those for whom English is a second language may need materials written at an elementary school reading level.
- Include a strong outreach component. People who are unfamiliar with U.S. culture may be unaware that substance abuse treatment is available or how to access it.
- Hire counselors and administrators and appoint board members from the diverse populations that the program serves. Section 2 provides more information about recruiting and hiring diverse staff members.
- Incorporate elements from the culture of the populations being served by the program (e.g., Native-American healing rituals or Talking Circles).

- Partner with agencies and groups that deliver community services to provide enhanced services, such as child care, transportation, medical screening and services, parenting classes, English-as-a-second-language classes, substance-free housing, and vocational assistance. These services may be necessary for some clients to be able to stay in treatment.
- Provide meals at the program facility. This may bring some clients (e.g., those who are elderly or homeless) into treatment and induce them to stay.
- Make case management services available for clients who need them.
- Emphasize structured programming, as opposed to open-ended discussion, in group therapy settings.
- Base treatment on clients' strengths. Experienced providers report that this approach works well with clients from many cultures and is the preferred approach for clients struggling with self-esteem or empowerment.
- Use a motivational framework for treatment, which seems to work well with clients from many cultures. Basic principles of respect and collaboration are the basis of a motivational approach, and these qualities are valued by most cultures.
- Encourage clients to participate in mutual-help programs to support their recovery. Although the mutual-help movement's roots are in White, Protestant, middle-class American culture, data show that members of minorities benefit from mutual-help programs to the same extent as do Whites (Tonigan 2003).

Sketches of Diverse Client Populations

The following demographic sketches focus on diverse clients who may be part of any treatment caseload. These descriptions characterize entire groups (e.g., number of people, geographic distribution, rates of substance use) and include generalized cultural characteristics of interest to the clinician. This type of cultural overview is only a starting point for understanding an individual. To serve adequately clients from the diverse groups described here, providers need to get to know their clients and educate themselves. Appendix A contains an annotated list of resources on cultural competence in general, as well as resources listed by population group. These resources include free publications available from government agencies — in particular the Center for Substance Abuse Treatment and the Center for Substance Abuse Prevention — and describe population-specific treatment guidelines and strategies.

Hispanics/Latinos

Hispanics/Latinos include individuals from North, Central, and South America, as well as the Caribbean. Hispanic people can be of any race, with forebears who may include American Indians, Spanish-speaking Caucasians, and people from Africa. Great disparities exist among these subgroups in education, economic status, and labor force participation. In 2002, the Hispanic/Latino population totaled 37.4 million, more than 13 percent of the total U.S. population, and it is now the largest ethnic group in the Nation. Mexican Americans are the largest subgroup, representing more than two-thirds of all Hispanics/Latinos in the United States (Ramirez and de la Cruz 2003).

Two-thirds of the Hispanic/Latino people in the United States were born here. As a group, they are the most urbanized ethnic population in the country. Although poverty rates for Hispanics/Latinos are high compared with those of Whites, by the third generation virtually no difference in income exists between Hispanic/Latino and non-Hispanic/Latino workers who have the same level of education (Bean et al. 2001).

Celebrations and religious ceremonies are an important part of the culture, and use of alcohol is expected and accepted in these celebrations and ceremonies. In the interest of family cohesion and harmony, traditional Hispanic/Latino families tend not to discuss or confront the alcohol problems of family members. Among Hispanics/Latinos with a perceived need for treatment of substance use disorders, 23 percent reported the need was unmet — nearly twice the number of Whites who reported unmet needs (Wells et al. 2001). Studies show that Hispanics/Latinos with substance use disorders receive less care and often must delay treatment, relative to White Americans (Wells et al. 2001). De La Rosa and White's (2001) review of the role social support systems play in substance use found that family pride and parental involvement are more influential among Hispanic/Latino youth than among White or African-American youth. The 2000 Substance Abuse and Mental Health Services Administration's (SAMHSA's) National Household Survey on Drug Abuse (NHSDA) found that nearly 40 percent of Hispanics/Latinos reported alcohol use. Five percent of Hispanics reported use of illicit substances, with the highest rate occurring among Puerto Ricans and the lowest rate among Cubans (Office of Applied Studies 2001). Hispanics/Latinos accounted for 9 percent of admissions to substance abuse treatment in 2000 (Office of Applied Studies 2002).

Spanish-language treatment groups are helpful for recently arrived Hispanic/Latino immigrants. Programs in areas with a large population of foreign-born Hispanics/Latinos should consider setting up such groups, using Spanish-speaking counselors. AA has Spanish-language meetings in many parts of the country, especially in urban areas.

African-Americans

African-Americans make up 13 percent of the U.S. population and include 36 million residents who identify themselves as Black, more than half of whom live in a metropolitan area (McKinnon 2003). The African-American population is extremely diverse, coming from many different cultures in Africa, Bermuda, Canada, the Caribbean, and South America. Most African-Americans share the experience of the U.S. history of slavery, institutionalized racism, and segregation (Brisbane 1998).

Foreign-born Africans living in America have had distinctly different experiences from U.S.-born African-Americans. As one demographer points out, "Foreign-born African-Americans and native-born African-Americans are becoming as different from each other as foreign-born and native-born Whites in terms of culture, social status, aspirations and how they think of themselves" (Fears 2002, p. A8). Nearly 8 percent of African-Americans are foreign born; many have grown up in countries with majority Black populations ruled by governments consisting of mostly Black Africans.

The 2000 NHSDA found that 34 percent of African-Americans reported alcohol use, compared with 51 percent of Whites and 40 percent of Hispanics/Latinos. Only 9 percent of African-American youth reported alcohol use, compared with at least 16 percent of White, Hispanic/Latino, and Native-American youth (Office of Applied Studies 2001). Six percent of African-Americans reported use of illicit substances, compared with 6 percent of Whites and 5 percent of Hispanics/Latinos (Office of Applied Studies 2001). African-Americans accounted for 24 percent of admissions to substance abuse treatment in 2000 (Office of Applied Studies 2002). Among African-Americans with a perceived need for substance abuse treatment, 25 percent reported the need was unmet — more than twice the number of Whites who reported unmet need (Wells et al. 2001).

Native Americans

The Bureau of Indian Affairs recognizes 562 different Native-American tribal entities. (The term "Native American" as it is used here encompasses American Indians and Alaska Natives.) Each tribe has unique customs, rituals, languages, beliefs about creation, and ceremonial practices. On the 2000 census, about 2.5 million Americans listed themselves as Native Americans and 1.6 million Americans listed themselves as at least partly Native American, accounting for 4.1 million people or 1.5 percent of the U.S. population (Ogunwole 2002).

Currently only 20 percent of American Indians and Alaska Natives live on reservations or trust lands where they have access to treatment from the Indian Health Service. More than half live in urban areas (Center for Substance Abuse Prevention 2001). The 2000 NHSDA found that 35 percent of Native Americans reported alcohol use. Thirteen percent of Native Americans reported use of illicit substances (Office of Applied Studies 2001). Among all youth ages 12 to 17, the use of illicit substances was most prevalent among Native Americans — 22 percent (Office of Applied Studies 2001). Native Americans begin using substances at higher rates and at a younger age than any other group (U.S. Government Office of Technology Assessment 1994). Native Americans accounted for 3 percent of admissions to substance abuse treatment in 2000 (Office of Applied Studies 2002). More than three-quarters of all Native-American admissions for substance use are due to alcohol. Alcoholism, often intergenerational, is a serious problem among Native Americans (CSAT 1999b). One study found that rates for alcohol dependence among Native Americans were higher than the U.S. average (Spicer et al. 2003) but not as high as often had been reported. Thirty percent of men in culturally distinct tribes from the Northern Plains and the Southwest were alcohol dependent, compared with the national average of 20 percent of men. Among the Northern Plains community, 20 percent of women were alcohol dependent, compared with the national average of 8.5 percent. Only 8.7 percent of all women in the Southwest were found to be alcohol dependent.

Among Native Americans, there is a movement toward using Native healing traditions and healers for the treatment of substance use disorders. Spiritually based healing is unique to each tribe or cultural group and is based on that culture's traditional ceremonies and practices.

Asian Americans and Pacific Islanders

Asian Americans and Pacific Islanders are the fastest growing minority group in the United States, making up more than 4 percent of the U.S. population and totaling more than 12 million. They account for more than one-quarter of the U.S. foreign-born population. The vast majority live in metropolitan areas (Reeves and Bennett 2003); more than half live in three States: California, New York, and Hawaii (Mok et al. 2003). Nearly 9 out of 10 Asian Americans either are foreign born or have at least one foreign-born parent (U.S. Census Bureau 2003). Asian Americans represent many distinct groups and have extremely diverse cultures, histories, and religions.

Pacific Islanders are peoples indigenous to thousands of islands in the Pacific Ocean. Pacific Islanders number about 874,000 or 0.3 percent of the population. Fifty-eight percent of these individuals reside in Hawaii and California (Grieco 2001).

Grouping Asian Americans and Pacific Islanders together can mask the social, cultural, linguistic, and psychological variations that exist among the many ethnic subgroups this category represents. Very little is known about interethnic differences in mental disorders, seeking help, and use of treatment services (U.S. Department of Health and Human Services 2001).

The 2000 NHSDA found that 28 percent of Asian Americans and Pacific Islanders reported alcohol use. Only 7 percent of adolescent Asian Americans and Pacific Islanders reported alcohol use, compared with at least 16 percent of White, Hispanic/Latino, and Native-American youth (Office of Applied Studies 2001). Three percent of Asian Americans and Pacific Islanders reported use of illicit substances (Office of Applied Studies 2001). As a group Asian Americans and Pacific Islanders have the lowest rate of illicit substance use, but significant intragroup differences exist. Koreans (7 percent) and Japanese (5 percent) use illicit substances at much greater rates than Chinese (1 percent) and Asian Indians (2 percent) (Office of Applied Studies 2001). Asian Americans and Pacific Islanders accounted for less than 1 percent of admissions to substance abuse treatment in 2000 (Office of Applied Studies 2002).

Persons With HIV/AIDS

In the United States, more than 918,000 people are reported as having AIDS (Centers for Disease Control and Prevention 2004). HIV is still largely a disease of men who have sex with men and people who inject drugs; these groups together account for nearly four-fifths of all cases of HIV/AIDS (Centers for Disease Control and Prevention 2004). Minorities have a much higher incidence of infection than does the general population. Although African-Americans make up only 13 percent of the U.S. population, they accounted for 50 percent of new HIV infections in 2004 (Centers for Disease Control and Prevention 2004). HIV is spreading most rapidly among women and adolescents. In 2000, females accounted for nearly half of new HIV cases reported among 13- to 24-year-olds. Among 13- to 19-year-olds, females accounted for more than 60 percent of new cases (Centers for Disease Control and Prevention 2002). HIV/AIDS is increasing rapidly among African-American and Hispanic/Latino women. Although they represent less than a quarter of U.S. women, these groups account for more than four-fifths of the AIDS cases reported among women; African-American women account for 64 percent of this total (Centers for Disease Control and Prevention 2004). Gay people who abuse substances also are at high risk because they are more likely to engage in risky sex after alcohol or drug use (Greenwood et al. 2001).

426

The development of new medications — and combinations of medications — has had a significant effect on the length and quality of life for many people who live with HIV/AIDS. However, these new treatment protocols require clients to take multiple medications on a complicated regimen. Clients with HIV often present with a cluster of problems, including poverty, indigence, homelessness, mental disorders, and other medical problems.

Lesbian, Gay, and Bisexual Clients

LGB individuals come from all cultural backgrounds, ethnicities, racial groups, and regions of the country. Cultural groups differ in how they view their LGB members. In Hispanic culture, matters of sexual orientation tend not to be discussed openly. LGB members of minority groups often find themselves targets of discrimination within their minority culture and of racism in the general culture.

Because of inconsistent research methods and instruments that do not ask about sexual orientation, no reliable information is available on the number of people who use substances among LGB individuals (CSAT 2001). Studies indicate, however, that LGB individuals are more likely to use alcohol and drugs, more likely to continue heavy drinking into later life, and less likely to abstain from using drugs than is the general population. They also are more likely to have used many drugs, including such drugs as Ecstasy, ketamine ("Special K"), amyl nitrite ("poppers"), and gamma hydroxybutyrate during raves and parties. These drugs affect judgment, which can increase risky sexual behavior and may lead to HIV/AIDS or hepatitis (Centers for Disease Control and Prevention 1995; Greenwood et al. 2001; Woody et al. 1999).

Persons With Physical and Cognitive Disabilities

Nearly one-sixth of all Americans (53 million) have a disability that limits their functioning. More than 30 percent of those with disabilities live below the poverty line and generally spend a large proportion of their incomes to meet their disability-related needs (LaPlante et al. 1996). Most people with disabilities can and want to work. But those with skills tend to be underemployed or unemployed. The combination of depression, pain, vocational difficulties, and functional limitations places people with physical disabilities at increased risk of substance use disorders (Hubbard et al. 1996).

Those with cognitive or physical disabilities are more likely than the general population to have a substance use disorder but less likely to receive effective treatment (Moore and Li 1998). Many community-based treatment programs do not currently meet the Federal requirements of the Americans with Disabilities Act. Any treatment program is likely to have clients who present with a variety of disabilities. Experienced clinicians report that an appreciable number of individuals with substance use disorders have unrecognized learning disabilities that can impede successful treatment. People who have the same disability may have differing functional capacities and limitations.

Treating substance use disorders in persons with disabilities is an emerging field of study. Culture brokering is a treatment approach that was developed to mediate between the culture of a foreign-born person and the health care culture of the United States. This model helps rehabilitation providers understand the role that culture plays in shaping the perception of disabilities and treatment (Jezewski and Sotnik 2001). Culture brokering is an extension of techniques that providers already practice, including assessment and problem solving.

Rural Populations

In 2000, nearly 20 percent of the U.S. population (55.4 million people) lived in nonmetropolitan areas; the nonmetropolitan population increased 10.2 percent from 1990 to 2000 (Perry and Mackun 2001). The economic base and ethnic diversity of these populations, not just their isolation, are critical factors. This population includes people of Anglo-European heritage in Appalachia and in farming and ranching communities of the Midwest and West, Hispanic/Latino migrant farm workers across the South, and Native Americans on reservations.

Despite this diversity, rural communities from different parts of the country have commonalities: low population density, limited access to goods and services, and considerable familiarity with other community members. People living in rural situations also share broad characteristics that affect treatment. These characteristics are

- Overall higher resistance to seeking help because of pride in self-sufficiency
- Concerns about confidentiality and resistance to participating in group work because in small communities "everyone knows everyone else"
- A sense of strong individuality and privacy, sometimes coupled with difficulty in expressing emotions
- A culturally embedded suspicion of treatment for substance use and mental disorders, although this varies widely by area

Among adults older than age 25, the rate of alcohol use is lower in rural areas than in metropolitan areas. But rates of heavy alcohol use among youth ages 12 to 17 in rural areas are almost double those seen in metropolitan areas (Office of Applied Studies 2001). Women in rural areas have higher rates of alcohol use and alcoholism than women in metropolitan areas (American Psychological Association 1999). However, in one study, urban residents received substance abuse treatment at more than double the rate of their rural counterparts (Metsch and McCoy 1999). Researchers attribute this disparity to the relative unavailability and unacceptability of substance abuse treatment in rural areas of the United States (Metsch and McCoy 1999).

Homeless Populations

Approximately 600,000 Americans are homeless on any given night. One census count of people who are homeless found about 41 percent were White, 40 percent were African- American, 11 percent were Hispanic, and 8 percent were Native American. Compared with all U.S. adults, people who are homeless are disproportionately African-American and Native American (Urban Institute et al. 1999). Homeless populations include groups of people who are

- **Transient.** These individuals may stay temporarily with others or have a living pattern that involves rotating among a group of friends, relatives, and acquaintances. These individuals are at high risk of suddenly finding themselves on the street. For some, continued living in other people's residences may be contingent on providing sex or drugs.
- **Recently displaced.** Some people may be employed but have been evicted from their homes. Their housing instability may be related to financial problems resulting from substance use.
- **Chronically homeless.** These individuals may have severe substance use and mental disorders and are difficult to attract into traditional treatment settings. Reaching these individuals requires the program to bring its services to the homeless through a variety of creative outreach and programming initiatives.

Approximately two-thirds of people who are homeless report having had an alcohol, drug, or mental disorder in the previous month (Urban Institute et al. 1999). Three-quarters of people who are homeless and need substance abuse treatment do not receive it (Magura et al. 2000). For 50 percent of people who are homeless and admitted to treatment, alcohol is the primary substance of abuse, followed by opioids (18 percent) and crack cocaine (17 percent) (Office of Applied Studies 2003*b*). Twenty-three percent of people who are homeless and in treatment have co-occurring disorders, compared with 20 percent who are not homeless (Office of Applied Studies 2003*b*). People who are homeless are more than three times as likely to receive detoxification services as people who are not homeless (45 percent vs. 14 percent) (Office of Applied Studies 2003*b*).

In addition to the resources found in Appendix A, the following clinical guidelines will assist providers in treating people who are homeless:

- Clients who are homeless often drop out of treatment early. Meeting survival needs of clients who are homeless is integral to successful outcomes. A treatment program needs to provide safe shelter, warmth, and food, in addition to the components of effective treatment provided to other clients who use substances, including extensive continuing care (Milby et al. 1996).
- Individuals who are homeless benefit from intensive contact early in treatment. Clients who attend treatment an average of 4.1 days per week are more successful than those attending fewer days (Schumacher et al. 1995).
- The Alcohol Dependence Scale, the Alcohol Severity Index, and the personal history form have been found to be reliable and valid screening tools for this population (Joyner et al. 1996). Reliability is higher when items are factual and based on a recent time interval and when individuals are interviewed in a protected setting.
- Case management must be available to ease access to and coordinate the variety of services needed by clients who are homeless and abuse substances. Case management should arrange for stable, safe, and drug-free housing. The availability of housing is a powerful influence on recovery. Making such housing contingent on abstinence has been shown to be a useful strategy (Milby et al. 1996). Case management also should coordinate medical care, including psychiatric care, with vocational training and education to help individuals sustain a self-sufficient life.
- Providers should work with homeless shelters to provide treatment services. Strategies include (1) working with staff members at shelters and with public housing authorities to find and arrange for housing, (2) locating the program within a homeless shelter or at least providing core elements of treatment at the shelter, and (3) placing a substance abuse treatment specialist at the shelter as a liaison with the program.

Older Adults

The number of older adults needing treatment for substance use disorders is expected to increase from 1.7 million in 2001 to 4.4 million by 2020. This increase is the result of a projected 50-percent increase in the number of older adults as well as a 70-percent increase in the rate of treatment need among older adults (Gfroerer et al. 2003). America's aging cohort of baby boomers (people born between 1946 and 1964) is expected to place increasing demands on the substance abuse treatment system in the coming years, requiring a shift in focus to address their special needs. This older generation will be more ethnically and racially diverse and have higher substance use and dependence rates than current older adults (Korper and Council 2002).

As a group, older people tend to feel shame about substance use and are reluctant to seek out treatment. Many relatives of older individuals with substance use disorders also are ashamed of the problem and rationalize the substance use or choose not to address it. Diagnosing and treating substance use disorders are more complex in older adults than in other populations because older people have more — and more interconnected — physical and mental health problems. Barriers to effective treatment include lack of transportation, shrinking social support networks, and financial constraints.

Oslin and colleagues (2002) find that older adults had greater attendance and lower incidence of relapse than younger adults in treatment and conclude that older adults can be treated successfully in mixed-age groups, provided that they receive age-appropriate individual treatment. When treating older clients, programs need to be involved actively with the local network of aging services, including home- and community-based long-term care providers. Older individuals who do not see themselves as abusers — particularly those who misuse over-the-counter or prescription drugs or do not understand the problems caused by alcohol and drug interactions — need to be reached through wellness, health promotion, social service, and other settings that serve older adults. In addition, programs can broaden the multicultural resources available to them by working through the aging service network to link up with diverse language, cultural, and ethnic resources in the community.

Programs that develop geriatric expertise can provide an essential service by making consultation available to staff members at programs that face similar challenges, along with in-service training, coordination of interventions, and care conferences designed to solve problems and develop care plans for individuals. There also may be opportunities to make this expertise available to caregivers and participants in settings where older adults receive interdisciplinary care (e.g., a support group for family caregivers or a discussion group for participants at a social daycare or adult day health center).

Exhibit 1. Glossary of Cultural Competence Terms

Cultural diversity. Differences in race, ethnicity, nationality, religion, gender, sexual identity, socioeconomic status, physical ability, language, beliefs, behavior patterns, or customs among various groups within a community, organization, or nation.

Culture. Social norms and responses that condition the behavior of a group of people; that answer life's basic questions about the origin and nature of things; and that solve life's basic problems of human survival and development.

Discrimination. The act of treating a person, issue, or behavior unjustly or inequitably as a result of prejudices; a showing of partiality or prejudice in treatment; specific actions or policies directed against the welfare of minority groups.

Ethnicity. The beliefs, values, customs, or practices of a specific group (e.g., its characteristics, language, common history, and national origin). Every race has a variety of ethnic groups.

Ethnocentrism. The attitude that the beliefs, customs, or practices of one's own ethnic group, nation, or culture are superior; an excessive or inappropriate concern for racial matters.

Multiculturalism. Being comfortable with many standards and customs; the ability to adapt behavior and judgments to a variety of interpersonal settings.

Prejudice. Preconceived judgments, opinions, or assumptions formed without knowledge or examination of facts about individuals, groups of people, behaviors, or issues. These judgments or opinions usually are unfavorable and are marked by suspicion, fear, or hatred.

Race. The categorizing of major groups of people based solely on physical features that distinguish certain groups from others.

Adapted from Administration for Children and Families 1994, pp. 108–109.

Exhibit 2. Stages of Cultural Competence for Organizations

Stage 1. Cultural Destructiveness

• Makes people fit the same cultural pattern; excludes those who do not fit (forced assimilation).

• Uses differences as barriers.

Stage 2. Cultural Incapacity

• Supports segregation as a desirable policy, enforces racial policies, and maintains stereotypes.

• Maintains a paternalistic posture toward "lesser races" (e.g., discriminatory hiring practices, lower expectations of minority clients, and subtle messages that they are not valued).

• Discriminates based on whether members of diverse groups "know their place."

• Lacks the capacity or will to help minority clients in the community.

• Applies resources unfairly.

Stage 3. Cultural Blindness

• Believes that color or culture makes no difference and that all people are the same.

• Ignores cultural strengths.

• Encourages assimilation; isolates those who do not assimilate.

• Blames victims for their problems.

• Views ethnic minorities as culturally deprived.

Stage 4. Cultural Precompetence

• Desires to deliver quality services; has commitment to civil rights.

• Realizes its weaknesses; attempts to improve some aspect of services.

• Explores how to serve minority communities better.

• Often lacks only information on possibilities and how to proceed.

• May believe that accomplishment of one goal or activity fulfills obligations to minority communities; may engage in token hiring practices.

Stage 5. Cultural Competence

• Shows acceptance of and respect for differences.

• Expands cultural knowledge and resources.

• Provides continuous self-assessment.

• Pays attention to the dynamics of difference to meet client needs better.

• Adapts service models to needs.

• Seeks advice and consultation from minority communities.

• Is committed to policies that enhance services to diverse clientele.

Stage 6. Cultural Proficiency

• Holds all cultures in high esteem.

• Seeks to add to knowledge base.

• Advocates continuously for cultural competence.

Source: Cross et al. 1989, pp. 13–18.

Cultural Competence Resources

Many resources listed below are volumes in the TIP and Technical Assistance Publication (TAP) Series published by CSAT. TIPs and TAPs are free and can be ordered from SAMHSA's National Clearinghouse for Alcohol and Drug Information (NCADI) at www.ncadi.samhsa.gov or (800) 729–6686 (TDD, [800] 487–4889). The full text of each TIP can be searched and downloaded from www.samhsa.gov/centers/csat2002/publications.html.

The Health Resources and Services Administration lists cultural competence assessment tools, resources, curricula, and Web-based trainings at www.hrsa.gov/culturalcompetence.

General

Cultural Issues in Substance Abuse Treatment (CSAT 1999*b*) — This booklet contains population-specific discussions of treatment for Hispanic Americans, African-Americans, Asian Americans and Pacific Islanders, and American Indians and Alaska Natives, along with general guidelines on cultural competence. Order from SAMHSA's NCADI.

Chapter 4, "Preparing a Program To Treat Diverse Clients," in TIP 46, *Substance Abuse: Administrative Issues in Outpatient Treatment* (CSAT 2006*f*) — This chapter includes an introduction to cultural competence and why it matters to treatment programs, as well as information on assessing a diverse population's treatment needs and conducting outreach to attract clients and involve the community. This chapter also includes a list of resources for assessment and training, in addition to culture-specific resources.

"Alcohol Use Among Special Populations" (National Institute on Alcohol Abuse and Alcoholism 1998) — This special issue of the journal *Alcohol Health & Research World* (now called *Alcohol Research & Health*) includes articles on alcohol use in Asian Americans and Pacific Islanders, African-Americans, Alaska Natives, Native Americans, and Hispanics/Latinos. Authors also address such topics as alcohol availability and advertising in minority communities, special populations in AA, and alcohol consumption in India, Mexico, and Nigeria. Visit pubs.niaaa.nih.gov/publications/arh22-4/toc22-4.htm to download the articles.

Mental Health: Culture, Race, and Ethnicity (U.S. Department of Health and Human Services 2001) — This publication describes the disparities in mental health services that affect minorities, presents evidence of the need to address those disparities, and documents promising strategies to eliminate them. Visit www.mentalhealth.samhsa.gov/cre/default.asp to download a copy of this publication.

Counseling the Culturally Different: Theory and Practice, Third Edition (Sue and Sue 1999) — This book offers a conceptual framework for counseling across cultural lines and includes treatment recommendations for specific cultural groups, with individual chapters on counseling Hispanics/Latinos, African-Americans, Asian Americans, and Native Americans and special sections on women, gay and lesbian people, and persons who are elderly and disabled.

The Cultural Context of Health, Illness, and Medicine (Loustaunau and Sobo 1997) — This book, written by a sociologist and an anthropologist, examines the ways in which cultural and social factors shape understandings of health and medicine. Although its discussions are not specific to substance abuse, they address the effect of social structures on health, differing conceptions of wellness, and cross-cultural communication.

Pocket Guide to Cultural Health Assessment, Third Edition (D'Avanzo and Geissler 2003) — This quick reference guide has individual sections on 186 countries, each of which lists demographic information (e.g., population, ethnic and religious descriptions, languages spoken), political and social information, and health care beliefs.

American Cultural Patterns: A Cross-Cultural Perspective, Second Edition (Stewart and Bennett 1991) — This book focuses on aspects of American culture that are central to understanding how American society functions. The authors examine perceptions, thought processes, language, and nonverbal behaviors and their effect on cross-cultural communication.

Hispanics/Latinos

CSAP Substance Abuse Resource Guide: Hispanic/Latino Americans (Center for Substance Abuse Prevention 1996*b* ; www.ncadi.samhsa.gov/govpubs/MS441/) — This resource guide provides information and referrals to help prevention specialists, educators, and community leaders better meet the needs of the Hispanic/Latino community. Order from SAMHSA's NCADI.

"Counseling Latino Alcohol and Other Substance Users/Abusers: Cultural Considerations for Counselors" (Gloria and Peregoy 1996) — This article discusses Hispanic/Latino cultural values as they relate to substance use and presents a substance abuse counseling model for use with Hispanic/Latino clients.

"Drugs and Substances: Views From a Latino Community" (Hadjicostandi and Cheurprakobkit 2002) — The researchers explore perceptions and use of licit and illicit substances in a Hispanic/Latino community. The primary concerns of the community are the increasing availability and use of substances among Hispanic/Latino youth.

"Acculturation and Latino Adolescents' Substance Use: A Research Agenda for the Future" (De La Rosa 2002) — This article reviews literature on the effects of acculturation to Western values on Hispanic/Latino adolescents' mental health and substance use, discusses the role that acculturation-related stress plays in substance use, and suggests directions for treatment and further research.

"Cultural Adaptations of Alcoholics Anonymous To Serve Hispanic Populations" (Hoffman 1994) — This article evaluates two specific adaptations to 12-Step fellowship: one adapts conceptions of machismo and the other is less confrontational.

African-Americans

Chemical Dependency and the African American: Counseling and Prevention Strategies, Second Edition (Bell 2002) — This book from the co-founder of the Institute on Black Chemical Abuse explores the dynamics of race, culture, and class in treatment and examines substance abuse and recovery in the context of racial identity.

Cultural Competence for Health Care Professionals Working With African-American Communities: Theory and Practice (Center for Substance Abuse Prevention 1998a) — This book provides tips for health care workers. Order from SAMHSA's NCADI or download at www.hawaii.edu/hivandaids/links.htm.

Relapse Prevention Counseling for African Americans: A Culturally Specific Model (Williams and Gorski 1997) — This book examines the way that cultural factors interact with relapse prevention efforts in African-Americans.

Native Americans

Health Promotion and Substance Abuse Prevention Among American Indian and Alaska Native Communities: Issues in Cultural Competence (Center for Substance Abuse Prevention 2001) — This volume frames the development of substance abuse prevention and treatment efforts in the context of health disparities that have affected Native-American and Alaskan-Native communities in rural and urban settings, as well as on reservations. Grounded in traditional healing practices, the volume examines innovative approaches to substance abuse prevention. Order from SAMHSA's NCADI.

Substance Abuse Resource Guide: American Indians and Native Alaskans (Center for Substance Abuse Prevention 1998b) — A substance abuse resource guide for American Indians and Alaska Natives, including books, articles, classroom materials, posters, and Web sites. Order from SAMHSA's NCADI.

Promising Practices and Strategies To Reduce Alcohol and Substance Abuse Among American Indians and Alaska Natives (American Indian Development Associates 2000) — This report collects descriptions of successful substance abuse prevention efforts by Native-American groups. It also includes a literature review and list of Federal resources. Visit www.ojp.usdoj.gov/americannative/promise.pdf to download the report.

"Morning Star Rising: Healing in Native American Communities" (Nebelkopf et al. 2003) — This special issue of the *Journal of Psychoactive Drugs* is devoted to healing in Native-American communities, with 13 articles on various aspects of prevention and treatment. Contact Haight-Ashbury Publications at (415) 565–1904.

Walking the Same Land — This videotape presents young Indians who are returning to traditional cultural ways to strengthen their recovery from substance abuse. It includes aboriginal men from Australia and Mohawk men from New York. Order from SAMHSA's NCADI.

Asian Americans and Pacific Islanders

Asian and Pacific Islander American Health Forum (www.apiahf.org/resources/index.htm) — This site provides links to information and resources.

Asian Community Mental Health Services (www.acmhs.org) — This site provides links to information and describes a substance abuse treatment program in Oakland, California.

Substance Abuse Resource Guide: Asian and Pacific Islander Americans (Center for Substance Abuse Prevention 1996*a*; www.ncadi.samhsa.gov/govpubs/MS408) — This guide contains resources appropriate for use in Asian and Pacific Islander communities. It also contains facts and figures about substance use and prevention within this diverse group.

Responding to Pacific Islanders: Culturally Competent Perspectives for Substance Abuse Prevention (Center for Substance Abuse Prevention 1999) — This book examines the culture-specific factors that affect substance abuse prevention in Pacific Islander communities. Order from SAMHSA's NCADI.

"Communicating Appropriately With Asian and Pacific Islander Audiences" (Center for Substance Abuse Prevention 1997) — This *Technical Assistance Bulletin* discusses population characteristics, lists cultural factors related to substance use in nine distinct ethnic groups, and presents guidelines on developing effective prevention materials for these populations. Visit www.ncadi.samhsa.gov/govpubs/MS701 to download the bulletin.

Opening Doors: Techniques for Talking With Southeast Asian Clients About Alcohol and Other Drug Issues — This program is available on videocassette in Vietnamese and Khmer with English subtitles. Order from SAMHSA's NCADI, and visit http://ncadistore.samhsa.gov/catalog/productDetails.aspx?ProductID=15136 to view it on the Web.

Persons With HIV/AIDS

TIP 37, *Substance Abuse Treatment for Persons With HIV/AIDS* (CSAT 2000*c*) — This TIP discusses the medical aspects of HIV/AIDS (epidemiological data, assessment, treatment, and prevention), the legal and ethical implications of treatment, the counseling of patients with HIV/AIDS, the integration of treatment and enhanced services, and funding sources for programs.

The Hawaii AIDS Education and Training Center has numerous resources available for download at www.hawaii.edu/hivandaids/links.htm.

LGB Populations

The Web site of the National Association of Lesbian and Gay Addiction Professionals is a clearinghouse for information and resources, including treatment programs and mutual-help groups, organized by State. Visit www.nalgap.org.

Substance Abuse Resource Guide: Lesbian, Gay, Bisexual, and Transgender Populations (Center for Substance Abuse Prevention 2000) — This publication lists books, fact sheets, magazines, newsletters, videos, posters, reports, Web sites, and organizations that increase understanding of issues important to lesbian, gay, bisexual, and transgender clients. Download the resource guide from www.ncadi.samhsa.gov/referrals/resguides.aspx?InvNum=MS489.

Addictions in the Gay and Lesbian Community (Guss 2000) — This volume includes personal experiences of substance use and recovery and research into the sources of and treatment for substance use disorders in gay and lesbian clients. The book also includes techniques for assessing and treating LGB clients, including adolescents.

Persons With Physical and Cognitive Disabilities

Programs should link with local groups that offer specialized housing, vocational training, and other supports for people who are disabled. The Centers for Independent Living (CILs) are organizations run by and for persons with disabilities to provide mutual-help and advocacy. CILs and Client Assistance Programs were developed to provide a third party to broker the interaction between clients and the service system. The Special Olympics may be able to help locate recreational activities appropriate for individual clients.

Coping With Substance Abuse After TBI — This report answers basic questions about substance use and traumatic brain injury (TBI) and includes recommendations from clients with TBI who are now abstinent. Download the publication at www.mssm.edu/tbicentral/resources/publications/tbi_consumer_reports.shtml.

TIP 29, *Substance Use Disorder Treatment for People With Physical and Cognitive Disabilities* (CSAT 1998*e*) — This volume discusses screening, treatment planning, and counseling for clients with disabilities. The book includes a compliance guide for the Americans with Disabilities Act, a list of appropriate terms to use when referring to people with disabilities, and screening instruments for use with this population, including an Education and Health Survey and an Impairment and Functional Limitation Screen.

Substance Abuse Resources and Disability Issues Program at Wright State School of Medicine (www.med.wright.edu/citar/sardi) — This Web site offers products for professionals and persons with disabilities, including a training manual with an introduction on substance abuse and the deaf culture, as well as a Web course on substance abuse and disability.

National Center for the Dissemination of Disability Research's Guide to Substance Abuse and Disability Resources (www.ncddr.org/du/products/saguide) — This Web site provides links to books, journal articles, newsletters, training manuals, audiotapes, and videotapes on substance abuse and individuals who are disabled.

Minnesota Chemical Dependency Program for Deaf and Hard of Hearing Individuals (www.mncddeaf.org) — This Web site includes links to articles on substance abuse treatment of individuals who are deaf and to manuals and videotapes for use in treatment.

Ohio Valley Center for Brain Injury Prevention and Rehabilitation (www.ohiovalley.org/abuse) — This Web site includes guidelines for treating people with substance use disorders and traumatic brain injury and links to other resources.

Center for International Rehabilitation Research and Information Exchange (www.cirrie.buffalo.edu/mseries.html) — This Web site includes downloadable versions of cultural guides that describe the demographics and attitudes toward disability of 11 countries, including countries in Asia, Central America, and the Caribbean. The site also includes a booklet that describes culture brokering, a practice in which counselors mediate between cultures to improve service delivery.

Rural Populations

TAP 17, *Treating Alcohol and Other Drug Abusers in Rural and Frontier Areas* (CSAT 1995*b*) — The papers in this volume describe providers' experiences across a variety of treatment issues relevant to rural substance abuse treatment, including domestic violence, enhanced service delivery, building coalitions and networks, and practical measures to improve treatment.

TAP 20, *Bringing Excellence to Substance Abuse Services in Rural and Frontier America* (CSAT 1996) — The papers in this volume examine innovative strategies and policies for treating substance use disorders in rural and frontier America. Topics include rural gangs and crime, needs assessment approaches, coalitions and partnerships, and minorities and women in treatment.

Rural Substance Abuse: State of Knowledge and Issues (Robertson et al. 1997) — This NIDA Research Monograph examines rural substance abuse from many perspectives, looking at substance use among youth and at the health, economic, and social consequences of substance use. The final section of the book addresses ethnic and migrant populations, including rural Native Americans, African-Americans, and Mexican Americans. Visit www.nida.nih.gov/PDF/Monographs/Monograph168/Download168.html to download the monograph.

Homeless Populations

National Resource Center on Homelessness and Mental Illness (www.nrchmi.samhsa.gov/pdfs/bibliographies/Cultural_Competence.pdf) — This Web site has an annotated, online bibliography of journal articles, resource guides, reports, and books that address cultural competence. Many resources discuss substance use disorders.

"The Effectiveness of Social Interventions for Homeless Substance Abusers" (American Society of Addiction Medicine 1995) — This special issue of the *Journal of Addictive Diseases* includes 11 articles that examine important aspects of treating people who are homeless, including retaining clients, residential versus nonresidential treatment, enhanced services, treating mothers who are homeless, and clients with co-occurring disorders.

The U.S. Department of Housing and Urban Development has compiled a list of local agencies by State and other resources to assist people who are homeless. Visit www.hud.gov/homeless/index.cfm.

The U.S. Department of Health and Human Services offers assistance and resources for people who are homeless. For example, the Health Care for the Homeless Program provides grants to community-based organizations in urban and rural areas for projects aimed at improving access for the homeless to primary health care, mental health care, and substance abuse treatment. Visit www.aspe.hhs.gov/homeless/index.shtml.

Substance Abuse Treatment: What Works for Homeless People? A Review of the Literature (Zerger 2002) — This report links research on homelessness and substance abuse with clinical practice and examines various treatment modalities, types of interventions, and methods for engaging and retaining people who are homeless. Download the report from National Health Care for the Homeless Council's Web site at www.nhchc.org/Publications/SubstanceAbuseTreatmentLitReview.pdf.

National Resource Center on Homelessness and Mental Illness (www.nrchmi.samhsa.gov) — This Web site lists trainings and workshops (such as the National Training Conference on Homelessness for People With Mental Illness and/or Substance Use Disorders), technical assistance, and fact sheets and other publications on homelessness.

Older Adults

TIP 26, *Substance Abuse Among Older Adults* (CSAT 1998*d*) — This volume discusses the relationship between aging and substance abuse and offers guidance for screening, assessing, and treating substance use disorders in older adults.

Substance Abuse Relapse Prevention for Older Adults: A Group Treatment Approach (CSAT 2005*c*) — This manual presents a relapse prevention intervention that uses a cognitive-behavioral and self-management approach in a counselor-led group setting to help older adults overcome substance use disorders. Order from SAMHSA's NCADI.

Substance Abuse by Older Adults: Estimates of the Future Impact on the Treatment System (Korper and Council 2002) — This report examines substance abuse treatment services for older adults in the context of increased demand in the future and calls for better documentation of substance abuse among older adults and prevention and treatment strategies that are tailored to subgroups of older adults, such as immigrants and racial and ethnic minorities. Download the report at www.drugabusestatistics.samhsa.gov/aging/toc.htm.

Alcohol and Aging (Beresford and Gomberg 1995) — This book for clinicians covers topics such as diagnosis and treatment, mental disorders, interactions of alcohol and prescription medications, and the biochemistry of intoxication for older adults.

Alcoholism and Aging: An Annotated Bibliography and Review (Osgood et al. 1995) — This volume surveys 30 years of research on older adults who use alcohol, providing abstracts of articles, books and book chapters, and research studies on the prevalence, effects, diagnosis, and treatment of alcohol use in older adults.

Administration on Aging (www.aoa.gov/prof/adddiv/adddiv.asp) — This Web site offers information on cultural competence, including resources on aging and ethnic minorities and the booklet, *Achieving Cultural Competence: A Guidebook for Providers of Services to Older Americans and Their Families,* which can be downloaded at www.aoa.gov/prof/adddiv/cultural/addiv_cult.asp.

Section 3, Chapter 3:
Co-Occurring Disorders

Introduction

Over the past few decades, practitioners and researchers increasingly have recognized the link between substance abuse and mental disorders. As a result, there is a great need in the treatment field for all counseling professionals to have an overview of diagnostic criteria, assessment, psychopharmacology, specific mental disorders, and the need for linkage between the mental health services system and substance abuse treatment system.

Research has provided a more in-depth understanding of co-occurring substance use and mental disorders – how common they are, the multiple problems they create, and the impact they have on treatment and treatment outcome. As knowledge of co-occurring disorders (COD) continues to evolve, new challenges arise: How do we treat specific populations such as the homeless and those in our criminal justice system? What is the role of housing? What about those with specific mental disorders such as posttraumatic stress disorder? Where is the best locus for treatment? Can we build an integrated system of care? The main purpose of this Section is to provide addiction counselors and other practitioners with this information on the rapidly advancing field of co-occurring substance use and mental disorders.

The Evolving Field of Co-Occurring Disorders

Today's emphasis on the relationship between substance use and mental disorders dates to the late 1970s, when practitioners increasingly became aware of the implications of these disorders, when occurring together, for treatment outcomes. The association between depression and substance abuse was particularly striking and became the subject of several early studies (e.g., Woody and Blaine 1979). In the 1980s and 1990s, however, both the substance abuse and mental health communities found that a wide range of mental disorders were associated with substance abuse, not just depression (e.g., De Leon 1989; Pepper et al. 1981; Rounsaville et al. 1982b ; Sciacca 1991). During this period, substance abuse treatment programs typically reported that 50 to 75 percent of clients had co-occurring mental disorders, while clinicians in mental health settings reported that between 20 and 50 percent of their clients had co-occurring substance use disorders. (See Sacks et al. 1997*b* for a summary of studies.)

Researchers not only found a link between substance abuse and mental illness, they also found the dramatic impact the complicating presence of substance abuse may have on the course of treatment for mental illness. One study of 121 clients with psychoses found that those with substance abuse problems (36 percent) spent twice as many days in the hospital over the 2 years prior to treatment as clients without substance abuse problems (Crome 1999; Menezes et al. 1996). These clients often have poorer outcomes, such as higher rates of HIV infection, relapse, rehospitalization, depression, and suicide risk (Drake et al. 1998*b*; Office of the Surgeon General 1999).

Researchers also have clearly demonstrated that substance abuse treatment of clients with co-occurring mental illness and substance use disorders can be beneficial – even for clients with serious mental disorders. For example, the National Treatment Improvement Evaluation Study (NTIES) found marked reductions in suicidality the year following substance abuse treatment compared to the year prior to treatment for adults, young adults, adolescents, and subgroups of abused and nonabused women. Of the 3,524 adults aged 25 and over included in the study, 23 percent reported suicide attempts the year prior to treatment, while only 4 percent reported suicide attempts during the year following treatment. Twenty-eight percent of the 651 18- to 24-year-old young adults had a suicide attempt the year before treatment, while only 4 percent reported suicide attempts during the 12 months following treatment. Similarly, the 236 adolescents (13 to 17 years of age) showed a decline in pre- and post-treatment suicide attempts, from 23 percent to 7 percent, respectively (Karageorge 2001). For the group as a whole (4,411 persons), suicide attempts declined about four-fifths both for the 3,037 male clients and for the 1,374 female clients studied (Karageorge 2001). A subset of women (aged 18 and over) were identified as either having reported prior sexual abuse (509 women) or reporting no prior sexual abuse (667 women). Suicide attempts declined by about half in both of these groups (Karageorge 2001), and both groups had fewer inpatient and outpatient mental health visits and less reported depression (Karageorge 2001).

Although many clients in traditional substance abuse treatment settings with certain less serious mental disorders than those described in NTIES appear to do well with traditional substance abuse treatment methods (Hser et al. 2001; Hubbard et al. 1989; Joe et al. 1995; Simpson et al. 2002; Woody et al. 1991), modifications designed to address those mental disorders can enhance treatment effectiveness and are essential in some instances.

Just as the field of treatment for substance use and mental disorders has evolved to become more precise, so too has the terminology used to describe people with both substance use and mental disorders. The term *co-occurring disorders* replaces the terms *dual disorder* or *dual diagnosis*. These latter terms, though used commonly to refer to the combination of substance use and mental disorders, are confusing in that they also refer to other combinations of disorders (such as mental disorders and mental retardation). Furthermore, the terms suggest that there are only two disorders occurring at the same time, when in fact there may be more. For purposes of this Section, *co-occurring disorders* refers to co-occurring substance use (abuse or dependence) and mental disorders. Clients said to have co-occurring disorders have one or more disorders relating to the use of alcohol and/or other drugs of abuse as well as one or more mental disorders. A diagnosis of co-occurring disorders occurs when at least one disorder of each type can be established independent of the other and is not simply a cluster of symptoms resulting from the one disorder.

New models and strategies are receiving attention and encouraging treatment innovation (Anderson 1997; De Leon 1996; Miller 1994*a*; Minkoff 1989; National Advisory Council [NAC] 1997; Onken et al. 1997; Osher and Drake 1996). Reflecting the increased interest in issues surrounding effective treatment for this population, the American Society of Addiction Medicine (ASAM) added substantial new sections on clients with COD to a recent update of its patient criteria. These sections refine criteria both for treating clients with COD and for establishing and operating programs to provide services for such clients (ASAM 2001).

In another important development, the National Association of State Alcohol and Drug Abuse Directors (NASADAD) began surveying its members about effective treatment of clients with COD in their States (Gustafson et al. 1999). In addition, NASADAD has joined with the National Association of State Mental Health Program Directors (NASMHPD) (NASMHPD-NASADAD 1999, 2000) and other collaborators in a series of national efforts designed to

- Foster improvement in treatment by emphasizing the importance of knowledge of both mental health and substance abuse treatment when working with clients for whom both issues are relevant.
- Provide a classification of treatment settings to facilitate systematic planning, consultations, collaborations, and integration.
- Reduce the stigma associated with both disorders and increase the acceptance of substance abuse and mental health concerns as a standard part of healthcare information gathering.

These efforts are slowly changing the way that the public, policymakers, and substance abuse counselors view mental illness. Still, stigma attached to mental illness remains. One topic worth mentioning is the public perception that people with mental illness are dangerous and pose a risk of violence. However, studies have shown that the public's fear is greater than the actual risk, and that often, people with mental disorders are not particularly violent; it is when substance abuse is added that violence can ensue. For example, Steadman et al. (1998) found that substance abuse symptoms significantly raised the rate of violence in both individuals with mental illness and those without mental illness. This research adds support to the importance of treating both mental illness and substance abuse.

In recent years, dissemination of knowledge has been widespread. Numerous books and hundreds of articles have been published, from counseling manuals and instruction (Evans and Sullivan 2001; Pepper and Massaro 1995) to database analysis of linkage among treatment systems and payors (Coffey et al. 2001). Several annual "dual diagnosis" conferences emerged. One of the most longstanding is the annual conference on The Person With Mental Illness and Substance Abuse, hosted by MCP Hahnemann University (now Drexel University), which began in 1988.

In spite of these developments, individuals with substance use and mental disorders commonly appear at facilities that are not prepared to treat them. They may be treated for one disorder without consideration of the other disorder, often "bouncing" from one type of treatment to another as symptoms of one disorder or another become predominant. Sometimes they simply "fall through the cracks" and do not receive needed treatment.

Definitions, Terms, and Classification Systems for Co-Occurring Disorders

Terms Related to Substance-Related and Addictive Disorders

According to APA (2013a), "a substance use disorder is a cluster of cognitive, behavioral, and physiological symptoms indicating that the individual continues using the substance despite significant substance-related problems" (p. 483). In severe and long-term use, these changes may be observed through underlying changes in brain circuits (Agrawal et al, 2012). The first four criteria for substance use disorders encompass impaired control, social impairment, risky use, and pharmacological criteria. Criteria 5 to 7 cover social, occupational, and interpersonal problems. Criteria 8 and 9 focus on risk taking surrounding use of the substance, and Criteria 10 and 11 are tolerance and withdrawal, respectively. Assuming an individual meets the general requirement for "clinically significant impairment or distress" related to pattern of use, just two specific criteria must be met to justify assignment of a clinical diagnosis.

The predominant change to the overall diagnostic criteria for substance use disorder is the inclusion of craving and the exclusion of recurrent legal problems. Craving is included in *ICD-10* criteria (WHO, 2007) and has been supported through epidemiological studies as a highly prominent and core feature of substance use disorders (Kavanaugh, 2013; Keyes et al., 2011; Ko et al., 2013; Mewton et al, 2011; Sinha, 2013). Functional magnetic resonance imaging (fMRI) has shown that there are certain brain regions directly related to craving (Ko et al., 2013). Presence of cues, negative moods, and stress reactions often lead to an increase in craving. Mindfulness training has been shown to reduce craving in that it can address awareness of the emotion and redirection of thoughts.

Diagnostic Criteria (Alcohol Use Disorder Example)

A. A problematic pattern of alcohol use leading to clinically significant impairment or distress, as manifested by at least two of the following, occurring within a 12-month period.

   1. Alcohol is often taken in larger amounts or over a longer period than was intended.

   2. There is a persistent desire or unsuccessful efforts to cut down or control alcohol use.

   3. A great deal of time is spent in activities necessary to obtain alcohol, use alcohol, or recover from its effects.

   4. Craving, or a strong desire to use alcohol.

   5. Recurrent alcohol use resulting in a failure to fulfill major role obligations at work, school, or home.

   6. Continued alcohol use despite having persistent or recurrent social or interpersonal problems caused or exacerbated by the effects of alcohol.

   7. Important social, occupational, or recreational activities are given up or reduced because of alcohol use.

   8. Recurrent alcohol use in situations in which it is physically hazardous.

9. Alcohol use is continued despite knowledge of having a persistent or recurrent physical or psychological problem that is likely to have been caused or exacerbated by alcohol.

10. Tolerance, as defined by either of the following:
    a. A need for markedly increased amounts of alcohol to achieve intoxication or desired effect.
    b. A markedly diminished effect with continued use of the same amount of alcohol.

11. Withdrawal, as manifested by either of the following:
    a. The characteristic withdrawal syndrome for alcohol (refer to Criteria A and B of the criteria set for alcohol withdrawal, pp. 499-500).
    b. Alcohol (or a closely related substance, such as a benzodiazepine) is taken to relieve or avoid withdrawal symptoms.

From *Diagnostic and Statistical Manual of Mental Disorders, Fifth Edition,* 2013, pp. 490-491. Copyright 2013 by the American Psychiatric Association. All rights reserved. Reprinted with permission.

Note: *The diagnostic criteria for alcohol use disorder are used as an example because the criteria are identical for all of the disorders with the exception of Criterion* **11***, which does not apply to hallucinogen-related and inhalant-related use disorders.*

Terms Related to Mental Disorders

The standard use of terms for non-substance use mental disorders, like the terms for substance use disorders, derive from the DSM-5 (APA 2013). These terms are used throughout the medical and mental health fields for diagnosing mental disorders. As with substance use disorders, this reference provides clinicians with a common language for communicating about these disorders. The reference also establishes criteria for diagnosing specific disorders.

The following information provides a brief introduction to some (not, by any means, all) of these disorders and offers advice to the addiction counselor and other practitioners for working with clients with these disorders. Addiction counselors are not expected to diagnose mental disorders. Clinicians in the substance abuse treatment field, however, should familiarize themselves with the mental disorders that co-occur with substance use disorders and/or that mimic symptoms of substance use disorders, particularly withdrawal or intoxication. The aim of providing this material is only to increase substance abuse treatment counselors' familiarity with the mental disorders terminology and criteria necessary to provide advice on how to proceed with clients who demonstrate these disorders.

Figure 3-1. Level of Care Quadrants

Alcohol and Other Drug Abuse (vertical axis)

high severity (top of vertical axis)

Category III
- Mental disorders less severe
- Substance abuse disorders more severe
- **Locus of Care** – Substance Abuse System

Category IV
- Mental disorders more severe
- Substance abuse disorders more severe
- **Locus of Care** – State hospitals, jails/prisons, emergency rooms, etc.

Category I
- Mental disorders less severe
- Substance abuse disorders less severe
- **Locus of Care** – Primary health care settings

Category II
- Mental disorders more severe
- Substance abuse disorders less severe
- **Locus of Care** – Mental health system

low severity ———————————————→ **high severity**

Mental Illness

Quadrant I: This quadrant includes individuals with low severity substance abuse and low severity mental disorders. These low severity individuals can be accommodated in intermediate outpatient settings of either mental health or chemical dependency programs, with consultation or collaboration between settings if needed. Alternatively, some individuals will be identified and managed in primary care settings with consultation from mental health and/or substance abuse treatment providers.

Quadrant II: This quadrant includes individuals with high severity mental disorders who are usually identified as priority clients within the mental health system and who also have low severity substance use disorders (e.g., substance dependence in remission or partial remission). These individuals ordinarily receive continuing care in the mental health system and are likely to be well served in a variety of intermediate level mental health programs using integrated case management.

Quadrant III: This quadrant includes individuals who have severe substance use disorders and low or moderate severity mental disorders. They are generally well accommodated in intermediate level substance abuse treatment programs. In some cases there is a need for coordination and collaboration with affiliated mental health programs to provide ongoing treatment of the mental disorders.

Quadrant IV: Quadrant IV is divided into two subgroups. One subgroup includes individuals with serious and persistent mental illness (SPMI) who also have severe and unstable substance use disorders. The other subgroup includes individuals with severe and unstable substance use disorders and severe and unstable behavioral health problems (e.g., violence, suicidality) who do not (yet) meet criteria for SPMI. These individuals require intensive, comprehensive, and integrated services for both their substance use and mental disorders. The locus of treatment can be specialized residential substance abuse treatment programs such as modified therapeutic communities in State hospitals, jails, or even in settings that provide acute care such as emergency rooms.

Personality Disorders

These are the disorders most commonly seen by the addiction counselor and in quadrant III substance abuse treatment settings (see **Figure 3-1** for a depiction of the four quadrants). Individuals with personality disorders have symptoms and personality traits that are enduring and play a major role in most, if not all, aspects of the person's life. These individuals have personality traits that are persistent and cause impairment in social or occupational functioning or cause personal distress. Symptoms are evident in their thoughts (ways of looking at the world, thinking about self or others), emotions (appropriateness, intensity, and range), interpersonal functioning (relationships and interpersonal skills), and impulse control.

Personality disorders are listed in the DSM-5 under three distinct areas, referred to as "clusters." The clusters are listed below with the types of symptoms or traits seen in that category. The specific personality disorders included in each cluster also are listed. For personality disorders that do not fit any of the specific disorders, the diagnosis of "personality disorder not otherwise specified" is used.

Cluster A: Hallmark traits of this cluster involve *odd or eccentric behavior.* It includes *paranoid, schizoid,* and *schizotypal* personality disorders.

Cluster B: Hallmark traits of this cluster involve *dramatic, emotional, or erratic behavior.* It includes *antisocial, borderline, histrionic,* and *narcissistic* personality disorders.

Cluster C: Hallmark traits of this cluster involve *anxious, fearful behavior.* It includes *avoidant, dependent,* and *obsessive-compulsive* personality disorders.

The prevalence of co-occurring substance abuse and antisocial personality disorder is high (Flynn et al. 1997). In fact, much of substance abuse treatment is targeted to those with antisocial personality disorders and substance abuse treatment alone has been especially effective for these disorders. Following is an Advice to the Counselor box on working with clients who have antisocial personality disorder.

Advice to the Counselor: Antisocial Personality Disorders

- Confront dishonesty and antisocial behavior directly and firmly.
- Hold clients responsible for the behavior and its consequences.
- Use peer communities to confront behavior and foster change.

Psychotic Disorders

The common characteristics of these disorders are symptoms that center on problems of thinking. The most prominent (and problematic) symptoms are delusions or hallucinations. Delusions are false beliefs that significantly hinder a person's ability to function. For example, a client may believe that people are trying to hurt him, or he may believe he is someone else (a CIA agent, God, etc.). Hallucinations are false perceptions in which a person sees, hears, feels, or smells things that aren't real (i.e., visual, auditory, tactile, or olfactory).

Psychotic disorders are seen most frequently in mental health settings and, when combined with substance use disorders, the substance disorder tends to be severe. Clients with psychotic disorders constitute what commonly is referred to as the serious and persistent mentally ill population. Increasingly, individuals with serious mental illness are present in substance abuse treatment programs (Gustafson et al. 1999).

Drugs (e.g., cocaine, methamphetamine, or phencyclidine) can produce delusions and/or hallucinations secondary to drug intoxication. Furthermore, psychotic-like symptoms may persist beyond the acute intoxication period.

Schizophrenia

This is one of the most common of the psychotic disorders and one of the most destructive in terms of the effect it has on a person's life. Symptoms may include the following: hallucinations, delusions, disorganized speech, grossly disorganized or catatonic behavior, social withdrawal, lack of interest, and poor hygiene. The disorder has several specific types depending on what other symptoms the person experiences. In the paranoid type there is a preoccupation with one or more delusions or frequent auditory hallucinations. These often are experienced as threatening to the person. In the disorganized type there is a prominence of all of the following: disorganized speech, disorganized behavior, and flat or inappropriate affect (i.e., emotional expression).

Advice to the Counselor: Psychotic Disorders

- Screen for psychotic disorders and refer identified clients for further diagnostic evaluation.

- Obtain a working knowledge of the signs and symptoms of the disorder.

- Educate the client and family about the condition.

- Help the client detect early signs of its re-occurrence by recognizing the symptoms associated with the disorder.

Mood Disorders

The disorders in this category include those where the primary symptom is a disturbance in mood, where there may be inappropriate, exaggerated, or a limited range of feelings or emotions. Everyone feels "down" sometimes, and everybody experiences feelings of excitement or emotional pleasure. However, when a client has a mood disorder, these feelings or emotions are experienced to the extreme. Many people with substance use disorders also have a co-occurring mood disorder and tend to use a variety of drugs in association with their mood disorder. There are several types of mood disorders, including depression, mania, and bipolar disorder.

Depression. Instead of just feeling "down," the client might not be able to work or function at home, might feel suicidal, lose his or her appetite, and feel very tired or fatigued. Other symptoms can include loss of interest, weight changes, changes in sleep and appetite, feelings of worthlessness, loss of concentration, and recurrent thoughts of death.

Mania. This includes feelings that are more toward the opposite extreme of depression. There might be an excess of energy where sleep is not needed for days at a time. The client may be feeling "on top of the world," and during this time, the client's decision-making process might be significantly impaired and expansive and he may experience irritability and have aggressive outbursts, although he might think such outbursts are perfectly rational.

Bipolar. A person with bipolar disorder cycles between episodes of mania and depression. These episodes are characterized by a distinct period of abnormally elevated, expansive, or irritable mood. Symptoms may include inflated self-esteem or grandiosity, decreased need for sleep, being more talkative than usual, flight of ideas or a feeling that one's thoughts are racing, distractibility, increase in goal-directed activity, excessive involvement in pleasurable activities that have a high potential for painful consequences (sexual indiscretions, buying sprees, etc.). Excessive use of alcohol is common during periods of mania.

Anxiety disorders. As with mood disorders, anxiety is something that everyone feels now and then, but anxiety disorders exist when anxiety symptoms reach the point of frequency and intensity that they cause significant impairment. In addiction treatment populations, the most common anxiety syndrome seen is that associated with early recovery, which can be a mix of substance withdrawal and learning to live without the use of drugs or alcohol. This improves with time and addiction treatment. However, other anxiety disorders that may occur, but need particular assessment and treatment, are social phobia (fear of appearing or speaking in front of groups), panic disorder (recurrent panic attacks that usually last a few hours, cause great fear, and make it hard to breathe), and posttraumatic stress disorders (which cause recurrent nightmares, anxiety, depression, and the experience of reliving the traumatic issues).

Advice to the Counselor: Mood and Anxiety Disorders

- Differentiate between mood disorders, commonplace expressions of depression, and depression associated with more serious mental illness.
- Conduct careful and continuous assessment since mood symptoms may be the result of substance abuse and not an underlying mental disorder.
- Combine addiction counseling with medication and mental health treatment.

Terms Related to Clients

Person-Centered Terminology

In recent years, consumer advocacy groups have expressed concerns related to how clients are classified. Many take exception to terminology that seems to put them in a "box" with a label that follows them through life, which does not capture the fullness of their identities. A person with COD also may be a mother, a plumber, a pianist, a student, or a person with diabetes, to cite just a few examples. Referring to an individual as a person who has a specific disorder – a person with depression rather than "a depressive," a person with schizophrenia rather than "a schizophrenic," or a person who uses heroin rather than "an addict" – is more acceptable to many clients because it implies that they have many characteristics besides a stigmatized illness, and therefore that they are not defined by this illness.

Terms for Co-Occurring Disorders

Many terms have been used in the field to describe the group of individuals who have COD. Some of these terms represent an attempt to identify which problem or disorder is seen as primary or more severe. Others have developed in the literature in order to argue for setting aside funding for special services or to identify a group of clients who may benefit from certain interventions. These terms include

- MICA – mentally ill chemical abuser. This acronym is sometimes seen with two A's (MICAA) to signify mentally ill chemically addicted or affected. There are regional differences in the meaning of this acronym. Many States use it to refer specifically to persons with serious mental disorders.

- MISA – mentally ill substance abuser.

- MISU – mentally ill substance using.

- CAMI – chemically abusing mentally ill, or chemically addicted and mentally ill.

- SAMI – substance abusing mentally ill.

- MICD – mentally ill chemically dependent.

- Dually diagnosed.

- Dually disordered.

- Comorbid disorders.

- ICOPSD – individuals with co-occurring psychiatric and substance disorders.

While all of these terms have their uses, many have developed connotations that are not helpful or that have become too broad or varied in interpretation to be useful. For example, "dual diagnosis" also can mean having both mental and developmental disorders. Counselors who hear these terms should not assume they all have the same meaning as COD and should seek to clarify the client characteristics associated with a particular term. Counselors also should realize that the term "co-occurring disorder" is not inherently precise and distinctive; it also may become distorted by popular use, with other conditions becoming included within the term. The issue here is that clients/consumers may have a number of health conditions that "co-occur," including physical health problems. Nevertheless, for the purpose of this Section, co-occurring disorders refers to substance use disorders and mental disorders.

Some clients' mental health problems may not fully meet the strict definition of co-occurring substance-related and mental disorders criteria for diagnoses in DSM-5 categories. However, many of the relevant principles that apply to the treatment of COD also will apply to these individuals. Careful assessment and treatment planning to take each disorder into account will still be important. Suicidal ideation is an excellent example of a mental health symptom that creates a severity problem, but alone doesn't necessarily meet criteria for a formal DSM-5 condition since suicidality is a symptom and not a diagnosis. Substance-induced suicidal ideation can produce catastrophic consequences. Some individuals may exhibit symptoms that could indicate the existence of COD but could also be transitory; for example, substance-induced mood swings, which can mimic bipolar disorder, or amphetamine-induced hallucinations or paranoia, which could mimic schizophrenia. Depending on the severity of their symptoms, these individuals also may require the full range of services needed by those who meet the strict criterion of having both conditions independently, but generally for acute periods until the substance-induced symptoms resolve.

Terms Related to Treatment

Levels of Care Placement

The American Society of Addiction Medicine's Treatment Criteria for Addictive, Substance-Related, and Co-Occurring Conditions (ASAM 2013) envisions treatment as a continuum within which there are ten levels of care. These levels of care are as follows:

- Level 0.5: Early Intervention

- OTP – Level 1: Opioid Treatment Program

- Level 1: Outpatient Services

- Level 2.1: Intensive Outpatient Services

- Level 2.5: Partial Hospitalization Services

- Level 3.1: Clinically Managed Low-Intensity Residential Services

- Level 3.3: Clinically Managed Population-Specific High-Intensity Residential Services

- Level 3.5: Clinically Managed High-Intensity residential Services

- Level 3.7: Medically Monitored Intensive Inpatient Services

- Level 4: Medically Managed Intensive Inpatient Services

Each level of care includes several levels of intensity indicated by a decimal point. For example, Level 3.1 refers to "Clinically Managed Low-Intensity Residential Services." A client who has COD might be appropriately placed in any of these levels of service.

Substance abuse counselors also should be aware that some mental health professionals may use another system, the Level of Care Utilization System for Psychiatric and Addiction Services. This system also identifies levels of care, including

- Level 1: Recovery Maintenance Health Management

- Level 2: Low Intensity Community Based Services

- Level 3: High Intensity Community Based Services

- Level 4: Medically Monitored Non-Residential Services

- Level 5: Medically Monitored Residential Services

- Level 6: Medically Managed Residential Services

These levels, like the ASAM levels, use a variety of specific dimensions to describe a client in order to determine the most appropriate placement.

Quadrants of Care

The quadrants of care are a conceptual framework that classifies clients in four basic groups based on relative symptom severity, not diagnosis.

- Category I: Less severe mental disorder/less severe substance disorder

- Category II: More severe mental disorder/less severe substance disorder

- Category III: Less severe mental disorder/more severe substance disorder

- Category IV: More severe mental disorder/more severe substance disorder (National Association of State Mental Health Program Directors [NASMHPD] and National Association of State Alcohol and Drug Abuse Directors [NASADAD] 1999)

For a more detailed description of each quadrant, see **Figure 3.1**.

The quadrants of care were derived from a conference, the National Dialogue on Co-Occurring Mental Health and Substance Abuse Disorders, which was supported by the Substance Abuse and Mental Health Services Administration (SAMHSA) and two of its centers – the Center for Substance Abuse Treatment (CSAT) and the Center for Mental Health Services – and co-sponsored by NASMHPD and NASADAD. The quadrants of care is a model originally developed by Ries (1993) and used by the State of New York (NASMHPD and NASADAD 1999; see also Rosenthal 1992).

The four-quadrant model has two distinct uses:

- To help conceptualize an individual client's treatment and to guide improvements in system integration (for example, if the client has acute psychosis and is known to the treatment staff to have a history of alcohol dependence, the client will clearly fall into Category IV—that is, severe mental disorder and severe substance use disorder). However, the severity of the client's needs, diagnosis, symptoms, and impairments all determine level of care placement.

- To guide improvements in systems integration, including efficient allocation of resources. The NASMHPD-NASADAD National Dialogue recognized that currently "there is no single locus of responsibility for people with COD. The mental health and substance abuse treatment systems operate independently of one another, as separate cultures, each with its own treatment philosophies, administrative structures, and funding mechanisms. This lack of coordination means that neither consumers nor providers move easily among service settings" (NASMHPD and NASADAD 1999, p. ii).

Interventions

Intervention refers to the specific treatment strategies, therapies, or techniques that are used to treat one or more disorders. Interventions may include psychopharmacology, individual or group counseling, cognitive-behavioral therapy, motivational enhancement, family interventions, 12-Step recovery meetings, case management, skills training, or other strategies. Both substance use and mental disorder interventions are targeted to the management or resolution of acute symptoms, ongoing treatment, relapse prevention, or rehabilitation of a disability associated with one or more disorders, whether that disorder is mental or associated with substance use.

Integrated Interventions

Integrated interventions are specific treatment strategies or therapeutic techniques in which interventions for both disorders are combined in a single session or interaction, or in a series of interactions or multiple sessions. Integrated interventions can include a wide range of techniques. Some examples include

- Integrated screening and assessment processes

- Dual recovery mutual self-help meetings

- Dual recovery groups (in which recovery skills for both disorders are discussed)

- Motivational enhancement interventions (individual or group) that address issues related to both mental health and substance abuse or dependence problems

- Group interventions for persons with the triple diagnosis of mental disorder, substance use disorder, and trauma, or which are designed to meet the needs of persons with COD and another shared problem such as homelessness or criminality

- Combined psychopharmacological interventions, in which an individual receives medication designed to reduce cravings for substances as well as medication for a mental disorder

Integrated interventions can be part of a single program or can be used in multiple program settings.

Episodes of Treatment

An individual with COD may participate in recurrent episodes of treatment involving acute stabilization (e.g., crisis intervention, detoxification, psychiatric hospitalization) and specific ongoing treatment (e.g., mental-health-supported housing, mental-health day treatment, or substance abuse residential treatment). It is important to recognize the reality that clients engage in a series of treatment episodes, since many individuals with COD progress gradually through repeated involvement in treatment.

Integrated Treatment

Integrated treatment refers broadly to any mechanism by which treatment interventions for COD are combined within the context of a primary treatment relationship or service setting. Integrated treatment is a means of actively combining interventions intended to address substance use and mental disorders in order to treat both disorders, related problems, and the whole person more effectively.

Culturally Competent Treatment

One definition of cultural competence refers to "the capacity of a service provider or of an organization to understand and work effectively with the cultural beliefs and practices of persons from a given ethnic/racial group" (Castro et al. 1999, p. 504). Treatment providers working with individuals with COD should view these clients and their treatment in the context of their language, culture, ethnicity, geographic area, socioeconomic status, gender, age, sexual orientation, religion, spirituality, and any physical or cognitive disabilities.

Cultural factors that may have an impact on treatment include heritage, history and experience, beliefs, traditions, values, customs, behaviors, institutions, and ways of communicating. The client's culture may include distinctive ways of understanding disease or disorder, including mental and substance use disorders, which the provider needs to understand. Referencing a model of disease that is familiar to the client can help communication and enhance treatment. The counselor acquires cultural knowledge by becoming aware of the cultural factors that are important to a particular ethnic group or client.

Cultural competence may be viewed as a continuum on which, through learning, the provider increases his or her understanding and effectiveness with different ethnic groups. Various researchers have described the markers on this continuum (Castro et al. 1999; Cross 1988; Kim et al. 1992). The continuum moves from cultural destructiveness, in which an individual regards other cultures as inferior to the dominant culture, through cultural incapacity and blindness to the more positive attitudes and greater levels of skill described below:

- *Cultural sensitivity* is being "open to working with issues of culture and diversity" (Castro et al. 1999, p. 505). Viewed as a point on the continuum, however, a culturally sensitive individual has limited cultural knowledge and may still think in terms of stereotypes.

- *Cultural competence*, when viewed as the next stage on this continuum, includes an ability to "examine and understand nuances" and exercise "full cultural empathy." This enables the counselor to "understand the client from the client's own cultural perspective" (Castro et al. 1999, p. 505).

- *Cultural proficiency* is the highest level of cultural capacity. In addition to understanding nuances of culture in even greater depth, the culturally proficient counselor also is working to advance the field through leadership, research, and outreach (Castro et al. 1999, p. 505).

It is important to remember that clients, not counselors, define what is culturally relevant to them. It is possible to damage the relationship with a client by making assumptions, however well intentioned, about the client's cultural identity. For example, a client of Hispanic origin may be a third-generation United States citizen, fully acculturated, who feels little or no connection with her Hispanic heritage. A counselor who assumes this client shares the beliefs and values of many Hispanic cultures would be making an erroneous generalization. Similarly, it is helpful to remember that all of us represent multiple cultures. Clients are not simply African American, white, or Asian. A client who is a 20-year-old African-American man from the rural south may identify, to some extent, with youth, rural south, or African-American cultural elements—or may, instead, identify more strongly with another cultural element, such as his faith, that is not readily apparent. Counselors are advised to open a respectful dialog with clients around the cultural elements that have significance to them.

Integrated Counselor Competencies

A counselor has integrated competencies if he or she has the specific attitudes, values, knowledge, and skills needed to provide appropriate services to individuals with COD in the context of his or her actual job and program setting.

Just as other types of integration exist on a continuum, so too does integrated competency. Some interventions and/or programs require clinicians only to have basic competency in welcoming, screening, assessing, and identifying treatment needs of individuals with COD. Other interventions, programs, or job functions (e.g., those of supervisory staff) may require more advanced integrated competency. The more complex or unstable the client, the more formal mechanisms are required to coordinate the various staff members working with that client in order to provide effective integrated treatment.

A number of service delivery systems are moving toward identification of a required basic level of integrated competency for all clinicians in the mental health and substance abuse treatment systems. Many States also are developing curricula for initial and ongoing training and supervision to help clinicians achieve these competencies. Other State systems (e.g., Illinois) have created career ladders and certification pathways to encourage clinicians to achieve higher levels of integrated competency and to reward them for this achievement.

Terms Related to Programs

A program is a formally organized array of services and interventions provided in a coherent manner at a specific level or levels of care in order to address the needs of particular target populations. Each program has its own staff competencies, policies, and procedures. Programs may be operated directly by public funders (e.g., States and counties) or by privately funded agencies. An individual agency may operate many different programs. Some agencies operate only mental health programs, some operate only substance abuse treatment programs, and some do both. An individual, licensed healthcare practitioner (such as a psychiatrist or psychologist) may offer her or his own integrated treatment services as an independent practitioner.

Key Programs

Mental health-based programs

A mental health program is an organized array of services and interventions with a primary focus on treating mental disorders, whether by providing acute stabilization or ongoing treatment. These programs may exist in a variety of settings, such as traditional outpatient mental health centers (including outpatient clinics and psychosocial rehabilitation programs) or more intensive inpatient treatment units.

Many mental health programs treat significant numbers of individuals with COD. Programs that are more advanced in treating persons with COD may offer a variety of interventions for substance use disorders (e.g., motivational interviewing, substance abuse counseling, skills training) within the context of the ongoing mental health treatment.

Substance abuse treatment programs

A substance abuse treatment program is an organized array of services and interventions with a primary focus on treating substance use disorders, providing both acute stabilization and ongoing treatment.

Substance abuse treatment programs that are more advanced in treating persons with COD may offer a variety of interventions for mental disorders (e.g., psychopharmacology, symptom management training) within the context of the ongoing substance abuse treatment.

Program Types

The ASAM Criteria (ASAM 2013) describes three different types of programs for people with COD:

- *Addiction only services.* This term refers to programs that "either by choice or for lack of resources, cannot accommodate patients who have mental illnesses that require ongoing treatment, however stable the illness and however well-functioning the patient."

- *Co-Occurring capable* programs are those that "address co-occurring mental and substance-related disorders in their policies and procedures, assessment, treatment planning, program content and discharge planning." Even where such programs are geared primarily to treat substance use disorders, program staff are "able to address the interaction between mental and substance-related disorders and their effect on the patient's readiness to change—as well as relapse and recovery environment issues—through individual and group program content."

- *Co-Occurring enhanced* programs have a higher level of integration of substance abuse and mental health treatment services. These programs are able to provide primary substance abuse treatment to clients who are, as compared to those treatable in DDC programs, "more symptomatic and/or functionally impaired as a result of their co-occurring mental disorder." Enhanced-level services "place their primary focus on the integration of services for mental and substance-related disorders in their staffing, services and program content."

Terms Related to Systems

A system is a means of organizing a number of different treatment programs and related services to implement a specific mission and common goals. A basic example of a system is SAMHSA. Single State Agencies are systems that organize statewide services. There may also be county, city, or local systems in various areas.

A system executes specific functions by providing services and related activities. It is often, but not always, a government agency. Systems may be defined according to a number of different characteristics: a section of government, a geographic entity, or a payor (e.g., the Medicaid system of care).

Systems work with other systems in a variety of ways and with different degrees of integration. The primary systems with which people with COD interact are the substance abuse treatment and mental health services systems. Other systems that frequently come into play are health care, criminal justice, and social services. Systems are usually the entities that determine funding, standards of care, licensing, and regulation.

Substance Abuse Treatment System

The substance abuse treatment system encompasses a broad array of services organized into programs intended to treat substance use disorders (including illegal substances, such as marijuana and methamphetamine, and legal substances, such as alcohol for adults over 21 years of age). It also includes services organized in accord with a particular treatment approach or philosophy (e.g., methadone treatment for opioid dependence or therapeutic communities). A system may be defined by a combination of administrative leadership (e.g., through a designated director of substance abuse treatment services), regulatory oversight (e.g., all programs that have substance abuse treatment licenses), or funding (e.g., all programs that receive categorical substance abuse funding, or, more rarely, bill third-party payors for providing substance abuse services).

In most substance abuse treatment systems, the primary focus is on providing distinct treatment episodes for the acute stabilization, engagement, active treatment, ongoing rehabilitation of substance use disorders, and relapse prevention. More intensive services are almost invariably targeted to the treatment of substance dependence. The primary focus of intervention is abstinence from illicit drugs for those who use illicit drugs and from alcohol for those who use alcohol excessively.

Mental Health Service System

The mental health service system includes a broad array of services and programs intended to treat a wide range of mental disorders. Like the substance abuse treatment system, the coherence of the mental health system is defined by a combination of administrative leadership (e.g., through a designated director of mental health services), regulatory oversight (e.g., all programs which have mental health licenses), and funding (e.g., all programs which receive categorical mental health funding or that primarily bill third party payors for providing mental health services).

In most mental health systems, services are provided for a wide range of mental disorders; however, in many publicly financed mental health programs, the priority is on acute crisis intervention and stabilization and on the provision of ongoing treatment and rehabilitative services for individuals identified as having

SPMI. Typically, the mental health system identifies a cohort of priority clients (identified by a State's definition of SPMI) for whom it assumes continuing responsibility, often by providing continuing case management, psychiatric rehabilitation services, and/or housing support services.

Interlinking Systems

Depending on the life area affected at a given moment, individuals with COD may present themselves at different venues. For example, a person who experiences an array of problems in addition to the COD—such as homelessness, legal problems, and general medical problems—may first be seen at a housing agency or medical clinic. Historically, the distinctive boundaries maintained between systems have impeded the ability of individuals with COD to access needed services (Baker 1991; Schorske and Bedard 1989).

Intersystem linkages are essential to a comprehensive service delivery system. Fundamental to effective linkage is the collaboration between substance abuse treatment and mental health systems, because they are the primary care systems for persons with COD. The coordination of these systems enhances the quality of services by removing barriers that impede access to needed services. For example, access to care and quality of care have been impeded historically by the failure to address issues of language and culture. Intersystem coordination can lead to cohesive and coordinated delivery of program and services, where the burden is not on the individual to negotiate services and the system's resources are used more effectively. The criminal justice system now plays a central role in the delivery of treatment for both mental health and substance use disorders, especially for those persons with COD, so it is important to ensure coordination with this system as well. Community health centers and other primary health providers also play critical roles in substance use disorder treatment and mental health treatment.

Comprehensive Continuous Integrated System of Care

The Comprehensive Continuous Integrated System of Care model (CCISC) is a model to bring the mental health and substance abuse treatment systems (and other systems, potentially) into an integrated planning process to develop a comprehensive, integrated system of care. The CCISC is based on the awareness that COD are the expectation throughout the service system. The entire system is organized in ways consistent with this assumption. This includes system-level policies and financing, the design of all programs, clinical practices throughout the system, and basic clinical competencies for all clinicians. This model derives from the work of the SAMHSA Managed Care Initiative Consensus Panel on developing standards of care for individuals with COD (Center for Mental Health Services 1998; Minkoff 2001*a*). CCISCs are grounded in the following assumptions:

- The four-quadrant model is a valid model for service planning.

- Individuals with COD benefit from continuous, integrated treatment relationships.

- Programs should provide integrated primary treatment for substance use and mental disorders in which interventions are matched to diagnosis, phase of recovery, stage of change, level of functioning, level of care, and the presence of external supports and/or contingencies.

This model has been identified by SAMHSA as an exemplary practice and is at various stages of implementation in a number of States. States in various stages of implementing the CCISC model include Alabama, Alaska, Arizona, Maine, Maryland, Massachusetts, Montana, and New Mexico, as well as the District of Columbia. Regional projects are underway in Florida, Louisiana, Michigan, Oregon, Texas, and Virginia.

Screening and Basic Assessment for COD

A basic assessment covers the key information required for treatment matching and treatment planning. Ideally, information needs to be collected continuously, and assessments revised and monitored as the client moves through recovery. Specifically, the basic assessment offers a structure with which to obtain

- Basic demographic and historical information, and identification of established or probable diagnoses and associated impairments
- General strengths and problem areas
- Stage of change or stage of treatment for both substance abuse and mental health problems
- Preliminary determination of the severity of the COD as a guide to final level of care determination

Note that medical issues (including physical disability and sexually transmitted diseases), cultural issues, gender-specific and sexual orientation issues, and legal issues always must be addressed, whether basic or more comprehensive assessment is performed. Treatment programs typically have appropriate procedures in place to address these and other important issues that must be included in treatment planning.

In carrying out the screening and assessment process for COD, counselors should understand the limitations of their licensure or certification authority to diagnose or assess mental disorders. Generally, however, collecting assessment information is a legitimate and legal activity even for unlicensed providers, provided that they do not use diagnostic labels as conclusions or opinions about the client. Information gathered in this way is needed to ensure the client is placed in the most appropriate treatment setting (as discussed later in this chapter) and to assist in providing mental disorder care that addresses each disorder.

In addition, there are a number of circumstances that can affect validity and test responses that may not be obvious to the beginning counselor, such as the manner in which instructions are given to the client, the setting where the screening or assessment takes place, privacy (or the lack thereof), and trust and rapport between the client and counselor. Throughout the process it is important to be sensitive to cultural context and to the different presentations of both substance use and mental disorders that may occur in various cultures.

The following *Advice to the Counselor* section gives an overview of the basic "do's and don'ts" for assessing for COD. Detailed discussions of these important screening/assessment and cultural issues are beyond the scope of this review.

Advice to the Counselor: Do's and Don'ts of Assessment for COD

1. *Do* keep in mind that assessment is about getting to know a person with complex and individual needs. *Do not* rely on tools alone for a comprehensive assessment.

2. *Do* always make every effort to contact all involved parties, including family members, persons who have treated the client previously, other mental health and substance abuse treatment providers, friends, significant others, probation officers as quickly as possible in the assessment process. (These other sources of information will henceforth be referred to as *collaterals*.)

3. *Don't* allow preconceptions about addiction to interfere with learning about what the client really needs (e.g., "All mental symptoms tend to be caused by addiction unless proven otherwise"). Co-occurring disorders are as likely to be under recognized as over recognized. Assume initially that an established diagnosis and treatment regime for mental illness is correct, and advise clients to continue with those recommendations until careful reevaluation has taken place.

4. *Do* become familiar with the diagnostic criteria for common mental disorders, including personality disorders, and with the names and indications of common psychiatric medications. Also become familiar with the criteria in your own State for determining who is a mental health priority client. Know the process for referring clients for mental health case management services or for collaborating with mental health treatment providers.

5. *Don't* assume that there is one correct treatment approach or program for any type of COD. The purpose of assessment is to collect information about multiple variables that will permit individualized treatment matching. It is particularly important to assess stage of change for each problem and the client's level of ability to follow treatment recommendations.

6. *Do* become familiar with the specific role that your program or setting plays in delivering services related to COD in the wider context of the system of care. This allows you to have a clearer idea of what clients your program will best serve and helps you to facilitate access to other settings for clients who might be better served elsewhere.

7. *Don't* be afraid to admit when you don't know, either to the client or yourself. If you do not understand what is going on with a client, acknowledge that to the client, indicate that you will work with the client to find the answers, and then ask for help. Identify at least one supervisor who is knowledgeable about COD as a resource for asking questions.

8. Most important, *do* remember that empathy and hope are the most valuable components of your work with a client. When in doubt about how to manage a client with COD, stay connected, be empathic and hopeful, and work with the client and the treatment team to try to figure out the best approach over time.

Source: Allen and Wilson 2003.

Screening

Screening is a formal process of testing to determine whether a client does or does not warrant further attention at the current time in regard to a particular disorder and, in this context, the possibility of a co-occurring substance use or mental disorder. The screening process for COD seeks to answer a "yes" or "no" question: Does the substance abuse (or mental health) client being screened show signs of a possible mental health (or substance abuse) problem? Note that the screening process does not necessarily identify what kind of problem the person might have or how serious it might be, but determines whether or not further assessment is warranted. A screening process can be designed so that it can be conducted by counselors using their basic counseling skills. There are seldom any legal or professional restraints on who can be trained to conduct a screening.

Screening processes always should define a protocol for determining which clients screen positive and for ensuring that those clients receive a thorough assessment. That is, a professionally designed screening process establishes precisely how any screening tools or questions are to be scored and indicates what constitutes scoring positive for a particular possible problem (often called "establishing cut-off scores"). Additionally, the screening protocol details exactly what takes place after a client scores in the positive range and provides the necessary standard forms to be used to document both the results of all later assessments and that each staff member has carried out his or her responsibilities in the process.

So, what can a substance abuse treatment counselor do in terms of screening? All counselors can be trained to screen for COD. This screening often entails having a client respond to a specific set of questions, scoring those questions according to how the counselor was trained, and then taking the next "yes" or "no" step in the process depending on the results and the design of the screening process. In substance abuse treatment or mental health service settings, every counselor or clinician who conducts intake or assessment should be able to screen for the most common COD and know how to implement the protocol for obtaining COD assessment information and recommendations. For substance abuse treatment agencies that are instituting a mental health screening process, the Mental Health Screening Form-III (Carroll and McGinley 2001) is a recommend tool to use. This instrument is intended for use as a rough screening device for clients seeking admission to substance abuse treatment programs.

Basic Assessment

While both screening and assessment are ways of gathering information about the client in order to better treat him, assessment differs from screening in the following way:

- Screening is a process for evaluating the possible presence of a particular problem.
- Assessment is a process for defining the nature of that problem and developing specific treatment recommendations for addressing the problem.

A basic *assessment* consists of gathering key information and engaging in a process with the client that enables the counselor to understand the client's readiness for change, problem areas, COD diagnosis(es), disabilities, and strengths. An assessment typically involves a clinical examination of the functioning and well-being of the client and includes a number of tests and written and oral exercises. The COD diagnosis is established by referral to a psychiatrist, clinical psychologist, or other qualified healthcare professional.

Assessment of the client with COD is an ongoing process that should be repeated over time to capture the changing nature of the client's status. Intake information consists of

1. Background – family, trauma history, history of domestic violence (either as a batterer or as a battered person), marital status, legal involvement and financial situation, health, education, housing status, strengths and resources, and employment
2. Substance use – age of first use, primary drugs used (including alcohol, patterns of drug use, and treatment episodes), and family history of substance use problems
3. Mental health problems – family history of mental health problems, client history of mental health problems including diagnosis, hospitalization and other treatment, current symptoms and mental status, medications, and medication adherence

In addition, the basic information can be augmented by some objective measurement, such as that provided in the University of Rhode Island Change Assessment Scale (URICA) (McConnaughy et al. 1983), Addiction Severity Index (ASI) (McLellan et al. 1992), the Mental Health Screening Form-III (Carroll and McGinley 2001), and the Symptom Distress Scale (SDS) (McCorkle and Young 1978). It is essential for treatment planning that the counselor organizes the collected information in a way that helps identify established mental disorder diagnoses and current treatment. The text box that follows highlights the role of instruments in the assessment process.

The Role of Assessment Tools

A frequent question asked by clinicians is

- What is the best (most valuable) assessment tool for COD?

The answer is

- There is no single gold standard assessment tool for COD. Many traditional clinical tools have a narrow focus on a specific problem, such as the Beck Depression Inventory (BDI) (Beck and Steer 1987), a list of 21 questions about mood and other symptoms of feeling depressed. Other tools have a broader focus and serve to organize a range of information so that the collection of such information is done in a standard, regular way by all counselors. The ASI, which is not a comprehensive assessment tool but a measure of addiction severity in multiple problem domains, is an example of this type of tool (McLellan et al. 1992). Not only does a tool such as the ASI help a counselor, through repetition, become adept at collecting the information, it also helps the counselor refine his or her sense of similarities and differences among clients. A standard mental status examination can serve a similar function for collecting information on current mental health symptoms. Despite the fact that there are some very good tools, no one tool is the equivalent of a comprehensive clinical assessment.

Careful attention to the characteristics of past episodes of substance abuse and abstinence with regard to mental health symptoms, impairments, diagnoses, and treatments can illuminate the role of substance abuse in maintaining, worsening, and/or interfering with the treatment of any mental disorder. Understanding a client's mental health symptoms and impairments that persist during periods of abstinence of 30 days or more can be useful, particularly in understanding what the client copes with even when the acute effects of substance use are not present. For any period of abstinence that lasts a month or longer, the counselor can ask the client about mental health treatment and/or substance abuse treatment – what seemed to work, what did the client like or dislike, and why? On the other hand, if mental health symptoms (even suicidality or hallucinations) resolve in less than 30 days with abstinence from substances, then these symptoms are most likely substance induced and the best treatment is maintaining abstinence from substances.

The counselor also can ask what the mental health "ups and downs" are like for the client. That is, what is it like for the client when he or she gets worse (or "destabilizes")? What – in detail – has happened in the past? And, what about getting better ("stabilizing") – how does the client usually experience that? Clinician and client together should try to understand the specific affects that substances have had on that individual's mental health symptoms, including the possible triggering of psychiatric symptoms by substance use. Clinicians also should attempt to document the diagnosis of a mental disorder, when it has been established, and determine diagnosis through referral when it has not been established. The consensus panel notes that many, if not most, individuals with COD have well-established diagnoses when they enter substance abuse treatment and encourages counselors to find out about any known diagnoses.

Treatment Planning

A comprehensive assessment serves as the basis for an individualized treatment plan. Appropriate treatment plans and treatment interventions can be quite complex, depending on what might be discovered in each domain. This leads to another fundamental principle:

- There is no single, correct intervention or program for individuals with COD. Rather, the appropriate treatment plan must be matched to individual needs according to these multiple considerations.

The following three cases illustrate how the above factors help to generate an integrated treatment plan that is appropriate to the needs and situation of a particular client.

Case 1: Maria M.

The client is a 38-year-old Hispanic/Latina woman who is the mother of two teenagers. Maria M. presents with an 11-year history of cocaine dependence, a 2-year history of opioid dependence, and a history of trauma related to a longstanding abusive relationship (now over for 6 years). She is not in an intimate relationship at present and there is no current indication that she is at risk for either violence or self-harm. She also has persistent major depression and panic treated with antidepressants. She is very motivated to receive treatment.

- ***Ideal Integrated Treatment Plan:*** The plan for Maria M. might include medication-assisted treatment (e.g., methadone or buprenorphine), continued antidepressant medication, 12-Step program attendance, and other recovery group support for cocaine dependence. She also could be referred to a group for trauma survivors that is designed specifically to help reduce symptoms of trauma and resolve long-term issues.
- Individual, group, and family interventions could be coordinated by the primary counselor from opioid maintenance treatment. The focus of these interventions might be on relapse prevention skills, taking medication as prescribed, and identifying and managing trauma-related symptoms without using. An appropriate long-term goal would be to establish abstinence and engage Maria in longer-term psychotherapeutic interventions to reduce trauma symptoms and help resolve trauma issues. On the other hand, if a local mental health center had a psychiatrist trained and licensed to provide Suboxone (the combination of buprenorphine and nalaxone), her case could be based in the mental health center.

Case 2: George T.

The client is a 34-year-old married, employed African-American man with cocaine dependence, alcohol abuse, and bipolar disorder (stabilized on lithium) who is mandated to cocaine treatment by his employer due to a failed drug test. George T. and his family acknowledge that he needs help not to use cocaine but do not agree that alcohol is a significant problem (nor does his employer). He complains that his mood swings intensify when he is using cocaine.

- ***Ideal Integrated Treatment Plan:*** The ideal plan for this man might include participation in outpatient addiction treatment, plus continued provision of mood-stabilizing medication. In addition, he should be encouraged to attend a recovery group such as Cocaine Anonymous or Narcotics Anonymous. The addiction counselor would provide individual, group, and family interventions. The focus might be on gaining the skills and strategies required to handle cocaine cravings and to maintain abstinence from cocaine, as well as the skills needed to manage mood swings without using substances. Motivational counseling regarding alcohol and assistance in maintaining medication (lithium) adherence also could be part of the plan.

Case 3: Jane B.

The client is a 28-year-old single Caucasian female with a diagnosis of paranoid schizophrenia, alcohol dependence, crack cocaine dependence, and a history of multiple episodes of sexual victimization. Jane B. is homeless (living in a shelter), actively psychotic, and refuses to admit to a drug or alcohol problem. She has made frequent visits to the local emergency room for both mental health and medical complaints, but refuses any follow-up treatment. Her main requests are for money and food, not treatment. Jane has been offered involvement in a housing program that does not require treatment engagement or sobriety but has refused due to paranoia regarding working with staff to help her in this setting. Jane B. refuses all medication due to her paranoia, but does not appear to be acutely dangerous to herself or others.

- ***Ideal Integrated Treatment Plan:*** The plan for Jane B. might include an integrated case management team that is either based in the shelter or in a mental health service setting. The team would apply a range of engagement, motivational, and positive behavioral change strategies aimed at slowly developing a trusting relationship with this woman. Engagement would be promoted by providing assistance to Jane B. in obtaining food and disability benefits, and using those connections to help her engage gradually in treatment for either mental disorders or addiction —possibly by an initial offer of help in obtaining safe and stable housing. Peer support from other women also might be of value in promoting her sense of safety and engagement.

All of these cases are appropriate examples of integrated treatment. The purpose of the assessment process is to develop a method for gathering information in an organized manner that allows the clinician to develop an appropriate treatment plan or recommendation.

Psychopharmacology

Many clients with COD require medication to control their psychiatric symptoms and to stabilize their psychiatric status. The importance of stabilizing the client with COD on psychiatric medication when indicated is now well established in the substance abuse treatment field. One important role of the psychiatrist working in a substance abuse treatment setting is to provide psychiatric medication based on the assessment and diagnosis of the client, with subsequent regular contact and review of medication. These activities include careful monitoring and review of medication adherence.

Pharmacologic effects can be therapeutic or detrimental. Medication often produces both effects. Therapeutic pharmacologic effects include the indicated purposes and desired outcomes of taking prescribed medications, such as a decrease in the frequency and severity of episodes of depression produced by antidepressants.

Detrimental pharmacologic effects include unwanted side effects such as dry mouth or constipation resulting from antidepressant use. Side effects perceived as noxious by clients may decrease their compliance with taking the medications as directed.

Some detrimental pharmacologic effects relate to abuse and addiction potential. For example, some medications may be stimulating, sedating, or euphorigenic and may promote physical dependence and tolerance. These effects can promote the use of medication for longer periods and at higher doses than prescribed.

Thus, prescribing medication involves striking a balance between therapeutic and detrimental pharmacologic effects. For instance, therapeutic antianxiety effects of the benzodiazepines are balanced against detrimental pharmacologic effects of sedation and physical dependency. Similarly, the desired therapeutic effect of abstinence from alcohol is balanced by the possibility of damage to the liver from prescribed disulfiram (Antabuse).

Side effects of prescription medications vary greatly and include detrimental pharmacologic effects that may promote abuse or addiction. With regard to clients with co-occurring disorders, special attention should be given to detrimental effects, in terms of (1) medication compliance, (2) abuse and addiction potential, (3) substance use disorder relapse, and (4) psychiatric disorder relapse (Ries 1993).

Advice to the Counselor: Some Common Side Effects

Tardive dyskinesia

- Involuntary movements of the tongue or mouth
- Jerky, purposeless movements of legs, arms, or entire body
- Usually seen with long-term treatment using traditional antipsychotic medications, sometimes seen with atypical antipsychotic medications
- More often seen in women
- Risk increases with age and length of time on the medication

Neuroleptic malignant syndrome

- Blood pressure up and down
- Dazed and confused
- Difficulty breathing
- Muscle stiffness
- Rapid heart rate
- Sweating and shakiness
- Temperature above normal

Diabetes mellitus

- Associated with atypical neuroleptics
- Excessive thirst
- Headaches
- Frequent urination
- Cuts/blemishes heal slowly
- Fatigue

Other

- Blurred vision
- Changes in sexual functioning
- Constipation
- Diminished enthusiasm
- Dizziness
- Drowsiness
- Dry mouth
- Lowered blood pressure
- Muscle rigidity
- Nasal congestion
- Restlessness
- Sensitivity to bright light
- Slowed heart rate
- Slurred speech
- Upset stomach
- Weight gain

Psychoactive Potential

Not all psychiatric medications are psychoactive. The term *psychoactive* describes the ability of certain medications, drugs, and other substances to cause acute psychomotor effects and a relatively rapid change in mood or thought. Changes in mood include stimulation, sedation, and euphoria. Thought changes can include a disordering of thought such as delusions, hallucinations, and illusions. Behavioral changes can include an acceleration or retardation of motor activity. All drugs of abuse are by definition psychoactive.

In contrast, certain nonpsychoactive medications such as lithium (Eskalith) can, over time, normalize the abnormal mood and behavior of clients with bipolar disorder. Because these effects take several days or weeks to occur, and do not involve acute mood alteration, it is not accurate to describe these drugs as psychoactive, euphorigenic, or mood altering. Rather, they might be described as *mood regulators.* Similarly, some drugs, such as antipsychotic medications, cause normalization of thinking processes but do not cause acute mood alteration or euphoria.

However, some antidepressant and antipsychotic medications have pharmacologic side effects such as mild sedation or mild stimulation. Indeed, the side effects of these medications can be used clinically. Physicians can use a mildly sedating antidepressant medication for clients with depression and insomnia, or a mildly stimulating antipsychotic medication for clients with psychosis and hypersomnia or lethargy (Davis and Goldman 1992). While the side effects of these drugs include a mild effect on mood, they are not euphorigenic. Nevertheless, case reports of misuse of nonpsychoactive medications have been noted, and use should be monitored carefully in clients with co-occurring disorders.

While psychoactive drugs are generally considered to have high risk for abuse and addiction, mood-regulating drugs are not. A few other medications exert a mild psychoactive effect without having addiction potential. For example, the older antihistamines such as doxylamine (Unisom) exert mild sedative effects, but not euphoric effects.

Reinforcement Potential

Some drugs promote *reinforcement*, or the increased likelihood of repeated use. Reinforcement can occur by either the removal of negative symptoms or conditions or the amplification of positive symptoms or states. For example, self-medication that delays or prevents an unpleasant event (such as withdrawal) from occurring becomes reinforcing. Thus, using a benzodiazepine to avoid alcohol withdrawal can increase the likelihood of continued use. *Positive reinforcement* involves strengthening the possibility that a certain behavior will be repeated through reward and satisfaction, as with drug-induced euphoria or drug-induced feelings of well-being. A classic example is the pleasure derived from moderate to high doses of opioids or stimulants. Drugs that are immediately reinforcing are more likely to lead to psychiatric or substance use problems.

Tolerance and Withdrawal Potential

Long-term or chronic use of certain medications can cause tolerance to the subjective and therapeutic effects and prompt dosage increases to recreate the desired effects. In addition, many drugs cause a well-defined withdrawal phenomenon after the cessation of chronic use. Clients' attempts to avoid withdrawal syndromes often lead them to additional drug use. Thus, drugs that promote tolerance and withdrawal generally have higher risks for abuse and addiction.

Nonpsychoactive Pharmacotherapy

Some medications are not psychoactive and do not cause acute psychomotor effects or euphoria. Some medications do not cause psychoactive or psychomotor effects at therapeutic doses but may exert limited psychoactive effects at high doses (often not euphoria, but sometimes dysphoria).

For practical purposes, all of these medications can be described as nonpsychoactive, since the psychoactive effect is not prominent. Medications used in psychiatry that are not euphorigenic or significantly psychoactive include but are not limited to the azapirones (for example, buspirone), the amino acids, beta-blockers, antidepressants, monoamine oxidase inhibitors, antipsychotics, lithium, antihistamines, anticonvulsants, and anticholinergic medications.

Psychoactive Pharmacotherapy

Some medications can cause significant and acute alterations in psychomotor, emotional, and mental activity at therapeutic doses. At higher doses, and for some clients, some of these medications can also cause euphoric reactions. Medications that are potentially psychoactive include opioids, stimulants, benzodiazepines, barbiturates, and other sedative-hypnotics.

The following is a list of some of the principal psychotherapeutic drugs currently used today. It is by no means an exhaustive list of compounds, but does list those found to be used in common practice. It is always advised that counselors speak with the program physician and/or psychiatrist to insure that they understand the drugs being used in their respective treatment program.

Advice to the Counselor: Principal psychotherapeutic drugs

<u>Psychiatric Disorder</u>	<u>Treatment</u>
Anxiety	benzodiazepines (e.g.,Valium, Librium, Xanax) buspirone (BuSpar)
Panic attack	alprazolam (Xanax)
Depression **Monopolar disorder**	tricyclic antidepressants (e.g., Tofranil, Elavil) MAO inhibitors (e.g., Nardil, Parnate) Selective Serotonin Reuptake Inhibitors (SSRI's) (e.g., Prozac, Luvox, Paxil, Celexa, Lexapro) trazodone (Desyrel) bupropion (Wellbutrin)

Bipolar disorder
    for treating
      depression:
	lithium (Eskalith, Carbolith, Cibalith-S, Duralith, Eskalith, Lithane, Lithizine, Lithobid, Lithonate, Lithotabs) carbamazepine (Epitol, Tegretol) lamotrigine (Lamictal) fluoxetine (Prozac) (for depression) ilmipramine (Janimine, Tofranil) tranylcypromine (Parnate)

for treating mania:	carbamazepine (Epitol, Tegretol) valporic acid (Depakene, Valproate, Valrelease) olanzapine (Zyprexa) risperidone (Risperdal) haloperidol (Haldol)

Psychosis (schizophrenia)
Short-acting: phenothiazines (e.g., Thorazine)
                     butyrophenones (e.g., Haldol)
                     clozapine (Clozaril)
                     trifluoperazine (Stelazine)
                     pimozide (Orap)
                     flupenthixol (Fluanxol)
                     chlorpromazine (Largactil)

Long-acting: flupenthixol (Fluanxol)
                     fluphenazine decanoate (Modecate)
                     pipotiazine (Piportil L4)
                     haloperidol decanoate (Haldol LA)

Source: "Drugs and Society," Eighth Edition. Hanson, Venturelli, and Fleckenstein. Jones and Bartlett Publishers, Boston, MA. 2004.

Section 3, Chapter 4:

HIV/AIDS Basic Information

Clean and Sober:

An addict with HIV kicks at the dark till it bleeds daylight

By Mike D.

New York City. July 10, 1985. Heading downtown from the Bronx on the No. 6 train to get my daily dose of methadone. I was 18 years old and addicted to heroin, running from a childhood of beatings and neglect. The heat was intense, but I wore a long-sleeved shirt to cover the little holes and black-and-blue marks on my arms.

That train ride to the city would be my last. I was at the end of my rope and couldn't take another day of the hustle to get "fixed." I picked up my dose and headed home. A scary feeling came over me: I was not going to survive another summer of shooting dope.

When I got home, the house was empty. I was high on methadone, along with some heroin, cocaine and various pills. I shot up, then lay down on my parents' bed. I rolled up my sleeves so they'd see the tracks on my arms. I thought, "They'll find me and then they'll know." I would wake up in a hospital where I'd be saved, or not wake up at all. Either way, it would end.

My parents found me passed out on their bed. They shook me into consciousness and rushed me to emergency. The doctor said if I kept it up, I'd be dead by September. So they took me to rehab. I went through withdrawal in a week, but got so sick that I couldn't walk for a month. I could hardly lift my head. After about 40 days, I was able to get around pretty well and even keep some food down. The most amazing thing is that I wanted to stay. For the first time ever, I felt safe. This guy Anthony came into my room 10 times a day and wiped my head with a wet towel and told me it was going to be OK. I believed him because he was a junkie, too, and he'd been clean for two months. Eventually I was able to sleep well and wake up without cramps or vomiting.

There is not enough paper in this magazine to describe the incredible journey of getting off -- and staying off -- dope, but I will tell you it was the hardest thing I've ever done. Not only did I have to give up my "best friend," I had to start dealing with why I did drugs in the first place.

After three years of exploring my deepest, darkest secrets, I graduated from the program. When asked to be a counselor, I jumped at the offer. AIDS was hitting home, as a few of my friends from treatment had tested positive. I wanted to know all I could about HIV. It wasn't easy, but I gained tons of knowledge. Unfortunately, it didn't come in handy two years later when I took the test myself.

Things were getting hot and heavy with this girl. It was several years since I'd been at risk, so I was pretty sure I was negative. Then again, why was I any different from Anthony, Chris, Fran and the other addicts I knew who had either died or were waiting to get sick?

I wasn't. When my test came back positive, my HIV training went out the window. I hadn't a clue to the numbness and fear. It was like being afraid of the dark even when the lights are on.

Here I was, 22, having spent the past few years getting my life together and now it seemed as good as over. Violent thoughts raced through my mind. I felt dirty, poisonous and wished I'd just die. I waited for the bogey man to get me.

Part of being an addict is thinking there's an easy way out of things. HIV proved to have no easy way out. It was so hard to stay clean back then. I didn't want to shoot up anymore, so I drank. A lot. But it only slightly dulled the pain. One night my buddies and I were at a bar when a real skinny man walked by. One woman we were with said, "Hey, look, the AIDS poster boy!" and laughed. It was too much to bear. A rage inside me was about to explode.

I jumped in my car and headed back to the only real relief I'd ever known. I got my dope and was right back where I left off. It only took a week to get as low as I had been right before I stopped using -- sitting in a puddle next to a garbage can with a needle in my hand. This guy walked over, kicked me and said, "Get the fuck off my block, junkie!" At that moment I knew I'd rather face the bogey man with dignity than die in the gutter with shame.

So I picked myself up and went to a 12-step group. I said, "My name is Mike and I'm an addict with HIV and I need help." About seven other people came up to me after and said, "Hey, I got it too." They turned on the lights and the bogey man went away.

HIV/AIDS AND SUBSTANCE ABUSE

Behavior associated with drug abuse is now the single largest factor in the spread of HIV infection in the United States. HIV is the Human Immunodeficiency Virus, which causes Acquired Immunodeficiency Syndrome, or AIDS. AIDS is a condition characterized by a defect in the body's natural immunity to diseases, and individuals who suffer from it are at risk for severe illnesses that are usually not a threat to anyone whose immune system is working properly. Although many individuals who have AIDS or carry HIV may live for many years with treatment, there is no known cure or vaccine.

Using or sharing unsterile needles, cotton swabs, rinse water, and cookers, such as when injecting heroin, cocaine, or other drugs, leaves a drug abuser vulnerable to contracting or transmitting HIV. Another way people may be at risk for contracting HIV is simply by using drugs of abuse, regardless of whether a needle and syringe are involved. Research sponsored by NIDA and the National Institute on Alcohol Abuse and Alcoholism has shown that drug and alcohol use interfere with judgment about sexual (and other) behavior, making it more likely that users have unplanned and unprotected sex. This places them at increased risk for contracting HIV from infected sex partners.

Currently, between 1.1 and 1.5 million people in the United States are injection drug users (IDU), costing society an estimated $58.3 billion each year. However, even more alarming than the numbers of injection drug users throughout the country is the rate at which this group is contracting HIV. According to the most recent Centers for Disease Control and Prevention (CDC) data, more than 200,000 reported AIDS cases in the United States, or 32%, are among injection drug users. Because laws exist restricting the possession, distribution and sale of any injection equipment in the United States, access to sterile needles is difficult and injection drug users across the country continue to share equipment, despite the risk of becoming infected with HIV.

Infection Rates

(NOTE: The statistical information that follows comes from the latest Centers for Disease Control and Prevention reports and is updated annually. Such reports are issued over the course of many months and years, and as such, reported information can be from two and up to five years in the past. You are encouraged to visit the CDC website at http://www.cdc.gov/hiv/ for the most recent reports as they become available.)

According to the most recent reports from the Centers for Disease Control and Prevention, an estimated 1,039,000 to 1,185,000 persons in the United States are living with HIV/AIDS, with 24-27% undiagnosed and unaware of their HIV infection.

The cumulative estimated number of diagnoses of AIDS in the United States is 944,305. Adult and adolescent AIDS cases total 934,862 with 756,399 cases in males and 178,463 cases in females. 9,443 AIDS cases were estimated in children under the age of 13.

Please note: These totals include persons of unknown race or multiple races and person of unknown sex.

Sharing syringes and other equipment for drug injection is a well-known route of HIV transmission, yet injection drug use contributes to the epidemic's spread far beyond the circle of those who inject. People who have sex with an injection drug user (IDU) also are at risk for infection through the sexual transmission of HIV. Children born to mothers who contracted HIV through sharing needles or having sex with an IDU may become infected as well.

Since the epidemic began, injection drug use has directly and indirectly accounted for more than one-third (36%) of AIDS cases in the United States. This disturbing trend appears to be continuing. According to a Center for Disease Control and Prevention (CDC) analysis of HIV surveillance data, of the 859,000 cumulative AIDS cases currently being reported, a total of 240,268 AIDS diagnoses were due directly to injection drug use, with males accounting for roughly 72 percent of these cases.

Among racial and ethnic groups, 43 percent of cumulative AIDS cases reported among adult and adolescent Hispanic males were directly or indirectly related to injection drug use, as were 42 percent among African American males. The percentages were greater among females, however. Fifty-eight percent of cumulative AIDS cases reported among adult and adolescent Hispanic females were directly or indirectly related to injection drug use, as were 57 percent of cases reported among White females and 51 percent among African American females. By comparison, only 18 percent of the cumulative AIDS cases reported among White males were directly or indirectly related to injection drug use.

The gradual decline over the last reporting period in the number of new AIDS diagnoses among IDUs contrasts with the steady to slightly increasing numbers of new AIDS diagnoses among men who have sex with men (MSM). However, the greater contrast is with the number of new AIDS diagnoses due to heterosexual contact, which has increased steadily for both adult and adolescent males (18 percent) and females (16 percent).

Noninjection drugs (such as "crack" cocaine) also contribute to the spread of the epidemic when users trade sex for money, or when they engage in high-risk sexual behaviors while under the influence of drugs. One CDC study of more than 2,000 young adults in three inner-city neighborhoods found that crack smokers were three times more likely to be infected with HIV than nonsmokers.

Infection Rates by Specific Populations

Trends among Gay, Bisexual, and Other Men who have Sex with Men (MSM)

Gay, bisexual, and other men who have sex with men (MSM)) represent approximately 2% of the United States population, yet are the population most severely affected by HIV. Young MSM (aged 13-24 years) accounted for 72% of new HIV infections among all persons aged 13 to 24, and 30% of new infections among all MSM. At the end of 2010, an estimated 489,121 (56%) persons living with an HIV diagnosis in the United States were MSM or MSM-IDU.

The Numbers

New HIV Infections

- MSM accounted for 63% of estimated new HIV infections in the United States and 78% of infections among all newly infected men. New HIV infections increased 22% among young (aged 13-24) MSM and 12% among MSM overall.
- Among all MSM, white MSM accounted for 11,400 (38%) estimated new HIV infections. The largest number of new infections among white MSM (3,300; 29%) occurred in those aged 25 to 34.
- Among all MSM, black/African American MSM accounted for 10,600 (36%) estimated new HIV infections in 2010. The largest number of new infections among black/African American MSM (4,800; 45%) occurred in those aged 13 to 24. New infections increased 20% among young black/African American MSM aged 13 to 24.

- Among all MSM, Hispanic/Latino MSM accounted for 6,700 (22%) estimated new HIV infections. The largest number of new infections among Hispanic/Latino MSM (3,300; 39%) occurred in those aged 25 to 34.

HIV and AIDS Diagnoses and Deaths

- In the United States, MSM accounted for 79% of 38,825 estimated HIV diagnoses among all males aged 13 years and older and 62% of 49,273 estimated diagnoses among all persons receiving an HIV diagnosis that year.
- Of the estimated 872,990 persons living with an HIV diagnosis, 440,408 (50%) were MSM. Forty-seven percent of MSM living with an HIV diagnosis were white, 31% were black/African American, and 19% were Hispanic/Latino.
- MSM accounted for 52% of estimated AIDS diagnoses among all adults and adolescents in the United States. Of the estimated 16,694 AIDS diagnoses among MSM, 39% were in blacks/African Americans; 34% were in whites; and 23% were in Hispanics/Latinos.
- An estimated 302,148 MSM with an AIDS diagnosis had died in the United States since the beginning of the epidemic, representing 48% of all deaths of persons with an AIDS diagnosis.

Prevention Challenges

The **large number of MSM living with HIV** means that, as a group, gay, bisexual, and other MSM have an increased chance of being exposed to HIV. Results of HIV testing conducted in 20 cities as part of the National HIV Behavioral Surveillance System indicated that 18% of MSM tested were HIV-positive and that HIV prevalence increased with increasing age.

In this study, the overall percent of gay and bisexual men with HIV who knew of their HIV infection increased from 56% in 2008 to 66%. Among those infected, 49% of young MSM aged 18 to 24 years knew of their infection, whereas 76% of those aged 40 and over were aware of their HIV infection. Fifty- four percent of black/African American MSM knew of their infection, compared with 63% of Hispanic/Latino MSM and 86% of white MSM. Persons who don't know they have HIV don't get medical care and can unknowingly infect others. The Centers for Disease Control and Prevention (CDC) recommends that all MSM get tested for HIV at least once a year. Sexually active MSM might benefit from more frequent testing (e.g., every 3 to 6 months).

Sexual risk behaviors account for most HIV infections in MSM. Anal sex without a condom (unprotected anal sex) has the highest risk for passing HIV during sex. It is also possible to become infected with HIV through oral sex, though the risk is significantly less than for anal or vaginal sex. For sexually active MSM, the most effective ways to prevent HIV are to limit or avoid anal sex, or for MSM who do have anal sex, to correctly use a condom every time. Gay men are at increased risk for sexually transmitted infections (STIs), like syphilis, gonorrhea, and chlamydia, and CDC recommends that all sexually active MSM be tested annually for these infections.

Alcohol and illegal drug use increases risk for HIV and other STIs. Using substances such as alcohol and methamphetamines can impair judgment and increase risky sexual behavior.

Homophobia, stigma, and discrimination may place gay men at risk for multiple physical and mental health problems and affect whether they seek and are able to obtain high-quality health services.

Trends among Injection Drug Users (IDUs)
Drug injection was identified as a risk factor for HIV/AIDS early in the epidemic. HIV is transmitted among IDUs who share injection drug equipment or have unprotected sex with an infected partner.

AIDS
Since the beginning of the epidemic, injection drug use has directly or indirectly accounted for more than one third (38%) of estimated AIDS cases diagnosed in the United States. This association appears to be continuing. Of all new cases of AIDS, nearly one quarter (22%) were in IDUs.

Racial and ethnic minority populations are most heavily affected. In 2003, injection drug use alone accounted for 25% of all AIDS cases diagnosed in black men and women and 24% of all AIDS cases diagnosed in Hispanic men and women, compared with only 16% in white men and women.

Among women, injection drug use accounts for a larger proportion of AIDS cases than it does among men. Since the epidemic began, 58% of all AIDS cases in women have been attributed to injection drug use or sex with partners who inject drugs, compared with 34% in men.

HIV
The good news is that new HIV diagnoses seem to be declining overall among IDUs, with a 53% decrease in estimated new HIV diagnoses from 1994 through 2003 in the 25 states with longstanding HIV reporting.

Data reported from 41 areas with confidential HIV infection reporting showed that among IDUs, blacks accounted for 40% of HIV infections, compared with Hispanics, 33%, and whites, 25%.

Trends among Heterosexual Adults

Historically, the HIV/AIDS epidemic has affected more men than women, but women are being increasingly affected. Since 1985 the proportion of estimated AIDS cases diagnosed among women has currently more than tripled, from 8% to 27%.

AIDS

The epidemic has increased most dramatically among women of color. Although black and Hispanic women together represent about one fourth of all US women, they account for more than three fourths of estimated AIDS cases diagnosed to date among US women. Currently, black and Hispanic women represent an even greater proportion (83%) of diagnosed cases in women.

Despite continuing decreases in HIV/AIDS-related deaths in men and women, HIV/AIDS remains the fifth leading cause of death in the United States for men and women aged 35–44 years and one of the top 10 leading causes of death for men and women aged 20–54. For blacks in these age groups, HIV/AIDS ranks even higher as a cause of death.

HIV

Although each year more men than women become infected with HIV, this gap is slowly closing. Data from the 25 states with longstanding HIV reporting show that new HIV diagnoses in men declined 27% since 1994.

Transmission routes differ by gender. Data shows that among men, HIV transmission is estimated to occur 63% through sexual contact with men, 14% through injection drug use, and 17% through sexual contact with women.

Among women, HIV transmission is estimated to occur 79% through sexual contact with men (many of whom are IDUs or also have sexual contact with men) and 19% through injection drug use.

Trends Among African Americans

African Americans have the most severe burden of HIV of all racial/ethnic groups in the United States. Compared with other races and ethnicities, African Americans account for a higher proportion of new HIV infections, those living with HIV, and those ever diagnosed with AIDS.

The Numbers

New HIV Infections

- African Americans accounted for an estimated 44% of all new HIV infections among adults and adolescents (aged 13 years or older), despite representing only 12% of the US population; considering the smaller size of the African American population in the United States, this represents a population rate that is 8 times that of whites overall.
- Men accounted for 70% (14,700) of the estimated 20,900 new HIV infections among all adult and adolescent African Americans. The estimated rate of new HIV infections for African American men (103.6/100,000 population) was 7 times that of white men, twice that of Latino men, and nearly 3 times that of African American women.
- African American gay, bisexual, and other men who have sex with men represented an estimated 72% (10,600) of new infections among all African American men and 36% of an estimated 29,800 new HIV infections among all gay and bisexual men. More new HIV infections (4,800) occurred among young African American gay and bisexual men (aged 13-24) than any other subgroup of gay and bisexual men.
- African American women accounted for 6,100 (29%) of the estimated new HIV infections among all adult and adolescent African Americans. This number represents a decrease of 21% since 2008. Most new HIV infections among African American women (87%; 5,300) are attributed to heterosexual contact. The estimated rate of new HIV infections for African American women (38.1/100,000 population) was 20 times that of white women and almost 5 times that of Hispanic/Latino women.

HIV and AIDS Diagnoses and Deaths

- At some point in their lifetimes, an estimated 1 in 16 African American men and 1 in 32 African American women will be diagnosed with HIV infection.
- From current reports, an estimated 15,958 African Americans were diagnosed with AIDS in the United States.
- By the end of 2011, an estimated 260,821 African Americans ever diagnosed with AIDS had died in the United States.

Prevention Challenges

African Americans face a number of challenges that contribute to the higher rates of HIV infection. The **greater number of people living with HIV (prevalence)** in African American communities and the fact that African Americans tend to **have sex with partners of the same race/ethnicity** means that they face a greater risk of HIV infection with each new sexual encounter.

African American communities continue to experience higher rates of **other sexually transmitted infections (STIs)** compared with other racial/ethnic communities in the United States. Having an STI can significantly increase the chance of getting or transmitting HIV.

Lack of awareness of HIV status can affect HIV rates in communities. During the latest reporting period, almost 85,000 HIV-infected people in the African American community were unaware of their HIV status. Diagnosis late in the course of HIV infection is common, which results in missed opportunities to get early medical care and prevent transmission to others.

The poverty rate is higher among African Americans than other racial/ethnic groups. The **socioeconomic issues** associated with poverty—including limited access to high-quality health care, housing, and HIV prevention education—directly and indirectly increase the risk for HIV infection, and affect the health of people living with and at risk for HIV. These factors may explain why African Americans have worse outcomes on the HIV continuum of care, including lower rates of linkage to care, retention in care, being prescribed HIV treatment, and viral suppression. New data indicate that 75% of HIV-infected African Americans aged 13 or older are linked to care, 48% are retained in care, 46% are prescribed antiretroviral therapy, and only 35% are virally suppressed.

Stigma, fear, discrimination, homophobia, and negative perceptions about HIV testing can also place too many African Americans at higher risk. Many at risk for HIV fear discrimination and rejection more than infection and may choose not to seek testing.

Trends among Latinos

HIV infection is a serious threat to the health of the Hispanic/Latino community. Hispanics/Latinos accounted for over one-fifth (21% or 9,800) of all new HIV infections in the United States and 6 dependent areas despite representing about 16% of the total US population.

The Numbers

New HIV Infections

- Hispanic/Latino men accounted for 87% (8,500) of all estimated new HIV infections among Hispanics/Latinos in the United States. Most (79% or 6,700) of the estimated new HIV infections among Hispanic/Latino men were attributed to male-to-male sexual contact.
- Among Hispanic/Latino men who have sex with men (MSM), 67% of estimated new HIV infections occurred in those under age 35.
- Hispanic women/Latinas accounted for 14% (1,400) of the estimated new infections among all Hispanics/Latinos in the United States.
- The estimated rate of new HIV infection among Hispanics/Latinos in the United States was more than 3 times as high as that of whites (27.5 vs. 8.7 per 100,000 population).

HIV and AIDS Diagnoses and Deaths

- At some point in their lives, an estimated 1 in 36 Hispanic/Latino men and 1 in 106 Hispanic/Latino women will be diagnosed with HIV.
- Hispanics/Latinos accounted for 22% (11,057) of the estimated 50,199 new diagnoses of HIV infection in the United States and 6 dependent areas. Of the 11,032 adult and adolescent Hispanics/Latinos diagnosed with HIV infection in 2011, 84% (9,256) were in men and 16% (1,776) were in women.
- Seventy-nine percent (7,266) of the estimated 9,256 HIV diagnoses among Hispanic/Latino men in the United States and dependent areas were attributed to male-to-male sexual contact. Eighty-six percent (1,522) of the estimated 1,776 HIV diagnoses among Hispanic/Latino women were attributed to heterosexual contact.
- Hispanics/Latinos accounted for 19% (220,400) of the estimated 1.1 million people living with HIV infection in the United States.
- An estimated 6,849 Hispanics/Latinos were diagnosed with AIDS in the United States and 6 dependent areas. This number has fluctuated since 2008.

- By the end of the most recent reporting period, an estimated 118,783 Hispanics/Latinos who had ever been diagnosed with AIDS had died in the United States and 6 dependent areas.HIV was the sixth leading cause of death among Hispanics/Latinos aged 25-34 in the United States and the eighth leading cause of death among Hispanics/Latinos aged 35-54.

Prevention Challenges

A number of factors contribute to the HIV epidemic in Latino communities.

- **There is a greater number of people living with HIV (prevalence)** in Hispanic/Latino communities and Hispanics/ Latinos tend to have sex with partners of the same race/ethnicity. This means that Hispanics/Latinos face a greater risk of HIV infection.
- While data suggest that most Hispanic/Latino men with HIV were infected through sexual contact with other men, the **behavioral risk factors for HIV infection differ by country of birth**. For example, men born in Puerto Rico have a higher percentage of diagnosed HIV infections attributed to injection drug use (IDU).
- The majority of HIV infections diagnosed among Hispanic/Latino men and women are attributed to **sexual contact with men**. Being unaware of a partners' risk factors (for example, IDU, multiple sexual partners, and male-to-male sexual contact) may place Hispanic/Latino men and women at increased risk for HIV.
- Research shows that the presence of a **sexually transmitted disease (STD)** makes it easier to become infected with HIV. Hispanics/Latinos have the third highest rates for STDs including chlamydia, gonorrhea, and syphilis.
- **Cultural factors** may affect the risk of HIV infection. Some Hispanics/Latinos may avoid seeking testing, counseling, or treatment if infected because of immigration status, stigma, or fear of discrimination. Traditional gender roles, cultural norms ("*machismo*," which stresses virility for Hispanics/Latino men, and "*marianismo*," which demands purity from Latina women), and the stigma around homosexuality may add to prevention challenges.
- **Socioeconomic factors** such as poverty, migration patterns, lower educational accomplishment, inadequate or no health insurance, limited access to health care, and language barriers may contribute to HIV infection among Hispanics/Latinos. Those factors may limit awareness about HIV infection risks and opportunities for counseling, testing, and treatment.
- Because of **fear of disclosing immigration status and possible deportation**, undocumented Hispanic/Latino immigrants may be less likely to access HIV prevention services, get an HIV test, or receive adequate treatment and care if they are living with HIV.

Trends among American Indians and Alaska Natives

HIV is a public health issue among the approximately 5.2 million American Indians and Alaska Natives (AI/AN), who represent about 1.7% of the US population. Compared with other racial/ethnic groups, AI/AN ranked fifth in estimated rates of HIV infection diagnoses, with lower rates than in blacks/African Americans, Hispanics/Latinos, Native Hawaiians/Other Pacific Islanders, and people reporting multiple races, but higher rates than in Asians and whites.

The Numbers

Overall, the effect of HIV infection on AI/AN is proportional to their US population size. However, within the overall statistics of new HIV infections and diagnoses, certain measures are disproportionate in this population group relative to other races/ethnicities.

New HIV Infections

- Fewer than 1% (210) of the estimated 47,500 new HIV infections in the United States were among AI/AN.

HIV and AIDS Diagnoses and Deaths

- AI/AN men accounted for 76% (161) and AI/AN women accounted for 24% (51) of the estimated 212 AI/AN diagnosed with HIV infection in the United States.
- Of the estimated 161 HIV diagnoses among AI/AN men in 2011, most (75%; 120) were attributed to male-to-male sexual contact.
- Of the estimated 51 HIV diagnoses among AI/AN women in 2011, the majority (63%, 32) were attributed to heterosexual contact.
- In the United States both male and female AI/AN had the highest percent of estimated diagnoses of HIV infection attributed to injection drug use, compared with all races/ethnicities. Among men, 11% (17) of new HIV diagnoses were attributed to injection drug use and 7% (12) were attributed to both male-to-male sex and injection drug use. Among women 37% (19) of new HIV diagnoses were attributed to injection drug use.
- An estimated 146 AI/AN were diagnosed with AIDS, a number that has remained relatively stable since 2008.
- By the end of the recent reporting period, an estimated 1,945 AI/AN with an AIDS diagnosis had died in the United States. HIV infection was the ninth leading cause of death among AI/AN aged 25 to 34.

Why Are American Indians and Alaska Natives Affected by HIV?

Race and ethnicity alone are not risk factors for HIV infection. However, AI/AN may face challenges associated with risk for HIV.

- **Lack of awareness of HIV status.** Overall, approximately one in six (16%) adults and adolescents living with HIV infection in the United States at the end of the recent reporting period were unaware of their HIV infection. However, by race/ethnicity, a greater percentage of adult and adolescent AI/AN (21%) were estimated to have undiagnosed HIV infection. This translates to an estimated 900 people in the AI/AN community living with undiagnosed HIV infection.
- **Sexually transmitted infections (STIs).** AI/AN have the second highest rates of chlamydia, gonorrhea, and syphilis among all racial/ethnic groups. STIs increase the susceptibility to HIV infection.
- AI/AN gay and bisexual men may face **culturally based stigma and confidentiality concerns** that could limit opportunities for education and HIV testing, especially among those who live in rural communities or on reservations.
- **Cultural diversity.** There are over 560 federally recognized AI/AN tribes, whose members speak over 170 languages. Because each tribe has its own culture, beliefs, and practices and can be subdivided into language groups, it can be challenging to create culturally appropriate prevention programs for each group.
- **Socioeconomic issues.** Poverty, including lack of housing and HIV prevention education, directly and indirectly increases the risk for HIV infection and affects the health of people living with and at risk for HIV infection. Compared with other racial/ethnic groups, AI/AN have higher poverty rates, have completed fewer years of education, are younger, are less likely to be employed, and have lower rates of health insurance coverage.

- **Mistrust of government and its health care facilities.** The federally funded Indian Health Service (IHS) provides health care for approximately 2 million AI/AN and consists of direct services delivered by the IHS, tribally operated health care programs, and urban Indian health care services and resource centers. However, because of confidentiality and quality-of-care concerns and a general distrust of the US government, some AI/AN may avoid IHS.
- **Alcohol and illicit drug use.** Although alcohol and substance use do not cause HIV infection, they can reduce inhibitions and impair judgment and lead to behaviors that increase the risk of HIV. Injection drug use directly increases the risk of HIV through contaminated syringes and works. Compared with other racial/ethnic groups, AI/AN tend to use alcohol and drugs at a younger age, use them more often and in higher quantities, and experience more negative consequences from them.
- **Data limitations.** Racial misidentification of AI/AN may lead to the undercounting of this population in HIV surveillance systems and may contribute to the underfunding of AI/AN-targeted services.

Trends among Asians

Despite being a rapidly growing population, Asians have experienced stable numbers of new HIV infections in recent years. Overall, Asians continue to account for only a small proportion of new HIV infections in the United States and dependent areas.

The Numbers

New HIV Infections

- Asians accounted for 2% (950) of the estimated 47,500 new HIV infections in the United States.
- From 2008 through the recent reporting period, the number of estimated new HIV infections among Asians remained stable.

HIV and AIDS Diagnoses and Deaths

- Asians accounted for 2% (982) of an estimated 50,199 HIV diagnoses in the United States and 6 dependent areas. Of the adult and adolescent Asians diagnosed with HIV infection, 84% (821) were men and 16% (153) were women.

- Eighty-six percent (705) of the estimated 821 HIV diagnoses among Asian men in the United States and dependent areas were attributed to male-to-male sexual contact. Ninety-two percent (141) of the estimated 153 HIV diagnoses among Asian women were attributed to heterosexual contact.
- Asians accounted for 1% (15,400) of the estimated 1.1 million people living with HIV infection in the United States and 6 dependent areas.
- An estimated 492 Asians were diagnosed with AIDS in the United States and 6 dependent areas (representing 2% of the estimated 32,561 AIDS diagnoses), a number that has remained relatively stable since 2008.
- An estimated 3,212 Asians with an AIDS diagnosis had died in the United States and 6 dependent areas.

Prevention Challenges

A number of unique factors contribute to HIV infection in Asian communities:

- **Sexual risk factors** are the main transmission route for HIV among Asians. Like other racial/ethnic groups, most of the Asians who are diagnosed with HIV infection are gay, bisexual, and other men who have sex with men (MSM). High-risk behaviors, including unprotected anal intercourse, multiple sexual partners, and substance use, may contribute to higher risk of infection in these groups. High-risk heterosexual contact is the main way Asian women become infected with HIV.
- **Substance use** can lead to sexual behaviors that increase the risk of HIV infection. Although substance use (with the exception of injection drug use) does not cause HIV infection itself, it is an associated risk factor because of its ability to reduce inhibitions and impair judgment. Asians, as a whole, have among the lowest rates of substance use compared with other racial/ethnic groups. However, higher rates of substance use have been reported among Asian lesbians, gay men, and bisexual men and women, compared to Asian heterosexual men and women.
- **Cultural factors** may affect the risk of HIV infection. Some Asians may avoid seeking testing, counseling, or treatment because of language barriers and/or fear of discrimination, the stigma of homosexuality, immigration issues, or fear of bringing shame to their families. Traditional Asian cultures emphasize male-dominated roles that highlight Asian women's lack of sexual negotiating power in female-male relationships and may contribute to heterosexual HIV transmission among Asian women.

- The **"model minority" stereotype** that assumes Asians always have high socioeconomic and educational achievement, obtain good medical care, and are in overall good health may have contributed to the lack of interest in studying this population and resulted in fewer studies and published literature.
- **Low HIV testing rates** and late testing among Asians have been reported despite this population's levels of HIV risk similar to other racial/ethnic groups. CDC reports that only 3 in 10 Asians have ever been tested for HIV. Low testing rates and late testing has been linked to short intervals between an HIV and AIDS diagnosis, which may indicate inadequate care and treatment among Asians because of poverty, acculturation and immigration issues, and language barriers.
- Due to the diversity among Asians, there may be **race/ethnicity misidentification** that could lead to the **underestimation of HIV infection rates** in this population. Similarly, HIV and AIDS diagnoses and deaths among Asians may be higher than reported. Inaccurate surveillance can result in fewer prevention programs that focus on key populations.

Trends among Native Hawaiians and Other Pacific Islanders

National estimates show that Native Hawaiians and Other Pacific Islanders (NHOPI) are not greatly affected by HIV. However, current estimates of HIV and AIDS diagnoses among NHOPI may be too low because of race/ethnicity misclassification and may mask the real impact of HIV on this population:

- The rate of HIV diagnoses per 100,000 people in the NHOPI population was more than twice as high as rates for whites in 2011.
- From 2008-2011, NHOPI ranked third in rates of HIV diagnoses by race/ethnicity in the United States, behind blacks/African Americans and Hispanics/Latinos.
- The proportion of NHOPI with late HIV diagnoses (AIDS diagnoses within one year of HIV diagnosis) was the highest of all races/ethnicities in the United States and dependent areas. Forty five percent of NHOPI developed AIDS within 12 months after a diagnosis of HIV infection, compared with 38% of American Indians/Alaska Natives diagnosed with HIV, 36% of Hispanics/Latinos, 35% of Asians, 32% of whites, and 31% of blacks/African Americans

The Numbers

New HIV Infections

- NHOPI accounted for less than 1% (70) of the estimated 47,500 new HIV infections in the United States and the District of Columbia.
- There was no statistically significant change in overall HIV incidence (the estimated total number of diagnosed and undiagnosed HIV infections) among NHOPI from 2008 through the most recent reporting period.

HIV and AIDS Diagnoses and Deaths

- Less than 1% (81) of 50,199 estimated diagnoses of HIV infection in the United States and 6 dependent areas were among NHOPI; 86% (70) of infections among NHOPI were in men, and 12% (10) were in women.
- 87% (61) of estimated HIV diagnoses among NHOPI men in the United States and dependent areas were attributed to male-to-male sexual contact, and 80% (8) of the estimated 10 HIV diagnoses among NHOPI women were attributed to heterosexual contact.
- At the end of this reporting period, an estimated 910 NHOPI were living with HIV in the United States and dependent areas.
- An estimated 51 NHOPI were diagnosed with AIDS in the United States and 6 dependent areas.
- By the end of the reporting period, an estimated 371 NHOPI ever classified with an AIDS diagnosis had died in the United States and 6 dependent areas.

Prevention Challenges

A number of unique factors contribute to HIV infection in NHOPI communities:

- **Sexual risk factors** are the main transmission route for HIV among NHOPI. Most of the NHOPI who are diagnosed with HIV infection are gay, bisexual, or men who have sex with men (MSM). High-risk behaviors in NHOPI gay and bisexual men, including unprotected anal intercourse, multiple sexual partners, and sexually transmitted diseases, may contribute to the higher risk of infection. High-risk heterosexual contact is the main way NHOPI women become infected with HIV.
- **Lack of awareness of HIV status** can affect HIV rates in communities. Nationally, approximately 18.1% of US adults and adolescents living with HIV infection were unaware of their HIV infection. However, 26.5% of adult and adolescent NHOPI with HIV were unaware of their infection.
- **Socioeconomic factors** such as poverty, inadequate or no health care coverage, language barriers, and lower educational attainment may contribute to NHOPI's lack of awareness about HIV risk and higher-risk

behaviors that may then lead to higher rates of infection and missed opportunities for testing, counseling, and treatmen.

- **Cultural factors** may affect the risk of HIV infection. NHOPI cultural customs, such as those that prioritize obligations to family (reputation and ethnic pride) and taboos on intergenerational sexual topics and sexual health discussion, may stigmatize homosexuality and interfere with HIV risk reduction strategies, such as condom use.
- **Limited research** about NHOPI health and HIV infection has resulted in few targeted prevention programs and behavioral interventions in this population.
- **The low number of HIV cases** among NHOPI may not reflect the true burden of HIV in this population because of **race/ ethnicity misidentification** that could lead to the **underestimation of HIV infection in this population.**

Trends among Transgender People

Transgender communities in the United States are among the groups at highest risk for HIV infection. The term *gender identity* refers to a person's basic sense of self, and transgender refers to people whose gender identity does not conform to a binary classification of gender based on biological sex, external genitalia, or their sex assigned at birth. It includes gender-nonconforming people with identities beyond the gender binary who self-identify as: male-to-female or transgender women; female-to-male or transgender men; two-spirit; and people who self-identify simply as women or men.

The Numbers

Because data for this population are not uniformly collected, information is lacking on how many transgender people in the United States are infected with HIV. However, data collected by local health departments and scientists studying these communities show high levels of HIV infection and racial/ethnic disparities.

- More than half of the HIV testing events among transgender people occurred at non-healthcare facilities (55.1%). The Centers for Disease Control and Prevention (CDC) reported that the highest percentage of newly identified HIV-positive test results was among transgender people (2.1%). For comparison, the lowest percentages of newly identified HIV-positive test results were among females (0.4%), followed by males (1.2%). Among transgender people, the highest percentages of newly identified HIV-positive test results were among racial and ethnic minorities: blacks/African Americans comprised 4.1% of newly identified HIV-positive test results, followed by Latinos (3.0%), American Indians/Alaska Natives and Native Hawaiians/Other Pacific Islanders (both 2.0%), and whites (1.0%).

- In New York City, since 2007 there were 191 new diagnoses of HIV infection among transgender people, 99% of which were among transgender women. The racial/ethnic disparities were large: approximately 90% of transgender women newly diagnosed with HIV infection were blacks/African Americans or Latinos. Over half (52%) of newly diagnosed transgender women were in their twenties. Also, among newly diagnosed people, 51% of transgender women had documentation in their medical records of substance use, commercial sex work, homelessness, incarceration, and/or sexual abuse as compared with 31% of other people who were not transgender.

- Findings from a meta-analysis of 29 published studies showed that 27.7% of transgender women tested positive for HIV infection (4 studies), but when testing was not part of the study, only 11.8% of transgender women self-reported having HIV (18 studies). In one study, 73% of the transgender women who tested HIV-positive were unaware of their status. Higher percentages of newly identified HIV-positive test results were found among black/African American transgender women (56.3%) than among white (16.7%) or Latino (16.1%) transgender women; and self-reported HIV infection in studies made up of predominantly of black/African American transgender women (30.8%) was higher than positivity reported in studies comprising mainly white transgender women (6.1%). Studies also indicate that black transgender women are more likely to become infected with HIV than non-black transgender women.

- A review of studies of HIV infection in countries with data available for transgender people estimated that HIV prevalence for transgender women was nearly 50 times as high as for other adults of reproductive age.

Prevention Challenges

Individual behaviors alone do not account for the high burden of HIV infection among transgender people. Many cultural, socioeconomic, and health-related factors contribute to the HIV epidemic and prevention challenges in US transgender communities.

- **Identifying transgender people within current data systems can be challenging.** Some transgender people may not identify as transgender due to fear of discrimination or previous negative experiences. Since some people in this community do not self-identify as transgender, relying solely upon gender to identify transgender people is not enough. Gender expression may fluctuate for some transgender people due to issues such as perceived safety or reluctance to identify as transgender in certain situations. The Institute of Medicine has recommended that behavioral and surveillance data for transgender men and women should be collected and analyzed separately and not grouped with data for men who have sex with men. Using the 2-step data collection method of asking for sex assigned at birth and current gender identity increases the likelihood that all transgender people will be accurately identified.

- It is important to avoid making assumptions about **sexual orientation** and **sexual behavior** based on gender identity because there is great diversity in orientation and behavior in this population, and some identify as both transgender and gay, heterosexual, bisexual, or lesbian. For example, transgender men claim a variety of sexual orientations and have sexual partners that include gay men and transgender women.
- **Transgender men's sexual health has been understudied.** Compared to transgender women, little is known about HIV risk and sexual health needs among transgender men. One meta-analysis of 29 studies involving transgender people showed that only 5 of them had separate data concerning transgender men.
- **Behaviors and factors that contribute to high risk of HIV infection** among transgender people include higher rates of drug and alcohol abuse, sex work, incarceration, homelessness, attempted suicide, unemployment, lack of familial support, violence, stigma and discrimination, limited health care access, and negative health care encounters.
- **Police policies can conflict with public health initiatives.** For example, some law enforcement officers and agencies view the presence of condoms as evidence of sex work, even though public health initiatives identify condoms as a way to prevent HIV infection.
- **Discrimination and social stigma** can hinder access to education, employment, and housing opportunities. In a study conducted in San Francisco, transgender people were more likely than men who have sex with men or heterosexual women to live in transient housing and be less educated. Discrimination and social stigma may help explain why transgender people who experience significant economic difficulties often pursue high-risk activities, including sex work, to meet their basic survival needs.
- Interventions that address multiple **co-occurring public health problems**—including substance use, poor mental health, violence and victimization, discrimination, and economic hardship—should be developed and evaluated for transgender people.

- **Health care provider insensitivity** to transgender identity or sexuality can be a barrier for HIV-infected transgender people seeking health care. Although research shows a similar proportion of HIV-positive transgender women have health insurance coverage as compared with other infected people who are not transgender, HIV-infected transgender women are less likely to be on antiretroviral therapy.
- **Additional research is needed to identify factors that prevent HIV in this population.** Several behavioral HIV prevention interventions developed for transgender people have been reported in studies, generally involving relatively small samples of transgender women. Most have shown at least modest reductions in HIV risk behaviors among transgender women, such as fewer sex partners and/or unprotected anal sex acts, although none have involved a control group. Behavioral HIV prevention interventions developed for other at-risk groups with similar behaviors have been adapted for use with transgender people; however, their effectiveness is still unknown.

Trends among Youth

Youth in the United States account for a substantial number of HIV infections. Gay, bisexual, and other men who have sex with men account for most new infections in the age group 13 to 24; black/African American or Hispanic/Latino gay and bisexual men are especially affected. Continual HIV prevention outreach and education efforts, including programs on abstinence, delaying the initiation of sex, and negotiating safer sex for the spectrum of sexuality among youth— homosexual, bisexual, heterosexual, and transgender—are urgently needed for a new generation at risk.

The Numbers

New HIV Infections Among Youth (Aged 13–24 Years)

- Youth made up 17% of the US population, but accounted for an estimated 26% (12,200) of all new HIV infections (47,500) in the United States.
- Young gay and bisexual men accounted for an estimated 19% (8,800) of all new HIV infections in the United States and 72% of new HIV infections among youth. These young men were the only age group that showed a significant increase in estimated new infections—22% from 2008 (7,200) through 2010 (8,800).
- Black youth accounted for an estimated 57% (7,000) of all new HIV infections among youth in the United States, followed by Hispanic/Latino (20%, 2,390) and white (20%, 2,380) youth.

HIV and AIDS Diagnoses and Deaths Among Youth (Aged 13-24)

- An estimated 10,456 youth were diagnosed with HIV infection in the United States and six dependent areas during the latest reporting period, representing 21% of an estimated 50,199 people diagnosed during that year. Seventy-eight percent (8,140) of these diagnoses occurred in those aged 20 to 24, the highest number and population rate of HIV diagnoses of any age group (36.3 new HIV diagnoses/100,000 people).
- Of the estimated 39,035 youth living with diagnosed HIV infection in the United States and 6 dependent areas: An estimated 27,621 HIV diagnoses were among young men. Of these, 77% of HIV diagnoses were attributed to male-to-male sexual contact and 13% to perinatal exposure.
- An estimated 11,413 HIV diagnoses were among young women. Of these, 56% were attributed to heterosexual contact and 34% to perinatal exposure.
- An estimated 3,004 youth in the United States and six dependent areas were diagnosed with AIDS, a number that has increased 29% since 2008.
- By the end of the reporting period, an estimated 11,731 youth with an AIDS diagnosis had died in the United States and six dependent areas since the HIV epidemic began.

Prevention Challenges

- **Low perception of risk.** A majority of 15- to 24-year-olds in the United States responding to a Kaiser Family Foundation survey said they were not concerned about becoming infected with HIV, which means they may not take measures to protect their health.
- **Low rates of testing.** It is estimated that since 2010, almost 60% of youth aged 13 to 24 with HIV in the United States were unaware of their infection, compared to 16% for all ages. In a 2011 survey, only 13% of high school students (22% of those who had ever been sexually active), and in a 2010 survey, only 35% of adults aged 18 to 24 had been tested for HIV.
- **Low rates of condom use.** In a 2012 survey in the United States, of the 34% of high school students reporting sexual intercourse in the previous 3 months, 40% did not use a condom.

- **High rates of sexually transmitted infections (STIs).** Some of the highest STI rates in the United States are among youth aged 20 to 24, especially those of minority races and ethnicities. The presence of an STI greatly increases a person's likelihood of acquiring or transmitting HIV.
- **Older partners.** Young gay and bisexual men are more likely to choose older sex partners than those of their own age, and older partners are more likely to be infected with HIV.
- **Substance use.** Nearly half (47%) of youth aged 12 to 20 reported current alcohol use, and 10% of youth aged 12 to 17 said they were current users of illicit drugs. Substance use has been linked to HIV infection because both casual and chronic substance users are more likely to engage in high-risk behaviors, such as sex without a condom, when they are under the influence of drugs or alcohol.
- **Homelessness.** Runaways, homeless youth, and youth who have become dependent on drugs are at high risk for HIV infection if they exchange sex for drugs, money, or shelter.
- **Inadequate HIV prevention education.** Young people are not always reached by effective HIV interventions or prevention education—especially young gay and bisexual men, because some sex education programs exclude information about sexual orientation.
- **Feelings of isolation.** Gay and bisexual high school students may engage in risky sexual behaviors and substance abuse because they feel isolated and lack support.

Trends among Older Americans

A growing number of people aged 50 and older in the United States are living with HIV infection. People aged 55 and older accounted for almost one-fifth (19%, 217,000) of the estimated 1.1 million people living with HIV infection in the United States in the recent reporting period.

The Numbers

New HIV Infections (Aged 55 and Older)

- Of an estimated 47,500 new HIV infections, 5% (2,500) were among Americans aged 55 and older. Of these older Americans:
    - 36% (900) of new infections were in white men, and 4% (110) were in white women;

- 24% (590) of new infections were in black men, and 15% (370) were in black women;
- 12% (310) of new infections were in Hispanic/Latino men, and 4% (100) were in Hispanic/Latino women.

- 44% (1,100) of the estimated 2,500 new HIV infections among people aged 55 and older were among gay, bisexual, or other men who have sex with men (MSM). Among MSM aged 55 and older, white MSM accounted for an estimated 67% (740) of new HIV infections, Hispanic/Latino MSM 16% (180), and black MSM 15% (160).

HIV and AIDS Diagnoses and Deaths

- People aged 50-54 represented 47% (3,951) of the estimated 8,440 HIV diagnoses among people aged 50 and older in the United States. From 2008-the present, the estimated annual numbers and rates of HIV diagnoses in this aged group remained relatively stable.
- The estimated rate (per 100,000 people) of HIV diagnoses for older blacks was 41.6, which was nearly 11 times the estimated rate for whites (3.9) and nearly 3 times the estimated rate for Hispanics/Latinos (15.4) in 46 states with confidential, name-based reporting.
- From 2007-the present, the estimated annual numbers of diagnosed HIV infections attributed to male-to-male sexual contact increased among men aged 50 and over (in 46 states with confidential, name-based HIV reporting).
- People aged 50 and older accounted for 24% (7,771) of the estimated 32,052 AIDS diagnoses in the United States.
- Of the estimated 19,343 deaths among people living with diagnosed HIV infection in the United States, 10,244 (53%) were among people aged 50 and older. In 2010, HIV was the 10th leading cause of death among men and women aged 50-54.

Prevention Challenges

Late HIV Diagnoses and Shorter HIV-to-AIDS Intervals

Older Americans are more likely than younger Americans to be diagnosed with HIV infection late in the course of their disease, meaning a late start to treatment and possibly more damage to their immune system. This can lead to poorer prognoses and shorter HIV-to-AIDS intervals. For instance, an estimated 24% of people aged 25-29 who were diagnosed with HIV infection in 2011 progressed to AIDS in 12 months, compared with an estimated 44% of people aged 50 to 59,

49% of people aged 60-64, and 53% of people aged 65 and older. One reason this may be happening is that health care providers do not always test older people for HIV infection. Another may be that older people mistake HIV symptoms for those of normal aging and don't consider HIV as a cause.

Sexual Risk Factors

Many older Americans are sexually active, including those who are infected with HIV, and have many of the same risk factors for HIV infection as younger Americans, including a lack of knowledge about HIV and how to prevent transmission, inconsistent condom use, and multiple partners. Older people also face unique issues, including:

- Many widowed and divorced people are dating again, and they may be less knowledgeable about HIV than younger people, and less likely to protect themselves.
- Women who no longer worry about getting pregnant may be less likely to use a condom and to practice safer sex. Age-related thinning and dryness of vaginal tissue may raise older women's risk for HIV infection.
- The availability of erectile dysfunction medications may facilitate sex for older men who otherwise would not have been capable of vaginal or anal intercourse.
- Although they visit their doctors more frequently, older Americans are less likely than younger Americans to discuss their sexual habits or drug use with their doctors, who in turn may be less likely to ask their older patients about these issues.

Stigma

Stigma is a particular concern among older Americans because they may already face isolation due to illness or loss of family and friends. Stigma negatively affects people's quality of life, self-image, and behaviors and may prevent them from seeking HIV care and disclosing their HIV status.

Trends among Women

At the end of the current reporting period, one in four people living with HIV in the United States were women. African American and Hispanic/Latino women continue to be disproportionately affected by HIV, compared with women of other races/ethnicities.

Not all US women who are diagnosed with HIV are getting the care they need. In 19 US jurisdictions with complete reporting, of all women who were diagnosed with HIV by year-end 2009 and alive in 2010, only 53% were staying in care in 2011, and 42% had viral suppression.

The Numbers

New HIV Infections

- Women made up 20% (9,500) of the estimated 47,500 new HIV infections in the United States in 2010. Eighty-four percent of these new infections (8,000) were from heterosexual contact.
- When comparing groups by race/ethnicity, gender, and transmission category, the fourth largest number of all new HIV infections in the United States (5,300) occurred among African American women with heterosexual contact. Of the total number of estimated new HIV infections among women, 64% (6,100) were in African Americans, 18% (1,700) were in whites, and 15% (1,400) were in Hispanic/Latino women.

HIV and AIDS Diagnoses and Deaths

- An estimated 10,257 women aged 13 years or older received a diagnosis of HIV infection in the United States (21% of the all estimated diagnoses during 2011), down from the 12,146 new diagnoses among women in 2008.
- Women accounted for 25% (7,949) of the estimated 32,052 AIDS diagnoses (including children) in 2011 and represent 20% (232,902) of the 1,155,792 cumulative AIDS diagnoses (including children) in the United States from the beginning of the epidemic through the end of 2011.
- Among women ever diagnosed with AIDS, an estimated 4,014 died during 2011, and by the end of the recent reporting period, an estimated 111,940 had died since the beginning of the epidemic.
- At some point in their lifetimes, an estimated 1 in 32 African American women will be diagnosed with HIV infection.

Why Are Women Affected by HIV?

- Some women may be **unaware of their male partner's risk factors** for HIV (such as injection drug use or having sex with other men) and may not use condoms.

- Women have a much higher risk for getting HIV during **vaginal sex without a condom** than men do, and **anal sex without a condom** is riskier for women than vaginal sex without a condom. More than 20% of women aged 20 to 39 who responded to a national survey reported anal sex in the past year.
- Women may be afraid that their partner will leave them or even physically abuse them if they try to talk about condom use.
- Some **sexually transmitted infections**, such as gonorrhea and syphilis, greatly increase the likelihood of getting or spreading HIV.
- Women who have been **sexually abused** may be more likely than women with no abuse history to engage in sexual behaviors like exchanging sex for drugs, having multiple partners, or having sex with a partner who is physically abusive when asked to use a condom.
- Some HIV infections among women are due to **injection drug and other substance use**—either directly (sharing drug injection equipment contaminated with HIV) or indirectly (engaging in high-risk behaviors while under the influence of drugs or alcohol).
- The greater number of **people living with HIV (prevalence)** in African American and Hispanic/Latino communities and the fact that people tend to have sex with partners of the same race/ethnicity means that women from these communities face a greater risk of HIV infection with each new sexual

---

Trends among Correctional Facility Inmates

Inmates in jails and prisons across the United States (US) are disproportionately affected by multiple health problems, including HIV, other sexually transmitted infections (STIs), tuberculosis (TB), and viral hepatitis. Each year, an estimated 1 in 7 persons living with HIV pass through a correctional facility. Most of them acquired HIV in the community, not while they were incarcerated. Compared with those who have not been incarcerated, incarcerated populations have more risk factors that are associated with acquiring and transmitting HIV, including injection drug and other drug use, commercial sex work, untreated mental illness, and lower socioeconomic status.

The Numbers

More than 2 million people are incarcerated in the US. At the end the Bureau of Justices' most recent report, 1,612,395 persons were in state and federal prisons; 748,728 persons were in local jails.

Men and women of color—particularly black men and women—are disproportionately represented in the US correctional system.

- Black males had an imprisonment rate that was nearly 7 times that of white males and almost 2.5 times that of Hispanic/Latino males.
- That same year, black females had an imprisonment rate that was nearly 3 times that of white females and almost 2 times that of Hispanic/Latino females.

In 2008 (the most recent year for which this information is available), 20,449 state prisoners and 1,538 federal prisoners (total, 21,987)—1.4% of the total prison population—were reported to be living with HIV or AIDS. Of the male inmates, 20,075, or 1.3%, were known to be living with HIV, compared with 1,912 female inmates, or 1.7%, who were living with the virus.

The rate of confirmed AIDS cases among state and federal prisoners was about 2.4 times the rate in the general US population. At year-end 2008, an estimated 5,733 inmates in state and federal prisons had confirmed AIDS. Of the 120 AIDS-related deaths in state prisons in 2007, nearly two-thirds, or 65%, were among black inmates, compared with 23% among white inmates and 12% among Hispanic/Latino inmates.

Prevention Challenges

HIV Testing

The correctional setting is often the first place incarcerated men and women are diagnosed with HIV and provided treatment. These settings are ideal for reaching persons who have HIV, other STIs, TB, and viral hepatitis, as well as for providing at least initial treatment and care for persons with these infections. They also offer an opportunity to provide risk-reduction interventions that help prevent infection among those at highest risk. Yet, correctional staff and health care providers in jails and prisons frequently confront challenges related to

- implementing testing, treatment, and prevention programs in these facilities; and
- providing effective linkages to care and support services that sustain clinical benefits for prisoners after their release.

The Centers for Disease Control and Prevention (CDC) recommends HIV testing as part of routine medical care. In correctional settings, CDC recommends that HIV screening be provided upon entry into prison and before release and that voluntary HIV testing be offered periodically during incarceration. Testing has both individual and public health benefits, given the importance of getting early

HIV care and the increased risk of HIV transmission among persons who do not know they have HIV. Although HIV testing is practical and acceptable in jails and prisons, inmates commonly are hesitant to be tested for a number of reasons, including

- fear of a positive diagnosis and the potential stigma associated with it; and
- concern that medical confidentiality will not be maintained.

Logistical, legal, and financial restrictions also have impeded HIV testing in correctional settings. Some of these logistical constraints—such as rapid turnover in jail inmates—have been addressed by using rapid HIV tests and testing within the first 24 hours after incarceration. Some correctional systems may be reluctant to provide HIV testing because it could mean increased laboratory and medical costs. Health care providers in correctional settings may face unique confidentiality and reporting requirements; they should be familiar with their local and state public health confidentiality laws and incorporate them into the HIV testing program.

Other HIV Prevention Interventions

In addition to HIV testing, CDC recommends that HIV education and prevention counseling be made available to inmates in correctional facilities. These programs should address risk inside and outside of the correctional setting. Prevention education programs delivered by peer educators are particularly effective in establishing the trust and rapport needed to discuss sensitive topics related to sexual practices, substance use, and HIV. Providing condoms and clean syringes to sexually active persons is an integral part of HIV prevention interventions outside prisons, but most US prisons and jails specifically prohibit the distribution and possession of these items. Although sex and substance use are forbidden in jails and prisons, the reality is that some incarcerated men and women have consensual or forced sex and that some use illicit drugs.

All inmates with HIV should have access to appropriate HIV medical care and treatment in addition to prevention counseling and, before release, should receive discharge planning and linkages to medical care in the community to ensure the continuity of HIV care and treatment. Such planning is crucial to sustain effective local HIV control efforts within the communities inmates return to.

Trends among People Worldwide
Though AIDS-related deaths have fallen by 30% since the peak in 2005, HIV and AIDS still pose one of the greatest challenges to global public health. Worldwide in the last reporting period, more than 1.6 million people died from AIDS. During that same period, an estimated 2.3 million people acquired HIV, bringing the number of people living with HIV to 35.3 million. Especially vulnerable are disadvantaged, marginalized, and unempowered populations such as commercial sex workers, IDUs, MSM, women and girls, and people living in poverty. Many people do not know that they carry the virus. Millions more know nothing or too little about HIV to protect themselves against it. Even those who do know about HIV prevention may not have the power to act on it, especially women and girls, who are often unable to say no to unprotected sex or to negotiate safer behaviors.

Sub-Saharan Africa
Approximately 25 million people are living with HIV/AIDS; an estimated 1.6 million were newly infected with HIV in this period. HIV/AIDS is the leading cause of death in sub-Saharan Africa. In the current reporting period alone, AIDS killed 1.2 million African people. Without adequate treatment and care, most of those living with HIV will not survive the next decade.

Asia and the Pacific
Approximately 4.8 million people are living with HIV/AIDS; an estimated 1.9 million were newly infected. The epidemic claimed over 261,000. High HIV infection rates in the region are being discovered among IDUs, MSM, and sex workers.

Latin America and the Caribbean
Approximately 1.5 million people are living with HIV/AIDS; an estimated 86,000 were newly infected. Driving the spread of HIV are unequal socioeconomic development and a highly mobile population. The region, however, has made admirable progress in providing treatment and care.

Western Europe, North America, Australia, and New Zealand
Approximately 2.8 million people are living with HIV/AIDS; an estimated 40,000 were newly infected. A larger epidemic threatens to develop in high-income countries. Unsafe sex and widespread injection drug use are propelling these epidemics, which are shifting more toward underprivileged communities.

Eastern Europe and Central Asia

Approximately 1.3 million people are living with HIV/AIDS; an estimated 130,000 were newly infected. Eastern Europe – especially the Russian Federation – continues to experience the fastest growing epidemic in the world. Because of high levels of other STDs and injection drug use among young people, the epidemic may grow considerably.

The Middle East and North Africa

Approximately 260,000 people are living with HIV/AIDS; an estimated 32,000 were newly infected. Poor surveillance systems in several countries hinder accurate assessment of and response to the epidemic.

"AIDS 101"

It is okay to start with little or no knowledge of AIDS, ARC, or safer sex. It is not okay to never find out. When it comes to AIDS prevention, knowledge really is power.

Since people approach AIDS with varying levels of education and understanding, this material, from the Harvard School of Medicine bulletin board service on Internet, provides the chemical dependency counselor with information on facts, issues, answers to common questions, and knowledge on testing and treatment of HIV and AIDS.

What is AIDS?

AIDS stands for Acquired Immune Deficiency Syndrome. First discovered in the United States in 1981, AIDS has spread rapidly, killing men, women and children, Blacks, whites, Latinos and Asians, heterosexuals, homosexuals, the rich and the poor. To date over 90,000 people in the United States have died from AIDS and the number of diagnosed AIDS case doubles every 13 to 15 months. There is no cure for AIDS: PREVENTION is the only way to stem the spread of this deadly virus.

Human immunodeficiency virus (HIV), the virus which causes AIDS, debilitates the immune system - that part of the body which normally protects against disease -leaving the individual vulnerable to rare infections which they could have easily fought off earlier. These infections can be deadly. More than half the people diagnosed with AIDS have already died from the disease.

Once a person is infected with HIV there is no way to destroy or rid the body of the virus. There is hope for effective treatments to thwart the effects of HIV. The drug AZT (Zidovudine) inhibits replication of the virus within the body. AZT may prolong the lives of people with AIDS and even prevent the appearance of symptoms related to HIV infection. Researchers are continuing to search for other ways to fight AIDS. Experimental vaccines to protect against HIV infection are now being tested. If one of these proves to be successful immunization against AIDS infection may begin in the 1990s.

AIDS is not contagious, that is, it is not spread by casual contact; therefore there is no need to fear people who have HIV or AIDS. You can not get AIDS by touching people, eating in restaurants, or being near someone who has AIDS. You won't get AIDS from your pets, toilets, swimming pools, dishes or bugs. AIDS is spread mainly through sexual intercourse and sharing drug needles with infected IV drug users. Women who are infected with the virus can also transmit the disease to their unborn child.

Why haven't we heard about it before? AIDS was not recognized or described as a disease until 1981. Tracking of AIDS only began when doctors had seen enough of it to recognize that they were faced with a serious, previously unknown disease. In 1981, 316 people in the United States had AIDS. Five years later (by August, 1986), over 23,000 cases were reported here. A tremendous growth in the rate of the disease has continued and today we have over 60,000 reported cases. This is alarming, and scientists, health professionals and the general public have all become extremely concerned about it.

The exact origins of AIDS are not known. Either it is a new human disease that developed recently, or it is a disease that was, until recently, isolated in a particular geographic group of people. The prevailing scientific opinion now is that the virus originated in Africa. A particular kind of monkey, the African green monkey, is known to carry a virus quite similar in structure to the human AIDS virus. The best scientific guess is that at some point in time, as a natural part of the process of all living organisms, there was a chance mutation of one of the simian (monkey) viruses, which make it possible for the virus to cross the species barrier from monkey to human. While mutations at the cellular level are fairly common, this particular type of mutation would be very unusual.

In certain areas of Africa, the green monkey is considered a food delicacy. Possibly through ingesting some uncooked organs, or through an accidental cut while preparing a carcass, the first human was infected. The disease may have begun in this simple, quiet manner, spreading to others from this point through sexual intercourse and shared needle use. We want to note that many African government representatives are sensitive about this view, understandably, since it is often set forth in a manner that seems to blame Africa for the appearance of the virus. While scientific events are not themselves racist, observations and reporting of them may be so. It is important to remember that no one person, nation or population is responsible for the development of AIDS, and we must all share the responsibility of stopping the spread of the virus.

What is ARC?

ARC stands for AIDS Related Complex, and is caused by the same virus which causes AIDS. People with ARC may show many of the same symptoms as a person with AIDS - ranging from persistent swollen lymph glands to extreme fatigue and rapid weight loss - though it differs from AIDS in that a person with AIDS also has an opportunistic infection. The most common opportunistic infections in people with AIDS are Pneumocystis carinii pneumonia (PCP) and Kaposi's sarcoma (KS), a rare skin cancer. "Immunosuppressed" or "immunocompromised" are other terms used to refer to people with a weakened immune system.

The effects of HIV (Human Immunodeficiency Virus) on the immune system may weaken the body so much that other health-related problems may lead to death for the person with ARC, making it no less serious as AIDS. Usually, persons with ARC lead active, productive lives, having only mild symptoms that don't normally affect daily activities.

People can also be without any symptoms for extended periods of time. Studies show some people with ARC may never go on to develop full-blown AIDS, and most do not progress to AIDS within five years. In a study conducted by researchers in New York City, 29% of people with ARC were diagnosed as having AIDS within 4 1/2 years. Public health officials estimate that there are between 100,000 and 200,000 persons with ARC in the United States.

How Does HIV Affect the Body?

Discovery of the virus which causes AIDS was first reported in May, 1983 by Dr. Luc Montagnier and fellow researchers at the Pasteur Institute in Paris. They named the virus lymphadenopathy-associated virus (LAV), because they had isolated it from the lymph node of a patient who had what is now known as ARC. At approximately the same time, Dr. Robert Gallo and his colleagues at the National Cancer Institute also identified the causative agent of AIDS. They named it human T-cell lymphotropic virus-III (HTLV-III), in light of its apparent similarity to other viruses isolated by Gallo and his staff, namely, HTLV-I and HTLV-II. Controversy surrounding the labeling of this newly identified virus led the International Committee on the Taxonomy of Viruses to give it the name human immunodeficiency virus (HIV). This is the designation which the medical community now uses to refer to the virus.

HIV is different from many other viruses. It belongs to a special family of viruses known as retroviruses. Like other viruses, retroviruses consist of a tightly packed core of genetic information and a protein coat. Retroviruses contain their genetic information in ribonucleic acid (RNA) rather than in deoxyribonucleic acid (DNA). In order to replicate, the retrovirus must use an enzyme known as reverse transcriptase to create DNA from viral RNA. This newly manufactured viral DNA is then inserted into the DNA of the host cell. The inserted viral DNA is termed the provirus. The provirus then uses the genetic machinery of the host cell to reproduce itself. In this way, retroviruses, like all viruses, depend upon the host cell to provide the mechanism for the production of new viral particles.

The primary target of HIV is a special type of white blood cell known as the T-4 helper cell, the cell responsible for directing the immune system's fight against invading organisms. When HIV enters the body, it seeks out the T-4 helper cell, attaches itself to this cell and then enters it. Once inside, it uses the genetic material of the T-4 helper cell to replicate. New viral particles are then released into the blood stream, where they can find new T-4 helper cells to infect.

The presence of HIV inside the T-4 helper cell can cause the cell to function poorly or destroy the helper cell completely. When the number of T-4 helper cells decreases drastically in the body, the immune system is unable to fight off many infections which normally pose no threat. Complications related to these opportunistic infections can lead to death for the person with AIDS.

Macrophages, another type of white blood cell, can also be infected by the AIDS virus. These cells often travel throughout the body, destroying invading organisms that may be present outside of the circulatory system. But macrophages can carry HIV into the brain. Once in the brain, HIV attacks the glial cells, the cells that provide structural support and insulation for neurons. If a large number of glial cells are destroyed, the intellectual functioning of the individual may be dramatically impaired.

The manifestations of HIV infection can vary widely from person to person. The range of infections seen is quite broad, with people being affected by fungal, bacterial, protozoal and viral disease as well as some cancers. Two diseases we hear most often about are Kaposi's Sarcoma (KS) and Pneumocystis carinii pneumonia (PCP).

KS is a cancer of the cells that line certain small blood vessels. People with KS develop purple lesions on the skin or possibly internally where they cannot be seen. In time, the lesions increase in both number and size, causing complications as they spread.

PCP is the most common opportunistic infection seen in people with AIDS. It is caused by a protozoan, a microscopic organism. People with PCP usually become quite ill at the time of diagnosis, with fatigue, weight loss, fevers, dry cough and difficulty breathing.

People with HIV may also suffer from infections that can lead to confusion, loss of memory, poor motor control, inability to speak clearly, seizures, or other manifestations of dementia. These problems may be caused by direct HIV infection of the brain, or by diseases such as toxoplasmosis or cryptococcal meningitis.

Other illnesses seen are either very unusual diseases rarely diagnosed in anyone who does not have HIV infection, or more common human illnesses that appear in unusually severe forms.

For example, a person with AIDS might have a thrush infection (Candida) which is not limited to the mouth but spreads throughout the esophagus and intestinal tract. An HIV infected individual might develop a herpes simplex infection that spreads well beyond the usual mucous membrane sites for herpes (mouth, genitals) over other skin surfaces, in spinal fluid, or in the lungs.

Estimates of the incubation period for AIDS have changed as research continues and we have more experience with the disease. The most recent research suggests the average length of incubation is seven to eight years, with people developing AIDS sooner than this and in some instances AIDS has appeared later than this. There are reported cases of people being infected with the AIDS virus for ten years and still show no symptoms.

What Are the Symptoms of ARC and AIDS?

Many of the symptoms associated with ARC and AIDS are the same as those associated with a cold or the flu; but for people with ARC or AIDS these symptoms are persistent and seem to have no apparent cause. The person just isn't able to overcome what ever is making them ill.

Only a health-care professional is qualified to diagnose the cause of the following symptoms:

- Unexplained, persistent fatigue that interferes with physical and mental activities.
- Weight loss greater than 10 pounds in less than 2 months not due to changes in diet or level of physical activity.
- Unexplained fever (greater than 100 degrees F) that lasts for more than several weeks.
- Night sweats that drench the individual's bedclothes and pajamas.
- Swollen glands (enlarged lymph nodes usually in the neck , armpits, or groin) which remain swollen for more than 2 months for no apparent reason.
- White spots or unusual blemishes on the tongue or roof of the mouth.
- Persistent diarrhea.
- A dry cough which has lasted too long to be caused by a common respiratory infection, especially if accompanied by shortness of breath.
- Pink to purple flat or raised blotches or bumps occurring on or under the skin. Initially they may resemble bruises but do not disappear. They are usually harder than the skin around them.

How is AIDS Transmitted?

Although the AIDS virus is found in several body fluids, a person acquires the virus during sexual contact with an infected person's blood or semen and possibly vaginal secretions. The virus then enters a person's blood stream through their rectum, vagina or penis. Small (unseen by the naked eye) tears in the surface lining of the vagina or rectum may occur during insertion of the penis, fingers, or other objects, thus opening an avenue for entrance of the virus directly into the blood stream; therefore, the AIDS virus can be passed from penis to rectum and vagina and vice versa without a visible tear in the tissue or the presence of blood.

Drug abusers who inject drugs into their veins are another population group at high risk and with high rates of infection by the AIDS virus. Intravenous drug users make up 25 percent of the cases of AIDS throughout the country. The AIDS virus is carried in contaminated blood left in the needle, syringe, or other drug related implements and the virus is injected into the new victim by reusing dirty syringes and needles. Even the smallest amount of infected blood left in a used needle or syringe can contain live AIDS virus to be passed on to the next user of those dirty implements.

Some persons with hemophilia (a blood clotting disorder that makes them subject to bleeding) have been infected with the AIDS virus either through blood transfusion or the use of blood products that help their blood clot. Now that we know how to prepare safe blood products to aid clotting, this is unlikely to happen.

If a woman is infected with the AIDS virus and becomes pregnant, she is more likely to develop ARC or classic AIDS, and she can pass the AIDS virus to her unborn child. Approximately one third of the babies born to AIDS-infected mothers will eventually develop the disease and die. Several of these babies have been born to wives of hemophiliac men infected with the AIDS virus by way of contaminated blood products. Some babies have also been born to women who became infected with the AIDS virus by bisexual partners who had the virus. Almost all babies with AIDS have been born to women who were intravenous drug users or the sexual partners of intravenous drug users who were infected with the AIDS virus. Many more such babies can be expected.

The AIDS virus has been found in blood, semen, urine, vaginal secretion, spinal fluid, tears, saliva and breast milk. Of these, only semen, vaginal secretions, and blood are implicated in transmission. There are a few reported cases in which babies have contracted AIDS through infected breast milk. Feces are also considered a risk because they may carry blood.

People are naturally concerned about some of the other fluids contact with tears or saliva is much more common in day-to-day life. Evidently, these other fluids do not carry a strong enough concentration of the virus to cause infection, even in the unlikely event one's blood system were to come into direct contact with them. In all reported U.S. cases so far, there is not a single case of transmission of the AIDS virus by saliva. Occasional news reports of such transmission, in the U.S. and elsewhere have all turned out to be incorrect.

So far, the AIDS virus has not been detected in sweat. Even if it is found here at a future time, sweat, like tears or saliva, would most likely not be implicated in transmission.

Finally, a small number of health care workers who have had unusual exposure to patient blood have become infected. For example, a lab technician, because of an equipment malfunction, was splashed in the eye with copious quantities of AIDS-infected blood. She has subsequently become infected herself. Instances such as these, while rare, remind health professionals to follow infection control guidelines carefully.

Who Gets AIDS?

Remember that anyone infected with the AIDS virus might develop AIDS; though people in the United State diagnosed with AIDS usually fall into one of several risk categories. It is behaviors, not membership in any particular group, which will put someone at risk for AIDS or HIV infection.

As of July 2005, the breakdown for source of infection in adolescents and adults with AIDS in the United States was as follows (while absolute numbers in these reports change weekly, the percentages represent more general trends and will not be likely to change significantly for some time):

Gay or bisexual men	61%
IV Drug Users	24%
Gay Male & IV Drug User	6%
Hemophilia/coagulation Disorder	1%
Heterosexual contact	3%
Blood Transfusion	1%
Undetermined	4%

How Does Someone Prevent AIDS?

Obviously, if someone avoids having sex they will not become infected with the AIDS virus through sexual contact. Abstinence can be a viable choice for many people at different times in their lives. It's a choice that many people seem to be making these days in the wake of AIDS.

The more people an individual has sex with - the greater the risk. Each new partner increases the chance that they will be exposed to the HIV virus: its like playing Russian Roulette with your life.

Latex condoms can provide effective protection against infection with the AIDS virus. Condoms act as a physical barrier which prevents the passage of the virus form one person to another. Using condoms reduces the risk associated with vaginal and anal intercourse. Condoms can also be used during oral sex to eliminate any possible risk associated with this activity.

By finding out which sexual activities are riskiest, you will be able to help clients make changes in their sex life so that they can reduce their own level of risk. There are many types of sexual expression that are not considered to be very risky. However, some activities, such as intercourse without a condom, can readily lead to transmission of the AIDS virus. Take the time to learn about making sex safer so that you can help clients protect themselves and the people they love from AIDS.

What is Safer Sex?

Safer sex means cutting the risk of being exposed to AIDS by changing sexual behavior. The following shows the various levels of risk associated with different sexual activities.

NO RISK

Dry Kissing: There have been no documented cases of an individual becoming infected from kissing.

Masturbation: You can not become infected by contact with your own body fluids. In order for infection with HIV to take place you must come in contact with the body fluids of someone who already has the virus inside his or her own body.

Protected Oral Sex: By using a latex condom or a rubber dam (a square piece of latex which can be placed over the vagina) during oral sex, individuals can reduce any possible risk associated with this activity. Both act as a physical barrier which prevents HIV from being passed from one partner to the other.

Touching: You won't get AIDS just by touching someone who carries the virus.

SOME RISK

Deep Kissing: Deep kissing is considered to be risky only when one or both persons has cuts or open sores in the mouth which could allow the virus to enter the blood stream.

Oral Sex: The risk of becoming infected with HIV through oral sex is much less than the risk associated with sexual intercourse. However, virus contained in semen or vaginal secretions can be transmitted during oral sex if there are open cuts or sores in the mouth.

Vaginal Intercourse: Although latex condoms have been shown to prevent transmission of HIV in the laboratory, they are not always 100% effective in real-life situations.

Anal Intercourse with Condom: If used properly, condoms can greatly reduce the risk associated with sexual intercourse.

HIGH RISK

Anal/Vaginal Intercourse without a Condom: Anal and vaginal intercourse WITHOUT a condom are the riskiest sexual activities that an individual can engage in. The virus can be passed by either anal or vaginal intercourse partner, although the receptive partner is at the greatest risk. You can give yourself protection by avoiding sexual intercourse outside of a mutually monogamous relationship with an uninfected person or by always using condoms.

Oral/Anal Contact: Some researchers have found oral/anal contact to be correlated with HIV infection. Others have not. Because many diseases such as hepatitis B, can be transmitted in this way, it is best to consider oral/anal contact a high risk activity.

Fact Sheet
10 Things to Know About HIV/AIDS

1. As of the end of 2012, an estimated 35.3 million people worldwide – including 2.1 million children younger than 10-19 years of ag - were living with HIV/AIDS. According to the World Health Organization (WHO), in 2012, an estimated 2.3 million individuals worldwide were newly infected with HIV. While cases have been reported in all regions of the world, 95% of new infections occur in individuals living in low- and middle-income countries. Sub-Saharan Africa is the most affected region, with nearly 1 in every 20 adults living with HIV. Sixty-nine percent of all people who are living with HIV in the world live in this region.

2. AIDS (acquired immunodeficiency syndrome) results from the late stage of infection with HIV (human immunodeficiency virus). In adults, the onset of AIDS can take up to 10 or more years, and new drug therapies can delay the progression of the disease into AIDS even longer. Thus, a person infected with HIV may look and feel healthy for many years, but he or she can still transmit the virus to someone else, which is why it is very important for individuals to get tested.

3. HIV is transmitted through the exchange of any HIV-infected body fluids. Transfer may occur during all stages of the disease. The HIV virus is found in the following fluids:

   - blood
   - semen (and pre-ejaculate fluid)
   - vaginal secretions
   - breast milk

   HIV does not survive long outside the body and therefore can only be transmitted when any of the above body fluids from an infected individual enters an uninfected individual.

4. HIV most frequently is transmitted sexually. The only way you can be completely sure to prevent the sexual transmission of HIV is by abstaining from all sexual contact. You can significantly reduce your risk of contracting HIV by:

   • correctly using a latex condom from start to finish, every time you have vaginal or anal intercourse and with each act of oral sex on a man.
   • being aware that HIV can be transmitted through oral sex. Use a dental dam or a condom cut open while performing each act of oral sex on a woman.
   • remembering all semen, even pre-ejaculate fluid, can carry the HIV virus.
   • engaging in safer sex practices that involve no penetration such as kissing, massaging, hugging, touching, body-rubbing and masturbation.

5. It is important to note that:

   • all blood, organs, and tissue used during transfusions or surgeries have been tested for HIV. All contaminated products are immediately and carefully disposed of by medical professionals.
   • all medical and surgical instruments, including those used for tattooing and body piercing, must be completely sterilized or discarded properly after each use in order to prevent HIV transmission.

   For information on HIV/AIDS in the work-place or referrals to organizations that handle the proper disposal of medical instruments call the CDC National HIV/AIDS Hotline at 1-800-342-AIDS.

6. Anonymous HIV testing is the only form of HIV testing that is not name based. If you receive a test from an anonymous testing center, no one but you will know the results of your test. Currently, 40 states plus the District of Columbia and Puerto Rico offer anonymous testing.

7. You do NOT get HIV from:

   • donating blood.
   • mosquito bites or bites from other bugs.
   • sneezes or coughs.
   • touching, hugging or dry kissing a person with HIV.
   • the urine or sweat of an infected person.
   • public restrooms, saunas, showers or pools.
   • sharing towels or clothing.
   • sharing eating utensils or drinks.
   • being friends with a person who has HIV/AIDS.

8. Young adults (under age 25) are quickly becoming the most at-risk age group, now accounting for an estimated 50% of all new HIV infections in the United States. Teenagers and young people here and around the world need to take an active role in changing the course of the HIV/AIDS pandemic by adjusting their behaviors and attitudes toward the disease.

9. Discriminating against people who are infected with HIV/AIDS or anyone thought to be at risk of infection violates individual human rights and endangers public health. Every person infected with and affected by HIV/AIDS deserves compassion and support, regardless of the circumstances surrounding their infection. Education is crucial in getting this message out.

10. You can help stop the spread of HIV! Get involved in community efforts. World AIDS Day is a special opportunity every year to focus attention on this urgent challenge that affects us all. It is marked around the world by thousands of different events designed to increase awareness and to express solidarity and compassion. This World AIDS Day -- and every day -- join the worldwide effort to stop the spread of HIV.

Should a Client Take the AIDS Antibody Test?

Soon after the virus (HIV) that causes AIDS was discovered, several tests were developed to test for HIV infection. The three tests that are used, ELISA, IFA, and Western blot, all work by detecting the presence of antibody to HIV. This antibody is developed by the immune system in response to the presence of HIV. The presence of this antibody indicates that a person has been infected with the virus. All three of the antibody tests are very accurate.

A positive test result indicates that antibody was present. A person who tests positive has been infected with HIV. A positive test result does not mean that a person has AIDS, or will become ill later. About 30 to 50 percent of persons who test positive go on to develop AIDS within seven years. Although a person receiving a positive test result may not go on to develop AIDS, he or she could spread the virus through sexual intercourse or by sharing an IV-drug needle.

A negative test result means that the antibody to HIV was not found. There are two possible explanations for a negative test result:

1. The person being tested has not been infected with the virus.
2. Infection may have occurred recently, and the body hasn't had enough time to develop antibody.

"Enough time" is about two to eight weeks, though in some cases it may take up to six months and possibly as long as a year to develop the antibody. If there is concern about recent exposure to the virus, re-test again in six months.

Since March of 1985, these tests have been used to screen all blood that is used in the United States. Blood that is found to be infected is discarded. The use of these tests has helped to make the nation's blood supply much safer.

Anyone concerned about their own possible exposure to the AIDS virus can ask their doctor to perform an AIDS antibody test (it is against the law for a physician to give this test without the individual's permission). In many states, the AIDS-antibody test is also available at Alternative Testing Sites, established to provide free testing in an anonymous and confidential setting. The individual's identity is protected, as well as the results of the test. If you have a client that engages in any of the previously mentioned high risk behaviors, it is strongly recommended by the Center for Substance Abuse Treatment that such clients be given education and awareness about the risk features, and to be encouraged to take an AIDS antibody test.

Anyone infected with the AIDS virus has HIV infection. Such people fall into one of three categories:

1. Some people infected with the virus do not appear or feel ill. They are able to pass the virus on to others through unsafe sexual contact or the sharing of needles in intravenous drug use. These people are said to have asymptomatic HIV infection. Sometimes they are called asymptomatic carriers because they carry the virus without showing symptoms.

2. Some people infected with the virus develop mild to severe symptoms caused by the infection, but do not meet the criteria set by the CDC for an AIDS diagnosis. These people are said to have AIDS Related Complex, or ARC.

3. Finally, some people who have HIV infection and symptoms of illness do meet the criteria for an AIDS diagnosis, and so have AIDS, by definition.

528

In 1981, when AIDS was first described, we did not know what caused the disease and we had no way to test for infection. The CDC developed a definition of AIDS so it could monitor the number of cases occurring. Their scientists described AIDS by listing common symptoms of the disease in its most serious state. These were the cases coming to the attention of physicians. This definition said a person had AIDS if he or she had no underlying cause of immune system problems, but did have one or more of the following:

1. Kaposi's sarcoma (KS),
2. Pneumocystis carinii pneumonia (PCP), or
3. Other opportunistic infections (OI). (These diseases are explained further below.)

This definition left out a lot of people affected by HIV infection, but it was several years before the broader range of HIV infection was understood. The CDC has make a few changes in its definition since 1981, but feels that broadening the definition too much will invalidate the data they have already collected on AIDS.

There are some difficulties with this situation. For one thing, people with ARC often are not eligible for the same benefits and services as people with AIDS, though they may need such assistance. For another, the uncertainties of having ARC are many (Will I die? Will I be able to continue working? Will I recover my health?), and numerous studies have shown people with ARC experience greater anxiety than people with AIDS or those who are well. Finally, the official CDC surveillance of the disease caused by the AIDS virus only counts a small percentage of those actually affected, and the concerns of people with ARC are often neglected in health policy and research planning.

Today the CDC estimates that 1.1 million Americans are infected and living with HIV. The CDC updated its definition of AIDS in August, 1987. People showing signs of direct brain infection with the virus and those who have "wasting" disease (severe and persistent loss of weight associated with AIDS virus infection) are now also considered to have AIDS. In 1986, a four-tier system of classifying all stages of HIV infection was developed. Many people working in the aids field now talk more generally of people having HIV infection or disease rather than making many distinctions between "AIDS," "moderate ARC," "severe ARC," "mild AIDS-related symptoms," and so forth.

Does Everyone Infected with the AIDS Virus Die

At this point, most of the people in the U.S. who are infected with the AIDS virus are not ill. However, in studies of people who have been infected for some time, rates of illness are quite high. In one well-known San Francisco study, a group of men who are known to have been infected since 1978 or 1979 has been followed carefully. After seven years, about 75% of these men had AIDS, ARC, or lymphadenopathy (swollen lymph glands) presumed to be related to infection with the AIDS virus. As time goes on, this number is likely to grow.

These findings are startling. If they hold true in other groups, it means that most people infected will become ill. And, while it is true that some people are only mildly ill or have episodes of illness alternating with periods of health, AIDS-related infections overall appear to be progressive in nature—that is, over time the state of health deteriorates. There is a very small number of individuals who may have recovered some of their immune functioning (their immune systems have become stronger), but most people have not done so once they become ill.

The answer to this question, then, is that we do not know if everyone infected with the AIDS virus will die. We certainly hope this is not the case. Out of respect for the thousands of people living with this disease today, it seems inappropriate to make any sort of blanket statements to this effect without better evidence than we currently have.

THE HIV CHALLENGE TO AOD TREATMENT

Alcohol and other drug (AOD) abuse and human immunodeficiency virus (HIV) infection can be viewed as "twin" epidemics. They often coexist in the same individual, who is at risk from exposure to other infectious diseases such as tuberculosis (TB) and sexually transmitted diseases (STDs) as well. The capacity of AOD abuse treatment programs to address these multiple health problems has expanded greatly in recent years, but there remains a need for comprehensive guidelines for screening, treatment, and referral of AOD patients with HIV and other infectious diseases.

Most AOD abusers with HIV infection or AIDS are injecting drug users (IDUs) in inner cities. They are poor, hard to reach through traditional public health methods, and in need of a spectrum of services. Collaborative, efficient approaches must be developed among AOD specialists, public health officials, mental health specialists, and private treatment providers to prevent further spread of disease and to assure delivery of high-quality care to infected individuals. In the treatment of patients with HIV disease, members of different disciplines must put aside all issues of turf and responsibility.

Overcoming the historical fragmentation of services among different disciplines and institutions is an enormous challenge. A further challenge involves overcoming misunderstanding and lack of communication based on differences in ethnicity, culture, economic status, sexual orientation, and lifestyle. Chemical dependence and HIV infection are both chronic diseases with remissions and exacerbations. "A framework of providing a spectrum of services for long-term healthcare is needed when conceptualizing the treatment of either or both illnesses" (Karan, 1990). Treatment may include both pharmacologic therapies and nonpharmacologic modalities such as individual counseling, group therapy, support groups, family therapy, cognitive and behavioral therapies, psychotherapy, and psychodrama. Nonclinical activities such as attendance at Alcoholics and Narcotics Anonymous meetings, spiritual development, stress management, and relaxation are also important elements of successful treatment.

Prevention and treatment of AOD abuse and HIV disease require a multidisciplinary approach that relies on the strengths of a variety of providers and treatment settings to provide a comprehensive range of effective services.

Obstacles to the Provision of Integrated Care to HIV-Infected AOD Abusers

Staff of most AOD abuse treatment programs have faced the need to provide medical treatment of HIV infection and AIDS to patients in the populations they serve. Treatment options in an individual case will depend on factors such as the availability of hospital and outpatient treatment for HIV infection and nonhospital residential facilities and halfway houses for those who are medically stable but need structure and support away from their home environments. Intensive outpatient counseling is often needed, along with home visits and nursing home and hospice care.

However, the life circumstances of many HIV-infected AOD abusers make continuity of care difficult or impossible to achieve. AOD abusers often suffer from poor health and nutrition and inadequate living conditions as well as a stressful lifestyle and lack of self-care. They may be very ill by the time they seek treatment. Individuals who live in poverty, in homeless shelters, on the street, or in correctional facilities generally lack access to good medical care, especially good primary care. Without financial resources, they have difficulty following dietary advice. Exposure to TB and STDs is common. A variety of factors, including lifestyle stressors and the effects of drug use, may cause individuals to deny their need for treatment for AOD abuse or HIV and to resist seeking or remaining in treatment.

The most important features of any program providing primary care to HIV-infected patients are minimal barriers to access and a "user friendly" environment. Patients may be deterred from adhering to care if they have to travel a long distance from the referral point to the source of primary care, or if the primary care providers are unfamiliar with or unresponsive to their needs. Language barriers and financial barriers may also exist. Special resources such as transportation and case management services facilitate patient follow-up of medical care if primary care is delivered offsite.

> *The most important features of any program providing primary care to HIV-infected patients are minimal barriers to access and a "user friendly" environment.*

Systemic barriers to care for HIV-infected AOD abuse patients result from the separate functioning of treatment and prevention programs for AOD abuse and HIV infection, as well as the separation of funding streams for such programs. Consequently, program design and organizational and staffing structures may be inadequate and unidimensional when the demographic profile of the treatment population demands a multidimensional approach.

Multiple service needs are the norm for HIV-infected persons with AOD abuse problems. The AOD abuse treatment program may be able to play a lead role in coordinating care for HIV-infected AOD abusers, given their understanding of the preexisting substance use disorder and the fact that the client may trust and identify more with the AOD abuse treatment program than with other providers. However, AOD treatment programs can only take on such responsibility if they achieve competence in providing case management services. Historically, AOD programs have not provided case management services or have done so poorly. This situation could be improved by redefining the mission of AOD agencies beyond narrow recovery goals and allocating resources to professional social-work or trained counselor/case management staff.

For example, access to mental health and social services will vary depending on whether treatment programs have established linkages with providers of such services. Obtaining housing or homemaker services for a patient with AIDS can be a logistical nightmare for AOD abuse treatment staff. Even when services are finally located, the patient may not have access to transportation to go to the specified clinic or agency. Other barriers to integrated care include lack of healthcare coverage and a lack of entitlement programs directed at the specific problems of HIV-infected AOD abusers.

Physicians and their staffs often lack the knowledge and experience needed to access social service resources for AIDS or AOD abuse patients. No systems exist to coordinate the provision of medical services with other services outside the medical setting. A further problem is that AOD abuse treatment program staff who lack expertise in HIV issues may fail to refer patients to appropriate HIV treatment services.

Philosophical differences between substance abuse treatment and primary healthcare providers may cause confusion for patients and providers alike. For example, a patient's physician may prescribe an antidepressant to treat the patient's severe depression. However, a substance abuse treatment provider, overly concerned about the danger of addiction, may tell the patient not to take the medication even though it is not addictive and it may improve the patient's quality of life.

Whereas a primary care provider may consider any decrease in drug use as an improvement in the patient's health status, a substance abuse provider may view anything short of total abstinence from drug use as a continuation of the patient's addiction. By contrast, the primary care provider, focusing on the need to bring about an improvement in the patient's health status, may fail to appreciate the effect of addiction on the patient's behavior.

For example, an individual may do well in a residential detoxification program, a very structured setting. Outside of that setting, however, and without the support of AOD detoxification staff, the individual may have difficulty staying motivated to continue treatment. If the individual stops attending Narcotics Anonymous meetings, misses outpatient appointments, and perhaps slips back into drug-seeking behavior, continuity of care suffers.

Preferential Admission to AOD Abuse Treatment for HIV-Infected Patients

When the number of treatment slots is inadequate for the numbers of AOD abusers seeking treatment, programs are faced with deciding whether to give priority to the admission of HIV-positive patients in order to try to stop the use of needles and halt the further spread of HIV. Alternatively, they may decide to admit non-HIV-infected patients in the hope of preventing them from being exposed to the virus through continued needle use. Where preferential admission is practiced, non-HIV-infected AOD abusers may claim to be HIV positive in order to get into highly valued treatment slots, particularly for methadone treatment.

> *Programs are sometimes faced with deciding whether to give priority to the admission of HIV-positive patients to try to stop their use of needles and halt the further spread of HIV. Or, they may decide to admit non-HIV-infected patients in the hope of preventing them from being exposed to the virus through continued needle use.*

Under the 1993 substance abuse block grants interim final rule, programs receiving block grant funds must create a waiting list for patients who are seeking AOD treatment and are at risk for HIV, sexually transmitted diseases, and tuberculosis. Patients on the waiting list are to be given preferential treatment in the following order: pregnant IDUs, other pregnant substance abusers, other IDUs, and all others. People with HIV infection are not specifically identified in the Federal regulations as a group mandated to receive preferential treatment.

The appropriateness of a preferential admission policy for HIV-infected AOD abuse patients will depend upon the HIV seroprevalence rate among the population served by a treatment program. Programs should consult with local health departments and other community agencies when deciding whether to adopt a preferential admissions policy.

Cultural Competence of Providers

AOD abuse treatment staff need to be sensitive to the culture in which their patients live. However, cultural sensitivity by itself is not enough. Staff also must be competent in providing services to people from cultures other than their own. Cultural sensitivity and competence are crucial to the recruitment and retention of HIV-infected AOD abuse patients in treatment. Acquiring this competence may require staff to participate in training courses that focus on developing skills in cultural competence.

> *Cultural sensitivity and competence are crucial to the recruitment and retention of HIV-infected AOD abuse patients in treatment.*

Staff must be able to provide services that are acceptable within the context of the culture of the persons they serve. Treatment staff who understand how patients define and regard sexual orientation, family, community, gender, and religion or spirituality are best able to develop positive relationships with patients and help empower them to overcome high-risk behavior. The treatment staff's understanding of and sensitivity to issues related to sexual orientation are very important. Staff should be aware of the pressures experienced by gay, lesbian, and bisexual patients in the employment setting and in the local community. Some treatment staff may have limited ability to deal with matters of sexual orientation, and this limitation can be a barrier to access to treatment for gay, lesbian, or bisexual patients.

The fact that many AOD treatment providers are themselves recovering from AOD abuse and are members of the ethnic and cultural communities they serve is an important element of cultural competence. Training and affirmative action hiring can help to ensure that therapists, counselors, and group leaders are sensitive to patients' culture, ethnicity, and language or language style. Cultural compatibility between group leaders and patients facilitates group interaction and discussion of sensitive issues -- effective counseling about HIV risk reduction must take account of both drug-using and sexual behaviors. Patients may have significant socioeconomic problems related to housing, employment, and legal and entitlement issues; these problems can be identified and addressed in culturally competent programs. It is also important for treatment staff to be prepared to provide appropriate treatment to women. Alcohol is often the link in transmission of HIV disease to women, since it can lead to sexual disinhibition. A similar effect on sexual feelings is associated with the use of cocaine and crack cocaine.

Care providers need an understanding of the nature and role of the family in minority cultures. This understanding includes acceptance of the family as defined by the patient. Sometimes, the patient's family may include or consist entirely of persons who are not related to the patient by blood or marriage. The notion and understanding of family take on added importance in view of the fact that rates of heterosexual and perinatal transmission of HIV are highest in African American and Hispanic communities. Thus, the families with whom AOD treatment staff come into contact are likely to be of low socioeconomic status, particularly in urban areas. Such families may be headed by women, often very young women with children. An extended family may be in place that assists with the provision of shelter, childcare, and emotional support. Care providers should seek to involve family members appropriately in information sharing and in education about HIV and AOD abuse.

> *Care providers should understand and accept how the patient defines his or her family. Sometimes, the patient's family may include or consist entirely of persons who are not related to the patient by blood or marriage.*

Appropriate utilization of AOD and other health services can be increased when services are sited in affected communities and when local resources such as clergy and traditional healers are involved in activities such as outreach, advocacy, and the promotion of healthy lifestyles. Involving patients in program evaluation through the use of consumer satisfaction surveys can help to ensure that services are meeting patients' self-identified needs in a culturally appropriate way.

Finally, an understanding of the place of spirituality and religion in patients' communities is important. Leaders and members of churches and other sources of spiritual counseling and support can be important allies in bringing patients into treatment and gaining their compliance with treatment regimens.

Conclusion

To provide comprehensive, coordinated care to HIV-infected AOD abusers, treatment programs must assess their existing resources and identify gaps. Ideally, a multidisciplinary professional team -- including a family physician or an internist, an obstetrician-gynecologist, a psychiatrist, a midlevel practitioner such as a physician's assistant or a nurse practitioner, a nurse, an AOD abuse treatment counselor, and a social worker -- should be available and should work together to meet patients' needs.

Case management at both hospital and community levels is important in achieving coordinated care. Increasingly, staff in AOD abuse treatment programs are finding that they need to conduct case management. Tracking and outreach teams composed of community volunteers are also vital, as is a telephone "hotline" to increase access to care. Developing programs to provide outreach to affected communities, providing home care, and furnishing transportation to health and AOD services can promote AOD abstinence and increase compliance with treatment regimens.

Substance abuse treatment, particularly opioid substitution therapy, of HIV-infected AOD abusers has been shown to be effective in reducing the spread of HIV (Ball et al., 1988; Hartel et al., 1988). In addition, addiction treatment can improve HIV-infected AOD abusers' quality of life by increasing their self-esteem, improving their sense of well-being, and helping them develop spiritually. Treatment can help them gain strength in making peace with themselves and their families and in determining how they want to spend the remaining portion of their lives.

> *Substance abuse treatment of HIV-infected AOD abusers has been shown to be effective in reducing the spread of HIV. In addition, addiction treatment can improve HIV-infected AOD abusers' quality of life by increasing their self-esteem, improving their sense of well-being, and helping them develop spiritually.*

HIV/AIDS Education and Resources

National Library of Medicine AIDS Portal

A collection of links to a wide variety of resources for patients, health care providers and researchers. Includes links to information en Español.

National Library of Medicine
http://sis.nlm.nih.gov/HIV/HIVMain.html

Questions About HIV Testing and Prevention?

The CDC National AIDS Hotline can answer questions about HIV testing and provide referrals to testing centers in your area. The hotline is open 24 hours a day, 7 days a week.

1-800-342-2437
1-800-243-7889 (TTY)
1-800-344-7432 (Español)

Centers for Disease Control and Prevention
http://www.ashastd.org/nah/index.html

Directory of Health Organizations Online (DIRLINE)

A database of approximately 10,000 records focused primarily on health and biomedicine. Follow these steps to search for organizations supporting HIV/AIDS services:
1. In the search box enter "hiv aids" (without the quotation marks).
2. Click on "any of the words" under Search.
3. Click on "MeSH Headings/Keywords" under Fields.
4. Click on the Search button.

National Library of Medicine
http://dirline.nlm.nih.gov/

Toll-Free Numbers for Health Care Organizations

A list of health-related organizations offering toll-free telephone services.

Includes TTY and Español services, when available.

National Library of Medicine
http://sis.nlm.nih.gov/cgi-
bin/hotlines/FindOrg?IndexString=Acquired+Immunodeficiency+Syndrome

Other U.S. Government Resources

Department of Defense - HIV/AIDS Prevention Program
http://www.nhrc.navy.mil/programs/dhapp/background/management.html

Department of Veterans Affairs
http://vhaaidsinfo.cio.med.va.gov/

Office of National AIDS Policy
http://www.whitehouse.gov/onap/aids.html

The White House HIV/AIDS Initiatives
http://www.whitehouse.gov/infocus/hivaids

Presidential Advisory Council on HIV and AIDS
http://www.pacha.gov/

U.S. Agency for International Development (USAID)
http://www.usaid.gov/pop_health/aids/index.html

U.S. Census Bureau
http://www.census.gov/ipc/www/hivaidsd.html

U.S. Department of Housing and Urban Development
http://www.hud.gov/offices/cpd/aidshousing/index.cfm

U.S. Department of State
http://www.state.gov/g/oes/hlth/

U.S. Environmental Protection Agency
http://www.epa.gov/safewater/crypto.html

Section 3, Chapter 5:

Ethics

According to Webster's Dictionary, ethics is defined as "the discipline dealing with what is good and bad and with moral duty and obligations - ethics are the principles of conduct governing an individual or group."

The subject of ethics and ethical behavior is important to every professional group. The ethical considerations define the way in which a group or profession conduct themselves. Unfortunately, the chemical dependency field, being a relatively young profession, still struggles with defining the principles that guide the practice of the professional in the field. At the present time there is no clear cut accepted national group or a consistent national credential for professionals in the field. Therefore, each state that credentials chemical dependency professionals has developed their own guidelines. While most are modeled after the code of ethics developed by the National Association of Alcoholism and Drug Abuse Counselors (NAADAC), confusion still exists among treatment professionals. (to view the current NAADAC code of ethics, visit their website at www.NAADAC.org)

Ethical considerations can typically be viewed from three different perspectives: (1) moral/professional judgments; (2) legal or regulatory considerations; and (3) ethical implications.

(1) Moral/professional judgments refer to the individual counselor's own value system. Within the therapeutic relationship, counselors need to ask themselves "Do I feel comfortable doing _____?" If a particular situation is morally uncomfortable for the counselor, but still legal and ethical, then the responsibility of the counselor is to help the client obtain the desired service in the most expeditious manner. For example, it is not uncommon to have a client in the chemical dependency field that has been or is currently involved in dealing drugs to support their habit. While the counselor may have strong feelings about this activity, legally and ethically the counselor may not disclose this information to law enforcement authorities. The counselor is obligated to provide services to the client (though a referral to another counselor may be appropriate if the counselor feels they cannot provide adequate service to the client).

(2) Legal or regulatory aspects relate to whether or not there are laws governing a specific activity. For example, counselors must determine whether they are qualified to provide services within their scope of practice. Licensure laws, currently being developed by many states, specify the types of activities the chemical dependency professional may perform. In states that do not provide licensure, certification standards do much of the same thing. Chemical dependency counselors must not engage in activities beyond the scope of their training. For example, a counselor may feel that a client would benefit from marital counseling in their recovery program. While the skill and training of the counselor may allow him or her to provide basic services to the spouse, including educational, awareness building services and referral to such programs as Al-Anon, marital counseling should be performed by a qualified marriage and family therapist. It would be illegal as well as unethical for the chemical dependency counselor to do otherwise.

(3) Ethical implications refer to the principles set forth by the ethical standards governing a particular profession. When considering ethical implications, the counselor should always remember the following:

   a. It is the counselor's responsibility to know and understand the ethical principles that guide them, whether they are state or national guidelines;

   b. It is necessary to consider all of these ethical principles to determine how they apply to each client the counselor serves;

   c. All variables, including legal responsibilities and medical considerations, must be reviewed for each case;

   d. Confidentiality is a critical area of concern and this ethical standard is frequently involved in clinical dilemmas - the primary justification for breaking confidentiality occurs when a person is a danger to self or others.

   e. Counselors need to be sensitive to the moral and social codes of the community;

   f. When making decisions involving ethics, counselors should usually be conservative in their judgment and frequently consult with other treatment professionals;

   g. Counselors should always have a keen awareness of their areas of competence and an appreciation of their limitations - regardless of personal belief, a counselor can not provide every service that a client needs.

ETHICAL AND PROFESSIONAL ISSUES FOR COUNSELORS

It is essential for the alcohol and drug abuse counselor to have a detailed understanding of the responsibilities and consequences associated with ethical principles and, in some cases, be familiar with laws that relate to them. In addition, alcohol and drug abuse counselors must be aware of several professional issues relevant to alcohol and drug abuse field and the mental health field in general.

Patient Rights

There have been a number of legal cases related to the rights of involuntarily committed patients. In the case of Wyatt v. Stickney, a U.S. District Court ruled that involuntarily committed patients are constitutionally entitled to treatment; commitment without such treatment constitutes indefinite punishment and violates the fundamentals of due process. Moreover, involuntarily committed patients must be treated in the least restrictive environment available. In a related issue, some states have passed laws that give involuntarily committed patients the right to refuse treatments associated with negative side effects and the right to refuse to take psychoactive drugs.

In some ways, the substance abuser does not enjoy the same legal protections as a person who has been involuntarily committed. Many users are pressured by the court, their employers, or even family members to undergo "voluntary" treatment. Although these patients sign voluntary consent to treatment forms, they often do not have the opportunity to give truly informed consent. Of course, chemical dependencies are often characterized by denial and self-delusion and in these cases it is almost certainly necessary to use some coercion, especially in the early stages of treatment, to get help to users who pose a danger to themselves or others. However, substance abuse professionals need to take it upon themselves to offer as much freedom of choice and the least restrictive treatment alternatives possible.

A problem often exists in that the decision as to where and how the patient should be treated is not always undertaken with the patient's best interests in mind. For instance, in some situations, the person who forces a patient into a treatment program may be the person who runs the program. In addition, employee organizations sometimes make contractual arrangements with a single treatment facility, and some employers and unions have gone into the business of providing treatment for their own employees. Such arrangements can potentially create conflicts of interest, reduce patient choice, and lower the quality of care provided.

In the past two decades, the field has seen a significant loss of private care facilities. Many abuses were uncovered by various states in1992 that suggested some of the larger national treatment chains were involved in questionable practices. Inappropriate admissions, failure to provide the least restrictive (and less costly) level of care, paying counselors for referrals, and inappropriate lengths of stay seemed to be acceptable practice. As a result, newer, more stringent guidelines have been developed by many states, and several of the national chains have closed facilities due to declining revenue and increased litigation costs. While there exists a need to allow clients to choose among several acceptable treatment facilities, choices are becoming fewer.

Substance abuse professionals should act in line with the principles that "the alcoholism and drug abuse counselor should define for self and others the nature and direction of loyalties and responsibilities and keep all parties concerned informed of these commitments" and "the alcoholism and drug abuse counselor, in the presence of professional conflict should be concerned primarily with the welfare of the client." Thus, in situations where there is only one source of treatment for in a particular place or for a particular organization, counselors should strive to ensure that clients are informed as to the nature of any agreements involved, that treatment is sufficiently individualized, and that treating facilities are checked intermittently to the quality and timeliness of care. In addition, there should be no opportunity for the counselor to profit from his/her referral in any way.

Confidentiality of Alcohol and Drug Abuse Patients

Confidentiality between a counselor and a client is crucial to the success of the counseling relationship. The client's beliefs about confidentially will determine the extent and the nature of the information revealed during the course of care. The basic principle of confidentiality is that no information divulged by patients in the course of treatment even the fact that a particular person is (or is not) a patient in a treatment facility may be revealed to an outside source without the written consent of the patient when he/she is rational and drug-free. Professional handling of information means that it will never be divulged in a careless, casual, or irresponsible way, discussed in social conversations, or revealed in casual inquiries.

The privacy of persons receiving alcohol and drug abuse prevention and treatment services is protected by federal laws. The legal citation for these laws is 42 U.S.C. 290dd-3 and ee-3. The regulations directing the implementation of these statutes were issued in 1975 and revised in 1987. They are found in the Code of Federal Regulations: 42 C.F.R. Part 2. A complete copy of these regulations can be found in Appendix C.

Many States also have confidentiality laws that apply to substance abuse treatment. These may afford individuals even greater privacy than the federal law. However, State laws may not be less stringent than federal laws. If they are, the federal law (or the more rigorous one) prevails. Violation of the regulations may result in fines up to $500 for a first offense and up to $5,000 for subsequent offenses.

The federal confidentiality law applies to all programs providing alcohol or drug abuse diagnosis, treatment, or referral for treatment that are federally assisted. Included are the following:

- programs receiving any type of federal funding;

- programs receiving tax exemption status through the Internal Revenue Service;

- programs authorized to conduct business by the federal government, such as those licensed to provide methadone or those certified as Medicare providers; and

- programs conducted directly by the federal government or state or local governments that receive federal funds.

The primary intent of the confidentiality law is to prevent disclosure of information "both written records and verbal information "that would identify a person as a patient receiving alcohol or drug treatment." This protection is even extended to those who have applied, but were not admitted to the program for treatment, and to former patients and deceased patients. Not only are programs prohibited from disclosing information, except under certain conditions to be discussed later, but they also are not allowed to verify information that is already known by the person making an inquiry.

According to these regulations, the very fact that a person is a patient in a treatment facility cannot be revealed, or denied, without the patient's expressed written consent. Thus, in response to inquiries about whether a particular person is a patient in such a facility, one can only answer "according to Federal law, I can neither confirm nor deny the presence of any client in our facility." In addition, these regulations set forth a strict standard for signed consents to disclose information - consent forms must specify what information will be disclosed, to whom the disclosure will be made, and set a time limit for such release of information. Too often, release of information forms used by facilities are too general, in essence granting a blanket release of what information is released without regards to time limitations. This is never appropriate.

Patients are entitled to notification of the federal confidentiality laws and regulations. Programs should provide a written summary of these provisions upon admission. The written summary should include:

- information about the circumstances in which disclosure can be made without the patient's consent;

- a statement that violations of the regulations may be reported as a crime;

- a warning that committing or threatening a crime on the program's premises or against program staff can result in release of information;

- notification that the program must report suspected child abuse or neglect; and

- reference to the federal law and regulations.

Programs must keep patient records in a secure room, a locked file cabinet or other similarly protected places. There should be written procedures concerning who has access to patient records. A single staff member, often the director, should be designated to handle inquiries and requests for information about patients.

Confidentiality vs. Privilege

"Privilege" is a legal term that refers to an individual's right not to have confidential information revealed in court or other legal proceedings. Most states have laws which establish the "professional-patient privilege." Thus, while the legal concept of privilege is similar to the ethical concept of confidentiality, it is much narrower in scope and applies specifically to situations involving court or other legal proceedings.

Ordinarily, the client is the "holder of the privilege", which means that a therapist cannot reveal confidential information in a legal proceeding unless the privilege has been waived by the client. Privilege is waived when the client has consented to disclosure of the information, when the client has disclosed a significant part of the information to a third person, and in certain legally-defined situations, which vary from state to state, such as when a client sues a counselor. Once the client has waived privilege, the therapist has no grounds for withholding relevant information if asked to do so in court.

Even though chemical dependency counselors have a confidential relationship with their clients, most states do not view this as privileged. Thus, when a chemical dependency counselor is subpoenaed to testify in court or release a patient's records to the court, they usually cannot be excused from these obligations under the laws relating to privilege. In some states, the law regarding privilege does apply to a person whom the patient reasonably believes to be a licensed professional. Thus, under this stipulation of law, communication between a patient and a licensed substance abuse counselor may be privileged in some cases and in some states. It is the responsibility of the counselor to be aware of state laws regarding privilege.

Exceptions to the General Confidentiality Conditions

Sometimes the good of the client, the protection of the public, and/or the law require or permit a substance abuse counselor to breach a client's confidentiality. Confidentiality is not an absolute requirement. Such issues as suicide, child abuse, or elderly abuse would be grounds for breaching confidentiality.

Although the degree to which one should, if ever, breach confidentiality in the counseling relationship is a matter of great controversy, there is general agreement on one point: the client has a right to know the limits that may exist with regard to the confidentiality of information discussed in treatment. Ideally, a discussion of the limits of confidentiality should take place during the intake or orientation process in the counseling relationship. In addition, a facility's staff policy manual should indicate the limits of confidentiality.

Under certain conditions, programs may disclose information about persons receiving or applying for substance abuse treatment. These are described in the following sections.

Patient Consent

Patients may sign a consent form allowing for the release of information. However, consent forms must contain specific information, including the following:

- program name;
- person or individual to receive the information;
- patient's name;
- purpose or need for the disclosure;
- the specific amount and kind of information to be released;

- a statement that the patient may revoke the consent at any time;
- date, event, or condition upon which the consent will expire;
- signature of the patient; and date upon which the consent is signed.

Only information that is necessary to accomplish the purpose stated in the form may be released. Even if a properly-signed consent form is in force, programs are allowed discretion about disclosing information, unless the form is accompanied by a subpoena or court order. It is usually necessary for patients to sign separate consent forms for each type of disclosure and for each person or organization to whom information is to be released. However, if similar information will be released to the same person/organization during the period the consent form is valid, signing a form for each release is not required. This might occur with funding sources requiring verification of treatment provided over the course of a person's enrollment in a treatment program. On the other hand, if a different type of information is requested by the same person/organization, a new consent form would be required.

Patients may revoke their consent at any time, either verbally or in writing. This does not require the program to retrieve information disclosed when the consent form was valid. If a patient revokes a consent form permitting disclosure of information to a third- party payer, the program still may bill the payer for any services provided during the time the consent form was valid. However, after revocation of consent, the program may not release information to third-party payment sources. If services continue to be provided, the program risks not receiving reimbursement.

The expiration date of consent forms should be at a time that is reasonably necessary to achieve the purpose for which they are signed. Rather than a specific date, consent forms may expire when a certain event or condition occurs. For example, if information is released to a physician the patient will see one time, the consent form may indicate that it is valid until the patient's appointment with the doctor. On the other hand, a consent form to provide verification of enrollment in the treatment program for an employer, who has placed the person on probation pending treatment, may be in effect until the end of the probationary period.

State laws are relied upon to determine the definition of minors and whether or not the consent of a parent (or guardian or other person legally responsible for the minor) is required for them to obtain substance abuse treatment. The regulations concerning consent for release of information follow state laws: If state law requires parental consent for treatment, then consent of both the minor patient and the parent (or guardian) must be obtained to disclose information. However, regardless of the requirement for parental consent, programs must always obtain the minor's consent for disclosure. The parent's signature alone is not sufficient.

In states requiring parental approval for the treatment of minors, programs must obtain the minor's consent before contacting a parent/guardian to obtain his or her permission for treatment. However, if the program director determines that certain conditions exist, s/he may contact the parent/ guardian without the minor's consent. In such cases, all of the following conditions must be present:

- the minor is not capable of making a rational choice because of extreme youth or mental or physical impairment;

- the situation presents a threat to the life or physical well-being of the youth or another person; and

- the risk may be reduced by communicating relevant facts to the minor's parent/guardian.

If these conditions are not present, the program personnel must inform the minor of his or her right to refuse consent to communicate with a parent/guardian. However, the program cannot provide services without such communication and parental consent. If state law does not require parental permission for treatment, programs still may withhold services from minors who will not authorize a disclosure so the program can obtain financial reimbursement for treatment, as long as this does not violate a state or local law.

Similarly, for adult patients who have been adjudicated incompetent, consent for disclosure may be made by the person's guardian or authorized representative. In situations in which a person has not been adjudicated incompetent but the program director determines that his or her present medical condition interferes with the ability to understand and take effective action, the director may authorize disclosure without patient consent only to obtain payment for services from a third-party payment source.

For deceased patients, disclosure may be authorized by the executor or administrator of his/her estate, spouse, or a family member. Without such consent, programs may make limited disclosures to comply with state or federal laws concerning collection of vital statistics or to respond to inquiries into the cause of death.

Any time a program releases information about a patient, it must be accompanied by a written statement indicating that the information is protected by federal law and the recipient cannot make further disclosure unless permitted by the regulations.

At times, patients may consent to disclosure of information to employers. Often, this can be limited to verification of treatment status or a general evaluation of progress. The program should limit disclosure to only information that is related to the particular employment situation.

Persons may be required to participate in treatment as a condition of probation or parole, sentence, dismissal of charges, release from incarceration, or other criminal justice dispositions. These patients also are entitled to protection of confidentiality, but some special qualifications apply concerning the duration and revocability of consent.

Whenever a person moves from one phase of the criminal justice system to another, a substantial change in status occurs. Until such a change occurs, consent forms cannot be revoked. Criminal justice system consent forms can be irrevocable so that individuals who agree to treatment in lieu of prosecution or punishment can be monitored. However, the irrevocability of consent ends with the final disposition of the criminal proceedings. Information obtained by criminal justice agencies can be used only with respect to a particular criminal proceeding. It may be advisable for judges or criminal justice agencies to require that the individual sign the necessary consent forms before referral to a treatment program. If not, and the program is unable to obtain the individual's consent for disclosure, it may be prevented from providing information to the criminal justice agency that referred the patient to the program. Treatment programs are allowed to apprise criminal justice agencies, without obtaining patient consent, if a person referred for treatment by such agencies fails to apply for or receive services from the program.

Because of the potential for abuse of methadone, these programs must take precautions that patients are not enrolled in multiple programs. Patients can be required to sign a consent form before they enter treatment to release information to a central registry. If the registry receives information about the same person in more than one program, each program may be notified so the problem can be resolved. Such consent remains in effect as long as the patient is enrolled in the program.

With a proper consent form, programs may release information to a patient's attorney. However, the program may use discretion to limit its response. Some programs may be concerned about potential law suits, but if they refuse to disclose information, attorneys may subpoena the records.

Internal Communications

Information about a patient may be shared among staff within a program only if there is a legitimate need for them to know it. When there is a need for internal communications, information that is shared always should be specifically related to the provision of substance abuse services being delivered.

When a program is part of a larger organization, such as a general hospital, community mental health center, or school, necessary information may be disclosed to other departments, such as central billing or medical records. However, any information that is not necessary to other departments should not be disclosed.

Releasing Information to Other Professionals

Releasing information to professionals outside of a treatment setting can pose a number of ethical difficulties for counselors. One reality of good clinical care is that in many situations, clients are referred from one professional or agency to another for testing or special services, or for follow-up care. Sharing of information among professionals or agencies is often in the best interest of the client and, indeed, is necessary to bring the optimum resources to aid the client's recovery. Many times, information is also shared in this way with spouses, parents, teachers, and other significant people. This kind of information sharing should be done only with the client's full knowledge and informed consent.

Disclosures Without Identification of Patients

Programs may release information that does not identify an individual as a substance abuser or verify someone else's identification of a patient. Reports of aggregate data about a program's participants may be provided. Individual information may be communicated in a manner that does not disclose that the person has a substance abuse problem. For example, the program may disclose that a person is a patient in a larger organization (e.g., general hospital, community mental health center, school) without acknowledging that s/he has a substance abuse problem. Information may be disclosed anonymously without identifying either the individual's status as a substance abuse patient or the name of the program. Finally, an individual's case history may be reported anonymously, provided information about the patient and the agency are disguised sufficiently that the person's identity cannot be determined by a reader.

Medical Emergencies

In a situation that poses an immediate threat to the health of the patient or any other individual, and requires immediate medical intervention, such as a dangerous drug overdose or an attempted suicide, necessary information may be disclosed to medical personnel. Such a disclosure must be documented in the patient's records, including the name and affiliation of the person receiving the information, the name of the person making the disclosure, the date and time of the disclosure, and the nature of the emergency. Programs should ask participants in advance to indicate a person to be notified in the event of an emergency, and the patient should be asked to sign a consent form allowing the program to notify the named person if an emergency should arise. Even without patient consent, information may be disclosed to the federal Food and Drug Administration if an error has been made in packaging or manufacturing a drug used in substance abuse treatment and this may endanger the health of patients.

Court Orders

State and federal courts may issue orders authorizing programs to release information that otherwise would be unlawful. However, certain procedures are required when such court orders are issued. A subpoena, search warrant or arrest warrant alone is not sufficient to permit a program to make a disclosure. First, a program and a patient whose records are sought must be given notice that an application for the court order has been made. The program and the individual must have an opportunity to make an oral or written statement to the court about the application. If the purpose of the court order is to investigate or prosecute a patient, it is only necessary to notify the program.

Before an order is issued, there must be a finding of good cause for the disclosure. If the public interest and need for disclosure outweigh possible adverse effects to the individual, the doctor-patient relationship, and the program's services, the order may be issued. Information that is essential for the purpose of the court order is all that may be released. Only persons who need the information may receive it. A court order may require disclosure of confidential communications if one of the following conditions exist:

- disclosure is necessary to protect against a threat to life or of serious bodily injury;

- disclosure is required to investigate or prosecute an extremely serious crime; or
- disclosure is necessary in a proceeding in which the patient has already provided evidence about confidential communications.

Before a court order can be issued to release patient information for a criminal investigation or prosecution, five criteria must be met. These are:

1. the crime is extremely serious (e.g., threatening to cause death or serious injury);
2. the records sought will probably contain information that is significant to the investigation or prosecution of the crime;
3. there is no other feasible way to acquire the information;
4. the public interest in disclosure outweighs any harm to the patient, doctor-patient relationship, and the agency's ability to provide services; and
5. the program has an opportunity to be represented by independent counsel when law enforcement personnel seek the order.

Ethical responsibilities regarding confidentiality often come into direct conflict with legal requirements when a counselor or agency is served with a subpoena (a summons to appear in court or release records to the court). Subpoenas may require a person to appear to give testimony or to bring documents to a hearing. Although they may be signed by a judge or other legal officials, subpoenas are not the type of court order required by the confidentiality regulations. Thus, federal confidentiality laws and regulations prohibit treatment programs from responding to subpoenas by disclosing information concerning current or former patients. However, if the person about whom the information is requested signs a proper consent form authorizing the release, the program may do so. If a court order is issued after giving the program and patient an opportunity to be heard, and after making a good cause determination, treatment programs may respond to subpoenas.

In most cases, any part of a client's formal file or record can be subpoenaed and placed in evidence in a court of law. Counselors should be aware that such notes or reports are not completely private. Caution should be taken when entering speculative remarks or assigning labels to clients. If a counselor wishes to maintain privacy of certain interview notes or other case materials, he/she should address notes as "memoranda to myself" and not include them in the formal record. Such memoranda are not generally subjects to subpoena although a counselor may be ordered in court to testify about their contents.

Various authorities have attempted to resolve this complex issue. The following guidelines are offered to chemical dependency counselors if their records are subpoenaed:

1. Never ignore a subpoena - but this does not mean that you automatically respond by releasing the information being requested;

2. Contact the lawyer who has issued the subpoena and determine the nature of the subpoena (e.g., does it require attendance by the therapist and/or production of records?);

3. After talking the matter over with the attorney, it may become apparent to the lawyer that the information contained within your records would not be helpful to the matter - in such cases, you will probably be asked to destroy the subpoena and you will not have to follow its request;

4. If the subpoena is requesting records protected by the federal confidentiality guidelines covering chemical dependency information, a subpoena will not be sufficient to force releasing information - a court order, based upon a hearing, will have to be issued before the records could be released;

5. Regardless of the nature of the subpoena, therapists should initially assert the privilege not to reveal confidential information, if this is an available option - again, a hearing would need to be held and a court order would allow you to release such information;

6. Therapists should immediately contact the client or client's attorney. If the client wants the therapist to testify or release the requested records, written consent from the client should be obtained - if the attorney requesting information is not representing your client, again it may be best to force the court to order the release of any records - this is for your protection and for the protection of the client.

Search warrants, similarly, may not be used to allow law enforcement officers to enter the program's facilities. However, arrest warrants do permit law enforcement personnel to search for a particular patient who has committed or threatened a crime on the premises of the program or against program personnel. Unless the arrest warrant is accompanied by a court order, the program may not cooperate with a search for a patient who committed a crime elsewhere.

The "Duty to Warn"

The concept of the "duty to warn" stems from the California Supreme Court's decision in Tarasoff v. Regents of the University of California. In this case, a psychotherapy client at U.C. Berkeley told his therapist that he intended to kill his girlfriend, Tanya Tarasoff. Although Tarasoff was out of the country at the time, the therapist notified the police, who took no action. The therapist subsequently destroyed his notes and did nothing further to prevent the crime. When Tanya Tarasoff returned to the States, the client did, in fact, kill her. Tarasoff's parents sued on the grounds that the therapist and the University had not adequately protected their daughter. They won the suit - the court ruled that a psychotherapist must breach patient confidentiality when he/ she determines that a patient is a danger to another person.

The "duty to warn" implies that when a therapist's client is threatening violence to a specific victim the therapist has a responsibility to warn both the intended victim and the appropriate police officials of the danger. Although the therapist in the Tarasoff case notified the police, he did not warn Tarasoff herself; this case, then, extended a therapist's responsibility to also include warning the intended victim.

This law only covers situations in which there is a "reasonably identifiable victim or victims." Sometimes a therapist may encounter a client who seems generally dangerous, but a potential victim cannot be precisely identified. In such cases, there is no clear legal guidance, but a breach of confidentiality, if necessary to protect the public or the client, is usually considered to be ethically justifiable. If the client's dangerousness is due to a mental disorder, involuntary hospitalization is also an option.

That the duty to warn exists only when the client him/herself is the violent party - if a client were to tell his/her therapist that he/she knew someone else who intended to commit murder, the therapist's legal obligation under duty to warn laws would not exist. However, the therapist in such a case should encourage the client to report the threat to the police or to take other appropriate action.

The Tarasoff decision intensified the ethical discussion within the professional helping disciplines regarding the rights of clients to confidentiality and the rights of potential victims to be warned of threats to their physical safety. This tension between client privacy and community safety continues today. Since the Tarasoff decision, the "duty to warn" has become both an ethical obligation and a keystone within the ethical standards of most helping professions. The "duty to warn" is generally operationalized as follows:

- All clients, as part of the informed consent process, are fully informed of both the scope and limits of confidentiality.
- A reasonable assessment of the client's potential for violence is conducted as a component of the intake assessment process.
- "Duty to warn" is activated when a client makes a threat of physical harm to an identified individual or individuals.
- A more intensified evaluation of the client's potential for violence is conducted in response to the verbal threat of aggression. Duty to warn applies where a threat of harm is deemed to be imminent.
- The warning constitutes direct contact of the threatened individual by the helper with a concise explanation of the nature of the threat that was made.
- The helper should initiate all other possible actions to reduce the likelihood of harm to others. These actions may include dealing with the client's anger in counseling, increasing the frequency of client counseling, referring the client for psychiatric assessment, hospitalizing the client, asking the client to relinquish weapons, and initiating a no-contact contract between the client and the potential victim. (VandeCreek and Knapp, 1989).
- The details of the client's threats, the assessment findings of the client's potential for violence, the management options considered by the counselor/agency, and the actions taken are documented in detail within the client's clinical record.

Although the "duty to warn" laws originated in California, many states now have similar requirements. It is important that you check your state laws and counselor licensing statutes for specific state guidance on duty to warn which may differ from the general common law principles articulated by Tarasoff.

If a Client is Dangerous to Self

When a client threatens suicide, a therapist is ethically justified in breaking confidentiality in order to protect the client - in other words, in such situations, a counselor is ethically justified in disclosing confidential information if such disclosure is deemed necessary to prevent the threatened danger.

Although there is no specific procedure outlined in the law, such as exists for child abuse and elderly abuse reports or threats of violence to identifiable victims, because the client is "dangerous to self," substance abuse professionals are generally acting within acceptable boundaries if they break confidence when a client is at risk for suicide. Note that this option is generally interpreted to mean the therapist has a RIGHT rather than a duty to disclose confidential information.

When a client is suicidal, a counselor's ethical obligation is to do everything within reason to prevent a suicide, with as little violation of the client's privacy as possible. In some cases, it may only be necessary to involve another professional or a family member. In more extreme cases, a counselor or other member of an agency may need to notify the police or an emergency psychiatric facility. If a substance abuse counselor is not qualified or is unable to deal with a suicidal client, he/she should consult with another professional when a client threatens suicide.

If a Client is Dangerous to Others

Ethical principles permit a breach of confidentiality when a client poses a danger to others. In situations where a client has threatened violence towards an identifiable victim, a counselor or agency may be bound by "duty to warn" laws, as previously noted. If these laws do not apply, counselors are still ethically justified in breaching confidentiality if such a breach can prevent the threatened danger. If a client is considered dangerous but a specific victim cannot be identified, a counselor is ethically justified in choosing to breach confidentiality if such a breach can prevent the threatened danger. As with threats of suicide, a breach of confidentiality in these cases is an option rather than a legally-mandated duty.

In both of these situations, any breach of confidentiality should respect the privacy of the client to the greatest degree possible. For example, a substance abuse counselor might contact another professional with more expertise before calling the police. If the police are brought in, they should only be given information that is necessary to prevent the threatened danger.

Crimes at the Program or Against Program Staff

A program may report, or seek assistance from law enforcement agencies, when a patient commits or threatens to commit a crime on the program's premises or against program personnel. Information that may be disclosed includes the suspect's name, address, last known whereabouts, and status as a patient in the program.

Information a patient may divulge about crimes or threats to persons away from the program present special dilemmas. In some states therapists are liable if they fail to warn someone that a patient has threatened to harm him or her. At the same time, the federal regulations, which override state laws, prohibit disclosures that identify substance abuse patients unless they are made pursuant to a court order or without identifying the patient. Such circumstances require knowledge of the applicable state and federal laws and a balancing of moral and legal obligations. If possible, the best solution may be for the program to try to make the warning in a manner that does not identify the individual as a substance abuser.

Public Presentation of Client Information

Counselors must obtain prior consent and/or disguise all identifying data before publicly presenting information gained in a professional relationship. If, for example, a counselor functioning as both a counselor and an instructor at a training institute, college or university were to substantiate lecture material with case examples using actual client information, he/she would need to carefully disguise all information that might identify individual clients. If possible, a signed release or consent would also be advisable.

Third Party Payers

Frequently, the costs of treatment are paid by someone other than the client, such as parents, spouses, employers, and insurance companies. Often such individuals or organizations feel that they have a right to obtain information about the client or even to influence the course of treatment. While certain information may be necessary, clearly their involvement does not provide them with any rights of access to confidential information. Information should be made available only at the client's request, or when the client consents to have it released at the request of another, and when it is in the client's best interests. In addition, the counselor should clarify with all involved parties the conditions surrounding the release of information. This clarification should take place at the beginning of the counseling relationship.

This issue becomes somewhat sticky when it comes to insurance companies. Insurance forms are processed in a variety of ways, involving many persons and agencies. These forms may be seen by clerks and agents of insurance companies and/or their intermediaries. They may also be processed through the client's employer. There is, therefore, no way to assure confidentiality in the usual sense. A DSM diagnosis usually must appear on the insurance claim form. This requirement mandates involving the client in a discussion of the availability of his/her diagnosis to others and of the issue of confidentiality in general. Practitioners must take every precaution regarding who will see such information. However, there is no absolute guarantee of confidentiality by either employers or insurance companies. Again, these issues should be discussed with clients and the client's signed consent to release information should be obtained.

Research and Audits

Researchers may obtain patient-identifying information if certain precautions are applied. The research protocol must ensure that information will be securely stored and not redisclosed except as allowable under the federal regulations. Confidentiality safeguards must be approved by an independent body of three or more persons. Researchers are strictly prohibited from redisclosing patient information. Reports of the research must not identify a patient, directly or indirectly.

Government agencies, third-party payers and peer review organizations may need to review program records without patient consent to conduct an audit or evaluation. Those persons involved in such activities must agree in writing that they will not redisclose patient identifying information unless it is pursuant to a court order to investigate or prosecute the program (not a patient). A government agency that is overseeing a Medicare or Medicaid audit or evaluation also may receive patient information.

Child Abuse/Elderly Abuse

As indicated, substance abuse professionals are legally obligated to breach confidentiality when, in a professional capacity, they acquire knowledge or suspicion of child abuse or neglect or elderly abuse or neglect. Reports are made to the appropriate state agencies or authorities. Laws related to child abuse and elderly abuse reporting generally include penalties for failure to report and provide immunity for the reporter from criminal and civil liability. Note that when reporting suspected child abuse or elderly abuse, the professional must report only the information required by law.

Laws pertaining to the reporting of abuse are somewhat controversial. It has been noted that determination of abuse or potential for abuse is subjective, that the potential breach of confidentiality can have detrimental effects on the therapeutic relationship between a therapist and the abuser or abused individual, and that such laws create the ethical dilemma of whether or not a therapist must warn clients of the limits of confidentiality prior to treatment. In addition, some have argued that these laws make abusers reluctant to seek treatment and therefore fail to result in a long-term reduction in child abuse and elderly abuse. Regardless, counselors must follow the law and report known or suspected incidents of child abuse or elderly abuse to appropriate state authorities.

Qualified Service Organization Agreement

A service organization is a person or agency providing services to the program. Examples include data processing, dosage preparation, laboratory analyses, vocational counseling, accounting, and other professional services. A Qualified Service Organization Agreement (QSOA) is a written agreement, between two parties only, acknowledging that the service organization is fully bound by the confidentiality regulations when dealing with information about patients from the program. It further must promise to resist efforts to obtain access to information about patients, except as permitted by the regulations.

Confidentiality and Other Diseases

Doctor-patient privilege is an accepted practice in medical treatment. In most cases, medical personnel are ethically bound not to divulge information about their patients' medical conditions. However, confidentiality requirements for most medical situations are not nearly as stringent as those that apply to substance abuse treatment programs. For example, generally, physicians are not restricted from acknowledging that an individual is a patient, as is the case with substance abuse treatment.

For substance abuse treatment programs, there are some special considerations when patients have specific diseases. The medical emergency exception to confidentiality does not apply to reporting the results of venereal disease tests to public health officials, as this does not present an immediate medical danger. Thus, these diseases are not reportable by substance abuse treatment programs (Legal Action Center, 1991).

There are some special considerations related to HIV disease, which is also a highly stigmatized illness requiring strict patient confidentiality. All states mandate that cases of AIDS be reported to public health authorities who subsequently report them to the federal Centers for Disease Control and Prevention. Some states also require that positive tests for HIV be reported. Sometimes information is used for tracing and contacting persons who might have been exposed to HIV by the patient, constituting a duty to warn. This may pose conflicting legal obligations for programs to report such information and maintain patient confidentiality. In some cases, anonymous reports can be made using codes rather than patient names. It also may be possible to get patient consent to make mandated reports. Some programs enter into qualified service organization agreements, and the necessary information is reported by a laboratory or medical care provider without identifying the individual as a recipient of substance abuse treatment. In the event that substance abuse treatment records must be released with patient consent or by a court order, programs may need to take precautions not to reveal HIV status inadvertently. Such release of information about HIV status to insurers, employers, and others could have serious ramifications for the infected individual. Ways to avoid unnecessary release of HIV information include maintaining a separate medical file which is not released, releasing the file without the HIV-related information, or having the individual sign a consent form authorizing the release of HIV-related information (Legal Action Center, 1991).

Client Welfare and Client Relationships

Clarifying the Nature of Professional Relationships

Counselors must take responsibility for clarifying all relationships when other parties have an interest in the client-counselor relationship. This requirement can apply in a variety of situations, including the provision of services to employees through EAP's, the treatment of one member of a family at the request of another member, or the treatment of a client whose therapy is being paid for by someone else. In each situation, the counselor has an obligation to clarify the nature of the relationships between all parties concerned. For example, if an organization referred an ineffective employee to a counselor for evaluation, the counselor has an obligation to inform the employee of the nature of the evaluation and the possible implications it may have for his continued employment. Conversely, if a counselor is treating an adult client whose treatment is being paid for by a family member, the client, as an adult, has a full right to a confidential relationship with the counselor. The fact that another family member is paying for treatment does not affect the confidential nature of the client-counselor relationship.

Terminating Counseling Relationships

Counselors must terminate clinical or counseling relationships when clients are not benefiting from them. The two issues related to this requirement include the treatment of particularly difficult clients and the failure of counselors to terminate a nonbeneficial therapeutic relationship. Counselors have a responsibility to recognize their professional and personal limitations. They must know when not to accept clients they are not prepared to treat and when to refer clients elsewhere. In cases where counselors are confronted with patients they are unable to treat, it is essential that they minimize the risk and discomfort to clients. In these situations, referrals should always be made appropriately and quickly.

Ethical problems also arise when the client is encouraged or allowed to remain in treatment beyond the point of benefiting from it. Counselors should be aware of issues such as dependency on the part of a client or personal bias on their part in making decisions for appropriate termination. When legitimate doubts arise regarding the client's therapeutic needs, they should be discussed with the client and often, the client should be referred elsewhere for consultation. When a client does not show improvement or seems to be getting worse, the counselor should seek consultation and/or an appropriate means to terminate therapy and arrange for referral.

Sexual Intimacies with Clients

The statement "the alcoholism and drug abuse counselor should not engage in any type of sexual activity with a client" (Principle 9d) implicitly recognizes that any behavior of this nature represents taking advantage of a position of power.

Clearly, any sexual relationship with a client is unethical. There are no ethically valid exceptions to this Principle. Yet this area continues to be one of the highest areas of ethical violations. A combination of a professional and sexual relationship with a client represents a "dual relationship," which violates both professional and ethical obligations. Such relationships are likely to have adverse consequences on the client. A survey of mental health professionals conducted by a task force of the California State Psychological Association found adverse effects stemming from these types of sexual relationships for over one-third of the clients involved. Sexual relationships with clients increase a counselor's vulnerability to malpractice suits as well as criminal charges. Many states have laws that explicitly prohibit sexual relationships between psychotherapists and clients.

Another related aspect of client exploitation is sexual harassment. Unwanted attention, remarks, gestures, "off-color" jokes, or unwanted touching can all be interpreted as sexual harassment. Conduct by a professional that may be interpreted as sexual harassment is unethical and unprofessional, and it serves to bring both the counselor and the profession into disrepute.

A particularly problematic issue is whether or not it is ethical for a counselor to become sexually involved with a former client. While such a relationship is not clearly prohibited by either legal or ethical provisions, sexual intimacies between therapists and "terminated" clients seem questionable for several reasons - for example, it is difficult to determine when a "terminated" client is actually terminated (former clients may relapse and return for counseling), and it may be impossible for the counselor-client relationship to be transformed into a personal relationship where each person has an equal voice in determining the direction the relationship takes.

Other Dual Relationships

Providing therapy to friends, relatives, students, and colleagues represents another type of dual relationship cautioned against in Principle 9c. Sometimes, the performance of multiple functions in an organization can pose problems with regard to this prohibition. Clearly, a counselor can retain his/her objectivity if he/she is an administrator as well as a counselor. However, if a counselor has been hired to train and supervise interns and to provide counseling to the organization's staff and their families, then dual relationships will exist that can compromise the effectiveness of treatment.

Socializing with clients presents another ethical dilemma. If the opportunity to enter into a social relationship with a client exists, a counselor should reject this opportunity. This serves to protect the counselor's objectivity in the therapeutic relationship as well as to reduce potential harm to the client. Counselors need to be aware of the dynamics of transference and counter transference, and strive to avoid fostering a dependent relationship that, while flattering to the counselor, could stunt the patient's growth and recovery.

Social relationships with clients may be somewhat difficult to avoid if the counselor is a recovering addict and participates in the same 12-step or similar group as his/her clients. If this is the case, the counselor should use common sense and try to keep social contact to a minimum and under no circumstance should a counselor act as a sponsor for a client.

Competence and Responsibility

The Beginning Counselor

The issue of competence is a difficult one for the beginning counselor. A lack of experience with a wide variety of treatment issues is unavoidable in the early stages of professional development. Beginning counselors must be aware of and sensitive to this issue and determine when consultation and clinical supervision will allow them to adequately treat clients versus when co-therapy or referral is required.

An important issue that is sometimes overlooked centers around informed consent for treatment – it is imperative that clients know the credentials of the counselor they are working with, especially if the counselor is an intern or counselor-in-training. Program staff must clearly identify roles and responsibilities of counselors to clients, and clients should also know the chain of command inside the program. Some states, e.g. New Jersey, require this information be made in writing, signed by the client, and placed in the patient's chart.

Limitations of Therapeutic Techniques

The alcoholism and drug abuse counselor should recognize boundaries and limitations of the counselor's competencies and not offer services or use techniques outside of these professional competencies. This issue is of growing concern for the profession. Various controversial therapies, treating such issues as repressed memory and post traumatic stress syndrome, have gathered a great deal of attention. Many professionals, without adequate training or supervision, are attempting to perform such treatment, causing great harm to their clients. In addition, many counselors, in an attempt to increase caseloads, are providing care in areas outside their scope of practice. With the expansion of "addiction" definitions, including such areas as gambling, sexual behaviors, and eating, many chemical dependency counselors are attempting to use techniques from their knowledge of alcohol and drugs in these areas as well. It is important that chemical dependency counselors recognize their limitations and not attempt to perform services for which they have no training or clinical experience.

Continuing Education

Addiction counseling is a rapidly changing and highly complex profession. Thus, substance abuse counselors must take it upon themselves to keep up with new developments in the field by, for example, reading professional journals and new books regularly, attending conventions and workshops, and taking additional courses.

Licensure laws or certification standards require counselors to complete a certain amount of continuing education coursework in order to remain licensed and/or certified. Unfortunately, many counselors delay their education until absolutely necessary. Even though most relicensure or recertification standards require a minimum number of educational hours be taken, remember that the word is minimum. If more hours are needed to stay current of new information and techniques, it is the responsibility of the counselor to upgrade their skills and knowledge on an ongoing basis.

Working with Unfamiliar Populations

Limitations to professional competence can at times include unfamiliarity with the population one is treating or researching (e.g.. a cultural minority, a member of a particular religious group). Counselors are obligated to obtain the necessary guidance and/or additional training required to assure competent treatment or research related to such populations. If a counselor feels uncomfortable, for whatever reason, working with a member of a particular group, the counselor should seek consultation or make an appropriate referral. Coursework in cultural awareness or on special populations should be a must for all counseling professionals.

Personal Problems and Professional Effectiveness

Counselors must "recognize the effect of professional impairment on professional performance and should be willing to seek appropriate treatment for oneself or a colleague." When personal problems impair professional performance, it is critical that professionals take the appropriate steps to ensure that clients and colleagues are protected and that the impaired counselor receives the rehabilitation he or she needs. Chemical dependency, mental illness or emotional problems on the part of a counselor do not justify ethical misconduct - there are many counselors with emotional problems who seek treatment without committing an ethical violation.

A special concern for substance abuse counselors is the possibility of relapse, since many counselors are themselves recovering addicts. This issue is discussed in the section titled "The Recovering Addict as Counselor."

Interprofessional Relationships

Conflict Situations

Principle 10a discusses the counselor's duty to other professionals when situations arise that may cause conflict. This concern arises in cases where treatment is sought from a counselor but the client is already in similar therapy with another mental health professional. Although the client has the right to chose a professional he/she is comfortable with, this Principle stipulates that the alcohol and drug abuse counselor should not offer services "except with the knowledge of the other professional or after the termination of the client's relationship with the other professional." It is advisable in these situations to encourage the client to discuss his/her dissatisfaction directly with the other therapist. If the client will not agree to this course of action, the therapist should seek authorization from the client to contact the other professional and discuss the problem. The counselor should not offer services if the client is unwilling to take steps to terminate the other relationship or to allow the two therapists to work cooperatively.

Alcoholics Anonymous

AA is an organization which has much to offer to recovering alcoholics and asks in return only that its customs and traditions be respected and followed. Thus, in referring a patient to AA, a counselor should consider the patient's needs in the context of AA's overall well-being.

One highly-valued AA tradition is anonymity - AA members are forbidden to identify themselves as such through the media, and are forbidden to identify others as members at all. This tradition is intended to reassure newcomers who might fear for their reputations, protect the fellowship from adverse publicity if a member relapses, and prevent individuals from appointing themselves as spokespersons. All addiction professionals should strive to protect this tradition.

In addition, counselors should think carefully about whom they refer to AA. For example, a large number of referrals, especially all at once, could be damaging to a chapter that has very few members. Another problem exists when programs require AA participation as a part of the treatment program. This can mean that many angry and hostile individuals descend on an AA group which can also be damaging. Many times, such referral occurs without clients having the benefit of learning about the customs and traditions of AA. Counselors should be familiar with the nature and the ways of their local chapter, insure that clients are informed as to the customs and traditions of AA, and act with understanding and respect at all times.

Health Insurance/Third Party Payments

Systems of Health Care Coverage and Reimbursement

Health care costs, especially mental health care costs, have been rising dramatically in recent years. Health care coverage and reimbursement that enable consumers to use health care services take a variety of forms in addition to traditional coverage by private companies thorough clients' employers. Many states have recently mandated that coverage for substance abuse problems be included in insurance policies, and that reimbursement occurs at a level that is reasonable and comparable to traditional health care coverage.

The substance abuse counselor, especially if he/she works in a treatment facility, may play a variety of roles that would require him/her to be familiar with systems of third-party payment - especially Medicaid. Such roles include helping clients and their families make care-related decisions by interpreting information for them, making necessary social and environmental changes to ensure that the patient continues to receive the services he/she needs, and case management which would require the counselor have the ability of following utilization requirements for reimbursement.

While many options currently exist and continue to emerge with the trend towards a national health care system, three of the most common systems of health care coverage and reimbursement - Medicaid, Medicare, and Health Maintenance Organizations (HMOs), are discussed below.

a. Medicaid: Medicaid is a federal and state government funded, means-tested program that provides payment for medical and hospital services to people who cannot afford them. In most areas, Medicaid is managed through local public assistance offices. Persons receiving SSI may be helped with applications for Medicaid at their local Social Security offices.

    The Tax Equity and Fiscal Responsibility Act of 1982 (TEFRA) allowed states to charge persons receiving Medicaid benefits small co-payments for some required and optional services. Exceptions to this include emergency services, family planning and pregnancy-related services, services to categorically needy minors, and services to the categorically needy in skilled nursing or intermediate care facilities or enrolled in HMOs.

b. Medicare: Medicare, a part of Social Security, is a federal entitlement program that guarantees benefits to persons over age 64 and to persons with long-term disabilities. It consists of two parts: Part A is hospital insurance that covers hospital care, skilled nursing facilities, home health agencies, and hospices. Part A is financed through Social Security payroll taxes. Part B is voluntary supplemental insurance obtained partly through premium payments and partly through government financing. It covers outpatient and inpatient physician services, hospital outpatient and laboratory services, durable medical equipment, treatment for end-stage renal disease, and medical supplies.

c. HMOs: The Health Maintenance Organization Act of 1973 is an alternative to the traditional fee-for-service delivery system. HMOs deliver wide-ranging health services to their enrolled members for a fixed, prepaid fee, covering a particular time period. Most HMO members are healthy middle-class working people and their families. HMOs include basic and supplementary services such as physician, outpatient and inpatient. mental health, emergency, family planning, immunization, physical exams, etc.

With HMOs, staff, records, and facilities are more centralized. The following advantages of HMOs have also been noted: (1) they reduce the cost of health care by relying less on hospitalization; (2) they rely more on ambulatory and preventative services by offering increased access to primary care: (3) because of higher quality, continuity of care is improved and less unneeded surgery is performed; and (4) they make productive use of auxiliary health professionals.

Issues in the Use of Third Party Payment

It is only recently that third-party payers have begun, on a widespread basis, to reimburse patients for treatment for substance use disorders. In the past, insurance fraud occurred in the form of using a medical diagnosis to provide care for the chemically dependent client, for example, a physician might list the diagnosis of a patient being treated for substance abuse as "cirrhosis of the liver," or something similar, on insurance forms. Today, however, the potential for insurance fraud exists in fitting the diagnosis of a client to fit the type of coverage. For example, a client may have coverage for alcohol related problems, but not for a drug such as cocaine. It would be tempting to create an alcoholism diagnosis, even though the client doesn't use alcohol, and cite it as primary, thus allowing treatment for the cocaine problem. Another example might be that many insurance companies will not reimburse family members of a chemically dependent individual for family therapy, unless the family members have received a psychiatric diagnosis. Thus, an addiction professional, with the patient's best interests in mind, may at times be tempted to assign an unwarranted diagnosis.

Substance abuse counselors should act as advocates for any efforts which strive to institute changes in public policy and legislation that benefit their clientele. At the same time, addiction professionals must remember that all forms of insurance fraud - which includes misleading an insurance company in any way - are not only illegal but also unethical.

The Recovering Addict as a Counselor

One of the unique aspects of the chemical dependency field is the fact that a significant number of alcohol and drug abuse counselors are themselves recovering addicts. As counselors, such individuals offer the advantage of serving as role models for their clients. These counselors can offer hope to their clients that a life free from substance use is not only possible but can be rich and fulfilling as well.

The use of recovering addicts as counselors, however, raises the question of how long the would-be counselor should maintain sobriety before he or she Is hired. The AA Guidelines For AA Members Employed in the Alcoholism Field (New York; 1987) suggest that members remain abstinent for three to five years before working in the field. Bissell and Royce (Ethics for Addiction Professionals) recommend at least two to three years of continuous sobriety as the standard. However, according to Bissell and Royce, the field is plagued with individuals who present themselves as qualified counselors after only a few weeks of abstinence. Agencies are often eager to hire such individuals, since their salary demands are often low and their level of enthusiasm and dedication is high. However, hiring such individuals poses risks such as relapse to the counselor and a low quality of service to clients.

Regardless of how long a recovering addict has maintained sobriety before beginning work as a counselor, the risk of relapse is always present. The relapse of a counselor raises many difficult issues for an agency, such as what should happen to a counselor, and what patients should be told. Bissell and Royce recommend that this problem be discussed before it happens, so that employees know what to expect and management knows what to do if a relapse occurs. The agency's policy regarding relapse should be made known to new staff when they are hired. Although the relapse of a counselor will always have profound effects on an institution, thoughtful advance policy planning helps keep the distress to a minimum.

Guidelines for the Counselor

While it would be nice and easy if all ethical concerns and considerations were able to be listed in terms of absolute guidelines, reality is that this is impossible. Every situation brings with it special issues and needs that must be addressed as it relates to that issue, not how it should be in the real world. Counselors would be best served if they all understood and followed the dictum "Primum non nocere" (Latin for "do no harm").

In an effort to provide some better guidelines for ethical practice, below are a set of guidelines for ethical practice adapted from the work of Gerald Corey in his book "Theory and Practice of Counseling and Psychotherapy, 4th edition, 1991. They are followed by some guidelines for ethical decision making.

Guidelines for Ethical Practice

1. Counselors must at all times be aware of what their own needs are, what they are getting from the work they perform, and how their needs and behaviors influence their clients. It is essential and critical that the therapist's own needs not be met at the expense of the client's well-being.

2. Counselors must have the training and experience necessary for the assessments they make and the therapeutic interventions they attempt. New skills and applications must be studied and perfected in educational settings, then under proper supervision prior to using such skills with a client.

3. Counselors must always be aware of the boundaries of their professional competence and either seek qualified supervision or refer clients to other practitioners when they recognize that they have reached their limit. They are required to be familiar with community resources so that they can make appropriate referrals when necessary.

4. Although practitioners know the ethical standards of their professional organizations, they must exercise their own judgment in applying these principles to each particular case they work with. The counselor needs to realize that many problems which occur may not have clear-cut answers or solutions, and they accept the responsibility of finding appropriate answers.

5. It is important for counselors to have some theoretical framework of behavioral change to guide them in their practice.

6. Counselors must update their knowledge and skills through various forms of continuing education. Such updating should occur in an ongoing and timely fashion to insure that the best possible care is always offered to the client.

7. Counselors must avoid any relationships with clients that are clearly a threat to the therapeutic relationship. If any potential harm can occur to the client due to a business or personal relationship, it should be avoided. Under no circumstance is a sexual relationship with a client acceptable during the course of care, and such intimacy after the end of the therapeutic relationship is also ill advised.

8. Counselors must inform clients of any circumstances that are likely to affect issues of confidentiality in the therapeutic relationship and of any other matters that are likely to negatively influence the relationship.

9. Counselors must be aware of their own values and attitudes, recognizing the role that their personal belief system plays in the relationships with their clients. Counselors must avoid imposing personal beliefs on their clients, in either a subtle or a direct manner.

10. Counselors must inform their clients about matters such as the goals of counseling, techniques and procedures that will be employed, possible risks associated with entering the therapeutic relationship, and any other factors that are likely to affect the client's decision to enter therapy. To make an informed decision for care, the client must be aware of all such considerations.

11. Counselors need to realize that they are teaching their clients through a modeling process. Thus, they need to practice in their own life what they encourage in their clients. "Do as I say, not as I do" doesn't work in parenting and it doesn't work in therapeutic relationships. If a counselor is unwilling to recognize this, they create potential harm to the client.

12. Counselors must realize that they are bringing their own cultural background to the counseling relationship. Likewise, their clients' cultural values are also operating in the counseling process. Awareness and understanding of such issues is vital to positive outcomes of the therapeutic relationship.

13. Counselor must learn and apply a process for thinking about and dealing with ethical dilemmas, realizing that most ethical issues are complex and defy simple, easy solutions. The willingness to seek consultation is a sign of professional maturity, not professional inadequacy.

Guidelines for Ethical Decision Making

1. Identify the problem or dilemma. Know your professional guidelines and always think in terms of "how am I applying these guidelines to each client I deal with," not "I'll deal with it if an ethical lapse occurs."

2. Define the potential issues involved. Do the issues center around cultural issues? Are there professional complications/implications involved? What is the counselor's liability to the individual and to society?

3. Obtain consultation from a clinical supervisor or peer. Such consultation will provide the counselor with constructive feedback, allow for perception checking, and provide the opportunity of looking at any hidden issues.

4. Consider all possible and probable courses of action. Don't be satisfied with only one solution. List all options which may be available.

5. Enumerate the consequences of various decisions. What is the potential harm to the client, someone close to the client, or society in general.

6. Decide on what appears to be the best course of action and take action. Simply waiting and hoping that the dilemma will pass can cause harm to the client and damage to the professional integrity of the counselor.

Ethics are something that the drug and alcohol professional must always be aware of and look at in each therapeutic relationship. By being proactive in knowing the professional responsibilities and applying them to each and every case handled, the counselor can be assured of performing their job in the highest ethical manner possible.

Section 3, Chapter 6:

12-Step Information for Counselors

Much of the information found in this Chapter comes from the official A.A. website at http://www.alcoholics-anonymous.org/index.cfm. The information is used by permission of Alcoholics Anonymous World Services, Inc., Grand Central Station, P.O. Box 459, New York, N.Y. 10163. Other references can be found at the end of the Chapter.

The following is the definition of A.A. appearing in the Fellowship's basic literature and cited frequently at meetings of A.A. groups:

Alcoholics Anonymous is a fellowship of men and women who share their experience, strength and hope with each other that they may solve their common problem and help others to recover from alcoholism.

The only requirement for membership is a desire to stop drinking. There are no dues or fees for A.A. membership; we are self-supporting through our own contributions. A.A. is not allied with any sect, denomination, politics, organization or institution; does not wish to engage in any controversy; neither endorses nor opposes any causes. Our primary purpose is to stay sober and help other alcoholics to achieve sobriety.

Alcoholics Anonymous can also be defined as an informal society of more than 2,000,000 recovered alcoholics in the United States, Canada, and other countries. These men and women meet in local groups, which range in size from a handful in some localities to many hundreds in larger communities.

In the United States, many public and private substance use disorder treatment programs subscribe to the 12-Step-based approach organized around the philosophy of Alcoholics Anonymous (A.A.). A.A. is an organization that began as a fellowship devoted to helping those who wish to stop drinking. From its original two members in 1935--Bill W., a stockbroker, and Dr. Bob, a surgeon-- it has become an international organization consisting of more than 73,000 groups worldwide, with an estimated membership in the United States and Canada of approximately 800,000. Certainly, any discussion of contemporary treatments for adolescents with substance use disorders must include a review of 12-Step models because of their great influence on substance use disorder treatment.

Interestingly, there is a notable lack of research on 12-Step-based programs, which have for nearly five decades been the most prevalent model of treatment. Yet family-based models, which are relatively new, have been impressively evaluated with controlled studies. This is partly because most 12-Step-based programs do not have a research tradition due to their emphasis on preserving the anonymity of their members.

Although A.A. does not view itself as a treatment modality, it plays a prominent role in the design and implementation of 12-Step-based programs in two important ways: (1) It fosters relationships with the local treatment facilities, and (2) its philosophy, methods, and materials are formally integrated into the treatment activities. Practically speaking, some 12-Step-based treatment programs are headed by private physicians or affiliated with a hospital, whereas others, often led by mental health professionals, are "self-standing." Although generally characterized as aftercare, 12-Step-based programs are sufficient treatment for millions of people, young and old, around the world.

Historical Data: The Birth of A.A. and its Growth

A.A. had its beginnings in 1935 at Akron, Ohio, as the outcome of a meeting between Bill W., a New York stockbroker, and Dr. Bob S., an Akron surgeon. Both had been hopeless alcoholics. Prior to that time, Bill and Dr. Bob had each been in contact with the Oxford Group, a mostly nonalcoholic fellowship that emphasized universal spiritual values in daily living. In that period, the Oxford Groups in America were headed by the noted Episcopal clergyman, Dr. Samuel Shoemaker. Under this spiritual influence, and with the help of an old-time friend, Ebby T., Bill had gotten sober and had then maintained his recovery by working with other alcoholics, though none of these had actually recovered. Meanwhile, Dr. Bob's Oxford Group membership at Akron had not helped him enough to achieve sobriety. When Dr. Bob and Bill finally met, the effect on the doctor was immediate. This time, he found himself face to face with a fellow sufferer who had made good. Bill emphasized that alcoholism was a malady of mind, emotions and body. This all-important fact he had learned from Dr. William D. Silkworth of Towns Hospital in New York, where Bill had often been a patient. Though a physician, Dr. Bob had not known alcoholism to be a disease. Responding to Bill's convincing ideas, he soon got sober, never to drink again. The founding spark of A.A. had been struck.

Both men immediately set to work with alcoholics at Akron's City Hospital, where one patient quickly achieved complete sobriety. Though the name Alcoholics Anonymous had not yet been coined, these three men actually made up the nucleus of the first A.A. group. In the fall of 1935, a second group of alcoholics slowly took shape in New York. A third appeared at Cleveland in 1939. It had taken over four years to produce 100 sober alcoholics in the three founding groups.

Early in 1939, the Fellowship published its basic textbook, *Alcoholics Anonymous.* The text, written by Bill, explained A.A.'s philosophy and methods, the core of which was the now well-known Twelve Steps of recovery. The book was also reinforced by case histories of some thirty recovered members. From this point, A.A.'s development was rapid.

Also in 1939, the *Cleveland Plain Dealer* carried a series of articles about A.A., supported by warm editorials. The Cleveland group of only twenty members was deluged by countless pleas for help. Alcoholics sober only a few weeks were set to work on brand-new cases. This was a new departure, and the results were fantastic. A few months later, Cleveland's membership had expanded to 500. For the first time, it was shown that sobriety could be mass-produced.

Meanwhile, in New York, Dr. Bob and Bill had in 1938 organized an over-all trusteeship for the budding Fellowship. Friends of John D. Rockefeller Jr. became board members alongside a contingent of A.A.s. This board was named The Alcoholic Foundation. However, all efforts to raise large amounts of money failed, because Mr. Rockefeller had wisely concluded that great sums might spoil the infant society. Nevertheless, the Foundation managed to open a tiny office in New York to handle inquiries and to distribute the A.A. book — an enterprise which, by the way, had been mostly financed by the A.A.s themselves.

The book and the new office were quickly put to use. An article about A.A. was carried by *Liberty* magazine in the fall of 1939, resulting in some 800 urgent calls for help. In 1940, Mr. Rockefeller gave a dinner for many of his prominent New York friends to publicize A.A. This brought yet another flood of pleas. Each inquiry received a personal letter and a small pamphlet. Attention was also drawn to the book *Alcoholics Anonymous*, which soon moved into brisk circulation. Aided by mail from New York, and by A.A. travelers from already-established centers, many new groups came alive. At the year's end, the membership stood at 2,000.

Then, in March 1941, the *Saturday Evening Post* featured an excellent article about A.A., and the response was enormous. By the close of that year, the membership had jumped to 6,000, and the number of groups multiplied in proportion. Spreading across the U.S. and Canada, the Fellowship mushroomed.

By 1950, 100,000 recovered alcoholics could be found worldwide. Spectacular though this was, the period 1940-1950 was nonetheless one of great uncertainty. The crucial question was whether all those mercurial alcoholics could live and work together in groups. Could they hold together and function effectively? This was the unsolved problem. Corresponding with thousands of groups about their problems became a chief occupation of the New York headquarters.

By 1946, however, it had already become possible to draw sound conclusions about the kinds of attitude, practice and function that would best suit A.A.'s purpose. Those principles, which had emerged from strenuous group experience, were codified by Bill in what are today the Twelve Traditions of Alcoholics Anonymous. By 1950, the earlier chaos had largely disappeared. A successful formula for A.A. unity and functioning had been achieved and put into practice.

During this hectic ten-year period, Dr. Bob devoted himself to the question of hospital care for alcoholics, and to their indoctrination with A.A. principles. Large numbers of alcoholics flocked to Akron to receive hospital care at St. Thomas, a Catholic hospital. Dr. Bob became a member of its staff. Subsequently, he and the remarkable Sister M. Ignatia, also of the staff, cared for and brought A.A. to some 5,000 sufferers. After Dr. Bob's death in 1950, Sister Ignatia continued to work at Cleveland's Charity Hospital, where she was assisted by the local groups and where 10,000 more sufferers first found A.A. This set a fine example of hospitalization wherein A.A. could cooperate with both medicine and religion.

In this same year of 1950, A.A. held its first International Convention at Cleveland. There, Dr. Bob made his last appearance and keyed his final talk to the need of keeping A.A. simple. Together with all present, he saw the Twelve Traditions of Alcoholics Anonymous enthusiastically adopted for the permanent use of the A.A. Fellowship throughout the world. (He died on November 16, 1950.)

The following year witnessed still another significant event. The New York office had greatly expanded its activities, and these now consisted of public relations, advice to new groups, services to hospitals, prisons, loners, and Internationalists, and cooperation with other agencies in the alcoholism field. The headquarters was also publishing "standard" A.A. books and pamphlets, and it supervised their translation into other tongues. Their international magazine, the A.A. Grapevine, had achieved a large circulation. These and many other activities had become indispensable for A.A. as a whole.

Nevertheless, these vital services were still in the hands of an isolated board of trustees, whose only link to the Fellowship had been Bill and Dr. Bob. As the co-founders had foreseen years earlier, it became absolutely necessary to link A.A.'s world trusteeship (now the General Service Board of Alcoholics Anonymous) with the Fellowship that it served. Delegates from all states and provinces of the U.S. and Canada were forthwith called in. Thus composed, this body for world service first met in 1951. Despite earlier misgivings, the gathering was a great success. For the first time, the remote trusteeship became directly accountable to A.A. as a whole. The A.A. General Service Conference had been created, and A.A.'s over-all functioning was thereby assured for the future.

A second International Convention was held in St. Louis in 1955 to celebrate the Fellowship's 20th anniversary. The General Service Conference had by then completely proved its worth. Here, on behalf of A.A.'s old-timers, Bill turned the future care and custody of A.A. over to the Conference and its trustees. At this moment, the Fellowship went on its own; A.A. had come of age.

Had it not been for A.A.'s early friends, Alcoholics Anonymous might never have come into being. And without its host of well-wishers who have since given of their time and effort — particularly those friends of medicine, religion, and world communications — A.A. could never have grown and prospered. The Fellowship here records its constant gratitude.

It was on January 24, 1971, that Bill, a victim of pneumonia, died in Miami Beach, Florida, where — seven months earlier — he had delivered at the 35th Anniversary International Convention what proved to be his last words to fellow A.A.s: "God bless you and Alcoholics Anonymous forever."

Since then, A.A. has become truly global, and this has revealed that A.A.'s way of life can today transcend most barriers of race, creed and language. A World Service Meeting, started in 1969, has been held biennially since 1972. Its locations alternate between New York and overseas. It has met in London, England; Helsinki, Finland; San Juan del Rio, Mexico; Guatemala City, Guatemala; Munich, Germany; Cartagena, Colombia; and Auckland, New Zealand.

From A.A. to Treatment

Different ways of incorporating the 12-Steps into treatment have evolved over the years. A major adaptation of the model initially developed at Willmar State Hospital, Minnesota, in 1954 has become known as the Minnesota model. By the 1980s, it was the linchpin of almost all programs treating alcoholic and other substance-dependent patients. The goals of the Minnesota model include moving away from the simple custodial care of alcoholics, clarifying the distinction between detoxification and treatment, and identifying a variety of elements of care within one program. The continuum of care components generally includes a diagnostic and referral center, a primary residential rehabilitation program, an extended care program, residential intermediate care (e.g., halfway houses), outpatient care (diagnostic, primary, and extended), aftercare, and a family program.

The Hazelden Foundation further modified this model of care, which preceded enrollment in a primary care program with several days of detoxification in a separate facility. The Minnesota model tried to develop an environment of recovery in a setting removed from daily life, often in the country, for a few months.

The approach that evolved was highly structured and included detoxification, psychological evaluation, general and individualized treatment tracks, group meetings, lectures, and counseling, as well as referral to medical, psychiatric, and social services, as needed. Group counseling was considered the main therapeutic technique. Emphasis was on using older, more advanced residents to share experiences and to pass on knowledge and values to patients. The 12-Steps were carefully studied, and A.A. meetings were held within the treatment framework. The primary care program was intended to last up to 60 days in a residential setting in the hope that a caring and low-stress environment removed from traditional daily life would facilitate the recovery process.

In the early 1960s, Hazelden developed a 21-day version; insurance companies then set 28 days as a reimbursement guideline in order to ensure sufficient coverage. This abbreviated version viewed intensive treatment as a multidisciplinary endeavor, in which the physician, nurse, psychiatrist, psychologist, counselor, and administrators were involved in a hospital setting. Rehabilitation was provided after intensive treatment by nonmedical staff and coordinated by the counselor. Participation in A.A. for patients and in Al-Anon for family members got started during treatment and ideally continued for 2 years after treatment. More specifically, treatment components included

- Strong A.A. orientation
- Skilled alcoholism counselors as primary therapists
- Psychological testing and psychosocial evaluation
- Medical and psychiatric support for coexisting disorders
- Therapists trained in systematized methods of treatment including Gestalt, psychodrama, reality therapy, transactional analysis, behavior therapy, activity therapy, and stress management
- Use of therapeutic milieu and crisis intervention
- Systems therapy, especially with employers, and later including a family component
- Family- and peer-oriented aftercare

For many years, some in the treatment field considered the Minnesota model the only "workable" method of treatment for substance use disorders. Then, as the nation's attention in the 1970s and 1980s focused on the use of illicit drugs (e.g., cocaine), three trends in service delivery occurred. First, treatment programs expanded their curriculum to address substances other than alcohol. Second, new programs were developed that specifically addressed individuals with nonalcohol substance use disorders. Third, both types of programs eventually discovered that alcoholism and substance use disorders overlapped, and thus most programs oriented themselves to the treatment of both.

As the years passed, additional types of treatment approaches emerged, including social model programs and programs based in psychology, such as family-based therapy in its many forms. Parts of the 12-Step-based approach were incorporated into these treatment programs. Since the advent of managed care, outpatient programs of all approaches are becoming the norm. Residential programs within the public or private sector have become less common and often have diminished lengths of stay. Those that remain are often located within institutions, such as correctional institutions or hospital-based psychiatric units.

EARLY BEGINNINGS

A variety of other programs were operating and experimenting with the integration of treatment programming and 12-Step services during this crucial period of growth and development of alcoholism treatment. Some of these programs are listed below.

- <u>Mrs. Pink's Place</u> – located in Dallas, Texas, this program provided what was commonly called the "St. Louis Treatment." For $125 paid in advance, alcoholics were detoxified through a regimen of whiskey every four hours, along with honey and milk to settle the stomach, and lots of encouragement from visiting A.A. members.
- <u>Bridge House</u> – located in New York City, this residential setting provided outpatient programming that viewed alcoholism treatment as an educational process. Residents were referred to as "students" and treatment involved four-weeks of lectures, discussion groups, and written and oral examinations.
- <u>Beech Hill Farm</u> – located in Dublin, New Hampshire, this program was known as "a post-hospitalization rest home for recovering alcoholics."
- <u>Alina Lodge</u> – located in Kenvil, New Jersey, this program was known for its "non-permissive approach" designed to instill discipline and a sense of self-responsibility in each alcoholic. A.A. attendance was mandatory and heavily influenced treatment services offered.
- <u>Portal House</u> – located in Chicago, Illinois, this program was established by the Chicago Department of Welfare, through assistance from the Chicago Committee on Alcoholism.
- <u>Brighton Hospital for Alcoholism</u> – located in Brighton, Michigan, it was founded by a member of the Michigan State Liquor Commission who "enticed" liquor dealers in the state to assist in soliciting funds from their patrons to support alcoholism treatment. While Brighton's treatment approach emphasized A.A. and utilized recovered counselors, it was one of the more medically oriented programs of that time.
- <u>The Georgian Clinic and Rehabilitation Center for Alcoholics</u> – located in Atlanta, Georgia, and founded by the Georgia Commission on Alcoholism (one of the first state agencies dedicated to alcoholism services founded in 1951), the programs offered utilized one of the first interdisciplinary models for alcoholism treatment.
- <u>Chit Chat Foundation</u> – located in Reading, Pennsylvania, this program had similar roots to Hazelden in that Richard and Catherine Caron opened their home to alcoholics and family members in need of support during early recovery. The bull sessions around a kitchen table were called "Chit Chats" – a name that would eventually be associated with a large alcoholism treatment complex that is still in operation today.
- <u>Mt. Carmel Hospital for Alcoholics</u> – located in Paterson, New Jersey, this was the first hospital licensed by the State in one of "Dutch Schultz's illegal breweries from the Prohibition era." Located on the corner of "Straight & Narrow Streets," admission required an A.A. sponsor and patients were discharged to the sponsor, who would take the patient to their first community based A.A. meeting that same day/night to begin their 90/90 (ninety meetings in ninety days).

The Twelve Steps of Alcoholics Anonymous

The 12-Steps were written in 1938 by the founders of the fledgling A.A. and originally appeared in what is known to legions of recovering adults as the Big Book. In A.A., sobriety is maintained by carefully applying this 12-Step philosophy and by sharing experiences with others who have suffered similar problems. Many clients who are involved with A.A. find another A.A. member who will serve as a sponsor and provide guidance and help in times of crisis when the return to substance use becomes overwhelming. This sharing and group support approach has spawned a number of self-help programs, such as Al-Anon (for families and friends of the alcoholic) and Narcotics Anonymous (NA) (for persons addicted to substances other than or in addition to alcohol). Learning and practicing the 12-Steps, which are listed below, is the main focus of A.A. and NA. NA programs change some wording in the first and last steps to make them appropriate to users of illicit drugs and other substances; these appear in parentheses.

1. We admitted we were powerless over alcohol (our addiction)--that our lives had become unmanageable.
2. We came to believe that a Power greater than ourselves could restore us to sanity.
3. We made a decision to turn our will and our lives over to the care of God as we understood Him.
4. We made a searching and fearless moral inventory of ourselves.
5. We admitted to God, to ourselves, and to another human being the exact nature of our wrongs.
6. We were entirely ready to have God remove all these defects of character.
7. We humbly asked Him to remove our shortcomings.
8. We made a list of all persons we had harmed and became willing to make amends to them all.
9. We made direct amends to such people wherever possible, except when to do so would injure them or others.
10. We continued to take a personal inventory and when we were wrong promptly admitted it.
11. We sought through prayer and meditation to improve our conscious contact with God as we understood Him, praying only for knowledge of His will for us and the power to carry that out.
12. Having had a spiritual awakening as the result of these steps, we tried to carry this message to alcoholics (addicts) and to practice these principles in all our affairs.

A. A. Traditions

During its first decade, A.A. as a fellowship accumulated substantial experience which indicated that certain group attitudes and principles were particularly valuable in assuring survival of the informal structure of the Fellowship. In 1946, in the Fellowship's international journal, the A.A. Grapevine, these principles were reduced to writing by the founders and early members as the Twelve Traditions of Alcoholics Anonymous. They were accepted and endorsed by the membership as a whole at the International Convention of A.A., at Cleveland, Ohio, in 1950.

1. Our common welfare should come first; personal recovery depends upon A.A. unity.
2. For our group purpose there is but one ultimate authority — a loving God as He may express Himself in our group conscience. Our leaders are but trusted servants; they do not govern.
3. The only requirement for A.A. membership is a desire to stop drinking.
4. Each group should be autonomous except in matters affecting other groups or A.A. as a whole.
5. Each group has but one primary purpose—to carry its message to the alcoholic who still suffers.
6. An A.A. group ought never endorse, finance or lend the A.A. name to any related facility or outside enterprise, lest problems of money, property and prestige divert us from our primary purpose.
7. Every A.A. group ought to be fully self-supporting, declining outside contributions.
8. Alcoholics Anonymous should remain forever nonprofessional, but our service centers may employ special workers.
9. A.A., as such, ought never be organized; but we may create service boards or committees directly responsible to those they serve.
10. Alcoholics Anonymous has no opinion on outside issues; hence the A.A. name ought never be drawn into public controversy.

11. Our public relations policy is based on attraction rather than promotion; we need always maintain personal anonymity at the level of press, radio and films.
12. Anonymity is the spiritual foundation of all our traditions, ever reminding us to place principles before personalities.

While the Twelve Traditions are not specifically binding on any group or groups, an overwhelming majority of members have adopted them as the basis for A.A.'s expanding "internal" and public relationships.

A. A. Meetings

The two most common kinds of A.A. meetings are:

OPEN MEETINGS: As the term suggests, meetings of this type are open to alcoholics and their families and to anyone interested in solving a personal drinking problem or helping someone else to solve such a problem. It doesn't matter whether the person feels that he or she is in need of the fellowship, or is a friend or loved one of a member, or is merely curious. The only obligation placed on attendance is that of honoring the anonymity of others by not disclosing their names outside the meeting. The views expressed at these meetings are those of the individuals attending, in that all A.A. members speak only for themselves. All members are free to interpret the recovery program in their own terms, but none can speak for the local group or for A.A. as a whole.

During the meeting there is usually a period for local A.A. announcements, and a treasurer passes the hat to defray costs of the meeting hall, literature, and incidental expenses. The meeting adjourns, often followed by informal visiting over coffee or other light refreshments.

CLOSED MEETINGS: In contrast, closed meetings are limited to members of the local fellowship group and visitors from other groups within the fellowship. These meetings safeguard members' anonymity and provide a forum for the discussion of specific phases of the members' problems that may be understood best by fellow members of the specific fellowship. The meetings are usually informal and highly participatory. All members are encouraged to participate in discussions. Closed meetings can be particularly helpful for newcomers, especially those who may be concerned about their anonymity in the community. They also provide a forum for airing questions that may trouble a beginner, or even an old-timer, that may seem inappropriate for an open meeting but do merit serious discussion.

Groups composed of individuals with like interests, such as health professionals, may opt for a closed meeting format. This allows them to address specific issues that involve a professional interface within their fellowship that are important within the group but would not be appropriate to pursue in depth in an open meeting. For example, for recovering counselors, the closed format provides a means of escaping the counselor/client identity that can reassert itself if a client is encountered at an open meeting.

Meeting Types

Within the two types of 12-Step meetings, there are several primary meeting formats and a variety of sub-formats that meetings may adopt. These include the following.

DISCUSSION MEETINGS

Discussion meetings and speaker/discussion meetings are the two most common A.A. meetings, and similar formats are used by other 12-Step fellowships as well. In a discussion meeting, the secretary usually presides, either supplying a topic or asking if anyone in the group has a topic that they wish to discuss. Topics usually involve recovery and fellowship issues. They may vary considerably, although certain themes, such as exercising spirituality, dealing with fear, anxiety, and other personal recovery problems, interpersonal and other life problems, and dealing with the disease frequently recur. Anyone and everyone at the meeting is encouraged to speak, either on the topic or on their own particular concerns or issues. Each speaker, when recognized by the secretary. introduces him or herself by first name and fellowship designation. i.e., Jan, alcoholic; John. addict; Richard, junkie and drunk; Alice, a grateful alcoholic. The rest then say, `Hi Jan." or whoever, and the person says his or her piece. This process continues until the end of the meeting. In most meetings, "cross-talk," i.e., sustained dialogues between two individuals, is discouraged in the interest of making sure that the meeting time is not dominated by one or two members and that everyone who wants to can have their say.

SPEAKER AND SPEAKER/DISCUSSION MEETINGS

At a speaker or speaker/discussion meeting, a member of the fellowship is asked to speak at the meeting. In some situations, the speaker may occupy the center for the entire meeting, but in most cases it is understood that the speaker's story will be limited to half an hour. Speakers may be regular attendees at the meeting, or they may have never attended the meeting at which they are speaking. Secretaries often work for a balance of the familiar and the new. There is no rule to this effect, but it is generally thought that an individual should have at least 6 months in the fellowship before being a formal speaker.

The format most often used in a speaker's story can be expressed as, "what it was like, what happened, and what it is like now." In other words, the speakers are expected to talk about their life as dominated by addictive disease, how they came into the fellowship, and how their life has changed as a result of the fellowship. When they are done. the secretary will ask them to provide a topic for discussion, and the speaker acts as moderator for the rest of the meeting, which now has the same format as a discussion meeting.

The first time a member speaks at a meeting is an important personal occasion, a valedictory that marks a passage within the fellowship. Although speakers may find the experience difficult, it is nearly always a positive experience and an aid in strengthening one's program of recovery and sobriety.

STEP MEETINGS

The 12 Steps provide a blueprint for developing individual spiritual maturity with the fellowship, and as such have a special type of meeting all their own. These are the step meetings. When a step meeting is initiated, it usually starts work on Step 1 at its first session and continues to focus on a step at a time through number 12. Then it starts back on Step 1 again. Some meetings may work their way through the Twelve Traditions as well.

In A.A. step meetings, the meeting will usually start with passing around and reading aloud the appropriate step in its long form from the "Twelve by Twelve," Twelve Steps and *Twelve* Traditions." The step, itself, then becomes the topic for discussion and the meeting follows a discussion format. A variation on this is a step/speaker meeting. in which the speaker is asked to organize the talk in relation to the step, and again, the step is the discussion topic.

BOOK MEETINGS

Book meetings are similar to step meetings but involve initiatory serial readings from the "Big Book," or other fellowship publications, such as *Living Sober:* Some *methods A.A. members have used for not drinking* or *Came to Believe ... : The spiritual adventure of A.A. as experienced by individual members.* Once more, passages are read by those attending the meeting, and these provide the topic for discussion.

CHIP OR BIRTHDAY MEETINGS

These are meetings at which fellowship birthdays are acknowledged. Members' birthdays are measured from their entry into the fellowship and are maintained as long as the member remains sober. Members who have a relapse typically admit this when they reenter the fellowship and set a new birth-date on their re-entry. Although a great deal of emphasis is placed on staying sober or drug-free "one day at a time," cumulative time in sobriety is encouraged and recognized through ceremonial recognition and the awarding of "chips," often literally poker chips that are engraved with the fellowship logo on one side and length of sobriety on the other. These are awarded by the meeting secretary or designee at the end of the meeting with general applause and encouragement. Chip meetings are usually open meetings and those close to a member receiving a chip are encouraged to attend.

Given the critical nature of early recovery, these tokens of accomplishment are given more frequently than the first year. Although there is no rule on this, the usual periods are: 24 hours, 30 days, 6 months, 1 year, and then at the end of each year thereafter. It is interesting to note that these intervals correspond with times that have been recognized as when the newly recovering individual is most vulnerable to relapse.

Frequent meetings other than chip meetings will set aside a few minutes at the last meeting of the month to recognize attendees who have birthdays in that month. Often special refreshments, such as a cake, are served as celebration of all members being a month older in sobriety.

Most often a meeting will adopt one format and use it every week. The meeting name may reflect the format, such as "Sunday Night Big Book Study," "Tuesday Night Step," "12 by 12 Study," or "Noon Discussion." Other meetings may vary their format, such as 3 weeks of speaker/discussion and once a month step study. There are no hard and fast rules on meeting format, and meetings vary to some extent between fellowships, regions, and groups.

The Importance of Anonymity

Traditionally, A.A. members have always taken care to preserve their anonymity at the "public" level: press, radio, television, and films.   In the early days of A.A., when greater stigma was attached to the term "alcoholic" than is the case today, this reluctance to be identified — and publicized — was easy to understand.

As the Fellowship of A.A. grew, the positive values of anonymity soon became apparent.

First, many problem drinkers might hesitate to turn to A.A. for help if they thought their problem might be discussed publicly, even inadvertently, by others. Newcomers should be able to seek help with assurance that their identities will not be disclosed to anyone outside the Fellowship.

Then, too the concept of personal anonymity has a spiritual significance for the A.A. program – that it discourages the drives for personal recognition, power, prestige, or profit that have caused difficulties in some societies. Much of the programs relative effectiveness in working with alcoholics might be impaired if it sought or accepted public recognition.

While each member of A.A. is free to make his or her own interpretations of A.A. tradition, no individual member is ever recognized as a spokesperson for the Fellowship locally, nationally, or internationally. Each member speaks only for himself or herself.

An A.A. member may, for various reasons, "break anonymity" deliberately at the public level. Since this is a matter of individual choice and conscience, the Fellowship as a whole obviously has no control over such deviations from tradition. It is clear, however, that such individuals do not have the approval of the overwhelming majority of members.

The Spiritual Experience

One of the most common misconceptions about Alcoholics Anonymous is that it is a religious organization. New members especially, confronted with A.A.'s emphasis on recovery from alcoholism by spiritual means, often translate "spiritual" as "religious" and shy away from meetings, avoiding what they perceive as a new and frightening set of beliefs. By the time they walk into their first meeting, many alcoholics have lost what faith they might once have possessed; others have tried religion to stop drinking and failed; still others simply want nothing to do with it. Yet with rare exceptions, once A.A. members achieve any length of sobriety, they have found a source of strength outside themselves — a Higher Power, by whatever name — and the stumbling block has disappeared.

A.A.'s Twelve Steps, which constitute its program of recovery, are in no way a statement of belief; they simply describe what the founding members did to get sober and stay sober. They contain no new ideas: surrender, self-inventory, confession to someone outside ourselves, and some form of prayer and meditation are concepts found in spiritual movements throughout the world for thousands of years. What the Steps do is frame these principles for the suffering alcoholic — sick, frightened, defiant, and grimly determined not to be told what to do or think or believe.

The Steps offer a detailed plan of action: admit that alcohol has you beaten, clean up your own life, admit your faults and do whatever it takes to change them, maintain a relationship with whatever or whoever outside of yourself can help keep you sober, and work with other alcoholics.

'God As We Understood Him'

As previously noted, the basic principles of Alcoholics Anonymous were worked out in the late 1930s and early '40s, during what co-founder Bill W. often referred to as the Fellowship's period of "trial and error." The founding members had been using six steps borrowed from the Oxford Groups, where many of them started out. Bill felt that more specific instructions would be better, and in the course of writing A.A.'s basic text, *Alcoholics Anonymous,* he expanded them to twelve. But he was dealing with a group of newly sober drunks, and not surprisingly his new version met with spirited opposition. Even though the founding members were in many ways a homogeneous bunch (white, middle-class, almost exclusively male, and primarily Christian in background), they represented the full spectrum of opinion and belief. Bill tells us in *Alcoholic Anonymous Comes of Age,* a history of the Fellowship's early years that "the hot debate about the Twelve Steps and the book's content was doubled and redoubled. There were conservative, liberal, and radical viewpoints." Some thought the book ought to be Christian; others could accept the word "God" but were opposed to any other theological proposition. And the atheists and agnostics wanted to delete all references to God and take a psychological approach.

Bill concludes: "We finally began to talk about the possibility of compromise. . . . In Step Two we decided to describe God as a 'Power greater than ourselves.' In Steps Three and Eleven we inserted the words *'God as we understood Him.'* From Step Seven we deleted the words 'on our knees.' And, as a lead-in sentence to all the steps we wrote these words: 'Here are the steps we took, which are suggested as a program of recovery.' A.A.'s Twelve Steps were to be *suggestions* only."

More than sixty years later, those crucial compromises, articulated after weeks of heated controversy, have made it possible for alcoholics of all faiths, or no faith at all, to embrace the A.A. program of recovery and find lasting sobriety.

Spiritual Awakening

Nevertheless, the phrase "spiritual awakening," found in the Twelfth Step and throughout A.A. literature, remains daunting to many beginners. For some, it conjures up a dramatic "conversion" experience — not an appealing idea to an alcoholic just coming off a drunk. To others, beaten down by years of steady drinking, it seems completely out of reach. But for those who persevere, ongoing sobriety almost invariably brings the realization that — in some wonderful and unexpected way — they have indeed experienced a spiritual change.

Spirituality, A.A. style, is the result of action. Step Twelve begins, "Having had a spiritual awakening *as the result of these Steps. . .*" (italics added), and in the book *Twelve Steps and Twelve Traditions*, Bill W. describes what happens: "Maybe there are as many definitions of spiritual awakening as there are people who have had them. But certainly each genuine one has something in common with all the others. . . . When a man or woman has a spiritual awakening, the most important meaning of it is that he has now become able to do, feel, and believe that which he could not do before on his unaided strength and resources alone. He has been granted a gift which amounts to a new state of consciousness and being. He has been set on a path which tells him he is really going somewhere, that life is not a dead end, not something to be endured or mastered. In a very real sense he has been transformed, because he has laid hold of a source of strength which, in one way or another, he had hitherto denied himself."

Groups and Their Customs

If the Steps are the program of recovery, the A.A. group is where alcoholics learn to live the program and practice it "in all their affairs." Virtually all group meetings in the U.S. and Canada begin with a reading of the A.A. Preamble, a brief description of what the Fellowship is and is not. Its last two sentences make it clear that A.A.'s purpose has nothing to do with religion: "A.A. is not allied with any sect, denomination, politics, organization or institution; does not wish to engage in any controversy; neither endorses nor opposes any causes. Our primary purpose is to stay sober and help other alcoholics to achieve sobriety."

Group customs that appear to be religious sometimes discourage new people from coming back. Professionals who refer people to A.A. may help by advising them to attend a variety of meetings, especially in the first year of sobriety, and to find a home group where they are comfortable. According to A.A.'s Fourth Tradition, each group is autonomous, which means in practical terms that every group is unique, with a flavor all its own. Thus, even if a shaky alcoholic finds himself one night in a meeting where the members feel at home with traditional religious language, he or she can try again the next night and find a group where even the most doubting or cynical soul will fit right in.

Similarly, A.A. members generally deal with the question of a Higher Power by assuring new members that they are free to find their own. Men and women who shy away from what is known in A.A. vernacular as the "God bit" can still identify a much-needed source of support outside themselves. For some, it is their A.A. group; others eventually choose a traditional idea of God, while still others rely upon an entirely different concept of a higher power. To show the variety of spiritual searches in A.A. the booklet *Came to Believe* was published in 1973. It is a collection of the various spiritual experiences of a wide range of members, from adherents of traditional religion to atheists and agnostics, with all stops in between.

Using the Lord's Prayer

The practice of ending meetings with the Lord's Prayer, once almost universal, is still common in many areas. Where it still exists, the leader normally asks attendees to join in only if they choose to. North American groups today have found a variety of ways to close their meetings. Use of the Lord's Prayer is rare in Spanish groups in the U.S. and groups outside the United States. Many recite the Serenity Prayer or A.A.'s Responsibility Statement; others use some other informal prayer or phrasing, or simply a moment of silence. And whatever the specific wording, the group conscience makes the decision.

Groups that continue to close with the Lord's Prayer are following a custom established in the Fellowship's earliest days, when many of the founding members found their support in meetings of the Oxford Groups. The practice of closing with the Lord's Prayer very likely came directly from those meetings. At the time, there was no A.A. literature, and so the founders leaned heavily on Bible readings for inspiration and guidance. They probably closed with the Lord's Prayer because, as Bill W. explained, "it did not put speakers to the task, embarrassing to many, of composing prayers of their own." Meeting formats became more inclusive once A.A. began to spread throughout North America and then the rest of the world, and it became obvious that the program of recovery could cross all barriers of creed, race, and religion.

In *Alcoholics Anonymous Comes of Age,* the Rev. Samuel Shoemaker, one of the nonalcoholic friends who was instrumental in shaping the Fellowship in the very beginning, reflects on the founders' fundamental decision not to define a set of beliefs. He says: "A.A. has been supremely wise, I think, in emphasizing the reality of the experience, and acknowledging that it came from a higher Power than human, and leaving the interpretation part pretty much at that. . . . If A.A.'s had said more, some people would have wanted them to say a great deal more, and define God in a way acceptable and congenial to themselves. It would have taken only two or three groups like this, dissenting from one another, to wreck the whole business. . . . So they stuck to the inescapable experiences and told people to turn their wills and their lives over to the care of God *as they understood Him.* That left the theory and the theology. . . to the churches to which people belong. If they belonged to no church and could hold no consistent theory, then they had to give themselves to the God that they saw in other people. That's not a bad way to set in motion the beginnings of a spiritual experience."

One Person's View

Prior to AA I had had contact with religion, but no spirituality or understanding of it. (I was a drunk.) As a drunk I had attended many different churches with many different congregations, in hopes of getting something right, but it made no sense to me. And of course, as a result of my lack of trust, of understanding and of faith, it didn't work for me. There was no end of frustration and despair, because I could see it working for others.

On coming to AA, and being told it was a spiritual program, my confusion was such that I finally asked a clever old man: "What is the difference between religion and spirituality?"

He said: *"Bob, let's put your particular concept of the creator aside for a moment and compare the difference between religion and spirituality. The way I see it, religion is man made by man to suit the needs of man. Religion talks the talk, and spirituality walks the walk. In spirituality we honor the existence of all creation including ourself. In AA, as we practice the 12 Steps in all our affairs, we are walking the talk..."*

Now that makes sense to me, now I can walk the talk of my religion.
It works, it really does!!!

Other Community Resources for Drug & Alcohol Clients

Although the focus of this Chapter is 12 Step Recovery, it would be incomplete if I did not draw your attention to the mutual-aid alternatives available that have been used for recovery. For these alternatives, I have included information submitted directly from the founders of 5 of the largest non-professional secular alternatives available for recovery: Rational Recovery (RR), Women For Sobriety (WFS), Secular Organizations For Sobriety (SOS), Moderation Management (MM), and Self Management And Recovery Training (S.M.A.R.T).

Rational Recovery®: A Guide for Professionals

Rational Recovery® provides a means for self-recovery from addiction to any mind/mood altering substance, Addictive Voice Recognition Technique® (AVRT). Based on the successful experience of self-recovered people, AVRT is not a form of counseling, therapy, or part of any psychological theory, nor does it contain spiritual or religious guidance. AVRT is simply the lore of self-recovery in a brief, educational format. The following facts support the use of AVRT:

- The large majority (+/- 70% to 80%) of those who actually recover from serious substance addictions do so on their own, without the aid of recovery groups or professional consultation. They get fed up with the outcome of drinking and quit for life.
- Recovery is not an outcome of a process of self-improvement, but personal growth is usually an outcome of a commitment to lifetime abstinence. Following a personal commitment to permanent abstinence, complete recovery is typically accomplished within a matter of weeks, or, with drugs that have a persistent withdrawal syndrome, within months.
- Addiction recovery, regardless of the substance involved, the age of onset, the duration of an addiction, or whatever other problems may co-exist, is much easier and simpler than currently imagined or made out to be.

- The ideal role of any professional person is to encourage individuals that they are capable of self-recovery, and to make available accurate information on planned abstinence through AVRT.
- The group format is inappropriate to the purpose of any individual's prompt recovery.
- The notion of addictive disease is discouraging to addicted people. Self-recovery is based on an understanding that addiction is an expression of survival drives associated with intense physical pleasure, and that self-restraint of these drives is well within human capability.
- The act of self-intoxication is an individual, moral issue once a pattern of self-destruction or antisocial behavior is established.
- Persons who make a commitment to permanent abstinence and acquire the abstinence skill of AVRT become highly confident in their ability to abstain, giving rise to uplifted feelings. These feelings are predictable, authentic, and vital to the regeneration of life following an episode of addiction. The goal of self-recovery is self-identification as a normal, healthy person who simply never drinks or uses for reasons that are nobody¹s business but one¹s own.

For obvious reasons, comprehensive information on planned abstinence (AVRT) must be the very first consideration when substance abuse appears, and the logical choice when other approaches first appear difficult, unhelpful, or objectionable.

AVRT is educational material subject to laws governing copyright and trademark laws. Although anyone may distribute Rational Recovery® materials and refer individuals to our Website for Self-Recovery http://www.rational.org/recovery, AVRT is not a professional tool and may not lawfully be provided by any professional person as a service to clientele. Even the language of AVRT is protected under the same laws. The reason for this protection is twofold:
- To prevent AVRT from being changed by parties other than Rational Recovery.
- To prevent AVRT from becoming an instrument of the recovery group movement and its business arm, the addiction treatment industry. Rational Recovery is self-recovery, not mandated recovery, institutional recovery, politically correct recovery, or recovery facilitated by parties other than Rational Recovery itself.

Rational Recovery Systems, Inc. Box 800, Lotus CA 95651
National office - 530-621-2667, 8 AM - 4 PM, PST
Recover online at http://www.rational.cc/recovery/
We believe in people -- not programs.
-Jack Trimpey, Founder of Rational Recovery

Women for Sobriety

Women for Sobriety has been providing services to women alcoholics since July, 1976. Based upon a Thirteen Statement Program of positivism that encourages emotional and spiritual growth, the "New Life" Program is effective in helping women overcome their alcoholism by learning a whole new lifestyle. WFS came forth with the belief that women alcoholics require a different kind of program in recovery than the kinds of programs used for male alcoholics. The success of the WFS "New Life" Program has shown this to be true. The psychological and emotional needs for women in recovery are very different from those of the male alcoholic and the WFS Program recognizes and addresses these needs.

To receive a copy of the WFS Program, please contact: Women for Sobriety, Inc., P.O. Box 618, Quakertown, PA 18951 - voice/fax: 215-536-8026, Internet: http://www.womenforsobriety.org - Email: NewLife@nni.com
-Dr. Jean Kirkpatrick, Founder of Women for Sobriety

SECULAR ORGANIZATION FOR SOBRIETY

The Secular Organization for Sobriety (also known as SOS or Save Our Selves) is an abstinence human support movement. Its effective self-empowerment method for achieving and maintaining a lasting sobriety, The Sobriety Priority Program, has helped thousands of alcoholics and addicts achieve and maintain sobriety many of whom could not have done so in other programs.

WHAT IS SOS?
SOS is an alternative recovery method for those alcoholics or drug addicts who are uncomfortable with the spiritual content of widely available 12-step programs. SOS takes a reasonable, secular approach to recovery and maintains that sobriety is a separate issue from religion or spirituality. SOS credits the individual with achieving and maintaining his or her own sobriety. SOS respects recovery in any form, regardless of the path by which it is achieved. It is not opposed to or in competition with any other recovery programs. SOS supports healthy skepticism and encourages the use of the scientific method to understand alcoholism.

GENERAL PRINCIPALS

All those who sincerely seek sobriety are welcomed as members in any SOS group. SOS is not a spin-off of any religious group. There is no hidden agenda--SOS is concerned with sobriety, not spirituality. SOS seeks only to promote sobriety amongst those who suffer from alcoholism or other drug addictions. As a group, SOS has no opinion on outside matters and does not wish to become entangled in outside controversy.

Although sobriety is an individual responsibility, life does not have to be faced alone. The support of other alcoholics and addicts is a vital adjunct to recovery. In SOS, members share experiences, insights, information, strength, and encouragement in friendly, honest, anonymous, and supportive group meetings. To avoid unnecessary entanglements each SOS group is self-supporting through contributions from its members and refuses outside donations. Sobriety is the number one priority in an alcoholic's or addict's life. As such, he or she must abstain from all drugs or alcohol. Honest, clear, and direct communication of feelings, thoughts, and knowledge aids in recovery and in choosing nondestructive, non-delusional, and rational approaches to living sober and rewarding lives. As knowledge of drinking or addiction might cause a person harm or embarrassment in the outside world, SOS guards the anonymity of its membership and the contents of its discussions from those not within the group. SOS encourages the scientific study of alcoholism and addiction in all their aspects. SOS does not limit its outlook to one area of knowledge or theory of alcoholism and addiction.

James R. Christopher, Founder - Secular Organization for Sobriety
More information about SOS can be obtained at:
http://www.unhooked.com/meetings/clghouse.htm

Moderation Management

For People Who Want to Cut Back or Quit Drinking

Moderation Management (MM) is a new national support group network for people who have made the healthy decision to reduce their consumption of alcohol. The main purpose of MM is to help problem drinkers reduce their drinking to a level which no longer causes life problems. Research indicates that many *nondependent* problem drinkers can be successful with a recovery goal of moderation.

MM encourages people to recognize and to do something about, a drinking problem as *early* as possible—before serious health and personal problems develop. Unfortunately, many problem drinkers today actively and purposefully avoid traditional treatment approaches. This is because they know that most traditional programs will label them as "alcoholic" (permanently), strongly suggest or even force A.A. attendance, and prescribe lifetime abstinence as the only acceptable recovery goal. They may also have real concerns about how their participation in these programs will affect their jobs and ability to attain future medical and life insurance. MM is seen as a less threatening option, and one that beginning problem drinkers are more likely to attempt *before* their problems become nearly intractable. This is when the likelihood of attaining full recovery, whether through abstinence or moderation, is still encouragingly high.

One of the most significant benefits of having both moderation and abstinence-based programs available is that more people seek help when they are given real options. It is probably not necessary to mention that the great majority of problem drinkers, whether their drinking problems are mild or severe, will try to moderate or reduce their consumption *before* they attempt total abstinence. When a problem drinker tries to moderate and is not successful, even after attending a program like MM where they receive support to cut back, they are more likely to accept that the most workable solution for them is to quit drinking entirely. With their dignity intact and their intelligence respected, they are empowered to commit to the recovery goal they have chosen for themselves.

Professionals in the field, who offer moderation training in addition to traditional abstinence-based treatment, employ a thorough assessment as part of a motivational intervention. The client is advised of his or her chances of success, the risks and benefits involved with both recovery goals are discussed, and information about free community self-help programs for follow-on support is provided. In this client-centered approach, the therapist does not force compliance with a predetermined recovery goal because this would rob the client of choice, raise resistance, and very likely create a great deal of denial.

The MM program offers mutual support in a self-help setting (meetings are typically held for one hour once per week), and a nine-step professionally reviewed program which provides information about alcohol, moderate drinking guidelines and limits, drink monitoring exercises, goal setting techniques, and self-management strategies. In addition, members work actively to achieve balance and moderation in many other areas of their lives.

MM recognizes that the same kind and level of treatment, the same recovery goal, and the same self-help group does not work for everyone with a drinking problem. New options are needed to address the needs of more people all along the continuum of alcohol abuse problems. All MM group meetings are anonymous, there are no fees, and Moderation Management Network, Inc. is a nonprofit, tax-exempt organization.

-Audrey Kishline, Founder of Moderation Management - Web site: http://www.moderation.org/

SMART

SMART Recovery (Self Management And Recovery Training) was incorporated as a non-profit organization in 1992. SMART sponsors support groups and other services for individuals desiring to abstain from any type of addictive behavior (substances or activities). SMART's program is significantly different from 12-step groups such as Alcoholics Anonymous. In SMART addictive behavior is viewed as a complex maladaptive behavior (i.e., a bad habit) rather than as a disease. SMART encourages increasing self-reliance rather than reliance on a higher power (although SMART does not in any way oppose belief in a higher power). SMART discourages use of the all-or-none labels "alcoholic" and "addict," and prefers to consider addictive behavior as lying on a continuum. SMART does not have a sponsor system (individuals who meet privately with newcomers to guide the recovery process), but encourages individuals who might want this level of individual involvement to seek psychotherapy.

The SMART recovery program is called the 4-Point Program: 1) Enhancing and maintaining motivation to abstain; 2) coping with cravings; 3) solving old problems by rationally managing thoughts, feelings, and behaviors; and 4) developing and maintaining lifestyle balance. Many of the methods of teaching the 4-Point Program are drawn from cognitive-behavioral psychotherapy, especially Rational Emotive Behavior Therapy.

SMART sponsors about 275 weekly support groups, including some in correctional facilities and some outside the US. SMART also publishes several publications, has a quarterly newsletter, has a recommended reading list, sponsors chat rooms via its website, and sponsors an internet listserv.

SMART assumes that almost any approach to recovery will be beneficial to some individuals. SMART encourages an individual who is seeking recovery to explore available options to determine the best one for that individual.

SMART opposes any effort to require an individual to adopt a particular approach to recovery.

-A. Thomas Horvath, Ph.D., President, SMART Recovery
        Web site http://www.smartrecovery.org/

Section 3, Chapter 7:

Motivational Interviewing as a Counseling Style

Motivational interviewing is a way of being with a client, not just a set of techniques for doing counseling. Miller and Rollnick, 1991.

Motivational interviewing is a technique in which you become a helper in the change process and express acceptance of your client. It is a way to interact with substance-using clients, not merely as an adjunct to other therapeutic approaches, and a style of counseling that can help resolve the ambivalence that prevents clients from realizing personal goals. Motivational interviewing builds on Carl Rogers' optimistic and humanistic theories about people's capabilities for exercising free choice and changing through a process of self-actualization. The therapeutic relationship for both Rogerian and motivational interviewers is a democratic partnership. Your role in motivational interviewing is directive, with a goal of eliciting self-motivational statements and behavioral change from the client in addition to creating client discrepancy to enhance motivation for positive change (Davidson, 1994; Miller and Rollnick, 1991). Essentially, motivational interviewing activates the capability for beneficial change that everyone possesses (Rollnick and Miller, 1995). Although some people can continue change on their own, others require more formal treatment and support over the long journey of recovery. Even for clients with low readiness, motivational interviewing serves as a vital prelude to later therapeutic work.

Motivational interviewing is a counseling style based on the following assumptions:

- Ambivalence about substance use (and change) is normal and constitutes an important motivational obstacle in recovery.
- Ambivalence can be resolved by working with your client's intrinsic motivations and values.
- The alliance between you and your client is a collaborative partnership to which you each bring important expertise.

- An empathic, supportive, yet directive, counseling style provides conditions under which change can occur. (Direct argument and aggressive confrontation may tend to increase client defensiveness and reduce the likelihood of behavioral change.)

This section briefly discusses ambivalence and its role in client motivation. Five basic principles of motivational interviewing are then presented to address ambivalence and to facilitate the change process. Opening strategies to use with clients in the early stages of treatment are offered as well. The section concludes with a summary of a 1997 review by Noonan and Moyers that studied the effectiveness of motivational interviewing.

Ambivalence

Individuals with substance abuse disorders are usually aware of the dangers of their substance-using behavior but continue to use substances anyway. They may want to stop using substances, but at the same time they do not want to. They enter treatment programs but claim their problems are not all that serious. These disparate feelings can be characterized as ambivalence, and they are natural, regardless of the client's state of readiness. It is important to understand and accept your client's ambivalence because ambivalence is often the central problem--and lack of motivation can be a manifestation of this ambivalence (Miller and Rollnick, 1991). If you interpret ambivalence as denial or resistance, friction between you and your client tends to occur.

The motivational interviewing style facilitates exploration of stage-specific motivational conflicts that can potentially hinder further progress. However, each dilemma also offers an opportunity to use the motivational style to help your client explore and resolve opposing attitudes. Examples of how these conflicts might be expressed at different stages of change are provided in **Figure 7-1**.

Figure 7-1: Stage-Specific Motivational Conflict

Stage of Change	Client Conflict
Precontemplation	I don't see how my cocaine use warrants concern, but I hope that by agreeing to talk about it, my wife will feel reassured.
Contemplation	I can picture how quitting heroin would improve my self-esteem, but I can't imagine never shooting up again.
Preparation	I'm feeling good about setting a quit date, but I'm wondering if I have the courage to follow through.
Action	Staying clean for the past 3 weeks really makes me feel good, but part of me wants to celebrate by getting loaded.
Maintenance	These recent months of abstinence have made me feel that I'm progressing toward recovery, but I'm still wondering whether abstinence is really necessary.

Five Principles of Motivational Interviewing

In their book, Motivational Interviewing: Preparing People To Change Addictive Behavior, Miller and Rollnick wrote,

> [M]otivational interviewing has been *practical* in focus. The strategies of motivational interviewing are more persuasive than coercive, more supportive than argumentative. The motivational interviewer must proceed with a strong sense of purpose, clear strategies and skills for pursuing that purpose, and a sense of timing to intervene in particular ways at incisive moments (Miller and Rollnick, 1991, pp. 51-52).

The clinician practices motivational interviewing with five general principles in mind:

1. Express empathy through reflective listening.
2. Develop discrepancy between clients' goals or values and their current behavior.
3. Avoid argument and direct confrontation.
4. Adjust to client resistance rather than opposing it directly.
5. Support self-efficacy and optimism.

Express Empathy

Empathy "is a specifiable and learnable skill for *understanding* another's meaning through the use of reflective listening. It requires sharp attention to each new client statement, and the continual generation of hypotheses as to the underlying meaning" (Miller and Rollnick, 1991, p. 20). An empathic style

- Communicates respect for and acceptance of clients and their feelings
- Encourages a nonjudgmental, collaborative relationship
- Allows you to be a supportive and knowledgeable consultant
- Sincerely compliments rather than denigrates
- Listens rather than tells
- Gently persuades, with the understanding that the decision to change is the client's
- Provides support throughout the recovery process

Empathic motivational interviewing establishes a safe and open environment that is conducive to examining issues and eliciting personal reasons and methods for change. A fundamental component of motivational interviewing is understanding each client's unique perspective, feelings, and values. Your attitude should be one of acceptance, but not necessarily approval or agreement, recognizing that ambivalence about change is to be expected. Motivational interviewing is most successful when a trusting relationship is established between you and your client.

Expressing Empathy

- Acceptance facilitates change.
- Skillful reflective listening is fundamental to expressing empathy.
- Ambivalence is normal.

Although empathy is the foundation of a motivational counseling style, it "should not be confused with the meaning of empathy as *identification* with the client or the sharing of common past experiences. In fact, a recent personal history of the same problem area...may compromise a counselor's ability to provide the critical conditions of change" (Miller and Rollnick, 1991, p. 5). The key component to expressing empathy is reflective listening.

Expressing Empathy With Native American Clients

For many traditional Native American groups, expressing empathy begins with the introduction. Native Americans generally expect the clinician to be aware of and practice the culturally accepted norms for introducing oneself and showing respect. For example, when first meeting a Navajo, the person often is expected to say his name, clan relationship or ethnic origin, and place of origin. Physical contact is kept to a minimum, except for a brief handshake, which may be no more than a soft touch of the palms.

If you are not listening reflectively but are instead imposing direction and judgment, you are creating barriers that impair the therapeutic relationship (Miller and Rollnick, 1991). The client will most likely react by stopping, diverting, or changing direction. Twelve examples of such nonempathic responses have been identified (Gordon, 1970):

1. *Ordering or directing.* Direction is given with a voice of authority. The speaker may be in a position of power (e.g., parent, employer) or the words may simply be phrased and spoken in an authoritarian manner.
2. *Warning or threatening.* These messages are similar to ordering but they carry an overt or covert threat of impending negative consequences if the advice or direction is not followed. The threat may be one the clinician will carry out or simply a prediction of a negative outcome if the client doesn't comply--for example, "*If you don't listen to me, you'll be sorry.*"
3. *Giving advice, making suggestions, or providing solutions prematurely or when unsolicited.* The message recommends a course of action based on the clinician's knowledge and personal experience. These recommendations often begin with phrases such as, "What I would do is...."
4. *Persuading with logic, arguing, or lecturing.* The underlying assumption of these messages is that the client has not reasoned through the problem adequately and needs help to do so.
5. *Moralizing, preaching, or telling clients their duty.* These statements contain such words as "should" or "ought" to convey moral instructions.
6. *Judging, criticizing, disagreeing, or blaming.* These messages imply that something is wrong with the client or with what the client has said. Even simple disagreement may be interpreted as critical.

7. *Agreeing, approving, or praising.* Surprisingly, praise or approval also can be an obstacle if the message sanctions or implies agreement with whatever the client has said. Unsolicited approval can interrupt the communication process and can imply an uneven relationship between the speaker and the listener. Reflective listening does not require agreement.

8. *Shaming, ridiculing, labeling, or name-calling.* These messages express overt disapproval and intent to correct a specific behavior or attitude.

9. *Interpreting or analyzing.* Clinicians are frequently and easily tempted to impose their own interpretations on a client's statement and to find some hidden, analytical meaning. Interpretive statements might imply that the clinician knows what the client's *real* problem is.

10. *Reassuring, sympathizing, or consoling.* Clinicians often want to make the client feel better by offering consolation. Such reassurance can interrupt the flow of communication and interfere with careful listening.

11. *Questioning or probing.* Clinicians often mistake questioning for good listening. Although the clinician may ask questions to learn more about the client, the underlying message is that the clinician might find the right answer to all the client's problems if enough questions are asked. In fact, intensive questioning can interfere with the spontaneous flow of communication and divert it in directions of interest to the clinician rather than the client.

12. *Withdrawing, distracting, humoring, or changing the subject.* Although humor may represent an attempt to take the client's mind off emotional subjects or threatening problems, it also can be a distraction that diverts communication and implies that the client's statements are unimportant.

Ethnic and cultural differences must be considered when expressing empathy because they influence how both you and your client interpret verbal and nonverbal communications.

Expressing Empathy with African-American Clients

One way I empathize with African-American clients is, first and foremost, to be a genuine person (not just a counselor or clinician). The client may begin the relationship asking questions about you the person, not the professional, in an attempt to locate you in the world. It's as if the client's internal dialogue says, "As you try to understand me, by what pathways, perspectives, life experiences, and values are you coming to that understanding of me?" Typical questions my African-American clients have asked me are

- Are you Christian?
- Where are you from?
- What part of town do you live in?
- Who are your folks?
- Are you married?

Develop Discrepancy

Motivation for change is enhanced when clients perceive discrepancies between their current situation and their hopes for the future. Your task is to help focus your client's attention on how current behavior differs from ideal or desired behavior. Discrepancy is initially highlighted by raising your clients' awareness of the negative personal, familial, or community consequences of a problem behavior and helping them confront the substance use that contributed to the consequences. Although helping a client perceive discrepancy can be difficult, carefully chosen and strategic reflecting can underscore incongruities.

Separate the behavior from the person and help your client explore how important personal goals (e.g., good health, marital happiness, financial success) are being undermined by current substance use patterns. This requires you to listen carefully to your client's statements about values and connections to community, family, and church. If the client shows concern about the effects of personal behavior, highlight this concern to heighten the client's perception and acknowledgment of discrepancy.

Once a client begins to understand how the consequences or potential consequences of current behavior conflict with significant personal values, amplify and focus on this discordance until the client can articulate consistent concern and commitment to change.

One useful tactic for helping a client perceive discrepancy is sometimes called the "Columbo approach" (Kanfer and Schefft, 1988). This approach is particularly useful with a client who prefers to be in control. Essentially, the clinician expresses understanding and continuously seeks clarification of the client's problems but appears unable to perceive any solution. A stance of uncertainty or confusion can motivate the client to take control of the situation by offering a solution to the clinician (Van Bilsen, 1991).

Tools other than talking can be used to reveal discrepancy. For example, show a video and then discuss it with the client, allowing the client to make the connection to his own situation. Juxtaposing different media messages or images that are meaningful to a client can also be effective. This strategy may be particularly effective for adolescents because it provides stimulation for discussion and reaction.

You can help your client perceive discrepancy on a number of different levels, from physical to spiritual, and in different domains, from attitudinal to behavioral. To do this, it is useful to understand not only what an individual values but also what the community values. For example, substance use might conflict with the client's personal identity and values; it might conflict with the values of the larger community; it might conflict with spiritual or religious beliefs; or it might conflict with the values of the client's family members. Thus, discrepancy can be made clear by contrasting substance-using behavior with the importance the clients ascribe to their relationships with family, religious groups, and the community.

Developing Discrepancy

- Developing awareness of consequences helps clients examine their behavior.
- A discrepancy between present behavior and important goals motivates change.
- The client should present the arguments for change.

The client's cultural background can affect perceptions of discrepancy. For example, African-Americans may regard addiction as "chemical slavery," which may conflict with their ethnic pride and desire to overcome a collective history of oppression. Moreover, African-Americans may be more strongly influenced than white Americans by the expressed values of a larger religious or spiritual community. In a recent focus group study with adolescents, African-American youths were much more likely than other youths to view cigarette smoking as conflicting with their ethnic pride (Luke, 1998). They pointed to this conflict as an important reason not to smoke.

The Columbo Approach

Sometimes I use what I refer to as the Columbo approach to develop discrepancy with clients. In the old "Columbo" TV series, Peter Falk played a detective who had a sense of what had really occurred but used a somewhat bumbling, unassuming Socratic style of querying his prime suspect, strategically posing questions and making reflections to piece together a picture of what really happened. As the pieces began to fall into place, the object of Columbo's investigation would often reveal the real story.

Avoid Argument

You may occasionally be tempted to argue with a client who is unsure about changing or unwilling to change, especially if the client is hostile, defiant, or provocative. However, trying to convince a client that a problem exists or that change is needed could precipitate even more resistance. If you try to prove a point, the client predictably takes the opposite side. Arguments with the client can rapidly degenerate into a power struggle and do not enhance motivation for beneficial change. When it is the client, not you, who voices arguments for change, progress can be made. The goal is to "walk" with clients (i.e., accompany clients through treatment), not "drag" them along (i.e., direct clients' treatment).

A common area of argument is the client's unwillingness to accept a label such as "alcoholic" or "*drug abuser.*" Miller and Rollnick stated that

> [T]here is no particular reason why the therapist should badger clients to accept a label, or exert great persuasive effort in this direction. Accusing clients of being *in denial* or *resistant* or *addicted* is more likely to increase their resistance than to instill motivation for change. We advocate starting with clients wherever they are, and altering their self-perceptions, not by arguing about labels, but through substantially more effective means (Miller and Rollnick, 1991, p. 59).

Although this conflicts with some clinicians' belief that clients must be persuaded to self-label, the approach advocated in the "Big Book" of Alcoholics Anonymous (AA) is that labels are not to be imposed (AA, 1976). Rather, it is a personal decision of each individual.

Avoiding Arguments

- Arguments are counterproductive.
- Defending breeds defensiveness.
- Resistance is a signal to change strategies.
- Labeling is unnecessary.

Roll With Resistance

Resistance is a legitimate concern for the clinician because it is predictive of poor treatment outcomes and lack of involvement in the therapeutic process. One view of resistance is that the client is behaving defiantly. Another, perhaps more constructive, viewpoint is that resistance is a signal that the client views the situation differently. This requires you to understand your client's perspective and proceed from there. Resistance is a signal to you to change direction or listen more carefully. Resistance actually offers you an opportunity to respond in a new, perhaps surprising, way and to take advantage of the situation without being confrontational.

Adjusting to resistance is similar to avoiding argument in that it offers another chance to express empathy by remaining nonjudgmental and respectful, encouraging the client to talk and stay involved. Try to avoid evoking resistance whenever possible, and divert or deflect the energy the client is investing in resistance toward positive change.

How do you recognize resistance? **Figure 7-2** depicts four common behaviors that indicate that a client is resisting treatment. How do you avoid arguing and, instead, adapt to resistance? Miller and colleagues have identified and provided examples of at least seven ways to react appropriately to client resistance (Miller and Rollnick, 1991; Miller et al., 1992). These are described below.

Figure 7-2: Four Types of Client Resistance

Arguing

The client contests the accuracy, expertise, or integrity of the clinician.

- *Challenging.* The client directly challenges the accuracy of what the clinician has said.
- *Discounting.* The client questions the clinician's personal authority and expertise.
- *Hostility.* The client expresses direct hostility toward the clinician.

Interrupting

The client breaks in and interrupts the clinician in a defensive manner.

- *Talking over.* The client speaks while the clinician is still talking, without waiting for an appropriate pause or silence.
- *Cutting off.* The client breaks in with words obviously intended to cut the clinician off (e.g., "Now wait a minute. I've heard about enough").

Denying

The client expresses unwillingness to recognize problems, cooperate, accept responsibility, or take advice.

- *Blaming.* The client blames other people for problems.
- *Disagreeing.* The client disagrees with a suggestion that the clinician has made, offering no constructive alternative. This includes the familiar "Yes, but...," which explains what is wrong with suggestions that are made.
- *Excusing.* The client makes excuses for his behavior.
- *Claiming impunity.* The client claims that she is not in any danger (e.g., from drinking).
- *Minimizing.* The client suggests that the clinician is exaggerating risks or dangers and that it really isn't so bad.
- *Pessimism.* The client makes statements about himself or others that are pessimistic, defeatist, or negative in tone.
- *Reluctance.* The client expresses reservations and reluctance about information or advice given.
- *Unwillingness to change.* The client expresses a lack of desire or an unwillingness to change.

Ignoring

The client shows evidence of ignoring or not following the clinician.

- *Inattention.* The client's response indicates that she has not been paying attention to the clinician.

- *Nonanswer.* In answering a clinician's query, the client gives a response that is not an answer to the question.
- *No response.* The client gives no audible verbal or clear nonverbal reply to the clinician's query.
- *Sidetracking.* The client changes the direction of the conversation that the clinician has been pursuing.

Source: Miller and Rollnick, 1991. Adapted from a behavior coding system by Chamberlain et al., 1984. Reprinted with permission.

Simple reflection

The simplest approach to responding to resistance is with nonresistance, by repeating the client's statement in a neutral form. This acknowledges and validates what the client has said and can elicit an opposite response.

Client: I don't plan to quit drinking anytime soon.

Clinician: You don't think that abstinence would work for you right now.

Amplified reflection

Another strategy is to reflect the client's statement in an exaggerated form--to state it in a more extreme way but without sarcasm. This can move the client toward positive change rather than resistance.

Client: I don't know why my wife is worried about this. I don't drink any more than any of my friends.

Clinician: So your wife is worrying needlessly.

Double-sided reflection

A third strategy entails acknowledging what the client has said but then also stating contrary things she has said in the past. This requires the use of information that the client has offered previously, although perhaps not in the same session.

Client: I know you want me to give up drinking completely, but I'm not going to do that!

Clinician: You can see that there are some real problems here, but you're not willing to think about quitting altogether.

Shifting focus

You can defuse resistance by helping the client shift focus away from obstacles and barriers. This method offers an opportunity to affirm your client's personal choice regarding the conduct of his own life.

Client: I can't stop smoking reefer when all my friends are doing it.

Clinician: You're way ahead of me. We're still exploring your concerns about whether you can get into college. We're not ready yet to decide how marijuana fits into your goals.

Agreement with a twist

A subtle strategy is to agree with the client, but with a slight twist or change of direction that propels the discussion forward.

Client: Why are you and my wife so stuck on my drinking? What about all her problems? You'd drink, too, if your family were nagging you all the time.

Clinician: You've got a good point there, and that's important. There is a bigger picture here, and maybe I haven't been paying enough attention to that. It's not as simple as one person's drinking. I agree with you that we shouldn't be trying to place blame here. Drinking problems like these do involve the whole family.

Reframing

A good strategy to use when a client denies personal problems is reframing--offering a new and positive interpretation of negative information provided by the client. Reframing "acknowledges the validity of the client's raw observations, but offers a new meaning...for them" (Miller and Rollnick, 1991, p. 107).

Client: My husband is always nagging me about my drinking--always calling me an alcoholic. It really bugs me.

Clinician: It sounds like he really cares about you and is concerned, although he expresses it in a way that makes you angry. Maybe we can help him learn how to tell you he loves you and is worried about you in a more positive and acceptable way.

In another example, the concept of relative tolerance to alcohol provides a good opportunity for reframing with problem drinkers (Miller and Rollnick, 1991). Many heavy drinkers believe they are not alcoholics because they can "hold their liquor." When you explain that tolerance is a risk factor and a warning signal, not a source of pride, you can change your client's perspective about the meaning of feeling no effects. Thus, reframing is not only educational but sheds new light on the client's experience of alcohol.

Rolling With Resistance

- Momentum can be used to good advantage.
- Perceptions can be shifted.
- New perspectives are invited but not imposed.
- The client is a valuable resource in finding solutions to problems.

Siding with the negative

One more strategy for adapting to client resistance is to "side with the negative"--to take up the negative voice in the discussion. This is not "reverse psychology," nor does it involve the ethical quandaries of prescribing more of the symptom, as in a "therapeutic paradox." Typically, siding with the negative is stating what the client has already said while arguing against change, perhaps as an amplified reflection. If your client is ambivalent, your taking the negative side of the argument evokes a "Yes, but..." from the client, who then expresses the other (positive) side. Be cautious, however, in using this too early in treatment or with depressed clients.

Client: Well, I know some people think I drink too much, and I may be damaging my liver, but I still don't believe I'm an alcoholic or in need of treatment.

Clinician: We've spent considerable time now going over your positive feelings and concerns about your drinking, but you still don't think you are ready or want to change your drinking patterns. Maybe changing would be too difficult for you, especially if you really want to stay the same. Anyway, I'm not sure you believe you could change even if you wanted to.

Support Self-Efficacy

Many clients do not have a well-developed sense of self-efficacy and find it difficult to believe that they can begin or maintain behavioral change. Improving self-efficacy requires eliciting and supporting hope, optimism, and the feasibility of accomplishing change. This requires you to recognize the client's strengths and bring these to the forefront whenever possible. Unless a client believes change is possible, the perceived discrepancy between the desire for change and feelings of hopelessness about accomplishing change is likely to result in rationalizations or denial in order to reduce discomfort. Because self-efficacy is a critical component of behavior change, it is crucial that you as the clinician also believe in your clients' capacity to reach their goals.

Discussing treatment or change options that might still be attractive to clients is usually helpful, even though they may have dropped out of other treatment programs or returned to substance use after a period of being substance free. It is also helpful to talk about how persons in similar situations have successfully changed their behavior. Other clients can serve as role models and offer encouragement. Nonetheless, clients must ultimately come to believe that change is their responsibility and that long-term success begins with a single step forward. The AA motto, "one day at a time," may help clients focus and embark on the immediate and small changes that they believe are feasible.

Education can increase clients' sense of self-efficacy. Credible, understandable, and accurate information helps clients understand how substance use progresses to abuse or dependency. Making the biology of addiction and the medical effects of substance use relevant to the clients' experience may alleviate shame and guilt and instill hope that recovery can be achieved by using appropriate methods and tools. A process that initially feels overwhelming and hopeless can be broken down into achievable small steps toward recovery.

Self-Efficacy

- Belief in the possibility of change is an important motivator.
- The client is responsible for choosing and carrying out personal change.
- There is hope in the range of alternative approaches available.

Five Opening Strategies for Early Sessions

Clinicians who adopt motivational interviewing as a preferred style have found that the five strategies discussed below are particularly useful in the early stages of treatment. They are based on the five principles described in the previous section: express empathy, develop discrepancy, avoid argument, adjust to rather than oppose client resistance, and support self-efficacy. Helping clients address their natural ambivalence is a good starting point. These opening strategies ensure your support for your client and help the client explore ambivalence in a safe setting. The first four strategies, which are derived from client-centered counseling, help clients explore their ambivalence and reasons for change. The fifth strategy is specific to motivational interviewing and integrates and guides the other four.

In early treatment sessions, determine your client's readiness to change or stage of change. Be careful to avoid focusing prematurely on a particular stage of change or assuming the client is at a particular stage because of the setting where you meet. As already noted, using strategies inappropriate for a particular change stage or forming an inaccurate perception regarding the client's wants or needs could be harmful. Therefore, try not to identify the goals of counseling until you have sufficiently explored the client's readiness.

Ask Open-Ended Questions

Asking open-ended questions helps you understand your clients' point of view and elicits their feelings about a given topic or situation. Open-ended questions facilitate dialogue; they cannot be answered with a single word or phrase and do not require any particular response. They are a means to solicit additional information in a neutral way. Open-ended questions encourage the client to do most of the talking, help you avoid making premature judgments, and keep communication moving forward (see **Figure 7-3**).

Figure 7-3: How To Ask Open-Ended Questions

Closed Question	Open Question
So you are here because you are concerned about your use of alcohol, correct?	Tell me, what is it that brings you here today?
How many children do you have?	Tell me about your family.
Do you agree that it would be a good idea for you to go through detoxification?	What do you think about the possibility of going through detoxification?
First, I'd like you to tell me some about your marijuana use. On a typical day, how much do you smoke?	Tell me about your marijuana use during a typical week.
Do you like to smoke?	What are some of the things you like about smoking?
How has your drug use been this week, compared to last: more, less, or about the same?	What has your drug use been like during the past week?
Do you think you use amphetamines too often?	In what ways are you concerned about your use of amphetamines?
How long ago did you have your last drink?	Tell me about the last time you had a drink.
Are you sure that your probation officer told you that it's only cocaine he is concerned about in your urine screens?	Now what exactly are the conditions that your probation officer wants you to follow?
When do you plan to quit drinking?	So what do you think you want to do about your drinking?

Listen Reflectively

Reflective listening, a fundamental component of motivational interviewing, is a challenging skill in which you demonstrate that you have accurately heard and understood a client's communication by restating its meaning. That is, you hazard a guess about what the client intended to convey and express this in a responsive statement, not a question. "Reflective listening is a way of checking rather than assuming that you *know* what is meant" (Miller and Rollnick, 1991, p. 75).

Reflective listening strengthens the empathic relationship between the clinician and the client and encourages further exploration of problems and feelings. This form of communication is particularly appropriate for early stages of counseling. Reflective listening helps the client by providing a synthesis of content and process. It reduces the likelihood of resistance, encourages the client to keep talking, communicates respect, cements the therapeutic alliance, clarifies exactly what the client means, and reinforces motivation (Miller et al., 1992).

This process has a tremendous amount of flexibility, and you can use reflective listening to reinforce your client's positive ideas (Miller et al., 1992). The following dialog gives some examples of clinician's responses that illustrate effective reflective listening. Essentially, true reflective listening requires continuous alert tracking of the client's verbal and nonverbal responses and their possible meanings, formulation of reflections at the appropriate level of complexity, and ongoing adjustment of hypotheses.

Clinician: What else concerns you about your drinking?

Client: Well, I'm not sure I'm concerned about it, but I do wonder sometimes if I'm drinking too much.

Clinician: Too much for...?

Client: For my own good, I guess. I mean it's not like it's really serious, but sometimes when I wake up in the morning I feel really awful, and I can't think straight most of the morning.

Clinician: It messes up your thinking, your concentration.

Client: Yes, and sometimes I have trouble remembering things.

Clinician: And you wonder if that might be because you're drinking too much?

Client: Well, I know it is sometimes.

Clinician: You're pretty sure about that. But maybe there's more...

Client: Yeah, even when I'm not drinking, sometimes I mix things up, and I wonder about that.

Clinician: Wonder if...?

Client: If alcohol's pickling my brain, I guess.

Clinician: You think that can happen to people, maybe to you.

Client: Well, can't it? I've heard that alcohol kills brain cells.

Clinician: Um-hmm. I can see why that would worry you.

Client: But I don't think I'm an alcoholic or anything.

Clinician: You don't think you're that bad off, but you do wonder if maybe you're overdoing it and damaging yourself in the process.

Client: Yeah.

Clinician: Kind of a scary thought. What else worries you?

Summarize

Most clinicians find it useful to periodically summarize what has occurred in a counseling session. Summarizing consists of distilling the essence of what a client has expressed and communicating it back. "Summaries reinforce what has been said, show that you have been listening carefully, and prepare the client to move on" (Miller and Rollnick, 1991, p. 78). A summary that links the client's positive and negative feelings about substance use can facilitate an understanding of initial ambivalence and promote the perception of discrepancy. Summarizing is also a good way to begin and end each counseling session and to provide a natural bridge when the client is transitioning between stages of change.

Summarizing also serves strategic purposes. In presenting a summary, you can select what information should be included and what can be minimized or left out. Correction of a summary by the client should be invited, and this often leads to further comments and discussion. Summarizing helps clients consider their own responses and contemplate their own experience. It also gives you and your client an opportunity to notice what might have been overlooked as well as incorrectly stated.

Affirm

When it is done sincerely, affirming your client supports and promotes self-efficacy. More broadly, your affirmation acknowledges the difficulties the client has experienced. By affirming, you are saying, "I hear; I understand," and validating the client's experiences and feelings. Affirming helps clients feel confident about marshaling their inner resources to take action and change behavior. Emphasizing their past experiences that demonstrate strength, success, or power can prevent discouragement. For some clients, such as many

African-Americans, affirmation has a spiritual context. Affirming their inner guiding spirit and their faith may help resolve their ambivalence. Several examples of affirming statements (Miller and Rollnick, 1991) follow:

- I appreciate how hard it must have been for you to decide to come here. You took a big step.
- I think it's great that you want to do something about this problem.
- That must have been very difficult for you.
- You're certainly a resourceful person to have been able to live with the problem this long and not fall apart.
- That's a good suggestion.
- It must be difficult for you to accept a day-to-day life so full of stress. I must say, if I were in your position, I would also find that difficult.

Elicit Self-Motivational Statements

Engaging the client in the process of change is the fundamental task of motivational interviewing. Rather than identifying the problem and promoting ways to solve it, your task is to help the client recognize how life might be better and choose ways to make it so.

Remember that your role is to entice the client to voice personal concerns and intentions, not to convince him that a transformation is necessary. Successful motivational interviewing requires that clients, not the clinician, ultimately argue for change and persuade themselves that they want to and can improve. One signal that the client's ambivalence and resistance are diminishing is the self-motivational statement.

Four types of motivational statements can be identified (Miller and Rollnick, 1991):

- Cognitive recognition of the problem (e.g., "I guess this is more serious than I thought.")
- Affective expression of concern about the perceived problem (e.g., "I'm really worried about what is happening to me.")
- A direct or implicit intention to change behavior (e.g., "I've got to do something about this.")
- Optimism about one's ability to change (e.g., "I know that if I try, I can really do it.")

Figure 7-4 illustrates how you can differentiate a self-motivational statement from a countermotivational assertion. You can reinforce your client's self-motivational statements by reflecting them, nodding, or making approving facial expressions and affirming statements. Encourage clients to continue exploring the possibility of change. This can be done by asking for an elaboration, explicit examples, or more details about remaining concerns. Questions beginning with "What else" are effective ways to invite further amplification. Sometimes asking clients to identify the extremes of the problem (e.g., "What are you most concerned about?") helps to enhance their motivation. Another effective approach is to ask clients to envision what they would like for the future. From there, clients may be able to begin establishing specific goals. **Figure 7-5** provides a useful list of questions you can ask to elicit self-motivational statements from the client.

Figure 7-4: How To Recognize Self-Motivational Statements

Self-Motivational Statements	Countermotivational Assertions
I guess this has been affecting me more than I realized.	I don't have any problem with marijuana.
Sometimes when I've been using, I just can't think or concentrate.	When I'm high, I'm more relaxed and creative.
I guess I wonder if I've been pickling my brain.	I can drink all night and never get drunk.
I feel terrible about how my drinking has hurt my family.	I'm not the one with the problem.
I don't know what to do, but something has to change.	No way am I giving up coke.
Tell me what I would need to do if I went into treatment.	I'm not going into a hospital.
I think I could become clean and sober if I decided to.	I've tried to quit, and I just can't do it.
If I really put my mind to something, I can do it.	I have so much else going on right now that I can't think about quitting.

Figure 7-5: Sample Questions To Evoke Self-Motivational Statements

Problem Recognition

- What things make you think that this is a problem?
- What difficulties have you had in relation to your drug use?
- In what ways do you think you or other people have been harmed by your drinking?
- In what ways has this been a problem for you?
- How has your use of tranquilizers stopped you from doing what you want to do?

Concern

- What is there about your drinking that you or other people might see as reasons for concern?
- What worries you about your drug use? What can you imagine happening to you?
- How much does this concern you?
- In what ways does this concern you?
- What do you think will happen if you don't make a change?

Intention to Change

- The fact that you're here indicates that at least part of you thinks it's time to do something.
- What are the reasons you see for making a change?
- What makes you think that you may need to make a change?
- If you were 100 percent successful and things worked out exactly as you would like, what would be different?
- What things make you think that you should keep on drinking the way you have been? And what about the other side? What makes you think it's time for a change?
- I can see that you're feeling stuck at the moment. What's going to have to change?

Optimism

- What makes you think that if you decide to make a change, you could do it?
- What encourages you that you can change if you want to?
- What do you think would work for you, if you needed to change?

Source: Miller and Rollnick, 1991. Reprinted with permission.

Effectiveness of Motivational Interviewing

A recent review of 11 clinical trials of motivational interviewing concluded that this is a "useful clinical intervention...[and] appears to be an effective, efficient, and adaptive therapeutic style worthy of further development, application, and research" (Noonan and Moyers, 1997, p. 8). Motivational interviewing is a counseling approach that more closely reflects the principles of motivational enhancement, and it also links these basic precepts to the stages-of-change model.

Of the eleven studies reviewed, nine found motivational interviewing more effective than no treatment, standard care, extended treatment, or being on a waiting list before receiving the intervention. Two of the 11 studies did not support the effectiveness of motivational interviewing, although the reviewers suggested that the *spirit* of this approach may not have been followed because the providers delivered advice in an authoritarian manner and may not have been adequately trained (Noonan and Moyers, 1997). Moreover, one study had a high dropout rate. Two studies supported the efficacy of motivational interviewing as a stand-alone intervention for self-identified concerned drinkers who were provided feedback about their drinking patterns but received no additional clinical attention. Three trials confirmed the usefulness of motivational interviewing as an enhancement to traditional treatment, five supported the effectiveness of motivational interviewing in reducing substance-using patterns of patients appearing in medical settings for other health-related conditions, and one trial compared a brief motivational intervention favorably with a more extensive alternative treatment for marijuana users.

Motivational Interviewing and Managed Care

In addition to its effectiveness, motivational interviewing is beneficial in that it can easily be applied in a managed care setting, where issues of cost containment are of great concern. Motivational interviewing approaches are particularly well suited to managed care in the following ways:

- **Low cost**. Motivational interviewing was designed from the outset to be a brief intervention and is normally delivered in two to four outpatient sessions.
- **Efficacy**. There is strong evidence that motivational interviewing triggers change in high-risk lifestyle behaviors.
- **Effectiveness**. Large effects from brief motivational counseling have held up across a wide variety of real-life clinical settings.
- **Mobilizing client resources**. Motivational interviewing focuses on mobilizing the client's own resources for change.
- **Compatibility with health care delivery**. Motivational interviewing does not assume a long-term client-therapist relationship. Even a single session has been found to invoke behavior change, and motivational interviewing can be delivered within the context of larger health care delivery systems.
- **Emphasizing client motivation**. Client motivation is a strong predictor of change, and this approach puts primary emphasis on first building client motivation for change. Thus, even if clients do not stay for a long course of treatment (as is often the case with substance abuse), they have been given something that is likely to help them within the first few sessions.
- **Enhancing adherence**. Motivational interviewing is also a sensible prelude to other health care interventions because it has been shown to increase adherence, which in turn improves treatment outcomes.

Section 3, Chapter 8:

Stages of Change

A Transtheoretical Model of Change

Adapted from "Enhancing Motivation for Change in Substance Abuse Treatment," *Treatment Improvement Protocol (TIP) Series* 35. Center for Substance Abuse Treatment, DHHS Publication No. (SMA) 99-3354. Printed 1999.

Theorists have developed various models to illustrate how behavioral change happens. In one perspective, external consequences and restrictions are largely responsible for moving individuals to change their substance use behaviors. In another model, intrinsic motivations are responsible for initiating or ending substance use behaviors. Some researchers believe that motivation is better described as a continuum of readiness than as separate stages of change (Bandura, 1997; Sutton, 1996). This hypothesis is also supported by motivational research involving serious substance abuse of illicit drugs (Simpson and Joe, 1993).

The change process has been conceptualized as a sequence of stages through which people typically progress as they think about, initiate, and maintain new behaviors (Prochaska and DiClemente, 1984). This model emerged from an examination of 18 psychological and behavioral theories about how change occurs, including components that compose a biopsychosocial framework for understanding addiction. In this sense, the model is "transtheoretical" (IOM, 1990b).

This model also reflects how change occurs outside of therapeutic environments. The authors applied this template to individuals who modified behaviors related to smoking, drinking, eating, exercising, parenting, and marital communications on their own, without professional intervention. When natural self-change was compared with therapeutic interventions, many similarities were noticed, leading these investigators to describe the occurrence of change in steps or stages. They observed that people who make behavioral changes on their own or under professional guidance first "move from being unaware or unwilling to do anything about the problem to considering the possibility of change, then to becoming determined and prepared to make the change, and finally to taking action and sustaining or maintaining that change over time" (DiClemente, 1991, p. 191).

As a clinician, you can be helpful at any point in the process of change by using appropriate motivational strategies that are specific to the change stage of the individual. In this context, the stages of change represent a series of tasks for both you and your clients (Miller and Heather, 1998).

The stages of change can be visualized as a wheel with four to six parts, depending on how specifically the process is broken down (Prochaska and DiClemente, 1984). Here, the wheel (**Figure 8-1**) has five parts, with a final exit to enduring recovery (the sixth part is recurrence or relapse). It is important to note that the change process is cyclical, and individuals typically move back and forth between the stages and cycle through the stages at different rates. In one individual, this movement through the stages can vary in relation to different behaviors or objectives. Individuals can move through stages quickly. Sometimes, they move so rapidly that it is difficult to pinpoint where they are because change is a dynamic process. It is not uncommon, however, for individuals to linger in the early stages.

For most substance-using individuals, progress through the stages of change is circular or spiral in nature, not linear. In this model, recurrence is a normal event because many clients cycle through the different stages several times before achieving stable change. The five stages and the issue of recurrence are described below.

Figure 8-1: Five Stages of Change

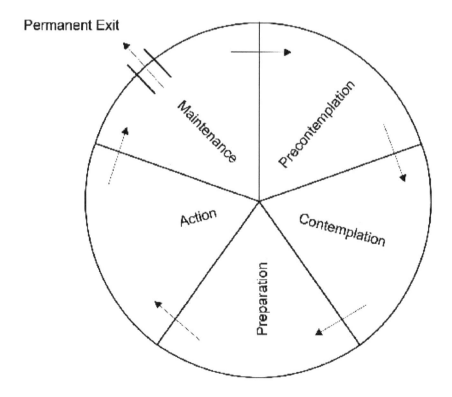

624

Clients need and use different kinds of motivational support according to which stage of change they are in and into what stage they are moving. If you try to use strategies appropriate to a stage other than the one the client is in, the result could be treatment resistance or noncompliance. For example, if your client is at the contemplation stage, weighing the pros and cons of change versus continued substance use, and you pursue change strategies appropriate to the action stage, your client will predictably resist. The simple reason for this reaction is that you have taken the positive (change) side of the argument, leaving the client to argue the other (no change) side; this results in a standoff.

From precontemplation to contemplation

According to the stages-of-change model, individuals in the precontemplation stage are not concerned about their substance use or are not considering changing their behavior. These substance users may remain in precontemplation or early contemplation for years, rarely or never thinking about change. Often, a significant other finds the substance user's behavior problematic. There are a variety of proven techniques and gentle tactics that clinicians can use to address the topic of substance abuse with people who are not thinking of change. Use of these techniques will serve to

(1)   create client doubt about the commonly held belief that substance abuse is "harmless" and

(2)   lead to client conviction that substance abuse is having, or will in the future have, significant negative results.

(*For all stages, this numbering (1) and (2) will be used to identify these two issues*)

It is suggested that clinicians practice the following:

- Commend the client for coming to substance abuse treatment (2)
- Establish rapport, ask permission to address the topic of change, and build trust (2)
- Elicit, listen to, and acknowledge the aspects of substance use the client enjoys (2)
- Evoke doubts or concerns in the client about substance use (2)
- Explore the meaning of the events that brought the client to treatment or the results of previous treatments (2)

- Obtain the client's perceptions of the problem (2)
- Offer factual information about the risks of substance use (2)
- Provide personalized feedback about assessment findings (2)
- Help a significant other intervene (2)
- Examine discrepancies between the client's and others' perceptions of the problem behavior (2)
- Express concern and keep the door open (2)

The assessment and feedback process can be an important part of the motivational strategy because it informs clients of how their own substance use patterns compare with norms, what specific risks are entailed, and what damage already exists or is likely to occur if changes are not made.

Giving clients personal results from a broad-based and objective assessment, especially if the findings are carefully interpreted and compared with norms or expected values, can be not only informative but also motivating. (1) Providing clients with personalized feedback on the risks associated with *their own* use of a particular substance--especially for their own cultural and gender groups--is a powerful way to develop a sense of *discrepancy* that can motivate change.

Intervening through significant others

Considerable research shows that involvement of family members or significant others (SOs) can help move substance-using persons toward contemplation of change, entry into treatment, involvement and retention in the therapeutic process, and successful recovery. (1) Involving SOs in the early stages of change can greatly enhance a client's commitment to change by addressing the client's substance use in the following ways:

- Providing constructive feedback to the client about the costs and benefits associated with her substance abuse (2)
- Encouraging the resolve of the client to change the negative behavior pattern (2)
- Identifying the client's concrete and emotional obstacles to change (2)
- Alerting the client to social and individual coping resources that lead to a substance-free lifestyle (2)
- Reinforcing the client for employing these social and coping resources to change the substance use behavior (2)

The clinician can engage an SO by asking the client to invite the SO to a treatment session. Explain that the SO will not be asked to monitor the client's substance use but that the SO can perform a valuable role by providing emotional support, identifying problems that might interfere with treatment goals, and participating in activities with the client that do not involve substance use. To strengthen the SO's belief in his capacity to help the client, the clinician can use the following strategies:

- Positively describe the steps used by the SO that have been successful (define "successful" generously) (2)
- Reinforce positive comments made by the SO about the client's current change efforts (2)
- Discuss future ways in which the client might benefit from the SO's efforts to facilitate change (2)

Clinicians should use caution when involving an SO in motivational counseling. Although a strong relationship between the SO and the client is necessary, it is not wholly sufficient. The SO must also support a client's substance-free life, and the client must value that support. (1) An SO who is experiencing hardships or emotional problems stemming from the client's substance use may not be a suitable candidate. (1) Such problems can preclude the SO from constructively participating in the counseling sessions, and it may be better to wait until the problems have subsided before including an SO in the client's treatment. (1)

In general, the SO can play a vital role in influencing the client's willingness to change; however, the client must be reminded that the responsibility to change substance use behavior is his/hers. (2)

Motivational interventions and coerced clients

An increasing number of clients are mandated to obtain treatment by an employer or employee assistance program, the court system, or probation and parole officers. Others are influenced to enter treatment because of legal pressures. The challenge for clinicians is to engage coerced clients in the treatment process. A stable recovery cannot be maintained by external (legal) pressure only; motivation and commitment must come from internal pressure. If you provide interventions appropriate to their stage, coerced clients may become invested in the change process and benefit from the opportunity to consider the consequences of use and the possibility of change--even though that opportunity was not voluntarily chosen. (2)

From contemplation to preparation

Extrinsic and intrinsic motivators should be considered when trying to increase a client's commitment to change and move the client closer to action because these motivators can be examined to enhance decision-making, thereby enhancing the client's commitment. Many clients move through the contemplation stage acknowledging only the extrinsic motivators pushing them to change or that brought them to treatment. Help the client discover intrinsic motivators, which typically move the client from contemplating change to acting. (2) In addition to the standard practices for motivational interviewing (e.g., reflective listening, asking open-ended questions), clinicians can help spur this process of changing extrinsic motivators to intrinsic motivators by doing the following:

- Show curiosity about clients. Because a client's desire to change is seldom limited to substance use, he/she may find it easier to discuss changing other behaviors. This will help strengthen the therapeutic alliance. (2)
- Reframe a client's negative statement about perceived coercion by re-expressing the statement with a positive spin. (2)

Clinicians can use decisional balancing strategies to help clients thoughtfully consider the positive and negative aspects of their substance use. (1) The ultimate purpose, of course, is to help clients recognize and weigh the negative aspects of substance use so that the scale tips toward beneficial behavior. Techniques to use in decisional balancing exercises include the following:

- Summarize the client's concerns. (2)
- Explore specific pros and cons of substance use behavior. (1)
- Normalize the client's ambivalence. (2)
- Reintroduce feedback from previous assessments. (1)
- Examine the client's understanding of change and expectations of treatment. (1)
- Reexplore the client's values in relation to change. (2)

Throughout this process, emphasize the clients' personal choices and responsibilities for change. The clinician's task is to help clients make choices that are in their best interests. This can be done by exploring and setting goals. Goal-setting is part of the exploring and envisioning activities characteristic of the early and middle preparation stage. The process of talking about and setting goals strengthens commitment to change. (1)

During the preparation stage, the clinician's tasks broaden from using motivational strategies to increase readiness--the goals of precontemplation and contemplation stages--to using these strategies to strengthen a client's commitment and help him/her make a firm decision to change. At this stage, helping the client develop self-efficacy is important. (2) Self-efficacy is not a global measure, like self-esteem; rather, it is behavior specific. In this case, it is the client's optimism that he/she can take action to change substance-use behaviors.

From preparation to action

As clients move through the preparation stage, clinicians should be alert for signs of clients' readiness to move into action. There appears to be a limited period of time during which change should be initiated. (2) Clients' recognition of important discrepancies in their lives is too uncomfortable a state to remain in for long, and unless change is begun they can retreat to using defenses such as minimizing or denying to decrease their discomfort. (2) The following can signal a client's readiness to act:

- The client's resistance (i.e., arguing, denying) decreases. (2)
- The client asks fewer questions about the problem. (2)
- The client shows a certain amount of resolve and may be more peaceful, calm, relaxed, unburdened, or settled. (2)
- The client makes direct self-motivational statements reflecting openness to change and optimism. (2)
- The client asks more questions about the change process. (2)
- The client begins to talk about how life might be after a change. (2)
- The client may have begun experimenting with possible change approaches such as going to an Alcoholics Anonymous meeting or stopping substance use for a few days. (2)

Mere vocal fervor about change, however, is not necessarily a sign of dogged determination. Clients who are most vehement in declaring their readiness may be desperately trying to convince themselves, as well as the clinician, of their commitment.

When working with clients in the preparation stage, clinicians should try to

- Clarify the client's own goals and strategies for change. (2)
- Discuss the range of different treatment options and community resources available to meet the client's multiple needs. (2)
- With permission, offer expertise and advice. (2)
- Negotiate a change--or treatment--plan and a behavior contract (2); take into consideration
  - Intensity and amount of help needed
  - Timeframe
  - Available social support, identifying who, where, and when
  - The sequence of smaller goals or steps needed for a successful plan
  - Multiple problems, such as legal, financial, or health concerns
- Consider and lower barriers to change by anticipating possible family, health, system, and other problems. (2)
- Help the client enlist social support (e.g., mentoring groups, churches, recreational centers). (2)
- Explore treatment expectancies and client role. (2)
- Have clients publicly announce their change plans to significant others in their lives. (2)

From action to maintenance

A motivational counseling style has most frequently been used with clients in the precontemplation through preparation stages as they move toward initiating behavioral change. Some clients and clinicians believe that formal, action-oriented substance abuse treatment is a different domain and that motivational strategies are no longer required. This is not true for two reasons. First, clients may still need a surprising amount of support and encouragement to stay with a chosen program or course of treatment. Even after a successful discharge, they may need support and encouragement to maintain the gains they have achieved and to know how to handle recurring crises that may mean a return to problem behaviors. (2) Second, many clients remain ambivalent in the action stage of change or vacillate between some level of contemplation--with associated ambivalence--and continuing action. (2) Moreover, clients who do take action are suddenly faced with the reality of stopping or reducing substance use. This is more difficult than just contemplating action. The first stages of recovery require only thinking about change, which is not as threatening as actually implementing it.

Clients' involvement or participation in treatment can be increased when clinicians

- Develop a nurturing rapport with clients (2)
- Induct clients into their role in the treatment process (2)
- Explore what clients expect from treatment and determine discrepancies (2)
- Prepare clients so that they know there may be some embarrassing, emotionally awkward, and uncomfortable moments but that such moments are a normal part of the recovery process (2)
- Investigate and resolve barriers to treatment (2)
- Increase congruence between intrinsic and extrinsic motivation (2)
- Examine and interpret noncompliant behavior in the context of ambivalence (2)
- Reach out to demonstrate continuing personal concern and interest to encourage clients to remain in the program (2)

Clients who are in the action stage can be most effectively helped when clinicians

- Engage clients in treatment and reinforce the importance of remaining in recovery. (2)
- Support a realistic view of change through small steps. (2)
- Acknowledge difficulties for clients in early stages of change. (2)
- Help the client identify high-risk situations through a functional analysis and develop appropriate coping strategies to overcome these. (2)
- Assist the client in finding new reinforcers of positive change. (2)
- Assess whether the client has strong family and social support. (2)

The next challenge that clients and clinicians face is maintaining change. With clients in the maintenance stage, clinicians will be most successful if they can

- Help the client identify and sample substance-free sources of pleasure-- i.e., new reinforcers (1)
- Support lifestyle changes (2)
- Affirm the client's resolve and self-efficacy (2)
- Help the client practice and use new coping strategies to avoid a return to substance use (2)
- Maintain supportive contact (2)

After clients have planned for stabilization by identifying risky situations, practicing new coping strategies, and finding their sources of support, they still have to build a new lifestyle that will provide sufficient satisfaction and can compete successfully against the lure of substance use. A wide range of life changes ultimately needs to be made if clients are to maintain lasting abstinence. Clinicians can help this change process by using competing reinforcers. (1) A competing reinforcer is anything that clients enjoy that is or can become a healthy alternative to drugs or alcohol as a source of satisfaction.

The essential principle in establishing new sources of positive reinforcement is to get clients involved in generating their own ideas. Clinicians should explore all areas of clients' lives for new reinforcers. Reinforcers should not come from a single source or be of the same type. That way, a setback in one area can be counterbalanced by the availability of positive reinforcement from another area. Since clients have competing motivations, clinicians can help them select reinforcers that will *win out* over substances over time.

Following are a number of potential competing reinforcers that can help clients:

- Doing volunteer work, thus filling time, connecting with socially acceptable friends, and improving their self-efficacy (2)
- Becoming involved in 12-Step-based activities and other self-help groups (2)
- Setting goals to improve their work, education, exercise, and nutrition (2)
- Spending more time with their families and significant others (2)

- Participating in spiritual or cultural activities (2)
- Socializing with nonsubstance-using friends (2)
- Learning new skills or improving in such areas as sports, art, music, and other hobbies (2)

Contingency reinforcement systems, such as voucher programs, have proven to be effective when community support and resources are available. (1) Research has shown that these kinds of reinforcement systems can help to sustain abstinence in drug abusers. The rationale for this type of incentive program is that an appealing external motivator can be used as an immediate and powerful reinforcer to compete with substance use reinforcers. Not all contingent incentives have to have a monetary value. In many cultures, money is not the most powerful reinforcer.

Recurrence

Most people do not immediately sustain the new changes they are attempting to make, and a return to substance use after a period of abstinence is the rule rather than the exception (Brownell et al., 1986; Prochaska and DiClemente, 1992). These experiences contribute information that can facilitate or hinder subsequent progression through the stages of change. *Recurrence*, often referred to as relapse, is the event that triggers the individual's return to earlier stages of change and recycling through the process. Individuals may learn that certain goals are unrealistic, certain strategies are ineffective, or certain environments are not conducive to successful change. Most substance users will require several revolutions through the stages of change to achieve successful recovery (DiClemente and Scott, 1997). After a return to substance use, clients usually revert to an earlier change stage--not always to maintenance or action, but more often to some level of contemplation. They may even become precontemplators again, temporarily unwilling or unable to try to change soon. Resuming substance use and returning to a previous stage of change should not be considered a failure and need not become a disastrous or prolonged recurrence. A recurrence of symptoms does not necessarily mean that a client has abandoned a commitment to change.

Triggers to Change

The multidimensional nature of motivation is captured, in part, in the popular phrase that a person is *ready, willing,* and *able* to change. This expression highlights three critical elements of motivation--but in reverse order from that in which motivation typically evolves. *Ability* refers to the extent to which the person has the necessary skills, resources, and confidence (self-efficacy) to carry out a change. One can be able to change, but not willing. The *willing* component involves the importance a person places on changing--how much a change is wanted or desired. (Note that it is possible to feel willing yet unable to change.) However, even willingness and ability are not always enough. You probably can think of examples of people who are willing and able to change, but not yet ready to change. The *ready* component represents a final step in which the person finally decides to change a particular behavior. Being willing and able but not ready can often be explained by the relative importance of this change compared with other priorities in the person's life. To instill motivation for change is to help the client become ready, willing, and able.

Figure 8-2 provides examples of appropriate motivational strategies you can use at each stage of change. Of course, these are not the only ways to enhance motivation for beneficial change.

Figure 8-2: Appropriate Motivational Strategies for Each Stage of Change

Client's Stage of Change	Appropriate Motivational Strategies for the Clinician

Precontemplation
 	
The client is not yet considering change or is unwilling or unable to change.
	• Establish rapport, ask permission, and build trust.
	• Raise doubts or concerns in the client about substance-using patterns by
	   ○ Exploring the meaning of events that brought the client to treatment or the results of previous treatments
	   ○ Eliciting the client's perceptions of the problem
	   ○ Offering factual information about the risks of substance use
	   ○ Providing personalized feedback about assessment findings
	   ○ Exploring the pros and cons of substance use
	   ○ Helping a significant other intervene
	   ○ Examining discrepancies between the client's and others' perceptions of the problem behavior
	• Express concern and keep the door open.

Contemplation
 	
The client acknowledges concerns and is considering the possibility of change but is ambivalent and uncertain.
	• Normalize ambivalence.
	• Help the client "tip the decisional balance scales" toward change by
	   ○ Eliciting and weighing pros and cons of substance use and change
	   ○ Changing extrinsic to intrinsic motivation
	   ○ Examining the client's personal values in relation to change
	   ○ Emphasizing the client's free choice, responsibility, and self-efficacy for change
	• Elicit self-motivational statements of intent and commitment from the client.
	• Elicit ideas regarding the client's perceived self-efficacy and expectations regarding treatment.
	• Summarize self-motivational statements.

Preparation	• Clarify the client's own goals and strategies for change.
The client is committed to and planning to make a change in the near future but is still considering what to do.	• Offer a menu of options for change or treatment.
	• With permission, offer expertise and advice.
	• Negotiate a change--or treatment--plan and behavior contract.
	• Consider and lower barriers to change.
	• Help the client enlist social support.
	• Explore treatment expectancies and the client's role.
	• Elicit from the client what has worked in the past either for him or others whom he knows.
	• Assist the client to negotiate finances, child care, work, transportation, or other potential barriers.
	• Have the client publicly announce plans to change.

Action The client is actively taking steps to change but has not yet reached a stable state.	<ul><li>Engage the client in treatment and reinforce the importance of remaining in recovery.</li><li>Support a realistic view of change through small steps.</li><li>Acknowledge difficulties for the client in early stages of change.</li><li>Help the client identify high-risk situations through a functional analysis and develop appropriate coping strategies to overcome these.</li><li>Assist the client in finding new reinforcers of positive change.</li><li>Help the client assess whether she has strong family and social support.</li></ul>
Maintenance The client has achieved initial goals such as abstinence and is now working to maintain gains.	<ul><li>Help the client identify and sample drug-free sources of pleasure (i.e., new reinforcers).</li><li>Support lifestyle changes.</li><li>Affirm the client's resolve and self-efficacy.</li><li>Help the client practice and use new coping strategies to avoid a return to use.</li><li>Maintain supportive contact (e.g., explain to the client that you are available to talk between sessions).</li><li>Develop a "fire escape" plan if the client resumes substance use.</li><li>Review long-term goals with the client.</li></ul>

Recurrence	• Help the client reenter the change cycle and commend any willingness to reconsider positive change.
The client has experienced a recurrence of symptoms and must now cope with consequences and decide what to do next.	• Explore the meaning and reality of the recurrence as a learning opportunity.
	• Assist the client in finding alternative coping strategies.
	• Maintain supportive contact.

Section 3, Chapter 9:

DSM Information for Counselors

UTILIZING DSM-5

Regardless of background, training, or theoretical orientation, professional counselors need to have a thorough understanding of the fifth edition of the *Diagnostic and Statistical Manual of Mental Disorders (DSM-5),* published by the American Psychiatric Association (APA; 2013). The *DSM-5* and its earlier editions have become the world's standard reference for client evaluation and diagnosis (Eriksen & Kress, 2006; Hinkle, 1999; Zalaquett, Fuerth, Stein, Ivey, & Ivey, 2008). Most important, the manual allows professional counselors to break down the complexity of clients' presenting problems into practical language for practitioners and clients alike. Sometimes referred to as the "the psychiatric bible" (Caplan, 2012; Kutchins & Kirk, 1997; Perry, 2012), the *DSM* is intended to be applicable in various settings and used by mental health practitioners and researchers of differing backgrounds and orientations.

Because of the prevalent use of the *DSM,* professional counselors who provide services in mental health centers, psychiatric hospitals, employee assistance programs, detention centers, private practice, or other community settings must be well versed in client conceptualization and diagnostic assessment using the manual. For those in private practice, agencies, and hospitals, a diagnosis using *DSM* criteria is necessary for third-party payments and for certain types of record keeping and reporting. Of the 50 states and the U.S. territories, including the District of Columbia, that have passed laws to regulate professional counselors, 34 include diagnosis within the scope of practice for professional counselors (American Counseling Association [ACA], 2012). Even professionals who are not traditionally responsible for diagnosis as a part of their counseling services, such as school or career counselors, should understand the *DSM* so they can recognize diagnostic problems or complaints and participate in discussions and treatment regarding these issues. Although other diagnostic nomenclature systems, such as the World Health Organization's (WHO; 2007) *International Statistical Classification of Diseases and Related Health Problems (ICD),* are available to professional counselors, the *DSM* is and will continue to be the most widely used manual within the field. For these reasons, the ability to navigate and use the *DSM* responsibly has become an important part of a professional counselor's identity.

BRIEF HISTORY OF THE *DSM*

- *DSM-I* was first published by the American Psychiatric Association (APA) in 1952 and reflected a psychobiological point of view.

- *DSM-II* (1968) did not reflect a particular point of view. Many professionals criticized both *DSM-I* and *DSM-II* for being unscientific and for encouraging negative labeling.

- *DSM-III* (1980) tried to calm the controversy by claiming to be unbiased and more scientific. Even though many of the earlier problems still persisted, these problems were overshadowed by an increasing demand for *DSM-III* diagnoses being required for clients to qualify for reimbursement from private insurance companies or from governmental programs.

- *DSM-III-R* (1987) utilized data from field trials that the developers claimed validated the system on scientific grounds. Nevertheless, serious questions were raised about its diagnostic reliability, possible misuse, potential for misdiagnosis, and ethics of its use.

- *DSM-IV* (1994) sought to dispel earlier criticisms of the *DSM*. The book included additional cultural information, diagnostic tests, and lab findings and was based on 500 clinical field trials.

- *DSM-IV-TR* (2000) does not change the diagnostic codes or criteria from the *DSM-IV;* however, it supplements the current categories with additional information based on the research studies and field trials completed in each area.

- *DSM-5* (2013) is released after more than a decade's worth of work. APA's goal in developing *DSM-5* was to create an evidence-based manual that is useful to clinicians in helping them accurately diagnose mental disorders.

DSM-5: THE NEWEST REVISION

While counselors will undoubtedly benefit from the knowledge found in the DSM-5 for all categories, the focus here is on the impact and use of the DSM within the drug/alcohol treatment field. We will first explore a broad overview of the structural changes made to the entire DSM-5 before moving in to the specifics of changes made that impact the drug/alcohol treatment field.

The *DSM-5* includes approximately the same number of disorders as the *DSM-IV-TR.* This goes against a popular trend within health care to increase, rather than decrease, the number of diagnoses available to practitioners (APA, 2013). Despite being similar in number, several major changes affect the manual as a whole. Unlike the previous version that was organized by 16 diagnostic classes, one general section, and 11 appendixes, the *DSM-5* is divided into three sections, 20 diagnostic classes, two general sections for medication-induced problems and other conditions that may be a focus of clinical attention, and seven appendixes. It also lists two sets of *ICD* codes, using *ICD-9-CM* (CDC, 1998) codes as the standard coding system with *ICD-10-CM* (CDC, 2014) codes in parentheses. *ICD-10-CM* codes are included because as of October 1, 2014, all practitioners must be in alignment with HIPAA, which requires use of *ICD-10-CM* codes.

DSM Section Overview

Section I of the *DSM-5* provides a summary of revisions and changes as well as information regarding utilization of the revised manual. Section II includes all diagnoses broken into 20 separate chapters ordered by similarity to one another. Because comorbid symptoms are clustered together, counselors can now better differentiate between disorders that are distinctively different but have similar symptom characteristics or etiology (e.g., body dysmorphic disorder vs. obsessive-compulsive disorder; acute stress disorder vs. adjustment disorder). Section III includes conditions that require further research before they can be considered for adoption in an upcoming version of the *DSM,* dimensional assessment measures, an expanded look at how practitioners can better understand clients from a multicultural perspective, and a proposed model for diagnosing personality disorders.

Cultural Inclusion

Section III (see pp. 749-759 of the *DSM-5)* includes special attention to diverse ways in which individuals in different cultural groups can experience and describe distress. The manual provides a Cultural Formulation Interview (pp. 750-757 of the *DSM-5)* to help clinicians gather relevant cultural information. Expanding on information provided in the *DSM-IV-TR,* the Cultural Formulation Interview calls for clinicians to outline and systematically assess cultural identity, cultural conceptualization of distress, psychosocial stressors related to cultural features of vulnerability and resilience, cultural differences between the counselor and client, and cultural factors relevant to help seeking. The *DSM-5* also includes descriptions regarding how different cultural groups encounter, identify with, and convey feelings of distress by breaking up what was formerly known as culture-bound syndromes into three different concepts. The first concept is *cultural syndromes,* a cluster of co-occurring symptomatology within a specific cultural group. The second is *cultural idioms of distress,* linguistic terms or phrases used to convey suffering within a specific cultural group. The third concept is *cultural explanation or perceived cause,* mental disorders unique to certain cultures that serve as the reason for symptoms, illness, or distress. This breakdown improves clinical utility by helping clinicians more accurately communicate with clients, so that they are able to differentiate disorders from nondisorders when working with clients from varied backgrounds.

Personality Disorders

Section III of the *DSM-5* also provides an alternative model for diagnosing personality disorders. This model is a radical change from the current diagnostic structure, introducing a hybrid dimensional-categorical model, which evaluates symptomatology and characterizes five broad areas of personality pathology. As opposed to separate diagnostic criteria, this proposed model identifies six personality types with a specific pattern of impairments and traits.

Adoption of a Nonaxial System

One of the most far-reaching structural modifications to the *DSM-5* is the removal of the multiaxial system and discontinuation of the Global Assessment of Functioning (GAF) scale. Table 1 includes a comparison of the traditional multiaxial and the new nonaxial system. Axes I, II, and III are now combined with the assumption that there is no differentiation between medical and mental health conditions. Rather than list psychosocial and contextual factors affecting clients on Axis IV, counselors will now list V codes or 900 codes (used for conditions related to neglect, sexual abuse, physical abuse, and psychological abuse) as stand-alone diagnoses or alongside another diagnosis as long as the stressors are relevant to the clients mental disorder(s). An expanded listing of V codes is included in the DSM-5. Although the DSM-5 does not include direction for formatting, counselors may also use special notations for psychosocial and environmental considerations relevant to the diagnosis. Similarly, counselors will no longer note a GAF score on Axis V. Rather, the DSM-5 advises that clinicians find ways to note distress and/or disability in functioning, perhaps using the World Health Organization Disability Assessment Schedule 2.0 (WHO- DAS 2.0; WHO, 2010) as a dimensional assessment of functioning. Again, the manual does not include directions for formatting or presenting this assessment.

> **Note:** *Counselors are not qualified to diagnose medical conditions. However, it is important to record all historical medical information. Counselors must work closely with medical professionals to identify any medical conditions.*

> *Once* ICD-10-CM *is implemented (October 2014), all codes in the Other Conditions That May Be a Focus of Clinical Attention chapter of the* DSM-5 *will change. Z codes will replace V codes, and T codes will replace 900 codes. The only exception is V62.89 borderline intellectual functioning, in which the* ICD-10-CM *code is R41.83. (See APA, 2013, pp. 715-727.)*

Table 1: Comparison of Multiaxial Versus Nonaxial Systems

DSM-III *and* DSM-IV *Multiaxial System*	DSM-5 *Nonaxial System*
Axis I: Clinical disorders and other conditions that are the focus of treatment *Axis II:* Personality disorders and intellectual disability (i.e., mental retardation) *Axis III:* General medical conditions	Combined attention to clinical disorders, including personality disorders and intellectual disability (i.e., mental retardation); other conditions that are the focus of treatment; and medical conditions continue to be listed as a part of the diagnosis.
Axis IV: Psychosocial and environmental stressors	Special notations for psychosocial and contextual factors are now listed by using V codes or *ICD-10-CM* Z codes. An expanded list of V codes has been provided in the *DSM-5.* In rare cases where psychosocial and contextual factors are not listed, counselors can include the specific factor as it is related to the client's diagnosis.
Axis V: Global Assessment of Functioning (GAF)	Special notations for disability are listed by using V codes or *ICD-10-CM* Z codes. The World Health Organization Disability Assessment Schedule 2.0 (WHODAS 2.0) has been included in Section III and is listed on APA's website (www.psychiatry.org) within the online assessment measures section.

The advantage to dropping the multiaxial system confirms what counselors from a wellness perspective have been claiming for decades – that differentiation among emotional, behavioral, physiological, psychosocial, and contextual factors is misleading and conveys a message that mental illness is unrelated to physical, biological, and medical problems. Combining these axes has the potential to be more inclusive, embracing more aspects of client functioning. However, practitioners will need to be intentional and systematic when incorporating more holistic assessments and notations into the diagnostic process so that their diagnoses do not become a simple listing of primary *DSM-5* disorders.

Note: *The* DSM-5 *has dropped the GAF scale because of a lack of clinical utility and reliability. The WHODAS 2.0 (WHO, 2010) has been included in Section III of the DSM-5 manual (745-748). This scale is used in the* ICD *as a standardized* *assessment of functioning for individuals diagnosed with mental disorders. The DSM-5 notes, however, that "it has not been possible to completely separate normal and pathological symptom expressions contained in diagnostic criteria" (APA, 2013, p. 21). Counselors who use the WHODAS 2.0 are responsible for ensuring they do so in accordance with the ACA Code of Ethics (ACA, 2014); this includes ensuring appropriateness of instruments through review of psychometric properties, appropriateness for client population, and appropriate use of interpretation. This is particularly important because the DSM-5 does not include information regarding the validity or reliability of the WHODAS 2.0.*

Critics of the multiaxial system argued that the system is cumbersome and ambiguous, thus providing poor clinical utility (Bassett & Beiser, 1991; Jampala, Sierles, & Taylor, 1986; Paris, 2013). Furthermore, many clinicians will agree that although the multiaxial system was well intentioned, client reports typically stopped at Axis I. In cases where Axis II was listed, some clients would feel stigmatized by their diagnostic label (Aviram, Brodsky, & Stanley, 2006; Fritz, 2012). Enhanced attention to V codes within the nonaxial system may also help counselors emphasize a client's entire worldview and systemic context in a way that informs the therapeutic process. If used intentionally, movement to a nonaxial system may help increase client understanding, remind counselors that medical and psychosocial issues are just as important as mental health diagnoses, and reduce stigma.

Challenges of moving to a nonaxial system include conceptual lack of clarity regarding how clinicians are going to implement the nonaxial system. If clinicians struggled to use holistic assessment within a multiaxial system that essentially required some attention to psychosocial and environmental issues and overall distress and disability, will they actually take the time to incorporate these elements into a more ambiguous format? We anticipate problems with interpretation, specifically regarding the combination of Axes I, II, and III, within the counseling profession and among interdisciplinary teams. Although counselors can include subjective descriptors next to the client's diagnosis, there is no telling whether these will carry over to the next clinician or if they will make sense to a different party. Other challenges include delays as insurance companies and governmental agencies update their claim forms and reporting procedures to accommodate *DSM-5* changes. Major challenges for both counselors and clients are to be expected as helping professionals, insurance and service providers, and public or private institutions move toward nonaxial documentation of diagnosis.

With these new changes, diagnoses will be cited listing the primary diagnosis first, followed by all psychosocial, contextual, and disability factors. For example, a client presents with depressive symptoms during withdrawal of a severe cocaine use disorder. She has just revealed that she is being sexually abused by her husband who just kicked her out of her home. This client would receive a diagnosis of 292.84 cocaine-induced depressive disorder, with onset during withdrawal. An additional diagnosis of 304.20 severe cocaine use disorder would also be recorded, as well as 995.83 spouse violence, sexual, suspected, initial encounter and V60.0 homelessness. Any subsequent notations related to a mental health diagnosis would follow.

DSM Chapter Organization

Overall organization of chapters within the *DSM* changed significantly to reflect a developmental approach to listing diagnoses. Diagnoses are now ordered in terms of similar symptomatology with presumed underlying vulnerabilities grouped together. This organization is indicative of the life-span (i.e., developmental) approach taken by the DSM-5 Task Force. Readers will notice that disorders more frequently diagnosed in childhood, such as intellectual and learning disabilities, are renamed as neurodevelopmental disorders and appear at the beginning of the manual. Diagnoses more commonly seen in older adults, such as neurocognitive disorders, appear at the end of the *DSM-5*. This modification more closely follows the *ICD* and was intended to increase practitioners' use of the manual for differential diagnosis.

Other structural changes include significant modifications to overall classification of disorders. The mood disorders section has been separated into two distinct classes: depressive disorders and bipolar and related disorders. Anxiety disorders have been broken out into three separate diagnostic chapters: anxiety disorders, obsessive-compulsive and related disorders, and trauma- and stressor-related disorders. In another large structural and philosophical change, the *DSM-5* eliminated disorders usually diagnosed in infancy, childhood, or adolescence. Disorders within this section were incorporated into a new neurodevelopmental disorders chapter or, if not presumed to be neurodevelopmental in nature, relocated to other specific section s of the *DSM-5*. The DSM-5 Task Force justified this change because many of the disorders in this section are also seen in adulthood (e.g., ADHD; Jones, 2013), and many disorders seen in childhood may be precursors to concerns in adulthood. This section, which was originally created for convenience, led clinicians to erroneously believe there was a clear distinction between "adult" and "childhood" disorders. Critics felt this division was confusing and prevented clinicians from diagnosing children with "adult" disorders such as major depression or posttraumatic stress disorder (PTSD). Likewise, adults diagnosed with disorders such as ADHD have reported feeling stigmatized with limited treatment options (Katragadda & Schubiner, 2007). In terms of structure, diagnoses that were removed from this section, such as childhood feeding and eating disorders, can now be found within their associated sections, just later in the manual. For example, the feeding and eating disorders section of the *DSM-5* now includes pica and rumination.

Other comprehensive structural changes include the removal of labeling disorders as *not otherwise specified* (NOS) so practitioners can be more specific and accurate in their diagnosis. As a replacement, the *DSM-5* has two options for cases in which the clients presenting condition do not meet the criteria for a specific category: other specified disorder and unspecified disorder. The use of *other specified disorder* allows counselors to identify the specific reason why the client does not meet the criteria for a disorder. *Unspecified disorder* is used when a clinician chooses not to specify a reason for not diagnosing a more specific disorder or determines there is not enough information to be more specific. This is also supportive of dimensional, rather than categorical, classification (this idea is expanded on in the next section, *DSM-5* Philosophical Changes). Finally, language throughout the *DSM-5* changed so that medical conditions, previously referred to as general medical conditions, are renamed *another medical condition.* This change reflects the philosophical assumption that mental health disorders *are* medical conditions.

> **Note:** *Clinical judgment is the driving force for whether the client's presenting condition should be "other specified" or "unspecified." APA is very clear in that the use of either is the decision of the clinician.*

Be sure to note that the *DSM-5* includes both *ICD-9-CM* and *ICD-10-CM* codes, something that many counselors are unfamiliar with or unaware of. This inclusion is a response to a mandate from the U.S. Department of Health and Human Services that required <u>ALL</u> health care providers to use *IDC-10-CM* codes by October 2014. To ease this transition, the *DSM-5* lists both code numbers in the Appendix section. This will aid in standardization among mental health care providers and will also allow for easier transition to the new *ICD-10-CM* codes and revised billing processes.

The following list is a summary of the major structural changes in the *DSM-5:*

- removal of the multiaxial system;
- modification to chapter order to reflect a developmental approach;
- division into three sections: Section I: *DSM-5* Basics; Section II: Diagnostic Criteria and Codes; and Section III: Emerging Measures and Models;
- replacement of the first diagnostic chapter of the *DSM-IV- TR,* Disorders Usually First Diagnosed in Infancy, Childhood, or Adolescence, with a new Neurodevelopmental Disorders chapter;
- inclusion of both *ICD-9-CM* and *ICD-10-CM* codes;
- modifications to the classification of disorders: Bipolar and related disorders and depressive disorders are now stand-alone chapters; anxiety disorders was separated into three distinct categories (anxiety disorders, obsessive-compulsive and related disorders, and trauma- and stressor-related disorders); and

- removal of NOS and inclusion of other specified and unspecified disorders.

Note: Whereas ICD code numbers were originally created for statistical tracking of diseases, not reimbursement, most medical systems within the United States use these codes for billing purposes. The DSM-III was coordinated with the development of the ICD-9. Other versions of the DSM continued to use the ICD-9 codes, despite that fact that the ICD-10 was first published in 1992.

Major Diagnostic Highlights

Although the focus here is on the issues related to substance-related and addictive disorders, it is important that counseling professionals who work with this population have a general idea of the major changes found in the *DSM-5*.

1. Mental retardation is now referred to as intellectual disability (intellectual developmental disorder). Severity of disability is now determined by adaptive functioning rather than IQ score. New criteria include severity measures for mild, moderate, severe, and profound intellectual disability. Intellectual developmental disorder is placed in parentheses to reflect the term used in the ICD.
2. Communication disorders have been restructured to include social communication disorder (SCD). SCD is intended to identify persistent difficulties in the social use of verbal and nonverbal communication. Individuals diagnosed under the DSM-IV-TR with pervasive developmental disorder NOS may meet criteria for SCD.
3. Two diagnostic categories have been added to communication disorders: language disorder and speech disorder. Language disorder combines DSM-IV-TR expressive and mixed receptive-expressive language disorders.
4. Phonological disorder is now referred to as speech sound disorder.
5. Stuttering is now referred to as childhood-onset fluency disorder.
6. Autism, Asperger's disorder, childhood disintegrative disorder, and pervasive developmental disorder have been replaced with one umbrella diagnosis: autism spectrum disorder. The purpose of this change is to improve diagnostic efficacy, accuracy, and consistency.
7. Specific learning disorders have been expanded to represent distinct disorders that involve problems with the acquisition and/or use of one of more of the following skills: oral language, reading, written, and/or mathematical operations. Now referred to as specific learning disorder, this diagnosis is intended to combine reading disorder, mathematics disorder, disorder of written expression, and learning disorder NOS.

9. Schizophrenia spectrum and other psychotic disorders remove special treatment of bizarre delusions and hallucinations involving conversations or commentary. Schizophrenia no longer includes attention to five subtypes.

10. Disruptive mood dysregulation disorder is added with the intent of addressing over-diagnosis of bipolar disorder in children. Symptoms include persistent irritability and persistent outbursts three or more times a week for a year.

11. Premenstrual dysphoric disorder is added to depressive disorders

12. The DSM-5 eliminates Criterion E, also known as the "grief exclusion," for a major depressive episode. Individuals who have experienced the loss of a loved one can now be diagnosed with depression if they meet other criteria for a major depressive episode.

13. Depressive and bipolar disorders include new specifiers such as with catatonia, with anxious distress, and with mixed features. These specifiers are intended to account for experiences often comorbid with mood disorders yet not part of standard criteria.

14. Anxiety disorders include separate diagnostic categories for agoraphobia and panic disorder. Clients no longer need to experience panic to be diagnosed with agoraphobia.

15. The anxiety disorders section includes diagnostic criteria for panic attacks. The specifier with panic attacks may now be used across all diagnostic categories of anxiety and within other sections of the DSM-5.

16. A new chapter on obsessive-compulsive and related disorders groups disorders such as obsessive-compulsive disorder, body dysmorphic disorder, and trichotillomania together as opposed to having them scattered throughout the manual. It also includes several new disorders including excoriation (skin-picking) disorder and hoarding disorder. Hoarding disorder is characterized by persistent difficulty disposing of possessions, regardless of monetary or personal value.

17. A new chapter on trauma- and stressor-related disorders groups disorders related to trauma and/or situational stress factors such as reactive attachment disorder, dis-inhibited social engagement disorder, PTSD, acute stress disorder, and adjustment disorder.

18. PTSD was revised to include four distinct diagnostic clusters (as opposed to three in the DSM-IV-TR); the section includes considerable attention to developmentally appropriate criteria for children and adolescents.

19. The feeding and eating disorders section includes a new disorder, binge eating disorder.

20. The personality disorders section has not changed and will maintain the same 10 categories as the DSM-IV-TR. However, Section III on emerging measures and models includes a framework for diagnosing personality disorders using trait-specific methodology.

22. The previous sexual and gender identity disorders section is now divided into three separate sections: sexual dysfunctions, gender dysphoria, and paraphilic disorders. Pedophilia disorder is now referred to as pedophilic disorder.

23. The sleep-wake disorders section includes revisions with enhanced attention to biological indicators for diagnosis of many disorders.

24. The substance-related and addictive disorders section is expanded to include addictive disorders; however, only gambling disorder falls in this category. Previous substance dependence and substance abuse criteria are combined into one overarching disorder: substance use disorders. Significant changes have been made to coding, recording, and specifiers for these disorders.

25. The chapter on neurocognitive disorders (previously cognitive disorders) removes language regarding dementia, includes enhanced attention to a range of impairment as evidenced by incorporation of major and mild neurocognitive disorders, and includes additional attention to neurological assessment and basis of the condition.

26. Section III includes several new disorders for study, such as attenuated psychosis syndrome (which describes individuals at high risk for psychosis who do not meet the criteria for a psychotic disorder), Internet gaming disorder, nonsuicidal self-injury, and suicidal-behavioral disorder.

27. Section III also contains a detailed discussion of culture and diagnosis, including tools for in-depth cultural assessment and a description of some common cultural syndromes, idioms of distress, and causal explanations relevant to clinical practice.

28. Within each diagnostic category, the NOS diagnosis has been replaced with other specified and unspecified diagnoses. The other specified category is used in situations in which the clinician chooses to communicate the specific reason that the presentation does not meet the criteria for the specific disorder.

Substance-Related Disorders

Substance-related disorders include 10 classes of drugs (alcohol; caffeine; cannabis; hallucinogens; inhalants; opioids; sedatives, hypnotics, and anxiolytics; stimulants; tobacco; and other/unknown substances) that activate the brain's reward system (APA, 2013a). Use of these substances often leads to impairments in multiple areas of functioning that occur at a clinical level and represent diagnosable disorders. There are three classifications: use, intoxication, and withdrawal (APA, 2013a). Prevalence rates of substance use are extremely high, with 22.6 million individuals in the United States reporting use of illegal substances within the past month; this represents 8.9% of the total population over 12 years of age (SAMHSA, 2011b). Additionally, according to SAMHSA (2011b), a staggering 131.3 million people (51.8%) ages 12 and older had used alcohol and 69.6 million (27.4%) had used tobacco in the past month. During the same year, 23.5 million people ages 12 or older needed treatment for an illicit drug or alcohol abuse problem; this represents 9.3% of the U.S. population age 12 or older (SAMHSA, 2011b).

According to the American Society of Addictive Medicine (ASAM, 2013):

Addiction is a primary, chronic disease of brain reward, motivation, memory, and related circuitry. Dysfunction in these circuits leads to characteristic biological, psychological, social and spiritual manifestations. This is reflected in an individual pathologically pursuing reward and/or relief by substance use and other behaviors, (para. 1)

Addiction is ongoing and often cyclical, with many negative effects on psychological and physiological wellness. Addiction is present and problematic within and across social, cultural, and economic groups (ASAM, 2013; SAMHSA, 2011b). The cost of addiction is enormous, with a price tag of $559 billion annually for illegal substances, alcohol, and tobacco (National Institute on Drug Abuse, 2011).

Because of the devastating impact and high prevalence rates of individuals with diagnosable substance-related and addictive disorders, virtually all counselors – regardless of their professional settings – will work directly with this population or provide services for the family members and loved ones of individuals with the disorders. Substance-related and addictive disorders appear throughout the life span in people of all socioeconomic status levels, educational attainment, gender, culture, ethnicity, and religion. It is critical that counselors possess a strong understanding of criteria for substance-related disorders. To help establish this framework, the following section provides an overview of the changes from the *DSM-IV-TR* to the *DSM-5*.

Major Changes from *DSM-IV-TR* to *DSM-5*

The *DSM-5* includes significant restructuring to the categorization of substance-related disorders. Undoubtedly the biggest change in the *DSM-5* is the removal of the distinction between abuse and dependence. The prior classification of abuse and dependence was based on the notion that there is a biaxial difference between the two and that abuse was a less severe form of dependence. The bimodal theory did not hold true in research and practice, so the classification was revised to address substance use disorders as existing on a fluid, continuous spectrum (APA, 2013a; Dawson, Goldstein, & Grant, 2013; Keyes, Krueger, Grant, & Hasin, 2011). This resulted in the new substance use disorders section.

Once clinicians note the presence of a substance use disorder, they may specify severity of the addiction using ratings of *mild, moderate,* and *severe.* Research supports an increasing spectrum of severity across addictions and addictive behaviors that occur as a continuous variable; this represents the predominant reason for the move from abuse versus dependence to severity ratings (APA, 2013a; Dawson et al., 2013; Keyes et al., 2011). In addition, the removal of the terms *abuse* and *dependence* supports the fluid and progressive nature of substance use disorders as conceptualized in the manual.

It is important to note that concerns related to specific substances in the Substance-Related and Addictive Disorders chapter of the *DSM-5* (and enumerated here) are viewed as distinctive disorders. For example, caffeine-related disorders are separate from cannabis-related disorders. However, despite being distinctly separate diagnoses, all substance use disorders are based on the same criteria. Substance use criteria are also separate from substance-specific intoxication and withdrawal criteria. For example, there is alcohol use disorder, alcohol intoxication, and alcohol withdrawal, which are all coded separately. The only exception is hallucinogen-related and inhalant-related disorders, because symptoms of withdrawal have not been sufficiently documented for these substances so the withdrawal criterion has been eliminated. All other criteria for hallucinogen-related and inhalant-related disorders are the same. This modification in the diagnostic process for substance use disorders represents one of the most substantive changes to a diagnostic category in the *DSM-5.*

Unlike the discrete categories in the *DSM-IV-TR,* many disorders within the *DSM-5* were revised to represent a continuum. In the Substance-Related and Addictive Disorders chapter of the DSM-5, this continuum is represented by replacing distinct categories of substance abuse and dependence with 11 standard enumerated criteria for substance use disorders (APA, 2013a). Two to three criteria must be present for the severity indicator of *mild,* four to five for *moderate,* and six or more for *severe.* Additionally, craving has been included as a criterion, and legal difficulties have been excluded as a criterion.

The APA Substance-Related Disorders Work Group found research that corroborates the development of the substance use spectrum (APA, 2013a). According to Compton, Dawson, Goldstein, and Grant (2013), 80.5% of individuals who met the criteria for alcohol dependence in the *DSM-IV-TR* also met the criteria for alcohol use disorder (moderate to severe) in the *DSM-5.* Dawson et al. (2013) and Keyes et al. (2011) also found support for this new unimodal, fluid approach.

A second substantive change is that other addictive disorders have been included as part of this chapter, although at this time the *DSM-5* only includes gambling disorder in this category. Pathological gambling was listed in the *DSM-IV-TR* in the Impulse-Control Disorders Not Elsewhere Classified section but has now been relabeled and classified with substance-related disorders. The addition of gambling disorder represents the first time a process-related addictive behavior has been included alongside use of substances. This is due to an abundance of research that shows that gambling activates the brain's reward system in ways that are consistent with substance use (APA, 2013a; Ko et al., 2013; Moran, 2013). The symptoms of gambling disorder also hold similarities to substance use disorders, and gambling disorder possesses similar etiology in terms of presentation, biological underpinnings, and treatment.

Internet gaming disorder, listed in Section III of the *DSM-5* under the chapter Conditions for Further Study, may be added as an addictive disorder to subsequent iterations of the manual. Other types of "behavioral addictions" such as exercise, shopping, or sex addictions have not yet been shown to identify a diagnostic profile or similar developmental course. These may also be considered for inclusion in future editions of the manual (APA, 2013a; Ko et al., 2013; Moran, 2013).

Some scholars have taken umbrage with the wordsmithing of the chapter title, pointing out that Substance-Related and Addictive Disorders implies that being diagnosed with a substance use disorder means the client has an addiction (Kaminer & Winters, 2012). There has also been concern over the removal of the abuse category. Kaminer and Winters (2012) posited that the category of abuse is particularly applicable for adolescents; they discussed a body of knowledge coined the "biobehavioral developmental perspective" that asserts the course of the substance use is heterogeneously progressive and fits a categorical model of abuse versus dependence. The authors worried that removal of the abuse category in the *DSM-5* will affect treatment services for this population. However, other scholars believed modifications will increase access to services (Dawson et al., 2013; Keyes et al., 2011; Mewton, Slade, McBride, Grove, & Teeson, 2011). Several other changes are reflected in the Substance-Related and Addictive Disorders chapter. Specifically, *early remission* is now defined as at least 3 but not more than 12 months' absence of meeting diagnostic criteria for substance use disorders. Craving can still be present as a symptom, even with remission, because individuals continue to experience craving, or a strong desire, for the substance. The specifier *with physiological dependence* is not included in the *DSM-5* nor is the diagnosis of polysubstance dependence. Newly included disorders that can now be coded are caffeine withdrawal and cannabis withdrawal (APA, 2013a).

Substance Use Disorders

Diagnoses associated with substance class			
	Substance Use Disorder	Substance Intoxication	Substance Withdrawal
Alcohol	X	X	X
Caffeine		X	X
Cannabis	X	X	X
Hallucinogens			
Phencyclidine	X	X	
Other Hallucinogens	X	X	
Inhalants	X	X	
Opioids	X	X	X
Sedatives, hypnotics, or anxiolytics	X	X	X
Stimulants	X	X	X
Tobacco	X		X
Other (or unknown)	X	X	X

The *DSM-5* includes specific criteria sets for each substance and applicable disorders related to that substance (e.g., use, intoxication, and withdrawal) as shown in the Table above. All diagnostic labels include the name of the specific substance, such as cannabis use disorder, cannabis intoxication, and cannabis withdrawal. If an individual meets the criteria for multiple substance-related diagnoses, they are all listed. The manual is explicit in noting the likelihood of comorbidity of substance-related disorders (APA, 2013a; SAMHSA, 2011b).

Essential Features

According to APA (2013a), "a substance use disorder is a cluster of cognitive, behavioral, and physiological symptoms indicating that the individual continues using the substance despite significant substance-related problems" (p. 483). In severe and long-term use, these changes may be observed through underlying changes in brain circuits (Agrawal et al, 2012). The first four criteria for substance use disorders encompass impaired control, social impairment, risky use, and pharmacological criteria. Criteria 5 to 7 cover social, occupational, and interpersonal problems. Criteria 8 and 9 focus on risk taking surrounding use of the substance, and Criteria 10 and 11 are tolerance and withdrawal, respectively. Assuming an individual meets the general requirement for "clinically significant impairment or distress" related to pattern of use, just two specific criteria must be met to justify assignment of a clinical diagnosis.

The predominant change to the overall diagnostic criteria for substance use disorder is the inclusion of craving and the exclusion of recurrent legal problems. Craving is included in *ICD-10* criteria (WHO, 2007) and has been supported through epidemiological studies as a highly prominent and core feature of substance use disorders (Kavanaugh, 2013; Keyes et al., 2011; Ko et al., 2013; Mewton et al, 2011; Sinha, 2013). Functional magnetic resonance imaging (fMRI) has shown that there are certain brain regions directly related to craving (Ko et al., 2013). Presence of cues, negative moods, and stress reactions often lead to an increase in craving. Mindfulness training has been shown to reduce craving in that it can address awareness of the emotion and redirection of thoughts.

Diagnostic Criteria (Example - Alcohol Use Disorder)

B. A problematic pattern of alcohol use leading to clinically significant impairment or distress, as manifested by at least two of the following, occurring within a 12-month period.
1. Alcohol is often taken in larger amounts or over a longer period than was intended.
2. There is a persistent desire or unsuccessful efforts to cut down or control alcohol use.
3. A great deal of time is spent in activities necessary to obtain alcohol, use alcohol, or recover from its effects.
4. Craving, or a strong desire to use alcohol.
5. Recurrent alcohol use resulting in a failure to fulfill major role obligations at work, school, or home.
6. Continued alcohol use despite having persistent or recurrent social or interpersonal problems caused or exacerbated by the effects of alcohol.
7. Important social, occupational, or recreational activities are given up or reduced because of alcohol use.
8. Recurrent alcohol use in situations in which it is physically hazardous.
9. Alcohol use is continued despite knowledge of having a persistent or recurrent physical or psychological problem that is likely to have been caused or exacerbated by alcohol.
10. Tolerance, as defined by either of the following:
    a. A need for markedly increased amounts of alcohol to achieve intoxication or desired effect.
    b. A markedly diminished effect with continued use of the same amount of alcohol.

11. Withdrawal, as manifested by either of the following:
   a. The characteristic withdrawal syndrome for alcohol (refer to Criteria A and B of the criteria set for alcohol withdrawal, pp. 499-500).
   b. Alcohol (or a closely related substance, such as a benzodiazepine) is taken to relieve or avoid withdrawal symptoms.

From *Diagnostic and Statistical Manual of Mental Disorders, Fifth Edition,* 2013, pp. 490-491. Copyright 2013 by the American Psychiatric Association. All rights reserved. Reprinted with permission.

Note: *The diagnostic criteria for alcohol use disorder are used as an example because the criteria are identical for <u>ALL</u> of the disorders with the exception of Criterion **11**, which does not apply to hallucinogen-related and inhalant-related use disorders.*

Substance Intoxication and Withdrawal

Substance intoxication is a syndrome that develops temporarily after ingestion of a substance. The subsequent psychological changes result from the physiological effects of the substance. Intoxication often includes alterations in attention, thinking, judgment, perception, interpersonal behavior, psychomotor behavior, and wakefulness. The diagnosis of substance intoxication is separate from substance use disorder, and the specific substance of intoxication is listed in the disorder. The *DSM-5* includes criteria sets specific to intoxication for each substance category, except for tobacco. *ICD-10-CM* coding will change on the basis of the comorbidity of a substance use disorder. For example, there are different codes for alcohol intoxication with comorbid alcohol use disorder, mild (F10.129), than for alcohol intoxication with comorbid alcohol use disorder, moderate (F 10.229), or alcohol intoxication without comorbid alcohol use disorder (F10.929).

Substance withdrawal includes physiological and psychological effects from stopping or reducing substance utilization after significant, prolonged use. Withdrawal can be distinctly unpleasant and trigger a cycle of renewed use to counterbalance the deleterious effects of the withdrawal. An individual can become intoxicated by, and have withdrawal from, more than one substance concomitantly. The *DSM-5* includes criteria sets specific to withdrawal from each substance; generally, withdrawal criteria are opposite what one would expect with substance intoxication for the substance. As with substance intoxication, the diagnosis of substance withdrawal can occur with or without the comorbid diagnosis of a substance use disorder (APA, 2013a).

Coding, Recording, and Specifiers

There are separate diagnostic codes for all substance-related disorders (see list below). In making a diagnosis for a substance-related disorder, counselors must identify specifiers accurately. In addition to specification of substance use disorders as *mild, moderate,* or *severe* as discussed earlier, specifiers include *in early remission, in sustained remission, on maintenance therapy,* and *in a controlled environment,* with the last being an additional specifier for remission. Jails, locked hospital units, and therapeutic living settings are examples of controlled environments.

Counselors use the codes that apply to the specific substances with the name of the specific substance included, for example, alcohol use disorder, mild *(ICD-9-CM,* 305.00; *ICD-10-CM,* F10.10). Other substance use disorder should be used if a substance does not fit into one of the enumerated classes.

Diagnostic Codes for Substance Use Disorders

Alcohol-Related Disorders

DSM Diagnosis	*ICD-9-CM (ICD-10-CM)*
Alcohol use disorder, mild	305.00 (F10.10)
Alcohol use disorder, moderate	303.90 (F10.20)
Alcohol use disorder, severe	303.90 (F10.20)
Alcohol intoxication with use disorder, mild	303.00 (F10.129)
Alcohol intoxication with use disorder, moderate or severe	303.00 (F10.229)
Alcohol intoxication without use disorder	303.00 (F10.929)
Alcohol withdrawal without perceptual disturbances	291.81 (F10.239)
Alcohol withdrawal with perceptual disturbances	291.81 (F10.232)
Unspecified alcohol-related disorders	291.9 (F10.99)

Caffeine-Related Disorders

DSM Diagnosis	*ICD-9-CM (ICD-10-CM)*
Caffeine intoxication	305.90 (F15.929)
Caffeine withdrawal	292.0 (F15.33)
Unspecified caffeine-related disorder	292.9 (F15.99)

Cannabis-Related Disorders

DSM Diagnosis	ICD-9-CM (ICD-10-CM)
Cannabis use disorder, mild	305.20 (F12.10)
Cannabis use disorder, moderate	303.90 (F12.20)
Cannabis use disorder, severe	303.90 (F12.20)
Cannabis intoxication without perceptual disturbance with use disorder, mild	292.89 (F12.129)
Cannabis intoxication without perceptual disturbance with use disorder, moderate or severe	292.89 (F10.229)
Cannabis intoxication without perceptual disturbance without use disorder	292.89 (F10.929)
Cannabis intoxication with perceptual disturbance with use disorder, mild	292.89 (F12.122)
Cannabis intoxication with perceptual disturbance with use disorder, moderate or severe	292.89 (F12.222)
Cannabis intoxication with perceptual disturbance without use disorder	292.89 (F12.922)
Cannabis withdrawal	292.0 (F12.288)
Unspecified cannabis-related disorders	292.9 (F12.99)

Hallucinogen-Related Disorders

DSM Diagnosis	ICD-9-CM (ICD-10-CM)
Phencyclidine use disorder, mild	305.90 (F16.10)
Phencyclidine use disorder, moderate	304.60 (F16.20)
Phencyclidine use disorder, severe	304.60 (F16.20)
Other hallucinogen use disorder, mild	305.30 (F16.10)
Other hallucinogen use disorder, moderate	304.50 (F16.20)
Other hallucinogen use disorder, severe	304.50 (F16.20)
Phencyclidine intoxication with use disorder, mild	292.89 (F16.129)
Phencyclidine intoxication with use disorder, moderate or severe	292.89 (F16.229)
Phencyclidine intoxication without use disorder	292.89 (F16.929)
Other hallucinogen intoxication with use disorder, mild	292.89 (F16.129)
Other hallucinogen intoxication with use disorder, moderate or severe	292.89 (F16.229)
Other hallucinogen intoxication without use disorder	292.89 (F16.929)
Hallucinogen persisting perception disorder	292.89 (F16.983)
Unspecified phencyclidine-related disorder	292.9 (F16.99)
Unspecified hallucinogen-related disorder	292.9 (F16.99)

Inhalant-Related Disorders
Specify the particular inhalant

DSM Diagnosis	ICD-9-CM (ICD-10-CM)
Inhalant use disorder, mild	305.90 (F18.10)
Inhalant use disorder, moderate	304.60 (F18.20)
Inhalant use disorder, severe	304.60 (F18.20)
Inhalant intoxication with use disorder, mild	292.89 (F18.129)
Inhalant intoxication with use disorder, moderate or severe	292.89 (F18.229)
Inhalant intoxication without use disorder	292.89 (F18.929)
Unspecified inhalant-related disorders	292.9 (F18.99)

Opioid-Related Disorders
Specify if on maintenance therapy or in a controlled environment

DSM Diagnosis	ICD-9-CM (ICD-10-CM)
Opioid use disorder, mild	305.50 (F11.10)
Opioid use disorder, moderate	304.00 (F11.20)
Opioid use disorder, severe	304.00 (F11.20)
Opioid intoxication without perceptual disturbance with use disorder, mild	292.89 (F11.129)
Opioid intoxication without perceptual disturbance with use disorder, moderate or severe	292.89 (F11.229)
Opioid intoxication without perceptual disturbance without use disorder	292.89 (F11.929)
Opioid intoxication with perceptual disturbance with use disorder, mild	292.89 (F11.122)
Opioid intoxication with perceptual disturbance with use disorder, moderate or severe	292.89 (F11.222)
Opioid intoxication with perceptual disturbance without use disorder	292.89 (F11.922)
Opioid withdrawal	292.0 (F11.23)
Unspecified opioid-related disorders	292.9 (F 11.99)

Sedative-, Hypnotic-, or Anxiolytic-Related Disorders

DSM Diagnosis	ICD-9-CM (ICD-10-CM)
Sedative, hypnotic, or anxiolytic use disorder, mild	305.40 (F13.10)
Sedative, hypnotic, or anxiolytic use disorder, moderate	304.10 (F13.20)
Sedative, hypnotic, or anxiolytic use disorder, severe	304.10 (F13.20)
Sedative, hypnotic, or anxiolytic intoxication with use disorder, mild	292.89 (F13.129)
Sedative, hypnotic, or anxiolytic intoxication with use disorder, moderate or severe	292.89 (F13.229)
Sedative, hypnotic, or anxiolytic intoxication without use disorder	292.89 (F13.929)
Sedative, hypnotic, or anxiolytic withdrawal without perceptual disturbance	292.0 (F13.239)
Sedative, hypnotic, or anxiolytic withdrawal with perceptual disturbance	292.0 (F13.232)
Unspecified sedative-, hypnotic-, or anxiolytic-related disorder	292.9 (F13.99)

Stimulant-Related Disorders

DSM Diagnosis	ICD-9-CM (ICD-10-CM)
Amphetamine-type substance use disorder, mild	305.70 (F15.10)
Amphetamine-type substance use disorder, moderate	304.40 (F15.20)
Amphetamine-type substance use disorder, severe	304.40 (F15.20)
Cocaine use disorder, mild	305.60 (F14.10)
Cocaine use disorder, moderate	304.20 (F14.20)
Cocaine use disorder, severe	304.20 (F14.20)
Other or unspecified stimulant use disorder, mild	305.70 (F15.10)
Other or unspecified stimulant use disorder, moderate	304.40 (F15.20)
Other or unspecified stimulant use disorder, severe	304.40 (F15.20)
Amphetamine or other stimulant intoxication without perceptual disturbance with use disorder, mild	292.89 (F15.129)
Amphetamine or other stimulant intoxication without perceptual disturbance with use disorder, moderate or severe	292.89 (F15.229)

Amphetamine or other stimulant intoxication without perceptual disturbance without use disorder	292.89 (F15.929)
Cocaine intoxication without perceptual disturbance with use disorder, mild	292.89 (F14.129)
Cocaine intoxication without perceptual disturbance with use disorder, moderate or severe	292.89 (F14.229)
Cocaine intoxication without perceptual disturbance without use disorder	292.89 (F14.929)
Amphetamine or other stimulant intoxication with perceptual disturbance with use disorder, mild	292.89 (F15.122)
Amphetamine or other stimulant intoxication with perceptual disturbance with use disorder, moderate or severe	292.89 (F15.222)
Amphetamine or other stimulant intoxication with perceptual disturbance without use disorder	292.89 (F15.922)
Cocaine intoxication with perceptual disturbance with use disorder, mild	292.89 (F14.122)
Cocaine intoxication with perceptual disturbance with use disorder, moderate or severe	292.89 (F14.222)
Cocaine intoxication with perceptual disturbance without use disorder	292.89 (F14.922)
Amphetamine or other stimulant withdrawal	292.0 (F15.23)
Cocaine withdrawal	292.0 (F14.23)
Unspecified amphetamine or other stimulant-related disorders	292.9 (F15.99)
Unspecified cocaine-related disorders	292.9 (F14.99)

Tobacco-Related Disorders

Specify if on maintenance therapy or in a controlled environment

DSM Diagnosis	ICD-9-CM (ICD-10-CM)
Tobacco use disorder, mild	305.1 (Z72.0)
Tobacco use disorder, moderate	305.1 (F17.200)
Tobacco use disorder, severe	305.1 (F17.200)
Tobacco withdrawal	292.0 (F17.203)
Unspecified tobacco-related disorder	292.9 (F17.209)

Other (or Unknown) Substance-Related Disorders

DSM Diagnosis	ICD-9-CM (ICD-10-CM)
Other (or unknown) substance use disorder, mild	305.90 (F19.10)
Other (or unknown) substance use disorder, moderate	304.90 (F19.20)
Other (or unknown) substance use disorder, severe	304.90 (F19.20)
Other (or unknown) substance intoxication with use disorder, mild	292.89 (F19.129)
Other (or unknown) substance intoxication with use disorder, moderate or severe	292.89 (F19.229)
Other (or unknown) substance intoxication without use disorder	292.89 (F19.929)
Other (or unknown) substance withdrawal	292.0 (F19.239)
Unspecified other (or unknown) substance-related disorder	292.9 (F19.99)

Implications for Counselors

The removal of the abuse and dependence categories allows counselors to assess severity on three levels, which lends to enhanced and tailored treatment options. The *mild* level of severity for substance use disorders (two to three criteria met) provides early intervention opportunities; individuals who present with *moderate* (four or five symptoms) or *severe* (six of more symptoms) substance use disorders may require more intensive treatments. In a study addressing the comparability of diagnoses between the *DSM-IV-TR* substance dependence and *DSM-5* substance use disorders, Compton et al. (2013) found excellent correspondence with alcohol, cocaine, cannabis, and opioid use disorders.

Initial substance use typically takes place during the mid-teens for most individuals, and conduct disorder is often comorbid with substance use disorders in adolescents (Crowley, 2007; Vandrey, Budney, Kamon, 8c Stanger, 2005). Considering the negative psychological, physiological, and environmental effects of substance-related disorders, it is critical to assess thoroughly and engage in treatment modalities early in the course of the disorder.

An important area for counselors to address in treatment is the lingering symptom of substance craving that can present a challenge for client relapse prevention. The desire and yearning for a specific substance or substances is a common symptom that can exist well beyond cessation of use (Sinha, 2013). Instillation of adaptive coping mechanisms and substitution of positive behaviors can be important elements of treatment in working with clients' residual craving. Mindfulness training has also been shown to be beneficial in treatment for substance-related disorders (Brewer, Elwafi, & Davis, 2013).

Specific Substance-Related Disorders Overview

The following sections provide brief descriptions and key elements of substance-related disorders outlined in the *DSM-5.* The manual also contains a section for other (or unknown) substance-related disorders that encompasses substances that fall outside of the specific types enumerated below.

Alcohol-Related Disorders

There is a high prevalence of alcohol use disorder in the United States, with approximately 12.4% of adult men and 4.9% of adult women afflicted (APA, 2013a). The highest prevalence is among Native Americans and Alaska Natives (12.1%) and the lowest is among Asian Americans and Pacific Islanders (4.5%). Age of onset peaks in the late teens, and most individuals who will develop alcohol use disorder do so by their late 30s (APA, 2013a).

Alcohol use and criminal activity are linked, with up to 40% of state prisoners reporting that they were under the influence of alcohol during commission of the crime for which they were incarcerated. Agrawal et al. (2012) found that genetic factors can contribute to alcohol craving, which makes certain individuals particularly vulnerable to alcohol use disorder since craving often exists after cessation of alcohol use (even after it is in sustained remission).

From an environmental standpoint, individuals living in cultures where alcohol availability and use are widespread are more prone to the development of the disorder. This is especially true if there are genetic predispositions to alcohol use disorder as is the case in almost 50% of individuals who develop the disorder. From a physiological standpoint, individuals with bipolar disorder, schizophrenia, and general impulsivity concerns have a heightened risk for alcohol-related disorders (APA, 2013a; Keyes et al., 2011).

Caffeine-Related Disorders

The *DSM-5* does not identify caffeine use disorder. Although evidence supports caffeine use as a condition, there is not yet sufficient information supporting impairment resulting from a problematic pattern of caffeine use. The United States has a high number of caffeine users – more than 85% of adults use caffeine regularly; among those, the average caffeine consumption is about 280 milligrams (two to three small cups of coffee) per day. Thus, caffeine use disorder is included in Section III of the manual as a condition for further study. The *DSM-5* includes caffeine intoxication and withdrawal as diagnosable disorders (APA, 2013a).

Caffeine withdrawal is a newly diagnosable condition and requires stopping caffeine use after prolonged daily consumption, with physical symptoms of headache, fatigue, dysphoric mood, difficulty concentrating, and possible flu-like symptoms that cause clinically significant distress. This is similar to withdrawal criteria for substance-related disorders listed in this chapter. It is interesting to note that excessive caffeine use is often seen in individuals with mental health disorders (e.g., eating disorders and other substance-related disorders) and incarcerated individuals (APA, 2013a). The growing popularity of energy drinks with high caffeine content poses a concern, especially because young people are frequent consumers of those beverages.

Cannabis-Related Disorders

Cannabis, or marijuana, has been known to be a "gateway" drug. According to the United Nations Office on Drugs and Crime (Leggett, 2006), cannabis is used more than any other illegal drug, with a definitive link found between cannabis use and mood disorders (Lynskey, Glowinski, & Todorov, 2004). Cannabis use is widespread in the United States, and the number of users is projected to increase over the next decade (Alexander & Leung, 2011).

Cannabis withdrawal is new to the *DSM-5* and includes physical symptoms arising after cessation of heavy use, which is defined as daily or almost daily use for a minimum of several months (APA, 2013a). Irritability, anger, aggression, nervousness, restlessness, and sleep disturbance are a few of the symptoms. The inclusion of cannabis withdrawal reflects the plethora of supportive empirical research (e.g., Budney, Hughes, Moore, & Vandrey, 2004; Budney, Moore, Vandrey, & Hughes, 2003; Crowley, 2007; Vandrey et al., 2005). Additionally, genetic factors can contribute to cannabis use and withdrawal, thus providing further rationale for their enumeration in the manual (Verweij et al., 2013).

Hallucinogen-Related Disorders

Hallucinogens are a heterogeneous grouping of substances that can have the same type of alterations of cognition and perception in users. These are most often taken orally, although some are smoked or injected. These types of drugs (e.g., ecstasy; lysergic acid diethylamide [LSD]; 3,4-methylenedioxy-methamphetamine [MDMA or ecstasy]; and psychedelic mushrooms) have a long half-life that can extend from hours to days. Hallucinogen use disorder has an annual prevalence rate of 0.1 % in adults, with men more likely than women to engage in use (APA, 2013a). Hallucinogens can have long-term effects on brain functioning. In diagnosing hallucinogen use disorder, counselors should identify the specific substance (e.g., "ecstasy use disorder" rather than the more general "hallucinogen use disorder"). Because withdrawal from hallucinogens has not been clearly documented, the withdrawal criterion is not present for hallucinogen use disorder (APA, 2013a; Kerridge et al., 2011).

Hallucinogens are sometimes used in religious practices (i.e., peyote in the Native American Church). Controlled use during religious observances is not to be considered a diagnosable condition. As with the diagnosis of any mental health disorder, cultural factors must be taken into account during assessment (Pettet, Lu, & Narrow, 2011).

Inhalant-Related Disorders

Inhalants such as glues, paints, fuels, and other "volatile hydrocarbons" are all included in this diagnostic classification. A small percentage (0.4%) of adolescents between the ages of 12 and 17 meet the criteria for inhalant use disorder, although usage rates for young people may be as high as 10% (Dinwiddie, 1994). This disorder is typically not seen in older children or adults (APA, 2013a).

Kerridge et al. (2011) used data from the National Epidemiological Survey on Alcohol and Related Conditions to assess fit for the unidimensional model of substance use disorders for inhalants. Their study found support for the *DSM-5* elimination of abuse and dependence for inhalants. Because of a dearth of documented physiological and psychological effects related to cessation of use, inhalant withdrawal is not included in the manual (APA, 2013a).

Inhalant use is quite dangerous and can be fatal. It is important for counselors to effectively identify inhalant-related disorders, especially counselors specializing in adolescent treatment. Counselors should be very concerned about reports of inhalant use. Even reports of "experimentation" can be fatal, as 22% of inhalant abusers who died of sudden sniffing death syndrome (i.e., cardiac arrest) were first-time users (J. E Williams & Storck, 2007). This problem afflicts children from all socioeconomic backgrounds and from families with both high and low levels of parental education.

Opioid-Related Disorders

Opioid use has multiple deleterious physical effects. Because opioids are frequently injected, there are many risks for infection and disease. Common opioids include morphine, oxycodone, and heroin (APA, 2013a). Counselors must be aware of the risks of needle sharing, which puts opioid users at higher risk for HIV, hepatitis, and tuberculosis. There is a heightened suicide risk and high mortality rate for opioid users (up to 2% yearly). Jim Morrison, Janis Joplin, John Belushi, Chris Farley, River Phoenix, Heath Ledger, and, most recently, Corey Monteith were all young, famous people who died from opioid overdoses. Even prescribed opioid use can be a problem; from 1999 to 2007, the rate of fatal prescription opioid overdoses in the United States increased by 124% (Bohnert et al., 2011).

Opioid use disorder typically develops in early adulthood and spans many years. Rates of opioid use are higher in males than females (APA, 2013a). Problems first occur in adolescence and early adulthood. Opioid use disorder is seen across ethnicities; tolerance and withdrawal are commonly evident criteria. Babies born to mothers who have used opioids during their pregnancy can be born physiologically dependent (APA, 2013a). The severity of negative health effects underscores the need for early and effective interventions for opioid users.

Sedative, Hypnotic, or Anxiolytic-Related Disorders

This class of substances includes all prescription sleeping medications and almost all anxiety medications. One great danger is the swift build-up of tolerance and withdrawal for these substances, often resulting in craving. Individuals in adolescence and early adulthood are at the highest prevalence for the disorder and often engage in concomitant use of other substances (APA, 2013a).

If sedatives, hypnotics, or anxiolytics are prescribed for specific medical purposes and the medication is taken as prescribed, an individual would not meet diagnostic criteria for the use disorder. Sometimes, individuals who receive a prescription will build tolerance and seek out additional access through use of multiple physicians; thus, counselors should be careful to assess for patterns of use even for clients who report accessing substances through medical providers. Sedative, hypnotic, or anxiolytic-related disorders are often comorbid with alcohol and tobacco use disorders, personality disorders, depressive disorders, anxiety disorders, and bipolar disorders (APA, 2013a).

Stimulant-Related Disorders

Substances included in this section include, but are not limited to, amphetamine, dextroamphetamine, methamphetamine, and cocaine. Stimulants can be taken orally, injected, or smoked and typically result in drastic changes in behavior and a concomitant feeling of subjective well-being. Violent and aggressive behavior occurs with stimulant use and can lead to interpersonal and legal difficulties. Withdrawal can cause significant depressive symptoms as well as medical conditions. Examples include cardiac difficulties, seizures, neurocognitive impairment, and respiratory problems, just to name a few. Stimulant-related disorders are likely to co-occur with other substance-related disorders and gambling disorder. It is notable that amphetamines are sometimes medically prescribed to treat ADHD, obesity, and narcolepsy (APA, 2013a).

There has been research supporting a higher diagnostic inclusion of individuals with stimulant-related disorders based on the revised diagnostic spectrum. This can help accurately identify those individuals in need of treatment for stimulant use disorders. Specifically, Proctor, Kopak, and Hoffmann (2012) found that the new criteria assist with inclusivity in meeting the needs of those with cocaine-related disorders.

Tobacco-Related Disorders

Approximately one in five adolescents in the United States will use tobacco on a regular basis; most individuals will develop tobacco use disorder prior to the age of 21. Many tobacco users attempt to quit, with most making multiple attempts before successfully stopping usage (APA, 2013a). Tobacco is linked to a plethora of physical health problems and accounts for approximately one in every five deaths in the United States. Tobacco smokers have a life-span projection that is about 10 years shorter than nonsmokers (CDC, 2008).

Tobacco intoxication is not included in the *DSM-5*. Tobacco withdrawal is a new diagnosis in *DSM-5* and involves symptoms of irritability, anxiety, difficulty concentrating, increased appetite, restlessness, depressed mood, and insomnia. There is a significant comorbidity (22% to 32%) of alcohol, anxiety, depressive, bipolar, and personality disorders (APA, 2013a).

Tobacco use has declined in the United States since the 1960s, in part from heightened awareness of the health risks and restrictions on smoking accessibility. However, the African American and Hispanic populations have seen less of a decline. Those from lower socioeconomic backgrounds are more likely to begin smoking tobacco and less likely to quit successfully (APA, 2013a; CDC, 2008).

Some Additional Considerations

In addition to the general symptoms, there are other physical signs and symptoms of substance use issues that are related to specific drug categories. You may wish to explore these areas when making an assessment:

- Signs and symptoms of alcohol intoxication are well-known; these include such physical signs as slurred speech, lack of coordination, unsteady gait, memory impairment, and stupor, as well as behavior changes manifesting themselves shortly after alcohol ingestion, including inappropriate aggressive behavior, mood volatility, and impaired functioning.
- Amphetamine users may exhibit rapid heartbeat, elevated or depressed blood pressure, dilated (enlarged) pupils, weight loss, as well as excessively high energy, inability to sleep, confusion, and occasional paranoid psychotic behavior.

- Cannabis users may exhibit red eyes with dilated pupils, increased appetite, dry mouth, and rapid pulse; they may also be sluggish and slow to react.
- Cocaine users may exhibit rapid heart rate, elevated or depressed blood pressure, dilated pupils, weight loss, in addition to wide variations in their energy-level, severe mood disturbances, psychosis , and paranoia .
- Users of hallucinogens may exhibit anxiety or depression, paranoia, and unusual behavior in response to hallucinations (imagined sights, voices, sounds, or smells that appear real). Signs include dilated pupils, rapid heart rate, tremors, lack of coordination, and sweating. Flashbacks, or the re-experiencing of a hallucination long after stopping substance use, are also a symptom of hallucinogen use.
- Users of inhalants experience dizziness, spastic eye movements, lack of coordination, slurred speech, and slowed reflexes. Associated behaviors may include belligerence, predisposition to violence, apathy, and impaired judgment.
- Opioid drug users exhibit slurred speech, drowsiness, impaired memory, and constricted (small) pupils. They may appear slowed in their physical movements.
- Phencyclidine users exhibit spastic eye movements, rapid heartbeat, decreased sensitivity to pain, and lack of muscular coordination. They may show belligerence, predisposition to violence, impulsiveness, and agitation.
- Users of sedative, hypnotic, or anxiolytic drugs show slurred speech, unsteady gait, inattentiveness, and impaired memory. They may display inappropriate behavior, mood volatility, and impaired functioning.

Other signs are related to the form in which the substance is used. For example, heroin, certain other opioid drugs, and certain forms of cocaine may be injected. A person using an injectable substance may have "track marks" (outwardly visible signs of the site of an injection, with possible redness and swelling of the vein in which the substance was injected). Furthermore, poor judgment brought on by substance use can result in the injections being made under dangerously unhygienic conditions. These unsanitary conditions and the use of shared needles are risk factors for major infections of the heart, as well as infection with HIV (the virus that causes AIDS), certain forms of hepatitis (a liver infection), and tuberculosis .

Cocaine is often taken as a powdery substance which is "snorted" through the nose. This can result in frequent nosebleeds, sores in the nose, and even erosion (an eating away) of the nasal septum (the structure that separates the two nostrils).

Overdosing on a substance is a frequent complication of substance use. Drug overdose can be purposeful (with suicide as a goal), or due to carelessness, the unpredictable strength of substances purchased from street dealers, mixing of more than one type of substance, or as a result of the increasing doses that a person must take to experience intoxicating effects. Substance overdose can be a life-threatening emergency, with the specific symptoms depending on the type of substance used. Substances with depressive effects may dangerously slow the breathing and heart rate, drops the body temperature, and result in a general unresponsiveness. Substances with stimulatory effects may dangerously increase the heart rate and blood pressure, produce abnormal heart rhythms, increase body temperature, induce seizures, and cause erratic behavior.

A FINAL WORD

Regardless of your thoughts or feelings about using DSM guidelines, or about the changes made in the latest revision, knowing how to use these diagnostic standards is important for all drug/alcohol professionals. There is a wealth of information to be found on a great number of areas that overlap the work performed by substance abuse professionals. Counselors are encouraged (at a minimum) to obtain a copy of the *DSM-5* and to become familiar with it. If possible, consider taking a class that covers the entire *DSM-5* manual – it will be well worth your time.

References - Section 3

Section 3, Chapter 1

Bandura, A. Principles of Behavior Modification. Holt, Rinehart, and Wintson. New York. 1969.

Belkin, G. Introduction to Counseling, 3rd edition. William C. Brown. Dubuque, IA. 1988.

Berne, E. Games People Play. Grove Press. New York, NY. 1964.

Corey, Gerald. Theory and Practice of Counseling and Psychotherapy, 6th Edition. Brooks/Cole Publishing Company, Monterey, CA. 2000.

Glasser, W. Reality Therapy: A New Approach to Psychiatry. Harper and Row. New York, NY. 1965.

Harris, T. I'm O.K., You're O.K. Avon Books. New York, NY. 1969.

Kahn, M. Basic Methods for Mental Health Practitioners. Winthrop Press. Cambridge, MA. 1981.

Marley, P. Positive and negative reinforcement. Unpublished, 2002.

Maslow, A. Toward a Psychology of Being. Van Nostrand Reinhold. New York, NY. 1954.

Patterson, C.H. Theories of Counseling and Psychotherapy. Harper and Row. New York, NY. 1980.

Perls, F. Gestalt Therapy Verbatim. Real People Press. Lafayette, CA. 1969.

Rogers, C. On Becoming a Person. Houghton Mifflin. Boston, M.A. 1961.

Skinner, B.F. About Behaviorism. Vintage. New York, NY. 1974, 1976.

Section 3, Chapter 2

American Psychiatric Association. *Diagnostic and Statistical Manual of Mental Disorders,* Fourth Edition (DSM-IV). Washington, DC: American Psychiatric Association, 1994.

Bean, F.D.; Trejo, S.J.; Crapps, R.; and Tyler, M. *The Latino Middle Class: Myth, Reality, and Potential.* Los Angeles, CA: Tomás Rivera Policy Institute, 2001.

Brisbane, F.L. Introduction: Diversity among African Americans. In: Center for Substance Abuse Prevention (CSAP). *Cultural Competence for Health Care Professionals Working With African-American Communities: Theory and Practice.* CSAP Cultural Competence Series 7. DHHS Publication No. (SMA) 98–3238. Rockville, MD: Substance Abuse and Mental Health Services Administration, 1998, pp. 1–8.

Center for Substance Abuse Prevention. *Substance Abuse Resource Guide: Asian and Pacific Islander Americans.* Rockville, MD: Substance Abuse and Mental Health Services Administration, 1996*a.* ncadi.samhsa/gov/govpubs/MS408 [accessed March 4, 2004].

Center for Substance Abuse Prevention. *Substance Abuse Resource Guide: Hispanic/Latino Americans.* Rockville, MD: Substance Abuse and Mental Health Services Administration, 1996*b.* www.ncadi.samhsa.gov/govpubs/MS441 [accessed March 4, 2004].

Centers for Disease Control and Prevention *HIV/AIDS Surveillance Report* 16:1–46, 2004.

Cross, TL.; Bazron, B.J.; Dennis, K.R.; and Isaacs, M.R. *Towards a Culturally Competent System of Care,* Vol. 1. Washington, DC: Georgetown University Child Development Center, National Technical Assistance Center for Children's Mental Health, 1989.

CSAT (Center for Substance Abuse Treatment). *A Provider's Introduction to Substance Abuse Treatment for Lesbian, Gay, Bisexual, and Transgender Individuals.* DHHS Publication No. (SMA) 01–3498. Rockville, MD: Substance Abuse and Mental Health Services Administration, 2001.

Fears, D. A Diverse — and Divided — Black Community. *Washington Post,* February 24, 2002, pp. A1, A8.

Gfroerer J, Penne M, Pemberton M, Folsom R. Substance abuse treatment need among older adults in 2020: The impact of the aging baby-boom cohort. *Drug and Alcohol Dependence.* 69((2)):127-135; 2003. (PubMed)

Greenwood G.L, White E.W, Page-Shafer K, Bein E, Osmond D.H, Paul J, Stall R.D. Correlates of heavy substance use among young gay and bisexual men: The San Francisco Young Men's Health Study. *Drug and Alcohol Dependence.* 61((2)):105-112; 2001. (PubMed)

Hubbard J.R, Everett A.S, Khan M.A. Alcohol and drug abuse in patients with physical disabilities. *American Journal of Drug Abuse.* 22((2)):215-231; 1996.

Jezewski, M.A., and Sotnik, P. *Culture Brokering: Providing Culturally Competent Rehabilitation Services to Foreign-Born Persons.* Buffalo, NY: Center for International Rehabilitation Research Information and Exchange, 2001.www.cirrie.buffalo.edu/cbrokering.html [accessed February 11, 2004].

Joyner L.M, Wright J.D, Devine J.A. Reliabilit and validity of the Addiction Severity Index among homeless substance misusers. *Substance Use & Misuse.* 31((6)):729-751; 1996. (PubMed)

Korper, S.P., and Council, C.L., eds. *Substance Use by Older Adults: Estimates of Future Impact on the Treatment System.* Analytic Series A-21. DHHS Publication No. (SMA) 03–3763. Rockville, MD: Office of Applied Studies, Substance Abuse and Mental Health Services Administration, 2002.

LaPlante, M.P.; Kennedy, J.; Kaye, H.S.; and Wenger, B.L. Disability and employment. *Disability Statistics Abstract.* Number 11. San Francisco: Disability Statistics Center, 1996.www.dsc.ucsf.edu/pdf/abstract11.pdf [accessed February 11, 2004].

La Veist, T.A.; Diala, C.; and Jarrett, N.C. Social status and perceived discrimination: Who experiences discrimination in the health care system, how, and why? In: Hogue, C.J.R.; Hargraves, M.A.; and Collins, K.S., eds. *Minority Health in America.* Baltimore: Johns Hopkins University Press, 2000, pp. 194–208.

Magura S, Nwakeze P.C, Rosenblum A, Joseph H. Substance misuse and related infectious diseases in a soup kitchen population. *Substance Use & Misuse.* 35((4)):551-583; 2000. (PubMed)

McKinnon, J. The Black population in the United States: March 2002. *Current Population Reports.* P20–541. Washington, DC: U.S. Census Bureau, 2003.

Metsch L.R, McCoy C.B. Drug treatment experiences: Rural and urban comparisons. *Substance Use & Misuse.* 34((4&5)):763-784; 1999. (PubMed)

Milby J.B, Schumacher J.E, Raczynski J.M, Caldwell E, Engle M, Michael M, Carr J. Sufficient conditions for effective treatment of substance abusing homeless persons. *Drug and Alcohol Dependence.* 43:39-47; 1996. (PubMed)

Moore D, Li L. Prevalence and risk factors of illicit drug use by people with disabilities. *American Journal on Addictions.* 7((2)):93-102; 1998. (PubMed)

Mulvey KP, Hubbard S, Hayashi S. A National Study of the Substance Abuse Treatment Workforce. *Journal of Substance Abuse Treatment.* 24:51-57; 2003. (PubMed)

Office of Applied Studies. *Summary of Findings From the 2000 National Household Survey on Drug Abuse.* NHSDA Series H–13. DHHS Publication No. (SMA) 01–3549. Rockville, MD: Substance Abuse and Mental Health Services Administration, 2001.http://oas.samhsa.gov/NHSDA/2kNHSDA/2kNHSDA.htm [accessed February 11, 2004].

Office of Applied Studies. *Treatment Episode Data Set (TEDS): 1992–2000, National Admissions to Substance Abuse Treatment Services.* DASIS Series: S-17, DHHS Publication No. (SMA) 02–3727. Rockville, MD: Substance Abuse and Mental Health Services Administration, 2002.wwwdasis.samhsa.gov/teds00/TEDS_2k_index.htm [accessed February 11, 2004].

Office of Applied Studies, Substance Abuse and Mental Health Services Administration (SAMHSA). *Treatment Episode Data Set (TEDS): 1992–2001. National Admissions to Substance Abuse Treatment Services.* DASIS Series S-12. DHHS Publication No. (SMA) 02-3778. Rockville, MD: SAMHSA, 2003*b.* wwwdasis.samhsa.gov/teds01/TEDS2K1Index.htm [accessed March 19, 2004].

Office of Applied Studies. *The DASIS Report: Characteristics of Homeless Admissions to Substance Abuse Treatment, 2000.* Rockville, MD: Substance Abuse and Mental Health Services Administration, August 8, 2003*b.*http://www.oas.samhsa.gov/2k3/homelessTX/homelessTX.htm [accessed February 11, 2004].

Ogunwole, S.U. The American Indian and Alaska Native population: 2000. *Census 2000 Brief.* C2KBR/01–15. Washington, DC: U.S. Census Bureau, 2002.

Oslin D.W, Pettinati H, Volpicelli J.R. Older age predicts better adherence and drinking outcomes. *American Journal of Geriatric Psychiatry.* 10:740-747; 2002. (PubMed)

Perry, M.J., and Mackun, P.J. Population change and distribution: 1990 to 2000. Census 2000 Brief. C2KBR/01-2. Washington, DC: U.S. Census Bureau, 2001.

Ramirez, R.R., and de la Cruz, G.P. The Hispanic population in the United States: March 2002. *Current Population Reports,* P20–545. Washington, DC: U.S. Census Bureau, 2003.

Schmidley, D. The foreign-born population in the United States: March 2002. *Current Population Reports,* P20–539. Washington, DC: U.S. Census Bureau, 2003.

Schumacher J.E, Milby J.B, Caldwell E, Raczynski J, Engle M, Michael M, Carr J. Treatment outcome as a function of treatment attendance with homeless persons abusing cocaine. *Journal of Addictive Diseases.* 14((4)):73-85; 1995. (PubMed)

Spicer P, Beals J, Croy C.D, Mitchell C.M, Novins D.K, Moore L, Manson S.M, the American Indian Service Utilization, Psychiatric Epidemiology, Risk and Protective Factors Project Team.. The prevalence of DSM-III-R alcohol dependence in two American Indian populations. *Alcoholism, Clinical and Experimental Research.* 27((11)):1785-1797; 2003.

Tonigan J.S. Project MATCH treatment participation and outcome by self-reported ethnicity. *Alcoholism, Clinical and Experimental Research.* 27((8)):1340-1344; 2003.

Urban Institute; Burt, M.R.; Aron, L.Y.; Douglas, T.; Valente, J.; Lee, E.; and Iwen, B. Homelessness: Programs and the People They Serve — Findings of the National Survey of Homeless Assistance Providers and Clients, Technical Report. Washington, DC: Interagency Council on the Homeless, 1999. www.huduser.org/publications/homeless/homeless_tech.html [accessed February 11, 2004].

U.S. Department of Health and Human Services. *Mental Health: Culture, Race, and Ethnicity — A Supplement to Mental Health: A Report of the Surgeon General.* Rockville, MD: Center for Mental Health Services, Substance Abuse and Mental Health Services Administration, 2001.www.mentalhealth.org/cre/default.asp [accessed February 11, 2004].

Wells K, Klap R, Koike A, Sherbourne C. Ethnic disparities in unmet need for alcoholism drug abuse and mental health care. *American Journal of Psychiatry.* 158:2027-2032; 2001. (PubMed)

Woody G.E, Donnell D, Seage G.R, Metzger D, Marmor M, Koblin B.A, Buchbinder S, Gross M, Stone B, Judson F.N. Non-injection substance use correlates with risky sex among men having sex with men: Data from HIVNET. *Drug and Alcohol Dependence.* 53((3)):197-205; 1999. (PubMed)

Section 3, Chapter 3

Allen, J.P., and Wilson, V.B. *Assessing Alcohol Problems: A Guide for Clinicians and Researchers,* 2d ed. Bethesda, MD: National Institute on Alcohol Abuse and Alcoholism, 2003.

American Psychiatric Association. *Diagnostic and Statistical Manual of Mental Disorders.* 4th ed. Washington, DC: American Psychiatric Association, 1994.

American Psychiatric Association. *Diagnostic and Statistical Manual of Mental Disorders* . 4th Text Revision ed. Washington, DC: American Psychiatric Association, 2000.

American Society of Addiction Medicine. *Patient Placement Criteria for the Treatment of Substance-Related Disorders: ASAM PPC-2R* . 2d Revised ed. Chevy Chase, MD: American Society of Addiction Medicine, 2001.

Anderson, A.J. Therapeutic program models for mentally ill chemical abusers. *International Journal of Psychosocial Rehabilitation* 1(1):21 –33, 1997. www.psychosocial.com/dualdx/rehabpub.html [Accessed March 18, 2002].

Baker, F. *Coordination of Alcohol, Drug Abuse, and Mental Health Services* . Technical Assistance Publication (TAP) Series 4. DHHS Publication No. (SMA) 00-3360. Rockville, MD: Center for Substance Abuse Treatment, 1991.

Carroll JFX, McGinley JJ. A screening form for identifying mental health problems in alcohol/other drug dependent persons. Alcoholism Treatment Quarterly 19(4):33-47. 2001.

Castro, F.G., Proescholdbell, R.J., Abeita, L., and Rodriguez, D. Ethnic and cultural minority groups. In: McCrady, B.S., and Epstein, E.E., eds. *Addiction: A Comprehensive Guidebook* . Oxford University Press, 1999. pp. 499 –526.

Center for Mental Health Services. *Co-Occurring Psychiatric and Substance Disorders in Managed Care Systems: Standards of Care, Practice Guidelines, Workforce Competencies, and Training Curricula* . 1998. www.med.upenn.edu/cmhpsr/pdf/cooccurringfinal.pdf [Accessed February 8, 2001].

Center for Substance Abuse Treatment. Treatment Improvement Protocol (TIP) #9 – *Assessment and Treatment of Patients with Coexisting Mental Illness and Alcohol and Other Drug Abuse* [DHHS Publication No. (SMA) 95-3061. Washington, D.C. 1995.

Center for Substance Abuse Treatment. *Substance Abuse Treatment for Persons With Co-Occurring Disorders.* Treatment Improvement Protocol (TIP) Series 42. DHHS Publication No. (SMA) 05-3922. Rockville, MD: Substance Abuse and Mental Health Services Administration, 2005.

Coffey, R., Graver, L., Schroeder, D., Busch, J., Dilonardo, J., Chalk, M., and Buck, J. *Mental Health and Substance Abuse Treatment: Results from a Study Integrating Data from State Mental Health, Substance Abuse, and Medicaid Agencies* . DHHS Publication No. (SMA) 01-3528. Rockville, MD: Substance Abuse and Mental Health Services Administration, 2001.

Crome IB. Substance misuse and psychiatric comorbidity: Towards improved service provision. Drugs: Education, Prevention & Policy 6(2):151-174. 1999.

De Leon G. Psychopathology and substance abuse: What is being learned from research in therapeutic communities. Journal of Psychoactive Drugs 21(2):177-188. 1989. (PubMed)

De Leon G. Integrative recovery: A stage paradigm. Substance Abuse 17(1):51-63. 1996.

Drake RE, Mercer-McFadden C, Mueser KT, McHugo GJ, Bond GR. Review of integrated mental health and substance abuse treatment for patients with dual disorders. Schizophrenia Bulletin 24(4):589-608. 1998b. (PubMed)

Evans, K., and Sullivan, J.M. *Dual Diagnosis: Counseling the Mentally Ill Substance Abuser*. 2d ed. New York: Guilford Press, 2001.

Flynn PM, Craddock SG, Hubbard RL, Anderson J, Etheridge RM. Methodological overview and research design for the drug abuse treatment outcome study (DATOS). Psychology of Addictive Behaviors 11(4):230-243. 1997.

Gustafson, J.S., Anderson, R., Sheehan, K., McGencey, S., Reda, J., O'Donnell, C., Strohl, J.B., Moghul, A., Clemmey, P., and Spencer, J. *State Resources and Services Related to Alcohol and Other Drug Problems: Fiscal Years 1996 and 1997.* Washington, DC: National Association of State Alcohol and Drug Abuse Directors, 1999.

Hanson, G., Venturelli, P., and Fleckenstein, A. *Drugs and Society*, Eighth Edition. Jones and Bartlett Publishers, Boston, MA. 2004.

Hubbard, R.L., Marsden, M.E., Rachal, J.V., Harwood, H.J., Cavanaugh, E.R., and Ginzburg, H.M. *Drug Abuse Treatment: A National Study of Effectiveness*. Chapel Hill, NC: University of North Carolina Press, 1989.

Hser Y, Grella C, Hubbard RL, Hsieh S, Fletcher BW, Brown BS, Anglin MD. An evaluation of drug treatment for adolescents in 4 US cities. Archives of General Psychiatry 58:689-695. 2001. (PubMed)

Joe GW, Brown BS, Simpson D. Psychological problems and client engagement in methadone treatment. Journal of Nervous and Mental Disease 183(11):704-710. 1995.

Karageorge, K. *Treatment Benefits the Mental Health of Adolescents, Young Adults, and Adults.* NEDS Fact Sheet 78. Fairfax, VA: National Evaluation Data Services, 2001.

McConnaughy EA, Prochaska J, Velicer WF. Stages of change in psychotherapy: Measurement and sample profiles. Psychotherapy: Theory, Research, and Practice 20(3):368-375. 1983.

McCorkle R, Young K. Development of a symptom distress scale. Cancer Nursing 1(5):373-378. 1978. (PubMed)

McLellan AT, Kushner H, Metzger D, Peters R, Smith I, Grissom G, Pettnati H, Argeriou M. The fifth edition of the Addiction Severity Index. Journal of Substance Abuse Treatment 9(3):199-213. 1992.

Menezes PR, Johnson S, Thornicroft G, Marshall J, Prosser D, Bebbington P, Kuipers E. Drug and alcohol problems among individuals with severe mental illness in south London. British Journal of Psychiatry 168(5):612-619. 1996.

Miller, N.S. Medications used with the dually diagnosed. In: Miller, N.S., ed. *Treating Coexisting Psychiatric and Addictive Disorders: A Practical Guide.* Center City, MN: Hazelden, 1994 *a*, pp. 143 –160.

Minkoff K. An integrated treatment model for dual diagnosis of psychosis and addiction. Hospital and Community Psychiatry 40(10):1031-1036. 1989.

Minkoff K. Developing standards of care for individuals with co-occurring psychiatric and substance use disorders. Psychiatric Services 52(5):597-599. 2001a.

National Advisory Council, Substance Abuse and Mental Health Services Administration. *Improving Services for Individuals at Risk of, or with, Co-Occurring Substance-Related and Mental Health Disorders* . Rockville, MD: Substance Abuse and Mental Health Services Administration, 1997. www.toad.net/~arcturus/dd/peppdown.htm [Accessed December 27, 2000].

National Association of State Mental Health Program Directors and National Association of State Alcohol and Drug Abuse Directors. *National Dialogue on Co-Occurring Mental Health and Substance Abuse Disorders.* Washington, DC: National Association of State Alcohol and Drug Abuse Directors, 1999. www.nasadad.org/Departments/Research/ConsensusFramework/national_dialogue_on.htm [Accessed December 27, 2000].

National Association of State Mental Health Program Directors and National Association of State Alcohol and Drug Abuse Directors. *Financing and Marketing the New Conceptual Framework for Co-Occurring Mental Health and Substance Abuse Disorders: A Blueprint for Systems Change* . Alexandria, VA: National Association of State Mental Health Program Directors and National Association of State Alcohol and Drug Abuse Directors, 2000.

Office of the Surgeon General. *Mental Health: A Report of the Surgeon General* . Rockville, MD: U.S. Public Health Service, 1999. www.surgeongeneral.gov/library/mentalhealth/home.html [Accessed March 18, 2002].

Onken, L.S., Blaine, J., Genser, S., and Horton, A.M., eds. *Treatment of Drug-Dependent Individuals with Comorbid Mental Disorders* . NIDA Research Monograph 172. NIH Publication No. 97-4172. Rockville, MD: National Institute on Drug Abuse, 1997.

Osher FC, Drake RE. Reversing a history of unmet needs: Approaches to care for persons with co-occurring addictive and mental disorders. American Journal of Orthopsychiatry 66(1):4-11. 1996.

Pepper B, Kirshner MC, Ryglewicz H. The young adult chronic patient: Overview of a population. Hospital and Community Psychiatry 32(7):463-469. 1981.

Pepper, B., and Massaro, J. *Substance Abuse and Mental/Emotional Disorders: Counselor Training Manual* . New York: The Information Exchange, 1995.

Ries RK. The dually diagnosed patient with psychotic symptoms. Journal of Addictive Diseases 12(3):103-122. 1993.

Rosenthal RJ, Lesieur HR. Self-reported withdrawal symptoms and pathological gambling. American Journal on Addictions 1:150-154. 1992.

Rounsaville BJ, Weissman MM, Kleber H, Wilber C. Heterogeneity of psychiatric diagnosis in treated opiate addicts. Archives of General Psychiatry 39(2):161-168. 1982b. (PubMed)

Sacks S, Sacks J, De Leon G, Bernhardt AI, Staines GL. Modified therapeutic community for mentally ill chemical "abusers": Background; influences; program description; preliminary findings. Substance Use and Misuse 32(9):1217-1259. 1997b.

Schorske B, Bedard K. One State's role in building a continuum of care for severe mental illness and chemical dependency. Community Support Network News 6(2):10. 1989.

Sciacca K. Integrated treatment approach for severely mentally ill individuals with substance disorders. New Directions for Mental Health Services 50:69-84. 1991. (PubMed)

Simpson DD, Joe GW, Broome KM. A national 5-year follow-up of treatment outcomes for cocaine dependence. Archives of General Psychiatry 59:538-544. 2002. (PubMed)

Steadman H, Mulvey E, Monahan J, Robbins P, Appelbaum P, Grisso T, Roth L, Silver E. Violence by people discharged from acute psychiatric inpatient facilities and by others in the same neighborhoods. Archives of General Psychiatry 55:393-401. 1998. (PubMed)

Woody, G.E., and Blaine, J. Depression in narcotic addicts: Quite possibly more than a chance association. In: Dupont, R., Goldstein, A., and O'Donnell, J., eds. *Handbook of Drug Abuse* . Rockville, MD: National Institute on Drug Abuse, 1979. pp. 277 –285.

Woody, G.E., McLellan, A.T., O'Brien, C.P., and Luborsky, L. Addressing psychiatric co-morbidity. In: Pickens, R.W., Leukefeld, C.G., and Schuster, C.R., eds. *Improving Drug Abuse Treatment* . NIDA Research Monograph 106. Rockville, MD: National Institute on Drug Abuse, 1991. pp. 152 –166.

Section 3, Chapter 4

American Society of Addiction Medicine (ASAM). Guidelines for HIV Infection and AIDS in Addiction Treatment. ASAM. Chevy Chase, MD. 1998.

Centers for Disease Control and Prevention (CDC). HIV and AIDS - United States, 1981-2001. *MMWR* 2001;50:430-434. http://www.cdc.gov/mmwr/PDF/wk/mm5021.pdf

Centers for Disease Control and Prevention (CDC). HIV Prevention Strategic Plan Through 2005. January 2001. http://www.cdc.gov/nchstp/od/hiv_plan/default.htm

Centers for Disease Control and Prevention (CDC). HIV/AIDS Surveillance Report 2002;14:1-40. http://www.cdc.gov/hiv/stats/hasr1402.htm

Centers for Disease Control and Prevention. Revised Guidelines for HIV Counseling, Testing, and Referral. *MMWR,*2001. 47(RR-195):1-5841.

Centers for Disease Control and Prevention. Young people at risk--epidemic shifts further toward young women and minorities. 1999

Center for Substance Abuse Treatment. Substance Abuse Treatment for Persons with HIV/AIDS. Treatment Improvement Protocol (TIP) Series, Number 379. DHHS Pub. No. (SMA) 0094-34102078. U.S. Government Printing Office. Washington, DC. 2000.

Center for Substance Abuse Treatment. . Treatment for HIV-Infected Alcohol and Other Drug Abusers Treatment Improvement Protocol (TIP) Series, Number 15. DHHS Pub. No. (SMA) 95-3038. U.S. Government Printing Office. Washington, DC.

Center for Substance Abuse Treatment. . Gay, Lesbian, Bisexual, and Transgender Populations Technical Assistance Publication (TAP) Series. U.S. Government Printing Office, in press (b). Washington, DC. 2000

Fleming, P.L. et al. HIV Prevalence in the United States, 2000. 9th Conference on Retroviruses and Opportunistic Infections, Seattle, Wash., Feb. 24-28, 2002. Abstract 11. http://63.126.3.84/2002/Abstract/13996.htm

UNAIDS. 2004 Report on the Global AIDS Epidemic, July, 2004. http://www.unaids.org/bangkok2004/report.html

U.S. Department of Health and Human Services. 2001 USPHS/IDSA guidelines for the prevention of opportunistic infections in persons infected with human immunodeficiency virus. Rockville, MD: HIV/AIDS Treatment Information Service. Available at http://aidsinfo.nih.gov/guidelines.

U.S. Department of Health and Human Services. *Incorporating HIV Prevention into the Medical Care of Persons Living with HIV* (available at **http://aidsinfo.nih.gov**).

U.S. Food and Drug Administration. *Drugs Used in the Treatment of HIV Infection.* (available at: http://www.fda.gov/oashi/aids/virals.html) 2004.

Vittinghoff, E.; Scheer, S.; O'Malley, P.; Colfax, G.; Holmberg, S.D.; and Buchbinder, S.P. . Combination antiretroviral therapy and recent declines in AIDS incidence and mortality. *Journal of Infectious Diseases* 179(3):717-720, : 1999.

World Health Organization. HIV: A Review of HIV Transmission Throughout the World. Joint United Nations Programme on HIV/AIDS (UNAIDS) 2002.

Section 3, Chapter 5

Alcohol & Drug Abuse Counselor Home Study Course, 7th Series Edition. The Association for Advanced Training in the Behavioral Sciences. 1993.

Bissell, L., M.D., C.A.C., Royce, J., Ph.D. "Ethics for Addiction Professionals." Hazelden Educational Publishing Services. Center City, MN. 1989.

Corey, G. "Theory and Practice of Counseling and Psychotherapy," 4th Edition. Corey. Brooks/Cole Publishing Company, Monterey, CA. 1991.

Crowe, A.H., M.S.S.W., A.C.S.W., & Reeves, R., M.A. "Treatment for Alcohol and Other Drug Abuse: Opportunities for Coordination." DHHS Publication No. (SMA) 94-2075, Rockville, MD. 1994.

Corey, G., Corey, M.S., & Callanon, P. "Issues and Ethics in the Helping Professions." Brooks/Cole Publishing, Monterey, CA. 2002.

Duffay, K., ed. Personal Growth & Behavior. Duskin Publishing Groups, Inc., Guilford, CT. 1988.

Edelwich, J. with Brodsky, A. Burnout: Stages of Disillusionment in the Helping Profession. Human Sciences Press, New York, NY. 1980.

Girdano, D. & Everly, G. Controlling Stress and Tension A Holistic Approach. Prentice Hall, Englewood Cliffs, NJ. 1979.

Kahn, M. Basic Methods for Mental Health Practitioners. Winthrop, Cambridge, MA. 1981.

Legal Action Center. Confidentiality: A guide to the federal laws and regulations. New York: 1991

Okun, B. "Effective Helping: Interviewing and Counseling Techniques." Duxbury Press., North Scituate, MA. 1976.

O'Toole, P. "Access and equality: The Americans with Disabilities Act." The Counselor, 29-31, November/ December,1992.

Peterson, J.,& Nisenholz, B. "Orientation to Counseling." Allyn and Bacon, Boston, MA. 1987.

Powell, D., Ph.D. "Clinical Supervision: Trainee's Workbook." Human Sciences Press, New York, NY. 1980.

Powell D., Ph.D. "Clinical Supervision: Skills for Substance Abuse Counselors." Human Sciences Press, New York, NY. 1980.

Selye, H. "The Stress of Life." McGraw /Hill. New York, NY. 1 9 5 6.

Silverstein, L. "Consider the Alternatives." CompCare, Minneapolis, MN. 1977.

VandeCreek, L. and Knapp, S. "Tarasoff and Beyond: Legal and Clinical Considerations in the Treatment of Life-Endangering Patients." Professional Resource Exchange, Inc. Sarasota, FL. 1999.

Van Hoose, W.H., & Kottler, J.A. "Ethical and Legal Issues in Counseling and Psychotherapy," 2nd. edition. Jossey-Bass, San Francisco, CA. 1985

Watson, D., & Tharp, R. "Self-Directed Behavior Modification for Personal Adjustment," 5th ed. Brooks/ Cole Publishing., Monterey, CA. 1989.

Section 3, Chapter 6

Alcoholics Anonymous: *Alcoholics Anonymous Comes of Age: A Brief History of A.A.* New York: Alcoholics Anonymous World Services. 1957.

Alcoholics Anonymous: Alcoholics Anonymous: *The Story of How Many Thousands of Men and Women Have Recovered from Alcoholism.* 3rd ed. New York: Alcoholics Anonymous World Services. 1976.

Alcoholics Anonymous: *Twelve Steps and Twelve Traditions.* New York: World Services. Inc., 1953.

American Psychiatric Association: Committee on religion and psychiatry: guidelines regarding possible conflict between psychiatrists' religious commitments and psychiatric practice. *American Journal of Psychiatry*, 1990; 47:542.

DuPont RL, McGovern JP: A *Bridge* to *Recovery: An introduction to 12-Step Programs*. Washington, DC: American Psychiatric Press, Inc., 1994.

Gerstein J: Rational recovery, SMART recovery and non-twelve step recovery programs, in: Graham AW. Schultz TK, Wilford BB (eds.), *Principles of Addiction Medicine*, 2nd ed. Chevy Chase, MD: American Society of Addiction Medicine, 1998. p. 719.

McElrath D. *Hazelden: A Spiritual Odyssey.* Center City, MN: Hazelden, 1987.

Narcotics Anonymous: *Narcotics Anonymous*. Van Nuys: World Service Office. Inc., 1982.

Section 3, Chapter 7
Alcoholics Anonymous. . Alcoholics Anonymous: The Story of How Many Thousands of Men and Women Have Recovered From Alcoholism, 3rd ed. New York: Alcoholics Anonymous World Services, 1976.

Center for Substance Abuse Treatment. . Enhancing Motivation for Change in Substance Abuse Treatment. Treatment Improvement Protocol (TIP) Series, Number 35. DHHS Publication No. (SMA) 99-3354. Washington, DC: U.S. Government Printing Office, 1999.

Davidson, R. . Can psychology make sense of change? In: Edwards, G., and Lader, M., eds. Addiction: Processes of Change. Society for the Study of Addiction Monograph No. 3. New York: Oxford University Press, . 1994.

Gordon, T. . Parent Effectiveness Training: The No-Lose Program for Raising Responsible Children. New York: Wyden, 1970.

Kanfer, F.H., and Schefft, B.K. . Guiding the Process of Therapeutic Change. Champaign, IL: Research Press, 1988.

Luke, D. . "Teens' images of smoking and smokers." Paper presented at the annual meeting of the Society for Research on Nicotine and Tobacco, New Orleans, LA, . 1998.

Miller, W.R., and Rollnick, S. . Motivational Interviewing: Preparing People To Change Addictive Behavior. New York: Guilford Press, 1991.

Miller, W.R.; Leckman, A.L; Delaney, H.D.; and Tinkcom, M. . Long-term follow-up of behavioral self-control training. *Journal of Studies on Alcohol.* 53(3):249-261, :1992.

Noonan, W.C., and Moyers, T.B. . Motivational interviewing. *Journal of Substance Misuse.* 2:8-16, :1997.

Rollnick, S., and Miller, W.R. . What is motivational interviewing? *Behavioral and Cognitive Psychotherapy* . 23:325-334, :1995.

Van Bilsen, H.P. . Motivational interviewing: perspectives from the Netherlands with particular emphasis on heroin-dependent clients. In: Miller, W.R., and Rollnick, S. Motivational Interviewing: Preparing People To Change Addictive Behavior. New York: Guilford Press, 1991. pp. 214-235.

Section 3, Chapter 8

Bandura, A. Self-Efficacy: The Exercise of Control. New York: W.H. Freeman, 1997.

Blomqvist, J. Paths to recovery from substance misuse: Change of lifestyle and the role of treatment. *Substance Use and Misuse*. 31(13):1807-1852, 1996.

Brecht, M.L., and Anglin, M.D. Conditional factors of maturing out: Legal supervision and treatment. *International Journal of the Addictions*. 25:395-407, 1990.

Brownell, K.D.; Marlatt, G.A.; Lichtenstein, E.; and Wilson, G.T. Understanding and preventing relapse. *American Psychologist*. 41:765-782, 1986.

Chen, K., and Kandel, D.B. The natural history of drug use from adolescence to mid-thirties in a general population sample. *American Journal of Public Health*. 85(1):41-47, 1995.

DiClemente, C.C. Motivational interviewing and the stages of change. In: Miller, W.R., and Rollnick, S., eds. Motivational Interviewing: Preparing People To Change Addictive Behavior. New York: Guilford Press, 1991. pp. 191-202.

DiClemente, C.C.; Carbonari, J.P.; Montgomery, R.P.G.; and Hughes, S.O. The Alcohol Abstinence Self-Efficacy Scale. *Journal of Studies on Alcohol*. 55(2):141-148, 1994.

DiClemente, C.C., and Prochaska, J.O. Processes and stages of self-change: Coping and competence in smoking behavior change. In: Shiffman, S., and Wills, T.A., eds. Coping and Substance Abuse. New York: Academic Press, 1985. pp. 319-343.

DiClemente, C.C., and Prochaska, J.O. Toward a comprehensive transtheoretical model of change: Stages of change and addictive behaviors. In: Miller, W.R., and Heather, N., eds. Treating Addictive Behaviors, 2nd ed. New York: Plenum Press, 1998.

DiClemente, C.C., and Scott, C.W. Stages of change: Interactions with treatment compliance and involvement. In: Onken, L.S.; Blaine, J.D.; and Boren, J.J., eds. Beyond the Therapeutic Alliance: Keeping the Drug-Dependent Individual in Treatment. NIDA Research Monograph Series, Number 165. DHHS Pub. No. (ADM) 97-4142. Rockville, MD: National Institute on Drug Abuse, 1997. pp. 131-156.

Institute of Medicine. . Treating Drug Problems. Washington, DC: National Academy Press, 1990b.

Marlatt, G.A., and Gordon, J.R., eds. Relapse Prevention: Maintenance Strategies in the Treatment of Addictive Behaviors. New York: Guilford Press, 1985.

Miller, W.R., and Heather, N., eds. Treating Addictive Behaviors, 2nd ed. New York: Plenum Press, 1998.

Orleans, C.T.; Schoenbach, V.J.; Wagner, E.H.; Quade, D.; Salmon, M.A.; Pearson, D.C.; Fiedler, J.; Porter, C.Q.; and Kaplan, B.H. . Self-help quit smoking interventions: Effects of self-help materials, social support instructions, and telephone counseling. *Journal of Consulting and Clinical Psychology*. 59:439-448, 1991.

Prochaska, J.O., and DiClemente, C.C. Stages and processes of self-change of smoking: Toward an integrated model of change. *Journal of Consulting and Clinical Psychology.* 51:390-395, 1983.

Prochaska, J.O., and DiClemente, C.C. The Transtheoretical Approach: Crossing Traditional Boundaries of Therapy. Homewood, IL: Dow Jones-Irwin, 1984.

Prochaska, J.O., and DiClemente, C.C. Stages of change in the modification of problem behaviors. In: Hersen, M.; Eisler, R.M.; and Miller, P.M., eds. Progress in Behavior Modification. Sycamore, IL: Sycamore Publishing Company, 1992. pp. 184-214.

Prochaska, J.O; DiClemente, C.C.; and Norcross, J.C. Changing: Process approaches to initiation and maintenance of changes. In: Klar, Y.; Fisher, J.D.; Chinsky, J.M.; and Nadler, A., eds. Self-Change: Social, Psychological, and Clinical Perspectives. New York: Springer-Verlag, 1992a. pp. 87-114.

Prochaska, J.O.; DiClemente, C.C.; and Norcross, J.C. In search of how people change: Applications to addictive behaviors. *American Psychologist.* 47:1102-1114, 1992.

Prochaska, J.O., and Goldstein, M.G. Process of smoking cessation: Implications for clinicians. *Clinical Chest Medicine.* 12:727-735, 1991.

Prochaska, J.O.; Velicer, W.F.; Rossi, J.S.; Goldstein, M.G.; Marcus, B.H.; Rakowski, W.; Fiore, C.; Harlow, L.L.; Redding, C.A., Rosenbloom, D.; and Rossi, S.R. . Stages of change and decisional balance for 12 problem behaviors. *Health Psychology.* 13(1):39-46, 1994.

Robins, L.N.; Davis, D.H.; and Goodwin, D.W. Drug use by U.S. Army enlisted men in Vietnam: A follow-up on their return home. *American Journal of Epidemiology.* 99:235-249, 1974.

Sobell, L.C.; Sobell, M.B.; Toneatto, T.; and Leo, G.I. What triggers the resolution of alcohol problems without treatment? *Alcoholism: Clinical and Experimental Research.* 17:217-224. 1993.

Sobell, M.B., and Sobell, L.C. Guiding self-change. In: Miller, W.R., and Heather, N., eds. Treating Addictive Behaviors, 2nd ed. New York: Plenum, 1998. pp. 189-202.

Sutton, S. Can stages of change provide guidelines in the treatment of addictions? In: Edwards, G., and Dare, C., eds. Psychotherapy, Psychological Treatments and the Addictions. New York: Cambridge University Press, 1996.

Tucker, J.A.; Vuchinich, R.E.; and Gladsjo, J.A. Environmental events surrounding natural recovery from alcohol-related problems. *Journal of Studies on Alcohol.* 55:401-411, 1994.

Strang, J.; Bacchus, L.; Howes, S.; and Watson, P. Turned away from treatment: Maintenance-seeking opiate addicts at two-year follow-up. *Addiction Research.* 6:71-81, 1997.

Section 3, Chapter 9

Agrawal, A., Wethrill, L., Bucholz, K. K., Kramer, J., Kuperman, S., Lynskey, M. T., . . . Bierut, L. J. (2012). Genetic influences on craving for alcohol. *Addictive Behaviors, 38,* 1501-1508.

Alexander, D., & Leung, P. (2011). The *DSM* Guided Cannabis Screen *{DSM-G-CS):* Description, reliability, factor structure and empirical scoring with a clinical sample. *Addictive Behaviors, 36,* 1095-1100.

American Counseling Association. (2012). *Licensure requirements for professional counselors: A state-by-state report.* Alexandria, VA: Author.

American Counseling Association. (2013). *What is professional counseling?* Retrieved from http://www.counseling.org/learn-about-counseling/what-is-counseling

American Counseling Association. (2014). *ACA code of ethics.* Alexandria, VA: Author.

American Psychiatric Association. (1952). *Diagnostic and statistical manual of mental disorders.* Washington, DC: Author.

American Psychiatric Association. (1968). *Diagnostic and statistical manual of mental disorders* (2nd ed.). Washington, DC: Author.

American Psychiatric Association. (1980). *Diagnostic and statistical manual of mental disorders* (3rd ed.). Washington, DC: Author.

American Psychiatric Association. (2000). *Diagnostic and statistical manual of mental disorders* (4th ed., text rev). Washington, DC: Author.

American Psychiatric Association. (2000). *Diagnostic and statistical manual of mental disorders* (4th ed., text rev.). doi:10.1176/appi.books.9780890423349

American Psychiatric Association. (201 la). DSM-5: APA responds to American Counseling Association concerns. Retrieved from http://www.psychiatrictimes.com/dsm-5-0/dsm-5-apa-responds-american-counseling-association-concerns#sthash.PiLWpxod.dpuf

American Psychiatric Association. (2010). Protocol for DSM-5 field trials in academic/large clinic settings. Retrieved from http://www.DSM5.org/Research/Documents/Forms/AHItems.aspx

American Psychiatric Association. (2011b). Protocol for DSM-5 field trials in routine clinical practice settings. Retrieved from http://www.DSM5.org/Research/Documents/Forms/AHItems.aspx

American Psychiatric Association. (2012a). DSM: History of the manual. Retrieved from http://www.psychiatry.org/practice/DSM/DSM-history-of-the-manual

American Psychiatric Association. (2012b). DSM-5 development: Timeline. Retrieved from http://www.dsm5.org/about/Pages/Timeline.aspx

American Psychiatric Association. (2012c). DSM-5 field trials. Retrieved from http://www.dsm5.org/Research/Pages/DSM-5FieldTrials.aspx

American Psychiatric Association. (2012d). DSM-5 overview: The future manual. Retrieved from http://www.dsm5.org/about/Pages/DSMVOverview.aspx

American Psychiatric Association. (2013). The diagnostic and statistical manual of mental disorders (5th ed.). Arlington, VA: Author.

American Psychiatric Association. (2013a). *Diagnostic and statistical manual of mental disorders* (5th ed.). Arlington, VA: Author.

American Psychiatric Association. (2013c). *Highlights of changes from DSM-IV-TR to DSM-5.* Retrieved from http://www.psychiatry.org/practice/dsm/dsm5

American Psychological Association. (2007). Report of the APA Task Force on Socioeconomic Status. Retrieved from http://www.apa.org/pi/ses/resources/publications/index.aspx

American Society of Addiction Medicine. (2013). *Public policy statement: Definition of addiction.* Retrieved from http://www.asam.org/for-the-public/definition-of-addiction

Belle, D., & Doucet, J. (2003). Poverty, inequality, and discrimination as sources of depression among U.S. women. Psychology of Women Quarterly, 27, 101-113.

Bohnert, A. S., Valenstein, M., Bair, M. J., Ganoczy, D., McCarthy, J. R, Ilgen, M. A., & Blow, F. C. (2011). Association between opioid prescribing patterns and opioid overdose-related deaths. *Journal of the American Medical Association, 305,* 1315-1321.

Brewer, J. A., Elwafi, H. M., & Davis, J. H. (2013). Craving to quit: Psychological models and neurobiological mechanisms of mindfulness training as treatment for addictions. *Psychology of Addictive Behaviors, 27,* 366-379.

British Psychological Society. (2011). Response to the American Psychiatric Association: DSM-5 development. Retrieved from http://apps.bps.org.uk/_publicationfiles/consultation-responses/DSM-5%202011%20-%20BPS%20response.pdf

Budney, A. J., Hughes, J. R., Moore, B. A., & Vandrey, R. (2004). Review of the validity and significance of cannabis withdrawal syndrome. *American Journal of Psychiatry, 161,* 1967-1977.

Budney, A. J., Moore, B. A., Vandrey, R. G., & Hughes, J. R. (2003). The time course and significance of cannabis withdrawal. *Journal of Abnormal Psychology, 112,* 393-402.

Caplan, P. J. (2012, April 27). Psychiatry's bible, the DSM, is doing more harm than good. Washington Post Opinions. Retrieved from http://www.washingtonpost.com/opinions/psychiatrys-bible-the-DSM-Is-doing-more-harm-than-good/2012/04/27/gIQAqyO WIT_story.html

Centers for Disease Control and Prevention, National Center for Health Statistics. (2014). The international classification of diseases, 10th revision, clinical modification (ICD-10-CM). Retrieved from http://www.cdc.gov/nchs/icd/icd 1 0cm.htm

Centers for Disease Control and Prevention. (2008). Smoking-attributable mortality, years of potential life lost, and productivity losses: United States, 2000-2004. *Morbidity and Mortality Weekly Report, 57,* 1226-1228.

Centers for Disease Control and Prevention. (2011). Burden of mental illness. Retrieved from http:// www.cdc.gov/mentalhealth/basics/mental-illness/depression.htm

Compton, W. M., Dawson, D. A., Goldstein, R. B„ & Grant, B. F. (2013). Crosswalk between *DSM-IV* dependence and *DSM-5* substance use disorders for opioids, cannabis, cocaine, and alcohol. *Drug and Alcohol Dependence, 132,* 387-390.

Council for Accreditation of Counseling and Related Educational Programs. (2009). 2009 standards. Retrieved from http://www.cacrep.org/doc/2009%20Standards.pdf

Crowley, T. J. (2007). Adolescents and substance-related disorders: Research agenda to guide decisions about *DSM-V.* In J. B. Saunders, M. A. Schuckit, P. J. Sirovatka, & D. A. Regier (Eds.), *Diagnostic issues in substance use disorders: Refining the research agenda for DSM-V* (pp. 203-220). Washington, DC: American Psychiatric Association.

Dawson, D. A„ Goldstein, R. B., & Grant, B. F. (2013). Differences in the profiles of *DSM-IV* and *DSM-5* alcohol use disorders: Implications for clinicians. *Alcoholism: Clinical and Experimental Research, 37,* E305-E313.

Eriksen, K., & Kress, V. E. (2006). The DSM and the professional counseling identity: Bridging the gap. Journal of Mental Health Counseling, 28, 202-216.

Frances, A., & First, M. B. (2011). Hebephilia is not a mental disorder in DSM-IV-TR and should not become one in DSM-5. Journal of American Academy of Psychiatry and the Law, 39, 78-85.

Gever, J. (2012, May 10). DSM-5: What's in, what's out. Retrieved from http://www.medpager.oday. com/MeetingCoverage/ APA/32619

Grant,]. E., Schreiber, L. R., & Odlaug, B. L. (2013). Phenomenology and treatment of behavioural addictions. *Canadian Journal of Psychiatry, 58,* 252-259.

Groh, C. J. (2006). Poverty, mental health, and women: Implications for psychiatric nurses in primary care settings. Journal of the American Psychiatric Nurses Association, 13, 267-274.

Health Insurance Portability and Accountability Act of 1996, Pub. L. 104-191, 110 Stat. 1936.

Hinkle, J. S. (1999). A voice from the trenches: A reaction to Ivey and Ivey (1998). Journal of Counseling & Development, 77, 474-483.

Kaminer, Y, & Winters, K. C. (2012). Proposed *DSM-5* substance use disorders for adolescents: If you build it, will they come? *American Journal of Addictions, 21,* 280-281.

Keyes, K. M., Krueger, R. R, Grant, B. R, & Hasin, D. S. (2011). Alcohol craving and the dimensionality of alcohol disorders. *Psychological Medicine, 41,* 629-640.

Ko, C. H., Liu, G. C, Yen,). Y, Yen, C. R, Chen, C. S., & Lin, W. C. (2013). The brain activations for both cue-induced gaming urge and smoking craving among subjects comorbid with Internet gaming addiction and nicotine dependence. *Journal of Psychiatric Research, 47,* 486-493.

Kupfer, D. J., First, M. B., & Regier, D. A. (2002). A research agenda for DSM-V. Washington, DC: American Psychiatric Association.

Kutchins, H., & Kirk, S. A. (1997). Making us crazy: DSM: The psychiatric bible and the creation of mental disorders. New York, NY: Free Press.

Leggett, T. (2006). United Nations Office on Drugs and Crime: Review of the world cannabis situation. *Bulletin on Narcotics, 58,* 1-155.

Mannarino, M. B., Loughran, M. J., & Hamilton, D. (2007, October). The professional counselor and the diagnostic process: Challenges and opportunities for education and training. Paper presented at the Association for Counselor Education and Supervision Conference, Columbus, OH.

McLoyd, V. C. (1998). Socioeconomic disadvantage and child development. American Psychologist, 53, 185-204.

Mewton, L., Slade, T., McBride, O., Grove, R., & Teeson, M. (2011). An evaluation of the proposed *DSM-5* alcohol use disorder criteria using Australian national data. *Addiction, 106,* 941-950.

Miller, J. D., &Levy, K. N. (2011). Personality and personality disorders in the DSM-5: Introduction to the special issue. Personality Disorders: Theory, Research, and Treatment, 2, 1-3.

Moran, M. (2013). Gambling disorder to be included in addictions chapter. *Psychiatric News.* doi:10.1176/appi.pn.2013.4bl4

National Institute on Drug Abuse. (2011). *Drug facts: Treatment statistics.* Retrieved from http://www.drugabuse.gov/publications/drugfacts/treatment-statistics Nock, M. K., Kazdin, A. E., Hiripi, E., & Kessler, R. C. (2006). Prevalence, subtypes, and correlates of *DSM-IV* conduct disorder in the National Comorbidity Survey Replication. *PsychologicalMedicine, 36,* 699-710.

Paris, J. (2013). *The intelligent clinician's guide to the DSM-5.* New York, NY: Oxford University Press.

Perry, S. (2012, May 4). Last chance to comment on psychiatry's controversial diagnostic "bible." Minnesota Post. Retrieved from http://www.minnpost.com/second-opinion/2012/05/last-chance-comment-psychiatrys-controversial-diagnostic-bible

Potenza, M. N, Balodis, I. M., Franco, C. A., Bullock, S., Xu, J., Chung, T., & Grant, J. E. (2013). Neurobiological considerations in understanding behavioral treatments for pathological gambling. *Psychology of Addictive Behaviors, 27,* 380-392.

Proctor, S. L., Kopak, A. M., & Hoffmann, N. G. (2012). Compatibility of current *DSM-IV* and proposed *DSM-5* diagnostic criteria for cocaine use disorders. *Addictive Behaviors, 37,* 722-728.

Regier, D. A., Narrow, W. E., Kuhl, E. A., & Kupfer, D. J. (2009). The conceptual development of DSM-5. American Journal of Psychiatry, 166, 645-650.

Sinha, R. (2013). The clinical neurobiology of drug craving. *Current Opinion in Neurobiology, 23,* 1-6.

Substance Abuse and Mental Health Services Administration. (2011b). *Results from the 2010 National Survey on Drug Use and Health: Summary of National Findings* (NSDUH Series H-41, HHS Publication No. SMA 11 -4658). Rockville, MD: Author.

Vandrey, R., Budney, A. J., Kamon, J. L., & Stanger, C. (2005). Cannabis withdrawal in adolescent treatment seekers. *Drug and Alcohol Dependence, 78,* 205-210.

Verweij, K. J. H., Agrawal, A., Nat, N. O., Creemers, H. E., Huizink, A. C, Martin, N. G., & Lynskey, M. T. (2013). A genetic perspective on the proposed inclusion of cannabis withdrawal in *DSM-5. Psychological Medicine, 43,* 1713-1722.

Williams, J. R, & Storck, M. (2007). Inhalant abuse. *Pediatrics, 119,* 1009-1017.

World Health Organization. (2007). *International statistical classification of diseases and related health problems, 10th revision.* Geneva, Switzerland: Author.

World Health Organization. (2010). WHO Disability Assessment Schedule 2.0-WHODAS 2.0. Geneva, Switzerland: Author.

Zalaquett, C. P., Fuerth, K. M., Stein, C., Ivey, A. E., & Ivey, M. N. (2008). Reframing the DSM-IV-TR from a multicultural/social justice perspective. Journal of Counseling & Development, 86, 364-371. doi: 10.1002/j. 1556-6678.2008.tb00521.x

APPENDIX A:
BIBLIOGRAPHY &
ADDITIONAL RESOURCES

OTHER RECOMMENDED MATERIALS

American Psychiatric Association. Diagnostic & Statistical Manual of Mental Disorders – 5. APA. 2013.

American Society of Addiction Medication. The ASAM Criteria. The Change Companies, 2013.

Benshoff, J. & Janikowski, T. The Rehabilitation Model of Substance Abuse Counseling. Brooks/Cole, 1999.

Buelow, G. & Buelow, S. Psychotherapy in Chemical Dependence Treatment: A Practical and Integrative Approach. Brooks/Cole, 1997.

Corey, G., Corey, M.S. and Patrick Callanan. Issues and Ethics for the Helping Professions. 6th Ed. Brooks/Cole, 2003.

Corey, G. and Marianne S. Corey. Groups: Process & Practice. 6th Ed. Brooks/Cole, 2001.

Corey, Gerald. Theory and Practice of Counseling and Psychotherapy. 6th Ed. Brooks/Cole, 2000.

DiClemente, Carlo. Addiction and Change: How Addictions Develop and Addicted People Recover. Guilford Press, 2003.

DeLeon, George. The Therapeutic Community: Theory, Model, and Method. Springer Publishing Company, 2000.

Doweiko, Harold. Concepts in Chemical Dependency. 5th Ed. Brooks/Cole, 2001.

Fisher, G. & Harrison, T. Substance Abuse: Information for School Counselors, Social Workers, Therapists and Counselors, 2nd. Ed. Allyn & Bacon, 1999.

Herdman, John. Global Criteria: The Twelve Core Functions of the Substance Abuse Counselor, 2nd ed., Learning Publications, 2000.

Inaba, Darryl. Uppers, Downers, All-Arounders, 4th Ed. CNS Publications, 2000. Kinney, Jean. Loosening the Grip. 7th Ed. McGraw-Hill, 2003.

McCollum, E. & Trepper, T., ed. Family Solutions for Substance Abuse: Clinical and Counseling Approaches. Haworth, 2001.

Miller & Rollnick. Motivational Interviewing: Preparing People for Change, 2nded. Guilford Press, 2002.
Perfas, Fernando. Therapeutic Community: A Practice Guide. Universe, 2003.

Powell, David. Clinical Supervision in Alcohol and Drug Abuse Counseling: Principals, Models, Methods, Jossey-Bass, 2004

Ray, O. and Charles Ksir. Drugs, Society and Human Behavior, 9th Ed. WCB/McGraw-Hill, 2002.

WEBSITES FOR STAYING CURRENT ON ADDICTION INFORMATION

Please note – while website information was current at the time this book was printed, websites can and do change IP addresses. If any link is not correct, simply use a search engine such as Google to find the correct linkage.

NIDA Homepage

Excellent resource with a great deal of research information and many downloadable articles. Be sure to check out the NIDA Notes link, and be sure to sign-up for the monthly publication. NIDA also has a Resource/Link page with multiple links with NIDA constituent organizations, grantees and Government sites of interest.

http://www.nida.nih.gov/

Rx List

Reference to prescription medications. This directory of drugs has medical information about their use and side effects, as well as the ingredients found in each drug. This site can be searched by using either the brand or generic name of the drug.

http://www.rxlist.com/

The Lycaeum

An organization that is definitely dedicated to the promotion of "controlled substance use." A valuable resource, none-the-less, to gain insight into the mind set of the user thinking and to stay current with information that is on the street regarding the use and "benefit" of specific drugs. Check out the graphics link – an excellent resource with pictures, drawings, etc., of various natural and synthetic drugs. I've used this sight to obtain graphics for overheads for various presentations and trainings.

http://www.lycaeum.org/

The Texas Commission on Alcohol and Drug Abuse, Research Publications

Click on "Research Archives" then scroll down to "Other Research Reports and Briefs" to find the link to "A Dictionary of Slang Drug Terms, Their Generic and Trade Names, and Pharmacological Effects and Uses" (October 1997). Click and download – an excellent resource for counselors.

http://www.tcada.state.tx.us/research/index.shtml

The Indiana Prevention Resource Center at Indiana University

Articles, information, and links for prevention efforts across the United States. Also has an excellent graphics section for pictures and slides of various drugs of abuse.

http://www.drugs.indiana.edu/

The National Addiction Technology Transfer Center Website

Homepage for the ATTC project – valuable links to all of the online resources that are participating in this national project which is geared toward expanding the knowledge base of the professional addiction counselor. Scroll through and find the link to TAP #21 – *Addiction Counseling Competencies: The Knowledge, Skills, and Attitudes of Professional Practice.* See what is being endorsed by such groups as IC&RC, NAADAC, INCASE, and the American Academy of Health Care Providers in the Addictive Disorders as the needs for addiction professionals in the 21st century.

http://www.nattc.org/

Center for Substance Abuse Research (CESAR)

The Center for Substance Abuse Research (CESAR) is a research center within the College of Behavioral and Social Sciences, University of Maryland College Park. A primary mission of CESAR is to collect, analyze, and disseminate information on the nature and extent of substance abuse and related problems in Maryland and nationally.

http://www.cesar.umd.edu/

Treatment Improvement Exchange

The Treatment Improvement Exchange (TIE) is a resource sponsored by the Division of State and Community Assistance of the Center for Substance Abuse Treatment to provide information exchange between CSAT staff and State and local alcohol and substance abuse agencies. Numerous free publications for counselors in downloadable formats – check under "Documents."

http://www.treatment.org/index.html

The National Institute on Alcohol Abuse and Alcoholism (NIAAA)

The National Institute on Alcohol Abuse and Alcoholism (NIAAA) supports and conducts biomedical and behavioral research on the causes, consequences, treatment, and prevention of alcoholism and alcohol-related problems. NIAAA also provides leadership in the national effort to reduce the severe and often fatal consequences of these problems.

http://www.niaaa.nih.gov/

Substance Abuse and Mental Health Services Administration (SAMHSA)

SAMHSA's mission is to assure that quality substance abuse and mental health services are available to the people who need them, and to ensure that prevention and treatment knowledge is used more effectively in the general health care system. (Managed care is among the topics covered on this site.)

http://www.samhsa.gov/

The Office of National Drug Control Policy

ONDCP is authorized to develop and coordinate the policies, goals, and objectives of the Nation's drug control program for reducing the use of illicit drugs.

http://www.whitehousedrugpolicy.gov/

Drug Enforcement Administration

The mission of the Drug Enforcement Administration (DEA) is to enforce the controlled substances laws and regulations of the United States and bring to the criminal and civil justice system of the United States. Check our their Drug and Drug Prevention pages for up-to-date information.

http://www.dea.gov/

American Society of Addiction Medicine

The nation's medical specialty society dedicated to educating physicians and improving the treatment of individuals suffering from alcoholism or other addictions.

http://www.asam.org/

The Distance Learning Center for Addiction Studies

Staying current with addiction and treatment information is necessary to insure quality of care and service to the field. The DLCAS provides distance training via the internet in a variety of topic areas. Training hour allow you to maintain your credential without unnecessary travel and time away from your office and family.

http://www.dlcas.com/

ReadyToTest.com

Need more help in preparing for your credentialing examinations? Let us help you. Preparation materials are available to assist you with either the written or oral exams that are used by IC&RC and NAADAC. These materials can help you prepare your case history, self-critique your responses to oral exam questions, or provide you with written test samples to help you pinpoint your strengths and weakness in your knowledge base.

http://www.readytotest.com/

APPENDIX B:
Some Basic Definitions

To understand the problems of drinking and drug use, it is important to understand some of the special vocabulary of commonly used terms, as well as some of the concepts of dependency. The following is a list of some important terms and concepts that are used throughout this review/preparation manual.

DRUG - Any substance that enters the human body and can change either the function or structure of the human organism This includes such items as foods, vitamins, nutrients, minerals and the like.

PSYCHOACTIVE DRUG - A chemical substance that not only can change the function and structure of the body, but also changes one's thinking, feelings, perceptions and behavior. These changes are the result of the drug's action on the human brain. Among the psychoactive drugs are those chemicals classified as follows:

Depressants - drugs that slow down central nervous system function, relax or tranquilize the person, and may produce sleep.

Narcotics - powerful painkillers, analgesics that also produce pleasurable feelings and generally induce sleep.

Stimulants - chemical substances that generally speed up central nervous system function, resulting in alertness and excitability.

Hallucinogens - also called mind expanders or psychedelics, these drugs affect a person's perception, awareness and emotions, and can cause hallucinations as well as misinterpretations of reality.

Inhalants - volatile nondrug chemical solvents that have druglike effects when inhaled. It includes commercial solvents (gasoline, toluene, acetone, carbon tetrachloride), aerosols (freon, amyl nitrite, butyl nitrite), and anesthetics (chloroform, ether and nitrous oxide).

For the purposes of this manual, the term drug will include the psychoactive drugs.

DRUG USE - the use or consumption of a drug within some socially prescribed or ritualistic context. Some examples:

> A glass of wine with a meal, wine at communion;
>
> A cup of coffee and a cigarette at break time;
>
> Taking a prescription medicine under doctor's orders.

DRUG MISUSE - the unintentional or inappropriate use of prescribed or nonprescribed drugs resulting in the impaired physical, mental, emotional or social well- being of the individual. Some examples:

Discontinuing the use of a prescribed medicine (before the medicine is gone) without consulting one's physician;

Saving unused medicines for self-treatment at some future time;

Combining alcoholic beverages with depressant-like drugs, such as antihistamines, tranquilizers, sleeping pills, and pain-killing medicines;

Using alcohol for effects that are contrary to it's physical action:

> *Two drinks of alcohol before a meal stimulates digestion, more than that actually inhibits digestion;*
>
> *Two drinks of alcohol before bedtime aids sleep, more than that sedates the part of sleep that is necessary for recovery.*

DRUG ABUSE - the deliberate use of chemical substances for reasons other than their intended medical purposes which result in any degree of physical, mental, emotional or social impairment of the user, the user's family, or society in general. It involves using illegal as well as legal, "recreational" drugs that lead to problems. Some examples:

Driving while intoxicated;

Adolescents who use alcohol or nicotine under the legal age of use;

Any use of illicit drugs;

Taking more than the prescribed dose of a medicine.

DRUG DEPENDENCE - Psychological and/or physical need for a drug, characterized by compulsive use, tolerance to the drug, and physical dependence manifest by withdrawal syndrome. Since some drugs do not show identifiable signs of withdrawal (e.g. marijuana), or if the signs of withdrawal are often misinterpreted as something else (e.g. cocaine, stimulants), a drug can be viewed as creating dependence if it produces euphoria in the user, and if as a result of that euphoria, it creates a pattern of self-reinforced use.

In understanding the definition of drug dependence, there are some additional terms that need to be defined:

Tolerance - A state of progressively decreasing responsiveness to a drugs' effects. In other words, a condition that requires the user to take more and more of a drug to get the same, desired effect.

Physical Dependence - A state in which the presence of the drug is required for the user to function normally. The body has adapted to the presence of the drug and the body views this as normal and necessary.

Withdrawal - Also referred to as the Abstinence Syndrome or Withdrawal Syndrome - Drastic and characteristic changes in physical functioning and behavior (insomnia, tremors, nausea, vomiting, cramps, elevation of the heart rate and blood pressure, convulsions, anxiety, psychological depression) due to over-excitation of the nervous system. These effects are observed or experienced when the user stops taking, or the use of a drug is significantly decreased (in which physical dependence upon the drug has developed). There is a craving for the drug when one is abstinent, and these symptoms are relieved when the drug is again taken.

In order to understand the terms related to the range of issues from simple drug use through dependence, some additional terms need to be introduced at this time:

ADDICTION: A chronic, progressive, relapsing disorder characterized by compulsive use of one or more substances that results in physical, psychological, or social harm to the individual and continued use of the substance or substances despite this harm.

For many, the terms drug dependence and addiction are interchangable. For others, a distinction is made between the two terms in the issue related to physical, psychological, or social harm that occurs with continued use.

ALCOHOLISM: A primary, chronic disease with genetic, psychosocial, and environmental factors influencing its development and manifestations. It is often progressive and fatal. It is characterized by impaired control over drinking, preoccupation with the drug alcohol, use of alcohol despite adverse consequences, and distortions in thinking, most notable denial. Each of these symptoms may be continuous or periodic.

ABSTINENCE: Refraining from the use of alcohol or other drugs.

RELAPSE: The return to substance use after a period of abstinence.

Other Key Terms:

ROUTES OF ADMINISTRATION - This refers to the method a drug is taken. The route of administration has a direct impact on the intensity and speed in which a drug has its effect. The common methods are as follows:

Oral - a drug is taken into the mouth, where it passes into the stomach. In the stomach, absorption begins, with the process continuing in the small intestines. Once absorbed into the bloodstream, the drug makes its way to all body parts. Drugs taken orally generally take 20 to 30 minutes to have their effect. Some of the drug's effectiveness is lost by oral ingestion.

Inhalation - A drug is inhaled (by smoking) directly into the lung. In the lung, the alveoli (air sacs) absorb the drug and move into the capillary system in the lungs. From there the drug passes into the heart and then to the brain. Drugs taken by inhalation generally take only 7 seconds to have their effect.

Intravenous - A drug is injected directly into a vein, where it travels to the lungs, heart and brain. No other absorption is required. Drugs taken in this fashion take approximately 14 seconds to have their effects.

Intranasal - A drug is inhaled into the nasal cavity, where it is absorbed in the mucous lining of the cavity. It is then absorbed by the capillary system in the nose, travels through the veins, then to the lungs, heart and brain. Drugs taken intranasally take from one to three minutes to have their effect.

Instillation - A drug is absorbed directly through the skin, where it eventually reaches the bloodstream. The skin is designed to prevent such absorption, but a few drugs, most notably LSD, are able to enter the system in such a fashion. Drugs absorbed in this fashion may take up to 60 minutes to have their effect.

DRUG DOSE - Refers to the quantity or amount of a drug that is taken at any particular time. The greater the dose, the greater the drug effect.

The threshold dose or minimal dose refers to the smallest amount of a given drug which is capable of producing some detectable response.

The median effective dose describes the dose required to produce a specific response in 50% of test subjects.

The lethal dose is that dose which would result in death for the user, while the lethal dose 50%, or LD-50 is the level of use that would kill 50% of those who took that amount. The potential danger of a drug is measured by its LD-50.

In addition to the dose of a drug, the time required by the body to remove the drug is also a factor in the drug's effect. The half-life is an indication of the time required for half of the dosage of a drug taken to leave the body. In other words, if a drug has a half-life of one hour and you take 100 milligrams, 50 mg. leave the system the first hour, 50 mg. remain. In one more hour, 25 mg. leave (half the dose remaining) and 25 mg. remain. This continues until all of the drug is removed from the system.

DRUG EFFECTS - When drugs are taken in combination, the drug effects can result in unexpected or even dangerous chemical interactions inside the body. One drug may make another act faster or slower, or more powerfully or less powerfully than normal. The types of effects are described below:

Independent effect – the effect of the individual drug is not changed when combined with another drug, that is, neither drug effects the action of another (1+1 = 1 and 1).

Antagonistic effect – the effect of one drug blocks or reduces the action of either or both drugs in the system (1+1 = 0).

Agonist effect – the effect of one drug mimics the action of another drug in the system (1 = B)

Additive effect – when two or more drugs are present in the body that have similar effects, the impact of adding one drug's action to another effectively doubles the effects of the drugs. In other words, the effect is the sum of the effects of the individual drugs (1+1 = 2).

Potentiation or synergistic effect – the combination of two or more drugs produce an exaggerated effect - one that goes above and beyond what might be expected from simply adding the effect of one drug to another. In other words, the effect is greater than the sum of the parts. This effect is potentially the most dangerous, especially if one of the drugs present is alcohol (1+1 = 10).

DRUG SCHEDULES - Drugs and other controlled substances are regulated by the federal government according to the potential the drug has for abuse; whether or not it has benefit or use in the medical community; and whether they can produce psychological or physical dependence. Such drugs are divided into different groups or schedules, numbered I through V. The following is a description of each of the five schedules:

Schedule I - a) The drug or other substance has a high potential for abuse; b) The drug or other substance has no currently accepted medical use in treatment in the United States; c) There is a lack of accepted safety for use of the drug of other substance under medical supervision.

Schedule II - a) The drug or other substance has a high potential for abuse; b) The drug or other substance has a currently accepted medical use in treatment in the United States or a currently accepted medical use with severe restrictions; c) Abuse of the drug or other substance may lead to severe psychological or physical dependence.

Schedule III - a) The drug or other substance has a potential for abuse less than the drugs or other substances in Schedules I and II; b) The drug or other substance has a currently accepted medical use in treatment in the United States; c) Abuse of the drug or other substance may lead to moderate or low physical dependence or high psychological dependence.

Schedule IV - a) The drug or other substance has a low potential for abuse relative to the drugs or other substances in Schedule III; b) The drug or other substance has a currently accepted medical use in treatment in the United States; c) Abuse of the drug or other substance may lead to limited physical dependence or psychological dependence relative to the drugs or other substances in Schedule III.

Schedule V - a) The drug or other substance has a low potential for abuse relative to the drugs or other substances in Schedule IV; b) The drug or other substance has a currently accepted medical use in treatment in the United States; c) Abuse of the drug or other substance may lead to limited physical dependence or psychological dependence relative to the drugs or other substances in Schedule IV.